WERTHEIM PUBLICATIONS IN
INDUSTRIAL RELATIONS

THE RISE OF
THE NATIONAL
TRADE UNION

THE DEVELOPMENT AND SIGNIFICANCE
of Its Structure,
Governing Institutions,
and Economic Policies

By

LLOYD ULMAN

CAMBRIDGE, MASSACHUSETTS · HARVARD UNIVERSITY PRESS
1966

Second Edition

Distributed in Great Britain by
OXFORD UNIVERSITY PRESS
London

Library of Congress Catalog Card Number 56–5175

This book is dedicated to my mother and father.

This book is dedicated to my mother and father.

FOREWORD

The distribution of influence and authority within the different trade union movements of the world varies considerably. In some of them the influence and authority of the national federation of unions is very great; in many, the local unions have little autonomy and are mere instruments of the national. Sometimes they are almost devoid of function.

The trade union movement of the United States is distinguished by the conspicuously weak influence and authority of the national federations (the A.F. of L. and the C.I.O.) and by the considerable amount of influence and discretion possessed by the local unions—a condition quickly noticed by most visiting European unionists. But by far the most important organizations in the American trade union movement are the national unions which dominate the two federations (soon to be one federation) and exercise considerable control over local unions.

Of course, the national unions have not always been the most important organizations in the trade union movement. The movement began with local unions and the nationals were formed by locals. Indeed, the locals were not easily and quickly convinced of the desirability or the necessity of forming nationals. Furthermore, it was not immediately and completely apparent that the most effective way to support and control the activities of local unions in a given trade or industry or to deal with their common problems was a federation of locals in a trade or in a group of related trades or occupations or in an industry. The idea of a national federation of locals had to compete with the idea of geographical federations and even with the idea of one big union.

Once national unions were formed, there arose the question of how far to go in giving them authority over the locals and over the individual members and what means to give them for making their authority effective. The settlement of these issues has entailed vigorous conflict and controversy in many unions and the decisions, quite understandably, have not been the same in different unions. Furthermore, the decisions have been made by a trial and error process, one arrangement after trial giving way to another. But the decisions have not been the result of accident, or even of personalities. They have reflected the conditions under which unions have operated—particularly the kind of labor markets in which they operated, but other conditions as well. Even where centralization of authority in the hands of nationals has gone quite far, local unions in the United States have succeeded in retaining considerable discretion and autonomy. Especially in the field of the administration of trade agreements with employers have locals kept considerable control.

The emergence of strong national unions created the problem of relations between them and raised the question of what kind of an organization, if any, the national unions might desire to promote their common interests and possibly to resolve conflicts between them.

Professor Ulman's study of the rise of national unions in the United States prior to 1900 is by far the most thorough study that has yet been made of the structure and the government of the American trade union movement. He has explored with meticulous care what went on inside various unions during their formative period, when they lacked experience and precedents to guide them, and when they were wrestling with the elementary questions of what responsibilities and authority to confer on the national organization. The mere establishment of a national union, as Professor Ulman has shown, created certain inescapable problems—what to do about traveling members, members in defunct locals, differences in standards of admission among the locals, the control and support of strikes, and many others. The solutions of these problems that were workable or acceptable to the members have depended upon conditions. Professor Ulman has searched for the determining conditions and he has striven to push generalizations concerning these determinants as far as the evidence justified. Thus, on the foundation of his minute and scholarly exploration of the evidence he has constructed generalizations which enable the reader to see what was going on and why it was happening as it did.

There have been excellent histories of the development of a number of national unions and there have been good studies of different aspects of union government and of selected union policies. There has been lacking, however, a comprehensive study which brings together the facts about the development of union government and policies and which shows how the present national unions have come to be what they are. This important gap has been filled by Professor Ulman. His study, I am sure, will quickly win recognition as one of the most competent and distinguished books on American industrial relations.

Although local unions in the United States were led with some reluctance to set up national organizations which in many instances became more or less their masters, the national unions have been successful on the whole in limiting the influence and authority of the national federations. In this respect the trade union movement of this country differs markedly, at least in degree, from most of those of Western Europe. The explanation of how and why the national unions have been able to limit the influence and activities of the federations is an important story. It belongs, however, to a later period than that covered by Professor Ulman.

Sumner H. Slichter

September 15, 1955

CONTENTS

CONTENTS

TABLES

CHARTS

PREFACE

This is a study of the emergence and development of the national union in the latter half of the nineteenth and the early years of the twentieth century. By the end of the nineteenth century the national union had achieved maturity in three important respects. In the first place, its governing institutions—executive, judicial, and legislative—had become well established (although, in some cases, it was still to experiment with the referendum), and its relationships with its affiliated local unions had become fairly well settled. In 1899 a president of the Bricklayers told the convention that, "Our laws are good, almost without a flaw . . ."; two years earlier International Secretary Thomas O'Dea had observed:

We have good laws. They are all right and don't need changing unless it may be to correct a typographical error.

The second area of organizational maturity consisted in the relationships between the national union and other institutions in the labor movement. By the end of the last century the national union had become dominant over both the national and local federations of trades.

Finally the national union had, in many instances, developed an economic outlook, embodied in certain strike and wage policies and work rules, which was to serve it for many decades to come and which it has by no means relinquished yet, although old and young dogs alike have indeed learned new tricks.

Why should one study a phenomenon which occurred a half-century ago? Apart from the satisfaction of one's natural curiosity concerning past events —history is surely its own excuse for being—understanding past situations can be of great value in facilitating understanding of the present. This proposition is none the less true for being trite, and it holds especially when the object of study has been subjected to environmental changes as dramatic as those experienced by the American labor movement in the past twenty years. One usually has a better chance of inferring the existence of a logical relationship between a given attribute of an institution and a particular facet of its environment if the period of observation lies in the not-too-recent past. Then, armed with information concerning such a relationship, one can attack the present from one of two directions. Noting a change in the institution itself, one should be able to isolate certain environmental factors from the contemporary flux and ascribe to them particular significance for the problem involved. Or, noting a recent change in sign or value of one of the "independent variables" in an historical relationship, one is alerted for possible change of a particular variety in the institution under examination. Thus hindsight might aid in understanding the present—and such aid is not to be spurned, the availability of the modern social sciences notwithstanding.

There is at least one other reason why the contemporary student of American labor should be interested in the history of American labor. Several challenging hypotheses concerning union behavior have been offered in recent years. In some instances, attempts were made to validate these hypotheses with reference to behavior observed in our own time. It should prove interesting to attempt to check such theories against the record of the more distant past in order to determine whether the alleged phenomena to which they direct our attention are in fact historic constants.

Granted that the student of the American labor movement might reread American labor history with profit as well as with pleasure, why should he attempt to rewrite it? If the contemporary American labor movement owes much to the calibre of its early leaders, contemporary students of that movement are equally indebted to the extraordinarily gifted observers, led by Commons and Barnett, who first chronicled its history. Yet each generation of students must build upon the efforts of its predecessors. New historical data are uncovered which necessitate modification of early interpretations; thus fairly recent work which leads one to question the validity of the Turner theory of the frontier is relevant, as we shall see, to the interpretation of American labor history. New tools of analysis are at hand; in the following pages I occasionally attempt to employ certain basic economic concepts, some of which were not available twenty years ago. Moreover, some time-honored theories of the labor movement, although illumined with insight, are marred to some extent by ambiguities or contradictions. Finally, the contemporary student is interested in new problems which are suggested by changed conditions or by fresh theorizing; this may require him to search for new historical data, which then might also be used to check old hypotheses.

In the present instance, I have sought to supplement familiar material with data obtained from a detailed analysis of the constitutions, proceedings, and journals of five national unions: the Bricklayers', Carpenters', Printers', Molders', and Bottle Blowers'. In addition, rather extensive use was made of testimony reported in the hearings before the U. S. Industrial Commission of 1901 and of the reports in U. S. Commissioner of Labor, *Regulation and Restriction of Output*. It is hoped that the future will bring forth the results of examination of additional national unions, for each union's record is fascinating and distinctive and could yield new hypotheses and conclusions.

This book consists of seven parts. Part I deals with some important historical factors, including the relative scarcity of labor in American economic development, their interaction, and certain impacts of each upon the growth and structure of the trade union movement.

In Parts II, III, and IV, certain aspects of the internal development of the national union are discussed. Part II considers some of the ways in which power passed from the locals to the national unions and how this transition was affected by the geographic mobility of labor, personified by the traveling member who became the first rank-and-file "citizen" of the national union. The development of national control over strikes is discussed in Part III, in which an attempt is made to assess the significance of various controls and of certain factors which played a part in their emergence. In Part IV the development of the principal governing institutions in the national union is considered and compared with the development of national union government in Britain. In this part the rise of the chief executive officer is discussed and the attempts to establish other independent governing institutions—notably the convention, the referendum, and the executive board—are assessed.

Internal affairs of unions are, of course, intimately related to their external, or "foreign" affairs, that is, their relations with outside organizations. In Britain, for example, the absence of positive evidence of internal democracy might be construed as evidence of contentment, for union members can "vote with their feet."[1] In the American labor movement, however, secession was not traditionally regarded as an approved weapon of democracy, for it frequently ran counter to the principle of "exclusive jurisdiction." Internal affairs have also been shaped by the collective bargaining relationships into which the union, or its subordinates entered, as well as by the union's relations with other unions. Thus it is claimed that the necessity to maintain a united front at all times before a potential and powerful foe imposes certain restraints to which internal democracy must be subjected. The "foreign affairs" of the national union are discussed in Parts V and VI. Part V deals with certain aspects of jurisdiction and federation—the national union's relationships with other organizations in the labor movement. An attempt is made to uncover certain underlying determinants of jurisdiction, in particular craft and multicraft jurisdiction. Then, since we have considered both the territorial and occupational requirements of the "business union," we proceed to a consideration of its relations with—and ultimate dominance over—the federations, local and national.

We suggest in Part V that the national union sought to establish its jurisdictional bounds with reference to certain bargaining requirements; thus the two classes of "external" relations—relations with other labor organizations and relations with employers—were intimately related. In Part VI we proceed to a more direct examination of the bargaining strategy and policies of the early national unions. Chapter 14 deals with national strike policies, in connection with which we discuss the cyclical and seasonal timing of strikes, the relationship of the latter to the development of the firm annual (or longer) collective bargaining agreement, and (in tentative fashion) the deci-

[1] H. A. Clegg, *Industrial Democracy and Nationalization* (Oxford: Blackwell, 1951), p. 22.

sion concerning whom or where to strike—whether to give high-wage firms priority over low-wage firms, or *vice versa,* whether to conduct strikes on an individual-firm or on an area-wide basis. Chapters 15, 16, and 17 are devoted to a consideration, under a single framework, of union attitudes and reactions to certain employer wage and output practices, of national wage policies—including an examination of some conditions attending the rise of national collective bargaining in certain industries—and of certain union work rules. In these chapters an attempt is made to determine under what conditions the national union endorsed "equal pay" policies and whether, in so doing, it was motivated by egalitarian considerations, on the one hand, or by "business" considerations, on the other.

The last part (VII) draws on material presented earlier in the study in a reappraisal of two leading theories of the American labor movement (those of Commons and Perlman) and also in a sketch of a different hypothesis, in part alternative and in part supplementary to the other theories.

This study was begun when I was a graduate student at Harvard University where Professors Sumner H. Slichter and John T. Dunlop were my major advisers. Both were kind enough to maintain interest in this work after I left Cambridge, and I am greatly in their debt for their many valuable criticisms and suggestions, both detailed and of a general nature. This study owes much to Professor Slichter's incisive comments on and interpretation of union work rules and jurisdictional practices. It has profited greatly as a result of Professor Dunlop's suggestions concerning national union strike policies, rules, and governing institutions. I wish to express my warm thanks to Professors Slichter and Dunlop for having encouraged me to undertake this study and for subsequently advising me throughout all stages of the project. I hold fast, however, to my claim of authorship for all remaining errors of fact, judgment, or analysis.

I wish also to acknowledge my debt of gratitude to Professor Edwin E. Witte. This study was begun some years after I left the University of Wisconsin, where I had been a graduate student, but Professor Witte's influence over those fortunate enough to have been his students has never failed the stern tests of time and distance.

This study was made possible by the generosity of the Social Science Research Council. I was a Fellow of the Social Science Research Council during the period July 1, 1948–June 30, 1949 and a National Fellow in Economic History during the period July 1, 1949–June 30, 1950. As a National Fellow in Economic History, I received wise counsel and encouragement from Professor Arthur H. Cole of Harvard University, which I wish to acknowledge with gratitude.

I am also indebted to the Committee of the Jacob Wertheim Fellowship in Industrial Relations for their counsel and assistance in connection with the preparation and publication of this book.

Acknowledgement is also made of the helpfulness and warm coöperation on the part of the staff of The Johns Hopkins University Library—Drs. Homer Halvorsen and J. Louis Kuethe and Miss Margaret Laugh—and Miss Angela Lavarello, secretary of the Department of Political Economy of that institution. Through their courtesy, the facilities of the splendid Barnett collection of union documents were made available to me. I am also very grateful to Mrs. Ruth Whitman of Harvard University Press for her most competent and cheerful editorial assistance in preparing the manuscript for publication.

I am also indebted to my colleagues at the University of Minnesota who were kind enough not only to bear with me during conversations which frequently were closer to my heart than theirs but to make many valuable suggestions to me. In particular I should like to thank Professors John G. Turnbull, Leonid Hurwicz, Francis M. Boddy, Joseph P. McKenna, and Harlan M. Smith. Professor Dale Yoder kindly came to my assistance in furnishing references on payment in kind and related employee services during the latter part of the nineteenth century.

Finally, I wish to express my deepest gratitude to my wife who helped edit the work, made many valuable observations and suggestions, and typed an unconscionably bulky manuscript several times over.

Lloyd Ulman

ECONOMIC DEVELOPMENT AND THE NATIONAL TRADE UNION—

CHAPTER ONE

THE POSITION OF LABOR

IN EMERGING by the end of the nineteenth century as the dominant form of labor organization in the United States, the national union triumphed over powerful and determined opposition in the American labor movement. It was opposed by members of local unions who remained for a long time profoundly suspicious of the national organization and who consented to an extension of its powers at the expense of the locals only after considerable delay and with marked reluctance. It was opposed by leaders of organizations intent upon furthering the welfare of the unskilled, who preferred regional groupings of all trades—in which craftless men might enlist in their own cause the superior bargaining power of those whose special aptitudes had made them more essential to employers—to autonomous national unions organized on narrow craft lines in the selfish interests of their respective member groups. Finally, it was opposed by the proponents of political utopianism—that hitherto hardy perennial which had bloomed unfailingly in the cyclically recurring winters of labor's discontent, to whom any concept of jurisdiction narrower than the brotherhood of man was anathema.

Yet the national unions grew and multiplied. In the following section of this chapter we shall trace the record of this growth and identify the period in American history in which the national union achieved its position of dominance.

THE RECORD OF GROWTH, 1850–1900

The first national union was the National Typographical Union, established in 1852, and, as Table 1 indicates, it was followed by five other organizations in the decade of the eighteen fifties. The institution, however, showed no marked evidence of growth until the latter part of the Civil War; of the twenty-one new unions listed as having emerged in the sixties, eighteen were formed after 1863.[1] Thereafter growth was rapid, so that 120 national unions

1. Data on the number of unions have been derived from information in an unpublished compilation by Professor Sumner H. Slichter, "Historical Data on Trade Unions, 1850–1946."

TABLE 1

INCREASE OF AMERICAN TRADE UNIONS, 1850–1947[a]

	Formation of Unions in period				Disappearance of Unions in period				Total in exist- ence at end of decade
	Total formed	New unions	Formed by merger	Formed by se- cession	Total disap- peared	Disap- peared by ex- piring	Disap- peared by merger with parent	Disap- peared by merger with another body	
1850–59	6	6	0	0	0	0	0	0	6
1860–69	24	21	0	3	1	1	0	0	29
1870–79	20	19	1	0	20	16[b]	0	4	29
1880–89	62	56	0	6	12	8	4	0	79
1890–99	77	66	4	7	36	18	3	15	120
1900–09	95	76	5	14	44	22	6	16	171
1910–19	34	21	3	10	42	14	3	25	163
1920–29	17	8	1	8	28	15	4	9	152
1930–39	66	40	10	16	24	6	3	15	194
1940–47	19	16	1	2	15	1	0	14	198
Totals	420	329	25	66	222[c]	101[c,d]	23	98	

[a] Compiled by Professor S. H. Slichter.
[b] Includes 7 unions which "expired by 1880."
[c] Includes 10 unions for which no date is given for expiring.
[d] Of the 10 other unions which expired but for which no date is given, 7 were formed between 1850 and 1889 and 3 were formed between 1900 and 1947.

were in existence at the end of the century. The path they trod, however, must have been treacherous, for the casualty rate was high: for every four unions newly formed over the entire period, one "disappeared by expiring." The development of national unionism was sensitive to cyclical variations in business activity (see Table 2).

Cyclical sensitivity in the formation of new unions after 1863 is apparent in the accompanying chart (Chart 1). No precise yearly data on expirations are available, but the fact that thirty-four of the forty-three expirations recorded in the half-century under discussion took place in the decades marked by the occurrence of the two "major" depressions of 1873–1879 and 1893–1897 indicates a strong cyclical influence on the death rate as well as on the birth rate of the national unions. Responsiveness to industrial fluctuations, however, appears to have diminished toward the end of the period, in one respect: while the ratio of expirations to new unions was .84 in the depressed seventies, it was only .27 in the depressed nineties. The unions established before and

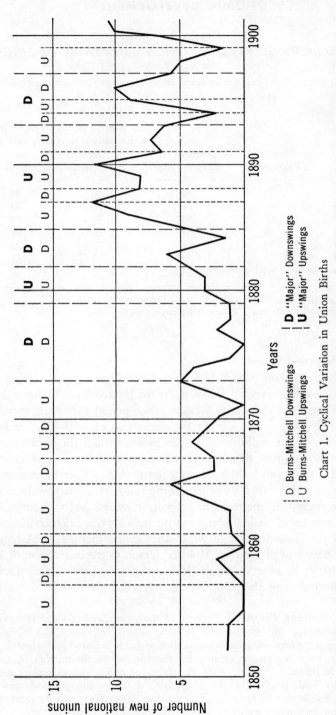

Years

D Burns-Mitchell Downswings   **D** "Major" Downswings
U Burns-Mitchell Upswings   **U** "Major" Upswings

Chart 1. Cyclical Variation in Union Births

Number of new national unions

Sources: Arthur F. Burns and Wesley C. Mitchell, *Measuring Business Cycles* (New York: National Bureau of Economic Research, 1946), pp. 78, 102–103; Alvin Hansen, *Fiscal Policy and Business Cycles* (New York: W. W. Norton, 1941), ch. i; S. H. Slichter, "Chronology of National Unions," manuscript.

TABLE 2

CYCLICAL RESPONSIVENESS OF UNION GROWTH BY DECADES,
1860-1929

(1) Decade	(2) Months of Expansion[a]	(3) Months of Contraction[a]	(4) Ratio of Months of Expansion to Months of Contraction	(5) Ratio of Expirations to New Unions[b]
1860–69	74	46	1.60	.05
1870–79	43	77	.56	.84
1880–89	69	51	1.35	.14
1890–99	68	52	1.30	.27
1900–09	72	48	1.50	.29
1910–19	65	55	1.18	.67
1920–29	66	54	1.22	.53

[a] Compiled from data presented in Arthur F. Burns and Wesley C. Mitchell, *Measuring Business Cycles* (New York: National Bureau of Economic Research, 1946), p. 78.
[b] Compiled from data in Table 1 above.

during the depressed period (or periods) in the nineties were considerably more durable than those which had been formed before and during the depressed period in the seventies. Thus, while the International Typographical Union lost 40 per cent of its membership in the period 1873–1878, membership fell by only 10 per cent during the depression of 1893–1897; and the latter loss included the withdrawal of the pressmen and the bookbinders.[2] By the end of the century the national unions, at least in terms of survival, had won their spurs; and although they were able neither to master the economic forces which called them into being nor even subsequently to prevent a drastic reversal in the trend of growth,[3] they retained without serious question the support of trade unionists as the only type of organization practicable under the circumstances in which they found themselves. A remark made by the president of the Iron Molders' Union to the convention of 1893 proved prophetic; he observed that, "It is noteworthy that, while in every previous industrial crisis the trade unions were literally mowed down and

2. James B. Kennedy, *Beneficiary Features of American Trade Unions* (Baltimore: Johns Hopkins, 1908), p. 14.
3. A turning point between growth and decline probably occurred in the first decade of this century, for although the greatest ten-year increase in the number of unions formed occurred between 1900 and 1909, the highest mortality also took place during those years. (See Table 1.) And, in view of the fact that the duration of good times was greater in this decade than in the preceding period, it is significant that the ratio of expirations to new formations registered a slight increase. (See Table 2.)

swept out of existence, the unions now in existence have manifested, not only the powers of resistance, but of stability and permanency."[4]

THE RELATIVE SCARCITY OF LABOR

The emergence and subsequent growth of the national unions paralleled developments which made their existence a condition of the survival of "business unionism" in this country. The dynamic forces in the economic environment, which greatly influenced the development of American trade unions, themselves formed part of a pattern of response to the country's original economic heritage: a low ratio of labor to natural resources and a trading area (later to be protected) capable of supporting a population large enough to constitute a mass market for manufacturing enterprise. The scarcity of labor, reflected since colonial times in a wage level higher than that prevailing abroad,[5] proved to be an extraordinarily persistent phenomenon, surviving the equilibrating tendencies which it stimulated and thereby serving as a continuing generator of economic progress. Broadly speaking, scarcity of labor contributed to two main lines of change: (1) an increase in population and (2) a widespread adoption of specialization and mechanical innovation.

The rate of population growth in the United States was extremely high until 1860, and much higher than that experienced in other Western countries. Since percentage increases in the number of gainful workers were even greater, this increase in population greatly augmented the country's work force.

Comparative percentages of increase, by decades, 1820–1900, were as follows:

	Population	Workers		Population	Workers
1820–30	33.5	36	1860–70	26.6	23
1830–40	32.7	35	1870–80	26.0	35
1840–50	35.9	43	1880–90	25.5	36
1850–60	35.6	37	1890–1900	20.7	23

The extent to which the relative scarcity of labor contributed to this increase is, of course, unknown, but there is reason to believe that two important sources of the growth in population—the high birth rate and immigration—

4. *Proceedings,* 1893, p. 12.

5. John R. Commons and Associates, *History of Labour in the United States* (New York: Macmillan, 1936), vol. I, pp. 34, 51, 305; Victor S. Clark, *History of Manufactures in the United States* (Washington, D. C.: Carnegie Institution of Washington, 1916 and 1928), vol. I (1607–1860), pp. 390–392; Chester W. Wright, *Economic History of the United States* (New York: McGraw-Hill, 1949), pp. 312, 333, 587, 589; "High Wages in Colonial America," *Monthly Labor Review,* v. 28, no. 1, January 1929, pp. 8–13; Karl-Erik Hansson, "A General Theory of the System of Multilateral Trade," *American Economic Review,* vol. XLII, March 1952, no. 1, pp. 59–68.

were appreciably motivated by economic as well as other considerations.[6] This rapid growth in the country's supply of labor was, however, offset in part by an accompanying increase in the supply of its already abundant resource, land. Since the latter increase was not as great as the former, population density rose,[7] but it did not approach the levels prevailing in England and western Europe. The result was that wages in the United States remained higher than those in Europe, with agriculture in this country providing "transfer earnings" for unskilled workers and skilled artisans alike.[8]

By 1860, however, our land area had ceased to grow, and, although great regions remained to be settled, land values rose sharply. But now the rate of increase in population fell (from over 35 per cent per decade between 1840 and 1860 to about 26 per cent from 1860 to 1890 and 21 per cent over the last decade of the century) so that the rate of increase in population density also declined, as the following percentages show:

	Density Increase	Population Increase		Density Increase	Population Increase
1840–1850	−19	35.9	1870–1880	26	26.0
1850–1860	34	35.6	1880–1890	25	25.5
1860–1870	26	26.6	1890–1900	21	20.7

Thus as in the previous period, "The density of population . . . still remained far below that of the the far more advanced countries of western Europe."

The relative scarcity of labor persisted and, persisting, continued to exert its magnetic effect upon people in lower-wage areas. For, although the rate of population growth declined, immigration increased in the last half of the nineteenth century. And "in the migration between 1860 and 1914, economic motives were even more dominant than before, though the desire for greater

6. "The demand for child labor on the expanding frontier provided an incentive, if any was needed, for the high birthrate and large families of colonial times." Richard B. Morris, *Government and Labor in Early America* (New York: Columbia University Press, 1946), p. 32. See also, *Statistical Abstract of the United States,* 1947, p. 5 and *Historical Statistics of the United States, 1789–1945* (Washington, D. C., 1949), p. 64.

7. In two decades, 1800–1810 and 1840–1850, the area of the United States increased more rapidly than its population. (See *Statistical Abstract of the United States,* 1947, p. 5.)

8. Clark, *History of Manufactures,* v. I, pp. 390–393, notes that unskilled labor in the mines and furnaces had to be lured away from the land. ("Our early manufacturers testified repeatedly that the compensation of industrial labor followed very closely rates paid in agriculture . . .") As for "expert operatives and artisans," their remuneration had to be raised sufficiently to induce them to emigrate to this country, since "Farmers had no inducement to apprentice their sons to trades, because they could employ them better at home, with the prospect of an independent life in agriculture." The "safety-valve" controversy is beside the point at hand: it was not necessary that workers themselves have the opportunity to leave industry for farming in order to provide a "floor" under their industrial earnings; it sufficed that the availability of cheap land prevented small farmers from leaving farming to take jobs in industry. See Louis M. Hacker, *The Triumph of American Capitalism* (New York: Columbia University Press, 1940), pp. 202–203.

political freedom and the wish to avoid military service or to escape religious persecution still exercised some influence."[9] The following phenomena reflect the operation of economic motives: the successful recruitment efforts of American agents abroad who sought to persuade their clients that better conditions awaited them across the Atlantic,[10] the high and increasing proportion of male to female immigrants (although the increase was most marked after 1899),[11] and a close relationship between immigration and cyclical movements in employment, which developed significantly after the disappearance of free land. This last phenomenon is especially interesting in view of the fairly close concurrence of good and bad times in the countries of emigration and immigration, suggesting that "the immigrant is attracted by unusually promising opportunities, rather than driven by the bitter necessity of seeking an adequate livelihood elsewhere."[12] The "new immigrant," however, proved to be numerically unreliable as an addition to this country's work force. Perhaps because he was more susceptible to the wage pull in the first place, he tended to return to his native land—and, often to his family—after he had accumulated his "pile" or after bad times in this country had disenchanted him. The result was a high ratio of emigration to immigration, which substantially offset the effect of the latter in increasing the supply of labor. (For the period 1870–1899 inclusive, for example, the average ratio of departing male steerage passengers to male immigrants was .31.)

The relative scarcity of labor and the relative abundance of land in the United States as compared to Europe affected the demand for labor as well as its supply. Two potential channels existed, through each of which reduction in demand for this relatively more expensive resource could be effected: the first was substitution of goods requiring a small amount of labor relative to land for their production in favor of those requiring a relatively high proportion of labor to land (for it was in the former that America's comparative advantage was greatest); the second, substitution of less costly resources for labor in the production of all goods. If the first type of substitution had been effected, the United States would have remained an agricultural country.[13] Actually, of course, the proportion of the gainfully employed engaged in agriculture has declined decade by decade, without interruption, since 1820, and the contribution of agriculture to national income, approximately steady throughout the 1820's and '30's, began a correspondingly sustained decline in

9. Wright, *Economic History*, pp. 450, 452.

10. John R. Commons, *Races and Immigrants in America* (New York: Macmillan, 1907), pp. 109–111, 122.

11. Wright, *Economic History*, pp. 452–454; *Historical Statistics*, p. 37.

12. Harry Jerome, *Migration and Business Cycles* (New York: National Bureau of Economic Research, 1926), p. 120. See also pp. 80, 82, 100, 103–105, 120, 169–177. See also pp. 239–243.

13. See Paul A. Samuelson, "International Trade and the Equalisation of Factor Prices," *Economic Journal*, v. LVIII, June 1948, pp. 163–184.

the following decade.[14] The increasing importance of manufacturing indicates that no reduction in demand for labor was effected indirectly through a relative reduction in production of nonagricultural goods.

It also indicates that the high cost of labor stimulated recourse to the second method of economizing on labor—the substitution of other resources for the scarcer factor. This substitution was effected primarily through the widespread adoption of innovations: that is, through changes in production functions (the quantitative relationship prevailing between inputs of resources and outputs of products) rather than changes in the proportions in which resources are employed in any one given state of the arts.

Innovation took the form of both specialization and division of labor, on the one hand, and the utilization of machinery, on the other. In either case, unit labor costs were reduced: in the former, because unskilled labor could be substituted for skilled labor; in the latter, because machinery could be substituted for labor. Due to the vigorous forces of growth in the economy and also, perhaps, to the nature of the innovations adopted (which we shall consider shortly) labor's displacement was on the whole relative rather than absolute: the proportion of labor cost to total unit cost declined. Innovations required the extensive employment of capital, which, like labor, had commanded a higher price on this continent than in western Europe and the British Isles. In this case, however, the stimulus of unequal reward brought about a more rapid increase in supply. Foreign investment in the United States, later supplemented by private domestic accumulation, "steadily reduced the difference between interest rates in this country and in western Europe," so that "by 1900, the difference was slight.[15] As a result, the supply of capital increased much more rapidly than the supply of labor.[16] Between 1880 and 1900, the value of equipment per gainfully employed worker (in constant 1929 prices) increased two-and-one-half times; the value of nonagricultural equipment (in constant prices) per gainful worker in nonagricultural pursuits increased about 2.2 times; and the value of manufacturing equipment (also in constant prices) per worker in manufacturing and hand trades almost tripled.[17]

Since most of the innovations in manufacturing during this period resulted in an increase in capital relative to output as well as to labor,[18] fixed costs

14. *Historical Statistics*, p. 63, pp. 13–14.

15. Wright, *Economic History*, p. 587.

16. Horsepower per wage earner in manufacturing increased from 1.14 in 1869 to 2.14 in 1899. See Harry A. Millis and Royal E. Montgomery, *Labor's Progress and Some Basic Problems* (New York: McGraw-Hill, 1938), p. 20 (Table 10).

17. Computed from Simon Kuznets, *National Product Since 1869* (New York: National Bureau of Economic Research, 1946), p. 219, Table IV 6, and *Historical Statistics*, p. 64.

18. See Alvin H. Hansen, *Fiscal Policy and Business Cycles* (New York: W. W. Norton, 1941), p. 356.

per unit of output rose. As a result of this greater "lumpiness," many innovations were predicated upon the expansion of the markets available to the firms which undertook them.[19] (This is not to deny that innovations which consisted simply in specialization were not also predicated upon the widening of market areas, as John R. Commons insisted.) The rapid increase in population, to which we have already referred in connection with the increase in the supply of labor, also increased the demand for labor, but existence of markets on a scale great enough to make feasible widespread innovation in manufacturing waited upon the development of the steam railway network.[20]

19. This phenomenon was described by Professor Schumpeter as "building ahead of demand." (Joseph A. Schumpeter, *Business Cycles,* New York: McGraw-Hill, 1939, vol. I, p. 91.) It should be noted that Lange's definition of innovations as "such changes in production functions . . . which make it possible for the firm to increase the discounted value of the maximum effective profit obtainable under given market conditions," is acceptable, since "discounted expected prices and schedules as well as current ones are included" in "given market conditions." (Oscar Lange, "A Note on Innovations," *Review of Economic Statistics,* vol. XXV, 1943, pp. 19–25. Reprinted in the American Economic Association, *Readings in the Theory of Income Distribution* (Philadelphia: Blakiston, 1946), pp. 185–186.) Schumpeter's definition: "We will simply define an innovation as the setting up of a new production function" (p. 87) is also relevant here, although the assumption of an increase in expected profits should be made explicit. Subject to this modification in his definition, Lange's hypothesis that most innovations are factor-using and output-increasing is acceptable (p. 190).

For an account of the role of the mass market in the development of the complex of innovations which has come to be known as mass production, see Samuel Rezneck, "Mass Production Since the War between the States," in Harold Williamson, *The Growth of the American Economy* (New York: Prentice-Hall, 1946), pp. 498–499. Also Wright, *Economic History,* p. 588.

20. See Edgar M. Hoover, Jr., "The Location of Economic Activities," in Williamson, *Growth of the American Economy,* pp. 586–587.

The relative contributions of the increase in population and of the development of the railway net are suggested by a brief reference to the careers of each of these phenomena in the periods in which modern industry emerged and developed in this country. Although innovations in manufacturing were certainly not unknown before 1840, modern industrial methods were first introduced on a significant scale in the fifties, a decade in which the value added by manufacturing also registered a very high rate of growth. During this period the rate of population growth was also very high as was the rate of increase in rail mileage. It was in the postwar decades of the seventies and eighties, however, that the most rapid growth of manufactures occurred (Wright, *Economic History,* p. 582) and in the second of these decades that the amount of capital employed per worker increased by half—a rate of growth surpassed only in the period 1910–1920. In this postwar period, the rate of growth in population continued a decline begun in the 1860's (although, of course, the population continued to grow absolutely and to contribute an annual increment to the nation's demand for the output of industry). At the same time, the spread of the rail net was phenomenal; mileage operated in 1890 was triple that in 1870. (*Historical Statistics,* p. 200.)

Of equal, if not greater importance was the change in the economic function of the railroads which did not begin to take place until the 1850's. Although the growth in railroad mileage was very great in the 1840's and 1850's, freight rates on canals and other

Thus innovations in manufacturing, stimulated in this country by a scarcity of labor,[21] were made feasible by innovations in transportation which contributed importantly to the creation of the modern mass market. (The railroads also made a more direct contribution to the market for the output of heavy industry as one of the largest and most dramatically growing consumers of some of its products—steel rails in particular.)

Innovation in transportation, however, could not ensure that markets would be widened, although it was a necessary historical condition of such occurrences. The fact that a product could now be sold throughout a wider geographic expanse did not necessarily mean that it actually would be sold throughout the area involved. Obviously it was necessary that the product in question be considered by the larger body of consumers to whom it was now accessible as a substitute for certain commodities which they had been purchasing before the newcomer's arrival, so that demand for the goods which had hitherto been produced under conditions of local monopoly now became more elastic. Standardized methods of production required standardized habits of consumption, or, as Schumpeter so well expressed it, "mass production . . . unavoidably means also production for the masses."[22]

American scholars have been inclined to take mass consumption for granted; yet it was almost peculiarly an American phenomenon. It has been observed that the area of Britain was large enough to support more efficient methods of production than were actually employed, but that British consumers, by clinging unreconstructedly to individualistic habits of consumption, prevented markets from becoming truly nationalized.[23] We shall return to this point in Chapter 12 when we attempt to draw certain comparisons between British and American trade unions.

---

waterways were lower than on the railroads, with the result that the latter served primarily as feeders to the waterways until the middle of the century. According to Wright, "It was not until the 1850's that anything like a real railroad system linked the trans-Appalachian region with the Atlantic coast states" (p. 478). Although some drop in rail rates occurred during the 1850's, "the most rapid drop in freight rates in the country's history took place between 1870–1885." This fall in freight rates, caused by intense competition among different lines and by the widespread introduction of improved techniques and materials (notably the standard-gauge track and the steel rail) in the seventies and eighties, enabled the railroads to supplant the waterways as freight carriers. (See Wright, pp. 287, 312, 478–9, 480–1, 487, 492.) Thus it was that the development of the railroad net and of manufacturing industry kept step with each other; both developed appreciably in the fifties, but did not really hit their stride until the postwar period.

21. Abroad, and especially in England, the scarcer factor and therefore irritant in the process of economic change, had been natural resources. See Louis C. Hunter, "Heavy Industries before 1860," in Williamson, *Growth of the American Economy,* p. 213; and Schumpeter, *Business Cycles,* vol. I, p. 85 (n).

22. Joseph A. Schumpeter, *Capitalism, Socialism, and Democracy* (New York: Harper, 2nd edition, 1947), p. 67.

23. In addition, Britain's production for export markets frequently precluded standardization; it was more like "custom" work. (See *The Economist,* January 3, 1953.)

An interesting attempt has recently been made to account for this international difference in consumer custom. A delegation of Danish trade unionists, upon completion of a tour of study in the United States, expressed the opinion that

The fact that American industry at an early stage had to pay a higher price for manpower made the American market different from that of Europe. The middle classes in Europe have always preferred individualized articles. It was not until after the First World War that the income of European workers became such as to have any decisive bearing on the demand for goods other than the barest necessities. In America, on the other hand, there was from the very beginning a much larger potential market among people who were prepared to buy mass-produced articles.[24]

Thus, according to this view, the scarcity of labor in this country created an effective demand by the lower income groups whose amenability to the purchase of standard products made national markets feasible.

These developments were paralleled by changes in the organization of economic activity. Nowhere, perhaps, did Adam Smith's observations on the relationship existing between specialization and the division of labor on the one hand, and the extent of the market on the other, receive more emphatic confirmation than in the United States in the nineteenth century. The growth of the railroad system made it possible for technological innovations to be adopted in agriculture in response to high labor costs, as well as in manufacturing, with the result that the farmer's conversion into a capitalist with high fixed charges (a capitalist, that is, in the literal sense of the word) accelerated the trend to agricultural specialization. The farmer received cash for his crop and, in turn, required cash to obtain many articles of consumption which he formerly had made for his own use. This decline in rural self-sufficiency, made possible by the extension of the market, in its turn further extended that market. Mechanized agriculture thus stimulated the mechanization of industry in the latter half of the century.[25]

Reduction in costs of transport and sufficiently acquiescent habits of consumption, by making profitable the adoption of modern methods of production, brought about the demise not only of rural household industry, but also of the putting-out system. Under the latter regime, the employing function

24. "America Is Different: A Report by Danish Federation of Labor Delegation on a Study Tour in the United States" (MS, 1949.) Bryce, in *The American Commonwealth* (New York: Macmillan, 1907) attributed what he termed "the uniformity of American life" in part to "the equality of material conditions, still more general than in Europe." He also cited the fact that nearly everyone was employed in agriculture, trade, or handicraft, "the diffusion of education," "the extraordinary mobility of the population," and "above all . . . the newness of the country, and the fact that four-fifths of it have been made all at a stroke, and therefore all of a piece. . . ." (v. II, p. 825).

25. Wright, *Economic History,* pp. 294, 501, and 503.

was typically performed by a merchant-capitalist who was more of a merchant than a capitalist; for work was performed in the homes of the workers, the latter owned the necessary tools and equipment, and they were often paid at least partly in produce. As markets widened and innovations were introduced, the modern industrial categories of employer and employee became more sharply differentiated.[26]

The disintegration of local monopolies, which had constituted the economic underpinning of the older institutions, was not followed by the emergence of a stable environment in which the forces of competition were given complete freedom. The agencies of economic change generated such momentum that the same forces which broke up the old monopolies gave rise to new ones—although it is possible that the "degree of monopoly" prevailing throughout the economy as a whole was permanently reduced in the process. Widening of market areas indeed made for greater competition, but it will be recalled that such widening also permitted the employment of capital-using innovations. With the increase in prospective profit created by the possibility of innovation in any given field, new firms followed hard on the heels of the pioneers,[27] or many existing firms innovated simultaneously. In many industries, excess capacity seems to have developed in the sense that, under existing conditions of demand, prices prevailed below a level at which all the firms could cover their total costs. Reduction in capacity was required, but reduction in capacity could take place only through a reduction in the number of firms. In the ensuing struggle for dominance (or survival), competition often took the form of spectacular price cutting. This was made possible by the capital-using nature of most innovations, which increased the proportion of fixed costs to total costs in the firms which had installed them. Since overhead need not be covered in the short run, the innovating firms had their technologically conservative competitors at a serious disadvantage.[28] In some instances, price cutting was deliberately embarked upon as a punitive measure; in other cases, the same effect was achieved by those businessmen

26. See Commons, *History of Labour,* vol. I, *passim,* but especially pp. 1–11, 56–58, 63–64, 73, 81, 91, 99–103, 106–107, 217, 278, 338–339. Commons assigned priority to the extension of markets as a causal agent: "Even the wonderful progress in the control of natural resources . . . appears as but an after effect proceeding from this extension of markets" (p. 6). Elsewhere in the same volume, Saposs wrote that, since many of the new processes and equipment installed here had originated abroad, "industrial evolution in colonial times was not the evolution of tools and processes, but the evolution of markets fitted to utilize the tools and processes already evolved." A somewhat different interpretation of the evolution of economic classes is given by L. M. Hacker, *Triumph of American Capitalism,* especially chapters 19 and 20.

27. See Lange, "Innovations," *Review of Economic Statistics,* p. 191: "the increase in the discounted value of the effective profit attracts new firms into the industry."

28. For examples of competition between "new" and "old" firms, see Arthur R. Burns, *The Decline of Competition* (New York: McGraw-Hill, 1936), pp. 33–34.

who assumed—either implicitly or explicitly but, in any event, mistakenly—
that their competitors would not react to their price cutting.[29] But the passage
of time and the ultimate necessity of covering overhead brought sophistication. Firms which could not beat their competitors decided to join them;
hence Mr. Dooley's definition of a trust as "somethin' for an honest, ploddin',
uncombined manufacturer to sell out to." Elimination of excess capacity by
merger being far more salubrious to survivor and vanquished alike than trial
by combat, the "trust movement" got under way following the end of the
depression of 1873–1879. It stalled through the depression years of 1893–1897
(following unfavorable judicial decisions and mounting antitrust sentiment
which had culminated in the passage of the Sherman Act of 1890) and resumed at its most rapid pace during the years 1897–1903.[30] As a result of all
this war and peace, a new institution arose, the large business unit with control over more than one industrial plant.[31]

An alternative explanation emphasizes "the development of the modern
corporation and the modern capital market" as a causal agent in the merger
movement of the late nineteenth century and denies the importance of economies of scale made possible by the adoption of modern industrial techniques.
The merit claimed for this approach is that it is compatible with the observed
fact that the merged firm's share of the market tended to decrease over time.[32]

The new economic groups which arose helped to create a political environment which favored the development of the forces to which they owed their
existence. With the successful conduct of the Civil War by the North, the
balance of political power swung away from the party dominated by Southern agrarian interests, and "All that two generations of Federalists and Whigs
had tried to get was won within four short years, and more besides."[33] Free
land was provided for settlers; railway construction was subsidized by grants
of public credit and land; tariffs, frankly protectionist in purpose, were raised

29. Edward H. Chamberlin, *The Theory of Monopolistic Competition* (Cambridge:
Harvard University Press, fifth edition, 1936), pp. 90–94.

30. Henry R. Seager and Charles A. Gulick, Jr., *Trust and Corporation Problems*
(New York: Harper and Brothers, 1929), pp. 51, 57–58, 60–62. Also Joe S. Bain, "Industrial Concentration and Government Anti-Trust Policy," in Williamson, *Growth of
the American Economy*, pp. 708–713.

31. The 318 companies listed by Moody as "important industrial trusts" acquired or
controlled 5288 plants. Not one of these companies controlled less than two plants. John
Moody, *The Truth About the Trusts* (New York: Moody, 1904), pp. 453–469. (For definition of "trust," see p. XIII.)

32. (See George J. Stigler, "Monopoly and Oligopoly by Merger," *Proceedings of the
American Economic Association,* 1949, pp. 23–34; also "Discussion" by Joe S. Bain, pp.
64–66.) We need not concern ourselves with the relative merits of these and other explanations of the merger movement, however, since we are concerned only with its by-
product, the multiple-plant firm.

33. Charles A. and Mary R. Beard, *The Rise of American Civilization* (New York:
Macmillan, revised edition, 1941), v. II, p. 105.

to unprecedently high rates; contract immigration was legalized for twenty years (the law of 1865 was repealed in 1885); a uniform currency was established, ending a multiplicity of bank notes convertible into one another at varying discounts; and, under cover of emancipation, the protection of "due process" was extended to the corporation, a business institution designed to attract the relatively large capital sums required for the formation of the new, large-scale enterprises. Without detracting from this impressive political achievement and with due acknowledgment of the role of the government's spending activities and of its inflationary fiscal policies during the war period, however, it must be noted that the economic developments roughly sketched in the preceding pages had been well under way while southern interests were still in a position to frustrate the ambitious successors of Webster and Clay.[34] The South, fearful of the growth of free soil political power, opposed federal subsidy of homesteaders and encouragement of immigration; but settlement and immigration proceeded unchecked. The South for the same reason opposed (after its disillusionment in 1850) government encouragement of railroad building; that activity, notwithstanding, accelerated greatly in the 1840's and 1850's. The South, an agrarian debtor region, prevented the enactment of high, protective tariffs; yet manufacturing (measured by net value added) took great forward strides in the 1850's. For the same reasons the South opposed "sound money"; yet foreign investment and the rise in the price level following the discovery of gold in California enabled the amount of capital per wage earner to increase during the 1850's at a rate surpassed in the nineteenth century only during the decade of the eighties.[35] All this does not at all deny the irrepressibility of the conflict or the importance of the Union victory to the continuation of economic development along lines which had already been established; it is intended only to demonstrate that the victory gained, although vital, was economically a defensive one. The rise to political power of the new economic groups ensured the continuing development of the underlying forces described in the preceding pages; it might also have accelerated that development to some extent.[36]

34. See Beard, *Rise of American Civilization*, pp. 166 and 105; Hacker, *Triumph of American Capitalism*, pp. 252, 256, 258, 323–324; Rezneck, "Mass Production," p. 501.
35. See Wilford I. King, *Raising the Workingmen's Standard of Living* (New York, 1945).
36. For confirmation of this view, see Wright, *Economic History*, pp. 426 and 428. G. D. H. Cole, in his *Introduction to Economic History, 1750–1950* (London: Macmillan, 1952), pp. 80–82, also 54–55, concludes that the resumption of protectionism during the 1860's probably accelerated the development of manufacturing and retarded the growth of agriculture, but he emphasizes that the American market was large enough to enable domestic industries to exploit economies of scale. Thus tariffs did not perform in this country the role of sheltering industries whose domestic markets were too small to enable them to achieve a degree of efficiency sufficient for survival in a free international market.

THE ORGANIZATION OF LABOR

The forces which conditioned the development of the first national unions emerged, in part, in response to the historical scarcity of labor on this continent, and they affected both the supply of and the demand for this scarce resource. The growth in population, to which immigration made a great contribution, increased the supply of labor, but not sufficiently to eliminate its relative scarcity. This was due partially to the fact that population growth increased demand as well as supply, and partly because of the increase in supply of the other two members of the economic triad, land and capital. The persistence of high wages in America also inspired the adoption of new industrial techniques which aimed at reducing the demand for labor and utilizing capital in its place. But these innovations in manufacturing, as we have remarked, were made practicable only when an innovation in transportation, the railroad, made it possible to extend market boundaries; they were for the most part "output-increasing," and such "saving" of labor as they effected was relative rather than absolute. Under such circumstances, the following developments over the period 1850–1900 (inclusive), remarkable as some of them may be, are understandable:

(1) America retained her wage supremacy.[37]
(2) Labor's relative share in the national income increased,[38] but this gain must be ascribed largely to the increasing proportion of the gainfully occupied in nonagricultural occupations,[39] as well as to the fact that the increase in supply of capital was more rapid than the increase in the labor force.
(3) National income itself increased prodigiously: by the end of the century it was eight times as high as it had been in 1850.[40]
(4) Although the population had more than tripled during the period, income per person increased about two and a half times.[41]
(5) Real per capita income increased virtually as much as did the unadjusted magnitude, since the cost-of-living index reversed a strong upward movement after 1865 and stood only a few points higher in 1900 than it had in 1850.

37. Wright, *Economic History*, p. 589.

38. From 36.4 per cent in 1850 the share of wages and salaries in the national income or aggregate payments per year increased to 48.7 per cent in 1900. Simon Kuznets, "Uses of National Income in Peace and War," *National Bureau of Economic Research Occasional Paper 6*, (March 1942), p. 38.

39. *Historical Statistics*, p. 63. Also Alvin H. Hansen, "Industrial Classes in the United States in 1920," *Journal of the American Statistical Association* (1922), vol. XVIII, pp. 503–506.

40. Bureau of Foreign and Domestic Commerce, *National Income, Supplement to Survey of Current Business*, July 1947, p. 19.

41. Computed by Professor Sumner H. Slichter, Harvard University, from data presented by Wilford I. King, *Wealth and Income of the People of the United States* (New York: Macmillan, 1917), adjusted to include annual value of rents from dwelling houses.

(6) Average hourly money earnings rose by nearly four-fifths, according to Hansen's estimate; real earnings, by more than three-fifths.[42]

(7) Real annual earnings, however, may not have risen as rapidly as did real hourly earnings; for the rise in the latter was offset in part by losses in wage income due to unemployment. The coexistence of rising real wage rates and declining employment frequently characterized periods of depression; in such situations, the increase in real wage rates resulted from prices falling more rapidly than money wage rates. This situation prevailed during the major depression of 1893–1897, which was characterized by a severe decline in employment, virtually stationary money wages, and a rise in real hourly wages. Indeed, money wage rates held constant and real wage rates rose in the downswing of 1882–1885, and the same phenomena characterized most of the other downswings in the latter half of the past century.

On the other hand, certain phenomena occurred during the period under discussion which would lead one to believe that the upward movement in real wage rates did not seriously exaggerate the increase in real wage incomes. In the first place, as Hansen observed, real wage rates fell in the long depression of 1873–1879 and it has been suggested elsewhere that the decline in employment during this period was very slight.[43] Thus the record of real wage rates during the depression of 1873–1879 does not imply any improvement in labor's real income. Furthermore, in the preceding period of prosperity (1867–1873), real wage rates rose, due primarily to a fall in the cost of living so that, in this period the rise in real wage rates was not offset by a decline in employment. Moreover, the wage lag seemed to manifest curious asymmetry in the post-Civil-War period. While, as we noted above, real wage rates tended to rise in most of the downswings, they did not fall during most of the upswings. In such upswings real wage rates held firm or actually increased; this was true especially in the strong prosperity of 1867–1873 when the cost of living declined drastically.

42. Alvin H. Hansen, "Factors Affecting the Trend of Real Wages," *American Economic Review* (March 1925), v. XV, no. 1, pp. 27–42.

43. Rendigs Fels, "The Long-Wave Depression, 1873–97," *Review of Economics and Statistics,* vol. XXXI, February 1949, no. 1, pp. 69–73; see also Fels, "American Business Cycles, 1865–79," *American Economic Review,* June 1951, v. XLI, no. 3, pp. 325–349, wherein the writer argues that the depression of 1873–1879, "Though exceedingly severe in monetary terms . . . was mild in real terms, partly as a result of price flexibility" (pp. 348–349). By "real terms" Fels means "in terms of output," and he cites Frickey's indices of production in support of his thesis. The inference that employment displayed a high and positive correlation with output—and that, therefore, unemployment was not too severe—is plausible. Since, however, it is generally held that labor's efficiency rises during the downswing as the more inefficient workers are laid off first, it is possible that the decline in employment was more severe than the decline in output. Nevertheless, the fact that real wage rates fell during this depression can be offered as additional evidence in support of Fels' view that the depression of 1873–1879 "was mild in real terms, partly as a result of price flexibility."

During the entire half-century, the greatest increases in real wage rates were associated primarily with declines in the cost of living rather than with increases in money wage rates. Furthermore, the post-Civil-War period in which virtually the entire increase in real wage rates occurred was characterized by chronic depression so that it is possible that gains in income from rising real wage rates were offset by losses in income from unemployment. However, the facts set forth above would suggest that, with the exception of the depression beginning in 1893, the typical depression of this period was not characterized by severe unemployment, with the result that data on real annual earnings—if such could be obtained— would probably reveal an increase comparable to the rise in real wage rates.

One further question remains in this assessment of the economic record of the period. To what extent was labor's progress in this period due to its own efforts in forming trade unions to improve its bargaining position? The answer is suggested by such data as are available on union membership (see Table 3).

TABLE 3

DEGREE OF UNION ORGANIZATION, 1870–1900

Period	Trade Union Membership (thousands)	Per Cent of Membership to Population, Age 15–64	Per Cent of Membership to Industrial Wage Earners
1870–1872	300.0	1.3	9.1
1880	200.0	.7	3.8
1890	372.0	1.0	5.0
1900	868.5	1.9	8.4

Sources: Data for 1870–72 and 1880, from Commons, *History of Labour*, II, 47 and 314; for 1890, from Emmanuel Stein and Jerome Davis, *Labor Problems in America* (New York: Farrar and Rinehart, 1940), p. 253; and for 1900, from Leo Wolman, *Ebb and Flow in Trade Unionism* (New York: National Bureau of Economic Research, 1936), p. 16.

The failure of the trade unions and especially the national unions to make any appreciable inroads into the working population is negative evidence in support of the view that labor owed its progress to the operation of the economic forces described in the preceding section rather than to the activity of its own institutions.

While there is some indication that union membership rose during the fifties (until 1857), the depressed postwar periods were not very conducive to a growth in unionism relative to the increase in the working population. In the 1890's, however, the absolute growth in membership was very great, and in the last two decades of the century, membership appears to have increased more rapidly than the work force. Absolute growth in membership also seems to have been great in 1864 and 1865 and during the upswing from 1870 to 1873, although data are not available.[44]

More positive evidence concerning the role played by the unions in the achievement of labor's gains consists in the fact that virtually the entire increase in real wages occurred during the period 1865–1900, when prices were falling sharply, while money wages rose very slightly over the entire period. These movements of money prices and wages are not typical of the longer trends. Over the period 1850–1940, prices moved slightly upward while money wages increased sharply. Real wages rose primarily because money wages rose more rapidly than prices from 1850 to 1940; real wages rose primarily because prices fell from 1865 to 1900. Whether unions were in fact responsible for the rise in real wage rates which occurred when money wages were rising sharply is debatable, but it is reasonable to conclude that they could claim little credit for the over-all increase in real wages which occurred in a period when money wages were rising much less rapidly and prices were falling.

However, while trade unionism was probably not responsible for the increase in the general average of real wages for the entire economy, it is possible that workers in unionized industries might have fared better than their unorganized colleagues. Indeed, Douglas concluded that "during the nineties and the early years of the present century the unionists were able to secure for themselves appreciably higher wages and shorter hours than the mass of wage earners."[45]

How can this conclusion be squared with the fact that even unionized trades, in many instances, were not thoroughly organized during the period under discussion? Wolman's data reveal that only five industries or occupations had as many as one-third of their employees organized in 1910.[46] Some of the most prominent of the early national unions reported disappointing progress along organizational lines. In 1900, for example, only one-quarter of the Printers' jurisdiction was organized. In 1898, the Bricklayers' secretary mentioned that only one bricklayer in seven was a union man. And when the Steel Workers were at their peak strength in 1891, less than one-fourth of the country's steel workers were unionized.

The existence of sizeable pockets of nonunionism in essentially local market jurisdictions did not necessarily prevent the more strongly organized jurisdictions (which, in the case of the printers, for example, were found in the larger cities)[47] from causing wages to rise more rapidly than they would

44. Commons, *History of Labour,* v. I, pp. 608–616; v. II, pp. 45–47.

45. Paul H. Douglas, *Real Wages in the United States* (Boston: Houghton Mifflin, 1930), p. 562.

46. Leo Wolman, *The Growth of American Trade Unions, 1880–1923* (New York: National Bureau of Economic Research, 1924), pp. 148–154.

47. George E. Barnett, *The Printers* (Cambridge, Mass.: American Economic Association, 1909), third series, v. X, no. 3, pp. 266–267.

have risen in the absense of unions. But if employers in strongly organized centers had to compete with nonunion employers elsewhere, how effectively could the strong union centers, with their flanks thus exposed, go about the business of pushing up wages and costs? Or, for that matter, how could unionized firms compete with nonunion establishments in their own localities?

The evidence presented by Slichter, although in part referring to periods later than the period with which this study is primarily concerned, suggests strongly that unionists succeeded in imposing upon their employers labor costs in excess of those prevailing in nonunion establishments.[48] In the period under discussion in this study the existence of certain working rules indicated, as we shall point out in Chapter 17, that early unions succeeded in raising wages above competitive levels. For more direct evidence of the occasional ability of unions to raise wages in the late nineteenth century consider the following excerpt from an article in the May 1893 issue of the Iron Molders' *Journal*:

The machinery and bench molders, of Chicago, Ill., have succeeded in establishing a minimum rate of wages in nearly all of the shops in the city and vicinity. The employers, however, instead of hiring all the members who were involved in the strike, claimed that they had not work for all, in consequence of which, there are a large number of our members idle.[49]

If we assume that wages were higher in union firms than they were in nonunion firms in the 1890's, it is not difficult to reconcile Douglas' finding that wages rose more rapidly in the union trades during that period with the fact that even many unionized trades were not thoroughly organized. Since the proportion of workers employed in union firms to the total work force in the industry increased more rapidly in the more unionized trades (especially building, printing, transportation, and mining), one would expect the average level of wages in those trades to have risen more rapidly than average wage levels in unorganized industries. Furthermore, the period under discussion was not characterized by "a strong sellers' market" for labor in which, according to Slichter, nonunion employers have tended to forestall unionism by matching, anticipating, or exceeding wage increases won by unions.[50] Hence a differential impact of unionism upon the wage structure could be observed.

But whatever differential advantages unions might have secured for their members during the entire period under review, it is nevertheless reasonable

48. Sumner H. Slichter, *Union Policies and Industrial Management* (Washington, D. C.: Brookings, 1941), ch. XII.

49. *Journal,* May 31, 1893, p. 3.

50. S. H. Slichter, "Do the Wage-Fixing Arrangements in the American Labor Market Have an Inflationary Bias?" *Proceedings American Economic Association,* December 29, 1953.

to assert that Douglas' conclusion that "the increase in *real* wages during the period studied (1890–1926) has been caused primarily by the increase in productivity rather than by unionization"[51] holds also for the three decades prior to 1900. The magnitude of earlier increases in productivity is suggested by data on capital-worker ratios which were set forth above; the latter, however, do not make full allowance for technological innovation. Woytinsky estimates that output per worker did not increase at all in the decade 1859–1869, but that it rose by 8 per cent in 1869–1879, by 17 per cent in 1879–1889, by 21 per cent in 1889–1899, and by 44 per cent in 1899–1909.[52]

51. Douglas, *Real Wages,* p. 564.
52. W. S. Woytinsky *et al., Employment and Wages in the United States* (New York: Twentieth Century Fund, 1953), p. 29, table 8.

CHAPTER TWO

THE ENVIRONMENT OF THE NATIONAL UNION

ALTHOUGH the influence of unionism upon labor's real income was of secondary importance in comparison with the influence exerted by certain non-institutional forces, the impact of the latter upon the development of the trade unions was nevertheless pronounced. From the brief account in the preceding chapter of certain outstanding economic developments in the latter half of the nineteenth century, we can single out the following phenomena in order to examine the nature of their impact upon the trade union movement: (1) immigration, (2) the extension of markets, (3) innovation, (4) the big firm, and (5) business conditions.

THE IMPACT OF IMMIGRATION

The increase in the volume of immigration which occurred after the Civil War contributed to the growth of an industrial work force in which, as we have seen, attempts to achieve effective trade union organization had met with relatively little success. Apart from its volume, however, the character of the postwar immigration created grave problems for the unions. During the eighties, the "new" immigration (from the southern and eastern countries of Europe) gained ascendancy over the "old" (from the northern and western regions and the British Isles).[1] Although predominantly of rural origin, these "new" immigrants did not take up farming in the new world to any great extent, as did the prewar foreign born (farmland was becoming increasingly expensive); they settled, for the most part, in the large cities and offered their services in the labor market. In view of their agrarian background, these services were preponderantly unskilled.[2] Thus they did not compete immedi-

1. See Paul H. Douglas, Curtice N. Hitchcock, and Willard E. Atkins, *The Worker in Modern Economic Society* (Chicago: University of Chicago, 1923), p. 190. Also, *Historical Statistics of the United States, 1789–1945* (Washington, D. C.: U. S. Department of Commerce, 1949), pp. 32–34.

2. Jeremiah W. Jenks and W. Jett Lauck, *The Immigration Problem* (New York: Funk and Wagnalls, 1912), pp. 182–183. Also John R. Commons, *Races and Immigrants in America* (New York: Macmillan, 1907), p. 123; and Douglas et al., *The Worker*, p. 192.

ately and directly with skilled union craftsmen; but such competition as they did offer was far more injurious than the obvious variety, for it threatened to undermine the most important element in the bargaining power of the craft union—the skill of its membership.

The new immigrants menaced craft skill from three directions. First, they furnished the greater part of the inexpensive bull labor employed in the construction of the railroads and canals which, by dissolving local market monopolies, stimulated technological innovation.[3] Second, by contributing heavily to the growth of the population, especially of the urban population, they helped to form the modern mass market, which likewise inspired the adoption of the newer methods of production. And finally, the existence of a large and growing supply of cheap unskilled labor contributed directly to specialization of occupations and the development of specialized machinery, both of which often shattered time-honored crafts into component fragments which could be handled by specialists working with or without new machines.

The effect of Jewish immigration upon the organization of the clothing industry is an excellent example of specialization. According to V. S. Clark,

The organization of this industry was in a state of almost continuous change, both on account of technical exigencies and the compulsion of manufacturing economies and because of the peculiar labor conditions affecting it. Between 1870 and 1890 this manufacture, at least in the larger centers, fell into the hands of immigrants, most of whom were Jews. The influx of these highly individualistic workers probably tended to preserve the dispersed and quasi-household system of production that had survived from an earlier period. Contractors and the sweat shops supplanted the family as outworker units. Indeed the small shop contractor became the manufacturer proper, while the nominal manufacturer confined himself increasingly to the purely commercial functions of buying raw materials and marketing finished goods. Simultaneously, processes of manufacture were so specialized as to dispense largely with highly skilled workers. Even in what would appear comparatively simple operations, such as the sewing of different seams in a coat, there was a subdivision of labor, the more experienced machine hands sewing the more difficult seams and their helpers the less difficult. Consequently this manufacture tended to concentrate at points of cheapest labor. This helps to explain why so large a share of the clothing manufactured in America is made at New York City, the debarkation point for most of our unskilled immigrants. It was largely for the same reason that the manufacture of certain grades of clothing became established on the Pacific coast. Practically no white labor was employed in the California factories, which were devoted largely to making shirts, cotton underwear, overalls and similar goods. Indeed, it was claimed in 1881 that duck and denim suits made in San Francisco by Chinese workmen could be sold at a profit in the eastern states.[4]

3. Commons, *Races and Immigrants,* p. 130. Jenks and Lauck, *Immigration Problem,* pp. 167–168.
4. Victor S. Clark, *History of Manufactures in the United States* (Washington, D. C.: The Carnegie Institution of Washington, 1916 and 1928), vol. II, pp. 446–448.

In coal mining, the operation of "shot-firing" emerged as a specialty, since it proved unsafe to allow inexperienced immigrant miners to do their own blasting, as miners always had done in the past.[5] In machinery also, and even in the building trades, specialists emerged, performing operations the relative simplicity of which obviated long periods of learning and apprenticeship.[6] Thus the new immigration presented American employers with a three-pronged fork which the latter forthwith pitched into the seat of trade union complacency.

Immigrant competition with native workers was intensified by the lower standards of living to which the newcomers had been accustomed. It would be more accurate, perhaps, to describe this competition as a conflict between customary and competitive standards of living, for the American workman conformed closely even in the nineteenth century to the Marshallian model of a consumer—a man in whom the satisfaction of any particular desire engenders not contentment but another unsatisfied want. Furthermore this "conflict of standards of living" (as one writer expressed it) was aggravated by the fact that a high proportion of the postwar immigrants were either single or unaccompanied by their families.[7] John R. Commons hailed the low ratio of child, aged, and female immigrants as evidence of "a population of working ages unhampered by unproductive mouths to be fed,"[8] but the young, unattached newcomers could get by on less than their coworkers and accordingly were able to offer their services for lower wages.[9]

Nowhere did the immigrant compete more effectively than in the anthracite coal industry. His modest wants, the ease with which he could be employed as a mine laborer (encouraged, at first, by the English-speaking miner who, under the contract system, paid his own helpers), and the ease with which the laborer could be trained to become a miner all contributed to a migration of the English-speaking miners from the Pennsylvania coal fields[10] and to the organizing difficulties of the struggling miners' unions which were already sorely beset from other quarters.

In addition to the threat which the unskilled immigrant represented to unions whose solid core of bargaining power consisted in craft skills, the immigrant at first seemed unpromising as union material. He was isolated from the English-speaking community by barriers of language and custom and for the most part worked and lived exclusively with fellow immigrants

5. Jenks and Lauck, *Immigration Problem*, pp. 187–188.

6. Commons, *Races and Immigrants*, pp. 124–126.

7. Douglas, *The Worker*, p. 234.

8. Commons, *Races and Immigrants*, pp. 120–122.

9. For a detailed and graphic account of this "conflict of standards of living" in the coal industry, see Frank J. Warne, *The Slav Invasion and the Mine Workers* (Philadelphia: J. B. Lippincott, 1904), pp. 65–84; also pp. 52–65.

10. See also Rev. William J. Walsh, *The United Mine Workers of America as an Economic and Social Force in the Anthracite Territory* (Washington, D. C.: National Capital Press, 1931), pp. 90–91.

from the same homeland.[11] Partly because it was convenient to do so, but also because they were aware of the obstacles which foreign language groups placed in the path of unionism, employers often encouraged and even solicited the importation of foreign labor.

But against these debit entries in the ledger of unionism one great contribution must be credited to the new immigration. From its ranks rose many of the ablest of the leaders in the trade union movement. The dynamic developments in the last half of the nineteenth century produced, as we have seen, great changes in the nature and structure of the economic classes in the country. Not only did the relative importance of farmers and farm laborers decline and that of industrial wage earners increase during this period, but the proportion of business proprietors and officials in the industrial population began to increase.[12] And while a recent study suggests that the captains of industry were not recruited from the ranks, as historians have led us to believe,[13] the line between employer and employee was not so sharply drawn in the nineteenth century as it is today; and the promise of opportunity, held out by the mushrooming of great fortunes, was sufficient to distract the attention of many of the more able or ambitious native workers from union affairs.

The preoccupation of union lawmakers of the period with the status of men who had crossed the line from employed to employer (a practice known among the Bricklayers as "bossing") is evidence of this unsettled temper; and the tendency of union officials to go into politics reveals the existence of another escape-hatch for labor's "elite." But these avenues of opportunity were largely barred to the talented foreign born, who were obliged to remain in the wage-earning ranks. For such men the trade union performed the same function as the church did in the middle ages for the outstanding leader in a far more rigidly stratified society: it provided an outlet for their ability. Moreover, many of these immigrant workers bore with them from their native lands a heritage of "class consciousness" and a tradition of devotion to the trade union movement, which was largely lacking in the New World; so that, even when language proved no barrier to economic mobility, as in the case of the English-speaking immigrants, they preferred to devote their energy and ability to "the movement." In discussing immigration in this light, Professor Slichter writes:

11. V. S. Clark described a large textile mill in Lawrence, Massachusetts, where more than thirty nationalities were represented in a work force of seven thousand. "These nationalities did not as a rule work together in the same departments and operations." (Clark, *History of Manufactures,* pp. 548–549.)

12. See Alvin H. Hansen, "Factors Affecting the Trend of Real Wages," *American Economic Review,* (March 1925) vol. XV., no. 1, pp. 27–42.

13. William Miller, "American Historians and the Business Elite," *The Journal of Economic History,* (November 1949) vol. IX, no. 2, pp. 184–208; "The Recruitment of American Business Elite," *Quarterly Journal of Economics* (May 1950), no. 2, pp. 242–253.

Immigration, however, has helped to supply the need. It has brought men of great ability who have been prevented by difficulties of language or by philosophies acquired in Europe, from holding managerial or political positions.[14]

THE IMPACT OF THE EXTENSION OF MARKETS

It is the thesis of John R. Commons that the division of labor, stimulated primarily by the continuous extension of the market in this country, sharpened the distinction between employer and employed and generated the modern economic classes. With functional specialization there developed distinctive group interests and, particularly on the part of the employed, organization of individuals to further those common interests. Thus the trade union is an institutional reflex of the expanding market. As an extension of this line of reasoning, it was urged that the national trade union is the child of the national market;[15] for once goods made elsewhere could be sold in the same market which provided an outlet for the product of his own labor, it was no longer possible for the local union member to ignore the conditions under which his fellow craftsmen in other bailiwicks marketed their services. An early historian of the Molders' Union illustrated the situation created by the interpenetration of markets:

A few of the locals had been able during the depression of 1861 to prevent any reduction in their wages; but on account of the disorganized condition of the trade in other cities, even these few were unable to enforce their demands for wages commensurate with the rising cost of living.[16]

The national union, as an organization created to cope with the growing interpenetration of different producing areas, was confronted with two formidable problems. The first was the problem of coördinating the actions and policies of the various local unions in different localities and regions of the country. One president of the Molders professed himself "strong in the belief that the large centers could not long maintain their advantages unless the smaller and lower paid localities were brought up more nearly to an equality with them," and advised "the distribution of the support of the organization as equitable as circumstances would permit in order, as it were, to preserve the balance and remove those inequalities in labor cost which are an important factor in the intense competition of the present day."[17]

The second problem concerned the organization of nonunionists to a degree sufficient to assure the national union of effective control of the work

14. Sumner H. Slichter, "The Worker in Modern Economic Society," *Journal of Political Economy* (1926), vol. XXXIV, pp. 119–120.

15. John B. Andrews, "Nationalization," in John R. Commons and Associates, *History of Labour in the United States* (New York: Macmillan, 1936), vol. II, ch. III.

16. H. E. Hoagland, "The Rise of the Iron Molders' International Union," *American Economic Review*, June 1913, p. 310.

17. *Proceedings of the International Molders' Union of North America*, 1902, p. 602.

force under its jurisdiction. So long as markets remained isolated, the profound indifference of the union member to the state of organization of the trade outside his local habitation was not too serious, but the "age of the railroad" required increased sophistication along these lines.

> Those of our members [complained the president of the Glass Bottle Blowers on one occasion] who are far removed from non-union localities cannot realize the magnitude of this evil as can those who are brought into personal contact with it, yet there is not a man but daily feels its influence.[18]

These two problems of national control and of organization were presented more uncompromisingly, perhaps, to the coal miners than to any other group. Experience kept an exceptionally hard school for the miners, with the result that the relationship between changes in the economic environment of the nature described in this section and developments in the organization of these workers was extremely close. For this reason, we shall conclude this section on the influence of the extension of markets on trade unionism with a digression on the developments preceding the formation of the United Mine Workers.

The Coal Miners—An Example

In the coal industry the development of the railway net not only drew geographically separate producing areas into the same competitive market, but also resulted directly in the emergence of new sources of supply. Competition between producing districts for markets along the Atlantic seaboard and the lower Mississippi River developed before the Civil War,[19] but, since the bulk of the freight was still shipped by water, this competition remained regional rather than national in scope. The seaboard markets were supplied primarily by the coal fields of eastern West Virginia, Maryland, central Pennsylvania, and the Pennsylvania anthracite regions; the consuming areas in the Lake and Northwest states, by western Pennsylvania, West Virginia, Ohio, Indiana, and Illinois; and the South, by western Pennsylvania, eastern Ohio, and West Virginia. "That these different markets drew their coal supply from these particular fields rather than from any others was due to the natural conditions of river outlets and mountain barriers. This explains briefly how it was that coal fields, lying next to each other, separated perhaps by only a mountain ridge, had their markets thousands of miles apart, and also why coal fields widely separated sent their product to a common market."[20] But with the rapid development of the railroad after the war, the

---

18. *Proceedings of the Glass Bottle Blowers' Association,* 1897, p. 10.

19. Edward A. Wieck, *The American Miners' Association* (New York: Russell Sage Foundation, 1940), pp. 57–60.

20. Frank J. Warne, *The Coal Mine Workers* (New York: Longmans, Green, 1905), pp. 197–198.

natural barriers no longer provided producing areas and markets with economic insulation. Some fields in West Virginia and Pennsylvania now were able for the first time to invade the Lakes and the Northwest; they, in their turn, faced competition in their old eastern markets from Ohio and also Kentucky, Tennessee, and Alabama; and the southern markets, as before, could buy coal from both of these producing areas, as well as from western fields. "Thus the hitherto widely separated coal markets were being bound so closely together that the least rise or fall in the price of the commodity in any of the sectional markets had its effect, directly and indirectly, upon the price of coal in all the others."[21]

At the same time, the expanding railroad net drew into production coal fields whose location had previously made their operation uneconomical. One of the most important of the new districts in this period was the coal field in southern Illinois. This development contributed to an expansion of capacity in excess of production, which intensified the competitive forces liberated by the railroads as described above.[22]

The extension of markets—and the emergence in depression as well as prosperity—of new producing areas, together with the increased productivity and greater burden of overhead costs (which constituted the contribution of mechanization to the problems of the industry) resulted in severe price- and wage-competition among the different producing districts. This development gained vigor in the last two decades of the century, with the revival of railroad construction after 1879, and the severity of the competition made imperative the coördination of the activities of the miners' unions in the various producing districts. While John Siney's call to action,[23] which preceded the formation of the Miners' National Association in 1873, made no specific reference to the necessity of coping with competition among operators, the pinch of interlocal competition was felt soon thereafter. In 1882, the preamble to the Ohio Miners Amalgamated Association noted that

For some years many of the most thoughtful minds among the miners of the state watched the gradual but sure approach of demoralization in the mining interests of the State, and with deep regret witnessed the utter indifference manifested by the miners of one district for the well being of those of another. It became evident that some step should be taken to check the evils that were fast accruing from insane competition, the heavy foot of which always rests upon the wages of the producer. It was found that the lines of connection between the

21. Warne, *Coal Mine Workers*, p. 89.

22. F. G. Tryon, "The Effect of Competitive Conditions on Labor Relations in Coal Mining," *The Annals of the American Academy of Political and Social Science* (January 1924), vol. CXI, no. 200, pp. 82–95. See also, Wieck, *American Miners'Association*, p. 60; and Walton H. Hamilton and Helen R. Wright, *The Case of Bituminous Coal* (New York: Macmillan, 1925), pp. 57–61.

23. Reproduced in Chris Evans, *History of the United Mine Workers of America* (Indianapolis, 1918), vol. I, pp. 26–27.

different mining districts of the State . . . were bound to be recognized or the utter ruin of the mining interests of the State would result, and complete degradation and misery of the miners would follow.[24]

The following year delegates from Pennsylvania, Maryland, and Illinois attempted to establish an organization (the Amalgamated Association of Miners of the United States) that would "recognize that fundamental principle that an injury to one district, locality or State shall be the concern of all." The attempt was unsuccessful, but the moral was driven home shortly thereafter in the famous Hocking Valley (Ohio) strike, when the operators sought a wage reduction apparently to offset relatively high costs of transportation.[25] The competitive effects of increasing rail mileage were intensified, until a "National Federation of Miners' and Mine Laborers of the United States and Territories" was formed in 1885 solely in response to this economic pressure. The preamble to this union's constitution stated its purpose:

As miners and mine laborers our troubles are everywhere of a similar character. The inexorable law of supply and demand determine the point where our interests unite. The increased shipping facilities of the last few years have made all coal-producing districts competitors in the markets of this country. This has led to indiscriminate cutting of market prices and unnecessary reductions in our wages, which for some time have been far below a living rate. . . . Local, district and State organizations have done much toward ameliorating the condition of our craft in the past, but today neither district nor State unions can regulate the market to which their coal is shipped. We know this to our sorrow. . . . In a federation of all lodges and branches of miners' unions lies our only hope.[26]

The initial convention of the new federation invited "the mine operators of the United States and Canada" to a joint meeting "for purpose of adjusting market and mining prices . . ." After two meetings at which representation of the operators was not sufficient to permit action to be taken, a joint conference was held in 1886 at which wage rates were established for specified "basing points" in Pennsylvania, Ohio, Indiana, Illinois, and West Virginia.[27] This agreement, however, covered only the so-called "Central Competitive Territory" and not even throughout this area was the union able to obtain compliance with its terms. "In order to justify those operators who are paying the scale of prices, and the necessity of maintaining a uniform rate for all miners," the federation raised funds to support strikes against those operators who refused to recognize the union and "pay the price."[28]

24. Evans, *United Mine Workers,* p. 97.
25. This appears to be Evans' version of the issues involved, pp. 109, 117.
26. Evans, *United Mine Workers,* p. 139, also p. 145.
27. Arthur E. Suffern, *The Coal Miners' Struggle for Industrial Status* (New York: Macmillan, 1926), pp. 39–40.
28. Evans, *United Mine Workers,* v. I, pp. 187–188.

The problem was further complicated by the active hostility of National Trades Assembly No. 135 of the Knights of Labor, which did not hesitate to undercut the federation scale in their effort to undermine its rival. The latter was unsuccessful in its attempt to control completely all competitive areas, with the result that, in the February 1887 Joint Conference, the operators agreed to an increase of five cents per ton to take place in May and to a further increase of equal amount in November, only on the condition that "the above shall not take effect until those districts named in the scale shall have complied with the provisions of such scale or are idle by reason of failure to comply." When the May deadline came, the operators granted the first increase despite the union's lack of complete success. Their decision was unanimous, although the Illinois operators were reluctant to take this action because the mines in the Southern part of their state were organized by the Knights of Labor. We have already made note of the fact that this region was one of the most rapidly growing new districts in the country.

Despite further organizing strikes throughout the area and the dispatching by the federation of "missionaries" into southern Illinois, no substantial progress was made; and when the operators of Indiana, Ohio, and western Pennsylvania agreed to grant the second increase, the Illinois employers withdrew from the conference. Next to leave were the Indiana operators, after demanding a reduction in order to meet competition from Illinois.[29] Then Ohio and western Pennsylvania sought reductions. The miners yielded to their demands in separate district agreements and the industry-wide wage setting disintegrated.[30]

By this time it was apparent that unionism, to be effective in the coal industry, had to be national and that the existence of more than one organization competing actively for the same trade jurisdiction was as unsatisfactory as the completely autonomous existence of local or district unions had proved to be. After several unsuccessful attempts at amalgamation (including the establishment of the abortive National Progressive Union), the United Mine Workers of America, "composed of N.T.A. 135, K. of L., and the National Progressive Union," was formed in 1890.

It was not until after the depression of 1893–1897, however, that this new national union furnished any evidence of possessing greater longevity than its predecessors. Such evidence was finally provided by two developments: the reëstablishment of the interstate joint conference in the central competitive territory, and the successful prosecution of an organizing drive in the western and southern producing areas which entered into competition with the central territory.

Thus the experience of the coal miners furnishes impressive evidence of

29. Evans, pp. 222, 228–230, 281, 307, 324, 327, 431, 437. "Illinois has been loose handed, and Indiana has been tied up and wants to be loose, too."
30. Suffern, *The Coal Miners' Struggle*, pp. 49–50.

the influence of the extension of market areas upon the development of trade unionism. Once local (or regional) producing areas lost their monopoly positions, local (or district) unionism was inadequate. It was necessary that miners in all competing districts be brought under unitary control. To achieve this result, the miners' leaders had to perform two tasks. First, all local and regional unions had to submit to control by a central organization, the national union. Second, it was necessary that miners in all regions be organized into local unions so that they, too, could be brought under national control.

THE IMPACT OF INNOVATION

"England is the land of strikes and holidays. Between the two the British manufacturer has a hard time, and he often wonders why England's quondam supremacy is being usurped by Germany, where the laboring man works like a machine and by America, where machines work like men."[31]

This wry observation of an embattled British manufacturer sheds considerable light upon the effect of technological change on a trade union movement (as well as it does, perhaps, upon certain differences in national temper). Of the many adjustments forced upon the economy by the process of innovation, (1) the struggle for survival between "old" and "new" firms and (2) the obsolescence of traditional skills made existence peculiarly precarious for the young trade unions in this country during the latter half of the nineteenth century, and especially in the period following the Civil War.

Technological innovation imparted to the otherwise vigorous competition of the time a quality accurately characterized as cut-throat. We have already referred to the struggle between the newer, large-scale establishments and the conservative firms which they sought to displace by adopting temporary policies of intensive price competition. Since in the short run it is theoretically necessary only that direct costs be covered, the older firms were often at a great disadvantage, because direct costs represented a far greater portion of their total costs than was the case with more mechanized concerns. Since direct costs had to be covered, their only recourse was to attempt to reduce them; and since labor costs form a high proportion of direct costs, price cutting was invariably attended by competitive wage reductions.

The position of a union which claimed jurisdiction over craft workers in the old firms was doubly embarrassing. In the first place, the employers' bargaining position in the labor market was strengthened; their backs were stiffened by developments in the markets for their products. And secondly, if the new machines or processes rendered obsolete the skills of their members employed in the "old" firms, the union often felt obliged to accede to demands for wage reductions. A classic example of a union which accepted wage cuts in order to meet the competition of unskilled labor operating new machines

31. Quoted in International Molders' Union, *Journal*, November 1899, p. 583.

was afforded by the Glass Bottle Blowers' Association, which agreed to a reduction in piece rates on those classes of ware that could be turned out successfully by the Owens automatic bottle machine.[32]

Another source of concern to the trade union movement was the solvent effect of technical change upon craft skills. Even an innovation which leaves unchanged the volume of employment measured in man hours in the industry in which it was introduced might result in the displacement of skilled workers. (Although the number of man hours employed remains the same, the number of "labor units" (defined by Keynes as "an hour's employment of ordinary labor") employed would be reduced. Thus, under given market conditions, the wage bill would be reduced after the installation of the new machine or process.) This menace to their livelihood might well motivate the formation or growth of unions of the skilled workers in jeopardy, but at the same time it threatens the foundation upon which such organizations are erected—their occupational jurisdiction. One of the main factors in the rapid growth of the Knights of St. Crispin was the competition offered by "green hands" in new shoe factories to the skilled craftsmen in the trade,[33] but the same phenomenon accounted for its equally rapid decline. Organized on a national basis in 1867, the Crispins were the largest union in the country by 1870 (with a membership estimated at 50,000); but by 1874 the organization was defunct. The fact that this precipitous downfall occurred in a period of general prosperity bears witness to the potential menace of technological change not only to the welfare of the skilled worker but to the trade union established to advance his welfare.

The policies which have been historically adopted by unions confronted with technological change were classified by Barnett and Slichter into three broad groups: obstruction, competition, and control.[34] It is not intended to discuss in any detail either the factors responsible for the adoption of these policies or the results achieved by them in terms of their objectives, but only to touch upon their efficiency in preserving the bargaining strength of a union which might adopt any one or more of them. Given the state of product demand and the conditions under which other resources (including other types of labor) were supplied, the strength of the typical national union (that is, its ability to raise wages above the nonunion level) during this period was largely dependent upon two conditions: (1) the skill of its members, which is one component of their "natural" bargaining power, and (2)

32. George E. Barnett, *Chapters on Machinery and Labor* (Cambridge: Harvard University Press, 1926), pp. 101–102.

33. Don D. Lescohier, "The Knights of St. Crispin, 1867–1874," *Bulletin of the University of Wisconsin,* no. 355, Economics and Political Science Series, vol. 7, no. 1, July 1910, pp. 25–30; pp. 5–10.

34. Barnett, *Machinery and Labor,* chapter VI; and Sumner H. Slichter, *Union Policies and Industrial Management* (Washington: The Brookings Institution, 1941), chapters VII, VIII, and IX.

the proportion of the workers in the same or related crafts organized by the union.

In view of the potentially disruptive effect of technological innovation upon craft skills, it is apparent that a campaign of obstruction, if successfully prosecuted, would be highly attractive to a union group. But obstruction, although an intensely popular policy with the rank and file, has been attended historically by a conspicuous lack of success. "When machinery is first introduced, the line between those displaced from the trade and the survivors has not yet been drawn. Every member of the union is potentially a displaced workman. The only policy, therefore, which fulfills the hope of every member is that of completely stopping the progress of the machine."[35] It has been observed that virtually complete control by the union over the workers in a competitive area is requisite for the success of such a policy, but it is doubtful whether even "100-per-cent organization" would suffice. As long as entry into the industry is free, there is nothing to prevent the formation of new firms, equipped with the machinery which the union seeks to bar. If such machines can be operated by unskilled or semiskilled labor, the new firms need not depend on the union for their labor supply. If, however, the services of the skilled workers are required on tasks which are "coöperant" with the machine operation, the union, by virtue of its control over the supply of skilled labor, could exclude the innovation. Professor Slichter notes that the policy of obstruction has probably met with greatest success in the building trades in which not only is organization quite complete throughout the competitive area, but "most of the changes opposed by these unions affect only a small part of the work done by the skilled craftsmen. The employer needs these men for other parts of the work."[36]

Unable directly to bar the entry of skill-displacing innovations, some unions have sought to accomplish the same end by accepting wage reductions for skilled workers on the old processes in order to make the adoption of the new techniques uneconomical. This is the policy of competition, of which the case of the Glass Bottle Blowers and the automatic bottle machine, discussed above, is an example. If successful (and permanent success is highly dubious), this policy would preserve the skill of the union's members; but the significance of skill lies in its ability to command a higher remuneration than the wage paid to less skilled labor. Thus the machine, although unable for a while to render the skill of the handworkers obsolescent, can strip it of its economic significance and effectively deprive the union of the bargaining power which it otherwise would provide. In opposition to the adoption of a policy of competitive wage-cutting, the President of the Typographical Union said, ". . . it is therefore futile to attempt to stay the tide of their (the linotypes') introduction by a reduction in the scale unless we are

35. Barnett, *Machinery and Labor*, p. 142.
36. Slichter, *Union Policies*, pp. 214, 223, and 228.

prepared to suffer level decreases amounting to 40 to 50 per cent, and at that figure *a better living could be secured at almost any unskilled vocation.* A serious reduction in the rate of hand composition is sure to affect the machine scale also."[37]

The effect of the policy of control upon the bargaining power of the union depends largely upon the circumstances under which control can be exerted. If the union, in order to control machine work, must admit semi-skilled workers to membership, its bargaining power is weakened on two counts: first, there is the danger that the balance of power within the union will shift in favor of the unskilled members,[38] and the union in effect will be transformed from a craft to an industrial organization;[39] and second, a surplus of skilled workers will, under given conditions of demand, result from exclusion of the latter from machine employment. If the union seeks to raise the wages of its semiskilled members in the new occupations in an attempt to make the new process less profitable, the nonunion firms will benefit from a competitive advantage over their organized rivals. Furthermore, the division of the semiskilled into high- and low-wage segments could be counted on to generate pressure for the elimination of this differential, so that it would be necessary for the union to organize and raise the wages of the semiskilled in all the occupations in which they are engaged.

If the new positions could be staffed by the skilled handworkers, the result would depend upon two circumstances: the degree of skill required to operate the machine, and "whether the number of jobs created by the new technique is large in relation to the number that it destroys."[40] (The latter includes two concepts: the technological fact of the number of man hours required to produce a unit of output—the reciprocal of average productivity—under the new method as compared with the old; and the economic fact of the elasticity of demand for the product.) The following situations can be distinguished:

(a) If none of the handworker's skill is required in the industry after the introduction of the machine, the employment of skilled workers would be contingent upon their acceptance of lower wages, and, as in the case of competition, the skill would become economically inoperative.

(b) If none of the skill of the handworkers is required to run the machine, but if that skill is still necessary in other essential productive operations, the union's ability to obtain a higher wage for the machine operation

37. Quoted in Barnett, *Machinery and Labor,* p. 16. My italics.

38. Slichter, *Union Policies,* p. 245. See also pp. 265–267.

39. This is one aspect of what Professor John T. Dunlop has termed the "key worker" problem, which will be discussed more fully in Chapter 11. See John T. Dunlop, "The Changing Status of Labor," in Harold Williamson, *The Growth of the American Economy* (New York: Prentice-Hall, 1946), p. 609. See also John T. Dunlop, "The Development of Labor Organization: A Theoretical Framework," in Richard A. Lester and Joseph Shister, *Insights into Labor Issues* (New York: Macmillan, 1948), pp. 179–183.

40. Slichter, *Union Policies,* p. 242. See also p. 249.

would be increased by the strategic position of its members, but it would be limited by any displacement of skilled labor which might result from the innovation. The nonunion firms, moreover, would gain an advantage; they would be able to employ skilled labor only where it was necessary and could relegate machine operations to the less skilled and lower paid.

(c) If the skill of the handworker enables him to operate the machine more efficiently than a semiskilled worker (and thus reduce overhead costs), it will probably be necessary for the union to accept some reduction in the differential between the wages paid to the skilled workers and their imperfect substitutes, in order to make the increased efficiency of skilled labor commensurate with its increased cost.[41] Under such circumstances, the ability of the union to negotiate wage increases for its members in excess of an increase in the wage level of the semiskilled substitutes is severely restricted.

(d) If the skill of the handworkers is essential to the operation of the machine, the craft skill remains secure, but if expansion of demand (for whatever reason) fails to overcome the "labor-displacing power of the machine," the union will be confronted with the alternative of accepting either unemployment among its members or a lower wage rate. If the former is chosen, the union might elect to spread the burden of idleness by reducing the length of the work day or week, but this policy might not eliminate internal dissension if an important proportion of the membership desired to work longer, at the union wage rate, than the number of hours specified as the union maximum. And if we assume (as we must, in the interest of historical accuracy) that the union had by no means organized its trade jurisdiction completely, the alternative of accepting unemployment really does not exist for the union. Nonunion firms, able to hire displaced skilled workers at lower wages, could drive their organized competitors from the market.

(e) Thus, only if the skill of the handworkers is essential to the operation of the machine and if the displacement of skill (according to the Slichter definition) were negligible, could a policy of control maintain the union's bargaining strength. The achievement of these two conditions lies entirely outside the union's discretion. In all other cases, the only policy which could maintain the bargaining strength would be obstruction, and this policy has invariably proved to be impracticable.

This hasty shortcut through a maze of possible circumstances was negotiated in order to demonstrate the unsettling effect of innovation upon a young trade union movement. Technological change presented a serious obstacle to the expansion of union organization, and it made the preservation of the economic significance of existing skills a very difficult matter. Furthermore, it was productive of dissension within the ranks of organized labor, for, as we shall note in Chapter 11, the blurring by technological innovation of traditional occupational boundaries frequently created job territories over which

41. Barnett, *Machinery and Labor*, p. 135.

members of more than one trade sought control. This was especially true if the innovation in question had seriously impaired the bargaining position of one or more groups of skilled workers and if it had deprived them of jobs. In this manner, technological change could produce internal dissension if the opposing groups were organized in the same union or, if they were members of different organizations, it could be a source of those jurisdictional disputes to which our national unions were addicted from infancy. Innovation was a tireless left jab, continually keeping the trade union sufficiently off balance to prevent it from fully organizing its forces.

THE IMPACT OF THE BIG FIRM

The large-scale business enterprise was the result of a number of phenomena considered briefly in our historical sketch of the period: the capital-using nature of innovations of the period, which required large-scale plants; the great accumulation of financial resources necessary to erect and operate such plants; the development of the corporation as an institution capable of amassing the requisite liquid capital; and finally, the "merger movement," which succeeded periods of competition between rival large-scale firms or between such firms and their older and smaller competitors.

In 1907 Samuel Gompers claimed that, "Organized labor has less difficulty in dealing with large firms and corporations today than with many individual employers or small firms."[42]

Since the trade union movement was hardly more successful in "trustified" industries than it was in atomistic trades, however, this statement suggests that the two extremes might have proved equally troublesome for different reasons. Any given industry is characterized by certain conditions which facilitate organization and by others which inhibit it so that its actual receptiveness (or resistance) to unionism depends on the relative strength of the opposing forces. These conditions include (1) the number of firms in the industry, (2) the severity of competition among the firms, (3) the potential endurance of the average firm in a struggle of attrition, (4) the prevailing proportion of labor cost to total direct cost, (5) the ease or difficulty of entry into or exit from the industry and (6) the average degree of skill required of the labor force employed. Since we are comparing large firm with small firm industries, we may omit (7) conditions of product demand and (8) conditions under which other resources are supplied, because there are no *a priori* reasons for believing that significantly different distributions of these elasticities of demand and supply exist in the two types of industry.[43] These factors

42. Samuel Gompers, *Labor and the Common Welfare,* ed. by Hayes Robbins (New York: E. P. Dutton, 1919), p. 91.

43. It will be noted the factors listed above include the conditions listed by Marshall "under which a check to the supply of a thing that is wanted not for direct use, but as a factor of production of some commodity, may cause a very great rise in its price." These conditions are: essentiality, inelastic demand for the final product, a small propor-

are obviously not all independent of one another, but each is nevertheless enumerated because it could exert one or more distinctive effects upon the "organizability" of the relevant jurisdiction.

Thus, when Gompers referred to the difficulty in "dealing with many individual employers or small firms," he might have been thinking of the following obstacles to organization: the large number of firms to be unionized (1); the high degree of competition (2) typical in atomistic industries, which makes complete organization most imperative just as it is most difficult to achieve; the high proportion of labor cost to total operating cost in such firms (4), making for a more elastic demand for labor; and the ease of entry or exit (5) resulting from a low ratio of fixed costs to total costs, so that it could be possible for a unionized employer to go out of business with little financial sacrifice and subsequently to reënter the industry as a nonunion employer. On the other hand, some conditions were favorable to the extension of organization, such as the relatively great vulnerability of a small firm in a highly competitive industry to a protracted shutdown (3) and the high incidence of skilled labor (6) in some (though not all) handicraft trades; but since they failed to outweigh the inhibiting factors, the progress of unionism in "small firms" was slow.

Similarly, when Gompers spoke more favorably (or less unfavorably) of relationships with "large firms and corporations," he probably was impressed by certain conditions, nonexistent in small-scale industry, which facilitated unionism in large enterprises. For one thing, the technological basis of many large concerns resulted in lower labor cost ratios (4), a situation resulting in lower elasticities of the demand for labor and, therefore, in greater bargaining power for the unions involved.[44] Again, the relatively small number of firms (1) in a large-scale industry reduced the difficulty and expense of organizing the workers employed in them. Furthermore, with few firms in an industry, competition was not likely to be so severe (2), since each unit was large enough to realize that its own price and production policies affected the market situation to a significant degree and that the penalty of price slashing was retaliation by the other firms (the oligopoly situation). Thus competitive pressure on wages would be less in the large firm situation than in small-scale industry. And, added to this lack of competitive pressure, the necessity of the large firm to cover its overhead by maintaining uninterrupted

---

tion of total cost to be borne by the factor in question, and inelastic supply of coöperant factors. Alfred Marshall, *Principles of Economics,* Eighth edition (London: Macmillan, 1938), pp. 385–386.

44. It has been observed that a lower ratio of labor to other resources constitutes a bargaining advantage provided that the elasticity of substitution of capital for labor is less than the elasticity of demand for the final product. See J. R. Hicks, *The Theory of Wages* (New York: Smith, 1948 edition), appendix (iii), pp. 241–246; Joan Robinson, *The Economics of Imperfect Competition* (London: Macmillan, 1948), pp. 257–262.

operation made for a "softer" bargaining situation.[45] Finally, it was frequently less easy for management to abandon a large-scale enterprise (5), provided that the scrap value of its real assets was low and that product price was sufficiently high to cover operating costs. Thus the problem of a high business mortality rate, coupled with a high birth rate, did not typically confront unions in heavy industries as it did in such industries as the garment trades.

These favorable conditions, however, were more than offset by factors which, in varying combinations, made it impossible for the trade unions to control to any appreciable extent any of the trustified industries which emerged during this period.

In the first place, since the large-scale firms invariably employed the most mechanized productive processes, the degree of skill required (6) was relatively low. This was an important deterrent to the organization of trade unions, especially of craft unions. Lack of skill not only deprived the workers of a "natural" bargaining asset, but it greatly simplified the problem of strike-breaking.

The relatively small number of concerns in large firm industries (1) probably proved to be more of an obstacle than a benefit to the unions. Fewness of numbers facilitated coöperative action against unions. The effectiveness of the time-honored blacklist, for example, could be increased greatly in an oligopolistic industry. This was especially true in the anthracite coal industry.[46] Formal organization was also encouraged. The fact that unionism for a long time was far less successful in the anthracite coal industry (concentrated in a relatively small and compact area) than in the bituminous trade (composed of widely scattered and competing producing areas), can be attributed in great measure to the acquisition of financial control over the anthracite mines by the railroads.

Nor is formal organization necessary when one large firm, by virtue of its dominant position in an industry, can achieve a position of "wage leader-

45. It was this latter consideration, incidentally, which prompted attempts by the early steel manufacturers to introduce the eight-hour day and a three-shift system. Curiously enough, this atypical move on the part of the employers was resisted by the Amalgamated Association of Iron and Steel Workers. Its members were on piecework, and were accustomed to a two-turn (shift) system, with an average of ten hours worked in each turn. They feared that an eight-hour turn would result in reduced daily earnings, and they were so opposed to its introduction that "in 1884 the national lodge actually revoked the charter of two lodges working three turns." Their president (Weihe) tried to persuade the membership that continuous operation would increase hourly earnings because the time lost at the beginning of each heat in warming the rolls (by rolling scrap) would be eliminated. His efforts, however, were unsuccessful; and after the union had been eliminated from the industry, the employers continued the two-turn system—but obtained twenty-four hour operations by lengthening each turn. (John A. Fitch, "Unionism in the Iron and Steel Industry," *Political Science Quarterly*, 1909, v. XXIV, no. 1, pp. 66–69.)

46. See Walsh, *United Mine Workers*, pp. 43–44; see also p. 41.

ship." This was the case in the steel industry. After the Carnegie Steel Company defeated the Amalgamated Association of Iron and Steel Workers at Homestead in 1892, "The other Pittsburgh steel mills that had been on strike also became nonunion. Where the great Carnegie Steel Company led, the others had to follow."[47]

Another disadvantage to trade unions in their relations with large firms is the relatively great ability of the latter to wage a campaign of attrition (3). In support of Gompers' statement, it was observed that, in many instances, the less elastic demand of large firms for labor and the more tepid competition with which they were confronted in the markets for their output lessened competitive pressure on wages. But while large firms could have been "softer" than the hard-pressed small units in their relationship with trade unions if they wished to avoid a contest, their armament was formidable, often so formidable in comparison with the resources of their opponents that they not infrequently provoked trials of strength. The conflict between the Steel Workers and the United States Steel Corporation, in which the basic issue was recognition of the union by the newly formed company,[48] was the most dramatic and decisive proof of the superior economic strength of the large business unit.

The greater reluctance of large-scale enterprises to go out of business under the conditions set forth above did not constitute an unalloyed advantage from the unionist's viewpoint. Supply having been probably greater than it would have been if more firms had withdrawn from the field, prices and profit margins tended to be held down, given conditions of demand. Under such circumstances, wage horizons narrowed, and, although employment in the trade was probably greater with more than with fewer firms in operation, the unionist was not likely to regard this effect upon employment as a satisfactory offset to the depressing effect upon wages exerted by "cutthroat competition." An editor of the Iron Molders' *Journal*, writing during the depression of the 1870's, attributed the unsatisfactory wage situation in his trade in large part to the low mortality rate among iron foundries:

> In its present condition, the business is not one to attract capital, and we have no doubt there are many now in it who would gladly withdraw if they could take out 50 per cent of all the money represented by their plant. It is doubtful, however, if many of them could realize 25 per cent upon anything except the real estate occupied by their foundries and stock yards. . . The only salvation for the founder who has not been able to accumulate a comfortable competence out of the net profits of past years of prosperity is to go on. . . Those who are in the business will probably find it to their interest to stay in it; those who are out of it will certainly find it to their interest to stay out. . . .[49]

47. Fitch, "Unionism," *Political Science Quarterly*, pp. 77–78.
48. V. S. Clark, *History of Manufactures*, vol. II, p. 622.
49. *Journal*, November, 1876, p. 143.

In the brief sketch of the major lines of economic development, reference was made to the multiple-plant business unit which rose to prominence in the period following the Civil War. In discussing the development of the trade union movement in 1926, Professor Slichter observed:

Because the market is often larger than can be economically served by one plant, many enterprises have several. But such firms are extremely difficult to unionize.[50]

In discussing the conditions which facilitated the organization of a firm or industry by a union, it was noted that the ability to survive lengthy stoppages on the part of firms subject to competitive pressure is severely curtailed. If two plants are operated by competing managements and one is struck by a union, the struck firm is likely to lose a considerable portion of its business to its competitor unless it comes to terms without much delay. But if these two plants are controlled by the same interests, and one of them is shut down, production may be diverted from the idle plant to the plant remaining in operation.

The diverse effects upon the conduct of strikes produced by competing and by coöperative managements were illustrated clearly in the anthracite coal industry. In the "long strike" of 1875, it was reported that the operators in the northern fields (which remained in operation) contributed financial support to the striking miners in the Lehigh and Schuylkill regions in the south. When another strike broke out in the Lehigh fields twelve years later, however, coal was diverted from the Schuylkill fields (which for a time remained operating under an agreement between the miners and the Reading Company to settle at the terms ultimately to be established in the Lehigh region) to the Lehigh operators to enable them to fill their orders.[51] The Congressional Committee investigating this strike found that virtually all the railroads serving the two regions were controlled by interrelated interests and that competition had been effectively eliminated throughout the entire area.

The steel industry may be summoned once more to furnish another example of the menace presented to unionism by unitary control over separate producing units. According to Fitch, the reaction of the union to rumors of consolidation in the industry in 1900 was prompted by the fear that the hostile Carnegie firm would emerge dominant in any amalgamation and would "insist on driving the union out of every mill in the combination." In 1901, the Amalgamated Association insisted that the American Tin Plate Company sign a new wage scale for its unionized and hitherto unorganized plants alike. The company agreed to do so, if the American Sheet Steel Com-

50. Slichter, "The Worker in Modern Economic Society," *Journal of Political Economy*, p. 120.
51. Walsh, *United Mine Workers*, pp. 60, 75–76, and Suffern, *The Coal Miners' Struggle*, pp. 54–57.

pany would follow the same practice. This proving impossible, the union struck both firms and the American Steel Hoop Company as well. Then the companies offered to sign contracts covering all but one of the tin mills, all hoop mills and sheet mills in which the union had been recognized during the preceding year, and four additional sheet mills. "This highly advantageous offer was foolishly rejected by the representatives of the union; they demanded all the mills or none."[52] If the union did act "foolishly," it nevertheless adhered consistently to its strategic concept of imposing control over all the mills controlled by the same group of interests. This concept found expression in the following provision in the union constitution:

"Should one mill in a combine or trust have a difficulty, all mills in said combine or trust shall cease work until such grievance is settled."[53]

The existence of "combines" required control by a national union over the activities of the various local unions in an industry, just as the existence of interregional competition did. Such control was exercised by the President of the Steel Workers' Union, when he revoked the charter of a local which refused to break its contract with the Illinois Steel Company and join the locals striking against the United States Steel Corporation in 1901.

But even a high degree of control over its locals could not secure the continued existence of the association. Its defeat and extinction by the biggest firm of all suggested that, when Gompers said that unions had less difficulty in "dealing" with large business units, he meant that they had less difficulty in bargaining with them after they had recognized the unions in their industries; for such firms were in a better position to grant bargaining concessions than small enterprises in highly competitive industries. He could not have meant, however, that unions had less difficulty in organizing large firms, for such a statement would have ignored the difficulties presented by the conditions which have just been reviewed: the relatively low degree of skill required of the large firm's employees; the staying power of the big concern; the facility with which a small number of large firms can coördinate their strategy; and the multiple-plant problem.

THE IMPACT OF BUSINESS CONDITIONS

In the section dealing with the relationship between labor's progress and the trade union movement, the marked prevalence of depression in the post-Civil-War years was mentioned as an obstacle to organization. In prosperous times the workers uniformly desired to form and join unions. It cannot be assumed, however, that similar unanimity obtained during depressions. The stimulus to organization might well have been accentuated among the unemployed, but the organizations which flourished during bad times were likely to be political protest movements rather than unions. And those remaining at

52. Fitch, "Unionism," *Political Science Quarterly,* p. 78; see also p. 71.
53. *Constitution,* 1900, Art. 17, Sec. 23.

work, while often subjected to an accelerated pace of work which tended to reduce their real effort wage might have benefited from a rise in their real time rates if the latter were not outweighed by part-time idleness. Most important, though, was their fear of retaliation for union activity by their employers.

Apart from this direct effect upon the workers themselves, depressed business conditions retarded the growth of trade unionism by intensifying competition among firms, with a resultant stiffening of employers' bargaining attitudes. As a partial offset to these unfavorable influences, however, immigration decreased appreciably during the downswings—although its lagging response to cyclical variations in business activity probably vitiated this beneficial effect.[54]

One might also add that with cyclical declines in investment, the unsettling influences of technological change and expansion of markets were damped down in bad times, but it would be putting the cart before the horse to classify such developments as mitigating by-products of business depression. For, whether one accepts the Schumpeterian view that innovation generates cycles or Hansen's contention that "the mere slowing down in the rate of growth (in new railroad construction) caused an absolute decline in the volume of new investment,"[55] and thereby induced a fall in income and employment, it is generally accepted that fluctuations in these dynamic developments produced cyclical variations in the national economy, and not *vice versa*. Thus it appears that the predominantly unfavorable effect of business contractions upon the development of trade unions might ultimately be ascribed to the operation of those dynamic factors the more immediate influences of which have been set forth in the preceding pages.

The need for national unionism arose in part from the operation of forces of expansion and change in the American economy, which enabled the output of producing units in widely scattered areas to appear for sale in the same markets. It arose also from labor's geographic mobility, which resulted in the creation of potential national markets for labor which often paralleled the national markets for products. These conditions made the welfare of any one group of workers dependent on that of others engaged elsewhere in similar lines of production. The task of the national union was therefore to adjust the conditions under which labor was sold in the different producing units of the industry in question so that an improvement in the situation of all local groups could be effected.

It was necessary that the following conditions be satisfied for the national union to perform its task efficiently:

(a) Sufficient control over the policies of the local unions in the trade

54. *Historical Statistics,* pp. 33–34; and Harry Jerome, *Migration and Business Cycles* (New York: National Bureau of Economic Research, 1926), pp. 91–93, 100, and 240.

55. Alvin H. Hansen, *Fiscal Policy and Business Cycles* (New York: W. W. Norton, 1941), p. 40.

jurisdiction to enable the national union to cope with the economic inter-relationships among the different producing areas.

(b) A degree of organization throughout the jurisdiction high enough so that the competition of nonunion firms and workmen could not menace the triad of union "wages, hours, and other conditions of labor."

(c) "Natural" bargaining advantages which, by eliminating possible substitutes for the services of its members, would enable them collectively to exploit a monopoly position. The most important natural bargaining advantage was the possession of an essential and not readily acquired industrial skill.

(d) Sufficient resources, financial and moral, to effect (a) and (b) and to supplement (c), especially in tests of strength with employers.

The achievement of the national unions fell short of its objectives, since the rise in the real price of labor which occurred in the latter part of the nineteenth century cannot be attributed to unionism. It is paradoxical that the gains of labor were largely achieved through the operation of equilibrating forces which were, in part, released by its historically high relative rate of return and which were intended to cheapen it as a commodity rather than by institutions expressly created for the purpose of raising its price.

The failure of national unionism to achieve its goal must be due to the absence, in each specific case of one or more of the conditions specified above, which were requisite to success. The historical environment in which the first national unions developed required the organization of national unions but, at the same time, opposed their prospects of success by creating conditions which were not at all conducive to effective unionism in general. The development of national unions was a historical phenomenon, and all the factors, favorable and unfavorable alike, which conditioned that development were related to each other as components of an indissoluble historical process. The extension of market areas, immigration, technological innovations in transportation, agriculture, and industry, and the rise of the big firm with control over more than one producing unit were not isolated phenomena; the existence of any one of these was affected vitally by the existence of all of the others. A study of the development of an institution requires that attention be directed not only to its growth but also and equally to the retardation of that growth.

The Commons theory that the "tri-century" extension of markets was primarily responsible for the growth and character of trade unions in America requires amplification. Extension of markets made national unionism only a necessary condition of the survival and growth of unionism in general, and it was but one component of a process of change which failed to provide the conditions sufficient for such growth and survival.[56] This explanation of

56. S. H. Slichter, in "The Worker in Modern Economic Society," *Journal of Political Economy*, pointed out that while Commons stressed the stimulating effect of the de-

the institution with reference to only one artificially isolated phenomenon cannot be expected to explain the whole truth. Specifically, it fails to account for the absence of national unions in some industries which had national markets. In such cases, local unionism was also nonexistent—or at least sporadic and ineffectual. It follows that where there could be no locals there could be no nationals. The outstanding examples were those industries in which big firms predominated and in which conditions were peculiarly unconducive to unionism with respect to organizability, bargaining power, and even industrial skill. Commons and his associates emphasize the intensifying effects of competition in discussing the widening of market areas, but they say little about the growing size of the business unit and the multiple-plant firm or "combination." Yet it is obvious that industries characterized by the latter phenomena were just as well qualified as more competitive industries, composed of smaller business units, if extension of markets is taken as the prime criterion of national unionism.

Commons' theory also fails to account for the presence of national unions in industries which did not have national markets. The oldest national union is the Typographical Union, and its strength has been concentrated in the newspaper branch of the industry, rather than in the book-and-job branch. The building trades also furnish an example of a localized industry in which national unions emerged. Such national unions owed their existence primarily to labor's geographic mobility—a phenomenon which will be considered in the chapter which follows.

---

velopment of a national market upon labor organization, he neglected the retarding influences of modern technology "which keeps so many of our workers in a semi-skilled class," and the multiple-plant firm, for both of which phenomena the national market "is responsible." J. T. Dunlop, "The Development of Labor Organizations: A Theoretical Framework," in Lester and Shister, *Insights,* also rejected the unitary interpretation and stressed "1. technology," "2. market structures and character of competition," "3. wider community institutions," and "4. ideas and beliefs" as determinants of labor organization. Robert F. Hoxie (*Trade Unionism in the United States,* New York: Appleton, 1917, p. 65) went even further than these two writers in assigning to "the temperamental characteristics of the workers involved" a role as important as that played by environment (however broadly the latter might be defined).

PART

II

THE TRAVELING MEMBER AND THE NATIONAL UNION

CHAPTER THREE

THE GEOGRAPHIC MOBILITY OF LABOR

In this part of the study we shall try to determine why the existence of a national market for labor—as distinct from a national market for products—proved in fact to have been a sufficient cause for the rise of national unions. What considerations should suggest, *a priori,* that the geographic mobility of labor might have been instrumental in inducing local unions to form national unions and to endow the latter with independent authority over their affiliates? Would these considerations lead one to believe that national unions formed in local product market industries were as strong as those formed in national product market industries? We shall also attempt to discover why, if labor migration was influential in forming national unions, the latter emerged when they did. What special incentives to the geographic mobility of labor existed in the latter half of the nineteenth century?

THEORETICAL EFFECTS OF MOBILITY ON NATIONAL UNIONISM

The appearance of national unions in industries in which well insulated local markets persisted has been explained with reference to the geographic mobility of their members. This explanation was championed most vigorously by T. W. Glocker, who wrote, "Probably the chief cause of the federation of local trade organizations has been the constant movement of journeymen from one part of the country to another."[1] J. B. Andrews attributed national unionism in local market industries to "competition for employment between migratory out-of-town journeymen and the locally organized mechanics."[2] In contrast to Glocker, however, he considered labor mobility to be considerably less important as a nationalizing influence than product mobility; and even Glocker ascribed the weakness of national unionism in the building trades "partly to the fact that in these crafts collective bargaining is conducted locally."[3]

1. Theodore W. Glocker, *The Government of American Trade Unions* (Baltimore: Johns Hopkins, 1913), p. 32. See also p. 39.
2. J. R. Commons and Associates, *History of Labour in the United States* (New York: Macmillan, 1936), v. II, p. 44.
3. Glocker, *Government of American Trade Unions,* pp. 49–50. Also p. 129.

If national unionism is required when the economic position of any local group of workers cannot be maintained in the face of equilibrating forces originating from the outside, is there any reason, theoretically, why traveling workers should provide less incentive than traveling products for the establishment of national unions? If the same factor commands (*ceteris paribus*) different rates of return in different localities, equalization can be achieved by the movement of products produced by the lower paid units to markets in which products produced by the higher priced units were sold, or by the direct movement of units of the factor in question from lower paying to higher paying regions, or by the movement of units of "coöperant" factors from regions where the factor in question received a higher return to areas where its remuneration is lower, or by a combination of product and factor mobility (the typical theoretical case of a national market industry in a closed economy).[4]

Certain *a priori* considerations, however, indicate that the centripetal pull of nationalization upon the local unions would be stronger in industries in which goods are mobile and different producing areas compete with one another than in industries in which local markets can be monopolized by nearby producing areas.

In the first place, both labor and commodity mobility prevail in the former type of industry, while only labor is mobile in the latter; and, while the same final result can be achieved by either mode of adjustment in isolation as by both in combination, the rate of change is likely to be higher in the latter case. This assumes that labor mobility prevails to the same extent in national market as in local market industries. As a matter of fact, some of the conditions conducive to labor mobility during the historical period under consideration in this study were peculiar to particular local market industries. These conditions will be discussed in the following section; their existence is referred to here in order to qualify the conclusion that the rate of adjustment to geographic differentials in wages, hours, and so on, is, other things being equal, likely to be more rapid in national market than in local market industries.

Furthermore, it is conceivable that, under certain circumstances, the final adjustment brought about by labor mobility would be less perfect than that which commodity mobility would require. Since nonpecuniary merits and drawbacks enter into individual welfare considerations, and since such nonpecuniary factors might differ as between different jobs requiring identical skill and effort, wage differentials are compatible with equilibrium.

4. "It does not matter that the mountain will not go to Mahomet as long as Mahomet is able to go to the mountain." Abba P. Lerner, *The Economics of Control* (New York: Macmillan, 1946), p. 349. For a more precise and qualified formulation, see Paul A. Samuelson, "International Trade and the Equalisation of Factor Prices," *Economic Journal*, v. LVIII, June 1948, pp. 163–184.

Reluctance to move from familiar surroundings to a strange community is a source of friction to the forces of adjustment set in motion by unequal pecuniary rewards. Theoretically, different individual workers might be regarded as attaching unequal importance to the nonpecuniary deterrents to migration, thus requiring geographic differentials of varying magnitudes to induce each to endure the unpleasantness involved. Since, under given conditions, large differentials would induce more individuals to move to higher wage areas than would small inequalities in the rate of return, the total "degree of mobility" generated will be proportionate to the size of the geographic differential.[5] It is, of course, entirely possible that any given differential might attract enough new workers to a high wage area to result in its complete elimination, but, if it fails to do so, there is no reason why the mere persistence of a reduced differential should stimulate any additional migration on the part of individuals to whom the original higher difference proved to be an insufficient incentive. An equilibrium situation could then prevail, and it would be characterized by geographic differences in wages and (if all other conditions were identical in the different regions) in labor and total costs. Thus a local union could enjoy within certain limits a monopoly with reasonable security, although outside labor would be free to migrate to its jurisdiction. If commodity mobility obtained, however, the persistence under static conditions of geographic wage inequalities, resulting in differences in total costs among competing firms, would be incompatible with equilibrium.

Even if the number of migrants attracted to a high wage community were sufficient to eliminate a given geographic wage differential under competitive conditions in the labor market, the presence of a well organized local union in the area could prevent the wage rate from being depressed. Confronted with an increment to the supply of the type of labor over which it asserts local jurisdiction, a local union which desires to maintain the wage rate at its prevailing level must be prepared to cope with an amount of unemployment equal to the supply of labor offered by the newcomers, assuming that no unemployment existed prior to the influx of migrants. This it can do either by barring the migrants from work (thereby obliging them to shoulder the entire burden of unemployment) or by requiring that they offer their services to employers only at the union rate of compensation. The second method allows the employers a wider choice of workers. Either alternative is feasible

5. This is somewhat analogous to the process of deriving a market supply schedule from individual schedules, wherein additional individuals enter the market with successive rises in the supply price. In the present case, substitute the geographic differential for the supply price, and the number willing to migrate for the quantity offered. Net nonpecuniary advantages (disadvantages) of moving would be measured by the distance between the origin and the y-intercept of this supply curve. A positive (negative) value of the function at zero mobility indicates the presence of net nonpecuniary advantages (disadvantages).

provided that the local union has the local labor force well organized and the number of migrants, while theoretically sufficient to eliminate the existing geographic wage differential (in the absence of unionism) constitutes only a relatively small proportion of the total labor force. If these conditions prevail, an attempt by any of the newcomers to work for a lower wage than that established by the union could be frustrated by a strike of the local union members, who would refuse to work with the "scabs." And even if all the migrants were willing to undercut the union wage, the employers would be obliged to pay the union rate as long as the number of union members appreciably exceeded the number of migrants. Of course, we must note that the higher the geographic differential maintained by the local union, the greater the number of migrants which it might attract to the locality in question.

Where strong union control over the resident labor supply did exist in fact, it often found institutional expression in closed-shop agreements between the employers in the region and the local union, which cemented the latter's control over the local job market. The local union of bricklayers in Chicago, formed in 1868, was able to remain aloof from the national union (which originated in 1865) until 1899, although Chicago was described as "the dumping ground for all bricklayers going West, and those traveling East, thereby being subjected to a greater influx of men than other cities." For "the Chicago people were better able to protect themselves, as a local union," since the latter had been able to enter into and enforce exclusive contracts with the local employers. Traveling members of the international union who desired to secure employment in Chicago were obliged to pay to the independent local union "high and excessive initiation fees ('to the extent of $25.00') together with the imposed cost of hall construction bonds which they would not do if their Traveling Card was accepted."[6]

The experience of the bricklayers in Chicago illustrates an important peculiarity of national unionism in local market industry. In Chapter 2 it was suggested that the development of national unionism was retarded by conditions which inhibited the development of unionism in general. Such circumstances could prevail in national market and local market industries alike, and where they did exist weak national unionism was accompanied by weak local unionism. From the foregoing discussion of some of the characteristics of geographic labor mobility, however, it follows that weak national unionism could also be, and actually was associated with strong local unionism, that the weakness of the national union could be attributed to the strength and self-sufficiency of at least some of its constituent locals. Such a situation, of course, could prevail only in a local market industry; in industries characterized by competition among firms in different producing regions, national unionism became essential to the survival of local unionism.

6. *Proceedings of the Bricklayers, Masons and Plasterers' International Union of North America*: 1894, p. 48 (report of the secretary); 1895, p. 15; and 1899, p. 28.

Thus the existence and strength of any particular national union in a local market industry depends upon two conditions which are themselves interrelated: first, the degree of organization and control over the local labor markets achieved by the local unions, and second, the degree of geographic mobility of the labor force over which jurisdiction is claimed by the national union.

HISTORICAL INCENTIVES TO MOBILITY

The degree of mobility actually achieved during the period in which the first national unions emerged was determined by the presence of certain conditions which still exist, by the presence of others which no longer prevail, and by the absence of some conditions which are familiar characteristics of contemporary economic life.

Knowledge of Better Conditions Elsewhere

Knowledge by workers in a given craft of the existence of better terms of employment in other localities, need not, as we have seen, prompt them to migrate. The actual extent to which such economically oriented migration did occur is impossible to determine, but union records of the period indicate that knowledge of geographic wage differentials did in fact prompt mobility. As early as 1867, the president of the bricklayers' newly formed national union recommended

to all unions when they are located nearby to each other (the desirability) of equalizing the rate of wages, so as to be nearly as possible alike. It would, in my judgment, be highly beneficial and prevent much of the contentions and the low rate of wages that we are now receiving in many cities; with all the efforts of men to raise their wages, they cannot long be maintained without a corresponding increase in other cities adjacent to them, because there is an immediate rush to obtain the higher wages, and all our efforts are neutralized.[7]

The printers were confronted with the same problem during this period,[8] and Glocker quoted a writer in 1847 who observed that artisans in general were quick to move from adjacent communities into localities where local unions had succeeded in raising wage rates above the general level, with the result that "wages rise elsewhere and by degrees fall here."[9]

In 1905, nearly forty years after the Bricklayers' president had recommended equalization of wage rates as protection of union standards against the leveling influence of migration, some of the local unions sought an alternative solution to the challenge presented by the economic rationalism of the traveling members. It was, however, a solution as embarrassing to

7. *Proceedings*, 1867, p. 14.

8. George E. Barnett, *The Printers, A Study in American Trade Unionism* (Cambridge: American Economic Association, 1909).

9. Glocker, *Government of American Trade Unions*, p. 34. The quotation is from J. W. Alexander, *The American Mechanic and Workingman*, p. 127.

the international executive as the problem itself. It seemed that, due to "abnormally prosperous conditions," many localities experienced a shortage of bricklayers.

To remedy this condition, as well as to obtain employment for idle members of other localities, we gave notice in one of our monthly circulars that we should be pleased to publicly announce those places where a shortage of workmen existed, and requested subordinate unions to inform us of the number of workmen required . . . our Unions did not take kindly to our idea, or desire the fact that their particular locality was short-handed to be published in any way. Candidly, we cannot understand such a reluctant feeling.[10]

Advertising by Employers

In view of the alacrity with which so many workers responded to the knowledge of geographic differentials, it is not surprising that employers in high wage localities sought to disseminate such knowledge in regions where labor of the variety demanded was less liberally compensated. Advertising for workers from out of town was a venerable practice; Barnett cites a case affecting the New York printers in 1809.[11] The Carpenters' secretary, commenting on the singular exclusion of the journeymen carpenters from the recent prosperity of the construction industry in general (1886–1888) and of "the booming towns of the West and South" in particular, explained: "In these cases much of the overcrowding is due to the newspaper advertising done by scheming speculators and unprincipled contractors, whose sole desire is to overcrowd the labor market and reduce wages."[12] The Bricklayers' secretary made the following plea:

Subordinate Unions will please instruct their members to pay no attention to any advertisements which may appear in any of the newspapers, or be circulated by handbills, about Bricklayers being wanted in certain localities, as such advertisements are the work of Bosses, or Exchanges, who seek to flood such localities for the purpose of reducing the wages and creating trouble among our Unions.

Employers seemed especially prone to encourage migration as a strikebreaking technique. They did this both by advertising for workers in other localities[13] and by direct recruitment,[14] and, judging by the frequency with which union officials attributed defeat to "imported labor," both techniques

10. *Proceedings*, 1905, p. 334 (report of the secretary).
11. Barnett, *The Printers*, pp. 17–18.
12. *Proceedings of the Carpenters' and Joiners' International Union*, 1888, p. 13; also p. 10 (report of the secretary).
13. See e.g.: *Proceedings of the Bricklayers' and Masons' International Union*, 1885, p. 35; and Barnett, *The Printers*, pp. 16–18.
14. See e.g.: *Proceedings of the Glass Bottle Blowers' Association*, 1899, p. 28; *Proceedings of the United Brotherhood of Carpenters and Joiners*, 1890, p. 16; *Proceedings of the Bricklayers' and Masons' International Union*, 1888, p. 28.

were quite successful. The former method appears to have been commonly practiced before the introduction of the latter; direct recruitment often required some degree of organization—or at least of active coöperation among employers in different localities, which did not evolve until unionism had developed sufficiently to commend such coöperation to the employers in the industry affected. While employing printers, circa 1803, were content to advertise for "sober young men from the country who have been accustomed to press work" to fill the places of striking journeymen, in 1891 the Pittsburgh employers, organized into a "Typothetae," received workmen from similar organizations in other cities and cash from the United Typothetae (the national organization) in resisting a strike for the nine-hour day.[15] In the bituminous coal industry, organized importation of strikebreakers was resorted to as early as 1873 and played an important part in the defeat of the miners' union in the Hocking Valley strike of 1884.[16]

The building trades furnished a unique example of employer-induced migration in the operations of several large firms, each of which contracted for work over a wide area. These interstate firms apparently arose after the depression of 1873–1879 and might be considered the counterparts in the construction industry of the large-scale, multiple-plant concerns elsewhere, the effect of which upon unionism was considered in the preceding chapter. They generally specialized in large-scale construction projects, such as state or municipal buildings, and contracted for the entire job, subletting to local contractors operations which they did not perform themselves. Thus, the Massachusetts firm of Norcross Brothers, which owned and operated several granite and brownstone quarries and made their own brick, would contract for the erection of an entire building in some locality and would sublet all work except masonry. It retained in its own employ a large force of stonecutters, stonemasons, bricklayers, plasterers, and even architects and draughtsmen, some of whom it would dispatch to the site of operations each time the firm secured a contract. Norcross was large enough in 1888 to be engaged simultaneously in projects in Boston, Worcester, New York City, New Orleans, St. Louis, and Omaha. According to a report made to the Bricklayers' convention in 1889, this and other large firms (of which three were mentioned by name) "sometimes have work going on in most a dozen different cities at the same time."[17]

In some cases these firms hired local labor directly on work which they did not subcontract. In some instances (where the local unions were strong) they hired union labor, giving "as a reason that they do not want their reputation as builders assailed," but in others they sought nonunion workers, "and

15. Barnett, *The Printers*, pp. 16–17 and 337–338.
16. Chris Evans, *History of the United Mine Workers of America* (Indianapolis, 1918), v. I, p. 43; also pp. 118, 119, 125, 126, 129, 131.
17. *Proceedings*, 1889, p. 29. Also *Proceedings*, 1911, p. 417.

when pressed for men [would] borrow help from some of their other works, or else import them by means of advertisements in English and Scottish newspapers." Their own mobile task forces were, at first, nonunion, including "some of the best workmen in the country, some of whom were expelled from our organization in times past, while the great majority are those who will not join a union so long as they can obtain steady employment from these firms."

The ability of such firms to organize migration constituted a grave threat to local unions in every locality in which they obtained work. For example, when the Omaha local union of bricklayers entered into a general strike for the eight-hour day in 1888, the local bosses obtained the support of Norcross Brothers, which was currently engaged in the construction of a courthouse in Omaha ("a very large job"), and which found that it could not obtain local bricklayers to do the front-work on its building. The Norcross manager and the local contractors advertised for bricklayers "all over the country." Another incident reveals how such firms could avail themselves of the existence of lower standards in the localities in which they obtained contracts in order to depress the terms of employment of workers whom they hired directly elsewhere and whom they sent into the localities where the work was to be performed. In this case the Indianapolis local, which had enforced the nine-hour rule of the international union throughout its jurisdiction, permitted some of its members who were hired by Indianapolis employers for jobs in other localities to work ten hours in small towns outside the city. This dispensation (which was subsequently reversed by the president of the international union) was granted to the employers "as they had to compete with the contractors of these small towns and hire labor and pay them the same for nine hours as the other contractors of small towns paid for ten hours."[18]

Misconceptions About Conditions Elsewhere

It is possible that ignorance as well as knowledge of conditions prevailing in the various markets for a given type of labor stimulated worker migration. While knowledge of better conditions elsewhere could and did stimulate migration, ignorance of the fact that conditions in other localities were no better than those prevailing in the community where a dissatisfied workman was employed often failed to prevent him from moving on. For this reason, union officials continually accused employers of misrepresenting the true state of affairs in their own communities in order to attract a large supply of labor there and thus reduce wages. It is also probable that men, heeding only their dissatisfaction with whatever jobs they held, took to the road without forming any definite opinion of what awaited them in other regions. In any event, Thomas O'Dea, the observant and voluble secretary of the Bricklayers' and Masons' Union, reported, "It is a strange fact that men will leave

18. *Proceedings,* 1889, p. 90.

their localities where the rate of wages range from 40 to 50 cents per hour and go to these places mentioned (in the Southern states) and work 10 hours per day for wages running from 17½ to 35 cents per hour. But such is the fact."[19]

Dissemination of Information by the National Union

However, O'Dea's organization, as well as other national unions, did seek to combat ignorance on the part of their general membership of the true facts of supply and demand in each locality in which a local union was organized. Constitutions of national unions invariably required that local secretaries periodically furnish the national or international secretary with data concerning the number of traveling cards issued to members leaving their local jurisdictions and, in addition, with the local officers' estimate of the "condition of trade" in their home communities. The reports (for the most part monthly) of the locals were regularly printed in the national journals, so that any member contemplating migration could determine whether wages and employment opportunities at his intended destination were assessed as "Good," "Bad," or just "Fair." Local opinion could not always be taken at face value, of course, and it is to be expected that errors of pessimism prevailed, since, as O'Dea noted, local unions did not "desire the fact that their particular locality was short-handed to be published in any way." A reader with a sharp eye, however, could check the local secretary's report on trade conditions with his report on the number of travel cards issued, and if the latter figure was low, he might reasonably conclude that, if very few men chose to leave a locality during the preceding month, opportunities there could be considered "Good," even if they were officially designated only "Fair."

On the other hand, employers in a locality not infrequently erred on the optimistic side when they advertised for workers; hence the journals of the national unions might well have performed an important function in counteracting this type of exaggeration or, in some instances, misinformation. It is impossible to assess the effect of the dissemination of information by national unions upon the mobility of labor. If one accepts the proposition that migration was inhibited by positive knowledge to the effect that no employment opportunities existed at the intended destination and that, on the other hand, migration was stimulated by the dissemination of information concerning existence of employment opportunities in various localities, one might contend that the national union, allowing for the aforementioned bias of its local reporters, served the membership as a reasonably honest broker. To this extent, it contributed (together with truthful employer advertising) to a more satisfactory geographical allocation of the labor offered by its members. Whether or not this resulted in a net increase or a net decrease in the total volume of labor migration is, of course, impossible to state on *a priori*

19. *Proceedings,* 1900, p. 38 (report of the chief organizer).

grounds. Some national unions, including the Bricklayers, established employment bureaus, maintaining lists of unemployed members and, in some cases, attempting to require that locals report shortages of workers whenever excess demand occurred. The national employment bureau, however, did not prove to be a particularly popular institution, since the fortunate locals naturally preferred to eliminate any excess of demand over supply by raising wages rather than by augmenting the supply from the outside. In a study published in 1919, D. P. Smelser found that only fourteen national unions out of a total of 125 maintained employment bureaus; of these "only seven can be said to possess merit."[20]

One national institution which probably tended to increase the geographic mobility of union members was the traveling loan system, which was intended to facilitate the movement of workers from areas of unemployment to communities where job openings existed. The Cigar Makers pioneered in establishing a traveling loan system (1867) which provided for repayment by the traveling member to the local in which he found work. Like the employment bureau, however, the national traveling-loan system was not overly successful. Rates of repayment were low; moreover, the induced mobility was not always salutary from the viewpoint of the national union, for, although loans were supposed to be extended only to members who could furnish evidence of genuine employment opportunity at their intended destinations, such evidence could be easily falsified.

Although, as we shall see presently, the geographic mobility of labor was an important factor in the formation of national unions, the latter did not adopt policies which were intended to reduce labor's mobility. We can find, however, one important exception by which to prove our rule. In the event of a strike in any locality, publication of the fact in the journal of the national union was intended to deter members elsewhere from traveling to the struck community in search of work. Furthermore some national unions—all of which except one, incidentally, were organized in local product markets—permitted striking locals to refuse to accept traveling cards presented by migrant members.[21]

The Influence of Economic Growth

The term "journeyman" is descriptive of the migratory habits of the earliest craftsmen. Commons and Saposs (attempting to apply Bücher's theory of industrial development to American economic history) described the colonial artisan as "an itinerant, travelling laboriously to the farm or

20. D. P. Smelser, *Unemployment and American Trade Unions* (Baltimore: Johns Hopkins, 1919), pp. 75–90; see also pp. 94–106.

21. George M. Janes, *The Control of Strikes in American Trade Unions* (Baltimore: Johns Hopkins, 1916), pp. 76–79.

plantation of his employer who was also the consumer of his product."[22] With the widening of market areas, however, the locus of production shifted from the residence of the consumer to the residence of the worker and then to the shop or factory, so that, whatever economic class structures later emerged, geographic mobility no longer remained an essential concomitant of the employee function. Thus, insofar as the economic growth of the country was accompanied by the development of modern economic classes, one aspect of labor mobility tended to disappear. There remained, however, a tradition of itinerancy, the survival of which might be traced in part to the absence in this country of feudalistic, legal, and other institutional barriers which had enabled municipalities abroad to exclude migrant craftsmen from the practice of their calling. Saposs noted some isolated examples of this species of local protection in the colonial period. As in medieval times, such legal discrimination derived moral sanction from the alleged necessity of protecting the consuming public from the allegedly shoddy workmanship of strangers. Unlike their European forbears, however, the early American craftsmen possessed no decisive political power in the community and were therefore held rigorously to account by the local consumers who, in their capacity as farmers, dominated the political scene. Thus, according to Saposs, "Unless the farmer-consumer was certain this protection was to his benefit, he refused it."

Economic growth, moreover, was associated with other developments which in themselves served to increase the migratory activities of the workers. In the first place increasing industrialization, with resulting urbanization, accelerated the movement of country mechanics to the cities, where wages were normally higher than in the villages and small towns. "From the beginning of the century," wrote Barnett, "The employing printers, in any time of difficulty with the local unions, have customarily obtained a supply of workmen from the unorganized towns." And the Carpenters' secretary on one occasion called attention to "the disastrous results to our Unions centered in large cities by having a horde of non-Union men continually flocking in from the country."[23] In 1900, President Donnelly, of the Printers, observed, "The influence of our organization in the large cities has been such that the employers have been compelled to draw upon the smaller country towns for their force of non-union men."[24]

The building of new communities incident to the westward and industrial development of the country during the second half of the nineteenth century resulted in a chronic oversupply at the local level of certain types of labor (most notably in the construction industry), which provided a powerful stimulus to geographic mobility. The amount of building labor required to

22. Commons, *History of Labour,* v. I, pp. 6–7; see also pp. 45–47.
23. Barnett, *The Printers,* pp. 260–261.
24. *Proceedings of the International Typographical Union,* 1900, p. 47.

erect a boom town was ordinarily greater than that required by its subsequent rate of growth, so that a substantial portion of its initial construction force was released from employment. Stagnation of employment opportunities was confined to the local level, however, for while demand was destroyed in one locality it was being created in another booming area. Thus a portion of the country's supply of building labor was absorbed by such growth requirements, and the men comprising this segment were obliged to keep on the move in order to find work. The magnetic pull of a geographic wage differential which was measured entirely by the rate prevailing in the "new" regions (since the alternative to migration was unemployment) was great, and the possibility that demand in the new area would decline drastically before the migration in response to its original level had ceased presented a serious obstacle to the formation and survival of local unions in the construction industry. This situation was particularly troublesome to the Carpenters:

Our greatest loss in lapsed and suspended unions has been principally in the smaller towns of the Western and Southern States, mostly in new towns where building booms have been under way and collapsed. In a number of instances, the members of these lapsed unions have gone into other towns and organized new unions or joined those already existing.[25]

The proliferation of the railroads greatly increased the geographic mobility of labor during this period, just as the development of the automobile and the highway net stimulated migration after the first World War.[26] The railroad increased the traveler's range and reduced the cost of his transportation. In some instances, where the wayfarer was not too demanding with respect to accommodations en route, the cost of travel could be reduced virtually to zero. That such cases were not unknown is revealed in a warning issued by the president of the Bricklayers in 1892 to the effect that, if a strike currently in progress should fail, "Whatever men are in the town will be either blacklisted or scabbed, or else they will have to do the box-car act, and leave their families here until a fresher and better pasture is found."

It will be recalled that the admonition of the Bricklayers' president in 1867 to equalize wage rates in different localities in order to eliminate the undermining effects of migration (see page 53 above), was directed to unions "located nearby to each other." Two years later the first transcontinental railroad was completed with the driving of a gold spike into the ties at Promontory Point, Utah, and at the next convention of the Typographical Union it was reported that although trade was good in all other regions, the

25. *Proceedings*, 1898, p. 38; 1892, p. 16 (report of the secretary). Also *Proceedings*, 1888, p. 13; and 1890, p. 16. In the latter reference, the secretary speaks of "new towns where building 'booms' have spurted for one season and then collapsed."

26. Glocker, *Government of American Unions*, p. 33, and Thomas R. Smith, "The Analysis of Past Migration," in Carter Goodrich *et al.*, *Migration and Economic Opportunity* (Philadelphia: University of Pennsylvania Press, 1936), p. 683.

printers' locals on the Pacific Coast had been obliged to accept wage cuts because of the large influx of traveling printers who had reached the West on the new railroad.[27] And while (as we have noted) building trades unions in the eighties and nineties attributed the "overcrowding" in the "booming towns of the West and South" to the blandishments of "unprincipled" employers, it is unlikely that their "newspaper advertising" would have met with such prompt and emphatic response had not the expanding railway net permitted contemporary migrants to embark upon expeditions which their economic ancestors, journeymen though they were in name and in fact, had rarely contemplated.

The Influence of the Business Cycle

The influence of cyclical swings in business conditions is indicated in the following excerpts from the records of the Bricklayers' union. The first two observations were made in the depressed years 1895 and 1896; the third, in 1900, a good year in the construction industry.

The number of our men upon the "road" has been unusually large seeking employment, and the great numbers of western men arriving in eastern cities looking for work shows what the condition of the trade has been.

In some sections of the country, the far west and middle west, our trade has been remarkably poor, causing thousands to travel in search of work away from their homes.

In general, the supply of men of our trade has not been equal to the demand and great numbers of men belonging to northern and western unions, likewise some from Texas, have overrun the country jumping from place to place, and some, I am sorry to report, leaving in a disgraceful manner.[28]

From the above it would appear that migration occurred during both good and bad times, but that it was not independent of cyclical fluctuations. On the contrary, it seems that prosperity and depression each exerted some causal influence upon the geographic mobility of labor, each presumably for a different reason. An explanation is suggested by Slichter's analysis of the turnover of factory labor into the following components: (1) resignations; (2) layoffs; (3) discharges; and (4) miscellaneous causes (death, disability, sickness, superannuation, and so on.) Since turnover, defined as the termination of employment,[29] is frequently a prerequisite of geographic mobility, the latter may be considered to include the same elements in its compound. Resigna-

27. George A. Tracy, *History of the Typographical Union* (Indianapolis: International Typographical Union, 1913), p. 247.

28. *Proceedings,* 1895, p. 31; 1896, p. 89; 1900, p. 38.

29. Sumner H. Slichter, *The Turnover of Factory Labor* (New York: Appleton, 1919), p. 11; see also pp. 3, 30–33, 85.

tions being more frequent in prosperous times and layoffs and discharges reaching their cyclical peaks during downturns, it would follow that labor migration was stimulated in prosperity primarily by whatever factors made for resignations; and in depressions, primarily by layoffs and discharges. Slichter found that the turnover rate was lower in depression than in prosperity (over the period 1906–1916) and that "resignations constitute the most frequent source of terminations of employment."

However, one early study uncovered a strong negative relationship between unemployment and the number of members of the Pattern Makers' union transferred by traveling card during the period 1909–1915. This led the author to deny that "the poor condition of trade forced many workmen to move from one city to another" and to conclude instead that "the percentage of transfers is governed by the fluctuations of employment between individual labor markets."[30] But the writer attributed this result in large part to increasing reliance by potential migrants upon dissemination of employment information by the union; in earlier periods the relationship between transfers and unemployment might not have been so strongly negative.

The Influence of Intermittent Demand

In certain industries intermittency in the demand for labor occurred independently of cyclical fluctuations in business conditions. Since such irregularity was characterized by a more rapid alternation of peaks and troughs in employment than was the cyclical variety, industries in which it occurred were affected to a peculiar degree by the problem of migration.

Perhaps the most familiar examples of noncyclical intermittency in the demand for labor are seasonal patterns of employment. In seasonal industries the duration of the job might be short, with the result that the worker does not consider himself permanently attached to any particular employer. The work forces in such industries were characterized by relatively high proportions of "floaters," whereas in nonseasonal industries, "The high turnover rate in most plants is due to a few men changing rapidly while the great majority of the force is stable."[31] Habitual occupational restlessness, built up by the short duration of the job, not only stimulated migration but made it practicable by creating the job vacancies which it required. "The very fact that workers are changing rapidly renders it easier for them to change since the rapid vacation of positions creates numerous opportunities for employment." The result was a game of musical chairs—but a game in which the number of seats was equal to the number of players. Since the building trades have always been regarded as a seasonal industry *par excellence,* the unique preoccupation of the Bricklayers and the Carpenters with the problem of mobility is understandable.

30. Smelser, *Unemployment,* pp. 27–28.
31. Slichter, *Turnover of Labor,* p. 43. Also pp. 85, n. 2, 157; see also p. 35.

It should be recalled at this point that the building trades unions were also vulnerable to migration on another count: the boom-and-bust pattern of construction work in new localities. This was peculiarly conducive to migration, for stagnation in one locality might coincide with opportunity elsewhere, whereas cyclical and, to a lesser extent, seasonal slumps in employment affected all regions of the country simultaneously.

Busy periods in seasonal trades, however, did stimulate the migration of part-time workers who followed, for the most part, agricultural pursuits in the off seasons. This migration of part-time workers from the farms was facilitated when the industry in question was typically located within short distances of agricultural communities and when neither the industrial skill required nor the trade unions of the full-time workers presented formidable obstacles to the bucolic invaders. The coal miners were particularly vulnerable to the incursions of these "cornhuskers," so-called; the first convention of the United Mine Workers adopted the following resolution:

That men who only work part of the year in the mines must pay all dues and abide by all conditions of our organization, and should they fall in arrears during the time they are out of the mines, they must pay all arrears before they can be allowed to work.[32]

Intermittency in the employment of compositors was associated with the problem of peak demand, primarily in the job-printing branch of the trade. The printing industry has long been divided into the newspaper branch and the book-and-job branch. The former has been and still is essentially a local-market industry; the latter trade has grown more competitive, but in the period under discussion much of its business was "custom-order," in which a firm located in the vicinity of the customer enjoyed a preponderant competitive advantage. Due to this localized nature of the industry, extra work (often resulting from the requirements of legislative bodies, according to Barnett) was handled by the *ad-hoc* hiring of out-of-town printers.[33] This state of affairs was eminently compatible with the existence of an important degree of labor mobility, but since the printing industry (unlike the building trades) offered sufficiently steady employment to attract relatively permanent work forces to its establishments, this mobility was concentrated, at any one time, in a certain segment of the printer population. The tradition of "carrying the banner," however, remained a proud one throughout the trade, and the tramp printer became a character in American folklore. Even a most unsympathetic observer of the American labor movement of his time admitted that "never was there another such a shrewd, good-natured, hapless, and yet reckless class of strollers on earth." Mr. Pinkerton continues:

32. Quoted in Evans, *United Mine Workers*, v. II, p. 27.
33. Barnett, *The Printers*, p. 30.

Printers are not all tramps, but, as stated, there is scarcely a printer who has not at some time been upon the road. The fraternity are quite proud of their accomplishments in this direction. Half the chatting among the employees of an office is upon the adventures of certain of their number, or of some particularly chronic old walker who has made a national reputation for himself on account of some noteworthy achievement in the tramp line, or who has some interesting personal characteristics. There are often among these confirmed tramp-printers, many of most brilliant minds and winning manners. . . .[34]

THE EXTENT OF GEOGRAPHIC MOBILITY

No data are available for the precise determination of the magnitude of the geographic labor mobility in the United States in the period during which the first national unions arose. Statistics on interstate migration are available from 1850,[35] but they reflect primarily certain broad trends in internal migration, especially the westward migration (which was dominant up to about 1910) and the increasing industrialization of the nation (the farm-to-industry movement, which was appreciable as far back as 1850 and which dominated internal migration after 1920).[36] Although numerical data are lacking, there is some evidence that the geographic mobility of labor increased during the last half of the nineteenth century and was of greater concern to the labor movement in that period than it has been in recent times.

Some of the conditions enumerated in the previous section support the view that labor migration increased in the period 1850–1900. The extension of the railway net, the increasing industrialization and urbanization of the country (one concomitant of which was the movement of "country mechanics" to the larger labor centers), and the westward movement of the urban frontier (the boom town phenomenon) made for increased mobility. Increasing coöperation among employers and the appearance of the interstate firm in the construction industry also stimulated migration, although this might have been offset by the growth of trade unions during the period and by their more vigorous efforts to cope with the problem by organizing the migrants and by disseminating information concerning the state of trade throughout the country in labor newspapers and periodicals.

Some evidence of the trend of migration might be obtained by compiling a series of ratios of a union's issue of travel cards to its membership. This has been done with Typographical Union data for the period 1857–1892 inclusive, as here shown:

34. Allan Pinkerton, *Strikers, Communists, Tramps and Detectives* (New York: G. W. Carleton, 1882), pp. 52–53.

35. *Historical Statistics of the United States,* 1789–1945 (Washington, D. C.: U. S. Department of Commerce, 1947). More detailed information—on east-west and north-south differentials—is available from 1870.

36. Thomas R. Smith, "The Analysis of Past Migration," in Goodrich *et al., Migration,* pp. 682 and 679.

	Local Admissions by Card	National Membership	Ratio (per cent)
1857	191	1,306	14.62
1858	278	2,181	12.75
1859	—	2,362	—
1860	549	3,492	15.72
1861	—	—	—
1862	—	1,585	—
1863	224	1,875	11.95
1864	506	2,577	19.64
1865	643	2,477	25.96
1866	928	4,013	23.12
1867	1,236	5,224	23.66
1868	2,216	6,095	36.36
1869	2,250	7,563	29.75
1870	2,738	7,657	35.76
1871	3,163	8,725	36.25
1872	3,662	8,724	41.98
1873	4,263	9,797	43.51
1874	3,427	9,819	34.90
1875	3,705	9,245	40.06
1876	3,163	8,624	36.68
1877	2,323	6,900	33.67
1878	1,267	4,260	29.74
1879	985	5,968	16.50
1880	1,467	6,520	22.50
1881	2,487	7,931	31.36
1882	3,813	10,439	36.53
1883	4,993	12,273	40.68
1884	7,754	16,030	48.37
1885	7,006	16,183	43.29
1886	7,726	18,484	41.80
1887	8,588	19,190	44.75
1888	9,157	17,491	52.35
1889	11,647	21,120	55.15
1890	12,387	22,608	54.79
1891	16,268	25,165	64.65
1892	18,559	28,187	65.84

No data on admissions by card were available before or after those years.[37]

Since the period covered is long enough to embrace several complete cyclical swings (including the long depression of 1873–1879), the record indicates a decided upward trend in the ratio of local union admissions by traveling cards to total membership, this percentage being four times as great in the terminal year of the series as it was in the initial year. It is possible, however, that an upward trend in the cards-to-membership ratio does not indicate a secular upswing in migration. If the union had gained its initial

37. Data on admissions by card were taken from *Proceedings of the International Typographical Union.* (Reports of Subordinate Unions.) Data on national membership may be found in Barnett, *The Printers,* pp. 375–376.

strength among the sedentary compositors and later recruited an increasing percentage of its membership from the ranks of the footloose, the proportion of traveling cards to membership would rise over time without any corresponding upswing in migration. In the case of the printers, however, it is reasonable to assume that variations in the ratio of habitual wanderers to the total annual increment of new members was not significant, since so large a proportion of printers had "been upon the road" at some stage in their careers and since the most impelling factor in the formation and early career of the National Typographical Union was the desire to control migration. If this interpretation of the data is accurate, the increasing proportion of traveling cards to membership does represent a significant upward trend in migration.

Data for longer periods are lacking, but there are grounds for believing that the geographic mobility of labor was greater before the first World War than in more recent times. Although the development of the automobile probably facilitated migration after the first World War at least as much as the railroad had done in the prewar period, other factors existed which rendered the utilization of this mechanical advantage less complete than it might have been otherwise.

In the first place, with the passing of the western frontier, the building of new localities lost some importance as an inducement to migration.[38] Growth of existing communities of course continued, but, while such growth created job opportunities, it did not necessarily stimulate migration.

Of greater importance was the emphasis on job stability which characterized the interwar period, and which remains a matter of paramount concern. Employers themselves, whose interest in recruiting workers had tended to increase mobility in the nineteenth century, also made serious efforts to retain those already in their employ. During the 1920's, they introduced systems of personnel administration which were intended to reduce turnover. Unions also played an important part in reducing turnover. Their interest in job stability stemmed from their concern with economic security and was implemented by a vigorous advocacy of the principle of seniority. Although the Printers had adopted a "priority" rule in 1890, the seniority movement first became widespread during and after the depression which began in 1929. Seniority acts as a double deterrent to mobility: it makes the

38. According to Kuznets, the increase in the proportion of net capital formation to national product in the period covered by the last three decades of the nineteenth century (from 14 per cent in 1869–1878 to 16.3 per cent in 1889–1898) was due primarily to a rise in the proportion of net construction to national product (from 8.1 per cent to 12.9 per cent). Similarly, the subsequent decline in the share of net investment (to 10.6 per cent in 1919–1928) is attributed to a decline in the share of net construction (to 5 per cent). These findings are consistent with our hypothesis concerning the impact of the expanding frontier on the mobility of construction labor, but the possibility that these movements in construction were cyclical rather than secular must not be excluded. Simon Kuznets, "Proportion of Capital Formation to National Product," *American Economic Review* (*Papers and Proceedings*), v. XLII, May 1952, number 2, pp. 515–517.

unemployed man reluctant to leave his home community, first, because of the fear of losing his position on the seniority list of the firm by which he has been employed, and, second, because of the certainty that he personally will be among the last to be hired in a plant situated in another locality (even if employment opportunities there are generally better than in the home community) and the first to be laid off at some future date.[39]

The unions probably contributed at least one further deterrent to labor migration. Apart from any policies which they might have adopted, their growth and the legal protection extended to them during the New Deal period virtually eliminated the employer-induced, strike-breaking component of migration. And to the extent to which unions might have been successful in reducing or eliminating geographic differentials in wages and other terms of employment, the incentive to labor mobility was also reduced.

In the light of the foregoing considerations, Slichter's estimate that the resignation rate among manual workers in factories declined from about 67 per cent before the first World War to slightly in excess of 30 per cent in 1929 and to less than 15 per cent in 1936 and 1937, might well be indicative of a similar decline in the geographic mobility of labor. (However, since turnover is composed of layoffs and discharges as well as resignations, a decline in the rate of resignations, without additional information, does not necessarily imply a decline in the rate of turnover.)

It would appear from such sketchy evidence as we have been able to marshall that the geographic mobility of labor during the period in which the first national unions emerged was economically more important in terms of the geographic range of its effectiveness and the percentage of the working population engaged in migratory activity than it had been in preceding periods and than it proved to be in more recent times. If this conclusion is correct and if our theoretical reasoning in the first section is valid, it is possible that the mobility of labor alone, apart from the extension of product markets, might have been sufficient to induce the formation of national unions. The operation of this incentive has been blurred, however, by the historical coincidence that the national unions first emerged in a period strongly characterized by the development of national product markets. This phenomenon has led observers to emphasize the causal role of the latter development in explaining the rise of the national union. However, as we have pointed out, this period was also characterized by developments which stimulated wage-induced labor migration to a unique extent. Hence one could explain the timing of the emergence of national unionism by reference to the extension of markets in labor as well as in goods. It is pertinent, therefore, to inquire into the "nationalizing" influence of labor migration.

39. "Men who do not have work, but who have claims to jobs when work picks up, are less likely to move to new localities in search of work and to be drawn away by a rise of employment in other industries." (S. H. Slichter, *Union Policies and Industrial Management* (Washington: Brookings Institution, 1941), p. 152; see also pp. 100–101, 202.

CHAPTER FOUR

THE PROCESS OF NATIONALIZATION

THE LOCAL unions appeared reluctant to acknowledge the implications of the increased geographic mobility of labor. At first the local attempted to cope with this phenomenon singlehandedly. Where such unilateral attempts failed, they were succeeded by limited coöperation among the locals affected. Finally, it was recognized that the problem posed by the traveling worker could best be handled by a national union through the issuance and honoring of traveling cards.

THE SINGLE-HANDED APPROACH AND ITS FAILURE

Although the nomadic habits of their members had been sufficiently widespread to prompt coöperation among local unions in the same trade at a very early period in the country's history, these local bodies tried also to cope with the problem by various forms of unilateral action. The exclusion of outsiders by a policy of charging high initiation fees and by exclusive trade agreements with local employers constituted a frontal attack on the competitive effects of migration, but such a course of action was seldom feasible. It required, as we have seen, strong control over the local labor market, and such control was rarely achieved. Indeed, it was the prior existence of migration which often frustrated local attempts at organization and even overwhelmed the local bodies in some instances.

Many of the local unions received the traveling brethren fraternally, aiding them financially and helping them to obtain employment. The social standing of the migrant was somewhat equivocal. As a throwback to the olden times when itinerancy was essential to the practice of the trade, he received from his sedentary colleagues the sentimental affection which invariably accrues to antique objects and institutions. On the other hand, the impecuniousness of the wanderer and his constitutional disregard of legally incurred debt often put local hospitality to a stern test. The pages of union journals of the period are liberally sprinkled with the imprecations of local unions, the members of which had considered themselves obligated to settle the board and lodging accounts left unpaid by these "birds of passage." The social virtues of the traveling craftsmen were debated vigorously in many issues of the Iron Molders' *Journal* during the eighties and nineties, and, after one skeptical contributor had referred to the traveling membership as "the noble band of never-sweats," the sober international president considered himself obliged to intervene personally in behalf of his mobile constituents. His defense was dignified and comprehensive, but when he suggested at one point that the frequent intemperance of the lonely wanderer might be ascribed to melancholy, it was apparent to partisans in both camps that the president had tried to prove too much. He was challenged immediately by one of those whose cause he had championed, a traveling molder who denied with heat that he and his colleagues drank when they were sad. They were sad, according to this authority, only when they had nothing to drink.

In any event (perhaps because so many of the sedentary members had been travelers themselves and could reasonably expect to resume their migrant status on short notice), many of the locals extended to traveling journeymen what was later described in the traveling card of the Typographical Union as their "friendship and good offices." If no opportunity for employment existed in the locality involved, the local union might extend a traveling loan to the migrant, so that he could proceed to some community where job vacancies existed. This granting of traveling loans by individual local unions tended to stimulate migration, just as the practice of certain powerfully entrenched locals in excluding migrants tended to discourage it.

But if jobs were available, a local union might seek to find employment for traveling fellow craftsmen. Thus, the constitution of the New York Printers' union of 1850 listed as one of the objects of that organization "the relief of deserving printers who may visit our city in search of employment."[1] This practice probably stemmed from the obligation placed upon their members by many of the struggling typographical organizations in the first half of the nineteenth century to obtain employment for brother members "in preference to any other person."[2]

Efforts to cope with the immigration of potential strikebreakers were also made by local unions on a unilateral basis, and such efforts were continued long after the rise of the early national unions. Having found that the penniless newcomers could not easily be dissuaded from replacing their striking members, the locals often sought to back their moral appeal with direct provision for the support of the unwanted immigrants and even for their

1. Quoted in Ethelbert Stewart, *A Documentary History of the Early Organizations* of Printers (Indianapolis: International Typographical Union, 1907), p. 79.

2. *Constitution of the Baltimore Typographical Society,* 1832, reproduced in Stewart, *Documentary History,* p. 101. See also pp. 12–13, 98. See also George E. Barnett, *The Printers, A Study in American Trade Unionism* (Cambridge: American Economic Association, 1909), p. 21 and note.

transportation from strikebound communities. Evans records a successful instance of such reinforced discussion, which occurred during a strike conducted in 1873 by a lodge of the Miners' and Laborers' Benevolent Association in the Blossburg district of Pennsylvania:

After several weeks' idleness a number of Swedes, as strikebreakers, were brought into the field, placed in barracks at Arnot by the operators and given all the protection possible under the circumstances mentioned.

The old miners, not to be outdone, made persistent efforts to talk with the new men in order to explain the situation to them, but were refused this privilege. A Swedish interpreter, however, soon solved the problem, and in a very short time had all the strike breakers and strikers marching together on the road for Blossburg, about four miles distant, with a Scotch bagpipe artist leading them, and, to the inspiring tune of "McGregor's Gathering," landed them at Blossburg, where a mass meeting was held for jollification over their success. After the meeting closed the imported men were given food and shelter until the next day, when they left the field, with the result that satisfactory conclusions were entered into between the operators and miners that gave the miners all for which they had been contending. It was a manly effort and deserved well the victory achieved.[3]

The Bricklayers reported similar episodes. Conduct of the important eight-hour strike in New York City in 1869 was hampered by the necessity and expense of "sending strangers back to their homes that have been enticed to the City of New York by their employers." Seven years later one local in the same union complained that, "Our city, during this struggle was an asylum to that class of transient bricklayers, whose name is legion, at times when these struggles are going on. We had to care for them; we gave them permits to work . . . besides supported (them), while unemployed, at the expense of the Union."[4] This last report indicates that not all the potential strikebreakers from out of town were recruited directly by the employers. The president of the Glass Bottle Blowers' Association distinguished between recruits and soldiers of fortune, but found the distinction of little significance to the embattled local:

I believe that every floater and strike-breaker in the trade has been at Bridgeton within the last three months, and this class of people are more to be dreaded than the employer, because it is by their aid that employers have been able to break strikes in many trades. These men have come either to go to work, or else demand money, cards, railway tickets and, in many cases, admission to the Association; and they have had to be taken care of in order to prevent their being used against us. Agents of the glass companies have also brought non-union flint blowers from Indiana and from Tarentum (to Bridgeton, New Jersey). All of these we had to return to their homes, with the exception of one shop which is still at

3. Chris Evans, *History of the United Mine Workers of America* (Indianapolis, 1918), v. I, p. 43.
4. *Proceedings*, 1869, pp. 38 and 45 (report of the secretary); 1876, p. 24.

the Cumberland. No matter how good the times may be, every trade-union leader will find during a strike that there are lots of unemployed people in this country, and they are potent factors in the struggle.[5]

It might be noted in passing that, on one occasion at least, the Bottle Blowers financed the exodus of migrants in a peaceful industrial situation. In 1887 a Montreal firm arranged for the immigration of a number of Scotch glass blowers who were to be employed in a new black bottle factory, since American blowers were unable to work black glass properly. Upon their arrival, the Scotsmen were admitted into the local assembly of the Knights of Labor. (The two bottle blowers' unions at that time were organized as K. of L. district assemblies.) Shortly thereafter the factory was closed down permanently, and three of the Scotch blowers were sent back to their homeland by the Montreal local assembly which was permitted by District Assembly 149 (which had jurisdiction over the locals of bottle blowers in the eastern section of the country) to utilize funds obtained in a recent strike assessment for that purpose. Although the union raised no objection to the importation of these blowers, its acceptance was conditioned upon their employment as blowers of black glass only; once that form of employment was denied to them, the Knights were willing to finance their return to Scotland in order to prevent their competing with native craftsmen on work that the latter, as well as the former, were capable of performing.

Since most of the local unions of the period were not strong enough to enforce a policy of excluding migrants from employment, and since this policy could prove effective only in local market industries, it proved impossible to cope with the problem of migration by unilateral action alone. The practice of "buying off" (to quote the Bricklayers' candid secretary) outsiders during strikes was a stop-gap device at best and even aggravated the condition it was intended to counteract, since, as the president of the Glass Bottle Blowers observed, some migrants were invariably attracted to communities where it was known that local unions were purchasing neutrality from strangers. And while, as we have mentioned, this practice was continued well after the emergence of national unionism, it invariably overtaxed the treasuries of the local organizations which were obliged to resort to it. As a president of the Bricklayers described the situation,

The "scab boss" . . . would be advertising for men, and when they would arrive upon the scene of the strife the Union would be compelled to use whatever funds there were in their treasury, together with taxing its members, to either buy up the scabs to prevent them from going to work, or else pay them wages and send them away from the locality. With the large amount of this transient element in the country, it is almost impossible for a local union to bear such a strain upon its treasury for funds, and to have to depend on their own resources altogether.[6]

5. *Proceedings,* 1899, p. 28 (report of the president); see also 1887, president's report.
6. *Proceedings,* 1885, p. 35 (report of the president).

The insufficiency of the single-handed approach was demonstrated in the case of the Omaha local union of bricklayers which, during a strike in 1888, was confronted with an influx of craftsmen bearing the Brotherhood's traveling cards, which admitted them to membership in any affiliated local. The Omaha local advanced the cost of return transportation to most of these men "with the understanding that it would be collected by those Unions with whom they deposited their cards, and return it to No. 1, Omaha." While some local unions did coöperate with Omaha, others "positively declined to do so, thereby showing a very unfriendly disposition to their brothers who are in distress."[7]

It was apparent that, in the great majority of cases, the problems raised by the geographic mobility of labor could not be disposed of effectively by local unions acting in isolation. Coöperation of some sort was required.

COÖPERATION AND ITS DEFICIENCIES

Coöperation among the different local unions in the same trade consisted in the interchange of information effected by the correspondence of local secretaries, just as coöperation among the American colonies in the pre-Revolutionary period consisted in the lines of communication maintained by local Committees of Correspondence. The information exchanged concerned the condition of trade in various localities and the status of those men on the road who practiced the common calling.

With respect to the first type of information, the attitude of local organizations revealed, as we have already observed, a peculiar asymmetry. They were eager to correct any false impressions which local employers might have broadcast, but reluctant to report conditions the knowledge of which in other quarters might stimulate immigration. Thus this early correspondence was intended to reduce employer-induced migration, although, as the Glass Bottle Blowers learned to their sorrow, dissemination of information concerning strike situations sometimes stimulated the migration of unprincipled "free riders."

The bulk of the correspondence, however, consisted in the interchange of information concerning members who were regarded as *persona non grata* by local unions in communities from which they had departed. In many trades this took the form of an exchange of lists bearing the names of "unfair" members; the forthright printers referred to these as "rat lists." These lists were intended to be both preventive and punitive in effect. In their former capacity they were of advisory value to locals in communities which the blacklisted individuals might include in their itineraries, and the issuing local was regarded as having rendered a valuable service to her sister organizations. As disciplinary instruments, however, the blacklists were intended to lengthen the arm of local law, and for this reason the local which issued a

7. *Proceedings,* 1888, p. 28 (report of the secretary).

blacklist was in the debt of an organization wihch honored it by refusing admission to travelers whose names appeared thereon. Since the issuing and honoring of lists were considered mutual obligations of the coöperating local unions, it was expected that all debts would cancel out.

It was soon discovered, however, that the control of migration through this system of mutual aid implied the surrender by each participating local of some of its autonomy. As the early local unions developed, they sought to impose upon their members two obligations which they considered of vital importance. The first of these was the obligation to work for not less than the union wage. As an example, the constitution of the New York Typographical Association in 1833 required that presiding officers ask newly initiated members to support "the constitution and the scale of prices of this association." Elsewhere in the document the following section appears:

The scale of prices for labor, appended to this constitution shall, in all cases, be considered as a part thereof, and no member of this association shall, on any pretense whatever, work, either directly or indirectly, for prices less than those specified therein.[8]

The second obligation which the locals attempted to enforce as they grew stronger was the requirement that no member work in any establishment which employed nonmembers at the trade. Thus in 1850, the constitution of the Philadelphia printers' local provided that

In no case shall members of this union work in any office after the 2d day of September 1850, where hands are employed who refuse to join the union; and should any member do so, he shall be fined or expelled, at the option of the union.[9]

This closed (or, more accurately, union) shop requirement apparently evolved from the earlier obligation which made it incumbent upon a member to secure employment for a brother member in preference to any other craftsman. This requirement seems to represent a later stage of development than the first obligation (to maintain union standard conditions). Although both were doubtless often honored in the breach, their acceptance in principle reflected the adoption of a modern philosophy of trade unionism. How were these obligations affected by the coöperative attempts of the local unions to cope with worker migration?

Coöperation depended upon the refusal by each local to accept any traveling workmen who had been blacklisted by any other local union which was

8. *Constitution of the New York Typographical Society,* 1833, reproduced in Stewart, *Documentary History,* p. 104, 106. The same requirement appears in the *Constitution of the New Orleans Typographical Association,* 1839, (Stewart, p. 114) and of the Philadelphia Typographical Union, 1850, (Stewart, p. 119). See also p. 116 for the identical provision in the constitution of the New Orleans local union.

9. Stewart, *Documentary History,* p. 123.

a party to the agreement, or, as the Franklin Typographical Society of Cincinnati proposed in 1835, "That rats pronounced such by one society, be considered as such by all other societies."[10] This meant, for example, that a local union would be obliged to exclude a traveler who had been blacklisted elsewhere by an organization which had been able to enforce more rigorous standards than the local in question had established. The locals were willing to blacklist men convicted elsewhere for acts which they themselves considered illegal, but they were often reluctant to exclude travelers for behavior which would not have been regarded as offensive within their own jurisdiction, or which, if it was so considered, had been atoned for by exemplary behavior since its commission.

Their reluctance was understandable, since denial of admission to migrants threatened the security of the local unions by creating a force of untouchables in every community. Nor was this threat without practical significance. Since the blacklisting of a man who had since left the locality did not augment the supply of nonunion labor in that community, this form of discipline was resorted to unsparingly by many of the early local unions. Thus the Nashville Typographical Society decided (1837) that "No person published by the society as a 'rat' shall be released without the unanimous consent of the voting members present at a regular meeting."[11] But the cost of discipline, while avoided by the local which administered it, was shifted to the sister organizations on its mailing list, and so excessive blacklisting threatened interlocal coöperation. For example, in 1838 the St. Louis Typographical Association protested against the continued "ratting" of printers whose behavior had been exemplary after they had left the locality in which they had incurred official opprobrium. After the seventh convention (1858) of the National Typographical Union urged its local affiliates to refrain from irresponsible abuse of their power to blacklist and to impose lesser penalties whenever possible.[12]

Although the obligation of the local union member to offer his services at a wage no lower than the union rate implied that the local union was free to admit to membership those who were willing to abide by local standards, the local in question could not admit him if he had been declared unfair in some other locality. Thus interlocal coöperation brought into conflict different local standards of employment and of discipline.

Furthermore, while a local union had to refuse membership to a man who had been declared unfair by another, it was not obliged to receive a traveler who had been a member in good standing of his local of origin. It will be

10. *Minutes of the Columbia Typographical Society*, Stewart, *Documentary History*, p. 56.

11. *Constitution of the Nashville Typographical Society*, 1837, Art. XIV, Section 5. Reproduced in Stewart, *Documentary History*, p. 110. See also pp. 67–68.

12. George A. Tracy, *History of the Typographical Union* (Indianapolis: International Typographical Union, 1913), p. 110.

recalled that when the early organizations required of their members only that they obtain employment for their brethren in preference to nonunionists whenever possible, this courtesy of preferential hiring was extended to travelers who had been good trade unionists in other communities. Later, as the locals sought to forbid their members to work in the same establishments with nonmembers, it became necessary to accord membership status to traveling workers if the latter were to continue on a parity with the local men. Indeed, the welfare of the local union, as well as that of the migrant, was involved, for failure to admit the latter would result in the familiar menace of a body of competent workmen in the locality who were outside the local union fold. And, unlike those branded as unfair, these newcomers might violate local standards in good proletarian faith: according to Stewart, "Roving printers . . . claimed that if they did not work below the scale of the society they had originally joined they were not violating any obligation."[13] The result was that most of the locals which were not strong enough to exclude outsiders from employment did admit travelers to membership. The Philadelphia printers' union, the same organization whose prohibition against its members working with nonunionists has been quoted above, required traveling printers to join their organization and extended the prohibition to include working with nonunionists from out of town:

Strangers arriving in the city shall be allowed to work, until the next stated meeting of the union, when they must become members. Should he or they neglect or refuse to join the union, it shall be the duty of the hands employed in the office to quit work, and insist upon his or their discharge.[14]

However, the admission of migrants in good standing elsewhere necessitated the surrender of a portion of local autonomy. It meant that the receiving local had to accept standards of admission and discipline in effect elsewhere. Requirements similar to the provision in the constitution of the Columbia Typographical Society of Washington, D. C., in 1815, which specified that, "No person shall be eligible to become a member of this society, who is not, at the time of his application, a resident of the District of Columbia, and who shall not have served an apprenticeship satisfactory to the society,"[15] could no longer be maintained.

The inadequacy of coöperation as a method of mitigating the impact of

13. Stewart, *Documentary History,* p. 37. The local whose standards were threatened in this instance was the Washington, D. C. City Typographical Society. According to Tracy (*History of the Typographical Union,* p. 57), "The Washington society's scale was higher than that of any northern city, and as the government printing made the capital a sort of Mecca for 'tramp' printers, this society became the first serious victim of this subterfuge."

14. *Constitution of the Philadelphia Typographical Union* (1850), Art. IV, Sec. 5. Reproduced in Stewart, *Documentary History,* p. 123.

15. *Constitution of the Columbia Typographical Society,* Washington, D. C. (1815), Art. XI. Reproduced in Stewart, *Documentary History,* p. 94.

labor's geographic mobility lay in its incompatibility with the absolute sovereignty of the local unions which were parties to the agreement. The coöperating local had to accept as a condition of receiving the outside aid which it required an abridgement of those powers which were implicit in the obligations of its members to accept employment only under conditions specified by that local and only if all of their fellow employees were also members of the organization. As far as migrant workers within its territorial jurisdiction were concerned, the local had to accept in lieu of its own criteria certain standards of employment, admission, and discipline adopted by the other unions with which it had agreed to coöperate. Since sharp divergences in union standards were potentially as menacing as the competition of "unfair" workers, some mediating agency was required whose functions it would be, first, to provide for a uniform interchange of members as well as the mutual exclusion of undesirables, and, second, to impose some degree of uniformity on local discipline and policies. Thus, the majority report of a committee appointed in 1842 by the Columbia Typographical Society to examine "The expediency of either modifying, repealing, or more rigidly enforcing the apprentice regulations," recommended that those regulations be repealed because they "could only be beneficial by general adoption."[16] Only a national union could cope with the traveling worker.

THE NATIONAL UNION AND THE TRAVELING CARD

The Obligation to Receive.

The instrument which enabled the national unions to discharge the function of providing for an interchange of members by its affiliated local unions was the traveling card. This device underwent a tortuous evolution which proceeded from the local union's recognition of both its moral obligation and its selfish need to include migrants in its jurisdiction during their sojourn in town. A simple fiat, such as the Philadelphia organization's requirement (quoted above) that all "strangers" must join the union if they wish to work by the side of members thereof, could not be expected to accomplish the desired result, unless, of course, the local was powerful enough to enforce the threatened industrial ostracism. (In that event, as we have noted elsewhere, the local would have no need to join a compact to control migration; nor would it be obliged, for its own security, to require that migrants become members.) Even if every local in the coöperating group established identical entrance requirements, it is doubtful whether the traveling craftsman could have been persuaded or coerced sufficiently by his local of origin to join every other local union which he might come upon in the course of his wanderings.

Presumably the traveler became a member of the local union in his home

16. Committee report reproduced in Stewart, *Documentary History*, pp. 70–71.

community either because he believed that it would benefit him to do so or, if the home local was exceptionally powerful, because he could not obtain employment unless he held the union's card. In any event his reason for joining had to be important enough for him to incur the costs of union membership which, then as now, included an initiation fee, the periodic payment of dues, and occasional assessments. But whatever the advantage or compulsion involved, it applied to his own local situation at home. Equally compelling reasons might not exist at all in a town which he came upon while on the road, especially if he merely planned a brief stopover therein. In order, then, to assert jurisdiction over such transients, it was necessary that a local union desirous of according some official status to travelers admit them without requiring payment of an initiation fee (or at least of the full fee).

Under the circumstances—and especially since any given local union furnished recruits to the ranks of the migrants from its own membership at the same time that it served as a point of destination for travelers who had set out from other communities—it was natural that any local which was willing to accept members of other unions without the payment of an initiation fee should demand that the same privilege be accorded its own members by other local unions. The Baltimore printers' union in 1832 provided that, "Any person presenting a certificate of membership from any other typographical society to this, shall be entitled to a seat as a member, and shall enjoy all the benefits of this society, if the society from which he comes reciprocates the same privilege."[17] The obligation to admit accredited (that is, card-bearing) travelers—and to admit them without the payment of initiation charges—became the distinguishing characteristic of the traveling card systems which were adopted by the first national unions. In 1836 the abortive National Typographical Society had proposed to the various locals in the trade that, "Any person presenting a certificate from one society, under the jurisdiction of the National Society, to another society under the same jurisdiction, and paying the monthly dues called for by their constitution, shall be entitled to the trade benefits of said society."[18] Seventeen years later, the first national union, the National Typographical Union, adopted the following traveling card (or "certificate of membership") at its third annual convention:

This is to certify that the bearer hereof, whose signature appears on the margin of this ——— Typographical Union No. ——, state of ———, and is entitled to the confidence, friendship and good offices of all unions under the jurisdiction of the National Typographical Union.

17. *Constitution of the Baltimore Typographical Society*, 1832, Art. XVIII.
18. "Address to Local Societies by the Convention of the National Typographical Society in 1836", Art. 11, reproduced in Stewart, *Documentary History*, p. 130.

Given under our hands and the seal of the union at ——, this —— day of
——, 18——

———, President

———, Secretary.[19]

The Bricklayers' constitution in 1876 specified that it was the duty of any subordinate union to accept a member bearing a card issued by any other local "on payment of dues to the said subordinate."[20] No mention was made of the payment of an initiation fee. The first constitution of the United Brotherhood of Carpenters and Joiners stipulated that possession of a traveling card entitled the bearer to membership in any local upon payment of dues and "without further initiation fee"; and in 1880 the Printers provided that "any person admitted by such certificate shall be exempt from the usual initiation fee."[21]

Where local unions autonomously performed important benevolent functions, waiving payment of the initiation fee created serious problems if such locals were obliged to admit traveling card holders to full membership. Accordingly many of the locals in the Bricklayers' union adopted the practice of charging travelers a fixed sum for accepting their cards. The New York locals, for example, charged five dollars for this service and defended their action with vigor:

in the Unions here a member is entitled to full (death) benefits on payment of only one month's dues. And there are cases where death has ensued in less than a month, the Union burying him, and in conjunction with physical disease, accidents are also an important factor, and considering the case fairly, would any insurance company offer the same terms?[22]

The judiciary board of the international admitted the hardship involved, but it pointed to a provision in the constitution in which it was provided that "he (a card holder) shall be entitled to membership on payment of dues from date of issue of said card" and was entitled "to all working privilege." The five-dollar charge, in the opinion of the board, could not be regarded as "dues." The convention subsequently inserted in the constitution a provision specifically forbidding local unions to impose any charge upon members depositing traveling cards, and added the following penalty: "Any Union violating this section shall pay five dollars ($5.00) more than it charged for said Traveling Card."[23]

19. Tracy, *History of Typographical Union*, p. 151.
20. *Constitution*, 1876, Art. XIV, Sec. 1.
21. *Constitution*, 1881, Art. X. Although this exemption continued in effect, admittance to any local union of a member bearing a "Clearance Card" was later conditioned upon a majority vote of the ballots cast at a regular meeting of the local. The vote in each case followed the report of a committee which had been appointed by the president of the local to investigate the newcomer's fitness for membership (*Constitution*, 1897); *General Laws*, 1880, Sec. 1.
22. *Proceedings*, 1899, pp. 122–123. See also *Proceedings*, 1895, p. 46.
23. *Constitution*, 1900, Art. XIV, Sec. 5.

We have already observed that the obligation to honor traveling cards was sometimes suspended in time of emergency. The Cigar Makers, Freight Handlers, Stove Mounters, Steam Fitters, Bakery and Confectionery Workers, Bookbinders, Theatrical Stage Employees, Cement Workers, Horseshoers, Plasterers, and Painters granted permission to locals which were involved in strikes authorized by national authority to refuse to admit members on traveling cards. In all cases, however, it was understood that such dispensation was granted as an emergency device and only for a limited period of time.[24] The object of the national union was to control migration, not to restrict it; the practice of restriction implied what we have dubbed the single-handed approach and had failed as a long-run policy.

The Obligation to Deposit

Once the locals had agreed to exempt travelers from initiation charges, it was possible to demand that traveling members deposit their cards with local unions which were affiliated with the national organization whenever they entered communities in which such locals existed. The Bricklayers at first merely required that every member deposit his card "with the subordinate union to which he may go," but it later tightened this provision by requiring that the card must be deposited "at the first regular meeting of said Union," and in 1897 it imposed a fine of five dollars upon anyone failing to meet this deadline.[25] Other unions merely required deposit before the card holder began working in the community in question.[26] This second requirement, less stringent than the first, was adequate logically since a traveling workman was of economic interest to a local union only as an increment to the work force over which it claimed jurisdiction and not as an idle transient. However, the ease with which traveling unionists could work "with their cards in their pockets" in towns in which local unions were weak, depositing them only where the locals were powerful enough to make evasion difficult, created a serious problem for many of the national unions. According to Secretary O'Dea of the Bricklayers,

The country is [in 1886] full of members of different subordinate Unions who hold traveling cards in their possession, who do us more injury than good, and when they do deposit their cards in a Union, do so after having had them in their possession for sometimes two years. Invariably a dispute is raised about the

24. George Milton Janes, *The Control of Strikes in American Trade Unions* (Baltimore: Johns Hopkins, 1916), p. 78.
25. *Constitution*, 1876, Art. XIV, Sec 1; *Constitution*, 1883, Art. XIV, Sec. 1; *Constitution*, 1897, Art. XIII, Sec. 1.
26. United Green Glass Workers' Association of the United States and Canada, *Constitution*, 1888, Sec. 46; Iron Molders' Union of North America, *Constitution*, 1876, Art. X, Sec. 4, Art. IX, Sec. 4; United Brotherhood of Carpenters and Joiners of North America, *Constitution*, 1886, Art. XVIII.

reception of such a card, and hundreds of such have been referred to me for decision.[27]

This type of situation prompted some of the national unions either to supplement or to supplant with some variety of time limit the order to deposit immediately upon obtaining employment. In some cases, the traveling member was required to deposit his card within a specified period of time following his arrival in the community. The Bricklayers' rule concerning the deposit of cards at the first regular meeting of the local field after the visitor's arrival is an example of this type of regulation. Rules of this nature, however, sometimes proved no more effective than the requirements which they were intended to strengthen or to replace. Thus the same section of the Carpenters' constitution of 1881 (Art. X) which provided that traveling members must deposit their cards "immediately" upon obtaining employment contained another clause with the stern notice that "all cards not deposited within four weeks thereafter shall be annulled." The Printers, after originally requiring deposit upon employment, changed to a time limit of forty-eight hours after arrival in the jurisdiction of an affiliated local union, and then returned to their original rule.[28]

A more effective time limit was provided by setting some maximum effective duration to the traveling card, after it had been issued. The Carpenters sought a way out of their dilemma of 1881 by establishing a maximum duration of three months for their traveling cards. The Printers had adopted a maximum effective period of six months before they provided specifically for deposit by the card holder after each change of locale. The Bricklayers' card was good only for thirty days.[29] The Molders at first permitted their card to remain "active" indefinitely, provided only that the holder did not allow himself to fall one year in arrears to the international union, but subsequently this union reduced the period of grace to twelve weeks.[30]

The effectiveness of limiting the duration of the traveling card lay in the

27. Bricklayers' and Mason's International Union of America, *Proceedings*, 1886, p. 50 (report of the secretary). See also *Proceedings*, 1883, p. 12 (report of the president).

28. National Typographical Union, *General Laws*, 1858, Sec. 3; International Typographical Union, *General Laws*, 1894, Sec. 2.

29. *Constitution*, 1886, Art. XVII. At this time a two-card system was in effect: the "traveling cards," which were issued to members who intended to return to their local of origin, were effective up to a maximum period of three months; the "transfer cards," which were issued to members contemplating a permanent change in locale, were to be null and void after the date specified in each instance by the issuing local. The dual-card system was eliminated in 1888 with the establishment of a single "clearance card." This card, like the old travel card, was made effective for a maximum of three months after the date of issue (*Constitution*, 1888, Art. XVII); National Typographical Union, *General Laws*, 1857, Sec. 3; *Proceedings*, 1886, p. 103. (Adopted as amendment to Art. XIV, Sec. 1, *Constitution*.)

30. *Constitution*, 1888, Art. XI; *Constitution*, 1895, Art. XI.

fact that no law-abiding local union could admit a man whose card had expired. This was sometimes made explicit by national unions in constitutional provisions which altered the status of members who failed to deposit their cards within the required interval. The Glass Bottle Blowers, whose traveling cards were good for three months from the date of issue, deprived members who did not deposit their cards within the prescribed period of "any rights or benefits" which their possession conferred upon the holders.[31] The Carpenters in 1892 imposed a fine of five dollars upon any member who failed to deposit his card within thirty days from its date of issue and also suspended him for three months. They also provided that if a traveling member failed to deposit his card while working within the jurisdiction of another city or local, "all penalties shall be doubled." Two years later, however, these provisions were repealed.[32] In the Molders' union, the penalty for "holding an annulled card" and failing to pay taxes thereon was suspension until the offender became reinstated by clearing his record financially.[33] These and similar provisions adopted by other unions were intended to make it necessary for the traveler to deposit a card with a weak local union (in a community where union membership was not an effective prerequisite to employment) in order to maintain his eligibility for subsequent admission to a strong organization (which maintained effective control over the job opportunities in its jurisdiction).

However, this time limit was often sufficiently long to permit the holder to work and travel for a considerable period of time without depositing his card. This was especially true when the migrant planned to remain in a given community for only a short time and to arrive at some subsequent destination with his card unexpired. In 1869, the Bricklayers' president reported that he had received "several complaints from different unions respecting members from other unions coming to work amongst them, and refusing to deposit their travelling card in the union."[34] Accordingly, it was found necessary to impose penalties for nondeposit with local unions, in addition to those provided for nondeposit within the life span of the card itself. Some unions penalized offenders by fining them,[35] proceeding on the assumption that the crime was motivated in the majority of cases by the desire to evade the payment of dues and concluding that the most fitting punishment was a financial penalty. Other organizations, like the Carpenters,[36] suspended members for this offense.

31. *Constitution,* 1897, Art. V.
32. *Constitution,* 1893, Art. VI; *Constitution,* 1895, Art. V.
33. *Constitutions:* 1876, Art. X; 1888, Art. X; 1895, Art. X.
34. *Proceedings,* 1867, p. 18 (report of the president).
35. Thus the Molders and the Glass Bottle Blowers imposed a fine of five dollars upon fined members who had been convicted of working in the jurisdiction of any local union without depositing their cards. (Iron Molders' Union of North America, *Constitution,* 1882; United Green Glass Workers' Association, *Constitution,* 1893.)
36. *Constitution,* 1888, Art. XVII.

The Bricklayers, after receiving their president's report concerning the refusal of traveling members to deposit their cards during temporary sojourns, decreed that the offender "shall be amenable to laws of the local union under whose jurisdiction he may be at work." This having proved ineffective, it was later provided that "anyone failing to comply with the above article shall not be admitted into any other Union until he procures a traveling card from the Union under whose jurisdiction he has been working." This provision theoretically made it impossible for a member who had been issued a traveling card by one local to have it honored elsewhere if, in the meantime, he had worked in another jurisdiction without having deposited his card therein—provided, of course, that the offended local union was aware of his transgression, that it disseminated information concerning the offender, and that its blacklist was honored by the local with which he attempted subsequently to deposit his card. The Bricklayers later (1882) added the penalty of a fine "commensurate with the offense" of working illegally in another local union's jurisdiction, to be determined and imposed upon the guilty member by his home local. In 1892, this union provided that a member so convicted stand expelled from the international union until his fine was paid, and five years later it added a specific fine of five dollars for failure to deposit his card at the first regular meeting of the local union held after the traveler's arrival in town. Thus the Bricklayers finally incorporated both the fine and the possibility of loss of membership status into their body of disciplinary measures.[37]

Some of the national unions cited above overreached themselves in developing punitive measures. The Bricklayers, after strengthening the enforcement of their rules governing the deposit of traveling cards to the point where the penalty for failing to pay a fine imposed by a local union for nondeposit was expulsion, reduced that penalty to "dropped or suspended" at the same time that the judiciary board of the international was empowered to increase such a fine if it found that it was not "commensurate" with the offense committed. The Carpenters, who had bravely ordered (in 1892) that the penalties (a fine of five dollars and suspension for three months) imposed for nondeposit within the effective duration of the card be doubled when a member neglected to deposit his card (even though it had not expired) while working in the jurisdiction of any local union and that the double penalty be enforced by the issuing local "under pain of expulsion,"[38] eliminated all sanctions two years later.

37. *Constitution,* 1869, Art. XIV; 1872, Art. XIV; 1882, Art. XIV; 1892, Art. XXII; 1897, Art. XIV. In 1897, the penalty for nonpayment of the fine imposed by the member's local of origin was changed from expulsion to "dropped or suspended." At the same time, however, the Judiciary Board of the International was empowered to review the fine imposed and, if that body decided that it was not "commensurate" with the gravity of the offense, to "order such fine placed as on investigation they may deem commensurate." (*Constitution,* 1897, Art. XIV.)

38. *Constitution,* 1892 (effective 1893), Art. XVII.

The seeming reluctance of these unions to enforce their own laws can be explained in great part by Barnett's observation that, "The effectiveness of the card system in preventing violations of union rules depends chiefly on the power to exclude non-members from employment."[39] While traveling members were often prompted not to deposit their cards en route by their reluctance to incur the cost of union membership, it was, as we have observed, the widespread inability of the local unions to exclude them from employment that enabled them to economize in this manner. The local unions, organized into national unions, at first sought to secure compliance with their regulations by reducing the incentive to disobedience: they waived payment of initiation fees by travelers. However, since the inducement to evade the payment of dues and assessments remained, this method proved inadequate. Unwilling or unable to eliminate the motive for noncompliance by making membership free for travelers, the unions subsequently attempted to penalize them for not depositing their cards. But as long as it was possible to obtain work without a union card, the effectiveness of such disciplinary measures in deterring violations was limited.

Indeed, insofar as stringent penalties might deter offenders from seeking reinstatement, they would aggravate the situation which they were intended to improve by actually increasing the supply of nonunion workers in the craft in question. Having removed neither the incentive to noncompliance nor the condition which encouraged it, the national unions thus found themselves on the defensive. The International Typographical Union revealed its awareness of this dilemma by attempting further to reduce the pecuniary stimulus referred to above. In 1885 it forbade its affiliated locals to charge dues if a traveling member remained in any one jurisdiction less than ten days; in the following year, it lengthened the dues-exempt period to fifteen days. It had also been provided that "less than one month's dues cannot be paid or demanded." The Printers' sophistication was further evidenced in their choice of sanctions: a member who neglected either to draw or to deposit a "certificate of membership" was required to pay "the usual initiation fee" in order to be readmitted to any local union.[40]

Thus, the traveling member could be obliged either to deposit his card before it expired, to deposit it in every place in which he worked—or even in every community in which he tarried as a transient—provided that a local union of his fellow craftsmen existed in every such community, or to deposit it within a period of time which was determined by the regulations of his particular union (for example, to deposit it at the next regular meeting of the local union, or immediately upon obtaining employment, or before reporting for work). Disciplinary measures were adopted by the national unions in order to enforce these obligations, but their effectiveness was often limited by insufficient union control over local labor markets. Their adoption, how-

39. Barnett, *The Printers*, p. 31, n. 3.
40. *General Laws*, 1885, Sec. 5; 1886, Sec. 6; 1858, Sec. 1.

ever, is nevertheless significant, for the granting of such disciplinary authority to the national union implied a curtailment of the autonomy previously enjoyed by its affiliated locals. This partial surrender of sovereignty becomes evident when one considers that a local union which had granted a traveling card to one of its members could not readmit that member if he had lost his standing while on the road through failure to deposit his card in some other jurisdiction.

The Obligation to Exclude

The duty of the individual to deposit his traveling card was accompanied by a corresponding duty of the local union not to accept an individual who had failed to deposit his card elsewhere. The Bricklayers in 1872 decreed that any member failing to comply with regulations governing the deposit of traveling cards "shall not be admitted into any other Union until he procures a travelling card from the Union under whose jurisdiction he is now working."[41] Furthermore, the obligation of every local union to admit the members of any other affiliated local union without the payment of an initiation fee implied the further obligation to admit no migrants who came into its jurisdiction without valid traveling cards in their possession. The provision in the Molders' constitution that, "Each subordinate Union shall require a card from every journeyman obtaining employment under the jurisdiction of their Union"[42] is an example of this type of requirement.

There appears at first to have been some uncertainty concerning this duty to exclude. The essence of the card system was considered to be the privilege which it conferred upon card holders of obtaining admission to affiliated locals without paying their initiation fees. To some, therefore, it appeared that failure to produce a card merely deprived the traveler of this privilege and did not constitute a bar to his admission. Thus the Printers, as we have seen, regarded any member who did not deposit his card under specified conditions as "delinquent," but allowed him to be reinstated upon payment of "the usual initiation fee." In 1876, a delegate to the Bricklayers' convention moved that "any member who has been suspended or expelled from any local union for the nonpayment of dues, the term of two years, shall be received into new membership by any Union to which he may apply, by paying the regular initiation charged by said Union," but his resolution was not approved.[43]

Perhaps because of uncertainty regarding the scope of the card system, the blacklist was carried over from the era of interlocal coöperation as a means of definitely excluding undesirables. In 1867 the International Union of Bricklayers of North America, then two years old, adopted the following provision (Constitution, Art. XVIII):

41. *Constitution*, 1872, Art. XIV.
42. *Constitution*, 1876, Art. X.
43. *Proceedings*, 1876.

The subordinate unions shall keep a black list of all delinquent members of the I. U., said list to be posted in a conspicuous place in their several meeting rooms, the Secretaries of the subordinate unions posting their names immediately upon receiving the same from the Secretary of the International Union.

In our previous discussion of the blacklist as a method of coöperation among the early locals, a distinction was made between its advisory and its compulsory aspects. As the national unions matured, the compulsory implications received increasing emphasis. In 1872 President Moore of the Bricklayers was charged with having exerted pressure upon the Albany local to accept a man who had been expelled from a local union in New York City. The convention of the international sustained the charge and resolved that no local "shall have the power" to receive a man who had been expelled from another local union until he was reinstated and issued a traveling card by the latter organization. At the same convention Albany accused a New York local of having accepted a member who had not been issued a traveling card by the Albany union because of his refusal to liquidate his indebtedness. The convention voted to make the New York local accountable to Albany for the man's debt, and it provided that the man himself be expelled if he did not square his accounts with the local in Albany.[44] These decisions were made without explicit constitutional sanction; they represented a loose construction of the article quoted above. In 1891, however, the Bricklayers added an express mandate to the foregoing provision:

No Union shall receive into membership any person whose name may appear on the black-list, under any circumstances, until he shall first settle all dues, fines, etc., with the Union by whom he was blacklisted.

However, the obligation of a local union not to admit workers without traveling cards was more comprehensive than the duty to exclude only those whose names appeared on blacklists issued by other locals. It was possible for men to report without traveling cards who had not previously fallen from grace in the locals of which they had been members: instances of workers having left without drawing cards (although eligible to do so), or having lost them en route were reported frequently. Thus, in 1898, the president of the Bricklayers complained that some of the locals admitted travelers without cards and charged them fifty cents or one dollar per day until their cards arrived from their home locals.[45] For this reason, it was often found expedient to provide for the admission under specified conditions of members arriving in local jurisdictions without traveling cards. The Carpenters provided that, "A member traveling, or at a long distance from his L.U., can be reinstated in the nearest L.U. by consent of the L.U. to which he formerly belonged, on payment of all arrearages to said unions."[46] The

44. *Proceedings*, 1872, pp. 25, 30–31; *Constitution*, 1891, Art. XVIII.
45. *Proceedings*, 1898, p. 66 (report of the president).
46. *Constitution*, 1888, Art. XI.

Printers, indulging their overdeveloped propensity to legislate, smothered the problem under a flurry of amendments and repeals. At first they apparently provided that a traveler, arriving without a certificate of membership in some local union, could be admitted to another local if he submitted a satisfactory "statement in writing of reasons why he should be admitted" or if his application for admission received the endorsement of the local in the community from which he came.[47] Two years later (1859), it was provided that "An applicant without certificate may be admitted only by obtaining permission of the Union in the place which he left." In 1868, the president of the national union was empowered to grant permission to any local union to admit a member without a card if that member's home local refused to grant such permission itself and "if in his opinion the welfare of the organization demands it, and his decision shall be binding until revoked by the National Union." Six years later, however, this power was revoked and matters stood as they had been before it was granted. Then, in 1880, the following law was enacted:

Subordinate Unions have a right to take favorable action upon an application for membership of a printer who hails from a town or city where a Union exists in cases where, after repeated efforts, no response is received as to said applicant's former status.

This provision deprived the traveler's home local of the pocket veto which it had previously enjoyed, but it left untouched the local's authority to veto explicitly the admission of a traveling member into another local union. At the same convention, however, the latter power was abridged, and the president of the international union once again was empowered to grant cards directly to members who had lost their certificates, provided that they had not engaged in "anti-Union conduct." This power was shared with the secretary-treasurer, whose signature, together with that of the president, was required on the card. In 1892, the provision (quoted above), allowing locals "to take favorable action" when no response had been received from the issuing union, was deleted, probably because it was not intended that there should be an overlapping of the functions of the local unions and the international executive or that the former should be empowered to admit members under circumstances under which the latter was forbidden to issue cards—in cases, that is, involving "anti-Union conduct."

In some unions, therefore, it was possible for a traveler to be admitted to a local union without a card, but in one of the two examples cited, the consent of the local from which the cardless member set forth was necessary. In the other case, this consent was not required, but the issuing local could be

47. *Constitution,* 1857, Sec. 5; *General Laws,* 1857, Sec. 1; *General Laws,* 1859, Sec. 1; *General Laws,* 1868, Sec. 1; *General Laws,* 1874, Sec. 1; 1880, Sec. 18; 1889, Sec. 28.

by-passed only in cases involving loss of card. Thus the blacklist principle was maintained, and no local union was permitted to accept a member who had not been in good standing elsewhere without permission.

The Obligation to Issue

Since the traveling card system required that local unions surrender certain prerogatives when receiving migrant unionists into their respective jurisdictions, it is understandable that the locals were bound also by certain obligations which governed the issuing of cards. The local unions could not be expected to refuse applicants who did not carry cards unless the issue of such cards was made subject to regulation.

In the first place, it was expected that a traveling card would be granted upon request. Failure to possess a card could then be ascribed to the member's own negligence or ignorance or to any behavior which would have made him ineligible to receive a card. The Printers, for example, required that

When a printer loses his Certificate of Membership, it is the duty of the Union from which he received it to issue him another one; Provided, He has not worked in the jurisdiction of any other subordinate Union before making his loss known and receiving its permission to work, and there are no charges or objections made against him either by the Union from which his card was first issued or that in whose jurisdiction he desires to go to work, and his original card had not expired before he made its loss known.[48]

The Printers, as we know, also provided that their international president and secretary-treasurer could issue a card directly to replace one which had been lost in the event that "the Union which issued it refuses to renew it." Provision for human frailty, however, rarely resulted in the granting of such authority to the national executive, but the right of a member who had lost his card to obtain a replacement was generally accepted, if not always explicitly stated. Thus, although it was the custom of well disciplined locals to conclude their monthly reports to the Iron Molders' *Journal* with the terse warning, "No card, no work," even that organization acknowledged that a member who had lost his traveling card was entitled to a duplicate from the local which had granted it—with the proviso that "he must furnish proof to the Union that he has lost his card."[49]

The practice engaged in by some local unions of charging a fee for the issuing of cards could not be tolerated, since it induced members to depart without drawing cards, thereby placing them beyond the control of other local unions whose jurisdictions they might subsequently enter. If these organizations honored their obligation not to admit men without cards, the

48. *Constitution,* 1880, Sec. 22.
49. *Constitution,* 1890, Art. XI, Sec. 8.

practice of charging for cards would result in an increase in the supply of nonunion labor in the trade just as the practice of charging for the deposit of cards had done. This practice caused enough concern in the Bricklayers' union to warrant the passage of legislation designed to outlaw it explicitly. Before such legislation was enacted, the president had directed one of the locals to remit a "fine" of five dollars which it had placed upon one of its members because he had requested a traveling card. This action apparently failed to settle the issue, for, twelve years later (in 1895), the international secretary questioned the legality of the action of some locals in imposing charges upon members when they applied for and when they deposited traveling cards.[50] In 1897, the former practice was banned unambiguously in the following constitutional amendment:

No Union shall charge or receive money for issuing a Traveling Card; and any Financial Secretary or other officer or Union who violates this section shall pay a fine of twenty dollars, to be paid to the Treasurer of the I. U. and to go into the funds of the I. U.[51]

The Molders legislated on an allied issue. In specifying the right of a member who had lost his card to be issued a duplicate, they provided that the issuing local send the duplicate "without charge, except for postage and stationery."[52]

The most important obligation of the issuing local was its duty to issue traveling cards to its members upon application. This duty to issue cards complemented the duty to exclude applicants for admission who did not possess cards, for, if any local union refused consistently to issue traveling cards to members who were about to depart from its jurisdiction, it would burden the other locals with the necessity of refusing them admission. Thus it might contribute to the body of nonunion migrants to an extent which would nullify the operation of the entire system of mutual recognition and exclusion. The effect is identical with that which would be produced by an influx of travelers from nonunion localities.

The importance of the obligation of the local union to grant cards to its members was appreciated early in the history of unionism in this country. The constitution which was drawn up in connection with the unsuccessful attempt to establish a national union of printers in 1836 proclaimed it to "be the duty of the local societies to issue one of these cards to every member in good standing, when about to leave the section of country over which they may have jurisdiction," and in 1858 the National Typographical Union stipulated that "Members in good standing who are desirous of leaving the jurisdiction of the Union to which they belong shall be entitled to receive

50. *Proceedings,* 1883, p. 11; 1895, p. 46 (report of the secretary).
51. *Constitution,* 1897, Art. XIV, Sec. 1.
52. *Constitution,* 1890, Art. XI, Sec. 8.

the National Typographical Union Certificate . . ."[53] In 1867, the Bricklayers pronounced it "the duty of the subordinate unions to furnish (cards to) their members on proper application in open meeting, personally, by proxy or in writing."[54] The Carpenters didn't legislate on this point until 1900 (the United Brotherhood having been formed in 1881), but then they provided that, "It is compulsory for the Local Union to issue said card."[55]

The obligations of the local unions to issue cards upon request and to receive cardholding members comprised the essentials of the traveling card system. These duties, however, were not unqualified. The duty to issue cards was made conditional upon the good standing of the applicant. The traveling card adopted by the first national union in 1853 (see p. 69 above) introduces its bearer as "a member in good standing" of the issuing local before commending him to "the confidence, friendship and good offices of all unions under the jurisdiction of the National Typographical Union." The qualification of good standing was adopted in order to maintain discipline within the local union and to assist it in its perpetual struggle for solvency.

The deterrent to disobeying local rules and regulations would have been slight indeed if the individual had been given an opportunity to leave town, before retribution could be visited upon him, with a traveling certificate which would make him eligible for work under union auspices in any other locality. Thus, although the Bricklayers deemed it the "duty" of their local unions to furnish cards to their members upon request, they also provided that, "A member applying for a card must be clear from all charges on the books."[56] And for a while the Printers expressly provided that, "A subordinate Union cannot be compelled to grant a card to a member against whom charges are pending."[57]

Furthermore, it was imperative that no member be cleared for transfer unless he had discharged his financial obligations in full. Although this was actually only a special case of maintaining discipline, it happened to be a case of special importance to the local unions. The chronic migrant, by virtue of his mobility, was in an excellent position to make light of his obligations. Hence the dilemma of local unions which required the affiliation of the traveling workmen in order to soften the economic impact of their migrations, but which seldom possessed sufficient control over their respective labor markets to make affiliation a prerequisite to employment; it was necessary to induce the travelers to join. In deference to the travelers' thriftiness, the

---

53. *Constitution of the National Typographical Association*, 1836, as amended in 1837, Art. XII, Sec. 1. Reproduced in Stewart, *Documentary History*, p. 128; *General Laws*, 1858, Sec. 3 (italics mine).

54. *Constitution*, 1867, Art. XIV.

55. *Constitution*, 1900, Art. XVII.

56. *Constitution*, 1867, Art. XIV.

57. *General Laws*, 1889, Sec. 6. This provision did not appear after 1891.

locals admitted them without payment of an initiation fee. The Printers, as we have seen, extended the inducement to affiliate by requiring their local unions to waive the payment of dues by travelers who intended to remain in a particular jurisdiction for only a short while. For the most part, however, it was expected that, once the traveling worker was admitted to a local union, he would be subject to the same current expenses as his sedentary colleagues. Therefore the requirement that a member applying for a traveling card be "clear on the books" was devised in an attempt to match the migrant's peculiar ability to evade his financial responsibilities with an appropriate deterrent. (Despite their unusually liberal practice of dues exemption, the Printers enforced this requirement of solvency with vigor.)[58] Thus the policy of inducement which was adopted with respect to the traveler was tempered with an element of coercion; and the local unions, in order to maintain internal discipline, were obliged to accept the risk that their traveling members would prefer to face ostracism elsewhere than to maintain good standing in the community in which they were sojourning.

The duty of the local union to receive cards was also made conditional. It was modified by the duty of the holder himself to deposit his cards under specified conditions—the duty, that is, to observe the rules of good union behavior after his card has been issued to him.

The first convention of the National Typographical Union advised the constituent local societies to give assistance to the bearers of traveling certificates "provided said holders have done nothing in the meantime, by a course of intemperance or otherwise, to disqualify them from the same . . ." The Bricklayers tightened their regulations governing the depositing of cards in 1883, after President Cole suggested that a local union be privileged to exclude a man with a traveling card "when the member presenting it is known to be in bad repute in his own Union."[59] The Carpenters, who hitherto had admitted all card holders who were able to give the quarterly password when challenged, in 1896 conditioned admission in each case upon "a majority of the ballots" cast at a local meeting. Voting was to take place after a committee of three, appointed by the president of the local, had reported to the membership on the fitness of the cardholding applicant.[60] This development was carried to its extreme by the International Typographical Union, which, nearly forty years after it had exempted its local unions from assisting cardholders who had "disqualified" themselves, promulgated the following requirement:

When a man is declared "unfair," and is so published by any subordinate Union,

---

58. *Decisions,* 1893, No. 61.

59. *Proceedings,* 1883, p. 12 (report of the president).

60. *Constitution,* 1897, Art. XVII. This provision is mentioned in note 21 above as a modification of the requirement that cardholders be admitted without further qualifications.

it is the duty of every other Union to withdraw his card, if he holds one, or refuse him admittance without the sanction of the Union whose laws he has violated.[61]

"Good standing," then, became a condition on which traveling cards were both issued and received, because it was necessary to keep law and order within the local union. Insofar as this requirement modified the obligation to issue cards, it helped to maintain discipline in the local of issue; insofar as it modified the obligation to accept cards, it helped also to maintain discipline in the local of deposit. But however essential this requirement might have been, the obligations which it modified in the interest of the internal stability of the local organizations were themselves essential to the operation of the traveling card system. This conflict of objectives arose because different local unions had evolved different criteria of good standing, because each local union was sovereign within its own bailiwick and over its own members, and because the interval between the issuing and the depositing of a traveling card created a jurisdictional vacuum which was abhorred by all locals concerned.

When the judgment of any local union in issuing (or refusing to issue) or in receiving (or refusing to receive) a traveling card was challenged by a sister organization, at least one of the two following questions emerged from the welter of controversy which such issues invariably produced:

Whose criteria of good standing shall prevail? This follows from the qualification of the duty to issue traveling cards. The duty to issue was imposed upon local unions because they were obliged to receive all travelers to whom cards had been issued and to refuse admission to all who did not possess traveling cards. If, however, a local could either issue or refuse to issue cards on the basis of its own determination of what constitutes good standing, the protection afforded to receiving locals would be considerably less than had been intended. Must a local union admit to membership a man who had been issued a traveling card by some other organization, but whom it would not itself receive as an initiatory member? And must it refuse admission to a man whose qualifications it considers satisfactory, but who was *persona non grata* to some other local union?

The second primary question was which local union can assert authority over a traveling member? This question arose primarily because the local's duty to admit men with traveling cards was qualified by regulations governing the deposit of cards by their holders. If a man is charged with having committed an "unfair" act after he had received a card, should the determination of guilt or innocence be made by the local in whose jurisdiction the misdemeanor was allegedly committed or by the local which had issued a traveling card to him? Of which local, in other words, is the traveler to be considered a "citizen"?

61. *General Laws*, 1889, Sec. 23.

Since the traveling card systems adopted by the national unions made no explicit provision for differences in local definitions of good standing, we shall defer consideration of the first of these two questions until the next chapter and proceed at this point to the second.

The Question of Citizenship

Legal jurisdiction over a traveling member who had failed to deposit his card in the manner prescribed by his national union might have been awarded either to the local union which had issued the card or to the local union in whose jurisdiction the offense had been committed. In some instances certain historical and financial considerations imparted a bias in favor of the former, but neither choice proved satisfactory, either in terms of the financial or the disciplinary objectives involved.

The problem of citizenship goes back to the early tenet that no man could ever resign from a trade union as long as he desired to retain his employee status in the trade.[62] He could, of course, be expelled, but the act of expulsion represents the exercise of the union's discretion and, in theory, expulsion meant denial of employment opportunity within the union's jurisdiction. The relationship between member and union could not be terminated on the former's initiative. This followed from the basic premise that the union exercised sovereignty over all jobs in its jurisdiction and that only union members were entitled to hold such jobs. The rights of nonmembers were not admitted, for the union denied them recognition as neutrals. The idea that the member could not revoke his union affiliation was expressed by the Molders, who provided that "No member of any subordinate Union, or of this Union, shall be allowed to disconnect himself from this organization by resignation or otherwise."

This concept, however, antedated the national unions, for it was held by some of the first local unions in the country. And when these early local unions agreed upon the necessity of controlling the effects of migration through coöperative action, they did not abandon their early concept of union citizenship. Members who intended to leave the community permanently

---

62. Initially, no distinction was made between employers and employees in this respect. In the "merchant capitalist" periods it was expected that a journeyman had a good chance of becoming an employer in the normal course of events, and it was expected that he would remain in the union and observe its rules and regulations as an employer. (See e.g., Tracy, *History of Typographical Union,* p. 40.) Later, some unions created a special status for employer members, and others permitted them to draw "honorary withdrawal" cards and the like. This placed them in the same status as members who wished to withdraw from the trade, and even in this case regulations of local and national unions which governed the readmission on special terms of such members in the event that they resumed their employee status in the industry (a common occurrence in the building trades) indicates that the affiliation of such employers was not considered to have been terminated.

were permitted to withdraw; they were placed in the category of those who abandoned their employee status in the local union's trade jurisdiction. But a careful distinction was drawn between permanent and temporary absentees, and jurisdiction over the latter was maintained tenaciously, as examples cited in the following paragraphs will make clear. It may suffice at this point to present an excerpt from an early constitution of the Carpenters' Brotherhood, an organization which, for a while, formalized this distinction by providing two cards—a transfer card, to be issued to a member intending to make his permanent residence elsewhere, and a traveling card, for the member whose absence from the local of issue was expected to be temporary. Concerning the latter, the constitution provided:

the traveling member is entitled to admission as a visitor into any Local Union. But in no case can a Traveling Card transfer membership from one Local Union to another.[63]

A more immediate reason for the reluctance of many local unions and their national parent bodies to stipulate that an interchange of cards meant an interchange of members, however, was the importance of the benevolent character of the local organizations. Stewart records various instances of contests between "alimoners" and "industrialists" for the control of local organizations of printers.[64]

Tracy, on the other hand, stresses the "industrial" aspects of these early societies and seems to suggest that their benevolent activities might have been intended to divert public attention from their designs upon wages and allied matters. He says,

There is no disposition here to question or ignore this element in these societies, but to bring to light from the minutes the evidence that whatever livery of charitable clubs they wore in public, in their hall rooms they were labor organizations.[65]

Yet he notes that the New York local, in order to protect its benefit funds, accepted a corporate charter from the state legislature in 1818, in return for which it had to promise (in its constitution) that, "in no case shall the society interfere in respect to the price of labor." It is true that the "industrialists" ultimately did prevail over the "alimoners" in most unions—and their victory was perhaps more decisive in this country than anywhere else—but the issue was by no means settled when the problems raised by migrant workmen first became acute. Indeed, considering the numerical weakness of the early local unions and their consequent inability in many instances to achieve their stated aims "in respect to the price of labor," their benevolent provisions, however

63. *Constitution*, 1888, Art. XVII.
64. Stewart, *Documentary History, passim.*
65. Tracy, *History of Typographical Union*, "Early Organizations of Printers," p. 43.

modest, often provided the most tangible benefits to be derived from union membership.

Since the benefit systems of the early locals were run independently of one another and since their provisions and assessments were not uniform, the traveling member presented the coöperating unions with an awkward problem. While willing to extend "trade (that is, strike) benefits" to holders of travel cards, the local union was often reluctant to declare them eligible for the other types of benefit which were frequently subsumed under the head of "alimony" and for which its own members had to make financial provision.

It could be argued, however, that, if the local did extend benefit privileges to travelers from other locals, its own migratory members would receive similar courtesies from these other organizations. Thus the Baltimore Typographical Society (1832) allowed "any person presenting a certificate of membership from any other typographical society . . . to enjoy all the benefits of this society, if the society from which he comes reciprocates the same privilege." [66] Yet there was always the possibility that the benefits granted elsewhere were not as liberal, so that the local in question would lose by the exchange.

Nor were the locals any more willing to relinquish financial control over those to whom they had issued cards than they were to confer beneficiary status upon members of other organizations. For if the absence of their own cardholders proved to be only temporary, the latter could return to the fold as members with full beneficiary rights. Hence most locals wished such members to pay back dues on their return, or to pay dues in advance before they left. Of the ten constitutions of early printers' locals which Stewart has reproduced, only four are explicit on this subject. Three of these contain provisions which excuse members leaving the jurisdiction from paying dues for the period of absence, but in only one case was the exemption unqualified.[67] Of the other two, one provided for exemption only "on said member leaving and returning *at any distant period*" [68] (italics mine), and the other accepted the returned traveler without the payment of back dues "if he joined a similar association during his absence" and "provided he, on his return produce a certificate of uniform correct conduct from the president of an association, as aforesaid, while a member thereof." However, this document continues, "should a member leave the District in any other manner than as before specified, and, on his return, wish again to join the association, he shall be charged with his monthly dues, for and during the time he has been ab-

66. *Constitution*, Art. XVIII. Reproduced in Stewart, *Documentary History*, p. 103.

67. *By-Laws of the New Orleans Typographical Association* (revised),1839, Sec. 17. Reproduced in Stewart, *Documentary History*, p. 117.

68. *Constitution of the Nashville Typographical Society*, 1837, Art. XIII, Sec. 2. Reproduced in Stewart, *Documentary History*, p. 110.

sent . . . unless a majority of the membership find that he is unable to make this payment, in which case he must pay the amount of the initiation fee.[69] The fourth local to legislate on this subject provided categorically that, "Absence from the city shall in no case exonerate a member from dues during such absence. . ."[70]

Thus the benefit systems of local unions created powerful support for the view that the traveling cardholder remained a member of the local which issued his card for some period beyond the date of issue. As late as 1896, the description of the Printers' certificate of membership in their constitution was followed by the following words of restraint:

> The issuance of this certificate shall in no case work a forfeiture of membership in the subordinate union from which it was drawn until such certificate shall have been accepted by a sister subordinate union, or shall expire by limitation.[71]

This concept of citizenship often permitted the issuing local to charge dues beyond the date of issue. This practice was partly responsible for the fact that some national unions set time limits on their traveling cards. It was also motivated by the desire to enforce the holder's obligation to deposit his card. When the Carpenters abolished their two-card system in 1888 they provided that a single "Clearance Card" be issued for a three-month period only, with all dues to be paid in advance. At the following convention, the period for which dues were to be charged in advance was reduced to one month, but in 1898 it was increased to two months.[72]

But the practice of charging dues in advance was premised on the early return of the traveler to the local from which he drew his card. For if dues were paid several months in advance and if the traveler deposited his traveling card elsewhere within the paid-up period, he would be obliged to pay dues to the latter organization either upon deposit or shortly thereafter. This trade-union variant of double taxation would go a long way toward nullifying the inducement for the traveling member to remain a union man, which the national union sought to provide when it required its affiliates not to charge the cardholder any initiation fee. It was probably for this reason that some of the early national unions considered or actually experimented with the two-card system, which permitted a distinction to be made between permanent and temporary absentees by the issue of one-way tickets to the former and round-trip accommodations to the latter.

The Printers, Bricklayers, and Carpenters were among those organizations

69. *Second Constitution of the Columbia Typographical Society* (Washington, D. C.) 1818, Art. XII. Reproduced in Stewart, *Documentary History*, pp. 98–99.

70. *Constitution of the Philadelphia Typographical Union*, 1850, Art. III, Sec. 6. Reproduced in Stewart, *Documentary History*, p. 119.

71. *Constitution*, 1896, Art. XVII, Sec. 3.

72. *Constitution*, 1888, Art. XVII; 1891, Art. XVII; 1899, Art. XVII.

which, at one time or another, had paid some attention to the dual-card system. The first convention of the National Typographical Union recommended that the affiliated locals grant both "traveling certificates . . . to be legal for one year, which shall recommend the holders thereof to assistance and traveling expenses from the union in any city or town where they cannot obtain work. . ." and "certificates from one union to enable the members thereof to become attached to any other, without paying an initiation fee."[73]

In 1875 a delegate to the Bricklayers' convention proposed the adoption of a dual-card system. If a "permanent card" (similar to the traveling card actually in use) was issued, no dues would be paid beyond the date of issue. On the other hand, a member applying for a "visiting card" would be obliged "to pay his dues in advance up to the time his card run out, which shall not be for a less time than six months." The type and amount of benefit provided by the issuing local and for which the bearer was eligible would be stated on the card, and if the bearer should become entitled to receive such benefits after depositing his card, the local of deposit would pay him or his heirs the sum for which he was eligible. The issuing local would then refund this amount to the union which paid it. It was argued that this scheme would maintain the eligibility of members who had contributed to the beneficiary features of their locals before drawing traveling cards. The opposition, however, claimed that "the National Union had no right to interfere with the benevolence of local Unions," and the proposed amendment was defeated.[74]

The Carpenters, installing a two-card system in 1886, went further than the other two unions. Their "transfer card," for those who did not plan to return, was granted upon payment of one month's dues in advance (and, incidentally only by majority vote of the local's membership present at the meeting).[75] The "traveling card," on the other hand, which, we might recall, "in no case can . . . transfer membership from one Local Union to another," was issued "for a stated time, not to exceed three months," and the recipient had to pay "all dues for the full time in advance for which the card is granted." The holder, however, was protected from the possibility of "double taxation" by the following provision:

No Local Union shall have the right to collect dues again for the months paid for the Traveling Card. The Local Union issuing said card shall pay to the General Secretary the capita tax for the month his Traveling or Transfer Card holds good.[76]

This provision was intended both to protect the benefit status of the traveler and to remove any financial deterrent to the maintenance of his good

73. Quoted in Stewart, *Documentary History*, pp. 82–83.
74. *Proceedings*, 1875, pp. 21–22, 36–39.
75. *Constitution*, 1886, Art. XVIII.
76. *Constitution*, 1886, Art. XVII. The same provision in effect governed the collection of dues on the transfer card. (Art. XVIII)

standing while he was employed in the trade outside the jurisdiction of his home local. At the same time, the receiving local, which was unable to charge dues until the expiration of the period for which the traveler was "paid up" in the issuing local, was exempted from beneficiary obligations to the holder of a traveling card, because the latter received only the status of "visitor" in the receiving local. (As noted above, Art. XVII of the 1886 Constitution, stated that "in no case can a Traveling Card transfer membership from one Local Union to another.") Relief from all responsibility of a benevolent nature was likewise afforded the receiving local with respect to the holder of a transfer card, for it was provided that this card "does not entitle him to any benefits of the Local Union, to which he is transferred, only as prescribed in their By-Laws." Nevertheless, the dual-card system apparently proved unworkable, for it was eliminated at the next convention, in 1888.[77]

It is possible that uncertainty concerning the applicants' future plans was in part responsible for the failure of the two-card systems of the Printers and the Carpenters. There is good reason to believe that this was true in the latter case especially, since the applicant had to pay up to three months' dues in advance in order to receive a traveling card, whereas only one month's advance payment was required for the issue of a (permanent) transfer card. It is significant that the local to which the holder of a transfer card intended to transfer his membership had to be specified on the face of that card.

The Carpenters had always emphasized the beneficiary aspects of unionism; and they were dissatisfied with their original traveling card, which entitled the bearer to membership in a local union upon the payment of dues therein without specifying whether or not the issuing local was entitled to charge dues in advance and whether or not the local of deposit was required to charge the depositor any dues until the period already paid for had elapsed. Their desire to safeguard local benefit systems persuaded the Carpenters to substitute two traveling cards for one, and, although the dual system proved unsatisfactory, this objective was not abandoned. The single "clearance card" which was adopted in 1888 was virtually the same as the old traveling card: it was issued for a period not to exceed three months; dues were to be paid in advance for the entire period; the receiving local was denied "the right to collect dues again for the months paid for on a Clearance Card," and, in return, it was not obliged to consider the cardholder eligible for its benefits. Since the local of deposit could not charge a traveling member dues until his card had expired, it was provided that "he shall until then be considered a member of said union," said union being the issuing local to which dues had been paid in advance.

By these provisions the Carpenters hoped to protect their benefit systems and at the same time avoid double taxation. This could be accomplished, however, only by requiring the locals to admit paid-up cardholders to "trade

77. *Constitution,* 1888, Art. XVIII.

benefits" without charge for stated periods. This might have aroused resentment on the part of those sedentary members who were compelled to subsidize the economic benefits to which the cardholder was admitted, for at the next convention the maximum period for which dues could be charged in advance was reduced to one month. In 1898, however, this period was increased to two months.[78] Thus, in providing for the advance payment of dues as a condition of the issue of traveling cards, the Carpenters resolved the conflicting interests of benevolent and of business unionism in favor of the former.

Other national unions, however, forbade their locals to charge dues in advance. The Bricklayers, in 1870, made it "unlawful for any subordinate union to grant traveling cards with dues paid in advance of the date of such grant" and declared that "all laws conflicting with the above are hereby repealed. . . " Five years later, as we have already had the occasion to observe, they declined to adopt a dual-card system which would have provided for the advance payment of dues and for continued eligibility for benefits granted by the local of issue. And the following year they rejected an amendment proposed by a Kentucky local's delegation, which would have permitted members to pay dues in advance in order to maintain their eligibility for benefits,[79] thereby consolidating a definitive victory by "industrialism" over "alimony."

The Printers also had decided at an early date that a member in good standing was entitled to draw a National Typographical Union Certificate without the payment of advance dues. They did allow their locals to follow their usual practice and charge dues on the first of the month, however, so that it was possible for a traveler to be charged dues in advance, but for no longer in advance than the number of days remaining in the month from the date on which his card was issued.[80] The Molders, however, reduced the maximum period for which dues could be charged in advance by providing that a member must pay dues to the first of the following month only if he drew his card on or after the sixteenth of the month.[81]

If issuing locals were not allowed to charge dues beyond the date (or month) of issue, two possibilities existed for the collection of dues by local unions in which cards were deposited. The latter could either charge the bearer from the date of deposit or require him to pay back dues from the date of issue. In either case, the possibility of double taxation would be virtually nonexistent because the issuing local could not charge dues for periods substantially beyond the date of deposit. If, however, dues were

78. *Constitution,* 1888, Art. XVII; 1891, Art. XVII; 1899, Art. XVII.
79. *Constitution,* 1870, Art. XIV, Sec. 5; *Proceedings,* 1875, pp. 21–22, 36–39; *Proceedings,* 1876.
80. *General Laws,* 1858, Sec. 3; 1892, Sec. 3.
81. *Constitution,* Art. XI, Sec. 7.

charged by the receiving local from a date not earlier than the date of deposit, the period of time between issue and deposit would become a hiatus in the payment of dues, corresponding roughly to an interval in which the traveler was on the road and not employed. On the other hand, if the local of deposit was allowed to charge dues from the date of issue, the traveler would be taxed during a period in which he was not long enough in the jurisdiction of any local union to receive any benefit from membership therein.

The Iron Molders changed over from a system of payment to the receiving local from date of issue to one requiring payment from date of deposit, and then changed back again to the date of issue.[82] The unpopularity of the final choice with the traveling member was voiced by a correspondent to the Iron Molders' *Journal,* who signed himself "Constitutional Tramp" and who, in a communication published under the ringing caption of "Taxation Without Representation," divested himself of the following sentiments:

Now, Mr. Editor, I would like to ask some of our "Union Legislators" what, if any, benefits have been extended to the brother by the Union receiving his card while the brother was hunting employment? . . . I say most emphatically that no local Union extended any favors to me, yet, when it came to depositing my card for a few days' work, I had to pay four months' local dues and taxes into the Treasury of the Union holding my card.[83]

The practice complained of was adopted partly in order to ensure that the monthly per capita payments on traveling members would be received by the international union in an unbroken series. This was particularly important since the Molders had provided an international fund for the payment of death and disability benefits, and all members, whether or not in a traveling status, were eligible to receive these benefits. It was expected that a local union, upon receiving a traveler's card, would deduct the appropriate sum from the back dues which it collected and forward it to the international. The locals, however, while complying with the requirement to collect back dues, often overlooked the detail of mailing part of the proceeds to the parent union.

I find that when a card is drawn (President Fox complained) the I. M. U. of N. A. loses . . . the monthly tax the members owe on their cards, which may be from one to twelve months before again being deposited, and which money goes into the treasury of the local instead of the national Union, where it rightfully belongs. This deprives the national Union of considerable revenue, while being no fault of the member, who keeps himself in good standing for benefits by paying the tax due on his card. . .

82. *Constitution,* 1876, Art. X, Sec. 4; 1878, Art. X, Sec. 4; 1882, Art. XI, Sec. 4; 1890, Art. XI, Sec. 7.
83. *Iron Molders' Journal,* January, 1894, pp. 1–2.

And should any of these members die thirty days after paying said tax, the national organization must pay the funeral benefits of one hundred dollars to his heirs, thus making it possible for a member to retain his standing for years and the national organization not receive one dollar of the tax he paid in.[84]

The president then recommended that a member desiring to leave his local union be required to pay three months' dues in advance, whereupon he would receive a "receipt-card" which would entitle him "to go to work under the jurisdiction of any Union, and to be admitted to their meetings, with all the privileges except that of the right of debate or to vote on any question coming before the members." The convention did not adopt this suggestion, nor did it alter the practice of the local unions in collecting dues from the date of issue. The Molders did, however, establish a system of uniform dues of twenty-five cents per member per week, ten cents of which was to be forwarded to the national and the remainder retained by the collecting local union. One of the main reasons for this centralization of finance was the desire to remove the traveler's sense of injustice.

it so happens that if a member while traveling, deposits his card in a Union he pays five cents, but within a month afterwards, by depositing it in another local is compelled to pay sixty cents.[85]

Under the new system, the traveler still had to pay dues for the period during which he was on the road and out of work. But in most instances the sedentary member would be expected to maintain dues payments to his local union during his periods of idleness so that, in principle, the traveler was not being discriminated against. And not even Constitutional Tramp had objected to keeping up his payments to the international union: he claimed that the requirement that dues be charged from the date of issue when the card was deposited was intended to apply only to International dues and taxes, which he apparently was quite willing to pay. In the first place, unless his wanderings took him beyond the confines of the northern hemisphere, the traveler never left the jurisdiction of the international, as he did that of the local union through which he passed while "on his way." Furthermore, he never lost his beneficiary status by traveling, since the Molders had nationalized their benevolent functions. Thus the Molders, thanks to a centralized benefit system, were able to institute a uniform system of finance which made collection of dues from the date of issue of the traveling card more palatable to the holder thereof. The minimization of this unpleasantness, it should be emphasized, was made possible because the payment of dues from date of issue was required in the interest of the national union and was divorced from local considerations of a beneficiary and financial nature.

84. *Proceedings,* 1895, pp. 7, 13, (report of the president).
85. *Constitution,* 1895, Art. VIII; *Proceedings,* 1895, pp. 8–9 (report of the president).

Other national unions, however, did not go as far as the Molders did in centralizing either their finances or their benefits. The Bricklayers, and Printers fell far short of the Molders' accomplishments in this respect, and it is significant that both of these unions finally required their locals to assess travelers, at the point of arrival, for dues from the date of deposit rather than from the date of issue. The Bricklayers vacillated between the two policies— first, obliging travelers to pay dues "from date of card"; later, changing to "date of arrival"; next, returning to the date of issue; and finally, settling upon the date of deposit.[86] The Printers at first required that the traveler must deposit his card with a local union immediately upon obtaining employment and provided that the local in question charge him dues "(only) from date of said deposit or employment." Later, however, when they insisted that the bearer must deposit his card within forty-eight hours after entering the jurisdiction of any local union, they omitted the alternative date of employment and provided simply that "dues shall (only) be charged from the date of such deposit."[87]

Both the Printers and the Bricklayers combined the prohibition against dues being charged in advance by the issuing local with the requirement that the receiving local charge dues "only" from the date of deposit. The Carpenters, we know, provided for advance payment of dues: like the Molders they were committed to the protection of national benefit features. The system of charging from the date of deposit not only eliminated the possibility of double taxation of the traveling member but it exempted him from payment of dues for periods spent unremuneratively in actual travel. If one ignores, for the moment, the case of the Iron Molders, this system might be considered the national union solution to the financial problems raised by the traveling member. However, it must be borne in mind that the national union solution entailed some sacrifice of the beneficiary interests of the local unions and that it was incompatible with the assumption that the traveler remained a citizen of the local of issue at least until he deposited his card elsewhere. Nor was this solution any more consistent with the view that the traveler was a citizen of the local in which he subsequently deposited his card, for that is the implication of a system which authorized the local of deposit to collect dues from the date on which the traveler's card was issued.

If the assumption that the traveler remained for a while a citizen of the local union in which his card was issued proceeded originally from financial and beneficiary considerations, requirements of discipline favored the opposite view, namely, that he be regarded as subject to the jurisdiction of the local in which he was supposed to deposit his card. This disciplinary aspect of citizenship, it will be recalled, arose from the requirement that the travel-

86. *Constitutions:* 1868, Art. XIV, Sec. 1; 1870, Art. XIV, Sec. 1; 1882, Art. XIV, Sec. 1; 1883, Art. XIV, Sec. 1.
87. *General Laws,* 1858, Sec. 3; 1888, Sec. 3.

ing member deposit his card punctually. Thus it was essential that the traveler be subject to the discipline of the local in the community in which he arrived, at least as soon as he offered his services for hire therein. The local of destination was therefore authorized to refuse admittance to any member who had failed to deposit his card in the manner prescribed or who had "worked illegally" within its jurisdiction. Or if the traveler had left town before he could be brought to justice, it could blacklist him, so that no other local could admit him until he had redeemed himself in the eyes of the organization which he had offended.

Since denial of union status could not always bar the traveler from employment, however, the local's power to reject and to blacklist did not exclude less drastic sanctions. On the contrary, the powers of exclusion were often granted in order to give force to other penalties, notably fines, upon compliance with which the traveler could be considered eligible for admission to the local in question or could have his name removed from its blacklist. (It may be recalled that the Bricklayers forbade their local unions to receive any person named on a blacklist *"until* he shall first settle all dues, fines, etc. with the Union by whom he was blacklisted.") Now this latter form of punishment, the fining of work-and-run members, was commonly employed, but it entailed serious administrative difficulties. The local union could deal effectively with a wrongdoer who remained within its jurisdiction and desired to be included in its membership, and it could blacklist a man who had moved on, but how could it enforce some less drastic sentence upon a member no longer in its jurisdiction and possessed of a valid traveling card?

The solution most frequently adopted was to require the issuing local either to try the accused and sentence him if found guilty, or to require the issuing local to execute a penalty imposed by the local in whose jurisdiction the offense had been committed. In assuming that the local of issue was best able to discipline traveling members, it was implied that the traveler's absence from the local which granted him a card was typically a temporary absence and that he could be considered with some assurance to be a citizen of that local. Discipline by one's "home" organization at the request of some other group, however, could hardly be expected to be discipline at its impersonal best. The shortcomings of this awkward system were made embarrassingly obvious by certain locals in the Bricklayers' union, to which reference will be made below. Thus neither concept of the traveler's citizenship was adequate for the disciplinary task at hand, and, as a result, some of the early national unions became involved in a painful and largely unrewarding vacillation between the alternative approaches to this problem.

The special emphasis placed by the Carpenters on beneficiary activities resulted in their adherence to the practice of charging dues in advance of the date of issue, as noted above, and created a predisposition on their part in favor of regarding the traveler as a member of the local union from which he had received his card. Thus, it was initially provided, under the short-lived two-card system, that the traveling card did not transfer membership and that its bearer was to be considered only as a "visitor" in the local in which he deposited it. The exigencies of discipline, however, led them to modify this view considerably and to grant other locals considerable discretion in dealing with traveling members who had failed to deposit their cards. This is reflected in a constitutional section adopted in 1892, which, in providing that a member who failed to deposit his card within thirty days from date of issue be fined five dollars, stipulated that, "Said fine shall be collected by the Local Union in which the card is deposited."[88] It was realized, however, that this provision could hardly be operative if the member failed to deposit his card at all in the locality in question before moving on. For this latter offense, the Carpenters doubled all penalties, as we have noted elsewhere, and they also provided that "the fine shall be collected by the original Union issuing the Clearance Card. On notification (by the offended local) the latter Union shall enforce said penalty under pain of expulsion." Thus the example of the Carpenters illustrates the inadequacy of attempting to discipline the traveling member through the sole agency of the local of destination; it was necessary that some jurisdiction be retained by the local of issue. How coöperative the issuing locals were in collecting fines imposed by the other organizations cannot be ascertained in this instance, because the sanctions in question disappeared from the Carpenters' books two years after their adoption.

The Typographical Union, although it remained committed to the view that a traveling member was a member of the local of issue until he deposited his card, was also obliged to compromise this principle when the question of discipline arose. It was at first provided that, "When a man is declared 'unfair' and is so published by any subordinate Union, it is the duty of every other Union to withdraw his card . . ." This provision was dropped in 1892, and, as in the case of the Carpenters, no written explanation was offered. A mild companion section, stating that "any member neglecting his duty (to deposit his card within forty-eight hours after arrival) shall be regarded as a delinquent, and upon readmission into any subordinate union shall be required to pay the usual initiation fee,"[89] survived. Thus jurisdiction was finally placed in the hands of the local of destination, but its punitive powers were greatly reduced.

The Bricklayers were prone to regard the traveler as a member of the issuing local while en route to some other jurisdiction. At first, however, the following provision was considered sufficient for the disciplining of members who had failed to deposit their cards with local unions in whose jurisdictions they obtained employment:

88. *Constitution,* 1892.
89. *General Laws,* 1880, Sec. 23; Sec. 3.

Anyone failing to comply with the above article shall be amenable to laws of the local union under whose jurisdiction he may be at work.[90]

Under this regulation the power to decide whether or not to discipline a member who had worked in some community without having deposited his card with the appropriate local could be vested exclusively in another local, under whose jurisdiction the man was working in some subsequent period. In 1872 this provision was dropped and the following regulation, which granted disciplinary authority to the local in whose jurisdiction the infraction actually occurred, was adopted:

Anyone failing to comply with the above article shall not be admitted into any other Union until he procures a travelling card from the Union under whose jurisdiction he has been working.

This form of discipline, however, apparently proved unsatisfactory in at least some cases, perhaps because "other" unions were unwilling to exclude travelers on the complaint of locals which the travelers were alleged to have slighted. In 1876 President Carpenter reported to the convention that an Indiana local had tried and punished several of its members who had refused to deposit their cards with a Kentucky local.[91] This would indicate that the coöperation of the issuing union was being sought in cases where punishment less drastic than exclusion was desired. This participation of the local of issue in disciplinary matters was provided for explicitly (in 1882) in cases in which members of one local might "go into the jurisdiction of another Union on strike and accept work illegally." Under those circumstances, "the Union to which such offending members belong shall impose a fine commensurate with the offense, and the fine so collected shall be paid over to the Treasurer of the National Union and by him transferred to the Union so injured."

Despite a complaint by Secretary O'Dea that this requirement was illegal because, as he argued, once a local issued a traveling card to a member it surrendered jurisdiction over him and therefore could not legally punish him, the view that the traveler remained a citizen of the local of issue for disciplinary purposes apparently gained widespread acceptance. In 1891, the responsibility of the issuing unions was carefully limited to the assessment of fines upon guilty members; they were not expected to forward the amount to the complaining locals, unless they "collect said fines, which they must do if possible." And in 1892, the entire procedure for handling the case of a member accused of accepting work illegally in another jurisdiction was spelled out in detail[92] and might be summarized as follows:

90. *Constitution,* 1869, Art. XIV, Sec. 1; see also 1872, Art. XIV, Sec. 1.
91. *Proceedings,* 1876, p. 8 (report of the president); see also *Constitution,* 1882, Art. XIV, Sec. 7.
92. *Proceedings,* 1884, p. 27, *Constitution,* 1891, Art. XIV, Sec. 5; *Constitution,* 1892, Art. XXII.

(1) The injured local prefers charges against the member to his home local and estimates the amount of damages caused by his conduct.
(2) The home local notifies the accused of charges and instructs him either to appear for trial in person or to forward a statement of his defense by mail, within a maximum of twenty days from the date of notice. If no reply is received, the member is declared guilty.
(3) If, after the trial has been held, the accused is found guilty, the home local "shall impose a fine commensurate with the offense." If, after investigation, the judiciary board of the international union finds that the fine is not commensurate with the offense, it shall levy a fine in such amount as it deems appropriate.
(4) Until his fine is paid, the convicted member "shall stand expelled from the I. U." (After 1896, the words "as dropped or suspended," were substituted for "expelled.") [93]
(5) If collected, the fine shall be forwarded by the home local to the injured local which preferred the charges.

Since no record was kept of instances of voluntary compliance by locals to which complaints were addressed, it is not possible to arrive at an accurate conclusion concerning the degree of interlocal coöperation which was actually achieved. We have expressed skepticism on this count. This view derives some support from the reply which the corresponding secretary of Local Union No. 7 of New York sent to his opposite number in Toronto, who had recommended that No. 7 fine two of its members twenty dollars each for refusing to deposit cards in Toronto. The New Yorker's response is quoted in its entirety:

Dear Sir and Brother:—I am directed to inform No. 2 of Toronto, that at a meeting of our Union, the charges against Robert Scott and William Robinson, were tried before a committee, and were exonerated from all blame of working against No. 2.[94]

Two years later (in 1895) an even more disappointing case, involving two Massachusetts locals, was reported in the Bricklayers' convention. The Fall River local charged that the Brockton union had ignored completely a complaint that a Brockton member had refused to produce a traveling card while working in Fall River. The extreme of local parochialism, however, was achieved in another case involving Fall River as the plaintiff, which occurred in 1899. Fall River complained that a member of the Bricklayers' local in Boston had failed to deposit a traveling card after he had obtained employment in the Fall River jurisdiction. The following statement of the accused was offered in evidence:

I told Shawcross that I did not know that I was required to get out a Traveling Card for the short time I was to be on the job; that I had traveled all over the

93. *Constitution*, 1897, Art. XIV, Sec. 3.
94. *Proceedings*, 1893, pp. 73–77.

country, more or less, for the past eighteen years; that I never got out a Traveling Card, and was never asked for a Traveling Card before.[95]

This statement, remarkably enough, was offered by the Boston local in support of its refusal to discipline its member. It was accompanied by the following letter to Fall River:

Brothers—Enclosed you will find the evidence upon which Union No. 3, Mass., acquitted Bro. Michael Rady of the charge preferred against him by Union No. 11, Mass.

Said evidence being the affidavit of Michael Rady, an old and honored member of Union No. 3, Mass.

Fraternally yours,

Fortunately for them, however, the Bricklayers did not have to rely exclusively upon either the conscience or the sophistication of their local organizations. They had thoughtfully provided for appeal by the plaintiff local to the judiciary board of the international union from the verdict rendered by the issuing local, and they provided further that, in the event that the judiciary board found that the fine imposed by the issuing local was not "commensurate with the offense," it was supposed to levy one which it considered appropriate under the circumstances. Furthermore, power was granted to the judiciary board to reverse acquittals by local unions and to pass sentence directly in such cases. Presumably this power was considered implicit in the board's authority to increase fines to levels which it considered to be commensurate with the offense committed.

It was this recourse to higher authority which made possible effective disciplinary control over their traveling members; in two of the three cases cited above as examples of local noncompliance, the issuing local was reversed. In the first Fall River case (1895), the executive board allowed the Fall River local twenty-five dollars in damages, which was equal to the fine which that local had suggested that Brockton levy upon its member for working illegally in Fall River. And in the second case in which the embattled Fall River local appeared as plaintiff, the judiciary board reversed the decision of the Boston local, which had refused to convict a member who had admitted working in Fall River without a card, and ordered it to fine him five dollars and to pay the fine over to the Fall River union. In the remaining case, the grievance committee of the 1893 Convention recommended that the New York local, a committee of which had exonerated two of its members from charges of working without cards in Toronto, be required to assess a fine of twenty dollars on one of them, as the Toronto local had requested. But the convention (whose delegates always reflected the attitude of the locals more closely than did the executive branch of the national union) rejected the recom-

95. *Proceedings*, 1895, pp. 19–20 (report of the president); *Proceedings*, 1899, p. 125.

mendation of its grievance committee and tabled the question indefinitely. It should be noted, however, that this case was the earliest of the three considered and that, by the end of the century, even the convention had grown in sophistication. For, after the judiciary board had reversed the New York local in the second Fall River case (1899), New York appealed to the convention to override its decision, but the convention upheld the board.[96]

In the first part of this discussion of union citizenship, it was observed that certain beneficiary and financial considerations, not directly related to the problem of discipline, inclined some of the national unions to the view that the traveling member remained a member of the local which had issued him his card (at least until he deposited it elsewhere), although financial measures adopted in conformity with this assumption soon revealed its inadequacy. In this section, however, we indicated that the requirements of discipline created a predisposition in favor of the alternative theory of local citizenship—membership in the local of either immediate or ultimate destination. Since, however, no measure short of blacklisting could be undertaken unilaterally, in most cases, by the local of destination, the latter concept of citizenship proved as unsatisfactory for disciplinary reasons as it was for financial and beneficiary purposes.

Nor was the attempt to regard the traveler as a member of the local of issue any more successful from the disciplinary viewpoint than it was when measured against financial requirements. For participation by the issuing local in the initiation of sanctions against a traveling member involved the untenable assumption that a local union would discipline one of its own members on the complaint of another local as readily as it would discipline him for an offense committed within its own jurisdiction. To be workable, such a system of discipline required buttressing by the extralocal authority of the national union. This was demonstrated most strikingly in the case of the Bricklayers, who, in authorizing their judiciary board to find guilty and sentence individuals who had been acquitted by local unions of charges brought against them by other locals, bestowed upon their national judiciary powers far more sweeping than those granted in this country to superior tribunals over trial courts. The failure of disciplinary measures based upon the assumption that the traveler was a member of the local of destination, or that he was a member of the local of issue, or that he was in part a member of both meant, in effect, that the traveling card system, although it was a decided improvement over the mutual observation of blacklists by unaffiliated locals, was inadequate in the absence of some measure of control over individual members by the national union. The traveler was not exclusively a citizen of any local union; he had to be regarded also as a citizen of the national union.

96. *Proceedings,* 1895, pp. 19–20; 1893, pp. 73–77; 1899, pp. 125, 173.

CHAPTER FIVE

THE TRAVELING MEMBER AND NATIONAL CITIZENSHIP

In the previous chapter we discussed some of the implications of the traveling card system for local autonomy, ultimately arriving at the conclusion that, for purposes of discipline, the traveling member had to be regarded as a citizen of the national union rather than merely as a member of one particular local union, be it the local of origin or the local of destination. In the first section of this chapter we shall attempt to answer another question which was raised in Chapter 4: given that the local's obligation to issue traveling cards was qualified by the requirement that the member be in "good standing" and given that the local's obligation to accept members upon presentation of cards was similarly qualified, whose criteria of "good standing" would prevail if standards of admission and discipline varied from local to local? In addition, we will investigate the effect of labor migration upon the extension of national authority over organization and jurisdiction, and, finally, over collective bargaining.

EXTENSION OF NATIONAL AUTHORITY OVER THE INDIVIDUAL MEMBER

Recognition of the traveler as a national citizen was significant on two counts: first, because he was the first rank-and-file unionist to become a member of the national union; and, second, because some of the legislation which conferred this status upon him was generally applicable to the sedentary worker, as well as to the itinerant, and thus brought the individual member under the direct control of the national organization.

Since the first national unions began as little more than a federation of sovereign local bodies, its only members were the delegates to its convention and the officers which they elected.[1] The Molders, in 1859, held that "this

---

1. George E. Barnett, *The Printers* (Cambridge: American Economic Association, 1909), p. 59. See also Theodore W. Glocker, *The Government of American Trade Unions* (Baltimore: Johns Hopkins, 1913), p. 103.

Union shall be composed of its elective officers and the representatives of the subordinate Unions acting under this Constitution";[2] and eight years later the Bricklayers duplicated this definition, except for a puristic purging of the possessive, "its."[3] Indeed, in singling out national officers for special mention, this definition was somewhat redundant, for it was commonly provided that, to use the Printers' constitution as an example, "No one except a delegate shall be eligible to any of the above named offices. . . ."[4]

But this concept of the national union as nothing more than a federation of sovereign locals was unable to withstand the challenge presented in the person of the traveling member. The latter, who, as we have seen, could not be treated successfully as a member either of any one local union exclusively or of more than one jointly and simultaneously, finally took up a position alongside the "elective officers" of the parent organization and "the representatives of the subordinate Unions" as a member of the national union. His changed status was revealed in some of the regulations which were enacted in order to keep him in line. Thus we might recall that the detailed procedure which was worked out by the Bricklayers, for the guidance of their locals in prosecuting and sentencing members accused of accepting work illegally in another jurisdiction, provided that a guilty member "shall stand as expelled from the International Union" until he has paid the fine specified in his sentence.[5] It was also provided that any member who failed to return his card within thirty days from the date of issue, failed to forward one month's dues and assessments to his old local, and failed to make personal application for renewal within thirty days from the date of issue forfeited his membership in the same International Union. The Molders were most explicit on the subject of their travelers' membership:

Any member in good standing in a subordinate Union shall be entitled to a card; said member, when holding a card, shall be considered a member of this Union, and subject to all its laws, and upon depositing the same with any (local) Union, shall become subject to its laws.[6]

This was construed by President Martin Fox to hold that, "According to our present law, a member, when he draws and holds his card, ceases to be a

2. *Constitution*, 1859, Art. II, Sec. 1.

3. *Constitution*, 1867, Art. II, Sec. 1.

4. See e.g. *Constitution*, 1894, Art. IV, Sec. 3. This was the last of the I.T.U. Constitutions in which this provision appears. The problem of eligibility for the holding of national office is discussed more fully in Chapter 8. It might be noted here, however, that the inclusion of national officers along with local union delegates is not entirely redundant, since some unions for a while made it possible for ex-delegates not only to retain their direct affiliation with the national union and to participate in convention proceedings, but also to be elected to national office.

5. *Constitution*, 1897, Art. XIV, Sec. 3 (italics mine); see also *Constitution*, 1897, Art. XIII, Sec. 1.

6. *Constitution*, 1876, Art. X, Sec. 3.

member of a local Union, and is therefore a member only of the I.M.U. of N.A."[7]

Issuing of Traveling Cards to Members of Defunct Locals

One phenomenon which was in part responsible for the traveler's special status was the high mortality rate of the early locals. After a local union had disbanded or had been suspended, it was only through the direct intervention of the national union that the affiliation of the individual members of the defunct organization could be salvaged. The Carpenters, early in their collective career, provided that a member of a lapsed or suspended local could transfer to the nearest local union in the vicinity, "upon application to the General Secretary by and with the consent of the Executive Board. And if no other Local Union is in the same city, he may send 25 cents per month as dues to the General Secretary, and be retained as a member of the Brotherhood."[8] Not all groups, however, were so prompt in affiliating members of defunct locals with the national union; the local unions looked uneasily upon the establishment of a direct relationship between the individual and what they had desired would be nothing more than a loose federation of independent locals. Nevertheless, they appreciated the necessity for intervention by the national organization, for the position of active local unions would have been imperiled had no provision been made for those members of suspended or disbanded locals who took to the road in search of employment in other communities.

The result was that locals often empowered their national unions to issue traveling cards directly to such orphaned union men, although they were inclined to drag their feet in the process. Thus, it was not until 1901 that the Printers saw fit to provide that

Any member of a suspended union, upon furnishing the Secretary-Treasurer with sufficient proof of membership, shall, upon payment of all arrearages owed the International Union, be entitled to receive from the Secretary-Treasurer of the International Typographical Union a certificate of membership, which must be deposited with the nearest local of his craft.[9]

The Bricklayers were obliged to take action at a much earlier stage in their history, but, as their subsequent record of backing and filling indicates, they too accepted the inevitable with poor grace. At first they permitted a member, who had been suspended from a local which subsequently disintegrated, to receive a traveling card from the international secretary "upon his application . . . in writing, signed by the President of the nearest union to where said person may reside," accompanied by a remittance of one dollar and fifty cents. Later (in 1867) this fee was raised to five dollars, but it was

7. *Proceedings*, 1895, p. 7 (report of the president).
8. *Constitution*, 1886, Art. XVII.
9. *Constitution*, 1901, Art. XVIII, Sec. 3.

also provided that, "The International Union may grant a traveling card to any member in good standing of a disbanded union, on his producing evidence of his former membership and paying a fee of fifty cents." It is interesting that the power of the international to issue cards to members who had been in good standing in locals which subsequently disbanded was permissive rather than mandatory, in view of the stated "duty" of the local unions to furnish their members with traveling cards.

Two years later, the Bricklayers restricted the issue of cards without the five-dollar penalty fee to members who had been "square on the books" of their old locals—a development which paralleled a similar prerequisite for the issue of cards by active local unions. In 1875, eligibility for an international card was further restricted by a presidential decision to grant a traveling card only if the disbanded local had surrendered its books to the international union, so that direct evidence on the standing of the applicant might be made available. If the disbanded union had not forwarded its records to the central organization, the member in question was required to pay dues to the local to which he subsequently applied for membership from the date of the disbanding.[10]

But the locals were not satisfied with these restrictions upon the power of the international to grant traveling cards, and in 1876 they withdrew it completely. Instead it was provided that members who had been in good standing in a suspended or disbanded local, but who did not hold traveling cards which were issued by that local before its suspension or disbandment, could be received into "new membership" by any local to which they applied; and that members who held cards which had been issued before the date of suspension could be admitted to other locals by card. Opponents of this measure argued that it would require some members to pay initiation fees in order to retain their union status and thus "would be punishing a good member for the faults of others, and cut him off from all means of holding his membership in the National Union." Its supporters, however, pointed out that under the old system a member of a disbanded local could join another local at less cost than a cardbearing traveler who came from an actively affiliated union, because the former was required to pay only fifty cents to the international for a card while the latter had to pay back dues to the date on which his traveling card was issued. But since these new regulations made no specific provision for the member who had been suspended (for nonpayment of dues) from a local which itself was subsequently suspended or disbanded, the international secretary's former power to issue traveling cards to individuals in this category was restored in 1882.[11] Five years later, however,

10. *Constitution*, 1866, Art. XIV; 1867, Art. XIV; 1869, Art. XIV; Proceedings, 1875, p. 7 (report of the president).

11. *Constitution*, 1876, Art. XIV; *Proceedings*, 1876, p. 28; Constitution, 1882, Art. XIV.

this authority was again revoked, and the system of administration by local unions exclusively once more prevailed.

Under this new system it seemed that a local union was not obliged to admit a member of a suspended or disbanded local, whether or not he had been in good standing therein: the law provided merely that such a member "can" be admitted into any other local under the conditions noted above. That this ambiguity proved fatal was demonstrated when, in 1888, the Newport, Rhode Island local refused to receive the traveling cards presented to it by the entire membership of the Fall River, Massachusetts, local which had issued these cards prior to its suspension from the international. The Fall River organization was suspended for failure to comply with a mandatory nine-hour rule which had been adopted by the convention of the national union, and, when International Secretary O'Dea ordered its members to deposit their cards with the Newport local, the latter claimed that "the Fall River men wanted Newport to fight the nine-hour battle for them." O'Dea and President Darragh of the international finally persuaded two Boston locals to accept the cards, but the convention, in rejecting a claim presented by a Fall River member against the Newport local for lost time and additional expenses, in effect decided that no local union was obliged to admit the members of a defunct organization.[12] With this episode in mind, the Bricklayers finally concluded that the issuing of travel cards by the national union was the price which had to be paid in order to retain the affiliation of members of former local unions, who otherwise would have been indistinguishable from any other nonunion migrants and would have presented the same competitive threat to the security of active locals in other communities. Thus, in 1891, the following amendment was enacted:

Discretionary power is vested in the Executive Board to grant Traveling Cards to any member or members who may apply for same within thirty days, but who cannot obtain such card from their Subordinate Union by reason of the withdrawal, disbandment, or suspension of subordinate Union.[13]

The reluctance of local unions to place the members of a defunct sister organization under the immediate jurisdiction of the national union was probably motivated less by a scrupulous adherence to contemporary canons of union citizenship than it was by distaste for the growth of the national union's authority over the locals, which was made possible by the extension of its authority over these individual members. For, since it was generally agreed that locals which were suspended from the national organization did not have the right to issue traveling cards,[14] it was to the interest of all locals in good standing that the national union avail itself sparingly of its power

12. *Proceedings:* 1888, p. 18 (report of the secretary); 1889, pp. 34–35, 89.

13. *Constitution,* 1891, Art. XIV.

14. See *Proceedings, Bricklayers,* 1875, p. 7. See also *Constitution,* International Typographical Union, 1880, Art. XVI, Sec. 1.

of suspension so long as no satisfactory provision was made for continuing the union status of travelers who came from suspended unions. Once it became possible, however, to control these migrants by authorizing the national union to issue cards directly to them, this deterrent to the suspension of local groups was eliminated, and the disciplinary authority of the national was consequently enhanced. The authority which was granted in 1901 to the secretary-treasurer of the International Typographical Union to issue traveling cards to members of suspended locals appeared in the constitution of that union as a new section in a long-standing article that provided for the suspension of any local union which fell three months in arrears in its financial obligations to the International.[15] The Bricklayers afford another example of the disciplinary value to the national union of its power to issue cards. It will be recalled that one local was able to refuse with impunity to accept the members of a suspended union in a period in which the international union was not empowered to issue cards directly to individual members. After this power had been restored (in 1891), another local union refused, on two occasions, to admit members of suspended unions: in one case, it refused to accept a card issued by the executive board of the international union; in another, it refused to accept a conventional traveling card which had been issued by another local to a member whom the latter had received on an international card. This time, however, the executive board was able to suspend the uncoöperative local, after which, the president reported happily to the convention, the local apologized and agreed to accept both cards.[16]

Admission and Discipline

More important to the development of national citizenship than the special status accorded to traveling members from disbanded or suspended locals was the assumption by the national union of a certain measure of control over the admission and discipline of individual members. This intervention was largely the historical outgrowth of differences which arose among the local unions over the admission or rejection of traveling members and which required the arbitration of a third party. Intervention was required, first, because local standards of admission and discipline—which governed the issuing and withholding of traveling cards—differed from community to community; and, second, because the disciplining of traveling members, usually requiring the efforts of more than one local, was difficult at best and often productive of friction, even when both locals concerned agreed that the behavior with which the individual was charged constituted a punishable offense.

This second cause of interlocal conflict, which raised the question of jurisdiction over the traveling member for the purposes of determining guilt and

15. *Constitution*, 1901, Art. XVIII; *Constitution*, 1880, Art. XVI.
16. *Proceedings*, 1891, pp. XCVII-CV (report of the president).

executing sentence, was sufficient to result in provisions for the judicial resolution by the national union of disputes between constituent locals.[17]

The existence of different standards of admission and discipline among the various locals in a national union, however, offered an even more serious threat to the system of controlling worker migration by traveling cards. It was in this connection that the following questions arose: must a local union admit to membership a man who had been issued a traveling card by some other organization, but whom it would not receive as an initiatory member? And must it refuse admission to a man whose qualifications it considers satisfactory, but who was *persona non grata* to some other local union? The conflict of standards involved in this latter question was expressed most frequently in cases involving the admission to one local union of a member who had been expelled from another.

In such cases it was uniformly decided that "an expelled member must be restored to membership in the expelling union before he may be admitted into any other local union."[18] The Carpenters, for example, broadened this principle to include rejected applicants for membership, in holding that "A person who has been expelled or suspended from, or rejected in any Local Union of this United Brotherhood, shall not be eligible to membership in any other Local Union, except by consent of the Local Union of which he was a member or in which he was rejected."[19] Any other course of action would have resulted in the complete frustration of the traveling card system, for the obligation of the local unions to refuse admission to those who had already been rejected or expelled by sister organizations was but part of their over-all duty to exclude all travelers who failed to present traveling cards, unless consent was obtained in each case from the appropriate local union.

Thus our second question was answered in the affirmative: a local union was obliged to refuse admission to an expelled, suspended, or rejected traveler even though he would have been completely acceptable as an initiate. Similarly, the first question received an affirmative answer: the local had to admit by card a man who could not have qualified for initiation. It will be recalled that these two questions arose because the "home" local's obligation to issue cards was modified by the requirement that the applicant be in "good standing" therein (see p. 89 above), but it is obvious that this qualification of the obligation to issue could not relieve the locals of their duty to receive those who came into their jurisdiction with traveling cards and to refuse admission to those who came without them.

17. See F. E. Wolfe, *Admission to American Trade Unions* (Baltimore: Johns Hopkins, 1912), p. 13. Reference has been made above to the provision in the Bricklayers' constitution which permitted the Judiciary Board of the International Union to review cases in which inadequate punishment of traveling members was alleged by plaintiff locals.

18. Wolfe, *Admission to Unions*, p. 157.

19. *Constitution*, 1892, Sec. 69.

But while it was necessary that the local unions honor one another's decisions to issue and to withhold traveling cards, it was possible (1) to eliminate conflicts of standards by imposing uniform policies concerning admission and discipline upon all the locals in a national union, and/or (2) to minimize such conflict by providing for judicial review by the national union of action taken by the locals in cases involving the admission or disciplining of members.

Since it is our purpose in this chapter to determine the contribution of the traveling member to the absorption of power by the national union, the material presented in the following discussion of national regulations governing these subjects is drawn exclusively from unions in local market industries, in which the influence of interlocality product competition was of minor importance. This crude attempt to hold other things equal by no means clears our historical test tube of foreign matter, for our sample of local market unions is inadequate to permit the cancelling out of all random and special factors which might have influenced the result in any one case. However, it does eliminate fairly well the influence of product competition, which was, of course, a major determinant in the evolution of national unionism.

National Standards

BALLOTING ON ADMISSION. Although it was customary for local unions to poll their members on application for admission, some of the national unions specified a minimum proportion of the total votes cast at a local meeting as both a necessary and sufficient condition for admission. The Carpenters, in 1886, provided that "a two-third vote shall be necessary to admit a member." [20] The object of such regulation was not to restrict membership in most cases, but, as Wolfe observed, "to secure uniformity among the locals and to check or prevent the easy rejection of applicants." [21] This bias in favor of inclusion rather than exclusion was implicit in the provision adopted by the International Typographical Union:

It shall be deemed illegal for a subordinate union to declare an applicant, who is not otherwise disqualified, rejected while three-fourths of the members present at the meeting at which said application was acted on voted in favor of his admission. [22]

This type of provision not only served to alleviate any dissatisfaction which a difference in voting requirements might have engendered, but, by restricting the locals' freedom to reject, it protected the weaker local unions from the competition of travelers who might have been excluded from stronger locals in other localities had the latter been free to follow a policy

20. *Constitution*, 1886, Art. VII.
21. Wolfe, *Admission to Unions*, p. 28.
22. *General Laws*, 1893, Sec. 73.

of rigorous exclusion. It must be noted, however, that not all national unions curtailed their locals' discretion in this respect. The Bricklayers, for example, left the determination of size of the vote necessary to reject an applicant to the constituent local unions.

INITIATION FEES. The one feature of the traveling card system which distinguished it most sharply from the more primitive exchange of blacklists by independent local unions was the obligation of the local union to admit any cardholder to membership without requiring him to pay an initiation fee. It is probable that no other waiver of local prerogatives which was implicit in the traveling card system was so apparent to the sedentary members of a local union, who quite frequently grew restive as they beheld outsiders being admitted without charge (other than the payment of dues) to the organization which had obliged them to pay an initiation fee prior to their admission. They realized, it is true, that the traveler who deposited a card had paid an entrance fee to some other local, but if their own charge was higher than that which the stranger had been required to pay to his home organization, they were apt to experience a strong feeling of injustice. It is not surprising, therefore, that attempts were occasionally made to oblige the duly accredited traveler to pay the difference between the higher initiation fee in effect in the local of deposit and the fee which was charged by the local which had issued his traveling card.

These attempts, however, usually met with resolute and successful opposition on the part of national officers, who foresaw the peril to which the traveling card system would be exposed by the toleration of such practices. The experience of the Carpenters with five of their locals in New York City is a case in point. These unions originally charged an initiation fee of five dollars, which was identical with the fee charged by locals in adjacent districts. Then, in 1900, they raised their fees to twenty dollars, which, as the general president observed, "they had the right to do." But they decided also to charge members who had been issued traveling cards by the outlying locals the difference between the fee of five dollars, which continued to prevail elsewhere, and the higher fee which they had just instituted. The general president refused to sanction this latter practice, and, after the New York local refused to abide by his decision, he suspended them.[23] Prior to this episode, some of the delegates to a convention of the Bricklayers tried to achieve by legislation what the Carpenters' locals had attempted by direct action. They introduced an amendment to the constitution which required that a traveling member pay the local with which he deposited his card a sum equal to the excess of its initiation fee over that of the issuing local. This measure, however, was rejected by the convention.[24] (But later on,

23. *Proceedings*, 1900, p. 15.
24. *Proceedings*, 1887, p. 143. (*Constitution*, 1891, Art. XIV.)

the Carpenters required that the difference between the fees charged by the local of deposit and the local of issue be paid by "an initiatory member drawing a traveling card within thirty days after date of initiation." This provision was repealed in 1900.)

This problem might have been eliminated by requiring that all the locals in a national union charge an initiation fee of a specified amount. Some unions did prescribe a uniform fee (such as the Molders, the Cigar Makers, the Granite Cutters, the Stone Cutters, and the Bookbinders), but a greater number did not impose this restriction upon their affiliates.[25] Sentiment in favor of the uniform fee indeed existed, but in most cases it yielded to the more powerful appeal of local autonomy. Thus, as early as 1872, the delegates from the Bricklayers' local in Troy, New York, moved "to have a general initiation fee in all Local Unions under the jurisdiction of the National Union," but the committee to which this motion was referred recommended "that the question remain as heretofore with the Local Unions, which was concurred in."[26] The issue remained alive, however, for in 1885 and 1886 proposals were made to establish a minimum fee, and the following year it was suggested that the convention adopt a flat fee of twenty-five dollars. None of these motions was adopted.

Some national unions, as Wolfe pointed out, established maximum fees; others set minimum fees; and still others prescribed both maxima and minima.[27] Considerations other than, or in addition to the desire to approach uniformity, however, motivated the adoption of such regulations. Thus the establishment of a maximum fee could be ascribed simply to the desire by the national officialdom not to exclude qualified workers from membership, although, to be sure, the most immediate danger of such exclusionist local fees to "the trade" as a whole lay in the stimulus which they provided for the worker who had been barred from membership and, possibly, employment in some community to migrate elsewhere as a nonunion man. To this extent, the imposition of maximum fees by national authority might have been motivated by a fear of augmenting the volume of nonunion labor migration; but this should be distinguished from the desire to establish a uniform initiation fee.

Nor was the same consideration solely—or even primarily—responsible for the prescription of a minimum fee. In some cases, the object of setting a minimum figure was to restrict membership, as was the case with the Hatters and Print Cutters, according to Wolfe. In others, minima were established in order to put an end to a variant of cutthroat competition which was sometimes practiced when different local unions in the same metropolitan area sought to attract members by competitive reductions in their initia-

25. See Wolfe, *Admission to Unions*, pp. 25–27.
26. *Proceedings*, 1872, p. 27; see also *Proceedings:* 1885, p. 67; 1886, p. 104; 1887, p. 72.
27. Wolfe, *Admission to Unions*, pp. 25–27.

tion fees. Thus the Bricklayers' and the Carpenters' unions, both of which prescribed minima, also provided that all locals in the same locality establish a uniform initiation fee.

The Bricklayers provided for a minimum fee—and a maximum, as well— in that article of their Constitution which enumerated the powers reserved to the local unions. The first section of this article declared that the subordinate union shall have the power "to establish its rate of initiation fee," and the fifth section modified this by stating, "but it shall not be less than ten ($10.00) dollars, or more than twenty-five ($25.00) dollars. . . ." In another article, in which the "general powers" of the international were spelled out, reference was made only to the minimum limit:

No Subordinate Union shall maintain, charge, or accept an initiation fee for membership of less than ten dollars ($10.00), unless special permission for a limited time (presumably as a concession to new locals in their first months of existence) has been granted by the Executive Board.[28]

They also provided for uniform wages, hours, and for "rules and regulations under which all can work in harmony."

The Carpenters established a minimum of one dollar in the first year of the United Brotherhood's existence (1881) and raised it to two dollars in 1888 and to five dollars ten years later. They likewise specified uniform wages, and they insisted that, in addition to the initiation fee, monthly dues be standardized.[29]

From the foregoing it is apparent that differences in local initiation fees did not necessarily eventuate in the erection of uniform standards by national unions. Some unions, as we have noted, did establish uniform fees, but none of these organizations had jurisdiction over local market industries. At the other extreme, there could be found national unions like the Typographical Union, which imposed no restraint at all upon their locals in this sphere of activity.[30]

APPRENTICESHIP AND COMPETENCE. National unionism in the typographical trade received a powerful impetus from the practice of employing runaway apprentices "for a small compensation. These were called two-thirds men, and have always proved a great pest to the profession."[31] They were called "two-thirds" journeymen because they were paid two-thirds of the qualified journeymen's rate of compensation. Others, who received half of

28. See *Constitution,* 1897, Art. XVI, Secs. 1 and 5, and Art. X, Secs. 1 and 5; 1883, Art. XII, Sec. 8.

29. *Constitution* 1881, Art. IV; 1886, Art. III, Sec. 3; 1888, Art. V; 1898, Sec. 55.

30. Barnett, *The Printers,* p. 325. Also Wolfe, *Admission to Unions,* p. 25.

31. From "Introductory Remarks" to the constitution adopted by the New York Typographical Association in 1831. Reproduced in Ethelbert Stewart, *A Documentary History of the Early Organizations of Printers* (Indianapolis: International Typographical Union, 1907), pp. 20, 43, 51–52.

the journeymen's wages, were known as "halfway journeymen." They invariably sought work in some community other than that in which they had served their truncated indentures, because their masters were legally entitled to compel them to return if they were caught. But when they left town, their apprehension was doubtful, not only because it was made difficult by the willingness of out-of-town employers to hire them to do journeymen's work "for a small compensation," but also because of the ease with which their old masters could take on new apprentices. Thus, the runaway apprentice problem reflected both a high degree of geographic labor mobility and an increased supply of newcomers to the printing trade.

The locals at first reacted to this competitive threat by raising their required terms of apprenticeship, but, as Stewart observed, "There was no effective means of preventing apprentices from running away, and the longer apprenticeship only increased the temptation to do so. . . ." Finally, the need for a coöperative approach to the problem was appreciated in some of the local unions, and the convention of the ill-fated National Typographical Society proposed that the local unions establish uniform apprenticeship regulations, that "no runaway apprentice shall be received into any office in the United States attached to the National Society, either as an apprentice or journeyman," and that a traveling-card system be adopted. The card system was proposed, according to the delegates from the Washington, D. C. local, expressly for the purpose of excluding "two-third apprentices."[32] What the failure of the projected National Society meant to local unions who had attempted to bring the apprenticeship problem under control can be gathered from the following excerpt from the majority report of a committee appointed by the local in Washington, D. C.:

That your committee consider the above-named regulations which were recommended by the general convention of printers, with the intention (in connection with other measures), to unite the societies of the different cities for the advancement of the interests of the craft; and could only be beneficial by general adoption. That such has not been the case is evident to everyone, for they have only been carried out by one society besides this. That, as said project of union has totally failed of success, this society is under no obligations to other society to enforce said regulations.[33]

After a durable national union of printers was finally formed in 1852, a traveling card system was instituted which was supposed to make it impossible for those who did not serve apprenticeships which were satisfactory to the locals in their home towns to be received into union membership—

32. "Address to Local Societies by the Convention of the National Typographical Society in 1836," Articles 1, 2, and 6. Reproduced in Stewart, *Documentary History*, pp. 127–128; *Constitution* of the National Typographical Society, Art. XII. Reproduced in Stewart, p. 128; see also p. 62.

33. Reproduced in George A. Tracy, *History of the Typographical Union* (Indianapolis: International Typographical Union, 1913), p. 99.

and, supposedly, to obtain work—elsewhere. If, however, a man had satisfied the apprenticeship requirements of his home local and was issued a traveling card by that organization, he had to be received into any other affiliate to which he presented that card, whether or not his apprenticeship was satisfactory to the latter union. Only through "general adoption" by all local unions of a uniform apprenticeship regulation could this situation be resolved.

Although the establishment of such uniform standards had been urged as early as 1836, it was not until 1902 that the International Typographical Union set a mandatory minimum term of apprenticeship. (Most of the locals, however, had required the four-year term prior to the enactment of the international regulation.) Nor was the Printers' union exceptional in its reluctance to legislate on this issue: of one hundred and twenty-five national unions investigated by Wolfe, fifty had no apprenticeship regulations on the books.[34]

The Bricklayers were among those unions which did not specify a uniform term. Originally the international union did prescribe a mandatory four-year term, but this was repealed in 1867, when the matter was left to the discretion of the various locals.[35] In 1887, a move to reëstablish the national standard term was defeated. The Bricklayers also decentralized control over apprenticeship in other respects. The international originally had required that no more than two apprentices be allowed to an employer or firm engaged in bricklaying. While never repealed, this regulation was not taken too seriously, for in 1870, when a local union sought authorization for a strike against the employers of Wilmington, Delaware, who sought to increase the number of apprentices from four to eight per firm, President O'Keefe, instead of either disciplining the local for admittedly allowing the employment of twice the maximum number of apprentices within its jurisdiction or throwing his support behind a move to reduce this number to the legal limit, refused to entertain the petition to strike. He gave as his reason, "the bad effect it would have on Unions who have those laws made in conformity with the laws of the National Union on the apprenticeship question, and in many cases have to struggle hard to maintain them." And in 1886, an omnibus motion which reaffirmed the limit of two apprentices to an employer and in addition proposed (a) that no firm be allowed an apprentice until it had been in existence for two years, (b) that all apprentices be legally indentured, and (c) that eighteen years be the maximum age of apprentices was rejected "after considerable discussion." It might also be added that, while the national union in 1867 took it upon itself to provide new employment for apprentices whose employers had gone out of business before their terms as apprentices had expired (a common development in the building trades), this task was transferred to the local unions in 1888.[36]

34. Wolfe, *Admission to Unions,* pp. 49–50; see also p. 39.
35. *Constitution,* 1867, Art. XVII, Sec. 1.
36. *Proceedings,* 1871, p. 9 (report of the president); 1886, pp. 103, 104; 1867, Art. XVII, Sec. 3; 1886, Art. XVII, Sec. 3.

Thus the annals of the Bricklayers reveal a movement away from national control over apprenticeship and in the general direction of local autonomy. As early as 1868, the Committee on General Good suggested to the convention that each local "regulate the apprenticeship system as is most conducive to their local interest." Eight years later, it was provided that, "Each local Union shall have power to regulate its apprentice laws, subject to the decisions of the Executive Officer."[37] And finally, in 1897, the defeat of the proponents of centralized control was officially conceded:

It being impossible for the International Union to formulate and maintain a general apprentice law within its jurisdiction, it hereby grants to each Subordinate Union the power to regulate its own apprentice laws. . . .

It is true that most national unions—including many which did not legislate on the subject of apprenticeship—insisted that no local union receive into membership an applicant who was not a competent journeyman. National pronouncements on worker competence, however, actually resulted in the imposition of little, if any, uniformity in local standards. Competence was subject both to economic and technical definition. The former is illustrated by the Carpenters' requirement that "No local Union shall admit to membership any carpenter or joiner who is not . . . competent to command a general average of wages."[38] Since conditions of demand for the labor in question (which reflected technological conditions) and union wage standards often differed considerably from locality to locality, it did not follow that a man who was adjudged "competent" by one local union on the basis of his ability to command the prevailing wage would have satisfied the same requirement elsewhere. And even if union wages had been equal, differences in the skill and knowledge required by employers in any two communities (that is, differences in conditions of demand) could have brought it about that a man who was worth the union (or prevailing) wage in one place was not worth the same wage in another.

Technical definition of competence was usually left expressly to the locals; the national unions did not spell out detailed standards of proficiency,[39] except in cases where national apprenticeship qualifications were made either synonomous with or a necessary ingredient of competence. The Typographical Union, for example, required that only "practical printers" be admitted to membership and directed each local to conduct "a rigid examination as to the competency of candidates,"[40] but, in leaving the details of the examination to each local, made the definition of "competency" a local matter.

Since the criteria of competence were determined largely on a local level,

37. *Proceedings*, 1868, p. 59; *Constitution*, 1876, Art. XVII, Sec. 1; 1897, Art. XII, Sec. 1.
38. *Constitution*, 1881, Art. IX, Sec. 1.
39. Wolfe, *Admission to Unions*, p. 68.
40. Barnett, *The Printers*, p. 303.

adoption of the traveling card system obliged local unions to accept by card men who might not have qualified for initiation. In many of the craft unions of this period, however, the mechanical qualifications of the membership were of vital importance to the organization, and the conflict of local standards in this area was often regarded seriously. Thus, after a local union of bricklayers had refused to accept a traveling card presented by a man whom it had considered incompetent, the international, on appeal, declared that a traveling card must indeed be accepted, but that the local was free to expel any member for incompetence immediately after it had admitted him on a card.[41] Nine years after this judgment was pronounced the Bricklayers added the following section to their constitutional requirements concerning membership:

He must be a practical bricklayer, mason or plasterer, and competent to command the existing scale pieces for work; and shall (if complaint is made as to his ability) be required to pass a satisfactory examination by a committee of the Union in whose jurisdiction he is working.[42]

FEMALE AND NEGRO WORKERS. The admission to union membership of female and colored workers was long subject to bitter debate. Where the employment of women became more widespread (after 1860 or thereabouts), their competition in the labor market prompted the national unions to take the lead in urging their affiliation.[43] Thus the Typographical Union which in 1854 had declared that it should not "encourage by its acts the employment of females as compositors," thirty years later cautioned its locals to "make no distinctions on account of sex in persons holding travelling cards." Furthermore, they upheld a decision of their international president which held that no local had the right to refuse admission to any female applicant who was otherwise qualified. In the ordinary run of cases, however, there appears to have been some divergence between national policy and local practice, with some local unions going to the extreme of refusing to accept cards presented by female travelers.[44]

In the case of negroes, two factors conspired to prevent the eradication by national authority of differences in local policy. In the first place, prejudice against admitting the negro workman was more intense than the prejudice against admitting white females. Second, as Wolfe observed in an excellent discussion of the subject, such prejudice could be indulged in because the competition of colored workers was not too serious in some of the more

41. Wolfe, *Admission to Unions,* p. 72.
42. *Constitution,* 1897, Art. X, Sec. 4.
43. Wolfe, *Admission to Unions,* pp. 80–92. See also Theresa Wolfson, *The Woman Worker and the Trade Unions* (New York: International Publishers, 1926), p. 74.
44. Barnett, *The Printers,* pp. 211, 215; Wolfe, *Admission to Unions,* p. 92; see also ch. VI, pp. 112–134.

skilled trades. For these reasons, some of the early national unions (notably the railroad brotherhoods) adopted an official policy of exclusion, while others, remaining neutral, made little attempt to oppose local unions which excluded negroes.

In the 1860's and 1870's according to Spero and Harris, the dominance of local autonomy accounted in considerable part for the failure of early national unions to insist upon the admission of negroes.[45]

As time wore on, however, national unions in occupations to which negroes were drawn in significant numbers took the lead in advocating their admission to membership, either in locals which were already in existence or in separate organizations to be composed of negroes exclusively. As usual, the first trials of strength between national and local union occurred when some locals in a national union which had not declared itself officially on the subject of negro membership refused to accept the traveling cards presented by negroes who had been admitted in other communities.

The position taken by the Printers on this issue was clearcut. While the Typographical Union never sought to oblige its locals to admit negro applicants by initiation, it was firm in requiring that they accept cards from negro printers who had been issued them by other locals. The problem, however, was of little practical importance to the printers, since the number of negroes working at their trade remained very small.[46]

This was not the case with the Bricklayers, whose national policy reflected in its evolution the growing economic importance of negroes in their industry. Thus in 1881, when an Ohio local inquired of the international secretary whether a local union was required to recognize a traveling card which had been granted to a member who was "a gentleman of color," the secretary and the president replied that the matter would be left to the discretion of each individual local.[47] Before the end of the first decade of the new century, however, this national union provided that any affiliated local or individual member found guilty of discriminating against any individual because of his race or color would be fined one hundred dollars. There is little doubt that this change in policy was made in response to the increased competition of negro bricklayers. As the president remarked in 1902, "The colored bricklayer of the south is going to lay brick, whether we take them under our care or not, and this fact being conceded, the Board maintains that his proper place is within our fold. . ."[48]

But the resistance which the national officials had to overcome in order

45. Sterling D. Spero and Abram L. Harris, *The Black Worker* (New York: Columbia University Press, 1931), pp. 17–22, 57–58.

46. Barnett, *The Printers*, pp. 321–322.

47. *Proceedings*, 1881, p. 7 (report of the president); *Constitution*, 1908, Art. VII, Sec. 19; see also Wolfe, *Admission to Unions*, pp. 124–125.

48. Quoted in Wolfe, pp. 124–125, from the report of the president, 1902, pp. 291–294.

to establish this requirement must not be ignored. An example is afforded by an incident which occurred in 1884, when fourteen members of a Missouri local asked the international president whether it was necessary for them to deposit their cards in the Houston, Texas union because "among the members of the Union, there were two (Negroes) and that they would not go into the meetings of the Union on that account."[49] The president replied in the affirmative, and the men from Missouri, having been shown, deposited their cards in the Texas local union.

In some unions (notably the Coopers', Cigar Makers', Bricklayers', Carpenters', and Iron and Steel Workers'), the national organizations were able to admit negroes by organizing them in separate locals where the established locals refused to admit them to membership. In others, however, local autonomy remained sufficiently strong so that a local which refused to admit negroes could also veto the proposed establishment of a negro local within its jurisdiction.[50]

STANDARDS OF DISCIPLINE. Attempts, whether successful or not, to create uniform local standards of admission with respect to balloting, initiation fees, apprenticeship and competence, and special classes of workers whose eligibility was subject to controversy were motivated in part by the desire to remove any grounds on which one local union might seek to refuse admission to a member who had been issued a traveling card by another. Attempts were also made to establish national standards of discipline in the interest of maintaining, as far as possible, effective union control over labor migration, but in this case the object was primarily to lessen a local's temptation to admit travelers without traveling cards, because they had been suspended or expelled from other local unions for the commission of acts which would not have deprived them of membership status in the local in question. With this aim in view, it was in the interest of the national union to take steps which would reduce the number of expulsions to what the national officers considered a minimum. Authority to achieve this result was sought as early as 1870 by the president of the Bricklayers, when he told the assembled delegates that

In my opinion many of the expulsions are unjust and result in no good to National or Local Unions. The National Union should specify the offense that may be punishable by expulsion and guarantee to every member a fair and impartial trial, and the Executive of the National Union should be vested with the power to set aside the action of a union by which such punishment has been inflicted without a legal trial; also to grant pardon in certain cases. I think this system would in certain instances prevent persecution and tend to secure your favorable consideration.[51]

49. *Proceedings*, 1884, p. 12 (report of the president).
50. Spero and Harris, *The Black Worker*, p. 22.
51. *Proceedings*, 1870, p. 32 (report of the president).

Favorable consideration, however, was not secured for more than twenty years after President Gaul had appealed to the convention to erect national specifications of offenses punishable by expulsion, to supply national standards of trial procedure, and to provide for judicial review and executive pardon by officers of the national union. With the exception of provisions for appeal, enactment of appropriate measures came only after a later national officer, Secretary Thomas O'Dea, had condemned the existing state of affairs in considerably stronger language:

From among the thousands of complaints and appeals that your Executive Officers have to consider, we find that an exercise of arbitrary authority bordering on despotism is practiced by some of our Unions towards its members, and acting on the theory of "might makes right," and no chance or opportunity for a defense is allowed to a member who may be charged with a supposed offense. This system is contrary to the laws of the land, and also to the spirit of our Constitution, which provides that the powers of this (national) union, besides being Executive and Legislative, are Judicial. The Judicial powers should therefore be defined by Code, so that all can be kept within the intent and meaning of the Constitution.[52]

In his report the following year, the secretary prefaced a submission of specific proposals to be incorporated in a "Code of Crimes and Penalties" with the observation that the Bricklayers' constitutional prohibition against the admission by any local union of a member who had been blacklisted by some other local union made it impossible to redress any injustices committed by the latter. It is interesting that every local practice of which he complained and every rectifying regulation which he proposed reflected preoccupation with the problem of keeping workers—especially traveling workers—in the fold. The specific "abuses" which he enumerated and the corrective legislation adopted by the convention (which, for the most part, adopted his proposals) follow:

Blacklisting members who had been suspended for nonpayment of dues. Although "the Executive Board have held that the matter of suspension for non-payment of dues is not a capital (sic) crime . . . exceptions have been taken from the ruling of the Executive Board in this matter." In 1897, the convention decided to adopt the interpretation of the executive board (of which the secretary was a member and moving spirit) and added to its "Code" the following section:

The names of members of a Subordinate Union, who may be dropped from the roll for non-payment of dues, will not be published in the delinquent list, as such is not considered a crime.

"Excessive fines or excessive special initiation fees." The latter were really readmission fees, which expelled members were obliged to pay as a condition of

52. *Proceedings,* 1891, p. 35 (report of the secretary); see also 1892, p. 26 (report of the secretary).

reëntry. They were normally higher than the regular initiation fee charged to initiates. O'Dea charged that, "We have men on the blacklist whose fines range from $5.00 up to $500.00 and we also have some against whom a special initiation fee of $500.00 has been placed." And then he made an observation which, in capsule form, expressed perfectly the viewpoint of the national union:

> It is our duty to build up the Union and keep members in it instead of keeping them out to the injury of the organization, and placing a barrier against men that they can never overcome.

O'Dea also expressed the fear that indiscriminate exclusion of individuals from membership might result in the union's being sued for damages in conspiracy cases and receiving "judgments for injury to character and prevention of work at the plaintiff's trade."

O'Dea then proposed, first, that the penalty for the nonpayment of fines and assessments be expulsion "without any recognition whatsoever" until such fines were paid, but he added a proviso that no additional financial penalties, other than the payment of accumulated dues, be added to the original fine or assessment. He also suggested that a member suspended for the nonpayment of dues be required to pay his local's initiation fee "only." These proposed regulations were not adopted, but, following another one of O'Dea's suggestions, the convention set a limit of twenty-five dollars over and above the regular initiation fee on the amount which any local could charge as a special initiation fee. Later, it was provided that "a fine and special initiation fee shall not be imposed on a member at one time as a punishment for one offense," and finally (in 1897) power to impose special initiation fees was confined to cases involving nonunion men "who refuse to join this organization." They could not be imposed on members. Furthermore, in order to curtail the locals' freedom of action in setting fines, the international established a schedule of offenses and corresponding penalties. Thus, while fines of fifty dollars each were prescribed for "inveterate or notorious scabs, for third offense or over," the "common scab, first or second offense" could be fined no more than twenty-five dollars (or less than ten).

Inadequate punishment by local unions of members. Greater leniency was advocated by O'Dea not as an end in itself but primarily in the interest of preventing the breakdown of the traveling-card system, which, he reasoned, would result from the creation by the locals themselves of a sizeable body of footloose and cardless expatriates. It was not inconsistent for him, therefore, to urge also that more severe measures be taken in cases where severity, rather than mercy, was required for the efficient operation of this system and for its respect by individual members and local unions alike. Thus there was no occasion for surprise when the Bricklayers' secretary deplored the fact that

> very rank injustice is done at times, owing to favoritism on the one hand, or malice on the other, according as the case may present itself, or the standing of the accused party may be with his or their respective Unions. For instance, a member of a Union might go into the jurisdiction of another Union that is on an authorized strike by the International Union and deliberately do scab

work there to the detriment of such Union, refusing all orders and commands to cease either from the Union on strike or his own Union. When in the end he is brought up on charges for his misdoings, he is in some cases, according to his standing or influence, let off with a nominal fine of $10.00 or so, when he should in reality be fined more for the premeditated injury that he done. . . .

The Executive Board, in the absence of any law on the matter, is as powerless as the injured Union is, for it cannot reverse such Union's action and impose a heavier amount.

O'Dea proposed that all "union wreckers" of this sort be assessed a mandatory fine of one hundred dollars, but the convention, unwilling to eliminate local discretion completely, set one hundred dollars as a maximum figure and also provided a minimum of twenty-five dollars. To remove any ambiguity concerning the type of offense to which this punishment was restricted, a "union wrecker" was subsequently defined as "one who deliberately and with evil intent goes into the jurisdiction of a Union that is on an authorized legal strike, knowingly accepts employment and persists in retaining it when he knows that he is doing so contrary to the law of the International Union and of the Union on strike, or, who resigns from or leaves a Union, (in opposition to the International Union) in order to defeat a legal strike."[53]

While the regulations governing "union wrecking" were undertaken in order to tighten local discipline, the national union's interest in maintaining its membership intact was not neglected. For, although union wrecking, as defined above, is about as heinous an offense as a union man might commit, the Bricklayers' secretary did not consider it a "capital crime," that is, one punishable by expulsion. This typically "national" attitude of opposition to expulsion finally found full expression in an amendment to the Bricklayers' constitution which was passed in 1897 and which provided that

It shall not be lawful for a Union to expel a member. The judgment shall be, fined, and to stand suspended or dropped from membership until paid.

The Carpenters embarked upon a program of national control over discipline at an earlier stage in their history than the Bricklayers did, and their catalogue of crimes and punishment was considerably longer. The United Brotherhood, for example, saw fit to enumerate and proscribe the following activities: drunkenness, or any offense bringing the Brotherhood into discredit (penalized by expulsion);[54] advocacy of the dissolution of any local union, or of the division of its funds, or of its separation from the Brotherhood (likewise grounds for expulsion); slander against any officer or mem-

---

53. *Constitution,* 1897, Art. XVIII, Sec. 2; *Proceedings,* 1892, p. 27 (report of the secretary); *Constitution,* 1893, Article XVIII, Sec. 2; 1896 and 1897, Art. XVIII, Sec. 2 and also Art. XIV, Sec. 3.

54. *Constitution,* 1886, Art. IV.

ber of the Brotherhood or fraudulent misapplication of funds (the punishment to be "fined, suspended, or expelled" at the discretion of the local union); violation of the constitution or by-laws (same local option as above); neglect of duty by local union officers or committeemen (to be fined twenty-five cents for each offense, subject to remittance "upon satisfactory excuse"); disturbance of a local union meeting by virtue of intoxication, profanity, or kindred conditions (a fifty-cent fine on the "second admonition," a fine of one dollar on the second offense, and suspension for three months for third offenders; in 1890, it was further provided that "the President shall strictly enforce this section "); bringing malicious charges against a member (suspension for three months; this particular offense was presumably specified because "any member having knowledge of the violation of any Article or Section of the Constitution or By-Laws . . . (was) in duty bound to prefer charges against the offending member" and was subject to a fine of one dollar if he failed in this duty); violation of the rule of privacy (punishable by a fine of not less than five dollars or by expulsion);[55] divulgence of the quarterly password (expulsion); and failure to keep the local's financial secretary informed of one's correct place of residence (fine of one dollar).

For the most part, however, the Carpenters concentrated on the same offenses to which the Bricklayers' national organization pretty well confined its regulatory efforts: "union wrecking" (the Carpenters did not avail themselves of this descriptive label, but defined the offense substantially as did the Bricklayers), scabbing, and delinquency in dues and assessments. But although both organizations singled out the same major categories for national control, they differed fundamentally with respect to the type of penalty specified.

The Carpenters availed themselves generously of the ultimate sanction of expulsion, while one of the prime objectives of the Bricklayers in imposing uniform standards of discipline was to put an end to the unrestricted recourse to capital punishment by its locals and, ultimately, to eliminate it completely. To that end, the latter organization set up a schedule of fines to be imposed upon members convicted of scabbing, and although they ultimately provided that any member convicted of "selling out our trade or protecting scabs" could be fined as much as one thousand dollars and no less than one hundred dollars, they did not countenance expulsion.[56] On the other hand, the Carpenters, although they, too, prescribed a fine (of not less than five dollars) for accepting work under nonunion conditions so as to jeopardize the job of any member, also specified expulsion as an alternative punishment available to the local unions.[57] "Undermining," as this offense was termed, was originally listed in the Brotherhood constitution as a "pun-

55. *Constitution*, 1890, Art. IV.
56. *Constitution*, 1903, Art. XVIII.
57. *Constitution*, 1886, 1890, Art. IX.

ishable act" in 1886, but no specific penalty was mentioned in connection with it until 1890.

As for strikebreaking, the penalty provided by the Carpenters in 1886 was a fine of not less than five dollars for each day the offender was so employed, but a member who had committed a "wilful violation of the Trade rules" of his locality could be "fined, suspended, or expelled," at the option of his local union. While the Carpenters considered what the Bricklayers had termed "union wrecking"—that is, strikebreaking in a jurisdiction other than one's home community—to be a particularly reprehensible act, it is doubtful whether their distaste for this offense exceeded that of O'Dea and his cohorts among the Bricklayers. Nevertheless, the Carpenters, while initially setting a financial penalty for "any member who goes into any city seeking work where a strike or lockout is pending" which was somewhat less stringent than the twenty-five-to-one-hundred-dollar fine prescribed by the Bricklayers, later added expulsion as either an alternative or a supplementary sanction—a measure which O'Dea had never advocated and doubtless would have opposed with vigor.[58] The Carpenters' mandatory fine of twenty-five dollars was equal to the Bricklayers' *minimum* figure. It is not intended to imply that the Carpenters capriciously provided the penalty of expulsion for an offense which they did not take too seriously. That they were anxious to cope effectively with union wreckers can be accepted as fact; in 1892—four years before expulsion was resorted to—it was provided that, "Any Local not charging the $25 fine shall be expelled."

It is true, however, that the general executive board of the United Brotherhood sought to reduce the number of expulsions when it held, in 1890, that, "A union cannot expel a member for owing a fine; it can only suspend him when with the fine his indebtedness equals the sum of dues calling for suspension."[59] But, on the other hand, the Carpenters invoked the penalty of expulsion for many acts which, as we have observed, the Bricklayers' national organization did not take the trouble to specify as offenses. These included advocacy either of dissolution of a local union or its secession from the United Brotherhood, slander of one's fellow members, and the divulgence of official secrets.

A further comparison might be made to illustrate the difference in the policies followed by the two organizations with respect to expulsion. Before they outlawed expulsion, the Bricklayers set a limit to the amount of the special initiation fee which any local could charge and also prohibited their locals from imposing both a fine and a special initiation fee in connection with the same offense. When expulsion was eliminated in 1897, they also made it illegal to levy a special initiation fee upon any member. The Carpenters, on the other hand, moved steadily in the opposite direction. At first

58. *Constitution*, 1886, Art. IV; 1890, Art. XX; 1892, 1896, Art. XX.
59. *Proceedings*, 1890, Standing Decisions of the General Executive Board.

they provided that any member who had been suspended for nonpayment of dues could be reinstated upon the payment of a ten-cent fee covering the notice of arrears plus the amount of his arrearage; and they further facilitated reëntry by prohibiting the collection of more than four months' back dues. Next, they decided to charge a suspended member a "reinstatement fine" of one dollar on his first reinstatement and five dollars on his second, and they removed the limitation on the amount of back dues which could be collected. A second change provided that any member who had failed to become reinstated within a period of six months following his suspension should be expelled, and that he had to pay six months' back dues plus the initiation fee of his local union in order to gain readmission. And finally, in 1896, they made his readmission "subject to such readmission fee as shall be determined by the Local Union or District Council and provided in their by-laws."[60] Thus the Carpenters' national union apparently shared neither the Bricklayers' extreme reluctance to expel members from their ranks nor the latter's anxiety to facilitate the return of their exiles.

The two national unions differed also in their treatment of financially delinquent members. The Bricklayers' constitution was silent on this subject, save for an admonition to the locals not to blacklist members for nonpayment of dues, "as such is not considered a crime." The Carpenters, however, regarded "indebtedness" as very much of a crime and spent more time legislating on this misdemeanor than they did on any of the acts of commission, listed above. Their record reveals vacillation between sterner and less stringent penalties for indebtedness, rather than a clearly discernible trend in either direction. In 1886, it was established that a member three months in arrears lost his good standing and was not entitled to any benefits. Furthermore, if he failed to settle his accounts after one month's notice, he was automatically suspended without vote of his local union, which meant (a) that a two-thirds vote of his local colleagues was required to reinstate him, (b) that he forfeited all of his previous rights and benefits, and (c) that he would not be eligible for any benefits until six months after reinstatement.[61] At the next convention, the penalty of suspension was reserved for those who were as much as six months in arrears, but, as we have observed in the preceding paragraph, reinstatement fines were provided for the first time. Moreover, if a member owed three months' back dues, he was not entitled to receive any benefits until three months after his arrearages were paid, and he was not entitled to learn the password or to hold office. In 1890, however, the convention reversed direction with respect to suspension, by making that penalty available for members who were in arrears only four months, instead of six—and it also provided for the expulsion of anyone who failed to become reinstated within six months after suspension. Its successor (in

60. *Constitution*, 1886, 1888, 1890, Art. X; 1896, Sec. 90.
61. *Constitution*, 1886, 1888, 1890, Art. X; 1892, 1894, 1896, Sec. 90

1892) restored the six months' period, and, although two years later the next convention restricted suspension to cases in which the offender owed one year's back dues, it also established that, "A member owing a sum equal to six months' dues shall remain debarred from benefits until six months after all indebtedness is paid in full." In 1896 it was again provided that arrearages covering half that period required suspension from membership.

These frequent reversals might well indicate that an influential group of delegates within the Brotherhood hesitated to invoke the penalty of suspension, or at least sought to restrict its use. If such was the case, their efforts did not prevent the Carpenters from making it mandatory for the locals to impose rather drastic penalties upon members who were behind in their dues payments. This penalizing of indebtedness, as well as the liberal recourse to expulsion for other offenses, on a national level, represented a considerable departure from the policy of restraint followed by the Bricklayers' and Masons' International Union. Since both unions operated in rather similar economic environments—both were building trades unions and the annals of both indicate preoccupation with problems created by their migrant membership—these distinctive disciplinary practices of the Carpenters cannot be attributed to the influence of the geographic mobility of labor.

The Carpenters' national beneficiary program suggests itself as a distinguishing factor which might have accounted for a good deal of the divergence between the policies of the two organizations. The emphasis placed by the United Brotherhood on the benevolent features of unionism makes plausible its provisions with respect to (1) the penalty of expulsion and (2) the offense of dues delinquency. In the first place, the penalty of expulsion might act as a greater deterrent to the commission of specified offenses when it carries with it the loss of accumulated beneficiary rights; and for that reason resort to exclusion might not expose a union with a centralized benefit system to as formidable a risk of creating a force of nonunion workers in the trade as that envisioned by O'Dea of the Bricklayers. Second, since an uninterrupted flow of premium payments (included in monthly dues payments) is vital to the solvency of any benefit plan, it is not surprising that the Carpenters, with their national plan, should have regarded member "indebtedness" as more of a "crime" than would a national union with no beneficiary provisions, and, therefore, that it should impose uniform —and relatively severe—disciplinary measures in connection with this offense.

In connection with this last point, it is certainly apparent that denial of eligibility to receive benefits was an important component in the discipline meted out to members in arrears. Indeed, a year after the convention denied eligibility to any member who was three months in arrears until three months after his obligations were paid, the general executive board held that, "A member owing a sum equal to three months' dues cannot pay part of his arrears and be in benefit. He must pay all he owes the Union and wait three months after that to be in benefit."[62] In 1898 it was further provided that no claim for benefit would be honored if it arose from sickness or accident occuring during a period in which the claimant was in arrears.[63]

The withholding of benefits also played a large part in the provision for suspension in cases involving delinquency of longer standing. In 1886, it will be recalled, the Carpenters provided that a suspended member not only forfeited his previous rights and benefits, but that he was not eligible to receive benefits until six months after his suspension had been lifted. From the point of view of benefit status, the two types of penalty for indebtedness —loss of good standing and suspension—can be regarded as interchangeable; it will be noted that, on two occasions in which the Carpenters lengthened the minimum period of arrearage for which suspension was prescribed (in 1888 and 1894), they also increased the period for which those offenders, whose delinqency did not warrant their suspension, were made ineligible for benefit payments.

However essential these rigorous disciplinary standards might have been to the success of the Carpenters' benevolent projects, they could not always be relied upon to achieve O'Dea's objective, which was "to keep members in it (the union) instead of keeping them out." It is significant that some of these measures were opposed emphatically by P. J. McGuire, who, although better known for his collaboration with Gompers in the formation of the American Federation of Labor, was the founder of the United Brotherhood and its General Secretary-Treasurer from its formation in 1881 until 1904. The basis of his opposition to the Brotherhood's disciplinary provisions was revealed in his report to the 1892 convention, in which he referred to the unsatisfactory progress made in organizing the trade, adding:

And were it not for the hardship of the laws enacted at our last convention, two years ago, particularly severe as to suspended members and their reinstatement, we would now number over 60,000 members in good standing.[64]

Although the difference in the nature of the disciplinary measures enacted by the Carpenters and by the Bricklayers might be traced to the benefit provisions of the former national union, it must not be supposed that the experience of the Bricklayers was typical of the experience of all local market national unions. Thus, although the Printers did list a number of offenses and penalties in their general laws, the nature of the offenses specified—such as the counterfeiting of dues stamps, applying to someone other than the foreman for employment, engaging in "speed contests," working more than six days or fifty-four hours in one week if a substitute is available, publishing

62. *Standing Decisions of the General Executive Board*, 1889.
63. *Constitution*, 1898, Sec. 89.
64. *Proceedings*, 1892, p. 15 (report of the secretary). The membership in 1892 was reported at 51,313.

"malicious or untrue articles" about any member of the I.T.U., or belonging to any "secret organization" within the union[65]—the listing of these offenses indicates greater interest in providing for the enforcement of regulations of peculiar importance to the national union than in establishing uniform standards of discipline among the locals.[66] Nor were the penalties which this national union did stipulate provided largely in order to restrict or eliminate recourse to expulsion, as was the case with the Bricklayers; of the six crimes enumerated above, three—counterfeiting dues stamps, publishing "malicious or untrue articles," belonging to a secret organization—were made punishable by expulsion, either exclusively or at the discretion of the local union. Furthermore, in 1882 it provided that "when a member has deliberately ratted, it is not necessary that he should be cited to appear for trial, but he may be summarily expelled."[67]

Indeed, aside from the Bricklayers, Wolfe mentioned only two national unions which forbade the expulsion of members, and he further observed that, "Offenses which entail suspension are not usually specifically enumerated. . . ."[68] Thus, notwithstanding the experience of the three local market unions examined in the preceding pages, the creation of uniform standards of discipline throughout a national union was by no means an inevitable organizational response to the problems which conflicting local standards had raised in connection with the traveling card system—just as the erection of uniform standards of admission was by no means standard practice in coping with issues of a similar nature.

Appeal and Amnesty

If conflicts in local laws and customs, which frequently subjected traveling card systems to considerable strain, could not be eliminated because

65. *General Laws,* 1901, Secs. 140, 103, 134, 109, 111, and 113 respectively. The last two measures were passed in an effort to eliminate the various cliques and caucuses, the influence of which was the subject of considerable controversy as far back as 1880, when the convention sought to outlaw a group known as the "Brotherhood of the Union of North America." See Tracy, *History of Typographical Union,* pp. 320–321, 354, 422–423, 518, 619, and 638–639 for references to the existence of "secret societies." The Typographical Union's experimentation with the referendum might have accounted for the renewed vigor of these cliques and for the spate of "malicious or untrue articles" at the end of the century, although International President Donnelly denied this.

66. In one respect, the Printers appear to have followed an example set by the Carpenters in punishing financially delinquent members. Not until 1909 did the International Typographical Union—as distinct from the locals—provide any penalty for dues delinquency (the penalty for any member four months in arrears was suspension—see Wolfe, *Admission to Unions,* p. 139), and this action was taken one year after the payment of pensions began in connection with an International old age pension plan. (See Barnett, *The Printers,* p. 104.)

67. *General Laws,* 1882, Sec. 48.

68. Wolfe, *Admission to Unions,* p. 140. These were the Metal Polishers, Buffers, Platers, and Brass Workers and the Wood Workers.

adoption of uniform standards of admission and discipline was not wide-spread, they could be mitigated through provision for judicial review by the national union of admission and disciplinary policies of the constituent locals. The right of a member who had been sentenced by his local union to appeal to national authority was invariably established at an early stage in the history of the national union. In time, provision was made for appealing first to the national president or executive board and then, if desired, to the convention, which was usually regarded as the ultimate authority in judicial, as well as legislative, matters.[69] This permitted judicial review of local decrees in the intervals between successive conventions, a step which became increasingly desirable as these intervals tended to lengthen.

The Bricklayers, in 1867, merely provided that, "Any subordinate union, or member thereof, shall have the right of appeal to this body [the convention]." Three years later, they granted the power of judicial review to "the judiciary of this Union" and further provided that, "The President may exercise commuting power with discretion." The convention was not powerless in judiciary matters, however, for review over presidential decisions was in effect exerted by the practice of voting on the recommendations of the committee on president's report, which urged either adoption or rejection of such decisions. Furthermore, in 1882 the clause granting the commuting power was deleted from the constitution. Finally, in 1897, it was formally set forth that a convicted member not only could appeal to the international's judiciary board, but that, "not being satisfied with the decision of the Executive or Judiciary Boards on the questions submitted to them for adjudication," he could carry his appeal to the convention.[70]

The Carpenters, after providing for "the right of appeal: first, to the Executive Board; second, to the Convention," inserted a new initial step in 1890, when they stipulated that, "The G. S. [general secretary] and the G. T. [general treasurer] shall . . . decide all points of law arising under the jurisdiction of the U.B.; also all grievances and appeals, subject to an appeal to the G. E. B. (general executive board), whose decision shall be final unless reversed by the Convention."[71] The Typographical Union also permitted three appeals: from the decision of a local union to the international president, from the president to the executive council, and from the council to "the International Union at a regular session, which judgment shall be final."[72]

<hr />

69. Glocker, writing in 1913, reported only five international unions which did not permit their members to appeal from the international officers or executive boards to the convention. These were: the Hotel and Restaurant Employees, the Paper Box Makers, the Paper Makers and Pulp, Sulphite and Paper Mill Workers, the Porters, and the Railway Conductors. Glocker, *Government of American Trade Unions*, p. 158.

70. *Constitution*, 1867, Art. XII; *Proceedings*, 1870, pp. 96, 98; *Constitution*, 1897, Art. XIV.

71. *Constitution*, 1881, Art. VIII; 1890, Sec. 28.

72. See *Constitution*, 1899, Art. VIII.

As was frequently true with respect to the attempted establishment of uniform standards of appeal and discipline by national unions, the provision for appeal from local decisions derived its original impetus from the need to enforce the essentials of the traveling card system. This accounts for the fact that the national union was usually empowered to resolve disputes involving two or more local unions exclusively, as well as those in which individual members appeared as appellants, since complaints about alleged infringements of traveling rules usually were made by local organizations. Barnett emphasized the importance of these interlocal disputes over traveling members in the following passage:

Nominally the National Union also had power to decide every question which a subordinate union might submit; but, for a considerable period, the Union refrained from deciding questions other than those concerning the card system. . . If one local union, for example, admitted to membership a printer who had been denounced as a "rat" by another local union, the offended union might appeal to the National Union. The appeals were thus, in effect, indictments for violations of the card system. Occasionally, also, a member of some local union complained to the National Union that he had been unjustly expelled, and thus secured from his local union a rehearing of the case.[73]

Wolfe, in a strikingly similar passage, claimed general validity for the conclusions which Barnett had drawn from his observation of the Printers' experience. After considering the appeal of one local from the refusal of another to admit a cardholding member in connection with the appeal of an individual against his expulsion from a local union, he added: "In this way every member came gradually to be recognized as having a right to appeal against any violation of his rights by the local union."[74]

Apart from alleged violations of the rules governing traveling members, however, the usual absence of national standards of admission and discipline made for an ambiguous situation. Granted the individual right of appeal, precisely what ruling of his local could be reversed? This question troubled the astute O'Dea and led him to propose his "code of crimes and penalties" to the Bricklayers. In support of his program he called attention to the following provision in the Bricklayers' constitution (which had counterparts in the laws of many other national unions):

Each Subordinate Union shall have power to arrange its local laws and local matters in its own way, but subject to the general laws and principles as laid down in this Constitution.[75]

Since the international union had no "general laws and principles" relating to disciplinary matters, O'Dea argued that it was "subject to the command of the Subordinate Union, which can place any penalty it likes upon

73. Barnett, *The Printers*, p. 33.
74. Wolfe, *Admission to Unions*, p. 13.
75. *Constitution*, 1892, Art. 16, Sec. 3.

members, without any reservation whatever."[76] And since no local union was permitted to admit a member who had been blacklisted by another local,[77] he continued, it was imperative that the international relieve the local of command. Thus the Bricklayers' secretary was convinced that the right of appeal to national authority was meaningless in the absence of national laws for the observance of which the locals could be held to account.

In addition to recommending the enactment of his "code," O'Dea successfully urged the Bricklayers to adopt a series of regulations governing the conduct of trials by local unions.[78] This recommendation followed his earlier assertion (see page 125) that many of the locals indulged in "an exercise of arbitrary authority bordering on despotism" and allowed "no chance or opportunity for a defense . . . to a member who may be charged with a supposed offense." And when, in 1897, the provisions governing appeal were rewritten, they appeared in the same article of the constitution in which trial procedure was set forth. Thus the Bricklayers promulgated procedural as well as substantive standards for compliance by their local unions and furnished their national executive officers with yardsticks by which they could determine the merit of an appeal by a member who claimed that he had not been given a fair trial by the local which had convicted him.

The Bricklayers did not pioneer in prescribing rules for the conduct of trials. The Carpenters had such regulations in effect as early as 1886.[79] Although the Printers did not provide uniform trial procedure until 1899,[80] their presidents had previously "held that not only must the rules of the subordinate union concerning trials be complied with, but also that the ordinary principles of jurisprudence governing the rights of accused persons must be observed."[81] When the Printers finally did insert in their general laws a group of sections entitled "Uniform Charges and Trials," they followed the Bricklayers in appending to the provisions governing trial procedure a section reaffirming the right of appeal "if the accused feel that an injustice has been done him."

Thus, although many national unions did not go as far as the Bricklayers in prescribing offenses and penalties, stipulation of trial procedure, in con-

---

76. *Proceedings*, 1892, p. 27; see also 1883, pp. 55, 57–59.

77. It was possible, however, for a man in the trade whose application for membership had been denied by one local union to be admitted as an initiatory member of another, even if the local which had rejected him withheld its consent to the arrangement. Under such circumstances, it was provided that "an appeal may be taken before the Judiciary Board of the International Union whose decision shall be final unless reversed by the International Union in Convention assembled." (*Proceedings*, 1883, pp. 55, 57–58, 59.)

78. *Constitution*, 1892, Art. XIV.

79. *Constitution*, 1886, Art. V.

80. *General Laws*, 1900, Secs. 29–41 inclusive.

81. Barnett, *The Printers*, p. 305.

junction with the right of appeal, enabled them to erect at least one barrier against indiscriminate resort to the penalty of expulsion by the local unions. The importance of this barrier to the Printers is indicated in Barnett's observation that "the chief protection that has been given the accused member has been the guarantee of a fair trial."

Some unions further restricted the availability of "capital punishment" by requiring that a specified proportion of the votes cast at a meeting of the local union be in favor of expulsion.[82] Both the Printers and the Carpenters, for example, required a two-thirds vote to expel a member.[83] This additional restriction on the local unions was a plausible extension of the guarantee of a fair trial. This guarantee assured the accused of the union's equivalent of a jury trial and made it illegal for guilt or innocence to be determined by committee.[84] The union jury consisted of the membership present at the local meeting, and a majority vote was usually required before the accused could be convicted. When, therefore, it was desired to discourage expulsion, it was often provided that a greater majority than that sufficient for a finding of guilt was required to expel a member.[85] Thus unions like the Carpenters and Printers, both of which required a majority of two-thirds to expel a member,[86] could, in the absence of a code of crimes and penalties similar to that adopted by the Bricklayers, impose a certain degree of uniformity upon the disciplinary practices of their affiliated locals. This was accomplished, first,

82. Wolfe, *Admission to Unions*, pp. 144–145.

83. *Constitution* of the International Typographical Union, 1868, Art. I, Sec. 3; *Constitution* of the United Brotherhood of Carpenters and Joiners, 1891, Sec. 75.

84. National unions which regulated the conduct of trials by their locals did not seek to eliminate all use of committees, but they did confine their functions to those of investigation and recommendation. The verdict was rendered by the local union's vote on the committee's report. Thus the advantages of a necessary division of labor were retained, while (it was hoped) any bias on the part of the committee would be counteracted by subjecting its conclusions to the approval of the entire local meeting. The Carpenters specified that the decision of the "Committee of Investigation" be voted on by the local union without debate, but it sought to assure the accused of a fair committee hearing (a) by having the local's vice-president draw the names for the five-man committee from a ballot-box containing ten or more slips, (b) by allowing the accused and (later) the accuser three challenges each, and (c) (later) permitting both accuser and accused, either in person or by representative, "to plead for, or state their side of the case" to the local meeting before the latter voted on the committee's recommendation. (*Constitutions:* 1886 and 1888, Art. V; *Constitution,* 1894, Sec. 170.) The Printers, on the other hand, allowed the local's president to appoint the committee, but they also provided that no committee would be appointed at all unless a majority present at the meeting decided that the charge was "cognizable." Furthermore they required the committee to "keep a correct record of the proceedings; which record shall be produced to the union on the call of any member, after the committee has reported." (*General Laws,* 1900, Secs. 30 and 36.)

85. *Constitution* of the United Brotherhood of Carpenters and Joiners, 1891, Sec. 75; *Constitution* of the National Typographical Union, 1868, Art. I, Sec. 3.

86. Printers' *Proceedings,* 1872, p. 6 (report of the president).

by the establishment of uniform procedural requirements and, second, by judicial review by national authority of appeals of individuals who alleged that the locals which convicted and expelled them did not comply with those procedural requirements.

Although the Bricklayers' action in providing substantive as well as procedural specifications in order to discourage expulsion was not widely followed, national officers in other unions did not share Secretary O'Dea's concept of judicial review as being restricted to cases in which local unions were alleged to have violated specific provisions in the national constitution. On the contrary, they tended to assume that provisions for appeal bestowed upon them the general authority to reverse local unions at their discretion—subject, of course, to the approval of the convention in every instance. For a while, it appeared that even the Bricklayers were veering in this direction. Thus President Meredith Moore of that union reported to the 1872 convention that an Ohio local had imposed a fine upon one of its members because he had worked overtime in violation of its law on the subject, although he had been requested to do so by his employer "in order to secure a bank which threatened to cave in at any moment," and although the overtime had been compensated at time-and-one-half. Considering the case upon appeal, President Moore remitted the fine, because as he explained in his report, "I did not think it just to impose a fine on any member under such circumstances." When the Committee on President's Report came to this case, it reported:

While your committee recognizes the faithfulness which has marked your presiding officer, in order that precedents may not be established which we consider dangerous to our fraternity, we would suggest as our judgment that he violated the Constitution to a certain extent (!) by remitting the fine of Patton, after being fined by law of Local Union.[87]

Three years later, in connection with another appeal by a member who had been fined and expelled until he paid his fine, it was recorded that, "Brother Hogen, No. 28, New York . . . was opposed to the National Union sustaining any members of Local Unions who should violate their laws. . . ."[88] Thereafter, the presidents tended to uphold local unions in appeals from fines imposed by them, and, although the right to appeal was not challenged, O'Dea, as we know, believed that it was of little value in the absence of specific standards of admission and discipline.

Other unions, however, found, in the exercise of judicial review by national authority, a substitute—imperfect, but workable—for some of the uniform standards of discipline and admission which were discussed in the preceding section. Reference has already been made to the fact that appeals from expulsion were the first to receive general recognition, since the ques-

87. *Proceedings*, 1872, p. 9.
88. *Proceedings*, 1875, pp. 23–24.

tion of expulsion was intimately related to the issue of blacklisting. Later, appeals were admitted from candidates who had been denied admission by local unions, even when a local alleged that membership was withheld because the applicant had failed to measure up to the standards of competence which it had established. This was foreshadowed, in the Bricklayers' union, by a rule which permitted appeal to the international's judiciary board in cases wherein certain locals had withheld their consent to the admission to membership in other local unions of applicants whom the former had previously rejected.[89] The Printers, in 1874, conferred the status of "general laws" upon presidential decisions which received the approval of the convention, and, although many of these "laws" were of little significance, Barnett concluded that, "the extension of the judicial activities of the Union had some effect in establishing a standard of usage for the subordinate unions." In 1898, the Printers provided for appeal by rejected applicants, and, according to Barnett:

This rule has practically made the president and the executive council the judges of the qualifications of candidates. The local union still retains the nominal right to pass upon candidates; but every applicant can secure a rehearing of his claim to membership before an International officer. Since the International Union has never defined the necessary qualifications of candidates, the officers are almost entirely free in interpreting the 'practice and law' of the union.

And while incompetence was acknowledged as grounds for rejection, and, "Competency must largely be judged by local standards," it was nevertheless true that "where incompetency has been alleged as a reason for not admitting a candidate, the president has required that the incompetency shall be proved."

Even before progress was achieved in curbing the locals' powers of rejection and expulsion—and such progress was not appreciable before the eighties[90]—the national unions resorted on occasion to the practice of declaring "amnesties" as a means of readmitting expelled members, or, as the Printers had it, of "white-washing rats."

From the earliest years in the history of national unions, the officers of these organizations sought to alert the local unions to the danger of creating a force of potential scabs and strikebreakers through indiscriminate resort to the capital punishment of expulsion. In 1858, for example, the National Typographical Union urged its locals "to exhaust all persuasive and mild measures previous to the ultimate resort of 'ratting' any member of the craft."[91] In view, however, of the unchallenged power of the locals to expel

89. Cf. footnote 77. See Wolfe, *Admission to Unions*, p. 37; Barnett, *The Printers*, pp. 323-325.
90. Wolfe, *Admission to Unions*, pp. 19-20 and *passim*.
91. Tracy, *History of Typographical Union*, p. 173.

members and of the prohibition against the admission by any local union of a member who had been expelled by any other without the latter's consent, such exhortations were not very effective. In the absence of national standards of discipline and admission, the amnesty was developed as a means of readmitting expelled members by suspending temporarily the obstacles to readmission. The first general amnesty in the Typographical Union was declared by the convention of 1868, on the advice of the national president. This amnesty was not particularly successful, since it was reported in the following convention that only 176 applications were received, and all but six of these came from New York City.[92] The Molders also employed this device on two occasions (in 1867 and 1876) in the early period of their history, as did the Steel Workers (in 1882).[93]

Amnesties were invoked either by individual local unions, with the consent of the parent body, or by the national unions in blanket pardons which applied to the entire trade jurisdiction. The former practice developed because locals on strike were often confronted with the alternative of conferring membership upon all nonunionists in the vicinity or of exposing themselves to serious strikebreaking activity.[94] In 1890, the Carpenters, by referendum vote of their membership, adopted a policy of granting amnesty to suspended members whose local unions specifically requested it. According to Secretary McGuire, this policy "has resulted in adding to our ranks many former members, who are now zealous workers in our cause." Following the passage, in 1890, of some of the severe disciplinary measures of which McGuire complained, many of the locals were granted what he referred to as "dispensations" to extend amnesties to suspended members and to reinstate them upon payment of a few dollars.[95]

General amnesties appear to have been resorted to most frequently in periods of industrial depression, when employment, earnings, and union membership declined. The Molders declared amnesties in 1867, 1876, and 1895;[96] the Carpenters, in 1893; and the Bricklayers, in 1894, remitted all fines which the international union had imposed upon locals and individual members during the past year.[97] During such times of hardship, the officials of the national unions perceived clearly what the men in the locals were often unable or unwilling to recognize—that they were faced with the unen-

92. Barnett, *The Printers*, pp. 307–308. Tracy, *History of Typographical Union*, pp. 228, 233, 236–237.

93. Wolfe, *Admission to Unions*, pp. 158–159.

94. Cf. Barnett, *The Printers*, pp. 308–309.

95. *Proceedings*, 1890, p. 19 (report of the secretary); 1892, p. 15 (report of the secretary).

96. Frank T. Stockton, *The International Molders Union of North America* (Baltimore: Johns Hopkins, 1921), pp. 65-69.

97. *Decisions of the General Executive Board*, 1893; *Proceedings*, 1894, p. 6 (report of the secretary).

viable choice of either maintaining discipline or maintaining their existence as an organization. In advocating amnesty, they abandoned local disciplinary prerogatives in favor of the survival of the national organization (which was equal to the sum of its local parts). For an accurate statement of the national union's position, we turn once more to Secretary O'Dea of the Bricklayers:

Unions should be very careful and conservative, and as a person is obliged to take medicine against his will, so will organized labor in the present crisis be forced to swallow matters that at other times it would instantly repudiate. Wherever it is deemed necessary I would recommend that the lines of discipline be loosened, and that Charity have a show as well as justice.[98]

This quotation appeared in a section of the Report entitled, "A WORD OF ADVICE." The president, at the same convention, said, "I would advise all Subordinate Unions to be very lenient with their members during this depression, and do not be so quick in placing fines upon them, and do more reprimanding and less firing."

ORGANIZATION AND JURISDICTION

From the viewpoint of the national union, it was desirable that the greatest possible number of workers in the trade jurisdiction throughout the nation be members of the national union. This objective was apparent in the provision by certain unions of requirements regulating the balloting for admission of new members. It was apparent in the setting of maximum initiation fees and in the leadership taken by certain national unions in urging their locals to admit women and negroes to membership. It was apparent in the various devices by which expulsions were discouraged, and it was especially evident in the granting of amnesties to those who had been expelled or whose good standing had been permitted to lapse for other reasons. Finally, it was manifest in a decision of the Bricklayers' judiciary board in a case concerning the eligibility of a candidate for membership whose apprenticeship qualifications were not quite in order. It was decided to admit him and subsequently to allow him to complete the requirements. "But by all means get him in somehow," the decision read, "he will be better in the union than out of it."[99]

Without the existence in every sizeable labor market of a fairly well organized local union, the traveling card system was of dubious value. For every local labor market was a potential tributary to the main stream of labor migration, and, if only one sizeable tributary was nonunion, the entire stream could be polluted. The limitation placed upon the potentialities of any blacklist or card system by the existence of unorganized areas was

98. *Proceedings*, 1893, p. 24 (report of the secretary).
99. *Report of the President*, 1900, p. 125; Wolfe, *Admission to Unions*, p. 53, note 2.

reflected in the following resolution, which was passed by the young National Typographical Union in 1857:

That the National Typographical Union do most earnestly recommend to Subordinate Unions, not to admit into their Unions, or give employment to, Printers coming without Cards from places *where there are Unions,* until all suspicion shall have been removed, by satisfactory evidence from the places or Unions whence they come.[100]

The Bricklayers' local in Chicago, which remained unaffiliated with the international union from its formation in 1868 until 1899, was feared by local unions everywhere as a menace to their security. Since bricklaying was definitely a local market occupation, there was not much danger of trade being diverted from other communities to Chicago; furthermore, the hours of work and the rate of pay prevailing in this independent local's jurisdiction were the same as those established in a neighboring community organized by an affiliated local union.[101] The explanation of the strenuous efforts of the international to bring the Chicago union into the fold lay entirely in Chicago's great potentiality as an importer and exporter of bricklayers. The situation was aggravated by the fact that a world's fair was in the process of construction in Chicago, and the demand for construction labor was abnormally high. This attracted bricklayers from all over the country, and those who came with the international union's traveling cards in their pockets resented the fact that they were obliged to pay high initiation fees to the unaffiliated local in order to secure work. The situation did not really become acute as far as the international was concerned, however, until the construction work on the fair was completed. For then "hundreds of bricklayers" were thrown out of work and were preparing to seek employment in other localities—including those in which affiliated locals were organized. These bricklayers could not possess traveling cards and thus threatened union standards wherever they went. The case for an affiliated local in Chicago was obvious:

We hold that if a Subordinate Union was organized in the city of Chicago, at least 90 percent of the bricklayers, who will be compelled to leave there, would do so with traveling cards, and come to our cities armed with them, ready and willing to live up to, support and maintain the rules, laws and regulations of said cities.[102]

The case of the Chicago bricklayers is especially interesting, because it illustrates the fact that, from the viewpoint of a national union, which administered an orderly interchange of members among its locals through the issuing and acceptance of traveling cards, an unaffiliated local union in a

100. *Proceedings,* 1857, p. 18. (Italics mine.)
101. *Proceedings,* 1896, pp. 24 and 25.
102. *Proceedings,* 1894, p. 91.

given locality was the equivalent of no local union at all. (Note that in the above quotation a "subordinate" union was desired, not merely a "local" union.) The problem of jurisdiction was closely allied with the problem of organizing the unorganized in local unions which were to be affiliated with a national organization. For this reason, it became customary for national unions to insist that their locals honor only those cards which were distributed to them by the national union in question. Thus, as early as 1858, the Printers provided that no subordinate of the National Typographical Union should honor cards issued by any association which was not chartered by the N.T.U.[103]

Since the welfare and security of the established local unions were affected by the migration of nonunion men from unorganized areas, the officers of the national unions urged that the national union be granted funds and manpower in order to organize those "backward" regions. Particularly troublesome to the locals were migrants from small towns, whose strikebreaking activities were notorious. These communities were very difficult to organize, since the number of workers in any one trade was frequently not large enough to permit the formation of a local union. Most national constitutions provided that a minimum number of workers, ranging usually from five to ten, be enrolled in a local union before it could receive a charter.

The nature of this organizing problem was well expressed by President Frost of the Bricklayers, who, as early as 1867, sought to convince the convention of the necessity "of bringing in Union men in different localities, when there are not sufficient numbers of our craft to form a union, and yet more than is desirable to leave without the pale of our organization." Two years later, the president's wisdom was proved, for an important factor in the defeat of three New York City locals in their major strike for an eight-hour day was the strikebreaking activities of "strangers" from "the outlying cities and villages," who had been "enticed to the City of New York by their employers." Locals affiliated with the Typographical Union were also very much aware of the value to their employers of "country printers" who were almost always available as a reserve of nonunion labor in times of strife.[104]

Yet little progress in organizing the unorganized was made by these and other national unions in local market industries. Unionism was strongest in the large metropolitan communities, a fact which suggests that most of the organizing activity which occurred during this period was of the "grass roots" variety, coming "from the bottom up," rather than "from the top down." Referring to the Printers, Barnett expressed the opinion that, "Speaking very broadly, it is hardly possible to maintain a local union in a city of

103. *General Laws*, 1858, Sec. 5.

104. *Proceedings*, 1867, p. 9 (report of the president); 1869, pp. 38 and 45; see Barnett, *The Printers*, pp. 260–261, 263; Tracy, *History of Typographical Union*, p. 209.

less than 10,000 population, unless, of course, one or more of the printing. establishments do something beyond a local business." The Printers and the Bricklayers did make some effort to organize workers in small towns, by authorizing their affiliation with the nearest local in the vicinity of such unorganized areas. The Printers at first (1864-1867) sought to admit country printers to "conditional membership," extracting from them the promise that they would not answer the siren calls of embattled employers, but this project failed, especially after the locals were directed to tax each of their members ten cents monthly in order to finance the work of organization.[105] The Bricklayers finally empowered their executive board to initiate applicants who resided "in the localities where there is not a sufficient number to form a Union," into the nearest established local, upon payment of the latter's initiation fee.[106] But this step was not taken until 1904, almost forty years after President Frost's plea for organization.

It was hoped by some harassed national officials that traveling members might assume the role of amateur organizers by sowing the seeds of unionism wherever they came to a town where no local existed. The Glass Bottle Blowers' provided that "any member going to work at a place where no Branch exists must notify the (National) President of the same, who shall appoint a factory committee of three . . ."[107] When we consider that much of the organizing activity of the time was of a spontaneous nature, there is little doubt but that many travelers were in fact carriers of unionism. In an official account of the origin of the Molders' union, it was observed that

With the development of our trade, the energy and eloquence of Neale and Sylvis, and last but not least the traveling propensities of a large portion of our craft (that portion commonly dubbed tramps, with whom most of us are familiar, having belonged to that especial fraternity ourselves in earlier days), the seeds of unionism were scattered broadcast over the continent.[108]

On the other hand, traveling members who refused to deposit their cards in towns where locals existed, if they could obtain work without so doing, were not the material of which missionaries were made. The deficiencies of the migrant bricklayers in this respect drew a heavy barrage from O'Dea:

To these men more than any other cause do I ascribe the fact that we did not get more unions than we have. As a rule they were opposed to the organizing of any unions, and did what they possibly could in some places towards having them formed (sic) . . . it was the influences of these men, these traitors to the organization, that prevented success. . . . Some of these men would boast of having traveling cards in their possession, while others, no doubt, were already

105. Barnett, *The Printers,* pp. 264–265.
106. *Constitution,* 1904, Art. V (8).
107. *Constitution,* 1892, Art. IV, Sec. 22.
108. *Journal,* May 1889, p. 8.

under the ban by being on the "delinquent list." The majority of such men were known by fictitious names, and were no doubt afraid of being "rounded up" if unions were started in the places named.[109]

O'Dea, as a matter of fact, distrusted the process of grass-roots organization and blamed the high mortality rate of the local unions on the lack of organizing activity of the national union:

I attribute the loss to our organization of all these Unions, and also our inability to create new ones to our lack of facilities for proper organization. Unions, like work, will not come looking for us. We must go look for them. Had we organizers in the field, our Report would be much different to what it is. . . We need organizers. . . We must have them in order to succeed. . . .[110]

But, while the local unions were willing to pass laws investing the national executive officers with the authority and duty to organize locals, and while they were even willing to provide, on occasion, for the appointment of "state" or "district" organizers, they invariably stopped short of providing funds for the payment of salaries and expenses. Thus, not until 1884 did the Printers employ a salaried "chief organizer" and reimburse his state deputies. The latter, however, were paid only for the time actually spent in organizing; and, in 1888, the functions of the chief organizer were transferred to the president of the international union. The latter urged the appointment of a paid, full-time traveling organizer, but without success.[111]

The Bricklayers were even more unrealistic. In 1867, President Frost observed that, "The Constitution states that each union organized shall pay the expense of the Deputy organizing it. This section has been the means of keeping a number of unions out of the organization, they not having funds on hand to pay the expenses of a deputy. . . ." And when, in 1883, the convention authorized the president to appoint state organizers, it did so with the proviso that, "The expenses incurred through traveling and loss of time shall be borne by the Union organized," although they generously added that, "Such expenses as may occur for stationery and postage shall be assumed by the National Union." Finally, in 1900, O'Dea decided to take the reins into his own hands. He resigned as secretary (because of ill health induced partly by "want of fresh air and exercise") and persuaded the executive board to appoint him chief organizer, so that he could devote full time to his organizing activities. Because this action was clearly unconstitutional, and because he drew compensation for services rendered, the convention, after much confusion, decided that it did not approve of the president's action. It disestablished the new office (which it had never authorized). It also defeated the incumbent president and replaced him with one who subse-

109. *Proceedings,* 1900 (report of the chief organizer).
110. *Proceedings,* 1898, p. 79 (report of the secretary).
111. Barnett, *The Printers,* pp. 262–263.

quently congratulated the convention on eliminating a "needless expense."[112]

The lack of progress made by the national unions themselves in organizing the workers in local market occupations, however, was not due solely to the shortsightedness and thrift of the locals, although those factors might well have been primarily responsible for this deficiency. In the last chapter, the observation was made that very well organized locals had less to gain from a national compact (including a card system) than weaker locals, because the former were able to impose unilateral control over their local labor markets and to prevent migrants from obtaining employment if they wished, especially if they had made closed shop agreements with the employers.

The Chicago Bricklayers' union was cited as an outstanding case of local independence. This was probably an exceptional case, but even if few other locals in the country satisfied the requirements of independence well enough not to participate in an interchange of traveling cards, it might be expected that, the more secure the control exerted by a local union over its territorial jurisdiction, the more reluctant it would be to approve the appropriation of funds for organizing adventures in remote regions. The more powerfully entrenched locals in a national union were usually numerically the largest organizations. Since, on a per capita basis, they contributed the lion's share of the national union's receipts (and would thus be obliged to contribute a proportionately great share of any organizing funds which might be appropriated), and since their combined voting power in the convention was frequently greater than that possessed by the smaller organizations, they were often in a position to give effective voice to their isolationist sentiment.

Although the organizing efforts of the national unions in local market industries were not impressive, the potentialities of national unionism in situations characterized by thorough organization of the relevant local labor markets were appreciated by the national officers. In one instance at least those potentialities were realized. It will be recalled that the large interstate construction firms were a source of concern to the Bricklayers, by virtue of their ability to import nonunion labor into any unionized localities in which they had been awarded contracts. These firms, in effect, organized the migration of nonunion labor, but their power to do so quite obviously depended on the availability of a sufficient supply of nonunion labor for the purpose at hand. In one instance (occurring in 1908) this supply proved inadequate, and, as a result, the international union was able to take the offensive. The Roebling Construction Company was obliged to seek union labor in the erection of a naval station in Illinois. Since this company had refused to employ union bricklayers on its cement work in Rochester, New York, however, the executive officers of the international persuaded the Illinois local to declare the naval project "unfair." In order to procure the

112. *Proceedings,* 1867, p. 9; 1883, pp. 43, 66–67; 1900, pp. 4–5, 44, 85, 225–226, 230; 1901, p. 4.

services of the Illinois union members, the company was obliged to agree to turn the Rochester cement work over to the union bricklayers in that city.

THE EXCLUSIVE LOCAL AGREEMENT

The nationalizing influence of geographic labor mobility rarely, if ever, resulted in the abridgment of local wage autonomy. Nevertheless there is some reason to believe that national authority was, on occasion, opposed to one particular local institution erected for the purpose of securing high local wage levels, and, further, that the geographic mobility of labor was a factor which contributed significantly to that hostility. The institution in question was known as the "closed" or "exclusive" local agreement, whereby the union either tacitly or explicitly agreed that its members would work only for members of the signatory employers' association on the condition that the latter's affiliated firms would hire only members of the local union involved. Thus the employers who were members of the association were assured of exclusive access to the supply of local union labor in the trade and, in the construction industry, could thereupon proceed to pool their bids on construction contracts instead of submitting them in competition with one another.[113] The union also benefited from the exclusion of outside competition —especially from the competition of nonunion or outside supply houses; in addition, the closed shop arrangement enabled it to institute a waiting list.

The exclusive agreement was found most frequently in the building trades. The following excerpts from an agreement entered into by the Plumbers' union of Troy, New York in 1900 are typical of arrangements which the obligations of the union's members, as well as the obligations of the employers, were set forth specifically:

That the party of the first part hereby agrees not to employ any plumber, steam and gas fitter who is not a member of Local Union No. 61, of the Plumbers, Gas and Steam Fitters, of Troy and vicinity, while the said Local Union No. 61 can furnish from among their members good, competent men....

In consideration of the above agreement on the part of the party of the first part the party of the second part agrees ... that the party of the second part also bind themselves and agree that no member of Local Union No. 61 shall accept employment to perform any work pertaining to plumbing, steam or gas fitting from any party or parties in the city of Troy or its vicinity who are not members of the Master Plumbers, Steam and Gas Fitters' Association of Troy and vicinity.[114]

113. These agreements were usually more effective where it proved possible to control the supply of material as well as labor; in such cases, it was usually agreed that union members would not be requested to work on materials produced by nonunion supply concerns or by concerns which were outside the local's jurisdiction. See U. S. Commissioner of Labor, *Regulation and Restriction of Output* (Washington: 1904), p. 275. On the practice of collusive bidding, see U. S. Industrial Commission, *Report* (Washington: 1901), v. VII, p. 965.

114. U. S. Industrial Commission, *Report,* v. VII, pp. 945 and 946.

Other examples might be found among the Bricklayers, Marble Cutters, Sheet Metal Workers, and Stone Cutters.[115] Secretary O'Dea of the Bricklayers inveighed against the exclusive local contracts on the grounds that it constituted an illegal and otherwise undesirable conspiracy in restraint of trade, and President Kelley of the Plumbers charged that they served only to enable the employers to police their collusive bidding arrangements. He also maintained that agreements designed to oblige manufacturers of building materials to sell only to members of the local master plumbers' association (as in Chicago) prevented journeymen plumbers from setting up in business for themselves; and, although he was careful to indicate his preference for bargaining with employers' associations rather than with firms on an individual basis, he characterized the exclusive agreement as "downright robbery . . . I consider a man just as honest that knocks you down and robs you of your watch—just as honest as that is." Finally, Kelley claimed that, due to the efforts of the national union, the number of exclusive agreements had been declining.[116]

It is unlikely that such vigorous national opposition was induced only by the factors mentioned above. It is probable that the national authorities feared that exclusive arrangements which at once restricted employment opportunities and secured the closed shop would result in denial of employment to traveling members. To that extent, the national fabric would be subjected to severe strain. It will be recalled that, from the viewpoint of some of the largest and most powerful locals, exclusion of outsiders from the local jurisdiction was an alternative to national unionism and the traveling card as a solution to the problem presented by traveling workers. It is interesting, therefore, that the Plumbers' president testified that the exclusive agreement "is going out in the small cities, but in the bigger cities they are fighting for it." It is interesting also that the exclusive agreement was found most frequently in the building trades, which were characterized by the absence of interregional product competition and which, therefore, need not have become "nationalized" had the locals been able to exclude outsiders by their individual efforts.

The testimony of a marble manufacturer reveals the type of "national" problem to which an exclusive local agreement could give rise:

The consideration for which they agree to work for only members of our association is that we are enabled to pay them higher wages. They are protected against the competition of marble workers in other localities where labor is cheaper. . . .

The marble cutters keep the membership of their union small, so that every

115. U. S. Industrial Commission, *Report*, v. XVII, pp. 380, 393, 394; Commissioner of Labor, *Regulation of Output*, pp. 275, 281, 334, 337.

116. Industrial Commission, *Report*, v. XVII, pp. 375, 389–390; v. VII, pp. 965, 967–969, 971.

member or as many as possible will always be supplied with work. . . . The marble cutters in localities outside of New York are opposed to the union here because it does not admit outsiders. Of course the union here can not afford not to supply the demand for labor, so when they can not supply cutters they issue probation cards to New York stonecutters or to marble cutters from outside New York. By paying a certain amount such men can get the privilege of working here on probation cards as long as New York cutters are not out of work, but when business becomes dull these probation cards are withdrawn.[117]

At that time (1904) the marble cutters had not formed a national union. Technically, the formation of a national union should have eliminated this problem, for, even if an exclusive local contract obliged the employers to hire only members of a particular local, the latter, by virtue of its subscription to the traveling card system, was obliged to admit outsiders to membership. In fact, however, adoption of such devices as the permit card and the waiting list—which, as noted above, were implemented by the exclusive agreement— tended to undermine the effectiveness of the national traveling card. When, in 1902, New York stonecutters, who were party to an exclusive agreement, flatly refused to honor traveling cards, the nature of the antagonism between the exclusive agreement and national unionism was clearly revealed. A special edition of the *Stonecutters' Journal* appeared, in which it was pointed out that "New York is the Benedict Arnold of trade unionism in America." The following resolution was submitted to referendum vote of the locals by the general secretary-treasurer of the national union:

Resolved, That unless the New York union opens her books to union stonecutters within 30 days, every branch of the general union, as well as every local in the United States and Canada, refuse to accept a New York card or permit a New York man to work in their jurisdiction for a period of 2 years after their books are finally opened; that we strike their name from the list of secretary addresses, refuse to allow them to subscribe to the Journal, or give them space in its columns for their official correspondence.

That the general secretary-treasurer be immediately instructed to establish a branch of the general union in New York City at the earliest opportunity.

That after the expiration of 2 years from the final opening of their books, a New York man will be charged $80 to join any branch of the general union or local.[118]

The threat of reprisal proved effective, for New York began to issue privilege cards to outside stonecutters before the balloting had been completed We do not know which of the threatened sanctions were most effective in securing victory (in principle, at least) for the national organization, but it is probable that the prospect of denial of employment to New York's own traveling members proved decisive.

117. Commissioner of Labor, *Regulation of Output*, p. 337.
118. Commissioner of Labor, *Regulation of Output*, pp. 341–342.

THE PRINTERS—A SPECIAL CASE

Although the local unions affiliated with the International Typographical Union maintained autonomy in the area of wage determination, the I.T.U. was exceptional among unions in local product market jurisdictions in that it did promulgate many regulations governing local economic affairs which were mandatory upon its affiliates. In one instance, at least—the rules governing the hiring practices of foremen—international authority can be traced in part to certain problems which arose out of the migratory propensities of a sizeable and influential body of the membership. Moreover, the ability of the international to enforce its working rules was underwritten by the esteem in which the locals held the international traveling card. But, as we shall observe later on, other factors contributed powerfully to the assumption of authority by the Printers' national union; we shall therefore defer consideration of these regulations until we discuss the economic policies and practices of national unions in chapter 16.

The geographic mobility of labor was great enough in the latter half of the nineteenth century to induce local unions in the same trade to form and join national unions and thus provide for an orderly interchange of members. The principal device whereby locals which had entered into national compacts sought to cope with labor migration was the traveling card system. Under this system, the local union was obliged to admit members with valid traveling cards without requiring them to pay any (or the full) initiation fee, to refuse admission to travelers who came from unionized localities without cards, and to issue cards to their own members in good standing upon application. Since the standards of admission and discipline adopted by the various local unions in a trade were not uniform, acceptance by a local of the first two of these obligations implied the surrender of a portion of its autonomy.

On the other hand, the obligation to issue was qualified by the issuing local's definition of "good standing" and the obligation to honor travel cards was made subject to the receiving local's concept of good standing. In order to minimize the friction resulting from different local standards and admission, it was suggested in some quarters that uniform requirements be established and made mandatory upon all member locals. In some unions certain national standards were provided, but, for the most part, local unions operating in isolated product markets were unwilling to surrender this much autonomy to national organizations. Thus, with certain exceptions, the determination of initiation fees, of requirements relating to apprenticeship and competence, and of the eligibility of women and negroes for membership were matters left to local discretion.

Nor were national unions in local market industries usually empowered to prescribe uniform standards of discipline (the Bricklayers were a notable exception), although the provision of such standards could have reinforced traveling card systems by furnishing acceptable criteria for the disposition of appeals and by minimizing recourse to the ultimate penalty of expulsion. Furthermore, these national unions made relatively little progress in organizing the unorganized; and complete organization of the trade jurisdiction was necessary in order to exclude from employment all workers without traveling cards.

And finally it should be noted that even the surrender of such prerogatives as were required by the traveling-card system, in its bare essentials, was by no means universally achieved. Local unions and individual members frequently violated the rules of the game. Secretary O'Dea complained to a Bricklayers' convention that

There has been more disputes and cases of reference of this nature come to my office this year than all other cases put together. It involved Unions in disputes with each other which culminates in charges, then trials, and perhaps suspension and creates bitter and personal feelings between members and Unions.[119]

Despite its many imperfections, however, the national union proved more effective in coping with traveling workers than did the average run of local unions, each acting in isolation. During strikes it was frequently the practice of the early locals to attempt to "buy off" potential strikebreakers from out of town, by defraying the expenses of their return journeys. While this practice continued into the period of national unionism, the national unions were able to adopt other and more effective tactics. In the first place, they frequently provided severe penalties for members who sought work in strike-bound jurisdictions, an offense which was termed "Union-wrecking" by the Bricklayers. In the second place, some national unions gave added effect to these sanctions by permitting struck locals to refuse to accept traveling cards. Finally, some national unions attempted policies of assisted migrations away from struck localities. The migration which these national unions sought to encourage, however, involved strikers and not strike breakers. Thus, during the eight-hour strike of the New York City bricklayers in 1869, Secretary Kirby of the national union requested each local to notify the striking New York locals "how many hands can be employed in your city."[120] The Glass Bottle Blowers, veterans of several bitterly contested organizational strikes, facilitated striker emigration by permitting the issue of traveling cards by striking locals to members in arrears and by denying strike benefits to any member "who refuses to work or fill a place in any factory not affected by such strike or lockout."[121] Furthermore, the national union was authorized

119. *Proceedings,* 1889, pp. 17–18 (report of the secretary). See also *Proceedings,* 1890, p. 45. See also D. P. Smelser, *Unemployment and American Trade Unions* (Baltimore: Johns Hopkins, 1919), pp. 90–93.

120. *Proceedings,* 1869, p. 35.

121. Provided they had been in good standing prior to strike—*Constitutions:* 1888, Art. VII; 1892, Art. VIII, Sec. 44; 1895, Art. V; 1896, Art. V.

to issue traveling cards to striking locals free of charge; the normal charge was ten cents per card.

In peaceful times, the isolated locals also did their bit to encourage migration by granting traveling loans to destitute "strangers." National unions, on the other hand, while they did not forbid this practice, usually indicated their disapproval by refusing to appropriate funds for such loans from their resources.[122]

The national union was also more effective than were independent local unions which coöperated with one another to the extent of exchanging pertinent information concerning trade conditions and individuals whom they wished to blacklist. In the first place, the national union's facilities for the collection and dissemination of information were superior to those at the disposal of the locals. Periodic reports to the national secretary containing such information as the outlook for employment in the community, the traveling cards issued and deposited, and the names of blacklisted members were usually required of the local unions. Furthermore, such information was often published in the union's own journal, a vast improvement over the hit-or-miss methods to which the early locals had to resort for the dissemination of vital information. The effect of the periodicals of national unions upon the direction and volume of worker migration cannot, of course, be assessed quantitatively, but its significance should not be ignored.

National unionism was superior to local coöperation in another respect: the traveling card system of the national union, by providing for the admission to local unions of cardholders, without the payment of initiation fees, represented a great advance over the blacklist, which could provide only for the exclusion of undesirables by the coöperating locals.

Finally, the blacklist brought different local standards into conflict with one another, and no provision for the resolution of such conflicts could be made by the unaffiliated local unions. The traveling card system involved the same conflict of standards, and, as we know, national unionism was not always able to provide uniform regulations governing admission and discipline which would have eliminated that conflict. Through their power of judicial review, however, the national unions were able to resolve disputes between local unions or between locals and individual members. Thus, cases involving alleged violation of the regulation governing the interchange of members under the traveling card system stimulated the development of judicial and, to some extent, legislative control by the national union over the individual member.

122. *Proceedings,* Bricklayers, 1873, p. 28. *By-laws,* Glass Bottle Blowers, 1892, 1894, 1896, 1897, 1898, 1899, 1900, 1901. The Bottle Blowers also provided for the discipline of delinquent borrowers by their local unions and specified that locals failing to administer such discipline would be fined.

PART

III

CONTROL OVER STRIKES: THE NATIONAL POWER AND THE NATIONAL PURSE

CHAPTER SIX

THE POWER OF THE NATIONAL PURSE

IN THE previous chapter, we traced the evolution of national authority over the individual member. This process involved a transfer of control from the local union to the national union, although it did not ensure the surrender of local power in such important areas as the determination of standards of admission. Now we shall consider the extension of national authority over one of the most vital activities of the local union, the initiation and conduct of strikes. In seeking the origins of this transfer of authority, we can expect no further help from the traveling member; indeed, in view of the *a priori* reckoning at the beginning of Chapter 3, we would not expect to find that so great an enlargement of control could be traced solely to the extension of the labor market. Turning elsewhere, therefore, we shall consider first the role of the emergence of the national strike fund in the development of national strike authority. We shall find that this increase in authority was associated with the presence of funds, but that by no means can all central control over strikes be traced to the national purse; furthermore, we shall find grounds for believing that the emergence of the national fund was not itself an independent development. Hence in the following chapter we shall consider the extent to which such factors as the degree of skill possessed by the members, the nature of the market structure which characterized the national jurisdiction, the emergence of national benefit systems, the age of the national union, and the emergence of regional and national union-employer relationships qualified as determinants both of funds and of controls. During the course of this discussion, we shall also seek to verify the hypothesis, suggested by our theoretical speculation in Chapter 3, that unions organized in national product markets could develop greater control over constituent locals than could national unions organized in local market jurisdictions.

In attempting to determine whether any relationship existed between the growth of financial aid extended to striking locals by national unions and the extension of national control over strikes, we shall adopt as the best available criterion of significant financial aid the presence of a national strike fund (although, as we shall see, it is by no means a completely acceptable criterion); and, we shall adopt provisionally as criteria of national control certain specific constitutional provisions which were discussed by George M. Janes in his study of *The Control of Strikes in American Trade Unions.* Janes' monograph was written in 1916 and refers to conditions which prevailed at the time of writing, but we shall obtain a fair picture of conditions which prevailed at the end of the century by applying these criteria to a group of ninety-three national unions, information concerning which was published by the Industrial Commission in 1901. Some of the data are summarized in Table 4.

This investigation reveals that none of the national controls enumerated in the table was confined to unions with strike (or, as they were frequently designated, "protective") funds. Furthermore, only three of the controls were employed by more than half the unions in the sample. Neither of these observations, however, necessarily invalidates the hypothesis that *de facto*

TABLE 4

SAMPLE OF 75 NATIONAL UNIONS IN 1901 CLASSIFIED ACCORDING TO PRESENCE OF STRIKE FUND AND TYPES OF STRIKE CONTROL

	(1) With Fund	(2) Without Fund	(3) Total
Total Number of Unions	40	35	75
Types of Control A. *Power to Initiate Strikes*			
1. Prior offer to arbitrate or negotiate required	30	17	47
2. Prior period of affiliation of local union required	12	6	18
3. Local union or members required to be in good standing	18	5	23
4. Strike vote in local prescribed	30	13	43
5. Consent by referendum required	9	10	19
6. Consent of national officer or executive board required	36	23	59
7. Specified maximum number of locals or members on strike simultaneously	5	3	8
B. *Power to Terminate Strikes*			
8. National executive authorized to stop benefits or proclaim end to strike	11	6	17
9. Same power conferred upon referendum . .	1	1	2

Source: *Reports of the Industrial Commission* (Washington, 1901): vol. XVII, Part II, pp. 1–324; Part III, pp. 821–847.

national control over strikes was associated with the presence of national strike funds. The presence of controls in the absence of funds might signify merely a manifestation of the fairly widespread tendency on the part of some unions to copy sections of the constitutions of older organizations. And the failure of all but three of the enumerated controls to command majority endorsement might well be explained by the fact that a number only slightly in excess of one-half of the national unions examined possessed strike funds. If a high degree of control was indeed associated with the establishment of funds, we should not expect that the proportion of the unions with controls would be higher than the proportion of the unions with funds.

In only three instances did 'the latter situation occur: 47 of the unions required that their locals make some offer to negotiate with the employer before going on strike; 43 either required merely that a vote be taken in the local prior to calling a strike or specified what majority was required for authorization; and 59 required prior consent of some member or members of the national executive.

Constitutional requirements that locals must offer to arbitrate before going on strike do not appear to have been of great significance. According to Janes,

The officers of the national union, wherever they have full control of strikes, can offer to arbitrate if that policy appears to be wise. Before the national union had acquired complete control of strikes an attempt was made to lessen the number of strikes by the adoption of rules requiring an offer of arbitration. Where such control exists an arbitrary rule of this kind is valueless. Consequently, the rule persists chiefly in unions in which the control of the national union is slight.[1]

Hence the fact that more unions required local arbitration than possessed funds does not by itself cast doubt upon the hypothesis that national funds and national power were closely associated.

The experience of the Molders casts light upon both the reason for the adoption and the inadequacy of this type of requirement. Before the establishment of their national strike fund, the Molders, like virtually all the national unions, attempted to aid striking locals by levying assessments upon locals which were not on strike. Since appeals for strike aid, however, were so numerous that the assessment system threatened to break down, the international convention of 1861 requested all the locals "to discountenance all strikes in their respective localities until every other remedy has been tried and has failed."[2] This recommendation was largely ignored, because the locals could circularize one another for aid without the intercession of the international, and because the locals were invariably more willing to support

1. George Milton Janes, *The Control of Strikes in American Trade Unions* (Baltimore: Johns Hopkins, 1916), p. 31.

2. *Proceedings*, 1861, p. 39. Quoted in Frank T. Stockton, *The International Molders Union of North America* (Baltimore: Johns Hopkins, 1921), p. 101. See also p. 106.

strikes than were the officers of the international. Furthermore, in the case of the Molders at least, sympathetic locals financed their donations at the expense of the international, for, as Stockton reports, "The money obtained in this manner consisted of funds taken out of the monthly tax due the International." Even when the international approved a strike and authorized assessments, the locals elected this painless method of financing their contributions; instead of assessing their members, they "used not only for strike purpose the monthly tax in their treasuries, . . . over which they had no control, but all their local funds."[3] Thus fiscal irresponsibility dulled their perception of the need to avoid battle whenever possible.

The locals, moreover, had good reason to ignore the requirement to arbitrate. The Molders' international required that no appeal for financial support be submitted to it until it had been referred to an arbitration committee consisting of two representatives of the local union, an equal number selected by the employer or employers involved in the dispute, and a neutral chosen by both sides. The committee was allowed five days in which to announce an award.[4] Now, under this, or any similar procedure, the assent of the employers, as well as of the locals, was required. Thus the procedure assumed recognition of the union by the employers, and when, as was most frequently the case, the latter withheld such recognition and refused to arbitrate, the only effect of an offer of arbitration was to give the employers advance notice of a strike and thus to deprive the conciliatory local of the advantage of surprise. In this connection, it is pertinent to report that the international constitution expressly limited arbitrable issues to "the question of wages or prices alone." In 1876, the national executive sent letters to the various employers in the trade, in which the latter were asked whether they would agree to submit henceforth to voluntary abitration. No replies were received, and, at the next convention (1878) the arbitration laws were repealed.[5]

The other two cases in which the proportion of unions possessing the control exceeded the proportion of unions with funds consisted in: (1) the requirement that ratification by a majority vote—usually some specified majority and most commonly a plurality of two-thirds—in a meeting of the local union be a necessary condition of authorization of the strike by the national union; and (2)—the required consent of the national president or executive board. Our 1901 data lend support to Janes' observation that, "the larger number of national unions require executive consent even in cases

3. *Proceedings*, 1878, p. 10. At that time, all tax money collected by the locals remained in their custody, subject to draft by the international president. (*Constitution*, 1876, Art. V, Sec. 1.)

4. *Constitution*, 1872, Art. VI.

5. F. W. Hilbert, "Trade-Union Agreements in the Iron Molders' Union," in *Studies in American Trade Unionism* (New York: Henry Holt, 1906), edited by Jacob H. Hollander and George E. Barnett.

when strike benefits are not paid by the national organizations."[6] Moreover, most unions which required a strike vote also insisted upon advance ratification by the national executive. Thus the Carpenters stipulated that, all attempts to arbitrate having failed, a grievance should be referred to the local meeting and, if sustained by a majority of two-thirds, could then be referred to the secretary of the Brotherhood and by him transmitted to the executive board for final approval or disapproval. By 1916, however, according to Janes, approval by the executive board was generally required before the strike vote could be taken.[7]

The fact that these two restrictions upon local autonomy were more widespread than the existence of national funds may indicate either that nationalization in this vital area of activity proceeded from causes other than requirements of solvency or merely that the presence of funds is too restrictive to serve as an indicator of the effect of financial aid upon the extension of strike control. It does not necessarily imply that the establishment of funds failed to entail an increased degree of centralization. Thus the need to coördinate the activities of different locals in the same community led to national specification of the strike vote. In the appendix on local jurisdiction, pp. 605–619, it is pointed out that, because of the necessity for establishing uniform economic policies within a given local market area, district organizations were established, usually upon the initiative of the national unions. One of the areas of activity in which the autonomy of the local within the district was curtailed consisted in the initiation of strikes. Since action taken by any single local union would be of great importance to its sister organizations in the same district, the area of the strike vote was broadened to include the members of all the locals in the district. Hence the following section in the Carpenters' constitution:

Should any trade difficulty arise in any locality where more than one Union exists, no application for aid shall be sustained unless all the Unions in the District have voted on the subject in their respective Locals, and then in such cases the D. C. shall act for and represent said Locals. . . .[8]

In some instances, district unions were formed from below, without the intervention of the national union, and they occasionally enjoyed a considerable degree of independence with respect to the initiation of strikes.[9] However, the national convention was frequently called upon to decide the manner of voting within the district council as well as the magnitude of the majority required for the authorization of strikes, since the interests of the

6. Janes, *Control of Strikes,* pp. 40, 43–44.
7. *Constitution,* 1881, Art. XI; Janes, *Control of Strikes,* p. 41.
8. *Constitution,* 1890, Sec. 126.
9. The Miners and the Molders furnish cases in point. See below, p. 613, n. 27 and p. 615, no. 31. In addition to the Miners and the Molders, Janes cites the Piano and Organ Workers, the Machinists, the Boiler Makers, and the Iron, Steel and Tin Workers.

large and the small locals often came into conflict. We therefore agree with Janes:

> The district councils and district unions limit the power of the local unions and extend the control of the national union over strikes. They have full power usually to adjust all differences between local unions and their employers subject to the approval of the general executive board, which usually has sole power to call a strike.[10]

To the extent, then, that the necessity to coördinate the economic policies of adjacent local unions required intervention by the national union through its control of the district union, the fact that, by the end of the century, the number of national unions which required approval of strikes by the executive board and which regulated the holding of strike votes exceeded the number which had adopted funds might well have signified that nationalization in these spheres of strike control proceeded from causes other than the growth of central financial support.

Janes, however, cites the increased payment of national strike benefits as one reason for extension of the power of the national over the district in unions in which the district organizations were reported as possessing a high degree of autonomy. Reference to the data of the Industrial Commission does not rule out the possibility that this tendency might have originated in the nineteenth century. Of the six unions singled out by Janes as granting an exceptional degree of control over strikes to their district councils, only the Mine Workers had made no provision for the payment of strike benefits by the national organization by 1901. Three of the six—the Piano and Organ Workers, the Molders, and the Iron and Steel Workers—possessed national "protective" funds in addition to paying out national strike benefits. The remaining two unions, the Machinists and the Boilermakers, did not have funds but disbursed strike benefits from the proceeds of *ad hoc* assessments.

Employment of the assessment system by the last two unions in the group recalls to mind our suggestion that the presence of a national fund is too restrictive a criterion of national financial support of strikes. Thus, while thirty-five of the seventy-five unions in the sample obtained from the Industrial Commission's Report had no national funds, only twenty-seven failed to report the existence of constitutional provisions which empowered the national union to raise money by special assessment or provided in some manner for the payment of strike benefits. Thus, as suggested above, the fact that more unions regulated the holding of local strike votes and required strike authorization by the national executive than possessed funds does not necessarily imply that national strike aid was not influential in the emergence of these controls. Nevertheless, we shall hold fast to the fund as our criterion, for, until the national was authorized to accumulate a fund, the locals could

10. Janes, *Control of Strikes*, pp. 42, 43.

never be sure of a regular source of support, constitutional regulations governing the payment of benefits notwithstanding.

Thus far we have merely cast doubt upon the hypothesis that central strike control emerged solely as a result of the prior establishment of funds. But even if the adoption of regulations governing the holding of strike elections and requiring advance approval by the national executive did not result, in every instance, from the establishment of funds, it does not necessarily imply, as we have already observed, that the establishment of funds did not result in some extension of the strike powers of the national union concerned, or that prior centralization in this direction was not conducive to the erection of funds. To obtain a better idea of the importance of the association between controls and funds, we should compare the prevalence of controls among the unions with funds with their prevalence among unions without funds or with their prevalence among all the unions examined. Such a comparison reveals that, with two exceptions, the relative incidence of controls among unions with funds was higher than it was among unions without funds; in six of the nine cases, the differences were of considerable magnitude.

Before considering the instances in which controls appeared to be associated with funds, let us attempt to assess the importance of those controls which were relatively less popular or hardly any more popular among unions with funds than among unions which did not have central funds.

Maximum Number of Locals or Members on Strike Simultaneously

It would appear that the regulation that no more than a specified maximum number of locals or members be permitted to strike simultaneously should definitely be related to the requirements of fiscal solvency. This prohibition would prevent too great a drain upon the central strike fund. Thus on one occasion, when the Molders' locals in Chicago were involved in a wage dispute, the executive board of the national union sought unsuccessfully to dissuade them from striking because, it claimed, if the Chicago locals struck, locals in twelve other cities would have been obliged to defer their own strike plans. These other locals had already been obliged to stand aside during a previous strike in Cleveland, and if Chicago had struck out of turn, the national would have had to withold support from the others in an effort to "redeem" still other districts which were relatively low-paid.[11] The Molders at this time possessed a national strike fund.

Nevertheless, it was also true that the maximum rule could serve a national union which had no central fund but which financed strike benefits by *ad hoc* assessments on locals. Since assessments could, in fact, be collected only from local unions the members of which were at work, the smaller the number of unions on strike at any one time, the more effective was the

11. *Proceedings,* 1902, p. 612.

assessment system; for, under such conditions, benefit requirements were held to a minimum while sources of revenue were maximized. Hence the Molders had instructed the national president and executive board to achieve a desirable balance between revenues from assessments and expenditures before they provided for a really solvent fund (in 1890), although they were obliged to retain these executive powers after that date in order to avoid overtaxing their fund, as noted above. In 1882, it was provided that the president and executive board

shall see that no more strikes are on hand at any time than the organization is able to handle. They shall concentrate the whole prestige and force of the National Union, financially and otherwise, in the direction most needed.[12]

The Carpenters originally decided that, "Not more than three strikes, in various cities, shall be permitted at the same time." Five years later, when they decided to increase the effectiveness of national strike aid by raising the regular monthly *per capita* assessment and by empowering the executive board to levy special assessments if the strike funds became exhausted, they reduced the maximum number of strikes which could be authorized to run simultaneously to one. It appeared, however, that the Brotherhood's power to proscribe reached no farther than its ability to pay, for, when the question arose whether the limit imposed in 1886 applied to striking locals which did not receive financial aid from the Brotherhood, the constitution was amended to provide that

All local strikes not requiring financial aid from the Reserve Fund can be conducted on the rules and usages laid down by the District Council or Local Union in that locality.[13]

This principle was reaffirmed in an additional amendment which abandoned the limitation upon the permissible number of strikes in favor of a partial limitation upon the number of striking members which could be tolerated at any one time:

When any strike or lockout, or any number of strikes, involves more than 3,000 members, no other strike shall be sustained or financially aided at the same time by the authority and under the jurisdiction of the United Brotherhood....[14]

In 1900, this limit was raised to 6,000 members.

The expedient of permitting strikes (or members on strike) in excess of the specified minimum, provided that the extra strikers received no support from the national union, could not, however, ensure the assessment system against a breakdown. It could keep expenditures within a specified minimum, but if additional locals were permitted to strike, could it be assumed that receipts from assessments would be maintained at a level sufficient to meet

12. *Constitution,* 1882, Art. VI, Sec. 2. (See below, p. 280.)
13. *Constitution,* 1881, Sec. 3; 1886, Art. XX; 1890, Sec. 124.
14. *Constitution,* 1890, Sec. 133; 1900, Sec. 133.

the obligations toward the members of the locals who, under the specified limit, were entitled to strike benefits? The Bricklayers were keenly aware of this problem; for, while they were no more willing than were the Carpenters to decree an absolute limit to the number of strikes permitted to run concurrently, they sought to ensure an adequate flow of receipts by insisting that striking locals, which were themselves not eligible for benefits, continue to pay assessments in support of striking locals which were eligible to receive financial support.

At first, indeed, the Bricklayers were unwilling to require that a striking local contribute to the support of another sister in distress; the convention of 1885 withheld endorsement from a recommendation by Union No. 3 of Missouri that no local be allowed to strike while another was on strike unless it was prepared to pay its share of the assessments ordered in support of the latter. Instead, the convention amended this resolution to provide "that such Union shall receive no aid from the International Union while on strike." The same convention also tabled, on the recommendation of the Committee on Constitution, a suggestion

That any Union that strikes against a reduction of wages, or an increase of hours, shall be exempt from assessments to support any Union who may be previously on strike, but shall pay all assessments due to the time up to date of their own strike.

Finally, the convention gave further evidence of its reluctance to infringe upon local strike autonomy by refusing to approve the following section of the report of its Committee on Officers' Reports:

We cannot too severely censure the Unions of the City of New York for entering into a strike while their brethren of No. 36, New York were fighting for a principle, thereby placing in jeopardy, not only the life of No. 36, but of the entire International Union.[15]

The next convention (1887) rejected a motion to prohibit more than one local from striking at the same time and also a subsequent move to enact a similar prohibition against more than two locals striking simultaneously. It did, however, go further than its predecessor in adopting a rule which provided that

No Union that requires assistance from this Union, shall be allowed to strike while three Unions are on a strike, unless said Union is prepared to pay its assessments to the Union on strike, and shall ask no aid or assistance from this Union....

However, this restriction on simultaneous strikes was vitiated by subsequent legislation (1888, 1889) which changed the word "Unions" in the above quotation to "cities," so that "All cities having two or more Unions, have the

15. *Proceedings,* 1885, pp. 63, 65, 66, 69. The "principle" for which No. 36 struck was a rise in wages.

same rights as individual unions, as far as getting permission to strike is concerned."[16] The wording was altered in 1892 in order to make the intent unambiguous: "All cities having two or more unions, shall be considered as one Union, when the same apply for permission to strike."

In 1897, however, the Bricklayers abandoned their ingenious attempt to reconcile financial requirements with local autonomy. They flatly forbade permission to strike to any local requesting such permission when three other locals were already out on strike. The inadequacy of arrangements which permitted local independence in this respect had been recognized by Secretary O'Dea some thirteen years earlier when he explained why it had been necessary to raise the *per capita* strike assessment after the petition of a New York local had received referendum endorsement:

Meanwhile the subordinate Unions had taken action on the bills of No. 5, Ontario and 2, Rhode Island, and had given their consent thereto. With their claims pending, together with that of No. 36, New York, it materially reduced the aggregate membership in the International Union that would be liable to taxation. I therefore advised that the amount would be increased to twenty cents. . . .

The experience of the Molders, the Carpenters, and the Bricklayers makes it evident why unions without funds, as well as those with them, should have sought to limit the number of locals on strike at the same time. Restrictions of this type were perhaps even more imperative where benefits were financed primarily by current assessment than where they were paid out of existing funds. However, funds were seldom of sufficient size to obviate the necessity of imposing a maximum rule of the type described in the preceding paragraphs, while national unions without funds frequently lacked authority to enforce a maximum rule.

AUTHORIZATION BY REFERENDUM VERSUS AUTHORIZATION BY EXECUTIVE

Authorization by referendum was required by a slightly larger proportion of national unions without funds (29 per cent) than it was by those unions which did possess central funds in 1901 (23 per cent). In contrast, the proportion of unions with funds which required prior consent of a national officer or executive board (90 per cent) was considerably greater than the proportion of unions without funds which provided for similar authorization (66 per cent). It is understandable that the referendum frequently accompanied the strike assessment, because under the assessment method funds were raised only when strikes were about to be called. Each strike furnished the occasion for a fresh financial decision. This was not the case under the fund system, which provided for regular and periodic collection of revenues, whether or not any local actually was on strike. Illustrative of the relationship between the *ad hoc* nature of the assessment system and the referendum

16. *Proceedings,* 1887, p. 135.

was the fact that some unions, which permitted their executive boards to levy strike assessments up to a stated amount, required that proposed assessments in excess of the stipulated maximum be submitted to referendum vote.[17]

Nevertheless, as we shall see in Chapter 10, the referendum failed to accomplish the purpose for which it had been designed. Locals, instead of seizing each opportunity to weigh the merits of the petition against available financial resources, tended either to take no action at all upon the issue or to sanction requests indiscriminately. Furthermore, obtaining authorization by referendum often involved delay which was regarded as intolerable by the petitioning local, with the result that striking local unions frequently refused to comply with authorized procedure and relied—in many instances with success—upon direct appeal to their sister locals for support of the strike in progress. For these reasons among others, a considerable number of national unions which did not possess central strike funds nevertheless did reserve to their national executives the power to authorize strikes. It should be noted that, in our sample, the proportion of national unions without funds which relied on referendum approval (29 per cent) was less than one-half the proportion of these unions which vested power to authorize in the national executive (66 per cent). Moreover, some of the national unions which vested strike authority in the referendum also empowered the national executive to authorize strikes; in such instances the referendum served primarily as an authority to which local unions could appeal from adverse rulings of their national executive boards.

As far as unions which did possess funds were concerned, the case for referendum approval did not apply, since each strike situation no longer furnished the occasion for a financial decision—while the case against it, which we have just reviewed, remained in full force. Nevertheless the proportions of unions with and without funds which adhered to the referendum differed very little. For unions with funds, however, the case for executive authorization became very strong, since it was virtually synonymous with the case for solvency. Thus, while about two-thirds of the unions without funds provided for authorization by the national executive, nine-tenths of the unions which did have funds made similar provision. The fact that so high a proportion of unions with funds required authorization by executive authority anticipates the conclusion, which we shall reach in Chapter 8, that the rise of the national executive was closely associated with an increase in the powers granted to the national union and that these powers lay in the area of the strike activities of the affiliated local unions.

TERMINATION BY REFERENDUM VERSUS TERMINATION BY EXECUTIVE BOARD

The final example of a type of control which was no more popular among unions with funds than it was among those without them is the termination

17. Janes, *Control of Strikes,* p. 98.

of strikes by referendum vote. The total number of unions which provided for this procedure, whether as the sole means whereby strikes, once authorized, could be terminated or as an appeal from termination by the national executive, was very small.

It should be noted that the power to terminate sometimes implied the power to refuse permission to a striking local to call a strike off as well as the authority to insist that a strike be called off. The former was more drastic than the authority to disapprove the calling of a strike. Disapproval could result only in refusal to permit a local to implement an expressed desire to strike; it did not imply the power to order a local to strike against its will. The difference in implied authority in the two cases might help to explain why the absolute and relative frequencies in Row 5 of Table 4 are greater than those in Row 9 and why the same inequality exists between Rows 6 and 8.

On the other hand, the power to terminate was most frequently confined to the power to cease payment of benefits, and it derived its real force therefrom. "The real power of the general executive board is found in its control of strike benefits."[18] The following section in the Molders' constitution is typical:

> The President, in conjunction with the Executive Board, shall have power, when satisfied from facts and information in their possession that a strike is lost, to declare the same at an end *so far as the financial aid to the I.M.U. of N.A. is concerned*. In all such cases at least two weeks notice shall be given to each union in which a strike may exist of the intention to declare the strike ended.[19]

An alternative explanation of the relatively small number of unions which provided explicitly for the power to terminate might consist in the fact that authority to cease benefit payments was implied in the power to authorize benefits and was effective whether or not it was spelled out in the national constitution.

Finally, it should be noted that the authority to terminate strikes, like the authority to authorize them, was conferred much more frequently upon the national executive than upon the referendum both by unions with funds and by those without them.

Having discussed three types of control which appear to have been nearly as popular, or even more popular, among unions which did not have funds as among those which did possess them, let us now consider those controls which were more popular among unions with funds.

In the first place, one might note that, of the six types of control in this category, only three were adopted by a majority of those unions which did have funds. This may merely mean, however, that in certain instances, the power involved, while not specifically authorized in a union's constitution,

18. Janes, *Control of Strikes,* p. 120.
19. *Constitution,* 1879, Art. VI, Sec. 3. My italics.

might have been generally accepted as implied and in fact exercised by the national union. The power of the national executive to terminate a strike might well fall in this category, especially in instances wherein the executive was authorized to initiate strikes and where the power to terminate implied little more than the authority to cease disbursement from strike funds.

Prior Offer to Arbitrate

Since we have already observed that the presence of the requirement of a prior offer to arbitrate is not a good indicator of national strike control, its greater absolute and relative frequency among unions with funds probably signifies nothing more than a somewhat greater concern on their part with the strike problem.

Prior Affiliation of Local Union

The requirement that a local union be affiliated for a specified length of time before being eligible to receive national strike benefits was obviously inspired in part by the belief that no local should be entitled to benefits if it had not made an appreciable prior contribution to the general fund, or, in the case of unions which relied upon assessments, if it had not at least run the risk of being assessed for the support of others on previous occasions. Janes attributes the adoption of this rule to "the general tendency among new local unions to agitate grievances which may result in strikes and exhaust the strike fund."[20]

Good Standing

Of greater interest is the requirement that the local union or its members on strike be in good standing as a condition of their receiving benefits from the national. Although adopted by only eighteen unions with funds (as against only five in the population of unions without funds, however), this type of requirement indicates that the greater ability of the national union to pay strike benefits could be employed to increase its power to collect revenue, including revenue destined for sources other than the payment of future strike benefits. This may be contrasted with the experience of the Molders (referred to above) under an assessment system, wherein the local unions diverted to the payment of assessments funds which should have been sent to national headquarters in payment of normal *per capita* charges.

Although the Bricklayers attempted to restrict eligibility for benefits to locals in good financial standing, they were unable to write vigorous legislation to that effect until they had provided for the establishment of a central fund of sorts. The original provision, passed in 1868, merely stipulated that strike benefits be paid "provided . . . that said local union has on hand, subject to order at the date of application for authority to act, the total amount of its

20. Janes, *Control of Strikes,* p. 102.

indebtedness to the National Union." In 1876, it was provided instead that "No local Union that is two or more quarters dues in arrears, or that is indebted to this Union, shall receive any assistance from this Union while on strike." After provision was made for the establishment of a central fund (in 1891 and 1897), however, all ambiguity was eliminated, and the convention, in 1897, decided simply that "No Subordinate Union that is indebted to this Union in any manner financially shall receive any assistance from this Union while on a strike." [21]

The Molders related a requirement that the individual member be in good standing to their rules governing strike votes taken by local unions. In 1886, their constitution was amended to provide that, "They (the members of the local union) shall take a secret ballot, and no member shall be allowed to vote who has not been in good standing three months." This amendment was passed at the convention following the one at which it was voted to establish a somewhat primitive strike fund by levying an assessment of one dollar for each member. [22]

The establishment of a strike fund might have been effective in reducing dues delinquency, for the greater the ability of a union to dispense strike aid, the more seriously regarded was its threat to withhold such aid. Nevertheless, discipline frequently had to be sacrificed to the requirements of victory once a strike was called, for observance of the picket line by all concerned was invariably a necessary condition of victory. Thus the Carpenters, after the apparent failure of attempts to devise efficient rules requiring "good standing" as a condition for eligibility for benefits, hit upon an ingenious method whereby the member would be dissuaded from falling in arrears but, if he did become delinquent, nevertheless would be induced to observe the strike rules. At the outset, and before a fund had been established, the Carpenters provided that a member had to have been in good standing for at least three months in order to be eligible for strike benefits. In 1890, the three months' time period was eliminated; good standing at the time of the strike became the sole qualification. In 1892, a central "Protective Fund" was established, and in 1894, the requirement of good standing was deleted entirely. In 1898, however, it was partially reinstated and the compromise between the requirements of strike participation and discipline, referred to above, was set forth in the following provision:

All members shall be entitled to strike pay, provided that a member who is in arrears shall out of his first strike pay square up his arrears in full. [23]

One interesting aspect of the "good standing" requirement is that the national union's ability to confer and withhold strike benefits placed it in a

---

21. *Constitution*, 1868, Art. XII, Sec. 2; 1876, Art XII, Sec. 3; 1897, Art. XVII.

22. *Constitution*, 1886, Art. VIII, Sec. 2; see also Stockton, *The Molders Union*, pp. 71 and 78.

23. *Constitution*, 1881, Art. XI, Sec. 9; 1890, Sec. 134; 1894, Sec. 134; 1898, Sec. 134.

direct relationship with the individual member and thus injected additional content into the concept of national citizenship. National authority was, in some cases, further endowed with sanctions other than the withholding or withdrawing of financial aid, but, in the case of the Molders and the Carpenters, it is fairly evident that such sanctions drew whatever strength they possessed from the power of the national purse. Thus the Molders, in their Constitution of 1888, provided that

While said grievance is pending, it shall be considered a violation of Union principles and laws of the organization for any member to go to work in said shop, for which violation he or she may be fined or expelled. No strike benefits shall be allowed by the I.M.U. of N.A. in such cases . . .

The Molders established a well financed strike fund in 1890, and, in 1907, the convention underscored the authority of the executive board to approve or disapprove local strikes in language which was considerably stronger than that found in the provision quoted above. For it was decided that, if a board order to return to work, in the event that a local grievance had been disapproved, was ignored, "it shall be the duty" of the president and the executive board to suspend the disobedient members.

The Carpenters' Brotherhood, when five years of age, had decided that, "Any member going to work on a job declared on strike or lockout in accordance with the laws of this Brotherhood shall be fined such sum as the Local Union may decide, but not less than $5.00 for each day so employed." In 1890, a mandatory fine of $25 was provided for "any member going into any city seeking work where a strike or lockout is pending." The fine was to be imposed by the errant member's home local. Six years later—a central strike fund had meanwhile been established—the penalty was raised to a "fine of $25 or expulsion or both". In 1898, the General Executive Board ruled that "Members violating trade rules and called out on strike are not entitled to strike pay."[24]

Strike Vote and Executive Authorization

It was pointed out above that the strike vote and the executive approval of the calling of a strike were required by more unions than possessed funds. At this point, however, we turn our attention to the fact that the incidence of these provisions and of executive authority to terminate was higher among unions with funds than among unions without funds. Thus, while there is no reason to relinquish the hypothesis, advanced above, that factors other than those related to the existence of funds might well have prompted national unions to install these controls, neither is there reason to reject the theory that the establishment of these controls, on the one hand, and provision for strike funds, on the other, were closely associated.

24. *Constitution*, 1886, Art. XX; 1890, Sec. 127; 1896, Sec. 127; General Executive Board, *Standing Decisions*, 1898.

It is not difficult to find examples which tend to support the latter view and, more specifically, the hypothesis that the establishment of strike funds resulted in an important increase in the authority of the national union.

In Chapter 8 we shall trace the increase in the authority of the national executive of both the Carpenters' and the Bricklayers' unions to the prior establishment of central funds. The power of the International Typographical Union to enforce its strike regulations also followed the creation of a strike fund. As early as 1876, this union stipulated that strike authorization required an affirmative vote of three-quarters of the members of the local who were eligible to vote, and eligibility was restricted to those who had been members of the local in question for at least six months.[25] Nevertheless, according to Barnett, "Since the local unions in case of strike were not aided by the International, disobedience to these rules carried no penalty." In 1885, the I.T.U. established a strike fund. For a long while thereafter, however, locals disregarded a rule that strikes had to be authorized by the executive council of the international.[26] But finally, following the failure of two unauthorized strikes in 1903-1904, the convention adopted a rule which required the executive council to "immediately disown all strikes occurring without its sanction and to guarantee protection to all members who remain at or accept work in the offices affected by the illegal strike."[27]

The Cigar Makers also found it possible to tighten strike control once they had established a fund. Following many unsuccessful strikes during the depression of 1873-1879, the convention provided for a national strike fund in 1879. At the same time, the executive board of the international was authorized to approve all strikes involving less than twenty-five members. Ratification of a strike involving more than that number required a simple majority of the votes cast in a referendum of all of the local unions; in case of a demand for a wage increase, a majority of two-thirds was necessary. Following some instances of violation of these rules, a law was passed, in 1885, which authorized the executive board to appoint an arbitration board which was empowered to compel the local strike committee to join with it and enter into negotiations. Furthermore, the local was obliged to abide by the results of the negotiations, provided that they were approved by a majority in a general referendum vote. In 1906, it was reported that two international representatives settled a strike over the protest of the local union involved, and in 1909 a similar settlement was approved by referendum vote.[28]

Before the establishment of a solvent national fund in 1890, the Molders' strike laws, which had included prescription of the local strike ballot and

25. *Proceedings,* 1876, p. 65.

26. George E. Barnett, *The Printers* (Cambridge, Mass.: American Economic Association, 1909), pp. 323, 327.

27. *Proceedings,* 1904, p. 50. Also Barnett, *The Printers,* p. 323; Janes, *Control of Strikes,* pp. 13, 55, 66, 89, and 94-95; Stockton, *The Molders Union,* pp. 65 and 68.

28. Janes, *Control of Strikes,* pp. 17-18, 90-91, 53-54, 117-118.

authorization by referendum, were frequently disregarded, and with impunity, by locals which apparently cherished a venerable tradition of independence and bellicosity. After the establishment of this fund, however, the president, Martin Fox, was able to enforce discipline. The power to authorize strikes was placed in the hands of the general executive board; unauthorized strikes were made punishable by the suspension of the offending local (a reënactment of an ancient and abandoned rule); and the president and the board were authorized to suspend any individual members who might refuse to return to work when their strike was declared illegal. On the other hand, greater incentive to comply with national authority was provided by the fact that, after the establishment of the fund, national benefits were actually disbursed on every authorized occasion.[29]

The Bottle Blowers provided for a fund in 1890 and, at the same time, authorized their executive board to suspend any local which failed promptly to pay a regular monthly assessment which might be imposed by the president and the executive board in the event that a strike or lockout occurred before the fund reached the capital sum of one hundred thousand dollars. In 1899, two local branches refused to pay a special assessment of ten per cent of each member's earnings at the trade, claiming that the levy was unconstitutional. President Hayes replied that the Association's constitution conferred upon him and the executive board "the entire powers of a convention between sessions," and the two branches were threatened with suspension if they did not pay the assessment within thirty days. One local moved "to expunge the words from the President's report that are of a personal nature and for the purpose of creating discord." "After a very lengthy discussion," this motion was defeated by a vote of 88 to 5. The next convention amended the constitution to grant express authority to the president, "with the consent of two-thirds of the Executive Board" to levy a maximum assessment of 10 per cent "on all moneys earned at the trade . . . when a strike is imminent or when a strike has been ordered by the President" and, when he, with the required majority of the board, "believes it necessary in order to maintain the funds in proper condition to carry on said strike."[30]

However persuasive the evidence might be to the effect that the establishment of funds paved the way for increased national control over strikes—and detailed examination of individual cases brings us closer to the truth of this matter than an over-all numerical analysis of constitutional provisions—it does not rule out the possibility that other factors might also have stimulated such control. Thus, even after the Printers had established their fund, many of the larger locals disregarded international authority because they were

29. Stockton, *The Molders Union,* pp. 106–107; A. M. Sakolski, *The Finances of American Trade Unions* (Baltimore: Johns Hopkins, 1906), p. 65; Janes, *Control of Strikes,* pp. 13–14, 52–53.

30. *Constitution,* 1892, Art. XI, Secs. 66, 67, 69; Art. III, Sec. 11; *Proceedings,* 1899, pp. 26–27, 49–50; *Constitution,* 1900, Art. VI, Sec. 33.

able to finance their own strikes. Later on, such insubordination ceased, but it is doubtful that the presence of the fund, although perhaps a necessary condition, was sufficient to establish local compliance with international regulation. According to Barnett,

As the interests of the union become more fully nationalized and a national policy developed, the members came to realize that a striking union, even though it paid its own expenses, might seriously imperil the success of an international policy.[31]

One must entertain similar reservations concerning the part played by the national fund in the evolution of one variety of strike control which we have not yet considered—the specific requirement that no local union declare a strike without prior authorization, even if it is prepared to finance the endeavor entirely from its own resources. The absolute prohibition of the so-called "independent strike" was not necessarily implied in the requirement of prior authorization by the national executive, for some national unions provided only that such authorization was prerequisite to eligibility for national strike benefits, and, therefore, striking without executive approval either was not unlawful *per se* or was punishable by no sanction other than the withholding of national funds.

Janes seems to have implied that the absolute prohibition of independent strikes was closely associated with the presence of national funds. In the first place, he observed, with respect to those unions which made no provision whatever for the restraint of their locals, that "The absence of any control by the national unions in this group may be explained by the fact that as there are no defense funds, the local unions must finance their own strikes." In the second place, he notes that, at the time of writing, the three national unions which had the largest balances in their strike funds (the Boot and Shoe Workers, the Locomotive Fireman, and the Operative Potters) "allow no independent strikes, have high dues, and exercise a larger degree of central control than do most of the others." On the other hand, the Barbers, Hotel and Restaurant Workers, and Painters, whose funds were much smaller than those possessed by the other unions, "allow a large measure of autonomy to their local unions."[32]

Thus Janes established (1) that national unions which did not forbid their locals to strike without prior authorization did not possess central strike funds and (2) that national unions which did have sizeable funds did prevent strikes. His findings, on the other hand, did not exclude the possibility

31. Barnett, *The Printers,* p. 32.
32. Janes, *Control of Strikes,* pp. 49, 51, 101–102. The Barbers' union was among those listed as exercising no restraint upon the strike activities of their locals; and the Hotel and Restaurant Workers, although they required approval by the general executive board as a condition of eligibility for national benefits, refused specifically to "deprive any of their local unions of the right to strike whenever they feel their interests can only be served by such a course."

that (3) some nationals which did have funds did not forbid independent strikes. The Barbers, Hotel and Restaurant Workers and Painters fall in this category; however, they are distinguished from the unions in the first category by the meagreness of their funds. Nor did Janes' analysis preclude the possibility (4) that nationals without funds did prohibit such strikes. Further analysis of Janes' data reveals that the last two, as well as the first two, categories actually existed. With respect to the third category, we find that almost one-half (31 of 64) of the national unions listed as possessing central strike funds in 1916[33] did not absolutely forbid their locals to strike without national authorization. And 13 of the 46 unions which prohibited such strikes did not possess national funds; these belong in the fourth category.

The importance of the strike fund in curtailing the local's autonomy in this respect is indicated by the fact that nearly three-fourths (33 out of 46) of all the unions listed as forbidding independent strikes had funds. On the other hand, the fact that such unions constituted barely over one-half the total number possessing central funds would indicate that the presence of a fund was not always sufficient to ensure the prohibition of independent strikes. In this connection, we might note that Janes refers to a group of "some twenty" national unions in the building trades "which allow their members working on a particular building to strike at once when a grievance arises." The reason given is that it is necessary because of the need of prompt action; if delayed, "the building will have been completed and the men scattered."[34] Since 5 of the 31 unions which did not forbid independent strikes but which did have national funds were in the building trades, it would appear that this special circumstance outweighed the influence of the strike fund in these cases.

33. Janes, *Control of Strikes*, pp. 99–100.
34. Janes, *Control of Strikes*, p. 50.

CHAPTER SEVEN

SOME OTHER FACTORS IN THE DEVELOPMENT OF STRIKE CONTROL

THE EVIDENCE considered in the last chapter suggests that the creation of central strike funds did contribute to the extension of national control over strikes. But this is not to say either that the establishment of strike funds was the sole cause of such power or that it was an independent causal agent. Analysis of our sample leads us to question both of these latter hypotheses because of, for example, the fact that, in three instances, the adoption of controls was more prevalent than the adoption of funds, and also the fact that most of the controls which were more prevalent among unions with funds than among unions without funds were not adopted by a majority of national unions which did have funds. Therefore we shall now consider briefly some factors which might have contributed directly to the extension of national strike control or which might have stimulated the development of central funds.

SKILL

Sakolski observed that unions in the more highly skilled crafts disbursed larger sums in strike benefits than did unskilled groups. Since highly skilled workers could not easily be replaced by strikebreakers, their unions were "apt to assume a more aggressive attitude" and to spend more money in the process. On the other hand, "unions composed exclusively of unskilled workmen . . . find it of little advantage to accumulate large defense funds, and unless aided by other organizations or assured of a very favorable public sympathy, can hope for little success by resort to a strike."[1] We might hold that the development of a well-insulated economic jurisdiction was a prerequisite to the establishment of strike funds because it was a necessary and yet not a sufficient condition for the winning of strikes. Without such a jurisdiction, well organized strikes could be broken by the employment of strike-

1. A. M. Sakolski, *The Finances of American Trade Unions* (Baltimore: Johns Hopkins, 1906), pp. 49–50.

breakers, and financial support to the strikers would be unavailing. But strikes could be lost in a campaign of attrition even if strikebreaking tactics were denied to the employers. Hence funds were of no avail to the unskilled, while they were necessary to the skilled. Moreover, the income status of the latter enabled them to shoulder a heavier burden of dues, out of which strike funds could be accumulated.

NATURE OF THE MARKET

In Chapter 3, we hazarded the opinion, on purely *a priori* grounds, that national unions organized in local product market industries would not have amassed as much authority as national unions organized in industries which were characterized by interregional product competition. Our discussion of the impact of the geographic mobility of labor upon union structure made it clear that such mobility was sufficient to account for the emergence of national unions, but no attempt was made to determine whether or not it was sufficient by itself to produce national unions which were as powerful with respect to their constituent locals as were those which were formed under the pressure of product competition. It is time that we make some effort to verify or disprove the conclusion reached earlier on theoretical grounds, although the evidence at hand is hardly conclusive.

If the theoretical considerations are relevant, one might expect to find some difference between the local product market union and the national product market union in the important area of national control over strikes. This would appear to follow, first, from the difference in the nature of strikes conducted in the two types of markets during the historical period under consideration, second, from the consequent difference in the nature of financial support required, and third, from the fact that the degree of central control was dependent upon the nature and extent of such financial support.

It was pointed out in Chapter 3, that it was possible for weak national unions and strong locals to exist together in the same local market industry, but that, where interregional competition was vigorous, powerful locals could not flourish in the absence of relatively powerful national organizations. In this connection, it is relevant to add that one would expect to find more strikes involving more than one locality at the same time in a national market industry than in a local market industry, although seasonal considerations might make it desirable for locals in economically isolated communities to strike simultaneously. In fact, there does appear to have been some difference between unions in the two types of market with respect to the variety of strike indigenous to each. Sakolski held that

As regards the character of their strike expenditures, American trade unions may be conveniently grouped under two heads: (1) those in which strikes are of considerable magnitude, usually covering a whole competitive district, but occurring only at considerable intervals, and (2) those in which strikes are frequent, but generally of a local character.[2]

As examples of the first type, he cites the United Mine Workers, the Amalgamated Association of Iron, Steel and Tin Workers, and the Glass Bottle Blowers' Association. It will be noted that none of these unions was organized in the local-market trade. Unions which specialized in frequent, local strikes included the Cigar Makers, the Carpenters and Joiners, the United Garment Workers, the Machinists, the Molders, the Painters and Decorators, and the Typographical Union. Three of these unions were in primarily local trades.

Although regional or nationwide strikes would rarely be expected in local trades, local strikes could occur in national trades. The local strikes conducted by the Molders were caused, somewhat paradoxically, by the nationwide scope of competition in their trade; they were organizing strikes, which were undertaken after the establishment of a system of national collective bargaining, in order to eliminate the competition of employers who were not members of the trade associations with which the union negotiated agreements.[3]

National unions whose locals struck independently of one another—provided, however, that the independent strikes were not staged simultaneously—had less need of accumulated national funds than did national unions whose strikes were on a nationwide or regional rather than local basis. The former could, theoretically, raise funds to support striking local unions by assessing those locals which remained at work, although it is not implied that funds might not have proved to be more satisfactory than assessments in situations in which the two methods could be considered as real alternatives. Where strikes frequently involved more than one local union as a matter of competitive necessity, however, the unions involved could not rely upon a method of financing strikes on a current basis. It was necessary for them to accumulate resources in periods of industrial peace, since strife was apt to embroil a sizeable portion of the national membership simultaneously.

If, therefore, the need for financing strikes on this type of insurance basis was an important factor underlying the establishment of strike funds, we should expect to find that the incidence of national funds was higher in the group of national product market unions than among the local product market unions. In fact, it was; 60 per cent or 32 out of the 53 national market unions in the Industrial Commission sample had funds, whereas only 36 per cent, or 8 of the 22 local market unions had funds. Of the total sample of 75 unions, 40, or 53 per cent, had funds (see Table 5).

It should be noted, however, that nearly 40 per cent of the national market unions in the group had no funds. This suggests that market structure, or,

2. Sakolski, *Finances of American Trade Unions*, pp. 55–57.
3. Sakolski, *Finances of American Trade Unions*, p. 61.

TABLE 5

BREAKDOWN BY TYPE OF MARKET OF 75 NATIONAL UNIONS IN 1901
CLASSIFIED ACCORDING TO PRESENCE OF STRIKE FUND AND TYPES
OF STRIKE CONTROL

	(1) National Market			(2) Local Market			(3) Combined		
	Fund	No Fund	Total	Fund	No Fund	Total	Fund	No Fund	Total
Total Number of Unions	32	21	53	8	14	22	40	35	75
Types of Control									
A. *Power to Initiate Strikes*									
1. Prior offer to arbitrate or negotiate required	23	11	34	7	6	13	30	17	47
2. Prior period of affiliation of local union required	8	3	11	4	3	7	12	6	18
3. Local union or members required to be in good standing	13	3	16	5	2	7	18	5	23
4. Strike vote in local prescribed	22	8	30	8	5	13	30	13	43
5. Consent by referendum required	8	6	14	1	4	5	9	10	19
6. Consent of National Officer or Executive Board required	28	14	42	8	9	17	36	23	59
7. Specified maximum number of locals or members on strike simultaneously	2	1	3	3	2	5	5	3	8
B. *Power to Terminate Strikes*									
8. National Executive authorized to stop benefits or proclaim end to strike	9	3	12	2	3	5	11	6	17
9. Same power conferred upon referendum	0	1	1	1	0	1	1	1	2
C. *Benefits, National*	16	4	20	6	6	12	22	10	32

Source: *Report of the Industrial Commission* (Washington, 1901); v. XVII; Part II, pp. 1–324; Part III, pp. 821–847.

more accurately, the nature of the product or service[4] was not the sole factor affecting, that is, stimulating or retarding, the development of national funds.

Since the incidence of national strike funds was somewhat higher among national market unions than among local market unions in our sample, one would expect that the incidence of any particular strike controls which were closely associated with the presence (or the absence) of funds would be higher (or lower) in the national market group. In this connection let us consider one class of strike control: regulations prescribing certain minimum and maximum conditions for eligibility for strike benefits.

Minimum conditions were implied in rules providing that no national benefits would be paid unless the strike in question was "general"—that is, unless it was directed against all the employers in the trade in locality, or unless it involved at least a stated number of members. Unions with such rules, according to Sakolski, spent more on strike aid than unions which did

4. It was not possible to determine, in each case, the actual geographic extent of competition prevailing at the end of the century. The criterion for assigning a particular union to either the "national product market" or the "local product market" group was, therefore, the nature of the product or service concerned. In some cases undoubtedly, industries which had not yet (in 1900) realized their potential development with respect to geographic extension were placed in the former category. The actual effects of the nationalization of product markets upon the development of both central strike funds and national control over strikes, as indicated in Table 4, may, therefore, be understated.

An outstanding example of an industry in which interlocal competition was manifested at a relatively late date (although before 1900) was the book-and-job branch of the printing trade. Barnett appeared at first to attribute the development of centralized authority within the Typographical Union to this interlocal competition, ("Collective Bargaining in the Typographical Union," in Jacob H. Hollander and George E. Barnett, editors, *Studies in American Trade Unionism* [New York: Henry Holt, 1906], p. 162), but later concluded that, "The increase since 1884 in the functions and power of the International has not been due chiefly to an increase in competition between the offices in different cities. Inter-city competition, though greater in many kinds of printing than formerly, is as yet slight in comparison with the total amount of work done." (George E. Barnett, *The Printers* [Cambridge, Mass.: American Economic Association, 1909], p. 40.)

It is also essential to point out that any classification of industries—and, therefore, of unions into "local product market" and "national product market" groups must be at least theoretically unsatisfactory in another respect. For interlocal competition prevails even within industries which have always been commonly regarded as "local" in nature, although such competition might be indirect and therefore not apparent to the naked eye. For example, if an interlocal differential in construction costs came to exceed a given magnitude, it would tend to retard the "development" of the high-cost community and favor the growth of the low-cost region and thus indirectly to generate a decline in the demand for construction (and other) labor in the former area and an increase in the demand for these types of labor in the latter area.

Nevertheless, differences in degree are of importance, and for this reason we have essayed the following classification. Within each product market group, the unions are listed in chonological order.

The following are classed as "national market" unions: Stone Cutters (1857); Iron Molders (1859); Cigar Makers (1864); Glass Bottle Blowers (1865); Iron, Steel and Tin Workers (1876); Granite Cutters (1877); Flint Glass Workers (1878); Boiler Makers

not impose this type of limitation.[5] Nevertheless it did not always follow that this type of regulation was positively associated with size of funds; in some instances it was adopted to protect limited funds from overstrain. The Cigar Makers did not impose any minimum rule after establishing a strike fund in 1879, but the Carpenters, who also had a fund, but a fund which was proportionately more slender than that of the Cigar Makers, paid benefits only to locals engaged in "general strikes."[6] The Bricklayers, however, having refused to sanction a minimum rule in the early period of their international's history, did pass such legislation some time after they had established a central fund. In 1868, the convention tabled a resolution providing that, "unless one-third of the members employed in any city refuse the demand of the local union this union will not recognize the said demand as a strike." Following—with a lag—the establishment of a national fund in 1891, however, the delegates, in a newly acquired spirit of fiscal responsibility, decided that

all strikes (in order to be eligible for the payment of benefits) must be of a general character, in which the Union is arrayed against the employer as a whole, and

---

and Iron Ship Builders (1881); Journeymen Tailors (1883); Wood Carvers (1883); Brewery Workmen (1886); Metal Polishers (1886); Pattern Makers (1887); Sheet Metal Workers (1888); Paper Makers (1888); Machinists (1888); Boot and Shoe Workers (1889); Blacksmiths (1889); Wire Weavers (1889); Mule Spinners (1889); United Mine Workers (1890); Coopers (1890); Potters ('1890); Carriage and Wagon Workers (1891); United Garment Workers (1891); International Textile Workers (1891); Bookbinders (1892); Longshoremen (1892); Stove Mounters (1892); Upholsterers (1892); Plate Printers (1893); Broom Makers (1893); Northern Mineral Mine Workers (1895); Tobacco Workers (1895); Wood Workers (1895); Hatters (1896); Coal Hoisting Engineers (1896); Leather Workers on Horse Goods (1896); Stogie Makers (1896); Box Makers and Sawyers (1896); Core Makers (1896); Metal Mechanics (1897); Meat Cutters (1897); Steam Engineers (1897); Stationery Firemen (1898); Tin Plate Workers (1898); Piano and Organ Workers (1898); Oil and Gas Well Workers (1899); Custom Clothing Makers (1899); Chain Makers (1900); Amalgamated Glassworkers (1900); Shirt, Waist, and Laundry Workers (1900); Watch Case Engravers (1900).

The following are classed as "local-market" unions: Typographers (1852); Carpenters, Amalgamated (1860); Bricklayers (1865); Horseshoers (1874); Carpenters, United (1881); Operative Plasterers (1882); Lithographers (1883); Bakers (1886); Barbers (1887); Painters (1887); Steam Fitters and Helpers (1888); Plumbers, etc. (1889); Printing Pressmen and Assistants (1889); Retail Clerks (1890); Hotel and Restaurant Employees (1890); Electrical Workers (1891); Street Railway Employees (1892); Theatrical Stage Employees (1893); Brickmakers (1896); Musicians (1896); Tile Layers and Helpers (1898); Team Drivers (1899).

5. Sakolski, *Finances of American Trade Unions,* p. 61, see also pp. 52–53.

6. The Cigar Makers, however, did distinguish between large and small strikes with respect to the method of obtaining authorization in each case. Strikes involving less than twenty-five members were sanctioned by the international executive board, while those involving more than that number were referred to referendum vote of all locals. George Milton Janes, *The Control of Strikes in American Trade Unions* (Baltimore: Johns Hopkins, 1916), p. 17.

vice versa. Any strike by a subordinate Union against an individual, firm, or a minority of the employers of its locality, shall not be considered an I.U. matter. . . .

And in 1903, it was established, as a condition for financial aid, that at least 75 per cent of the membership of the local must be on strike.[7]

Maximum conditions governing eligibility for strike benefits are found in regulations penalizing locals which declared strikes when a specified number of locals or members were already on strike. This type of regulation, it will be recalled from previous discussion, was adopted by some national unions which sought to protect their central funds from excessive strain, but it was also designed for unions which relied on the assessment system and which, therefore, sought to keep current expenditures in line with current receipts. Hence we found that only a few unions in all adopted this type of rule and that it was relatively not much more popular among unions with funds than it was among those without funds. In view of the fact that region-wide or nation-wide strikes could occur in national product markets, we should not expect that many national unions organized in such markets—even those without funds—would impose this type of maximum. As a matter of fact only three national unions, comprising 6 per cent of all the national market unions in the sample did. The remaining five national unions which provided for the maximum were organized in local market industries, and these comprised over 20 per cent of the total. It is of further interest to observe that, among unions with funds, the relative incidence of this control in the local market group (3 out of 8, or 38 per cent) was considerably higher than it was in the national market group (2 out of 32, or 6 per cent); this was also true among the unions without funds but the difference was not nearly so marked.

We may conclude tentatively from the evidence presented thus far in this section that the extent of national control over strikes was in some degree influenced by the geographic nature of the market over which the national union claimed jurisdiction. Strikes embracing more than one locality were more likely to occur in national than in local jurisdictions. As a result, central strike funds were more prevalent among national unions in national market industries (although the seasonal timing of independent local strikes and the inefficiency of the assessment system helped to account for their presence in a third of the local market unions), while regulations limiting the number of strikes which could be prosecuted simultaneously—which tended to reduce the scale of national financial support—were more prevalent in local market unions.

Turning now to other types of strike control, we note first (see Table 5) that the requirements that strikes be authorized and terminated by the

7. *Proceedings,* 1896, pp. 96 and 100–101; *Constitution,* 1897, Art. XVII; 1903, Art. XVII.

national executive were not much more prevalent among national market unions than they were among local market unions for the period 1850–1900. In Chapter 6 it was observed that the adoption of these regulations was frequently prompted by factors other than the existence of strike funds, although the incidence of executive authorization and termination was higher among national unions with funds than it was among national unions without funds. The data in each market group in Table 5 tend to substantiate these conclusions.

The incidence of referendum approval among unions with no funds was higher than it was among unions with funds in both market groups, confirming our previous suggestion that this type of control was not intimately associated with the presence of a strike fund. In this case, also, the control in question was nearly as popular relatively among local market unions as it was among national market unions. Termination by referendum belongs in much the same category.

With respect to the other areas of authority, we note that our earlier observation that, in each case, the relative incidence of the control was greater among unions with funds than among those without funds is confirmed by analysis within each market group. On the other hand, in no case is the relative incidence of a control appreciably greater in the national market group than in the local market group; hence we observe no evidence of the impact of market structure upon the distribution of these controls.

What might we conclude concerning the influence of market structure upon national control over strikes? First, a direct influence is observed, since the incidence of national strike funds was higher among national market unions than among local market unions. Second, our data do not reveal the presence of a strong indirect influence, via the impact of the establishment of strike funds upon the adoption of strike controls. The latter finding might be due to the fact that factors in addition to the presence of strike funds were conducive to the establishment of the strike controls in question and that the distribution of these additional influences was largely independent of market influences.

BENEFITS

In our investigation into the origins of national citizenship, we had occasion to point out that the benefit programs of the local unions, on occasion, impeded the adaptation of early unionism to expanding market areas. Locals which financed insurance schemes for their members were not likely to accept without qualification the essential feature of the traveling card system, which consisted in admission of the traveling member without the payment of any initiation fee (see above, pp. 93ff.). Moreover, some of them engaged in the practice of collecting dues in advance from members who were about to leave their home jurisdiction for a while and who wished to maintain their eligibility for benefits during their absence; this practice exposed the traveler to the hazards of double taxation and, therefore, it made more attractive the alternative of working with his card in his pocket while away from home (see above, pp. 95ff.). In addition to these barriers which the method of mutual insurance placed in the way of national unionism was an obstacle to the growth of union membership in general in the form of the high dues which locals were obliged to charge in order to finance their benefit programs. It was for this reason, according to J. B. Kennedy, that spokesmen of what the printers alluded to as the "industrialist" persuasion were strongly opposed to the establishment of benefit programs ("alimony") by trade unions.[8]

After the Civil War, however, their viewpoint underwent radical change. The great popularity and rapid growth of mutual insurance companies induced many national unions to establish benefit systems of their own. In discussions among unionists about the merits and drawbacks of union insurance, emphasis was now transferred from the deterrent effect of high dues upon recruitment (for was not the flourishing condition of the insurance companies proof that workers were not reluctant to pay premiums?) to the putatively adhesive influence of paid-up policies upon the existing membership. In his autobiography Gompers wrote that "we were convinced that the organization (the International Cigarmakers) could retain a stable membership by offering them benefits that would make it worth their while to pay dues regularly."[9] In particular, it was believed that reluctance to allow accrued benefit rights to lapse would help to maintain membership during bad times when other inducements of unionism were not always evident and when employer resistance to the institution reached maximum effectiveness.[10]

8. James B. Kennedy, *Beneficiary Features of American Trade Unions* (Baltimore: Johns Hopkins, 1908), pp. 10–12.

9. Samuel Gompers, *Seventy Years of Life and Labor* (New York: Dutton, 1925), v. I, pp. 144, 166. Gompers drew upon the experience of the British unions in formulating the proposals which he presented to the Cigar Makers. He was of English birth, although his family moved to this country when he was only "ten years and three months" of age.

10. For Gompers' views on this matter see American Federation of Labor, *Proceedings,* 1888, p. 12, and 1893, p 12. But Kennedy casts considerable doubt upon the accepted view that benefit systems were influential in maintaining membership during the depression of 1893–1897. It is true that "The Typographical Union lost about 10 per cent of its membership, the Brotherhood of Carpenters about 50 per cent, while the Cigar Makers with a highly developed system of benefits lost only 1½ per cent." It is also true that the Cigar Makers' had declined from 3771 in 1873 to 1016 in 1877, a period prior to the establishment of its celebrated national benefits in 1880. Nevertheless, the Typographical Union, which had suffered a loss of 40 per cent during the earlier depression—a loss of the same magnitude as the decline experienced by the Cigar Makers—also fared much better during the depression of 1893–1897, in which their ranks were depleted by only one-tenth; and the benefit program of the Printers was confined to a death payment of sixty-five dollars and a home for aged members. Furthermore, the Carpenters, with a better developed benefit program than the Printers, lost half of their membership during

Moreover, although benefit systems had somewhat impeded the development of national power in the pre-Civil War era, it appeared that this source of conflict, too, had been eliminated in the later period. It even seemed that mutual insurance might strengthen the authority of the national organization over its now more or less "subordinate" locals. It was primarily the local character of the early benefit systems which threatened the national traveling card; after the national unions had overcome this and other difficulties and had achieved a position of preëminence, the question became moot. Furthermore, the rise of national benefit systems followed closely the rise of national unions, and "the more highly developed the beneficiary functions of the national unions become, the less freedom the local unions are given in carrying on such functions."[11]

Moreover, it was possible for "benevolent features" actually to strengthen the disciplinary authority of the national organization over the individual member. We have already observed that, largely in order to protect their national benefit system, the Carpenters, unlike many other national unions, adopted a detailed uniform code of individual offenses and penalties, elevated dues delinquency to the status of a major transgression, and did not hesitate to prescribe the ultimate penalty of expulsion (see above, pp. 128ff.). Now it was in the interest of the union both as a bargaining institution and as a mutual insurance organization to include within its ranks as many men in its occupational and territorial jurisdictions as it possibly could; but, whereas the business union was better off with members who were financially (but not otherwise) delinquent than without them, the insurance union was not. Thus one might hold that such extention of its disciplinary authority as the national union owed to the requirements of its benefit plans did not strengthen its bargaining power at all. However, it might be argued that expulsion was a far more serious penalty to the member who had accumulated insurance credits than it was to one who had no such financial stake in

---

the depression in the 1890's. On the other hand, our author subscribes to the view that the compulsory insurance rules adopted by the railroad brotherhoods was instrumental "in securing and retaining members. . . . After the member has carried insurance for several years, his financial interest are bound up with the interests of the organization, and his loyalty to the union is increased." Kennedy, *Beneficiary Features,* pp. 12–15, 18, 27–28, 45.

11. Kennedy divided all national unions at the time of writing (1908) into three groups: the railway brotherhoods, which forbade locals to pay death and disability benefits but permitted them to pay other benefits; the Cigar Makers, German-American Typographia, Plumbers, Piano and Organ Workers, and others with death, sick, or out-of-work benefits, which prohibited their locals from paying similar benefits; and the "largest group," including the Printers, Carpenters, Painters, and Wood Workers, which permitted their locals to supplement national benefits with local payments. The national systems established by this latter group were not as well developed as were those in the unions in the first two categories.

membership. It is therefore possible to maintain that the value of provision for the penalty of expulsion as a deterrent to unlawful acts of commission or omission exceeded the disadvantages discussed above. Furthermore, some national unions exempted unemployed members from the payment of dues; the Molders did so in order to maintain their sick benefit rights, and they financed payment of the dues of unemployed members by a weekly per capita tax of one cent.[12] This combination of benefits and underwriting of a member's financial standing certainly tended to strengthen the cohesiveness of the union in bad times.

Finally, it was held that national benefits aided the national union in establishing authority over its constituent locals, just as it increased its ability to discipline individual members. It was claimed that national benefit systems extended national control over strikes, and it is for this reason that a discussion of some aspects of the "method of mutual insurance" is discussed in this chapter. At first sight it might appear that the diversion of a sizeable portion of monthly dues to benefit funds might stunt the growth of a union's war chest. However, if the national union's battery of benefit features included a fund for the payment of out-of-work benefits, any limitation upon the potential size of the national strike fund would be partially offset by the national's ability to disburse out-of-work benefits. But the funds set aside for the payment of out-of-work benefits were, of course, subject to drain by members who were unemployed for any reason (except, usually, dismissal for cause); thus not all the funds earmarked for out-of-work benefits could be considered available for strike purposes. Furthermore, only six national unions provided out-of-work benefits in 1907, whereas sixty-three paid death benefits, six paid benefits to members on the death of their wives, and twenty-four paid sick benefits. Nevertheless, funds diverted to these other purposes did not necessarily stay put, for the liquid assets of our early national unions often flowed freely, and funds accumulated for death benefits could be disbursed for strike benefits. On the other hand, where benefit systems were developed on an important scale, such an eventuality was not regarded lightly; and, if members' equities were to be safeguarded, their freedom to strike and thus to ensnare the total resources of the international union had to be curbed. Thus, the creation of national benefit funds not only increased the combat potential—and therefore, in the eyes of the local membership and officialdom, the prestige—of the national union; it could also lead directly to an increase in national control over strikes.

Before the Cigar Makers adopted their national benefit schemes, local unions in this trade could declare strikes on their own initiative. They could appeal to the international executive board for approval, but such a gesture was perfunctory since the board could not withhold approval. Gompers recalled to the 1883 convention that, "In the past the Executive Board of the

12. Kennedy, *Beneficiary Features,* pp. 92 and 93; see also 16–17.

International Union has been an automaton with the power of an affirmative nodding machine without the power of shaking its head in the negative."[13] But when, in 1879, the Committee on Constitution, of which Gompers was chairman, urged the adoption of uniform dues and traveling benefits, "as protection to the benefits proposed we (also) recommended that every union obtain permission from the Executive Board before inaugurating a strike." The recommendations of the committee were approved by the convention and subsequently ratified by referendum vote; it was established that the executive board could pass upon all strikes involving less than twenty-five members each, and that strikes involving more than that number had to be approved in a referendum vote of all locals.[14]

But greater national control over strikes was not the only alternative to the appropriation of accumulated benefit funds for strike purposes. There is evidence which seems to suggest that the establishment of mutual insurance programs, instead of limiting the resources available for the prosecution of strikes, actually stimulated the formation of central strike funds to some extent. Perhaps it convinced the membership of the soundness of collective thrift, or (more probably) perhaps strike assistance was considered to bear a family likeness to death, sickness, and, especially, out-of-work benefits; it can hardly be coincidental that, in many unions, strike payments were known as "trade benefits." Sakolski writes:

In most of the leading organizations, the obligation to pay all legitimate claims to the strike benefit is considered as binding as other obligations. In the Cigar Makers' Union, for instance, the strike benefit has been given equal rank with the benevolent features and is regarded as a form of beneficiary expenditure. The same is true of the strike benefit in the Iron Molders' Union, the International Association of Machinists, the Bricklayers' and Masons' International Union, the Granite Cutters' Union and the Stone Cutters' Association. In these organizations it early became the practice to pay strike claims long after the occasion for which they were presented had passed and even after the strikers had returned to work.[15]

In any event, further analysis of the data compiled from the report of the Industrial Commission indicates that unions with national benefit systems were more likely to possess central strike funds than were unions without such benefits. Thirty-two of the 75 unions in the sample examined paid national benefits of one variety or another. Of the 32 unions with benefits,

13. Gompers, *Seventy Years*, v. I, pp. 168, 172.
14. Janes, *Control of Strikes*, pp. 17–18.
15. It is more probable that benefit programs might have stimulated the formation of central strike funds for the reason elaborated above than for the other reason suggested, namely, that the accumulation of benefit funds made the members more amenable to the raising of funds in general. For, as referendum votes demonstrated, members of the rank and file showed a marked disposition to turn down the pleas of their national officers to raise dues in the interests of solvency. Sakolski, *Finances of American Trade Unions*, pp. 47–48, n. 7.

22 or 69 per cent had funds, while only 18 of the 43, or 42 per cent, of the unions without benefits possessed strike funds.

It is hardly necessary to point out that the above relationships between the existence of central strike funds and the existence of benefit systems do not establish the causal role of the latter; they are merely not inconsistent with the hypotheses set forth in the preceding paragraph. Thus, to cite two prominent counterexamples, the Bricklayers did not have a national benefit system but did establish a national strike fund, and the Printers established their benefit system (1891) after they had created a strike fund (1885).

Nor, *a fortiori,* do these relationships point to the method of mutual insurance as the sole generator of strike funds. If benefits were the sole cause of strike funds, we should expect to find that all of the unions with funds had benefit systems, even though unions without funds also had benefit systems. But the data reveal that only about one-half of those unions with strike funds had benefit systems (22 out of 40). This proportion is higher, however, than the percentage of unions without funds which had benefit systems: 10 out of 35, or 29 per cent.

Moreover, it appears that the apparent influence of the national benefit system upon the creation of the national strike fund was not independent of the nature of the product market involved. The proportion of national market unions with national benefit systems which had central strike funds was higher than the proportion of such local market unions which had strike funds: 80 per cent (or 16 out of 20) versus 50 per cent (or 6 out of 12) in the latter.

The foregoing, however, does not necessarily imply that the establishment of benefit systems had no effect upon the provision of national strike funds. Since the concentration of strike funds among unions with benefits was higher than it was among those without benefits, the greater prevalence of funds among national market than among local market unions might merely have signified that a larger proportion of the former had benefits. And since there is no reason to suppose that national market unions were more likely to acquire benefit systems than were local market unions, this would tend to support, rather than discredit, the hypothesis that the existence of national benefit systems stimulated the creation of national strike funds. Actually, however, the data reveal that the proportion of local market unions with benefits (55 per cent) was higher than the proportion of national market unions with benefits (38 per cent).

Nevertheless, one would still hesitate to reject out of hand the Gompers-Strasser thesis that the installation of national benefit systems furthered the development of business unionism by strengthening national authority and discouraging defection from the ranks. Even our meagre statistical evidence would tend rather to confirm than to deny that there was some truth in the claims of what we might call the new alimoners, although those claims were exaggerated. Granted that the influence of benevolence was not independent of the configuration of the market, one must take note of the fact that, if we eliminate the latter influence, the former stands revealed. For if we consider only those unions organized in national product markets, the proportion of the total number with central strike funds (60 per cent) was appreciably less than the proportion of those unions with benefit systems which had strike funds (80 per cent). Among the local market unions, the difference (36 per cent against 50 per cent) was in the some direction.

AGE AND DATE OF FORMATION

National strike funds, like national benefit systems, did not experience widespread popularity until the '80's and the '90's. It is possible that this late development can be accounted for by one or both of the following hypotheses. First, for whatever reason or reasons, the need for these national institutions was first manifested in this period. Second, it took time for the national unions to acquire sufficient prestige and authority to assume the degree of control over the individual member and his local union which the benefit and strike programs entailed. The latter explanation implies that the appearance of the institution in question marked a certain stage in the development of the individual national union.

The second hypothesis is suggested by the fact that many of the older unions did not establish these programs until the second or third decade following the end of the Civil War. The Printers, founded in 1851, did not establish a strike fund until 1885 and a benefit fund until 1891. The Molders, organized in 1859, established their benefit program in 1879 and a strike fund in 1882. The Cigar Makers, organized in 1864, established both their strike fund and their benefit program in 1879. The Bricklayers, organized a year after the Cigar Makers, delayed until 1891 before providing for a national strike fund.

On the other hand, some of the newer national unions lost little time in setting up these programs. Kennedy observes that the Granite Cutters (formed in 1877), Painters (1887), Metal Polishers (1890), and Wood Workers (1890) established beneficiary features at their inaugural conventions.[16] The Carpenters, established in 1881, created a benefit system the following year, although they did not provide for a central strike fund until 1892. The Flint Glass Workers, on the other hand, were formed in 1880 and established a strike fund in 1881.

The syncopation exhibited by the newer unions, with the result that new and old alike launched benefit and strike-support programs during the same period, tends to support our first hypothesis. It might be reconciled with the second, however, if one takes into account the imitativeness of the American

16. Kennedy, *Beneficiary Features*, p. 11. He might have added the Piano and Organ Workers (formed in 1898) and the United Metal Workers (formed in 1900).

national union. Just as the founders of the early nationals derived some part of their inspiration from the example of British trade unionism, so did the men who helped to form the later national unions seek to profit from the examples set by the American organizations already in the field. (Casual comparison between the early constitutions of the later national unions and the constitutions of organizations in other jurisdictions which were veterans at the time reveals the extent to which the fledgling national imitated its elders in drafting its governing rules.)

But in other instances what might pass for imitation, namely the more rapid adoption of certain institutions by younger unions, might really signify a change of attitude among trade unionists in new and old organizations alike toward the institution in question. Thus, as we know, we have reason to believe that the adoption of national benefit systems in the eighties and the nineties signified such a change in attitude rather than a stage in the evolutionary development of the older national unions, accompanied by prompt imitation on the part of their juniors.

On the other hand, in contrast to the development of national benefits, there is reason to believe that the emergence of national strike funds and certain concomitant extensions of national strike control were more a matter of evolution than of mutation. As long as the role of the national union was confined to the administration of the traveling card system and to the enforcement of such disciplinary authority over individual members as the locals were willing to concede to it—in other words, as long as national authority was exerted primarily over the individual rather than over the local union, the latter formulated its bargaining strategy and tactics in independence of the national union and did not rely upon the national treasury in financing its strikes. The locals were not always financially self-sufficient, however. In the period preceding the Civil War, and especially prior to the crash of 1837, striking local unions relied for aid upon their local trades assemblies (which collected regular *per capita* payments from their affiliates) and, in some instances, were required to obtain approval from the latter in order to be eligible for financial help.[17]

But when locals joined national unions of their own craft, they turned increasingly toward sister organizations in the same trade, rather than in the same community, for emergency funds. At first, they merely relied upon the appeal for donations, with the secretary of the embattled local circularizing his opposite numbers in other localities. Later, the national secretary or president undertook the job of appealing for aid in behalf of the striking local, whose secretary now needed to communicate only with national headquarters. Next, the national union itself raised funds by levying *per capita* assessments upon the locals on an *ad hoc* basis; but this entailed granting authority to

17. Janes, *Control of Strikes,* p. 11. John R. Commons and Associates, *History of Labour in the United States* (New York: Macmillan, 1918), v. I, pp. 350–380.

the national union, first, to levy such extra taxes and, next, to approve and to reject applications for aid. As a result, it took some time before the locals in the oldest national unions were willing to take this step; and, as noted elsewhere, local reluctance to delegate these powers, especially the second, could be measured by the persistence with which locals, whose appeals had been disallowed by national authority, continued to circularize their sister organizations, and by the invariably sympathetic responses which they received. The final step, of course, was the specification of regular strike benefits in the national constitution and the establishment of national funds;[18] and with this development came further national control over strikes.

Since, therefore, the development of strike funds and controls involved acceptance of a considerably broader concept of the role of the national union than had prevailed originally, it is not surprising that Sakolski found that "during the early history of the older national unions and in many of those more recently organized no effective measures were taken to accumulate central reserve funds for defense purposes," or that Janes observed that, "The abolition in this third group (of national unions) of the independent strike on the part of local unions has been brought about only after many years of effort and experimentation."[19] Presumably, even in those cases in which the formation of the national union was stimulated as much by the competitive pressures exerted by the extension of product markets (for example, the coal miners) as it was by the extension of labor markets, and where, therefore, less drastic reorientation of viewpoint concerning the nature of the national union was involved, it took some time for the locals to vest control over strikes and strike funds in the national authority. We shall return to this point presently.

The development of national strike funds and related controls took less time among some of the newer national unions, for, as in the case of the adoption of benefit and other provisions, these newer unions imitated the older organizations. According to Janes, "The tendency is toward centralized control (over strikes), and new unions usually copy the policies and rules of older unions."[20] Nevertheless, there was considerable difference between copying a clause from the constitution of an older union and translating that clause into action as effectively as the veteran organization was doing at the time. Note that Sakolski remarked upon the absence of strike funds not only "during the early history of the older national unions," but "in many of those more recently organized." And Janes, although we have quoted him (and

18. Sakolski, *Finances of American Trade Unions,* pp. 35, 46.

19. Janes, *Control of Strikes,* p. 52. Sakolski, however appears to assign to "the centralization of union functions in the national bodies" a causal role in the development of national funds, whereas the latter development, in many cases, *was* the "centralization" and "sufficient concentration of authority" (p. 46) in question.

20. Sakolski, *Finances of American Trade Unions,* p. 47; Janes, *Control of Strikes,* p. 19.

Sakolski) as indicating that imitation had taken place, observed elsewhere that, "In the newer and weaker unions local autonomy in strike control was complete."[21]

Table 6 yields one measure of the extent to which imitation by the newer unions actually occurred. It lists the number of national unions in the sample which was formed in each decade in the latter half of the nineteenth century, the number of unions in each decade which, by 1900, had installed national funds, and which had adopted each of the control measures discussed in the preceding chapter. If, by 1900, an appreciable number of the newer unions had adopted—even on paper—those institutions which the older organizations possessed in 1900, we should expect that the percentages of unions formed in each decade which adopted the specified provision would exhibit no marked trend. In most instances, however, the proportions of the older unions with controls are higher than the proportions of the newer unions with controls. The same trend is verified more readily in Columns (6) and (7), wherein the group of eleven unions formed before 1880 has been segregated from the remainder, which were organized after that date. It also holds, although less strongly, when the proportions of unions with funds are compared, although the incidence of provision for executive authorization is higher in the group of newer unions with funds. Finally, whereas all the unions in the sample which were formed before 1880 had central strike funds by the end of the century, less than half of the younger national organizations had funds.

By comparing the incidence of controls among the national market unions with the incidence of controls among the local market unions within each age group, the influence of age is eliminated. However, no clearcut market influences are revealed thereby; relative incidence is higher among the national market unions in Rows 3, 5, 10 in the 1850–1879 group and in Rows 1, 4, 6, 8 in the 1880–1900 group. Similarly, no pattern emerges from the data if we also eliminate the influence of strike funds by comparing the incidence of controls among the national market unions with funds with their incidence among the local market unions with funds within each broad age grouping. Within the 1880–1900 age group, however, the relative incidence of funds is clearly higher among the national market unions than among the local market unions. In the 1850–1879 group, all eleven unions had funds.

THE SCOPE OF EMPLOYER RELATIONS

The emergence of national regional trade agreements has also been cited as a cause of national strike control.[22] The national union itself was a party to such compacts, and, since both signatories usually agreed that no strike or lockout would occur before representatives of both sides had an opportunity

21. Janes, *Control of Strikes*, pp. 12–13.
22. Janes, *Control of Strikes*, pp. 34-37.

to settle the dispute in question, national control over strikes was obviously strengthened. It will be recalled that, in most instances, the constitutional requirement that the local union exhaust the possibilities of negotiation or arbitration before going on strike really indicated the absence rather than the presence of true national control over strikes. But where national agreements were in force, the national union itself could intervene in local disputes, and no local could strike before such intervention occurred without violating the collective agreement. In such instances, as Janes pointed out, where the national had effective control over strikes, formal requirements concerning local recourse to arbitration were unnecessary. But it is significant that the rules of the railroad brotherhoods, whose national agreements provided for a comprehensive chain of mediation under the Erdman Act, made members who violated collective contracts subject to discipline. Another indication of the influence of national or regional bargaining on the control over local strike activities consists in the fact that, of twenty-three national unions cited by Janes as having entered into national or regional bargaining arrangements up to the time of writing (1916), sixteen specifically forbade their affiliated locals to strike without express authorization from the national.[23]

Extension of the area of bargaining sometimes implied a widening of the possible area of economic conflict; and, if the former resulted in an increase in direct national control over strikes in order to enable the signatory organization to uphold the "sanctity of contracts," the latter was often associated with the emergence or enlargement of the central war chest. The Iron Molders' concern with employers' associations in their trade can be discovered as far back as 1866, when local unions were urged to be prepared to remit strike assessments to national headquarters without delay, since trouble was expected from the employer's combine. Following the formation of the Stove Founders' National Defense Association in 1886, the Molders established a new central strike fund (1890), and, as a result of some bitter struggles with the National Founders' Association in 1900 and 1904, their strike expenditures rose sharply. This rise, however, could also be traced to a desire to improve relations with organized employers, for, in the years 1899–1902, the Molders conducted a series of organizing strikes which were designed to enforce upon independent manufacturers the same conditions of employment which were observed by members of the associations.[24] The maintenance of relatively large "defense funds" by the Bottle Blowers, Iron and Steel Workers, Potters, Flint Glass Workers, Machinists, and railroad brotherhoods was also attributed (by Sakolski) to "the existence of a combination of the manufacturers in the trade."

Of the eight national unions which were parties to national or "district"

23. From data appearing in Janes, *Control of Strikes,* pp. 35-37, 51, 55, 90, and 99–100.

24. Sakolski, *Finances of American Trade Unions,* pp. 39–40, 60 and 61.

TABLE 6

BREAKDOWN BY TYPE OF MARKET AND PERIOD OF FORMATION OF 75 NATIONAL UNIONS EXISTING IN 1901 CLASSIFIED ACCORDING TO PRESENCE OF STRIKE FUND AND TYPES OF STRIKE CONTROL

	NATIONAL UNIONS FORMED IN																	
	(1) 1850–1859						(2) 1860–1869						(3) 1870–1879					
	National Markets			Local Markets			National Markets			Local Markets			National Markets			Local Markets		
	Funds	No Funds	Total	Funds	No Funds	Total	Funds	No Funds	Total	Funds	No Funds	Total	Funds	No Funds	Total	Funds	No Funds	Total
Total Number of Unions			3						4						4			
Number of Unions in	2	—	2	1	—	1	2	—	2	2	—	2	3	—	3	1	1	1
Types of Control																		
A. Power to Initiate Strikes																		
1. Prior offer to arbitrate or negotiate	2	—	2	1	—	1	—	—	—	2	—	2	3	—	3	1	1	1
2. Prior period of affiliation of local union required	1	—	1	1	—	1	—	—	—	—	—	—	1	—	1	1	1	1
3. Local union or members required to be in good standing	2	—	2	1	—	1	—	—	—	1	—	1	2	—	2	—	—	—
4. Strike vote in local prescribed	2	—	2	1	—	1	—	—	—	2	—	2	3	—	3	—	—	—
5. Consent by referendum required	1	—	1	—	—	—	1	—	1	1	—	1	2	—	2	—	—	—

6. Consent of National Officer or Executive Board required	1	—	1	1	—	1	2	—	2	2	—	2	1	—	1	2	—	2
7. Specified maximum number of locals or members on strike simultaneously	1	—	1	—	—	—	1	—	1	—	—	—	—	—	—	1	—	—
B. *Power to Terminate Strikes*																		
8. National executive authorized to stop benefits or proclaim end to strike	—	—	1	1	—	1	1	—	1	—	—	—	1	—	1	—	—	—
9. Same power conferred upon referendum	—	—	—	1	—	—	—	—	—	—	—	—	—	—	—	—	—	—
10. National benefit systems	—	—	—	1	—	1	1	—	1	2	—	2	1	—	1	2	—	2

TABLE 6 (Continued)

| | (4) 1860–1889 | | | | | | (5) 1890–1900 | | | | | | (6) 1850–1879 | | |
| | National Markets | | | Local Markets | | | National Markets | | | Local Markets | | | | | |
Total Number of Unions in → 22 (4); 42 (5); 11 (6)	Funds	No Funds	Total	Funds	No Funds	Total	Funds	No Funds	Total	Funds	No Funds	Total	Funds	No Funds	Total
Number of Unions in	9	4	13	4	5	9	13	20	33	—	9	9	11	—	11
Types of Control															
A. Power to Initiate Strikes															
1. Prior offer to arbitrate or negotiate	7	2	9	3	1	4	11	9	20	—	5	5	9	—	9
2. Prior period of affiliation of Local union required	—	1	1	2	1	3	6	2	8	—	2	2	4	—	4
3. Local union or members required to be in good standing	3	1	4	3	1	4	6	2	8	—	1	1	6	—	6
4. Strike vote in local prescribed	8	2	10	4	1	5	9	6	15	—	4	4	9	—	9
5. Consent by referendum required	1	1	2	—	1	1	3	5	8	—	3	3	5	—	5
6. Consent of National Officer or Executive Board required	9	2	11	4	4	8	14	12	26	—	5	5	9	—	9
7. Specified maximum number of locals or members on strike simultaneously	1	—	1	1	1	2	—	1	1	—	1	1	3	—	3
B. Power to Terminate Strikes															
8. National executive authorized to stop benefits or proclaim end to strike	4	—	4	—	1	1	4	3	7	—	2	2	3	—	3
9. Same power conferred upon referendum	—	—	—	1	—	1	—	1	1	—	—	—	—	—	—
10. National benefit systems	6	2	8	4	3	7	5	2	7	0	3	3	7	—	7

Types of Control	(7) 1880–1900 64			(8) 1850–1879 11						(9) 1880–1900 64					
				National Markets			Local Markets			National Markets			Local Markets		
	Funds	No Funds	Total	Funds	No Funds	Total	Funds	No Funds	Total	Funds	No Funds	Total	Funds	No Funds	Total
Number of Unions in	29	35	64	7	—	7	4	—	4	25	21	46	4	14	18
A. *Power to Initiate Strikes*															
1. Prior offer to arbitrate or negotiate	21	17	38	5	—	5	4	—	4	18	11	29	3	6	9
2. Prior period of affiliation of local union required	8	6	14	2	—	2	2	—	2	6	3	9	2	3	5
3. Local union or members required to be in good standing	12	5	17	4	—	4	2	—	2	9	3	12	3	2	5
4. Strike vote in local prescribed	21	13	34	5	—	5	4	—	4	17	8	25	4	5	9
5. Consent by referendum required	4	10	14	4	—	4	1	—	1	4	6	10	—	4	4
6. Consent of National Officer or Executive Board required	27	23	50	5	—	5	4	—	4	23	14	37	4	9	13
7. Specified maximum number of locals or members on strike simultaneously	2	3	5	1	—	1	2	—	2	1	1	2	1	2	3
B. *Power to Terminate Strikes*															
8. National executive authorized to stop benefits or proclaim end to strike	8	6	14	1	—	1	2	—	2	8	3	11	—	3	3
9. Same power conferred upon referendum	1	1	2	—	—	—	—	—	—	—	1	1	1	—	1
10. National benefit systems	15	10	25	5	—	5	2	—	2	11	4	15	4	6	10

systems of collective bargaining in 1900,[25] five had central strike funds. These were the Bottle Blowers, the Flints, the Potters, the Iron and Steel Workers, and the Molders. Those which did not possess such funds at that time were the Machinists, the Mine Workers, and the Longshoremen. The Machinists' agreement with the Metal Trades Alliance was a short-lived affair, which was entered into in 1900 and was terminated on the initiative of the Alliance the following year. The Mine Workers and the Longshoremen entered into district rather than national agreements. Five of the six unions which were parties to national agreements thus had funds; 63 per cent of the unions which were parties to regional and national agreements had funds; and 40 of the 75 unions in the Industrial Commission's sample, or 53 per cent, had funds.

It is also interesting that all six unions which were involved in nationwide bargaining in 1900 might be classified as "national market" (i.e., extralocal market) organizations. It will be recalled that 32 of the 53 national market unions in the sample, or 60 per cent had funds, as compared with 36 per cent of the local market unions. Now if, in place of the nature of the product or service, we were to substitute involvement in national (excluding district) collective bargaining as the distinguishing characteristic of a national market union, we would find that, of the 6 unions in this category, 5 had funds (as noted above), whereas of the remaining 69 in the other category, 35, or only about half, had funds. Thus, if we were to adopt the more restrictive criterion of national market unionism, we could claim that national strike funds were considerably more intimately associated with national market unions than they were with other organizations.

But if the old criterion was too inclusive, the new one is certainly too restrictive. In the first place, while not all potentially national jurisdictions had expanded into their wider frontiers by 1900, there were truly national markets in which employers' associations and regional or national collective bargaining did not emerge.[26] National unions organized in such markets merited our designation as "national market unions." In the second place, the opening decade of the present century saw the development of national agreements involving such predominantly "local market" unions as the Printers (1901), the Printing Pressmen (1901, 1902–'07), the Stereotypers and Electrotypers (1901), the Photo Engravers (1905), and the Lithographers (1904). Moreover, the Printers, the Pressmen, and the Photo Engravers not only had national strike funds, but they, along with the Stereotypers and Electrotypers (the latter did not possess a strike fund) specifically forbade their locals to embark upon independent strikes.

25. From data presented in George E. Barnett, "National and District Systems of Collective Bargaining," *Quarterly Journal of Economics,* v. 26, 1911–1912, pp. 425–443.

26. Thus McCabe mentions the following unions which, in 1912, maintained only local uniformity in piece rates but desired "lists of wider application": the Garment Workers, Hatters, Tailors, and Cigar Makers. David A. McCabe, *The Standard Rate in American Trade Unions* (Baltimore: Johns Hopkins, 1912), pp. 126–127.

No national agreements occurred in the building trades, but the rise of large contractors and of local employers' associations sufficed to extend the authority of the national union. The emergence of the large general contractor, with whom it proved possible to enter into collective agreements for periods exceeding the time required for the completion of one project and embracing all the projects undertaken by him, led the Bricklayers to prohibit their locals from engaging in sympathetic strikes on individual projects with other unions in the building trades.[27] Carpenters' locals became more dependent upon the United Brotherhood for strike support, because "the tendency for building employers to combine into association for the purpose of dealing collectively with the unions . . . resulted in a number of large and protracted strikes."[28]

Thus we may infer that the emergence of organized or large employers, apart from the geographic extent of the markets in which they operated, was often sufficient to account for an increase in the national purse or the national power. If we divide the unions which, in 1916 (the year in which Janes' work appeared), had engaged in national or district bargaining at one time or other in their careers into national market and local market groups, and if we compare the two groups with respect to the incidence of funds and the requirement that no local strike independently, no clearcut differences emerge. The incidence of funds is somewhat higher among the national market unions in this category; 12 out of 17 had funds, as against 3 out of 5 local market unions. On the other hand, relatively more local market unions (4 out of 5) forbade their locals to strike independently; the proportion in the case of the national market unions was again 12 out of 17. In each case, the proportion of unions with funds which had this requirement was higher than the corresponding proportion which did not have funds. But if this indicates that funds played a causal role in the development of this control, they appeared to do so to a slightly greater extent in the local market group, where all 3 of the unions with funds possessed the control, than they did in the national market group, where 5 out of 6 with funds had this requirement.

It appears, then, that we are justified in assigning to whatever forces were responsible for nationwide or regional—or even community-wide—employer relations an independent influence in the emergence of national strike control, or, put negatively, that such employer relations were not solely determined by market structure.

One power, however, was reserved to national—or, at least, to extralocal—market unions alone. Of those systems of national or district bargaining which, according to Barnett (in 1912), not only provided for the mediation of

27. Janes, *Control of Strikes*, p. 50. The peculiar nature of the construction industry is discussed in conjunction with the relationship of the national and local unions to the building trades councils in Chapter 12, together with the peculiar position of the Bricklayers within this industry.

28. Sakolski, *Finances of American Trade Unions*, p. 63.

disputes but also determined wage rates on either a national or a district level, none was established in a local market industry. Thus the power to set wages was concentrated exclusively, in this group, in the "national market" unions.

This rate-setting group consisted, in 1911, of twelve unions: the Iron, Steel and Tin Workers, the Molders, the Flint Glass Workers, the Window Glass Workers, the Glass Bottle Blowers, the Mine Workers, the Potters, the Longshoremen, the Stove Mounters, the Marine Engineers, the Coopers, and the Machine Printers.[29] Eight of these unions had funds and denied their locals the right to strike independently; one had a fund but did not specifically forbid the independent strike (the Stove Mounters); and three provided for neither fund nor prohibition (the Longshoremen, the Marine Engineers, and the Machine Printers). Of the group of 12, however, only 9 set wage rates on a nationwide basis. The Miners, Longshoremen, and Marine Engineers engaged only in regional, or "district," bargaining; and of these, the latter two had no funds and did not forbid independent strikes. The Miners' national union, on the other hand, qualified on both counts. Thus, of the 9 unions which entered into industry-wide wage negotiations, 8 had funds and 7 prohibited their locals to strike independently.

But national control over wages and other conditions of employment is less interesting as cause than as effect. As the former, it can probably be credited with exerting an independent influence upon the development of strike funds and controls; but, as noted above, it can hardly stand as surrogate for the national product market in so doing, and, furthermore, the same types of control appeared (if not with equal frequency) in national unions which did not intervene directly in the establishment of conditions of employment in their jurisdictions (and these included national unions organized in local product markets). But national control over the economic policies—as distinct from the tactics—of the local affiliate was a distinctive contribution of the national-market jurisdiction in the sense that, while not all "potential" national market unions possessed such controls, no local market unions did. Since these controls were confined to a minority in the national market group, however, it is probable that the presence of other conditions, in addition to a certain type of market structure, was required to produce them. But it is sufficient for the purpose of this chapter to record that the existence of a nation-wide product market appears to have been a necessary if not a sufficient condition of control over wages. For the theoretical argument which led us to look for some difference between the national market and the local market union with respect to the authority possessed by each hinged upon the degree to which each type of jurisdiction could tolerate wage differentials. Given that the emergence of national labor markets was sufficient to account for the appearance of the national union, if the degree of control which was ceded to that organization depended, in its early career, upon the urgency of

29. Barnett, *The Printers*, p. 427–428.

the need to coördinate local wage movements, we should not be surprised to find that the outstanding difference between the national union in the two types of product market appeared in the area of policy formation.

The incidence of strike controls among national unions with funds was higher than the incidence of such controls among unions without funds in every instance in which we found it reasonable to expect that the presence of a fund would be more likely to lead to the adoption of the control in question than would the absence of a fund.

However, only three controls—prior offer to negotiate or arbitrate, prescription of the strike vote, and authorization by the national executive—were adopted by a majority of the unions in the sample with funds. Moreover, many unions which did not have funds possessed one or more of the enumerated controls.

Thus it is fairly certain that the presence of a national fund, although in some cases sufficient, was not always necessary to bring about national strike controls; and it is possible that, even where controls seemed to be closely associated with the presence of funds, the latter was not a "final cause" of the former. It is therefore necessary to determine whether some other factors contributed either to the extension of national strike controls or to the creation of strike funds. Our findings may be summarized briefly as follows:

Strike funds were found more frequently in unions of skilled workers than in organizations of the unskilled, because the former had a better chance of winning strikes, given the necessary financial resources, and because, being a higher income group, they could afford to pay the higher dues which were necessary for the accumulation of financial reserves.

The incidence of strike funds was higher among national unions in national product markets than it was among those in local product markets. This may be explained in part by the fact that strikes embracing extended competitive areas were confined to the former type of jurisdiction, and such strikes could not be financed adequately by *ad hoc* assessments. Susceptibility to the region-wide strike may also explain why the national market unions were more reluctant to limit the number of local strikes which could be carried on at once. On the other hand, national market unions were somewhat more prone to forbid their locals to strike independently. However, authorization and termination of strikes by the national executive were not more prevalent among the national market unions; neither were most of the other controls enumerated in the tables.

While national benefit systems absorbed part of the limited income available to national unions, the desire to prevent the diversion of benefit funds to the financing of strikes in some cases resulted in an extension of national strike control. Moreover, the incidence of national strike funds among unions with benefit systems was higher than the incidence of funds among unions which did not have benefit systems. However, the fact that the proportion of unions with benefits which had funds was higher in the national market group than in the local market group might suggest that some of the influence upon the establishment of strike controls which might be attributed to the existence of national benefit systems was really due to market structure. On the other hand, the incidence of funds was higher among the unions with benefits than among those without benefits within each market group.

Although newer national unions frequently aped the practice of their elders, the incidence of funds and controls was higher, at the end of the century, among the older national unions than among the younger organizations. Thus the degree of strike control possessed by the national union was partly a function of its age and "maturity." However, breaking down the unions by age groups does not result in throwing into bold relief the contribution of market structure to the development of national strike control.

The emergence of union-employer relations on a regional or nationwide scope exerted a definite influence upon the development of national control over strikes, both directly and via its impact upon the creation and strengthening of national strike funds. Within the group of unions which had experienced district or national collective bargaining, no clearcut differences emerge, with respect to the incidence of funds or of the prohibition of the independent strike, between the national and the local market unions. However, only national market unions in this group had the power to determine wages.

In Part II we found that the rise of a national labor market alone was sufficient to induce the local unions to share their sovereignty over the individual member with a national organization. In this part we found that national unions organized in local market industries as well as those in national market industries acquired a considerable degree of control over the strike activities of their local affiliates, due in considerable measure to the establishment of national strike funds. The latter, it is true, were found to be somewhat more popular among unions organized in national product markets, so that there may be some reason to believe that the prestige and authority of those unions exceeded, to some extent (although no conclusive evidence was uncovered by the numerical analysis of the specific controls enumerated in our tables) the power of the local market unions. Moreover, we found no evidence that, at the end of the century, any national union in the latter group possessed control over the wage policies of its locals; that range of powers was concentrated in the national market jurisdictions.

Nevertheless, the degree of control ceded to the national union in the local market jurisdiction was sufficient to produce a pattern of authority within that national union which in its essentials, was no different from that which developed in the national market union. This will become apparent in the part which follows. Having considered the status of the national union with respect to (1) the individual member and (2) the affiliated local, we shall now turn to a different set of problems which are concerned with the locus of power within the national organization itself.

PART

IV

NATIONAL GOVERNMENT AND THE
POWER OF OFFICE

CHAPTER EIGHT

THE DEVELOPMENT
OF THE NATIONAL EXECUTIVE

In BOTH Britain and the United States, the activities and responsibilities of the officers of national unions grew apace with the importance and authority of their organizations. Authority drifted to the chief executive despite the fact that, in both countries, attempts were made to reserve certain powers to other agencies and thus to make the government of national unions conform to the requirements of constitutionalism, which has been defined succinctly by Friedrich as "dividing power."[1] While certain governing institutions were experimented with in both union movements, the British unionists apparently made a more determined effort than the Americans to retain control over matters of policy in the hands of the unpaid representatives of the rank and file. In view of this interesting divergence, it might prove fruitful to preface our account of the evolution of some of the governing institutions of the early national unions in this country with a highly condensed summary of the main lines of evolution traced by the British unions, as set forth by the Webbs in the first three chapters of *Industrial Democracy*.[2] Consideration of the British case will permit us to establish a frame of reference which should afford insight into American developments.

THE BRITISH EXPERIENCE

The Local Heritage

In the local unions, or "trade clubs," of the eighteenth century, government was of the town meeting variety. Final authority was vested in the "voices" of the members, and administrative duties were discharged by parttime, unpaid officers who served for very short terms. Indeed, the fact that

1. Carl J. Friedrich, *Constitutional Government and Democracy* (Boston: Little, Brown, 1941, revised edition), p. 20.
2. Sidney and Beatrice Webb, *Industrial Democracy* (London: Longmans, Green, new edition, 1911), chs. I, II, and III, pp. 7, 8.

offices were frequently rotated among the membership suggests that the institution of "equal and identical service" was a device for imposing upon each member a share in the task of running the club (somewhat akin to jury duty in our democracy) as well as insurance against the possibility that authority might tend to be concentrated in the hands of a few in their capacity as quasi-permanent officers. In other words this type of local government was designed to insure that the designs of the slothful and of the overambitious alike would be frustrated.

It was pointed out, to be sure, that "this form of democracy was compatible only with the smallest possible amount of business," and that, under "the exigencies of their warfare with their employers," the authority to determine and enforce policy was delegated by the "voices" to "a very small committee, in whom, on very particular occasions, all power resides, from whom all orders proceed, and whose commands are implicitly obeyed . . ."[3] Nevertheless, as a general rule, it was accepted that authority resided in the membership meeting and that it was not lightly to be delegated.

The "Governing Branch"

Although national "amalgamations" and "federations" could not be governed "by general meeting of all the members," the British sought to transfer to the regional and national spheres the essential features of their traditional system of local union government. This they did by designating the "voices" of one particular branch in the national union as surrogate for the membership in all the branches. Thus the first national organization was the "governing branch"; and the first national officers were the unpaid, part-time, and closely supervised officers of the governing branch. Furthermore, the powers and duties of national government were rotated at frequent intervals among the several branches so that no one local union served as the seat of national government for a protracted period.

To what motivations can experimentation with administration by rotation of the governing branch be ascribed? In the first place, the same considerations that impelled the adoption of town-meeting government of local unions prompted its acceptance in principle at the national level. These were, to repeat, first, the desire to oblige all members of the society to bear a hand in the work involved in running it and, second, the desire to safeguard against the monopolization of power by a minority of constituents. At the national level, however, the attempt to implement these two objectives implied the sacrifice of a government which was representative of the organization as a whole. As the Webbs put it, "the leading idea was not so much to get a government that was representative of the society as to make each section take its turn at the privileges and burdens of administration."

3. Francis Place, *The Gorgon*, No. 20, 1818, quoted by the Webbs in *Industrial Democracy*, p. 9.

The desire to adhere to time-honored principles of union government, however, could not account completely for the initial popularity of the governing branch. This institution also

had the advantage of being the cheapest machinery of central administration that could be devised. By it the national union secured its executive committee, at no greater expense than a small local society.[4]

The General Secretary

However, just as the town meeting served the local branch efficiently only when there was relatively little for the local branch to do, so the governing branch ceased to be an acceptable institution for national administration once the national union succeeded in exercising more than nominal authority over its local affiliates. The specific developments which exposed the inadequacy of rule by the rotating governing branch were, according to the Webbs, "the multiplication of branches and the formation of a central fund." The national union now required an executive more permanent and competent than the committee of its constantly changing headquarters local.

The discharge of continuing functions required both longer incumbency in executive office and the devotion of the executive's entire working day to the duties of his office. Hence the emergence of the "general secretary" as a full-time and (therefore) paid officer of the national union. The secretary of the national union was not selected by the "voices" of the governing branch as were his amateur colleagues. He was the only paid officer, and since his salary was paid out of a fund to which members in all branches contributed, the general secretary became the only officer to be elected by the entire membership of the national union.

With the emergence of the full-time general secretary, universal participation in administration was no longer feasible. "The setting apart of one man to do the clerical work destroyed the possibility of equal and identical service by all the members, and laid the foundation of a separate governing class." Now, mere increase in the volume of work was not sufficient cause for the emergence of "a separate governing class"; if the work could have been performed by any and every member of the rank and file, rotation in office perhaps could have been continued, with each member quitting the trade for a short period and being reimbursed by the union for time lost. However, the secretarial work grew in complexity as well as in volume, and the office soon required professional qualification on the part of its incumbent. Furthermore, the basic requirement of literacy made the overwhelming majority of "unlettered men" in the trade ineligible to hold this high office in their own organization.

Thus, with bureaucratic expertness in strong demand and short supply,

4. *Industrial Democracy*, p. 12–13. See also pp. 58–59, 72.

rotation in the office of general secretary was hardly feasible. In fact, although prescribed terms of office were initially short, incumbents were reëlected with little or no opposition. And protected incumbency generally widened the gap between officer and constituents, for the longer the incumbent remained in office, the more expert he became in his practice of the new art. Furthermore, opposition was discouraged:

even if some other member possessed natural gifts equal or superior to the ac-quired skill of the existing officer, there was, in a national organisation, no op-portunity of making these qualities known. The general secretary, on the other hand, was always advertising his name and his personality to the thousands of members by the printed circulars and financial reports, which became the only link between the scattered branches, and afforded positive evidence of his compe-tency to perform the regular work of the office.[5]

The upshot was that annual elections resulted in "permanence of tenure exceeding even that of the English civil servant." Furthermore, so widespread was the acceptance of this phenomenon as a fact of political life that some of the most important unions dispensed with reëlection; the Webbs quote the constitution of the Amalgamated Association of Operative Cotton-spinners which provided that the general secretary "shall continue in office so long as he gives satisfaction."

With the rise of the national union and its professional officer, the problem of union government changed in nature. From the attempt to ensure that each member in the organization perform "equal and identical service," emphasis shifted to devising institutions capable of "uniting efficient adminis-tration with popular control" over the incumbent professional.

Control by the Governing Branch

At first most of the national unions in Britain retained the governing branch and sought to subject the general secretary to the surveillance and authority of the unpaid, part-time, transient amateurs who were chosen by the "voices" of the branch to act as both local and national executive. Thus the governing branch was at once relieved of much of the work of adminis-tration and charged with the responsibility of supervision. It proved, how-ever, as inadequate in the latter capacity as it had been in the former.

With the rise of the general secretary, the rotation of national head-quarters became impractical. With the permanent secretary came the secre-tariat, and (the Webbs wrote in 1897) "though the desire periodically to shift the seat of . . . authority long manifested itself and still lingers in some trades, the growth of an official staff, and the necessity of securing accommodation on some durable tenancy, has practically made the headquarters stationary, even if the change has not been expressly recorded in the rules." Thus the repre-

5. *Industrial Democracy*, pp. 14–17.

sentative character of the governing branch was sacrificed to the requirements of administative efficiency.

Furthermore, the executive committee of the governing branch was unfit for the work of supervision for the same reason that it had proved unfit for the work of administration: it was composed of members who worked at the trade and who, therefore, possessed neither time nor skill enough to guide or criticize the general secretary.

Such inexperienced and casually selected committees of tired manual workers, meeting only in the evening, usually found themselves incompetent to resist, or even to criticise, any practical proposal that might be brought forward by the permanent trained professional whom they were supposed to direct and control.[6]

Control by Direct Election of the Executive Council

The failure of the governing branch to function competently and to represent fairly the interests of all groups in the national membership failed to diminish the popularity of the view which held that important policies should be determined by the rank and file. The British unionists now turned to the direct election of national officers as a device for ensuring that each important member of the national executive would remain responsive to the will of the entire membership.

As we have observed, the general secretary, as the first paid national officer, was elected by the entire membership and not by the governing branch alone. When it became necessary to expand the national executive and provide for more than one national officer—whether assistant secretary or district delegates—the principle of direct election was extended in each instance. By withholding from the chief executive officer the power to appoint his lieutenants and by electing the latter by popular vote either of the entire national union or of the districts which they represented, the possibility of personal dictatorship, based upon patronage, was excluded. Furthermore, the elected executive officers, like the general secretary, were full-time, paid officials and thus became professionals themselves in the course of their tenure in office, capable (it was hoped) of keeping the secretary under surveillance.

It was later hoped that this type of "representative executive" would constitute an effective check upon the general secretary, and many unions created executive councils composed in part of members elected, not by the entire national membership but on a territorial or trade basis. Thus some executive councils consisted of both full-time, paid executive officers, elected by the entire membership, and of part-time, "lay members," each elected by and therefore representative of a certain segment of the membership.

Nevertheless, control of the secretary by the executive council was not effective. In the first place, there was the danger of factionalism emerging

6. *Industrial Democracy,* p. 18. See also pp. 28, 49–52.

within the executive when the ambition of some member of the council to succeed to the office of the secretary might lead him to further his candidacy by a public campaign of criticism against the incumbent. The Webbs concede, however, that it is difficult to determine the precise point at which constructive criticism leaves off and factionalism begins.

The representative executive also exposed the British national union to a danger opposite to and, in the Webbs' opinion, graver than irresponsible factionalism, namely collusion.

More usually the executive committee, feeling itself powerless to control the officials, tends to make a tacit and half-unconscious compact with them, based on mutual support against the criticism of their common constituents. If the members of the committee are themselves salaried officials, they not only have a fellow-feeling for the weaknesses of their brother officials, but they also realise vividly the personal risk of appealing against them to the popular vote. If, on the other hand, the members continue to work at their trade, they feel themselves at a hopeless disadvantage in any such appeal. They have neither the business experience nor the acquaintance with details necessary for a successful indictment of an officer who is known from one end of the society to the other, and who enjoys the advantage of controlling its machinery. Thus we have in many unions governed by a Representative Executive the formation of a ruling clique, half officials, half representatives.[7]

Control by the Referendum

Many British unions resorted to government by written constitution. These union constitutions, which were designed, among other things, to enumerate and to limit the powers of the chief executive, were drawn up at conventions of delegates from the various branches. In form, therefore, these constitutional conventions resembled the later legislative conventions. In fact, however, they differed from such "representative" conventions because the branches sent to the early constitutional meetings instructed delegates who not only "were bound to decide according to the votes already taken in their respective branches," but who were, in some instances, denied the right to discuss, on their own initiative, items of business on which the "voices" of the locals had not instructed them beforehand.

Thus the early constitutional meeting resembled a referendum of the locals more closely than it resembled the modern convention. Consequently, when the constitutional meeting proved to be too expensive an institution to be supported by the impecunious young national unions, it was succeeded by the initiative and the referendum.

The initiative and the referendum prevailed in the period between 1834 and 1870, but they did not prove efficient in the government of national unions in Britain. The membership of the local branches tended to exercise the

7. *Industrial Democracy,* p. 52. See also pp. 19, 20.

power to initiate without discrimination, and this in time proved fatal to either the vitality or the integrity of the initiative. The "wild and absurd propositions . . . were almost uniformly rejected"; but, while this display of commonsense by the majority was reassuring, it was frequently followed by atrophy of the initiative. "Branches got tired of sending up proposals which uniformly met with defeat." Alternatively, in unions in which initial abuse of the initiative failed to engender apathy, attempts were made to curtail the employment of the initiative by either authorizing or permitting the executive to determine whether or not a proposal might be submitted to referendum vote. Furthermore, the executive himself was given the right of the initiative; this authority, in conjunction with his veto power over the questions submitted by the locals and the apathy referred to above, brought it to pass that "the right of putting questions to the vote came practically to be confined to the executive." Moreover, "any change which the executive desired could be stated in the most plausible terms and supported by convincing arguments, which almost always secured its adoption by a large majority."[8] The wheel had turned full circle; the initiative, devised as a means of retaining popular control over the determination of policy, came under the hand of the executive whom it was supposed to restrain.

The referendum, too, soon gave evidence of imperfection. Although, as we have seen, the membership commendably rejected proposals which were "wild and absurd," they were less cautious in adopting policies which were less obviously untenable in the long run or which were mutually exclusive. The short-comings of the referendum were revealed most clearly by the irresponsible measures voted in connection with the benefit systems. (It should be recalled that the "method of mutual insurance" was emphasized more by the British unions than by those in the United States.) In the first place, the electorates indulged their understandable determination to have their cake and eat it too; they were seldom averse to increasing benefits, but they were notably reluctant to raise contribution rates. Furthermore, the referendum was employed on behalf of individual claimants as an instrument of appeal from adverse rulings upon their eligibility which had been made by the officials in charge of the benefit systems. With an eye on their own uncertain future and in the interest of reciprocity, members tended to support one another in their appeals. So widespread was this practice that it imperiled the solvency of some of the benefit systems.

The British unionists' experience with the referendum—in particular, their fatal propensity to assent—suggested to the Webbs that the average man frequently failed to distinguish between the stated purpose of the proposal up for referendum and the foreseeable results of its adoption. On the other hand, it was not essential to democratic government that he do so, but only that he elect a lawmaker to legislate in his interest and that he subsequently

8. See *Industrial Democracy*, pp. 22–26.

be given the opportunity to pass judgment on the fruits of the labors of his representative. *"What Democracy requires is assent to results; what the Referendum gives is assent to projects."* Hence the Webbs rejected the referendum "as a legislative act"[9] and, by implication, as a legislative check upon the powers of the executive.

The British unionists had come to a similar conclusion. The scope of government was narrowed in some instances by prohibiting the revision of constitutional laws within some stated period following their passage. In some unions the referendum was completely abolished.[10] Even where it was retained, however, it failed to check the acquisition of power by the national executive; we have already noted the consequences of endowing the executive with both a veto power over the initiative and with the right to initiate proposals himself.

Control by the Representative Convention

Government by such contrivances as Rotation of Office, the Mass Meeting, the Referendum and Initiative, or the Delegate restricted by his Imperative Mandate, leads straight either to inefficiency and disintegration, or to the uncontrolled dominance of a personal dictator or an expert bureaucracy.

This was the verdict passed upon those forms of national government which reflected the opinion that "each citizen should enjoy an equal and identical share in the government." If any institution could be devised which would be capable of preventing the assumption of authoritarian control by the full-time professional officer, it would presumably reflect a different concept of government. An alternative concept was indeed found in representative government, as opposed to the town meeting; and an institutional alternative was discovered in the convention of popularly elected but uninstructed "representatives," in contrast to the early meeting of the "delegates" who were bound by the "imperative mandate" of their local branches. The Webbs could find only two national unions, the Cotton Operatives and the Coalminers, the governments of which were predominantly representative; and of these only the first met all of their specifications. Nevertheless, they were convinced that, "Trade Union history . . . points . . . to government by a Representative Assembly as the last word of democracy."

Representative government is characterized by the presence of a convention which, "like the British Parliament, is absolutely supreme. Its powers and functions are subject to no express limitations, and from its decisions there is no appeal." The particular convention referred to (the "Cotton-spinners' parliament") met frequently (every quarter) in regular session, and, in addition could be convened by the executive council in special sessions "at any time." Between sessions, this union was run by an executive

9. *Industrial Democracy*, pp. 61–62. Italics in original.
10. *Industrial Democracy*, p. 25. See also pp. 36, 39, 46, 54, 64–65.

council which was composed of three distinct groups of members. The first group was composed of the executive officers themselves—the president, treasurer, and secretary, all of whom were elected, not by the membership directly, but by the convention itself. The secretary, who was the principal executive officer, was elected for an indefinite tenure and therefore enjoyed "a permanence of tenure equal to that of the English civil service." Incidentally, he possessed authority to hire necessary office help. The next group in the council consisted in six permanent officials of the principal district unions of which the Cotton Operatives' federation was composed; they formed a "subcouncil" which performed "the daily work of administration." Finally, it was provided that seven additional members of the executive council be members who were working at the trade. Thus, the professional administrator was brought under amateur control, first, because of the presence of the "lay members" on the executive council and, second, because he himself was elected by and responsible to the convention.

It is evident that the Webbs believed that the Cotton Operatives had achieved the optimum admixture of efficiency (through its permanent civil service) and popular control (through its convention of unpledged "representatives" and the election of officers by the convention). Here was a union which had managed both to eliminate the futility of attempted direct government—whether by town meeting, referendum, instructed delegates, or rotation in office—and to retain popular control by representative government. Why, then, did the representative convention and its subordinate executive make its appearance as a late stage in the evolution of trade union government in Britain—and one which had not found majority acceptance even at the time that the Webbs wrote? "The workman," said the Webbs, "has been slow to recognise the special function of the representative in a democracy." Why was this true, if he had the example of the British parliament before him? More specifically, why didn't the early constitutional conventions of instructed "delegates" evolve into conventions of "representatives" instead of giving way to "primitive democracy" by referendum?

It will be recalled that the early constitutional meetings were abandoned in some instances because the expenses involved in paying for the transportation and maintenance of the delegates from the different locals were too burdensome. But if a convention was to be effective either as a formulator of policy or as a watchdog of the executive, it had to meet at frequent intervals, as did the Cotton-spinners' parliament. Indeed, in discussing the British parliament in connection with a different matter, the Webbs stated that, "the governing assembly of any important state must always demand practically the whole time of its members." Since, therefore, they could not afford to maintain a continuing parliament, the unions embarked upon their experimentation with various forms of direct government. Thus it is significant that the bulk of the membership of both the Cotton Operatives and the

Miners' Federation (which were the two great unions the governments of which conformed to parliamentary requirements) were clustered within very small areas, so that transportation costs could be minimized.

Nevertheless, the Webbs believed that the financial problem was neither permanent nor paramount. Convention costs were largely a function of the degree of industrial concentration and, "In view of the increasing uniformity of working conditions throughout the country, the concentration of industry in large towns, the growing facilities of travel and the steady multiplication of salaried local officials, we do not ourselves regard the geographical difficulty as insuperable."

The representative convention not only evolved late; it was not destined to become the lasting successor to the unworkable variants of direct government enumerated above. Instead, as the Webbs observed, "it is in the constitution of the central executive that the trend towards representative institutions is most remarkable." The Webbs, as we know, appreciated the virtues of the representative executive, which consisted primarily in (1) the independence of the elected executive officers with respect to one another and (2) the "representative" character which was imparted to the council by the inclusion thereon of members elected on a territorial and trade basis. Nevertheless, our authors believed that the executive officers should be selected by and responsible to the convention rather than to the electorate, and they placed little faith, as we know, in the ability of the "lay" representative simultaneously to become sufficiently conversant with the art and wiles of government and to maintain the viewpoint of the man at the bench. Contemporary British unionism provides some evidence, although it is fragmentary, that the Webbs' reservations concerning the lay member and the representative executive were not unfounded.[11] On the other hand, the experience of many American national unions suggests that the selection of the executive by the convention, which the Webbs apparently regarded as the strategic element in the "representative convention," failed to ensure that executive authority would be effectively contained. We shall now attempt to trace the evolution of some of the principal governing institutions in the American national union.

THE AMERICAN EXPERIENCE

Although the American unions encountered many of the same problems that their British counterparts did and although, in many instances, similar problems gave rise to similar institutional developments, the paths of evolution followed by the two movements diverged in several important respects. Such divergence was doubtless the product of many factors, including historical accident and differences in national temperament and political environment, but two distinguishing aspects of American unionism will be emphasized in the pages to follow which were of great importance in shaping the

11. See Joseph Goldstein, *The Government of British Trade Unions* (London: Allen and Unwin, 1952).

institutional development of the national unions in this country. These factors are, first, the persistence of a spirit of local separatism and autonomy and, second, the extensiveness of the territorial jurisdictions of the national unions.

Our discussion of the effect of the geographic mobility of labor upon the development of the national union established the reluctance of the local unions in this country to surrender some of their traditional prerogatives to national authority. To their tenacity might be attributed in part such distinguishing characteristics of our national unionism as the method of selecting executive officers, the early importance of the convention, and, in some instances, the later recourse to the referendum. Another important peculiarity in the American situation was the factor of distance. In connection with our discussion of the Knights of Labor below, it will be noted that, in many cases, the British federations and amalgamations were not really nation-wide unions, whereas the location of industry, interregional competition, and labor mobility in this country were more frequently of such a nature as to make truly nation-wide organization a condition of the existence of effective unionism. Furthermore the geographic extent of the United States is, of course, much greater than the area of Great Britain, so that the area covered by a national union in this country was correspondingly greater than that covered by a genuinely national union in Britain. This factor of distance undoubtedly contributed to American parochialism, mentioned above; but it also exerted a direct and important influence upon the governing institutions of the national unions here—notably upon the convention and upon the development of the national executive. We shall observe the influence of these two interrelated factors of parochialism and distance in the account of the early development of national government which follows.

The Convention and the Selection of the National Executive

In tracing the development of "national citizenship," it was noted that the first members of the national unions were the delegates sent by the local unions to the national conventions. Other individual unionists were originally regarded as members of their respective local unions only. This early restriction of national citizenship reflected the original concept of the national union as a federation of local organizations which retained a considerable measure of sovereignty. The early national conventions were thus regarded as meetings at which the representatives of the virtually autonomous locals would enter into compacts for the mutual advantage of their respective constituencies. In some early unions, the national union was not considered to possess an existence independent of the convention of local representatives; according to Barnett, for example, "The National Union (of Printers) was for many years not the name of the central organization regarded as a whole, but merely of the annual assembly of representatives."[12] And since the only

12. George E. Barnett, *The Printers* (Cambridge, Mass.: American Economic Association, 1909), p. 59, fn. 3.

constituents of the national union were the locals, the only flesh-and-blood members of the national were the representatives of the locals. Thus the Molders' constitution provided that, "This Union shall be composed of its elective officers and the representatives of the subordinate Unions acting under this Constitution."[13] In almost identical language it was established that the Bricklayers' union "shall be composed of elective officials, and the representatives of the subordinate unions acting under this Constitution."[14]

Who were the "elective officers"? If personal membership in the national union was restricted to the convention delegates, and if the organization restricted eligibility to office to its own membership, it followed that only delegates to the convention could serve as officers. For a time, however, some unions made ex-delegates eligible for election to national office. Others denied this privilege to all nondelegates, even though their position implied that an incumbent officer could not be retained in office if he had not been returned as a delegate by his local union. Thus, while, in 1858, the Printers had bestowed permanent membership upon their ex-delegates and endowed them with "all the rights of delegates, except that of voting," at the Convention of 1865 the chair was sustained in a ruling that ex-delegates be not permitted to hold office on the grounds that, if one of them were elected president, he would, by virtue of his office, be entitled to cast the tie-breaking vote.[15] Not until 1891 did the Typographical Union retreat from this position, and, as late as 1886, the national secretary was declared ineligible for reëlection because he was not a delegate.[16] Barnett maintained that this practice followed from "the theory that the National Union was a body distinct from the general membership." The Molders had adopted a similar rule, requiring that all officers be chosen from the ranks of active delegates; this had the effect of preventing William H. Sylvis from becoming either president or treasurer of the national union in 1861. Sylvis had not been elected as a delegate from his own local union, and his nomination for both national positions was successfully opposed on the grounds that he was ineligible for office.[17]

The Bricklayers, on the other hand, at first permitted ex-delegates to hold office. They did not, however, permit them to vote. The relevant section of their constitution reflects an interesting attempt to arrive at a compromise between the concepts of the national union as a federation, on the one hand, and as an organization of individual members, on the other:

Delegates to the International Union shall, after their term of service in that capacity expires, be permanent members of the same so long as they retain their

13. *Constitution*, 1876, Art. II, sec. 1.

14. *Constitution*, 1867, Art. II, sec. 1.

15. *Constitution*, 1858, Art. II, Sec. 2; *Proceedings*, 1865, p. 6. In 1869, the constitution was amended so as expressly to deny to ex-delegates the right to be elected to office. (*Constitution*, 1869, Art. II, Sec. 1.)

16. Barnett, *The Printers*, p. 65.

17. *Iron Molders' Journal*, December 31, 1888, p. 2.

membership in any subordinate union, proof of which they shall present, and said union retain its connection with this body. They may discuss any question or serve on a committee, not provided for by the Constitution, by permission of the Union, and may be elected to any office but shall not vote on any question on any occasion.[18]

If, as Barnett found, the practice of restricting eligibility for office to current delegates furnished evidence in support of the concept that the national union was distinct from the individual unionists in its jurisdiction, the extension of this eligibility to ex-delegates supports the view that the national union was also regarded as an organization distinct from its constituent locals. Although the national membership which was bestowed upon the individual delegate was originally intended merely to symbolize the autonomous status of the local union which he represented, the delegates themselves, once in convention assembled, apparently developed a certain *esprit de corps;* and a community of interest emerged, in the face of differing local backgrounds, which was, perhaps, not unlike the familiar phenomenon in our federal government known as senatorial courtesy. Indicative of this was an episode in the Bricklayers' convention of 1876. After having elected a delegate, one of the locals sought to reconsider its action. The delegate involved challenged the legality of the attempted recall, and President Carpenter of the international sustained him,

claiming that when a Delegate has been duly elected, as the law requires, that he then becomes a member of the National Union, and subject to its jurisdiction only, and therefore cannot be deprived of his office, only through charges for misdemeanors, in open Convention, or through the Judiciary Committee of the National Body, at its next session. Several instances of this nature having come under my observation, I desire an expression from your Honorable Body upon this question. . . .[19]

The convention sustained the president, but eight years later, the provision, quoted above, permitting ex-delegates to hold national office, was repealed. Although a move to revoke their premanent membership failed, it was later provided that" Subordinate Unions have the privilege to regulate their own laws with reference to the eligibility of members to be elected as Delegates.[20]

The decline of the ex-representative paralleled the growth in importance of the national union. As long as the latter was not much more than a debating club, it mattered little whom the "members" declared eligible for admission. But once the national convention began to exercise independent authority, its decisions became of greater importance to the affiliated locals, and the latter sought to strip their delegates of the slight measure of independent authority which they had previously permitted them to assume.

18. *Constitution,* 1867, Art. XIX.
19. *Proceedings,* 1876, pp. 8–9.
20. *Proceedings,* 1894, p. 15; *Constitution,* 1897.

Thus, the old basis for distinguishing the national union from its locals—that is, the eligibility of nonrepresentatives to hold office—disappeared with the emergence of a new and more significant individuality which was based upon acquired powers. At the same time, Barnett's distinction between the national union and "the general membership" also began to disintegrate, for, although constitutional clauses holding that "this International Union shall be composed of elective and appointive officers, and the legally elected representatives of the subordinate unions" persist to this day, direct membership in the national union in effect was bestowed upon the rank and file with the emergence of the national judiciary (see Chapter 4 above). Nevertheless, insofar as eligibility to hold national office continued to be restricted to delegates and/or ex-delegates, a distinction was drawn between the type of membership in the national union held by local representatives and the citizenship of those who did not represent their local unions, either as convention delegates or, in some instances, as local officers.

The same distinction holds when we turn from eligibility to hold office to a consideration of eligibility to participate in the selection of national officers. For the early concept of personal membership of the delegates and the practice of restricting to delegates the eligibility to hold office led logically to the election of national officers by the convention. Glocker, writing in 1913, observed that, "The American unions have been slow to adopt the method of electing officers by popular vote."[21] Before 1890 only the Stone Cutters, Granite Cutters, and "perhaps one or two other trades" held direct elections, and by 1913 the number of such unions had increased only to eighteen. The Printers joined this small group in 1896, and their experience illustrates the relationship between eligibility for office and the method of selecting the national officers. In the period during which nondelegates were not eligible candidates for national office, officers were elected by the convention. But when the Printers extended eligibility to all members of local unions, they also substituted direct election by referendum for election by the convention.[22] However, most unions retained the methods of officer selection which the Printers chose to abandon in 1896.

Thus the early reluctance of the local unions in this country to surrender prerogatives to national organizations was reflected in the restriction of national membership to local delegates, and this, in turn, led to the selection of the national executive by the convention rather than by the rank and file. It is interesting that selection of the national executive by the convention should have prevailed in this country, while direct election by the membership of the local unions was the method most widely adopted in Britain. For in the United States, the president is directly elected by the voters, while, under

21. Theodore W. Glocker, *The Government of American Trade Unions* (Baltimore: Johns Hopkins, 1913), p. 202.

22. Barnett, *The Printers*, p. 66.

the British system of parliamentary government, the cabinet is elected by and is responsible to parliament. Thus each movement adopted the system of executive selection which prevailed in the other's homeland.

It hardly follows, of course, that the American unionists decided upon executive selection by the convention out of preference for parliamentarianism over the system of separation of powers with which they were acquainted as citizens of this country. Nor does it follow that British unionists, for the most part, opted for direct election of the executive because they were convinced of the superiority of American over British governing institutions. If such relatively theoretical considerations had governed the decisions made by the union lawmakers, it is probable that each union movement would have copied the system prevailing in its own country. In fact, pragmatic conditions indigenous to the union movement in each country accounted for the choice made in each case. The American choice of selection of the chief national executive by the convention reflected the survival of a peculiarly hardy tradition of local autonomy. The popularity of direct election among the British unions, on the other hand, could be explained, as the Webbs pointed out, by their desire to make the only paid national official a direct representative of the entire body of taxpayers.

Salary, Morality, and Incumbency in Office

When the Typographical Union voted to hold direct elections, it supported the position of its president who had declared that, "the only explanation of why an entire convention is debarred from changing a word in the constitution, but a majority of the delegates can elect officers, is that the custom had its birth when the International offices were merely honorary positions . . ."[23] This statement reflects the historical fact that, in the earliest days, when, as in Britain, the national unions were no more than delegate conventions, the functions of national officers were largely confined to routine duties in connection with the holding of meetings. Glocker, describing this stage of development, observed that

In the local union the primary organ of government was the mass-meeting of members, and in the federal association it was the representative assembly. For the conduct of both the local-mass-meeting and the federal assembly the same officers were needed, namely, a president to act as chairman, a vice-president to take his place when he was absent, and a recording secretary to keep the minutes.[24]

As the rudiments of permanent organization emerged, however, it became necessary, as in Britain, to provide for officers who were charged with attending to the continuing activities of the national union and who were

23. *Proceedings*, 1896, p. 12. Quoted in Barnett, *The Printers*, p. 66.
24. Glocker, *Government of Unions*, p. 176.

supposed to perform duties between, as well as during, the periodic conventions. Nevertheless, the conventions were reluctant to install full-time salaried executive officers. The officers themselves, however, frequently refused to subscribe to the view that theirs were part-time jobs, which could be performed by men who worked full time at their trades. In 1867 the Bricklayers' president informed the convention that, "it was well for the International Union that the secretary was not working at his trade," although the secretary was not then a salaried official.[25] But for a more detailed and impassioned account of the officer's plight, we must turn once again to Secretary O'Dea of the Bricklayers, whose eloquence has already served us well. O'Dea was typical of many—if not most—of the American union leaders of his time in that, while he was perfectly willing to devote himself singlemindedly to the building of his union, he wanted to be paid for his efforts. In 1883, he advised the convention that

The duties of your officers are arduous and onerous, and to fulfill them acceptably they should receive that compensation which their positions would warrant. During the past year an immense amount of business has been transacted through my office, and were it not for the position in which I was placed, I tell you frankly I would not have done it; and anyone who imagines it is a sinecure, I will assure him never made a more grievous mistake in his life. During the past year I received 1,464 communications, all of which received proper attention. The amount of mail matter that left my hand is as follows: 1,566 letters, 984 postal cards, 1,071 circulars, 147 reports and thirteen charters, making a total of 4,058 . . . Through the rapid growth of this organization, the time has approached when, to have the duties of this office thoroughly attended to, you must take its occupant from the cares of earning his living by journey-work, and give him a salary that he can live upon, so that he can give his whole attention to its duties.[26]

The international president was equally disturbed and, referring to himself in the third person, told the convention of 1889 that

I believe that he now has to work night and day to complete his work, and would most earnestly recommend that your next presiding officer be paid a *salary* that will enable him to either stay home and do the work or else hire it done, as it is too much to expect your President to devote his entire time of *every evening* to the duties of his office.

It remained for O'Dea, however, to reduce the argument for executive compensation to more concrete terms:

I again recommend that your officers be paid suitable salaries to recompense them for their services to you. Your organization is an infant no longer. . . . . . . You work nine hours per day and have the balance of the day to yourself, without any responsibility upon you.

25. *Proceedings,* 1867, p. 13. He was paid $100 and expenses in 1866. The following year, however, his "salary" was raised to $500.
26. *Proceedings,* 1885, pp. 39–40.

I have worked on an average for the first six months of this year 14 hours per day. Is that Unionism? . . .

Now how does my salary compare with Union wages?

You pay me $1200 for a year. To pay that amount it comes to a fraction less than five cents on each member of the I.U. The wages paid to the members of my Union are 45 cents per hour.

I work every day in the year. Sundays and holidays find me at work in the office, as well as week days. My time is not my own, it is yours. Three hundred and sixty-five days at $4.05 per day of nine hours, amounts to $1,514.75. You don't pay me that much; you only pay me $1200. Then I must be a SCAB, for I am working *under wages,* and working *more hours* than the law calls for. Is that Unionism?

The Secretary did not pause for a reply:

The International Union in its convention made me a "Scab." Just think of it! The International Union makes one of its EXECUTIVE OFFICERS A SCAB. They require him to work for less wages, and to work longer hours than any other member in the entire organization, and at the same time require of him as an Executive officer, to suspend any Subordinate Union that will allow any of *its* members to do what *he* is doing.

And finally came the crux of the matter. Courageous and devoted as they were, the men who built our business unions could not be quite content with virtue's own reward. Zealots could, no doubt, but these men were not zealots; on the contrary

They are mortals as well as you are, are as good as you and have the same rights as you. . . .[27]

O'Dea's plea, however, was not persuasive to the convention, for not until 1900 was the international secretary's salary raised from $1200 to $1600 a year. Indeed, it took the Bricklayers twenty years to pay their secretary as much as $1,000. The international union was formed in 1865; in 1867, the secretary was voted a salary of $500, which was eliminated in 1871, restored to half its former amount in 1871, reduced to $150 in 1877, to $100 the following year, and eliminated in 1879. In 1882 it was decided, "That if it be found at the next Convention that more than sufficient money is on hand to defray the expenses of the Union for the year, Brother Carpenter, National Secretary, shall receive the surplusage, provided the same shall not exceed one hundred dollars." Brother Carpenter received $100 for his labor. In 1883 the salary was raised to $250; the following year, to $300; and in 1886, it was doubled so that, for the first time, it exceeded the level at which it stood in 1867. Nor had the heady inflationary process spent itself: the secretary was paid $800 in 1887, $1,000 in 1888, and $1,200 in 1889. With this bit of financial history behind them, some of the older members and delegates must have reacted

27. *Proceedings,* 1890, pp. 49–50; 1882, p. 27.

to O'Dea's request much as the Beadle did to Oliver Twist's petition for another helping of workhouse victuals.

Nor were the Bricklayers an isolated case. The Printers, founded in 1852, did not pay their national executive regular salaries until 1882.[28] Indeed, the examples of the Bricklayers and the Printers lend some support to Glocker's contention that it was the "decentralized" unions (presumably those operating in local product market industries), which clung most tenaciously to "the system of unpaid or nominally paid officials." In support of this thesis, one might cite the fact that the Iron Molders, a "centralized" union, founded in 1859, voted a salary of $600 to their president as early as 1864[29] and awarded subsequent increases so that, by 1876, the compensation of the chief executive stood at $1600. Furthermore, in 1890, the year in which O'Dea lamented the inadequacy of his $1200 salary, the Iron and Steel Workers paid their president at the rate of $1500 per annum.[30] The Glass Bottle Blowers, another union established in a national market, paid their president $2,000, reduced it subsequently to $1600, raised it once more to $2,000 in 1893–1894, and once again reduced it to $1600 at which figure it remained at the end of the century.

On the other hand, the Molders, despite their early tradition of generosity, had descended so far from the peak of 1876 that by 1890 their president received $1200, which was precisely equal to the stipend of Secretary O'Dea. Thus a national market union paid its president no more than the "decentralized" Bricklayers paid its secretary. Furthermore, the Carpenters, another example of a "decentralized" national union, had established a salary of $2,000 for Secretary P. J. McGuire, which was higher than that paid by both the Molders and the Iron and Steel Workers. (McGuire's salary was especially vexatious to O'Dea, for bricklayers were a higher-paid craft group than carpenters. "Verily," O'Dea protested, "a bricklayer should receive as much wages as a carpenter."[31])

On some occasions the early national unions paid dearly for their parsimony. Evidence to support O'Dea's observation that officers were mortal can be found in instances of embezzlement and neglect of duty by national executives in some of the most prominent unions of the period. The Molders, for example, developed a more powerful executive board in 1878 in part because their president had embezzled funds and it was therefore deemed advisable henceforth to exercise closer supervision over the highest office.[32] The Bricklayers' president and vice-president, both unpaid, on one occasion abdicated without the formality of advance notice, and neglected to circulate

28. Glocker, *Government of Unions,* p. 177.
29. *Journal,* February 1889, p. 6.
30. *Proceedings, Bricklayers,* 1890, p. 50.
31. *Proceedings,* 1890, p. 50.
32. Frank T. Stockton, *The International Molders Union of North America* (Baltimore: Johns Hopkins, 1916), p. 29.

among all the locals petitions to grant aid to some that were on strike. Where-upon the salaried International Secretary O'Dea "assumed those responsibili-ties . . . until the Subordinate Unions considered the trying situation in which I was placed, and by a majority vote placed the power of conducting the affairs of our Order into the hands of the Treasurer and myself, until the assembling of this body in convention."[33] During the year 1893–1894, Secretary Longstoft of the Glass Bottle Blowers' Association, one of the most powerful and respected of the national unions, absconded. Although the secretary was a paid official, receiving a salary of $1400, at the time, he was also doubling as treasurer. Since the treasurers' office paid only $200, it is possible that no incumbent could be found and that Longstoft's dual in-cumbency reflected the shortsighted influence of an economy bloc which had been pressing for a reduction in executive salaries.[34]

Perhaps the most tragic case involved the defalcation of P. J. McGuire, founder of the Carpenters' United Brotherhood and retained as its General Secretary-Treasurer from 1881 until 1902. McGuire, originally a Socialist, had also aided Gompers in the formation of the American Federation of Labor. Ironically enough, four years prior to his defection (which occurred in 1902) he had argued against the action of the convention in unanimously raising his annual salary to $2,000, objecting that, "labor organizations should not go to excess in the payment of officers' salaries." After McGuire had agreed to repay $1,000 of the $10,000 in official funds for which he had failed to give an adequate accounting, the union decided not to prosecute the case in court. "The further prosecution of Brother McGuire," sadly concluded the president, "would be a strong weapon in the hands of those antagonistic to Union Labor. It would hold Union Labor up to ridicule, and show that even the greatest leader of them all was not to be relied upon."[35] The Brother-hood did take one constructive measure, however; it promptly separated the offices of secretary and treasurer and provided for a full-time general treas-urer whose salary was set at $1500 per year, which was only five hundred dollars less than the salary which the general president received at the time.[36]

One further consequence of the early state of executive compensation ought briefly to be noted—its apparent effect upon incumbency in office. It is a fact that, in contrast to later developments, the early national unions were typically characterized by rapid turnover in their high offices. Thus Barnett, referring to the Printers, observed that, in the period 1850–1885, "only five presidents held office for more than one year, and of these, only one for more than two years. In thirty-five years the Union had twenty-eight presidents. The tenure of the other officers was equally short."[37] The Carpenters, in the

33. *Proceedings,* 1885, pp. 10–40.
34. *Proceedings,* 1894, p. 33; 1897, pp. 19 and 35.
35. *Proceedings,* 1888, p. 42; 1902, pp. 20-27.
36. *Constitution,* 1902, Sec. 30.
37. Barnett, *The Printers,* p. 61.

period 1886–1902, failed to reëlect a president; each incumbent held office for one two-year term. Other organizations shared this experience in their early years, but, as the union matured, terms of office typically lengthened. In the first twenty years of their history, (1865–1885), the Bricklayers elected fourteen presidents to office; none held office for more than two years consecutively. From 1886 to 1904, however, there were only five incumbents. Only one held office for no more than one year, two served three years each, one was reëlected four times, and one served seven terms. The Molders elected a different president in each of the first three years of their collective existence, but, from 1863 to 1903, only five men held office.

It will be recalled that the Webbs attributed the reduction in turnover among office-holders to an increase in the duties of office and, consequently, a greater demand for competent administration. Glocker adopted this explanation when he sought to account for the same phenomenon in the United States: "the older unions have tended to lengthen the term of office and to reëlect officials for several terms" because "the newly elected leader comes to his office as very raw and crude material, and attains efficiency only after some years of experience."[38] There is little doubt that the argument is plausible in both cases, but tenure in office depends upon supply as well as demand, and an explanation in terms of efficiency sheds light only on the demand for officers. To a considerable extent the supply of incumbents—like the supply of other commodities—must have been in part a function of price, if we are willing to lend credence to the voluble protestations, quoted above, of O'Dea.

Some evidence can be marshalled in support of this suggestion. In the first place, although presidential elections in the unions studied were generally contested in the early periods when turnover was high, there were also a sufficient number of unanimous elections to indicate that, in many instances, turnover was due to resignation of the incumbent. Apparently, the desire to hold an honorary but virtually unpaid office was not without a time limit. This view is supported by fairly numerous examples of an incumbent declining renomination.

The records of the Molders and the Bricklayers suggest the importance of the executive salary in providing a continuing supply of executive competence. The Molders' period of long incumbencies dates from 1863; their policy of paying a stipulated salary to their chief executive was adopted the following year. The Bricklayers also had initially provided for a salaried chief executive (in their case, the secretary), with the result that the first incumbent held office for five years. Subsequently, as we know, they reduced this compensation—ultimately (in 1878) to one-fifth of its original level—and did not restore it to the level at which it had stood in 1867 until 1886. At the same time, the period of incumbency in the office was reduced con-

38. Glocker, *Government of Unions*, p. 184.

siderably; none of the first secretary's successors held office for more than two years in the period 1870–1877. Secretary Carpenter was a noteworthy exception to the rule; he served for four years (1880–1883) and received a total of $350 in salary for the entire period. He had previously served one year as international president without pay. He was succeeded by O'Dea, however, whose views on this question were quite unequivocal. O'Dea remained in office from 1883 until 1900, and during his long incumbency the salary was increased from $250 to $1200.

The final bit of evidence which might suggest a relationship between compensation and willingness to hold office consists in a comparison, within the same union, of rates of turnover between salaried and virtually non-salaried executive offices. The Carpenters are a case in point. During a period (1886–1900) in which McGuire occupied the salaried post of secretary-treasurer without interruption, eight unpaid presidents served brief terms (the term was two years) in office.

The foregoing might be persuasive, but it hardly establishes a simple relationship between salary and the supply of offices. Furthermore, evidence can be offered in rebuttal. How, for example, to explain the fact, already referred to, that rotation in the presidential office in the Bricklayers' union underwent a notable reduction after 1885, while the office remained without compensation? During O'Dea's tenure, seven unsalaried presidents were elected, but in the previous seventeen-year period there were eleven presidents. Furthermore, the office of treasurer had a somewhat puzzling career, although it might appear to illustrate the relationship between compensation and willingnss to serve in office. It is true that, after a salary was established in 1885, the office was held by one and only one Patrick Murray whose uninterrupted tenure reached from 1882 until 1918. Nevertheless, Murray's unpaid predecessors in office had been few in number; there were only five treasurers (including two men who performed double duty as secretary-treasurer) between 1865 and 1882, while there were twelve presidents during the same period. Both offices were unpaid, but, while the treasurer's duties were routine and not especially onerous, the office of president was more time-consuming. In other words, granted the desire of both president and treasurer to serve their union, only the latter, able to work full-time at his trade, could afford to do so for any protracted period.

The Sedentary Secretary, the Perambulating President, and the Traveling Organizers

When the Bricklayers' Secretary O'Dea pleaded for more generous executive compensation, he argued that the duties of his office had been increasing. This was putting his best forensic foot forward, for, given the traditional parsimony of the delegates from the local unions, it is evident that past increases in pay had been in recognition of increased secretarial services rendered. As early as 1877 it had been moved and adopted, "that the Secretary's salary be set at $150 per annum and his work be diminished." In 1881, tribute was paid by the Bricklayers' president to another international secretary, Lewis Carpenter, who, it will be recalled, had served without pay. According to the president, "Too much credit cannot be given Brother Carpenter for his indefatigable efforts in behalf of the National Union. By and through him, are we principally indebted for the privilege of again meeting in National Council."[39]

The growing burden of administration which characterized the growth of national unionism in Britain was reflected in the emergence of the general secretary. The secretary was also the most important officer in some of the early national unions—notably in the building trades—in this country. In the Carpenters' and Bricklayers' unions, the secretary was the first paid, full-time national officer. As we observed in connection with the question of compensation, the secretaries of these unions, McGuire and O'Dea, received compensation while the presidents of the organizations were still unpaid. They also remained in office for longer periods and thus, through their greater familiarity with the problems and practices of national unionism, they became more influential and powerful than did the presidents.

In most unions, however, the president was the chief executive in fact as well as in name, but, in the early period of the national union's growth, there is some indication that the president's duties were, to a considerable extent, of a secretarial nature. Some unions which paid salaries to the presidents did not reimburse their secretaries, or, if they did, paid them at much lower rates. The Glass Botttle Blowers paid their president $400 a year in 1886, while the secretary received only $100; in 1888, the president received $2,000, but the secretary, whose pay had been raised to $200 in 1887 (the president's compensation was not increased at all that year) received an additional raise of only $100.[40] The Molders' president, in 1876, received $1600 a year, but the recording secretary's pay was limited to $4 per day during conventions. Since unions which provided for full-time paid secretaries did not pay their presidents equivalent sums, it would appear that the typical national union could not afford more than one full-time officer early in its career. And since it is reasonable to suppose that president-led nationals developed the same volume of administrative work as did those led by secretaries, it can be inferred that, in the former organizations, much of the secretarial work between conventions was performed by the presidents. This situation seems to have prevailed in the Molders' union. In 1886, the president was relieved of the duty of keeping accounts between the national union and each local, and this chore was transferred to the secretary who, at the same time, became a full-time officer with a salary only slightly under

39. *Proceedings,* 1877, p. 21; 1881, p. 6.
40. *Proceedings,* 1887, p. 67; 1888, p. 114; 1889, pp. 59, 92.

that received by the president. Prior to this time, that routine work had been performed by the president. Since the Constitution originally stated that, "The President shall have no clerk," a good portion of his working time must have been consumed by clerical duties.[41]

Nevertheless, one might well wonder why such administrative tasks were entrusted to the president rather than to the secretary. Why, in most unions, was the first full-time executive officer the president and not, as in Britain, the secretary? The records provide us with no direct answer. It might be held that the governing institutions of this nation furnished an example which most of the American unions chose to follow, although, as we have observed, they were not similarly influenced in their choice of a method for selecting their executive officers. One is tempted to inquire into the functions of the early American national presidents in order to ascertain whether they might not have performed, in addition to their routine tasks, some duties which were peculiar to their time and place.

We find that many of the early presidents did indeed engage in a decidedly nonsecretarial activity: they traveled about a good deal. To make national unionism effective, it was desirable that all the local labor markets within the national trade jurisdiction be organized and that all local organizations conform to national authority. Since this was a larger country than Britain, since its markets were frequently more thoroughly "nationalized," and since there was less concentration of industry within limited areas, the area embraced by a "national" union in the United States was greater than in Britain. Thus we find that the early national presidents were frequently great travelers, going from locality to locality, helping the uninitiated members and officers of local unions to master the complex arts of organization, negotiation, and striking, and, in the process, enhancing the influence of the presidential office throughout the national jurisdiction. Indeed so pressing were these roving assignments that the national secretaries often were obliged to discharge the judicial duties of the presidents in the absence of the latter.[42] Thus the president, who in the first instance was obliged to perform routine clerical work, soon was unable to discharge all these executive functions which had been explicitly delegated to him by constitutional authority.

Perhaps the most famous of the traveling presidents was William H. Sylvis of the Molders, the outstanding labor leader of his time. He was the Paul Revere of the trade union movement, and his travels in the years during and following the Civil War first built up the international and later, in the opinion of his most recent biographer, saved it from extinction.[43] This confirmed the earlier judgment of John P. Frey, who, as editor of the Molders' *Journal* in 1889, decribed Sylvis' achievement most graphically:

41. *Constitution,* 1886; 1876.
42. Glocker, *Government of Unions,* pp. 180–181.
43. Jonathan Grossman, *William Sylvis, Pioneer of American Labor* (New York: Columbia University Press, 1945), pp. 57-74, 181-189.

When the National Union appeared to be nearing its dissolution, in the fall of 1862, Sylvis again came to the front, and was mainly instrumental in reorganizing the institution. In his organizing tour he traveled over ten thousand miles of road in the States and Canada upon the ridiculously small sum of six hundred dollars. Through the mountainous districts of Pennsylvania, the hills and valleys of fair New England, and the prairie land of the west, he plodded his lonely toilsome way; into the foundries where his fellow-craftsmen were at work, he went till the homely plaid he wore bore the marks of molten iron. . . .[44]

On these tours, Sylvis not only organized new locals and "reorganized" some of those already in existence but approaching dissolution; he also intervened in local strikes and bargaining situations, thus furnishing the inexperienced local officers with expert leadership. In this informal manner, through the perambulations of its president, the national union came to exert great influence over its affiliated locals, and especially over those locals which owed their existence to the personal intervention of the national executive either in their international affairs or in their relationships with the employers with whom they sought to bargain collectively. Formal recognition of this presidential function was granted when the union specifically awarded to the chief executive the "Power to visit subordinate Unions, and inspect their proceedings, either personally or by deputy, upon proper information that his presence is required, and require compliance with the laws, rules, and usages of this Union."[45] This provision in the constitution of the Molders was typical of those adopted by virtually every national union shortly after its formation. Moreover, as the national union itself extended its authority over its affiliated locals, much of this increased power was vested in the office of the national president. Thus, in 1892, the Bottle Blowers decided that their president

shall have power to suspend any Branch in the Association for any violation of its laws, or for insubordination to any lawful command of himself or the Executive Board, and shall immediately report the same to the trade. . . . may suspend any Branch that refuses or neglects to pay within one month after notification of arrears, tax due the Association or assessment levied. . . .

When the suspension of a Branch has been ordered by the Board or President, either the President or some member of the Board duly authorized by him shall procure from the President of said Branch, the books, charter and other property, and deposit the same with the General Secretary. Any officer of a Branch refusing to deliver the property in his charge, in accordance with the demand of the President or Executive Board, shall be expelled from the Association. . . .

shall see . . . that the general workings of the Branches are in accordance with the laws of the Association, and shall by himself or some competent member visit and inspect the workings of each Branch as often as practicable.[46]

44. *Journal,* July 31, 1889, p. 7.
45. *Constitution,* 1876, Art. III.
46. *Constitution,* 1892, Sec. 13

Exercise of his authority to mediate in the affairs of the locals apparently consumed an increasing portion of the president's time and led to attempts to reduce his burden of work. In the first place, it was decided to furnish him with aid in discharging some of his duties which were of a more routine nature. Although, as we have seen, the Molders had originally stipulated that, "The President shall have no clerk," the convention, in 1886, finally relented and generously resolved that, "The President shall have a clerk, and, if required, he shall put an additional clerk to work, if absolutely necessary."[47] At the same time, the president was relieved of his routine financial tasks and, more important, the convention provided for a second full-time, paid official, the national secretary. Thus, in this president-led union, the elevation of the national secretary could be traced in part to the increase in the non-secretarial functions of the president.

Furthermore, it would appear that the office of secretary owed a measure of whatever prestige was attached to it to the higher office of president. For some national presidents had served as secretaries, an apprenticeship which doubtless prepared them well for the positions which they later attained. Martin Fox, who served as president of the Molders from 1890 until 1903, when ill health obliged him to resign, had begun his professional career in the national union as the clerk of a previous president and later (in 1886) became the first national secretary of his union. In the Potters' Brotherhood, the two presidents whose combined tenures extended from 1903 to 1922 had previously served as secretaries.[48] Of the eighteen unsalaried presidents of the Bricklayers between 1865 and 1900, two had been secretaries before serving as president, and one president had been vice secretary for one year. The Bricklayers, however, were a secretary-led union, and it is interesting that Secretary Lewis Carpenter, during whose term the office of secretary attained pre-eminence within the union's executive, should have reversed the apprentice-ship routine which we have been discussing, for he served three years as president before becoming international secretary.

In addition to relieving their president of the secretarial duties which he had originally assumed, the Molders sought to provide him with aid in his task of organizing local unions and assisting them in the performance of many of their vital activities. In 1878, the president and the executive board were given "full power to send out one or more organizers; if in their judg-ment it is necessary, they shall have power to fix compensation of organizers." The president himself was designated chief organizer and, in that capacity, was charged with "see(ing) that every locality capable of maintaining a Union is attended to, and a thorough and systematic effort . . . made to organize them."[49] It was not intended, however, that the president become

47. *Constitution*, 1886.
48. David A. McCabe, *National Collective Bargaining in the Pottery Industry* (Balti-more: Johns Hopkins, 1932), pp. 59–60.
49. *Constitution*, 1878, Art. I; 1888, Art. IV.

a sedentary overseer of his corps of organizers, for it was further provided that, "He shall visit in person, if practicable, such locality" for the purpose either of organizing or of aiding any local "involved in trouble in regard to prices or of principle." In the latter event, indeed, "it shall be the imperative duty of the President to visit said Union in person." Nevertheless, "should personal attendance be impossible, he shall instruct such other officer of this Union as he may deem advisable to act as his deputy . . ." To this end, the vice president was made assistant organizer, and the official specification of his duties in that capacity reveals the importance of the traveling official:

As Assistant Organizer he shall be subordinate to the President; he shall proceed to any section of the country designated by the former and use every effort to organize such localities to which he may be assigned; he shall visit all Unions on his route for the purpose of inspecting their workings and instructing the officers of said Unions; he shall report weekly to the Secretary all matters of interest appertaining to his office as Organizer, and perform such other duties as may be assigned to him by the President and Executive Board. He shall devote his entire time to the duties herein specified, and for the faithful performance of said duties he shall receive the sum of $1,000 per year (payable monthly) and properly itemized traveling expenses.

By 1900, the international had four vice presidents and had commissioned them all for service in the field at the discretion of the executive board. In 1899, however, the convention, on the recommendation of the president, had decided not to increase the staff of organizers because it was believed that prevailing boom conditions, which inspired great local demand for their services could not be expected to continue indefinitely.[50]

These early traveling organizers were the forerunners of the modern international representative, and the emergence of this body of national officials undoubtedly enhanced the prestige of the national union among the locals. For, while the latter were clearly reluctant to cede their jealously guarded autonomy to the former, they were quick to welcome the visiting experts when they were in trouble. These early international "representatives," following the example of Sylvis, devoted themselves to bargaining and strike-leading as well as to organizing. It will be recalled that, "trouble in regard to prices or of principle" was sufficient to require the visit of the president, or an officer deputized by him, to the locality afflicted. In 1892, the Molders' president told the convention that, "While the Vice-Presidents of the Union include organizing among their labors, it would be a misnomer to style them organizers, for they are chiefly the trained negotiators of the Organization, whose wide knowledge and tact are invaluable and indispensable aids in its work."[51] The Bottle Blowers also testified to the popularity of the services

50. *Proceedings,* 1902, p. 620; 1899, p. 10.
51. *Proceedings,* 1902, p. 620.

rendered by one of their traveling vice-presidents, a man who later became a most distinguished president of their association, when the convention of 1895 resolved

That it is the sense of this Convention that the itinerancy (sic) of Vice President Hayes during the past season was productive of the utmost good to our Association, organized labor, and the course of human liberty, progress and enlightenment, and we unanimously endorse and approve of his labors.[52]

The early organizers also increased the power of the executive within the national union. In the first place, they were made responsible to the president at whose discretion they acted, for they were originally regarded as an extension of the executive arm. Furthermore, the power of the president and the executive board to appoint paid officers on an *ad hoc* basis was not without political significance, since patronage has traditionally been the material with which political fences are mended and bureaucracies erected. Indeed, the reluctance of the Molders and other national unions to assume a heavy fixed cost of organizing played an indirect part in the increase in the power of national office, for most of the early national unions preferred to have their official "traveling" performed on an *ad hoc* basis by temporary officers hired by the president or the executive board rather than to maintain a staff of permanent salaried officials elected by the convention.[53]

Finally, insofar as they were able to translate into practice powers which the convention had formally granted to the president, the traveling officers augmented both the authority of the national executive and that of the national union. Such powers included the granting of charters, the inspection of local finances, the suspension of local unions, and, in some unions, the approval of strike petitions as a prerequisite to the dispensing of financial aid from the national treasury. When the Molders in 1878 authorized the president and executive board to send out and fix the compensation of organizers they also provided that the president have the power "to call in old charters in localities where officers are either incompetent to discharge their duties, or negligent in the performing of the same, or when the Union fails to be self-sustaining, and grant new charters, *upon the recommendations of the organizers.*"[54]

Control over Strikes and Control over Organizers

In the case of the Molders and the Bottle Blowers the hospitality with which the president and his emissaries were received by embattled local unions foreshadowed the willingness of the latter ultimately to cede a great measure of authority to their national unions. This authority consisted in the

52. *Proceedings*, 1895, p. 62.
53. Glocker, *Government of Unions*, p. 183.
54. *Constitution*, 1878, Art. I, Sec. 7. My italics.

creation of national strike funds and systems of collective bargaining on a national scale, directed by the parent unions. Both of these unions operated in jurisdictions which were characterized by the presence of nationwide product markets. Not all national unions, even in national product markets, were able to achieve a measure of control over the economic activities of their local affiliates which approximated the authority exercised by the Molders and Bottle Blowers, of course, but in general where the national union increased its control over the striking activities of the local unions, the authority of the chief executive within the national union was enlarged. The Bricklayers and the Carpenters, both of which operated in the local product markets which characterized the construction industry, had been led by secretaries until the turn of the century. Later they made their presidents their chief executive officers in fact as well as in name, and the president's rise to prominence followed the extension of national control over strikes in each case. It might be noted that the extension of national control over strikes often involved the chief executives of these local market unions in extensive travel, so that, as in the case of the Molders and Bottle Blowers, the president's prominence increased with his mobility. The extension of national strike control was instrumental in increasing the size and authority of the executive branch of the national union partly because it resulted in an enlargement of its duties and because it frequently obliged the national executive literally to be in more than one place at the same time.

The Carpenters, as we know, initially designated their secretary as their only paid national officer. Authority to send out organizers was vested in an executive board consisting of the president, three vice-presidents, secretary, treasurer, and three trustees. The president, vice-presidents and secretary were elected by the convention, but the treasurer and the trustees were selected by the local union or unions in the headquarters city. The executive board was also empowered to approve petitions for strike benefits by local unions, but its decision was subject to reversal by a majority vote of all members voting in a referendum held for the purpose. At this time, each local union was required to divert 10 per cent of its monthly receipts to a strike fund which could "not be used or appropriated for any other purpose." However, such funds remained in the custody of the local unions themselves.[55]

In 1886, the executive board was reorganized so as to increase the authority of the "governing branch." The number of members of the board who were selected by the headquarters local or locals was increased to five; the number of vice-presidents, who were chosen by the convention, was reduced to two and they were not made members of the board; the treasurer and the secretary both lost their power to vote on the board; and the president lost his membership thereon. Thus the new board consisted of seven members; of these, two—the secretary and the treasurer—were nonvoting members, and

55. *Constitution*, 1881, Arts. II and III; Art. XI.

the remaining five were voting members who were chosen by the local or locals in the headquarters city.

At the same time the power of the executive branch was strengthened and the spheres of authority of both the board and the president were redefined. The referendum vote required to overrule board decisions disallowing petitions for strike aid was increased from a simple majority to two-thirds of those voting. The president (as yet an unpaid official), in conjunction with the board, was authorized to declare any authorized strike "at an end, so far as the financial aid of the Brotherhood is concerned . . . when satisfied that a strike should cease." Finally, the board was authorized to appoint deputy organizers in each state and territory on the recommendation of the local unions—but only "when sanctioned by the General President." Presumably the president was regarded as the chief organizer, since reference was made to the appointment of deputies.

In 1888, however, the organizing duties were assigned to seven general vice-presidents in different geographic districts. Each vice-president had to belong to a local union in the district which he served; he was paid by the general executive board when on duty ("except when acting under orders of a Local Union"); and he reported to the general secretary. At the next convention (1890), the position of the secretary was further strengthened when he, instead of the board (which was once more reconstituted), was empowered to appoint the district organizers. The number of vice-presidents was reduced to two and they were relieved of organizing duties. However, the secretary's appointments were made subject to the approval of the president. At the same time, the secretary and the treasurer (the latter was now elected by the convention instead of the headquarters local) "in conjunction" were authorized to pass upon all rules and by-laws adopted by local unions and to decide all grievances and appeals, subject to appeal to the new board.[56] Finally, in connection with any local strike situation, the board could authorize the Secretary to

deputize some suitable member to proceed at once to the scene of the difficulty, with power to select three members of the Local Union or District Council involved, to go with him and visit the employers, and endeavor to adjust the trouble by negotiation or arbitration. Failing in this the Deputy shall telegraph or report in writing to the General Secretary a concise and full statement of the difficulty, his efforts at settlement, the answers of the employers, and also his recommendations as to what course should be pursued.[57]

Thus, the deputies of the Carpenters' secretary performed functions very similar to those of the deputies of the Molders' president. Indeed, to all intents and purposes, the Carpenters vested in their secretary the same powers which

56. *Constitution,* 1886, Art. XX, Art. XXVII; 1888, Art. XXIV; 1890, Sec. 30, Sec. 28.
57. *Constitution,* 1890, Sec. 131.

other American unions had assigned to their presidents. In so doing, they followed the British pattern of a union which, after seeking unsuccessfully to vest the authority to determine policy in an amateur executive board selected by a "governing branch," finally granted the power in question to a full-time secretary who originally had been intended to serve in a routine capacity. Nevertheless, the parallel was not maintained, for the Brotherhood ultimately became a president-led union. It is difficult to determine to what extent this change was induced by Secretary McGuire's defalcation, but, traumatic or not, that episode occurred in 1902, and the record reveals instances of transfer of duties from secretary to president before that date. Indeed, two important events which had occurred before this transfer of powers—and which could well have been of some importance in producing it—were, first, the elimination, in 1890, of all provision for appeal to referendum vote by local unions from adverse rulings by the executive board on strike benefits, and, second, the establishment, two years later, of a central "Protective Fund," "which shall be forwarded monthly to the General Secretary until said fund amounts to the sum of $12,000, when the General Secretary shall instruct the Locals to retain said fund in their treasuries until again called for by the General Secretaries in case it may be required at headquarters."[58]

The creation of the central fund increased the duties of the secretary, and he was authorized "to employ his own clerical assistance at reasonable salary" —just as the Molders' president had been permitted to do in 1886. Thus the analogy between the Carpenters' secretary and the presidents of other American unions held; and it continued to hold when, in the following convention, his position was strengthened through the merger of the offices of secretary and treasurer. At the same time, it was provided that a fixed percentage of all funds received by the secretary-treasurer be used exclusively as a strike reserve; no strike funds at all were to be retained in local treasuries.[59] Furthermore, the secretary-treasurer was then authorized to render decisions on all appeals and grievances, subject to appeal to the convention. This power was transferred from the president and vice-presidents. Thus the Carpenters' secretary acquired powers which elsewhere were reserved to the president, and his resemblance to a president appeared to be more striking than ever.

In other unions, however, when the president became unable to discharge all his obligations under the constitution, his judicial functions were frequently transferred to the secretary on a *de facto* basis in order to permit the chief executive to travel about the jurisdiction on missions of mercy or discipline. If the Carpenters had continued to vest in their secretary-treasurer the power which other national unions had lodged in their presidents, one might expect that McGuire would have granted first priority to his roving duties, if necessary, at the expense of his newly acquired fiscal and judicial tasks. Instead,

58. *Constitution*, 1892, Sec. 59.
59. *Constitution*, 1892, Sec. 31; 1894, Secs. 15, 26, 59.

the supervision of local accounts—a traveling assignment the importance of which was increased by the creation of the central fund—was reserved to the general president who was authorized "personally or by deputy, (to) examine all books, papers and financial accounts of any Local Union or District Council summarily, or when he may deem it necessary."[60]

Moreover, the president's long-standing authority to declare an authorized strike at an end "so far as the financial aid of the United Brotherhood is concerned" now assumed increased significance, although the convention decided that it should be shared with the general executive board. Furthermore, in 1898, the power to decide grievances and appeals, which had been granted to the secretary only four years before, was taken from him and conferred upon the president. Finally, in 1900, the power to appoint organizers (on the recommendation of any district council or local union) was conferred upon the president. And for the first time, it was provided that the general president should receive regular compensation.[61] Thus, as the functions of the national union increased, the activities of the national executive expanded to the point where they could no longer be discharged by only one full-time officer, and the more important powers of office were taken from the secretary of the United Brotherhood and vested in the president. The major difference between the experience of the Carpenters and that of most other unions was that in the latter the president was the first full-time officer and that his more routine duties were abandoned in favor of supervision and organization of locals, while in the former the secretary was the first full-time officer and that the duties which were taken from him were those which the presidents of the other organizations retained.

The emergence of the Bricklayers' president as chief executive was also associated with a genuine increase in power by the national union itself. At first, the president of this union shared with the vice-president the "executive power to determine all questions and all applications for assistance that shall be laid before them by the Presidents of subordinate unions." Strike benefits were financed by *ad hoc* assessments which were initiated by the locals' presidents following the approval of petitions by the national executive. This authority was withdrawn the following year, however, when ratification of petitions was made to depend upon a referendum of the membership of the affiliated local unions. It was also provided, in the first edition of the Bricklayers' constitution, that the president "shall have power to visit subordinate Unions, and inspect their proceedings, either personally or by deputy, and require a compliance with the laws, rules and usages of this union." This authority was not rescinded, but President White apparently was reluctant to travel about with no means of support, for he told the convention of 1867 that, "to increase our organization I would recommend that our next Presi-

60. *Constitution*, 1894, Sec. 20.
61. *Constitution*, 1896; 1898, Sec. 23; 1900, Sec. 24.

dent be allowed a salary and also a certain amount to pay his travelling
expenses, so that he can visit any section of the country where, in his judgment he may think fit, for the purpose of organizing unions." [62]

The convention refused to adopt the president's recommendation; and
the action which it did finally take could hardly have stimulated executive
travel, for it added to the section quoted above, which authorized the president to visit local unions, the phrase, "provided the expense incurred is
defrayed by the local union." Thus, the only important functions of the
Bricklayers' early national executive were clerical, and these were performed
by the secretary. This left little for the president to do, for, as the incumbent
himself frankly stated,

The work of the President for the past year has not been very severe, owing to
our worthy Secretary, who has always been willing to do my corresponding, and
relieved me all that lay in his power. [63]

The worthy secretary was well occupied, however, since the president, as we
know, reported that "it was well for the International Union that the Secretary was not working at his trade."

The president, at the outset, was empowered "to appoint a deputy for
each union to supervise the working of his respective union." The president,
however, was apparently restricted in the exercise of this power to appoint, for
the deputy for a particular local was also a member of that local. These
deputies, nevertheless, were supposed to function as representatives of the
international, since it was provided that

A subordinate union violating its Constitution, the deputy of said union shall
report such violation to the President of the I.U.; if he deems the violation of
sufficient cause for suspension of said union, he shall notify said union of his
decision assigning the reason thereof. [64]

But the executive authority of the international was not strengthened by this
provision, for the president of the Bricklayers did not possess the power—
which was granted to many of his colleagues in other organizations—to suspend local unions. He was authorized merely to submit the case to a referendum of the locals:

Should said union persist in the violation, the President of the I.U. shall issue a
circular through the Secretary of the I.U. to each subordinate union under the
jurisdiction of the I.U., stating clearly the case. The subordinate unions shall act
upon it at their next regular or special meeting; and should two-thirds of the

62. *Proceedings,* 1867, p. 13; see also *Constitution,* 1867, Art. XII; 1868, Art. XII;
1867, Art. IV.
63. *Proceedings,* 1867, p. 10.
64. *Constitution,* 1867, Art. XV, Sec. 1 and 2. In violating "its" own constitution,
a local presumably violated the law of the International, for the former had to be approved by the president of the International Union.

subordinate unions decide that the offense merits suspension, the President of the I.U. shall upon receiving notice of such decision from the Secretary of the I.U. declare said union suspended until the action of the I.U. can be had on the same.

Later (in 1876), the local deputies in each locality were also instructed to enforce another provision of the constitution, which required that all locals in the same community "establish a uniform rate of wages, together with rules and regulations under which all can work in harmony; their action to be subject at all times to the approval of the Judiciary of the National Union, acting in conformity with this Constitution."[65] This implied increase in the executive authority of the national body was more nominal than real, however, for the early presidents had taken care not to offend the local unions in their choice of deputies. In 1868, the president assured the convention that, "I have endeavored in selecting deputies to organize new unions to comply with the request of those organized . . . ," and in the following year he repeated this statement, adding that, "Some may have thought me partial in the selection, but it was because they were not acquainted with the circumstances of the case."[66] But the locals apparently were not reassured, and, in 1876—at the same time that the deputies were assigned to policing the coördination of district wage policies, the president's power to appoint the deputies was terminated. The deputy of each local was "nominated" by its delegates to the national convention, subject only to the approval of the national president.[67] The result was unfortunate from the viewpoint of the national officers, for, in 1890, we find the president complaining of the calibre of the local deputies:

It seems Subordinate Unions or the Delegates to Convention, name and recommend men to the Executive Board for this position without taking into consideration whether the man is capable or qualified in any way to fill the position, and without taking into consideration the importance of the office. I will say now to all Subordinate Unions: you had better have a poor set of officers all through your local offices, *than have an incompetent Deputy*. This office should be filled by a man as well posted in I.U. law as any officer on your Executive Board, or at least one, who, after being appointed, would interest himself enough to study I.U. law, and may be able to give his Union any information asked for, and be able to back up his opinion with good proof from the I.U. constitution. If this was carried out a vast amount of correspondence with your executive officers might be done away with. The idea seems to prevail with some Deputies that their chief duty is to take little trips and install new unions, and that duty is very poorly done at times.[68]

The locals, however, determined to maintain control over the officers who were supposed to be the instruments of national authority; and the following

65. *Constitution*, 1876, Art. XV, Sec. 3 and Art. XII, Sec. 8.
66. *Proceedings*, 1868, p. 13; 1869, p. 11.
67. *Constitution*, 1876, Art. XV.
68. *Proceedings*, 1890, p. V. (Italics in original).

year the constitution was changed to provide for the election of deputies by the membership of their respective locals, subject to the approval of the international president.[69]

Meanwhile, the national executive was attempting to secure the convention's assent to some important changes. In the first place, it was urged that the president be made a full-time salaried officer and that he serve as chief organizer of the union. The first president, after noting that his work had not been "severe," made the following proposal to the convention of 1867:

> to increase our organization I would recommend that our next President be allowed a salary and also a certain amount to pay his travelling expenses, so that he can visit any section of the country where, in his judgment he may think fit, for the purpose of organizing unions.[70]

In his later requests for increased executive compensation, Secretary O'Dea, as we know, was successful only in obtaining increased pay for his own office. The convention refused to create a second salaried official; in 1887, for example, it rejected the recommendation of its finance committee that the "office of President be made a salaried office, at the rate of $200 per year."[71]

Another objective of the Bricklayers' leaders was the creation of a central strike fund. As early as 1875, the national union was urged by President White to establish a "permanent Relief Fund, always, and instantly available." When, seven years later, Secretary Carpenter reiterated this recommendation, the Constitutional Committee, while agreeing "upon its merits," found, "upon consultation with others," that a strike fund "was wholly impracticable at the present time." A similar request by O'Dea, in 1884, was also turned down, but in order to expedite strike aid, the convention did provide that each local levy a *per capita* assessment of ten cents, to be held in its treasury as a strike fund "and used for no other purpose."[72]

This measure fell considerably short of providing for a central fund, for, in the first place, it did not require that the assessment be made more than once, and, second, the funds accumulated remained in the local treasuries. Nevertheless, it did strengthen the international's power to come to the aid of its striking locals. Furthermore, the advance levy was raised from ten cents to one dollar in 1887, and at the 1891 Convention, it was provided that, "On or before the first day of May, 1891, each Subordinate Union shall forward to the Treasurer of the B. and M.I.U. the sum of twenty-five (25) cents per member, the fund so raised to be used as a contingent fund for the support of any Union on an authorized strike or lockout." Thus, some moneys were finally accumulated by the central organization, although, as the 1894 conven-

---

69. *Constitution*, 1891, Art. XV.
70. *Proceedings*, 1867, p. 13.
71. *Proceedings*, 1887, p. 138. Also, *Proceedings*, 1886, pp. 50 and 109.
72. *Proceedings*, 1875, p. 8; 1882, p. 47; 1884, pp. 15, 63, and 71.

tion took pains to point out, payment was to be made thereafter only by each local "when installed. This is not to apply to Unions who have already paid." Later, this procedure was dropped in favor of a requirement that each local union assess every newly initiated member twenty-five cents, "the said tax being exclusively for the I.U. Reserve Fund, and when collected shall each quarter be forwarded to the Treasurer of the I.U."

Thus, although the executive officers of the national union failed to secure the provision of a central strike fund financed by a monthly assessment on all members, the ability of the international to render prompt aid was increased. As a result, international approval of strikes became more important to the locals petitioning for aid. Since international approval consisted in a favorable referendum vote, most petitions were approved, for any local union, its eye on the future, was hesitant to deny the request of an embattled sister organization.[73] And the executive board was powerless to remedy the situation, since it was obliged to accept the facts alleged in the petition at face value. According to O'Dea,

> The great fault lies with ourselves—with our own laws—for under these laws we are obliged to recognize any bill of grievance that may be sent to the Executive Board provided it is made out in what is termed the regular form. The circumstances may not be as they are represented, nevertheless we are forced to accept it. . . . the Board is just as ignorant of the state of affairs as the Subordinate Unions are. Whether a strike is legitimate or not, or whether it is beneficial or meritorious, the Board cannot go behind the returns as is stated in the bill of grievances as presented, and they have no alternative but to print and send out such bill, unless some positive proof, backed up with evidence, was presented, on which the Board could delay matters pending an investigation.

The power to investigate was granted to the board in 1896:

> All Unions, before declaring a strike, shall make application to the Executive Board, and said Board shall investigate, or deputize someone to investigate the matter, and report the result of the investigation to the Executive Board, before it is submitted to the Subordinate Unions, and the Executive Board shall report the result of such investigations to the Subordinate Unions for their final action.[74]

It is interesting that the executive was not made to rely upon the services of the regular deputies, who were elected by their respective local unions, for information concerning the facts in labor disputes. According to the provision quoted above, the board was instructed either to investigate the matter in person or to "deputize someone." In 1897, it was specifically provided that, on receipt of a local union's application, the executive board send a "Special Deputy" to the scene of action and that it submit his recommendation to the

73. *Proceedings*, 1887, p. 172; 1891, p. 176; 1894, p. 27; *Constitution*, 1897, Art. IX, Sec. 3; *Proceedings*, 1893, pp. 25–26.

74. *Constitution*, 1896, Art. IX.

locals for their final action.[75] Furthermore, the power to appoint all special deputies and to define their duties and their powers was vested in the president alone. They would be appointed at the discretion of the board "for the purpose of organizing or installing new Unions and for the investigation of strikes and lockouts or other special work." The deputy so appointed "shall hold himself in readiness at all times to perform any service or go on any mission that may be required by the President of the I.U."[76]

Thus the new deputy, appointed by the president, in part supplanted the old deputy, who was "elected" by and under the control of the local union, as the true representative of the international union. We recall that, in the opinion of the international secretary, the deputies whom the locals had elected were hardly outstanding as international representatives; the same official was able to furnish a much more favorable character report on the special officers whose appointments were controlled by the executive of the international:

> During the year the Executive Board has been required on several occasions to avail themselves of the services of special deputies to investigate matters of serious moment which tended to cause a breach of discipline, or create trouble of an International character. In all such cases the Board was fortunate in selecting good representatives who gave most faithful service and were highly successful in settling the questions at issue in their several missions, and thus again sustaining our position of several years past, that through personal investigation and arbitration we can overcome the questions of issue that may arise between Unions and their employers, and thus avoid costly and long-drawn strikes . . .[77]

At the same time that the president was authorized to appoint special deputies, the powers of the national executive (namely, the executive board, which consisted of all the international officers) were broadly described in the new constitution of 1897 as embracing

> . . . the *entire* control of *all* executive business of this Union, when not in session, *viz.,* all grievances relating to and all strikes and lockouts, the settlement of all disputes between bosses or exchanges and members of this or Subordinate Unions, and the concurrence in the appointment of *all* special deputies or committees. They shall have full and complete control of all strikes . . .[78]

Now "full and complete control" was a somewhat ambiguous concept, since the national executive's newly acquired powers were merely investigatory, the authority to approve strike petitions remaining in the hands of the local unions. But it was clarified when, in 1903, the strike referendum was eliminated. It was then provided that, upon submission by a local union of a

75. *Constitution*, 1897, Art. XVIII.
76. *Constitution*, 1897, Art. I.
77. *Proceedings*, 1897, p. 163.
78. *Constitution*, 1897, Art. I. (Italics in original).

"bill of grievance," the executive board should dispatch a special deputy to the scene of action to investigate and report the facts and his recommendations. If the special deputy's report supported the allegations in the local's bill and if his report was approved by the executive board, the special deputy was then authorized to "order a strike." If, on the other hand, the board disapproved its deputy's report, its members were obliged personally to visit the scene of trouble and, after investigation, either sanction or refuse permission to call a strike. In either event, "The decision of the Executive Board in the premises shall be final."[79]

Even before the hand of the national executive was further strengthened by the legislation of 1903, however, the authority of the president had been substantially enhanced. (Incidentally, most of the changes which were responsible for the rise of the national union's president and his subsequent position of dominance within the executive branch, were drafted and advocated by Secretary O'Dea near the end of his tenure in office.) The president was relieved of the routine work of granting charters to new locals and furnishing them with books and seals; this work was transferred to the secretary. Furthermore, the president was authorized to appoint an assistant secretary. The president was also empowered on his own initiative to suspend any local for any offense reported by its deputy (that is, the deputy whom its members had elected), subject to confirmation by the president. Formerly, the president could do nothing more than report the case to the other locals who alone, through referendum vote, could effect suspension of a sister affiliate. At the same time, it was provided that the president "shall examine all subordinate laws or rules, and see that they conform to I.U. laws before they meet with his approval." Finally, the president's authority to travel to local unions in order to secure compliance with international law was strengthened by the omission of the ancient proviso that, "the expense incurred is defrayed by the local Union."

All these changes occurred as a result of the constitutional revision of 1897. In 1902, the convention acknowledged the increased powers and responsibility of the presidency by voting its incumbent a regular annual salary for the first time. And in 1904, the president's position as chief executive was solidified by a series of provisions which subordinated the vice-presidents to the president. The first vice-president was to be stationed at international headquarters and to act as special deputy whenever requested to do so by the president "to whom he is at all times subject." The second vice-president was also required to act as special deputy at the discretion of the president. Furthermore, provision was made for the designation of two additional vice-presidents whose duties were to be defined by the executive board. Thus, although these "deputies" were not appointed by the president, they were subject to his control as absolutely as if they had been his own appointees.

79. *Constitution*, 1897, Art. XVII.

The process whereby the president succeeded the secretary as chief executive officer in the Bricklayers' union differed from the procedure adopted by the Carpenters' Brotherhood. The Carpenters' president owed his eminence largely to a shift of authority within the national executive; he acquired certain powers and duties which formerly had been granted to the secretary. The increased authority of the Bricklayers' president, on the other hand, was not achieved at the expense of the secretary of that organization; as in the case of the Molders and other unions which had been president-led from their inception, it came as a direct result of a fresh acquisition of power by the national union itself.

Nevertheless, it is doubtful whether this difference was significant in any basic sense, for the transfer within the executive branch of the Brotherhood was associated with an increase in the authority of that national organization similar to that which the Bricklayers experienced. Indeed, certain similarities in the two cases are more interesting than the divergence noted above. In both unions, the secretary was chief executive when the authority exercised by the national over the affiliated local unions was slight if not negligible. In both cases, the records fail to reveal acknowledgment by the locals of their need for the type of activity in which the traveling executives of other organizations engaged. Thus, although Sylvis' heroic services as the traveling representative—or, more accurately, the personification—of his national union must not be minimized, one should note that the Molders did recognize his service inasmuch as they provided a salary for their president. But when President White, only a few years later, requested the Bricklayers to provide him with funds for a similar mission, his petition was denied. As a result of their locals' apparent lack of interest in the services typically represented by national representatives, the so-called deputies of the early Bricklayers' and Carpenters' national organizations were controlled by the locals whom they were, in some instances, supposed to police. Although supposedly subject to presidential approval, the deputies of the Bricklayers' were "nominated" and later "elected" by their respective local unions. The state deputies of the Carpenters were appointed by the executive board, but the board followed the recommendations of the locals in each state jurisdiction; and these deputies were later succeeded by regional vice-presidents.

In both the Carpenters' and the Bricklayers' unions the shift in emphasis from secretary to president was symptomatic of increased control by the national body over the strike activities of its locals which, in turn, followed the former's acquisition of financial resources that were made available to local unions whose strikes had been approved by the appropriate national authority. With the increased capacity of these national unions to render aid there came a corresponding increase in the authority of their executives to pass upon local petitions for such aid. As a result of the increased authority vested in the national executive, the presidents of both unions were assigned increased duties, which ultimately resulted in their appointment as full-time, paid officials in their own right. Another consequence was the strengthening of the national's ability to ensure that the locals obey national law, for now expulsion or suspension from the national union meant potential deprivation of strike benefits. These increased powers of the national executive were vested in the president rather than the secretary. Still another prerogative of the president was the power to appoint deputies, for, since the national executive was authorized either to approve or disallow strike petitions, it was necessary that it be informed speedily and accurately of the facts in each case. At the same time, the power to employ deputies implemented the disciplinary control of the national union over its locals and widened its influence throughout the jurisdiction. Thus, as a result of the extension of national control over strikes, the presidents of these local market unions were able finally to select representatives of their own choosing.

In the Molders' and Bottle Blowers' unions, the emergence of the president as chief executive and of his corps of appointed deputies resulted from the awareness of the local unions, operating in national product markets, of the advantages to be obtained from the missionary work of the traveling representatives of the national union, as well as from the development of the national war chest. But this need for outside aid and control was not such a powerful stimulus to the local unions of Carpenters and Bricklayers, organized as they were in fairly distinct local product markets. In those unions, prior to the establishment of national strike funds, the primary activity of the executive, apart from clerical routine, was the exercise of their judicial power which, as we observed in Chapter 4, resulted from the recognized necessity of controlling the activities of traveling members—from the fact that the local labor markets involved were not nearly as isolated from one another as were the corresponding product markets.

Indicative of the attitude of the local market union was the repudiation by the Bricklayers' convention of O'Dea's attempted coup in 1900 whereby he had, on his own initiative, created the office of general organizer, filled it himself and departed on an organizing tour. Although the Bricklayers, three years earlier, had been willing to increase the authority of their executive branch in order to enable it more effectively to supervise the strike activities of the local unions, the convention was unwilling to finance an expansion of the executive for the purpose of organizing in nonunion localities. Confronted with O'Dea's *fait accompli,* it passed two resolutions, the first allowing bygones to be bygones, the second providing that what had gone by should not recur. The first resolution stated

that while the creation of the Office of Chief Organizer by the Executive Board is not clearly authorized by the Constitution, the Committee however after considering the matter most carefully and believing that the motive of the Executive Board was not the result of hasty action, but was dictated by a desire for the upbuilding of the B. and M.I.U.,

And taking into consideration the number of new Unions organized in sections heretofore barren of organization, thus adding materially to our fold and reviving renewed impetus and prestige to the B. and M.I.U.,

Resolved, we therefore concur in the action of a Chief Organizer for the remainder of the year 1900.[80]

The Committee on General Good, however, reported that it did "not agree" with President Klein, who created the office of chief organizer at O'Dea's instigation, and recommended that it be discontinued. This view was shared by the majority of delegates, and another motion was adopted unanimously to the effect, "that the Convention do not establish the office of chief organizer." The action of the convention can be interpreted as a repudiation of the retiring secretary, for the incumbent administration was unseated, and, in his report to the convention the year following, the new president congratulated the convention of 1900 on dispensing with the position of chief organizer as a needless expense.

To the record of the development of the executive in the Carpenters' and Bricklayers' unions one might add the experience of the Printers, as related by Barnett.[81] Although the Printers' executive was never characterized by long incumbencies in either major office, it followed the same pattern of development which was exhibited by the other two local market unions. Prior to provision for a central strike fund in 1885, "The only considerable expansion made in the functions of the National Union was an increase in its judicial activities"; and these activities consisted almost exclusively in deciding cases concerning traveling members. Some attention was given to the problem of organization; in 1882 the president appointed state and territorial deputies, but they were not paid officials. Two years later, the convention elected a chief organizer and paid him a salary of $1000. However, following the establishment of the strike fund, this office was eliminated and the president was directed to act as chief organizer. At the same time, the president and secretary were granted salaries for the first time in order to permit them to discharge the increased duties of office. But, although he was placed in charge of the organizing activities of the international in 1888, the president lost his power to appoint the organizers. The latter, representing districts instead of states and territories, were elected by the convention. This system proved unworkable. Since the delegates to the conventions selected district organizers from their own ranks, tenure in office was short; the incumbents, therefore, were not well qualified. At the same time, their duties increased in scope and complexity, for, as in the other unions discussed above, the Printers depended upon their organizers to investigate local strike situations after they had decided to maintain a central fund. As a result of this demand for expert negotiators and strike managers, the Printers finally followed the example of other organizations and granted their president the power to appoint salaried organizers on a full-time basis.

80. *Proceedings:* 1900, pp. 4–5, 44, 85, 225–226, 230, 109; 1901, p. 4.
81. Barnett, *The Printers,* pp. 66–67. See also pp. 33, 37, 61–62, 329–331.

CHAPTER NINE

THE CONVENTION

In both Britain and the United States acquisition of power by the early national unions frequently resulted in the enhanced authority of the executive within the national unions. In both countries, however, the unions sought to control their executive officers by vesting superior powers in a number of institutions which were immediately responsive to those sources from which the national organizations themselves derived their ultimate authority. Among these institutions was the convention of "delegates" or "representatives" from the affiliated locals. The representativeness of the early convention was indicated by the amount of discretionary authority granted to its delegates; the more representative the convention, the more rigidly "pledged" were the delegates to abide by the decisions of their constituents. Thus the Printers in this country at first provided that a constitutional amendment which had been proposed at one session could not be voted upon until the next;[1] the purpose was to give the locals sufficient time to consider the measure and instruct their delegates in accordance with their decisions. The Carpenters ruled that, "amendments or alterations must be submitted to the local unions at least two months before the Convention." The Glass Bottle Blowers, although permitting "any member" to "memorialize or petition the Annual or Special Sessions," insisted that, "Notice of the intended alterations must be made in writing to the President at least one month previous to the Annual Session; and the President shall notify all Branches that such alterations or amendments will be acted upon at the session."[2]

The British unionists, too, initially left very little to the discretion of their delegates when drafting constitutional law. However, it appears that their object differed from that of the Americans in one respect. The British were motivated primarily (according to the Webbs) by a desire to retain governing authority in the "voices" of the membership; the Americans, by the wish

1. George E. Barnett, *The Printers* (Cambridge, Mass.: American Economic Association, 1909), p. 62.
2. Carpenters' *Constitution*, 1881, Art. XII, Sec. 3; Glass Bottle Blowers' *Constitution*, 1892, Art. II, Sec. 9; Art. XII, Sec. 70.

to safeguard the powers originally held by the local unions. The latter position implied opposition to the extension of national authority; the former did not. It will be recalled that the British turned to what the Webbs called, "the elementary device of a written constitution" as "the most obvious check upon the predominant power of the salaried officials"[3] only after the device of the governing branch had failed to accomplish the same purpose. Now the governing branch, even if it rotated among the various locals, was at best representative of the sentiment of the individual members at large; it was not intended as a guardian of the parochial interests of the local unions. Hence it is no accident that the evolutionary process of national unionism in the United States failed to include a stage of serious experimentation with the governing branch. Where found in this country, the governing branch reflected a process of uncritical and unsuccessful importation from abroad, and, as in the case of the Carpenters, it existed along with rather than in place of the convention.

SYSTEMS OF REPRESENTATION

Another indication of the true concern of the Americans in the instructed convention was the principle underlying the systems of representation which were originally adopted. If the number of votes accorded to each local union had been in proportion to its membership, the convention would have been directly representative of the individual unionists themselves; but, if each local had received the same number of votes, the convention would have derived its real authority from the affiliated local organizations. Under the first system, equality among individual members for purposes of representation implied inequality among local unions of different sizes; under the second, or senatorial, system, equality among the local organizations implied unequal representation for members of different locals. Since the local unions were jealous of their independence, most of the early national conventions initially adopted the senatorial principle.

The first convention (in 1859) of the Molders' union was attended by one delegate from each of the participating locals; this practice was followed until 1863.[4] The Printers originally allowed each local union to be represented by three delegates each, each delegate receiving one vote.[5] The Bricklayers, at their first convention (1865), also provided that the number of delegates for each local be fixed at three, regardless of the size of the organization.[6] It was also intended that each representative be given one vote; this was in accordance with the original conception of the national union as an organization in which the delegates alone held personal membership. As

3. Sidney and Beatrice Webb, *Industrial Democracy* (London: Longmans, Green, new edition, 1911), p. 18.
4. Frank T. Stockton, *The International Molders Union of North America* (Baltimore: Johns Hopkins, 1921), p. 24.
5. Barnett, *The Printers*, p. 59.
6. *Constitution*, 1865, Art. II.

Barnett put it, "The Government of the National Union corresponded closely to the form of government to which the Printers had long been accustomed in their local unions—a meeting in which every member had a vote on all questions. . . ."

Now, if each local were allotted the same number of representatives, the fact that each representative was entitled to an equal voice in the convention's proceedings did not, theoretically, run counter to the principle of equal representation for all local unions. In practice, however, this principle was violated, for it was frequently impossible for locals—especially the smaller organizations—to send full delegations. The Bricklayers attempted to ensure maximum representation to their locals; in 1868, although their constitution affirmed the principle of allowing one vote to each regular representative, they provided that each local was entitled to three votes "without reference to the number of its representatives present."[7] Thus, as in the case of the decline of the ex-representative as a members of the national union, we find that, when the concept of the national union as an organization of individual delegates came into conflict with the concept of the national union as a federation of local unions, the prerogatives of the delegates were subordinated to the prerogatives of the organizations which they represented.[8]

As the national unions grew older, their conventions became more representative of the membership at large. Most of them abandoned the system of granting equal representation to all local unions, regardless of size.[9] The Printers held to the senatorial principle from 1852 to 1869; but the Molders abandoned it after a trial of four years (1859–1863), and the Bricklayers after only three (1865–1868). Some unions, like the Carpenters and the Glass Bottle Blowers, profited from the experience of the earlier national unions and provided from the outset that their larger locals be entitled to more delegates than the smaller ones. The record of the unions with which we have been primarily concerned is set forth in Table 7. In the case of the Molders, Printers, and Bricklayers, it covers the period between the elimination of equal representation for all locals and the end of the century; in the case of the Carpenters and Bottle Blowers, it begins with the founding of the national unions in question.

Aside from the fact, already mentioned, that all these unions decided to

7. *Constitution*, 1868, Art II.

8. The Bricklayers, however, might have preserved some of the early prerogatives of the delegates, for when the provision quoted above was amended in 1890, it read, "Each regular representative to the International Union is entitled to one vote; and *when a vote by Unions is taken,* each Union is entitled to three votes," etc. (Constitution, 1890, Art. II. Italics mine.) The italicized phrase suggests that two types of votes were taken, one by local unions, in which a representative might cast more than one vote if his local had not sent its full quota of delegates to the convention, and the other, by individual representatives, in which no delegate could cast more than one vote.

9. Theodore W. Glocker, *Government of American Trade Unions* (Baltimore: Johns Hopkins, 1913), p. 163.

TABLE 7

ALLOWED REPRESENTATION AT CONVENTIONS OF FIVE UNIONS

(1) Year	(2) Minimum No. of Members Required for 2 Delegates	(3) (2) ÷ 2	(4) Minimum No. of Members Required for 3 Delegates	(5) (4) ÷ 3	(6) Minimum No. of Members Required for 4 Delegates	(7) (6) ÷ 4	(8) Minimum No. of Members Required for 5 Delegates	(9) (8) ÷ 5	(10) (5) − (3)	(11) (7) − (5)	(12) (9) − (7)
1869[a]	101	50½	501	167	PRINTERS 1000	250	Max.: 4 delegates	—	116.5	83	—
1881[b]	101	50½	501	167	CARPENTERS 1000	250	Max.: 4 delegates	—	116.5	83	—
1868[c]	Min.: 3 delegates	—	—	—	BRICKLAYERS 800	200	1300	250	—	—	50
1891[d]	Min.: 3 delegates	—	—	—	500	125	750	150	—	—	25
1893[e]	Min.: 3 delegates	—	—	—	400	100	550	110	—	—	10

					Molders						
1863[f]	101	50½	301	100⅓	Max.: 3 delegates	—	—	—	49⅘	—	—
1876[g]	100	50	200	66⅔	300	75	400	80	16⅔	8⅓	5
1888[h]	151	75½	251	83⅔	351	87¾	451	$90\frac{1}{5}$	$8\frac{1}{5}$	$4\frac{1}{10}$	2½
					Glass Bottle Blowers						
1888[i]	35	17½	55	18⅓	75	18¾	95	19	⅘	½	¼
1892[j]	50	25	80	26⅔	110	27½	140	28	1⅔	⅘	½

[a] *Constitution*, 1869, Art. V:
Locals with 100 members or less—1 delegate
Locals with more than 100 and less than 500 members—2 delegates
Locals with more than 500 and less than 1,000 members—3 delegates
Locals with 1,000 or more members—4 delegates

[b] *Constitution*, 1881, Art. I: Same basis of representation as Printers.

[c] *Constitution*, 1868, Art. II: 3 representatives for any number of members in good standing up to 300 plus 1 additional representative or vote for each additional 500 members.

[d] *Constitution*, 1891, Art. II: 3 representatives for the first 250 members or less and 1 additional representative or vote for each additional 250 members.

[e] *Constitution*, 1893, Art. II: 3 representatives for the first 250 members or less and 1 additional representative for each additional 150 members.

[f] *Constitution*, 1863, Art. II:
Locals with less than 100 members—1 delegate
Locals with more than 100 and less than 300 members—2 delegates
Locals with more than 300 members—3 delegates

[g] *Constitution*, 1863, Art. II:
Locals with less than 100 members—1 delegate
Locals with 100 members—2 delegates
Locals with more than 100 members—1 additional delegate for every 100 members after the first 100.

[h] *Constitution*, 1888, Art. II:
Locals with 100 members or less—1 delegate
Plus 1 additional delegate for every 100 members after the first 100 or major fraction thereof.

Note: Between 1884 and 1886, delegates were elected by so-called District Unions, of which there was one in each state where there were three or more locals. (*Constitution*, 1886, Art. II.) However, an amendment to the Constitution, offered by the Connecticut State District, providing for a return to the old system of representation, was ratified by the locals. (*Proceedings*, 1888, pp. 10–11. See also Stockton, *Molders Union*, p. 24.)

[i] *Constitution*, 1888, Art. I, Sec. 6: One representative for every 20 members and a fraction of ¾ of 20, "provided this shall not be so construed as to debar any Local from representation having 10 members in good standing."

[j] *Constitution*, 1892, Art. II, Sec. 9: One representative for every 30 members and a fraction of ⅔ of 30 members. The minimum number of members in good standing required to qualify a local for 1 representative was lowered from 10 to 7.

allow their larger locals to be represented by more delegates than the smaller ones, what inferences are suggested by the data set forth in the table? In the first place, it is apparent that both the Molders and the Bricklayers moved in the direction of representation in proportion to membership during the periods under consideration. In the case of the Molders, this "progress" is revealed in columns 10, 11, and 12. These columns reveal the differences in the number of members per delegate in local unions, the membership of which is assumed to equal the minimum number of members required to entitle them to 2 (column 2), 3 (column 4), 4 (column 6), and 5 (column 8) delegates respectively. We are interested in whether a change in the system of representation narrowed the differences in the number of members per delegate between the larger and the smaller locals. In this connection, we note that, in the case of the Molders, the difference between a two-delegate and a three-delegate local with respect to the number of members per delegate declined from 49 4/5 in 1863 to 16 2/3 in 1876 and to 8 1/5 in 1888 (column 10). The difference between the four-delegate and the three-delegate local declined from 8 1/3 in 1876 to 4 1/10 in 1888 (column 11); and the difference between the five-delegate and the four-delegate union was reduced by half in the same period (column 12). Even more important was the elimination of the three-delegate maximum which had been enforced until 1876.

The Bricklayers' record reveals a similar trend in the narrowing of the differential between the five-delegate and the four-delegate local—from 50 in 1868, to 25 in 1891, to 10 in 1893. The reduction in the number of members per delegate in the four-delegate local (column 7) is also significant. The Bricklayers originally provided for three delegates for any number of members up to 300 plus one additional delegate for each additional 500 members; thus the maximum number of members per delegate in a three-delegate local was 100, while the minimum number of members per delegate in a four-delegate local was 200 (column 7). In 1891, this was changed to provide for three delegates for any number of members up to 250, with one additional delegate for each additional 250 members (footnote 15); now the maximum number of members per delegate in a three-delegate local fell to 83, but the minimum number of members per delegate in a four-delegate local was reduced to 125. The spread in members per delegate between the largest possible three-delegate local and the smallest possible four-delegate local was thus reduced from 100 to 42. It was further reduced in 1893, when one additional delegate was allowed for every 150 (instead of 250) members in excess of 250. The minimum number of members per delegate in a four-delegate local was reduced from 125 to 100 and, since the maximum number of members per delegate in a three-delegate local remained 83, the difference fell from 42 to 17. Thus a reduction in the per delegate load is significant of "progress" if it indicates a reduction of the difference between the maximum number of members required to qualify a local for representation by the minimum number of delegates and the minimum number of members required to entitle a local to the first additional delegate.

However, the table reveals failure to achieve a system of representation in exact proportion to numbers. If any union had established a single ratio of members to delegates, its per delegate load would not have increased with increases in the size of the local unions and its entries in columns 10, 11, and 12 would have been zero. On the contrary, all the unions examined experienced such increases in load. Furthermore, the great range of membership throughout which the number of delegates was set at a minimum (one delegate for the first 100 members) ensured underrepresentation of the medium-sized locals near the top of the bracket—that is, a local with 90 members had no more representation at the convention than one with 10 members. The Molders who, as we have noted, succeeded in reducing the load differential among locals with more than two delegates, actually discriminated against their smaller (although not their smallest) locals by raising the minimum number of members required for a second delegate in 1888 (column 2).[10] The Bottle Blowers, who most closely approached the zero limit in columns 10, 11, and 12, also increased the minimum number of members required for the first additional representative in their revision of 1892, and they further aggravated the situation of locals whose membership was just under that minimum by reducing the number of members required to qualify a local for one representative from 10 to 7. However, their minimum membership for the first additional delegate was greatly below the minima established by the others so that their very small locals did not have too disproportionate an advantage in representation.

Finally, we take note of the Printers and the Carpenters, whose development was arrested at an identical point which was considerably further removed from equiproportionate representation than any of the others. The Printers made only one move: from equal representation for all locals to the system described in Table 7, footnote a. The Carpenters, however, although they did not pass through the stage of equal representation for all locals, never did alter their initial system in the period studied. (Incidentally, it should be noted that the three unions in local market jurisdictions displayed appreciably less willingness to move in the direction of representation in proportion to membership than had the two organized in national markets, although the Bricklayers' progress was great enough to enable them to occupy a position midway between the two groups by the end of the century.)

A comprehensive survey by Glocker, who wrote in 1913, affords some basis for generalization of our findings.[11] Of a total of 123 national unions investi-

10. Stockton (*Molders Union*, p. 24) attributed this and subsequent changes which had the effect of increasing the per delegate load to the necessity for economy and to the need for keeping the size of the convention within manageable limits.

11. Glocker, *Government of Unions*, pp. 163–165.

gated, only 12 granted equal representation to all locals and of those 12, half were described as "young, decentralized associations," and 5 were railway brotherhoods whose local lodges were "of a more or less uniform size, since they do not embrace the workers in a certain locality, but those employed on a regular unit of the railway system." Fifty-six national unions were described as granting "representation proportional to membership"; however, according to the author, "The small local unions have still the advantage, since each society is allowed one delegate even though it have much fewer members than the maximum number which a single delegate may represent." Furthermore, in twenty-five unions, the "basis of representation increases as the delegates of a society increase in number," while the number of members per delegate decreased in only four cases. The basis of representation first increased and then decreased in two unions, while in only six did "each local union send one delegate who casts a number of votes proportional to the number of members he represents."

The foregoing suggests the presence of one or more forces which inhibited the development of the national convention as an institution which derived its authority from the membership at large rather than from relatively autonomous local groups. Furthermore, since one concomitant of "representation proportional to membership" was an increase in the voting power of the larger locals relative to that of the smaller unions, one might expect that one of the forces retarding the development of the convention consisted in the opposition of the small locals. Granted that any local, regardless of size, was reluctant to entrust its fate to a group of deputies of which its own representatives would invariably constitute a minority, changing the system of representation from one based on the senatorial principle to one based upon membership was bound to increase the smaller locals' opposition to nationalization at the same time that it reduced the hesitancy of the larger and now better represented groups. And, since most of the locals in a national union were small (although a large portion of the membership might have been concentrated in a few locals in the large cities), resistance to proposed revision of the basis of representation was frequently effective. Thus the larger locals probably owed whatever concession they did win to the high valuation which the smaller locals placed upon continued affiliation with their larger sister organizations.

After 1868, the Bricklayers rebuffed four attempts by the larger locals to make representation in conventions more proportionate to membership,[12] before adopting the change in 1891 which is discussed in Table 7, footnote d. One of these abortive plans, which contemplated one delegate for locals with up to two hundred members, two for two hundred, three for three hundred, and one additional delegate for each additional three hundred members, was

12. *Proceedings,* 1872, p. 7; 1882, p. 46; 1886, p. 102; 1889, p. 23, 95.

proposed by a large New York City local with 1038 members in good standing. In reporting adversely upon it, the Committee on Constitution noted that

If our representation is to be determined by mere numerical strength, a combination of two or three of the first-class cities would be enabled to dictate the policy of all the Unions now in existence. New York City alone would have the combined influence of from twelve to fifteen other cities who can afford but one small Union each. Such a measure, therefore, would be manifestly unjust. . . .

Brother Kenny's amendment would give to No. 4 New York one additional delegate, making five votes, seven Unions would retain their present representations of three each, five Unions would lose one delegate each and twenty-two Unions would lose two delegates each. . . . Thus it will be seen that but one Union would be benefited, seven Unions would not be affected, five Unions would lose five delegates, and twenty-two Unions would lose forty-four delegates, making a net total loss of forty eight delegates on present representation. Should such a change be made, it would, in our judgment, prove objectionable to a great majority of the local Unions, and be attended by the most serious consequences, introducing, as it would, dissension and discord, thereby imperiling our existence as a National organization. For that reason we decline to recommend any change.[13]

FREEING THE DELEGATES

In addition to revision of the basis of representation, a greater degree of independence allowed to the individual delegates was required in order to bring the national convention to maturity. It will be recalled that the Bottle Blowers, Printers, and Molders had sought originally to pledge their delegates by insisting that sufficient notice of proposed constitutional changes be provided so that the local unions might be able to instruct their representatives in advance. The Bottle Blowers adhered to this method, but, as Glocker observed, most of the national unions were obliged to abandon their early attempts to bind the convention in this manner. Since a convention of instructed delegates precluded the granting of facilitating concessions on the floor, the system proved unworkable.[14] The Bricklayers, like the Bottle Blowers, provided that the constitution could be amended only at conventions and that a vote of two-thirds of the delegates present was required, but, unlike the Bottle Blowers, they did not require that notice of proposed amendments be submitted to the locals in advance of action by the convention.[15]

SUBSTITUTING THE REFERENDUM

Unpledged delegates, however, did not make free conventions. Instructing the delegates was only one method of denying power to the convention; there remained the alternatives of removing certain types of activity from the

13. *Proceedings*, 1882, p. 46.
14. Glocker, *Government of Unions*, p. 211.
15. *Constitution*, Bricklayers, 1867, Art. XXI, Sec. 2; *Constitution*, Glass Bottle Blowers, 1892, Art. XII, Sec. 70.

competence of the convention or of requiring ratification of its decisions by a higher authority. In either instance, the convention was supplanted, in varying degrees, by the referendum. The Carpenters ultimately adopted both methods. At first they had provided that their constitution could be amended only by a two-thirds vote of the convention delegates and only if the proposed alterations had been submitted to the local unions at least two months before the convention was held. In 1886, they dropped the requirement of advance submission to the local unions, but provided in its stead that amendments which had gained the necessary two-thirds vote at the convention be submitted, within ten days following the adjournment of the convention, "to the local unions for their approval or rejection." A two-thirds vote of the membership voting was necessary to "sustain" the action of the convention. In 1890, a simple majority vote of the delegates was declared sufficient to report an amendment out of the convention, but the latter body was now required to share its initiatory authority with the general executive board which was given the power to "recommend a clause to the Local Unions to be voted on." Finally, in 1900, the locals were also allowed to submit amendments to referendum, provided that they secured the endorsement of the executive board or of "five Unions in as many states."[16]

Similar powers were appropriated by the Molders' locals. Originally, the Molders, too, had provided that the national constitution could be amended only by the convention, but, in 1868, the convention was obliged to share its authority with the locals. Initiative could be obtained through sponsorship of an amendment by five local unions; and such measures could then be enacted into law, without action by the convention, by an affirmative vote of three-quarters of the locals.[17]

The Printers' convention, on the other hand, seemed to be making progress in the direction of independence before it was undercut by the referendum. In 1876, the old rule that no amendment could be voted upon until the session following the one in which it was proposed was amended to permit immediate adoption of any amendment which secured unanimous approval of the delegates. In 1882, the required vote was reduced to four-fifths, and, two years later, to two-thirds. However, following the submission of some highly important issues to the membership in 1887 and 1888, the constitution was revised in 1889 to provide that all proposed amendments and increases in taxation be submitted to popular referendum, and for a period of six years thereafter, according to Barnett, "The initiative and the referendum seemed about to supplant the session entirely." In 1893, the power to initiate amendments to the constitution or "general laws" was extended to the local unions; the approval of twenty locals was required for a submission to referendum.

16. *Constitution,* 1881, Art. XII, Sec. 3; 1886, Art. VII, Sec. 1; 1890, Sec. 183; 1900, Sec. 183 (b).

17. Stockton, *Molders Union,* pp. 30–31.

In 1896, the required number of supporting locals was reduced to five. The power of initiative was also given to the national officers. At the same time, the interval between conventions was increased from one year to two years, and, finally, in 1896, it was decided that conventions should be held only when demanded by popular vote.[18] Thus the referendum so far supplanted the convention that the very existence of the latter came to depend upon the plebiscite.

After 1896, however, an effort was made to restore to the convention some measure of its former power. In 1897, regular biennial sessions were restored, and the following year saw a return to the original annual session. Meanwhile, the number of locals whose support was required to initiate proposed amendments was increased to fifty, and, in 1901, much of the constitution was redesignated as "general laws," amendment of which, with the exception of tax increases, did not require submission to referendum. As a result, the number of submissions to referendum originating in the convention declined sharply. Nevertheless, the convention still felt obliged to submit "every important legislative act" to referendum, even when it was not obliged to do so; Barnett made it clear that the restoration of the convention was little more than nominal.

Insofar as the adoption of the referendum signified a tightening of control by the local unions, it might be urged that the referendum was essentially a superior substitute for the pledged delegate and that the failure of the convention to mature merely reflected the failure of the national union to gain ascendancy over its affiliated locals. Thus, Glocker notes that "when the referendum was originally adopted by some of the older organizations, its form was not truly democratic, since each local union was allowed one vote irrespective of its size."[19]

Included among such unions were the Cigar Makers and the Molders. The former, however, subsequently changed their system to allow each local as many votes as it had members, and the Molders confined their use of the "not truly democratic" form to the strike referendum. When they first provided for constitutional amendment by referendum (in 1868), they stipulated that any amendment would be carried if it secured a three-fourths vote in favor, "each union to have as many votes as . . . representatives."[20] In 1879, this was reduced to a simple "majority of votes returned by the local Unions." Nor did the Carpenters allow an equal voice to all locals; when they introduced the referendum in 1886, they provided that "a two-thirds vote *of the members* voting shall be necessary to sustain .˙. . amendments or alterations." Later, they sought to eliminate any possible ambiguity by specifying that,

18. Barnett, *The Printers*, pp. 62–66.
19. Glocker, *Government of Unions*, pp. 205, 206.
20. Quoted in Stockton, *Molders Union*, p. 31. See *Constitution*, 1879, Art. XIV, Sec. 2.

"Whenever a general vote of the members is taken, it shall require a two-thirds vote of the members voting to decide. . . ."[21] The Printers, too, polled their membership rather than their locals.

Thus adoption of the referendum was by no means confined to organizations in which the process of nationalization was being resisted successfully by the smaller local unions. On the contrary, in the case of the Printers, "A prime motive in the introduction and extension of the referendum was the desire to further the movement toward centralization. By the use of the referendum, a direct bond was established between members of the local unions and the International Union."[22]

One must conclude, then, that the convention was obliged, in many instances, to surrender an important degree of authority primarily because it failed the national union as a governing device and not because the national union itself had failed to acquire increased powers with the passing of time. One reason for this failure might have consisted in the inadequate representation in the convention, which, as we have observed, was granted to the larger locals. Yet the Printers who, if we are to believe Barnett, switched to the referendum in order to accelerate the process of nationalization, were willing to abandon it and return to a convention whose basis of representation remained unchanged. Furthermore, any inadequacy due to overrepresentation of the larger locals indicated the persistence of localism and the consequent weakness of the national union itself, whereas our problem is to determine why it was generally true that the national convention waned as the national union waxed more powerful.

FAILURE OF THE CONVENTION AS A NATIONAL INSTITUTION

The convention failed as an institution of national government because of various imperfections, of which we shall consider only those which appear to have been the most serious.

Unwieldiness

In the opinion of many, the conventions of the larger unions, which sometimes numbered several hundred delegates, were too large to be efficient. The unions adopted the obvious remedy of having the important preliminary work performed by committees, but convention committees tended to proliferate at an alarming rate and their lines of jurisdiction were not carefully drawn. As a result, the convention not too infrequently voted more than once during a session upon the same subject if that topic was reported upon by more than one committee, and occasionally the convention would adopt the reports of two committees whose recommendations on the same item were diametrically opposed to one another.[23]

21. *Constitution*, 1886, Art. VII, Sec. 1 (Italics mine); 1890, Sec. 183.
22. Barnett, *The Printers*, p. 63.
23. Glocker, *Government of Unions*, pp. 159–160.

Lack of Flexibility

The national officers frequently contended that the convention did not possess sufficient flexibility to conduct strikes effectively. Glocker referred to a secretary of the Miners' Association of Western Pennsylvania who was hampered by what he termed the "iron jacket of orders from convention."[24]

Length of Sessions

Although the length of the convention session tended generally to increase over time—the Molders delegates, for example, spent nine days in session in 1874 and twenty in 1902[25]—the duties of the delegates grew even more rapidly. Glocker's verdict seems clearly justified:

Certainly a week or even two weeks seems a very short time in which to adopt needed legislation, clear the docket of judicial cases, elect officers, audit accounts, levy dues, appropriate funds, declare strikes, and transact the numerous other items of business which have been accumulating during the year or more since last convention.[26]

Frequency of Sessions

The longer the interval between conventions, the greater the power of the national officers (who were originally supposed to exercise independent authority only between convention sessions) and the more nominal the superior authority of the convention to review their executive and judicial activities *ex post facto*. The Webbs, who believed strongly in "government by a Representative Assembly as the last word of democracy" took pains to point out that the convention of one of their model unions, the Amalgamated Association of Operative Cotton-spinners, met quarterly in regular session and could be convened in special session at the will of the executive council. Furthermore, they noted that the "Miners Parliament," although it met regularly only once a year,

expects to be called together whenever any new departure in policy is required. In times of stress the executive committee shows its real dependence on the popular assembly by calling it together every few weeks.[27]

In contrast, no national union in this country held conventions more frequently than once a year,[28] although it was not uncommon for provision to be made for the calling of special sessions at the discretion of the executive, on the request of a specified number of local unions, or following a favorable

24. Glocker, *Government of Unions*, p. 173.
25. Stockton, *Molders Union*, p. 78.
26. Glocker, *Government of Unions*, p. 161.
27. *Industrial Democracy*, pp. 44–45.
28. Glocker, *Government of Unions*, pp. 160–161.

referendum vote.[29] Even more significant of the failure of the convention was the general tendency for sessions to be held less frequently during the last two decades of the nineteenth century. From Table 8 it is apparent that the annual convention, which was employed by a comfortable majority of national unions in existence in 1880, lost popularity steadily thereafter. It is

TABLE 8

I.

FREQUENCY OF CONVENTIONS IN UNIONS IN EXISTENCE IN 1920 WHICH WERE
ORGANIZED BEFORE OR SHORTLY AFTER 1880, BY DECADES

Convention Held	1880		1890		1900		1910		1920	
	No.	%	No.	%	No.	%	No.	%	No.	%
Annually	17	85.0	14	70.0	11	55.0	8	40.0	8	40.0
Biennially	1	50.0	4	20.0	8	40.0	10	50.0	3	15.0
Triennially					1	5.0			4	20.0
Quadrennially . . .							1	5.0	2	10.0
Quinquennially . . .							1	5.0	2	10.0
No Record	2	10.0	2	10.0					1	5.0

II.

FREQUENCY OF CONVENTIONS IN UNIONS IN EXISTENCE IN 1920 WHICH WERE
ORGANIZED BETWEEN 1880 AND 1890

Convention Held	1890		1900		1910		1920	
	No.	%	No.	%	No.	%	No.	%
Annually	20	60.0	14	48.3	9	31.0	8	27.6
Biennially	6	20.7	13	44.8	15	51.7	6	20.7
Triennially			1	3.4	1	3.4	6	20.7
Quadrennially					3	10.3	4	13.8
Quinquennially					1	3.4	2	6.9
No Record . . . . , .	3	10.3	1	3.4			3	10.3

Source: Lloyd G. Reynolds and Charles C. Killingsworth, *Trade Union Publications* (Baltimore: Johns Hopkins, 1944), v. I.

also interesting that, in 1890, 1900, 1910, and 1920 the relative frequency of the annual convention was lower among the unions formed between 1880 and 1890 than among the unions already in existence in 1880. Annual conventions were being abandoned in favor of biennial meetings in the closing decades of the past century; and the latter began to give ground to triennial and quadrennial sessions by the second decade of the twentieth century. Thus, while the length of the sessions increased as the national unions grew in numbers and authority, this trend was more than offset by the growing

29. Cf., e.g., Molders' *Constitutions:* 1879, Art. XV, Sec. 4; 1895, Art. XV, Sec. 6; 1902, Art. XV, Sec. 6. Also, Bottle Blowers' *Constitution,* 1892, Art. II, Sec. 6; Art. I, Sec. 2. Also, Carpenters' *Constitutions:* 1881, Art. I; 1886, Art. XXI; 1890, Sec. 5; 1900, Sec. 5.

tendency to hold fewer conventions. It will be recalled that one of the reasons why the early British constitutional conventions failed to evolve into permanent governing institutions was the expense involved in assembling periodic meetings of delegates. In this country an effort was made to govern by convention, but here, too, financial considerations threatened to sap the vitality of the legislative branch.

Representation of Locals

Although the systems of representation adopted by the national unions frequently permitted the smaller local unions to choose more delegates than they would have been entitled to on the basis of representation in strict proportion to membership, in practice the local unions were underrepresented at the conventions. They were frequently unable to afford the expense involved in sending delegates to the meetings.[30] The predicament in which Bricklayers' Union No. 4, Missouri, found itself in 1875 was far from atypical, although its official attitude was considerably more gracious than might have been expected under the circumstances:

We received your invitation to attend the Convention. After due consideration, knowing that our city will be ably represented by delegates from Unions No. 1 and 3, of Missouri, and also by James G. Hall, your worthy Treasurer, with due respect to the National Union, we resolved to omit sending a delegate to the Convention. . . .[31]

Of the foregoing defects of the national convention, the final two might be considered crucial. The first, unwieldiness, was not necessarily a fatal flaw. It presented a problem in scale: a convention could be made smaller by the simple expedient of increasing the prescribed number of members per delegate. The Molders, as we know, changed their basis of representation in order to hold down the size of the convention, and it is probable that the Bottle Blowers were similarly motivated when they changed their system in 1892. Of course, if the minimum number of members required to qualify a local for its first delegate were not raised *pari passu* with the minima required for additional representatives, the structure of representation would have been distorted in favor of the smallest locals by the process of altering the scale. However, since some distortion of this nature did occur as a result of the changes made by the Molders and the Bottle Blowers, it is not likely that the larger locals would have considered the alteration of sufficient importance to warrant serious protest.

In any event, size was not necessarily a crime, since, as the conventions themselves appreciated, a division of labor could be effected through the functioning of appropriate committees. That the early committee systems

30. Glocker, *Government of Unions*, pp. 165–166.
31. *Proceedings*, 1875, p. 32.

were not models of efficiency did not mean that they could not have been improved. It is true, as Glocker implied, that the conventions frequently tended to rubber-stamp the recommendations of their committees, but this defect resulted in great part from lack of time at the disposal of the convention. If sessions could have been longer, there would have been sufficient time for adequate debate.[32] Or, if the intervals between conventions could have been shortened, the agenda before any one session would have been reduced correspondingly. Thus much of the weakness associated with numbers can be subsumed under the problem of the length and the frequency of sessions.

The same holds for the objection that the convention did not constitute a mechanism of policy determination which was sufficiently flexible to cope with fluid industrial situations. If the convention could have been convened whenever the occasion for the initiation or revision of important policies arose, or if it could have remained in session more or less continuously for the duration of such emergencies, its orders need never have congealed into an "iron jacket." Once again we call to mind the quarterly and special sessions of the British Cotton-spinners, this time in contrast to the Miners' Association of Western Pennsylvania, whose unfortunate secretary was the man in the iron jacket.

From the above it is evident that the short sessions and growing infrequency of meetings were two aspects of the same situation. Ideally, or at least for maximum effective control over the executive, the convention should lead a more or less continuous existence. This holds *a fortiori* for the union convention which is also endowed with supreme judicial powers, for the appellate process must be speedy if it is to afford real relief. Obviously, if the convention had resembled the Congress more closely and remained in session more or less continually, the distinction between length of session and interim interval would have become academic. However, an important practical difference remains. A continual convention could have been composed only of full-time paid delegates, and the cost of maintaining professional union congressmen would have been prohibitive. The best compromise, and indeed a superior alternative if a legislature and judiciary of amateurs be preferred to one of professional, full-time representatives, was the British expedient (although by no means in general acceptance in the United Kingdom during the period under consideration) of making it possible for the convention to convene frequently. Thus, the third and fourth conditions were directly

32. The Carpenters sought to provide more time for debate by convening important committees in advance of the convention, so that their reports would be available earlier in the session. The Carpenters, in 1890, provided that their Committee on Constitution meet in the convention city four days before the convention's opening date. (*Constitution,* 1980, Sec. 5.) In 1896, similar provision was made for the meetings of the committees on Finance and on Grievances and Appeals. (*Constitution,* 1896, Sec. 13 [b].)

related: the greater the frequency of conventions, the less need for lengthy sessions.

Reduction in the interval between conventions, therefore, would have mitigated the adverse effects of the three preceding conditions—unwieldiness, inflexibility, and brevity of sessions. But the same relationship did not hold between frequency of meetings and the final defect noted, underrepresentation of the smaller locals. The latter condition, as noted above, was occasioned by lack of financial resources; hence the more frequently conventions were held the greater the strain upon exchequers and the less likely that the smaller unions would send representatives.

Various devices were discussed or adopted in the attempt to compensate for the inability of the smaller locals to finance convention delegations. Of these the most popular was the practice of holding the convention in a different part of the country each year. However, this practice did not increase the attendance at any one convention; it merely enabled the small local to send a delegate or two whenever the convention was held in its vicinity. Rotation of the convention site in this country served the same modest purpose that rotation of the governing branch had done in Britain; it spread the burden of unrepresentativeness more evenly over the entire jurisdiction.

Another extensively debated device was the vote by proxy, but this was successfully opposed, in most instances, by the claim that its adoption would facilitate control of the convention by small cliques with great voting power.[33] Thus the Printers in 1857 provided that no representative be allowed to vote unless he was present. In 1882, all ambiguity was removed when the Constitution provided instead that, "Each Union must be represented by its properly accredited delegates and no proxies allowed. Each delegate shall be entitled to one vote."[34] The Bricklayers, at their first convention, specifically ruled that, "No union shall be represented by proxy in convention."[35] The Carpenters, too, established at their first convention that no delegate be entitled to more than one vote. Later on, they sought to accommodate the smaller locals by providing that

A delegate to the convention of the U.B. must hold credentials from the Local of which he is a member, but several Locals can club together, or so can Unions in a D.C. (i.e. District Council) and elect a delegate, but he must hold credentials from the Union of which he is a member.[36]

This, however, was not tantamount to proxy voting, since the old rule, which restricted each delegate to one vote, remained in effect.

The Carpenters' attempted remedy suggested another possible solution

33. Glocker, *Government of Unions*, p. 166.
34. *Constitution*, 1857, Art. VII; 1882, Art. II, Sec. 1.
35. *Constitution*, 1865, Art. II.
36. *Constitution*, 1881, Art. I; General Executive Board, *Standing Decisions*, 1892.

to the problem of local representation, the system of electing delegates by districts. The Molders conducted a brief and unsuccessful experiment with this system in 1886–1888, and few unions in this country ever put it into effect at all.[37] The Molders' system was economically unrealistic, since they made their districts coextensive with the several states. There is, however, a more fundamental reason for the failure of the district system. It was not designed to solve the problem posed by the underrepresentation of the smaller locals, since, under the district system, the smaller locals would have suffered political submergence, if delegates had been chosen by popular vote of the combined membership. In the Appendix on local jurisdiction (pages 605–619), it will be pointed out that one of the main functions of the district organizations in this country was to help preserve the autonomy of the smaller locals, the existence of which was encouraged by some of the national unions. Hence the district union, in this country, was a local organization and usually remained without representation at any higher level. (The Miners, as we know from Chapter 2, were an exception.) Furthermore, in many cases, local jurisdictions were coextensive with local labor markets, so that the inclusion, for purposes of representation, of such locals in wider organizations might have resulted in the selection of district delegates whose constituency was composed of diverse local interests. The same observation holds of any attempt to include locals of different crafts (but in the same national union) in the same districts; no counterpart to the British "trade district" emerged in this country in the period under discussion.

Payment of delegates' expenses by the national union seemed to many to be an obvious solution. This alternative, however, merely transferred the financial burden from the locals to the national union, and it only served to make more evident the choice between conventions which were held frequently and conventions which were well attended. We have already remarked that, under a system of local financing, the more frequently conventions were held, the less able were the smaller locals to send delegates to the meetings. It is equally true that, under a system of national financing, the more frequently conventions were held, the greater the strain upon central funds. Hence one could find, on the one hand, national unions which paid part or all of the expenses of local delegations and which held conventions only at rather long intervals of time, and, on the other, national unions which held conventions rather frequently but which did not defray delegate expenses and whose conventions were rather poorly represented, as a result.

The Printers were an example of the latter type of national union. Although they returned to the biennial convention in 1897 and then restored the annual meeting a year later, "The Union has steadily defeated all proposals looking to the payment of representatives from the International treasury, and the small unions are for the most part unable to pay the expenses of

37. Glocker, *Government of Unions*, pp. 169–170.

delegates."[38] The Bricklayers were another case in point. They maintained annual conventions until 1908; at the same time the representation of smaller locals presented such a problem that, in 1869, they changed the requirement for a quorum at conventions from "a majority of representatives" to "the representatives of a majority of Unions represented and admitted to seats in Convention."[39] At the 1869 Convention, the secretary expressed the opinion that

Some plan should be decided upon to make the cost of sending delegates to our Convention fall more equal upon the unions—the cost to the small unions is so great that they cannot send a delegate. Some of them have never been represented in the Conventions and never will be under the present system. It will cost a union with 20 members $2.50 to send a delegate when $50 is required to send one,—and a union with 500 members it would cost only 10¢ a piece. I would recommend the making of our dues sufficiently large to pay the fare of the delegates by the most direct route to and from the Convention, and also to allow them so much per day for hotel expenses. It would not cost the unions as much as it does now, and we could have every union represented. This plan has been adopted by other trades organizations and found to work successfully, and much cheaper than that of each union paying the expenses of their delegate.[40]

But what the secretary failed to specify was that the per capita cost of delegates would be reduced only for the smaller locals and, for that reason, they certainly would be increased for the larger ones. Two years later, therefore, he changed his tack and, in so doing, made explicit the choice between the frequency of conventions and the extent to which they could be represented by qualified locals. He proposed that conventions henceforth be held only every two years and "from the amount that would be expended at the session to accrue a fund to pay the expenses of the Delegates of those small Unions whose funds will not permit them to be represented as by this means a more diversified opinion will be insured . . ." In reply, the convention adopted a recommendation of the Committee on General Good "that the sessions of this Union be held yearly as before." The following year, no recommendation was made that the international defray the expenses of the smaller and poorer locals, but the president did suggest the two-year interval because "this, to my mind, is essentially necessary, as it will be a great source of saving to the different Local Unions." This, too, failed of adoption, however, as did two subsequent recommendations in 1884 and 1891 that the convention be held every two years.[41] At the 1891 convention O'Dea estimated that a convention

38. Barnett, *The Printers*, p. 60.
39. *Constitutions:* 1865, Art. X; 1869, Art. X.
40. *Proceedings*, 1869, p. 44. This plan was rejected after a special committee, in reporting favorably upon it, also recommended that the number of delegates allowed to each local union be reduced to one! (P. 97.)
41. *Proceedings*, 1871, p. 15, pp. 25–26; 1872, pp. 7, and 16; 1884, p. 78; 1891, p. 36.

cost the national and local unions $20,000 in all, $15,000 of which was allotted for expenses of 150 delegates and officers.

In contrast to the Printers and the Bricklayers, the Molders' International Union always paid the mileage expenses of the delegates to its conventions and, beginning in 1882, it paid them per diem allowances of three dollars each "to defray expenses."[42] As a result, in only three of the ten conventions held between 1876 and 1902 did less than 60 per cent of the Molders' locals send delegates. This contrasts with the record of the Printers at whose conventions, according to Barnett (who wrote in 1909), "usually less than one-third of the local unions are represented."[43] On the other hand, the Molders are a flagrant example of a national union which permitted long intervals to elapse between conventions. Conventions were held annually from 1859 to 1868, biennially from 1868 to 1878, quadrennially from 1879 to 1886, biennially from 1886 to 1890, quinquennially from 1890 to 1899. The record of local union representation, 1876–1902, is shown in Table 9.

TABLE 9

MOLDERS' LOCAL UNION REPRESENTATION AT CONVENTIONS, 1876–1902

	Locals in Existence	Locals Represented	Per Cent Represented
1876	94	63	67
1878	91	44	48
1879	83	25	30
1882	151	49	32
1886	136	95	70
1888	171	119	70
1890	235	174	74
1895	231	146	63
1899	260	202	71
1902	383	339	89

It will be noted that, with the exception of the sharp increase in attendance following the decision of the international "to defray expenses" of the delegates in addition to their transportation costs in 1882, the percentage of locals represented did not increase with subsequent lengthenings of the interval between conventions. It is therefore pertinent to inquire whether convention expenses were responsible, in part at least, for the long intervals between conventions. There is evidence that this was the case. In the first place, convention costs increased sharply. From 1876 to 1902, the number of delegates increased from 78 to 385, the number of days in session increased from 9 to 20, and the mileage and per diem costs rose from $3,844.60 to $50,670.72.[44]

42. Stockton, *Molders Union*, p. 78; *Constitution*, 1882, Art. II, Sec. 3.
43. Barnett, *The Printers*, p. 60.   44. Stockton, *Molders Union*, table on p. 78.

Our second piece of evidence follows from the fact that the Molders left the decision concerning the holding of conventions to referendum vote. In 1879, it was established that the approval of two-thirds of the locals voting, in addition to the prior sanction of a majority of the executive board, was required to hold special conventions. There was no prescribed frequency for regular conventions until 1886, when President Fitzpatrick complained that, "four years is too long between conventions. I am of the opinion that we should meet at least once every two years." He then recommended that this be accomplished by reducing the number of convention delegates and by having the locals themselves defray either the mileage or per diem expenses of their delegates. The delegates responded by providing for mandatory sessions to be held every two years, but, exhibiting a failing not uncommon among legislators, they omitted to make provision for the increased financial burden involved, for they refused to adopt Fitzpatrick's recommendations. Accordingly, it was left to another president, Martin Fox, to remind the delegates to the 1890 convention of the unpleasant facts of life and to question once again the wisdom of payment of delegate expenses by the national union. Said President Fox,

We are all aware that our Conventions consume a large amount of the funds of the organization, and in many cases but very little benefit derived from long sessions. Many seem to think that the local Unions should pay the per diem and the National Union the railroad fare—however, this is a matter for you to decide.[45]

The assembly decided to leave all expenses to be borne by the national union, but it removed the mandatory feature of its 1886 legislation providing biennial conventions by inserting the following proviso:

unless decided otherwise by a majority of popular vote of the members of all local unions of the I.M.U. of N.A. In the month of March preceding intended convention all local Unions shall vote on the following proposition: "Shall the regular convention of the I.M.U. of N.A. convene this year?"[46]

Note that, unlike the provision for a referendum of local unions which had been adopted in 1879, this law called for a popular vote and thereby gave the larger locals, which bore the larger share of the expenses, a greater voice in deciding whether or not conventions would be held. The next convention, as we know, was not called until 1895. A referendum was held in 1892, and the corresponding representative of the local in Alleghany, Pennsylvania urged a negative vote on the grounds of the expense involved. The motion was defeated, as was a similar one the following year, by a "large majority." There is no record of the holding of a referendum the following year, and, although it was voted to hold a convention in 1895 over the protest

45. *Constitution,* 1879, Art. XV, Sec. 4; *Proceedings,* 1886, p. 8; *Constitution,* 1886, Art. II; *Proceedings,* 1890, p. 15.
46. *Constitution,* 1890, Art. II.

of another economy-minded local official, the vote cast was very light, as it had been in the previous referenda.[47] In 1895, the convention made it more difficult to call special sessions without the consent of the larger locals by changing the required affirmative vote from two-thirds of all locals to two-thirds of the membership voting.[48] At the same time, however, the delegates revoked an old rule to the effect that locals which were in arrears in their tax payments to the international should be denied representation in convention.[49] When, therefore, another referendum was about to be held in 1897, President Fox abandoned his efforts to shift the financial burden to local shoulders, noted the considerable mileage and per diem expenses entailed in holding the 1895 convention (which came to $15,000), observed that this expense would be exceeded in the future as a result of the suspension of the bar on account of indebtedness, and, for the first time, urged the locals not to vote for another convention. They followed his advice that year, and voted in the negative again in 1898.[50]

In 1899, Fox again advised against holding a convention. He said that it was necessary to finance the last convention out of surpluses belonging in the Strike, Death Benefit, and Out-of-Work Benefit Funds, and that, if a new convention were to be held, it would be necessary to do the same thing again. At the same time, an editorial in the *Journal* urged the establishment of a separate Convention Fund and a minimum interval of four years between conventions, to be followed by a referendum vote. In support of the latter proposal, the editor noted that, while the Printers recently voted for annual conventions and the Machinists held their sessions biennially, the

47. *Journal,* January 1892, pp. 3–4; March 1892, p. 6; May 1893, p. 4; March 1895, pp. 2–3, 9.

48. *Constitution,* 1885, Art. XV, Sec. 6.

49. *Journal,* January 1897, p. 32. This law was first passed in 1878 when it was declared that any local whose indebtedness to the International amounted to three dollars per capita was not entitled to representation at the convention. (*Constitution,* 1878, Art. II, Sec. 2.) In 1882, the year in which the convention voted to pay a per diem allowance of three dollars to each delegate, the minimum amount of indebtedness required to disqualify was reduced to two dollars per capita. (*Constitution,* 1882, Art. II, Sec. 2.) That year, however, the convention had refused to sustain its Committee on Claims which had ruled that a local which had exceeded the earlier debt limit should not be permitted representation. (*Proceedings,* 1882, pp. 31–32.) In 1886, some forty-five delegates from locals which owed more than two dollars per head to the international were seated "as they have promised to their utmost to place their Unions in good financial standing with the I.M.U. of N.A." (*Proceedings,* 1886, p. 49.) In 1888, the Committee on Credentials reported that it was "time that the law in regard to representation in this body should no longer remain a dead letter." Nevertheless, it recommended that the delegates of No. 2, Troy, N. Y., which had exhausted its line of credit, be seated because their local was "a large and influential Union (which) has done good service in the cause of our organization." The convention at first rejected this recommendation, but it later voted to seat the Troy delegates. (*Proceedings,* 1888, p. 47.)

50. *Journal,* January 1897, p. 32; April 1897, p. 172; March 1898, p. 123.

Cigar Makers, "which alone of these pays the mileage and per diem of the delegates as our does," met in convention only once every five years. But the administration was obviously embarrassed at having been forced into the position of opposing conventions, and Editor Black continued:

The one great objection that we can see to the present law is that when the time for issuing the voting circular comes round, the officers sometimes find themselves under the necessity of calling attention to the state of the treasury, and thus, indirectly, advising against the holding of a convention. While it should not be, still this leaves a disagreeable task, and leaves their advice open to all sorts of mean interpretations. We have some members who, through some prejudice, grudge, or inherent meanness, at once fly to the conclusion and spread the sentiment, so far as they can, that such a circular is only a scheme on the part of the officers to perpetuate themselves in office.[51]

Black's fears might have been well founded, for the 1899 referendum did favor a convention. In his report, President Fox once more alluded to his dilemma:

it becomes obligatory upon the officers to send out a voting circular, and at the same time give a detailed account of the finances of the organization. If there was always a handsome balance to our credit there would be no objection, but when circumstances over which we had no control had so drained our Treasury that there was clearly an insufficiency of funds to provide the expenses of a convention, it becomes an unpleasant duty so to state, and leaves ourselves open to the meanest insinuations that could be used against men in your service. I am satisfied that the great bulk of our membership appreciated our motives, but it is, nevertheless, most galling to a self-respecting official to endure the vile taunts and insinuations of the residue. I would, therefore, commend to you the policy of making provision for a Convention fund by setting aside a certain percentage of the weekly dues for that purpose. When a fund is assured at the end of whatever term may be specified in Article II, Section 1, it is then a very simple matter to call for a popular vote on the question of holding a Convention, and an equally simple matter for the members to decide.[52]

But if the president's good name was in jeopardy, the convention's very existence was apparently at stake. The delegates did establish a fund: it was provided that the financier withdraw 25 per cent of the balance of the Sick Benefit Fund once every year and deposit it to the credit of a Convention Fund; "and he shall be empowered to draw at any time upon the balance in the Sick Benefit Fund of any local Union for such sums as he may deem advisable, and deposit the same to the credit of the aforesaid Convention Fund." The President had complained that the convention was bankrupting the union; the convention thereupon adopted bankruptcy as a mandatory policy. Thus did the Molders of old unloose their Gordian knots. Then, its

51. *Journal*, March 1899, pp. 110–111.
52. *Proceedings*, 1899, p. 16.

fiscal flank secured, the convention addressed itself to the task of facilitating its future existence. It provided that, "If the (referendum) vote be negative, it shall be taken yearly until affirmative."[53]

The Convention Fund met an interesting fate. Deposits in the fund over the period 1900–1902 totaled $57,911.34. However, "the needs of the Sick Benefit Relief and Strike Funds . . . necessitated their assistance from the Convention Fund . . ."! Such assistance, together with expenses of administration, totaled $33,374.60, leaving a balance in the Convention Fund of $24,-536.74.[54] Since the expenses of the 1902 convention came to $50,670.72, the financial problem remained unsettled.

The membership, however, apparently remained determined to hold conventions more frequently, while the officers, with equal determination, opposed this viewpoint. A referendum held in 1901 failed to obtain a majority. However, noting both that many locals failed to vote at all and that a majority of the new locals, formed after the Convention of 1899 before which Fox had preached his edifying sermon, had not been able to pass on the measure, the editor of the *Journal* wrote that, "It is to be regretted that it is left for such a small minority to determine a matter which is of so much importance and involves the expenditure of so much money."[55] Later the same year, a Cleveland local issued a circular in which it requested a special convention. Standing upon his constitutional authority (since calls for special sessions had to be approved by a majority of the executive board), Fox declined to approve it and sent out a circular of his own informing the locals, as he later said, that "All calls for a referendum vote are issued by the National officers." Nevertheless, a convention was held in 1902, and it was provided that referenda on the calling of special conventions could be held if submitted "by at least five Local Unions, bearing the signatures of each local." It was also provided that regular conventions be held every three years, subject to approval by referendum vote.[56] The membership, however, apparently came to terms with financial reality, for their pious intention of holding triennial sessions—which was, incidentally, certainly inadequate to transform the convention into an efficient governing body—was never realized: after 1902, conventions were held quinquennially up to 1917, and thereafter five- and six-year intervals prevailed.[57]

Taken together, the contrasting experiences of the Printers and the Brick-layers, on the one hand, and the Iron Molders, on the other, suggest that the national union in this country was confronted with a choice between two

53. *Constitution*, 1899, Art. II, Sec. 1.

54. *Proceedings*, 1902, p. 646.

55. *Journal*, March 1901, p. 143.

56. *Proceedings*, 1902, p. 624; *Constitution*, 1902, Art. XV, Sec. 6; *Constitution*, 1902, Art. II. A simple majority of those voting sufficed for approval of regular sessions; special conventions required a majority of two-thirds.

57. Reynolds and Killingsworth, *Trade Union Publications*, p. 195.

conditions, both of which required fulfillment if the national convention was to function as an efficient organ of government. The Bricklayers and ultimately the Printers succeeded in holding conventions at fairly frequent intervals, or, more accurately, their success was measured by the fact that they prevented the interim periods from growing longer with the passage of time; but, in so doing, they sacrificed local representation to frequency of meeting. The Molders, on the other hand, gained representation at the expense of frequency. Some unions probably satisfied both conditions tolerably well; judging from a low ratio of members to delegates, a sustained record of annual conventions, and the absence of recorded debate over representation, the Bottle Blowers were probably a case in point. (However, as we shall see presently, the financing of conventions proved a problem to even this powerful group.) Yet, the general concensus that conventions were held too infrequently and that smaller locals were underrepresented suggests that most of the national unions failed satisfactorily to achieve either objective. Why were the American unions confronted with the necessity of choosing between two necessary conditions for the success of their conventions?

The two factors of local separatism and distance, which helped to explain some of the peculiarities in the development of the national executive in this country, can also account in part, at least, for the failure of the American convention. To the parochialism of their locals, the national unions owed the inability of district representation—which would have reduced the number of delegates and hence the cost of conventions—to take root here. Localism, too, was one of the factors underlying the extremely limited employment of the vote by proxy. As for the even more stubborn facts of geography and location of industry, it is obvious that transportation costs were necessarily high in this country, both because great distances were involved and because industries in which the early national unions were organized were seldom concentrated exclusively (although they might have been located preponderantly) in only a few localities. From the data on the number of delegates, number of days in session, and combined cost in mileage and per diem which are presented by Stockton, one can arrive at the proportion of the combined cost of the Molders' conventions which was accounted for by mileage expenses alone.[58] During the period 1886–1907, transportation charges appear to have accounted for slightly under one-half of total convention costs in most cases. (The percentages of mileage to combined costs were as follows: 1886, 22; 1888, 42; 1890, 81; 1895, 13; 1899, 46; 1902, 54; 1907, 42.)

Even the Bottle Blowers, whose convention met frequently and appeared to be adequately representative, felt obliged to take cognizance of the fact

58. Stockton, *Molders Union,* table, p. 78. Per diem cost was derived by multiplying the product of the number of delegates and the number of days in session by three dollars, which was the per diem allowance. Mileage cost is the difference between the combined mileage and per diem costs, which were published by the union, and the per diem costs as computed above.

that, as the national jurisdiction expanded, convention costs grew. Shortly before a national union of bottle blowers was formed within the Knights of Labor by the merger of the so-called Eastern and Western Leagues (District Assemblies 149 and 143 respectively) in 1889, the Eastern District provided, "That each Local Assembly shall pay their own delegates expenses to the D. A. sessions, except mileage, which shall be paid by the district."[59] After the merger took place, however, and the geographic jurisdiction of the union was greatly enlarged by the inclusion of the western (really midwestern) delegates, it was decided that the national union no longer should defray the travel expenses of the delegates but that, "Each Branch shall pay their own expenses for representation to the Annual Sessions."[60] Feeling on the subject must have been strong, for when, nine years later, a motion was made that the association resume payment of mileage expenses, a tie vote resulted in convention. No change occurred, for a two-thirds vote was required.

The British, too, we recall, were apparently deterred by the high cost of convention, for the reasons underlying the failure of their early constitutional assemblies of instructed delegates to mature into representative conventions were partly financial. Yet the comparatively few British unions which did adopt the convention in the late nineteenth century compared favorably with ours with respect to the frequency with which meetings were held and the adoption of devices which economized on representatives. The "Cotton-spinners Parliament" met regularly every quarter, and the "Miners' Parliament," although its regular meetings were annual, held "other meetings . . . as business requires."[61] In contrast, no prominent American parliament met more frequently than once every year. Furthermore, the delegates to the proletarian parliaments of Britain, to which the Webbs referred, not infrequently represented constituencies which embraced more than one local union.

These differences in structure can be traced in part to differences between the two countries with respect to the geographic and economic extent of trade jurisdictions and the location of industry. In the first place, representation by district delegates did not necessarily imply a spirit of cosmopolitanism on the part of members of British local unions which was lacking in the United States. For if local unions in the same product markets in Britain were willing to share common representation at the national convention as, generally speaking, they were not willing to do in this country, it must be recalled (as we shall note in Chapter 12) that the British national union itself was frequently more a "federation" than an "amalgamation," and that the different districts were accorded a significant degree of independence

59. *Constitution*, 1889, p. 59.
60. *Constitution*, 1892, Art. II.
61. *Industrial Democracy*, p. 44; see also pp. 55, 124–125.

which corresponded to the degree to which their geographic jurisdictions were economically distinct from one another.

Furthermore, geographic concentration of industry prevailed to a greater extent in Britain than in this country. The Cotton-spinners' national jurisdiction was narrowly circumscribed, even if we include within it all of its economically diverse "provinces." Thus "mileage" charges did not present to the British a problem comparable in magnitude to that which confronted the American unions.[62] According to the Webbs,

The Cotton Operatives enjoy the special advantage of having practically all their membership within a radius of thirty miles from Manchester. The frequent gatherings of a hundred delegates held usually on a Saturday afternoon entail, therefore, no loss of working time and little expense to the organisation. The same consideration applies to the great bulk of the membership of the Miners' Federation, three-fourths of which is concentrated in Lancashire, West Yorkshire, and the industrial Midlands. Even the outlying coalfields elsewhere enjoy the advantage of close local concentration, so that a single delegate may effectively represent the hundreds of lodges in his own county. And it is no small consideration that the total membership of the Miners' Federation is so large that the cost of frequent meetings of fifty to seventy delegates bears only a trifling proportion to the resources of the union.[63]

Finally, one should observe that where location of industry assumed similar characteristics in both countries, the convention suffered much the same fate. Instances of "close local concentration" could be found here, as in Britain, in the coal industry, and it is worthy of note that this coincidence of economic conditions was paralleled by a similarity in governing institutions, for the delegates to the United Mine Workers, and its earlier organizations, represented "districts" and "divisions" as well as local unions. On the other hand, where industry was decentralized in Britain, national unions were reluctant to adopt the convention at all. And although the Webbs believed that the "geographic difficulty" was bound to disappear with the growing concentration of industry and that, "The tardiness and incompleteness with which Trade Unions have adopted representative institutions is mainly due

62. According to Glocker's account, the New England Laster's Association must have been a counterpart to the type of regional national union found in Britain. When its affiliates were all located in Massachusetts, conventions were held quarterly. After locals had been established in Maine and New Hampshire, however, the interim interval was lengthened to six months. Finally, with the admission of local unions situated outside of New England, conventions were held annually.

63. *Industrial Democracy*, p. 53. See also fn. 3, pp. 40–41, wherein it is noted that, "More than half the total membership (of the Amalgamated Association of Operative Cotton-spinners)is included in two important 'provinces,' Oldham and Bolton, which possess elaborate federal constitutions of their own." For further examples of the effect of the "extreme localisation of the separate industries," see Sidney and Beatrice Webb, *The History of Trade Unionism* (London: Longmans, Green, 1894), p. 422.

to a more general cause," they nevertheless found it "easy to understand why, with so large a number of isolated branches, it has not yet seemed practicable to constitutional reformers in the building or engineering trades, to have frequent meetings of representative assemblies."

If the Webbs had found that there did exist a true family likeness between the early assemblies of "delegates" and the later conventions of "representatives," a clearer case could be established in favor of the "more general cause" on the basis of a comparison between the union movements in the two countries. For such a finding would have indicated that the convention had been adopted at the outset in both countries and, therefore, that it had suffered in Britain a fate even crueler than it did in the New World. Then, indeed it might be difficult (although not impossible), on the basis of international comparison alone, to assign high priority to transportation expenses as a causal influence, for to do so would imply that such costs proved a greater deterrent in the smaller country than in the larger one. Even so, however, the "geographic difficulty" could be subjected to a different interpretation and remain formidable, if not "insuperable." For when the editor of the Molders' *Journal* refused to concede that his organization should follow the example of many of the larger British unions and hold no conventions at all, he argued that the British could dispense with the convention only because the smaller geographic areas embraced by their jurisdictions resulted in uniformity of "needs and conditions."[64]

64. *Journal*, August 1901, p. 479.

CHAPTER TEN

THE REFERENDUM AND THE EXECUTIVE BOARD

CONTROL BY POPULAR VOTE

IN THE preceding chapter it was observed that, in this country, the convention was often superseded by the referendum as a device for adding to or amending the basic law of the national union. Therefore it has been remarked that the history of the use of the referendum by trade unions in the United States contrasts with its career in Britain, where it preceded the convention in time and where it was first used as the instrument for electing the chief executive officers of the national union. It is also true that, whereas the convention was at one time largely supplanted by the referendum in Britain, the convention continued in existence in the great majority of American unions after the latter had adopted the referendum.[1] Although the referendum was not resorted to here as widely as it was in Britain, it was used for a variety of purposes. Chief among these were (1) amendment of the constitution, as mentioned above, and (2) ratification of strikes. In conjunction with the referendum, we shall also discuss (3) the direct election of officers, which, while it differs from the referendum insofar as it implies an attempt by the electorate to delegate governing activity, nevertheless is akin to the referendum as a manifestation of a general intent to hold governing power closely in the hands of the governed.

Amendment by Referendum

It has already been pointed out that the referendum was adopted not merely to curtail the power of the national union, although this was, in some cases, the original purpose. For referenda in which all local unions were given equal voting strength were replaced by referenda in which each individual member received one vote, and the voting strength of each local was thus determined by its size. What purpose was the latter type of vote intended to serve? According to Glocker, "Primarily have they been em-

1. Theodore W. Glocker, *Government of American Trade Unions* (Baltimore: Johns Hopkins, 1913), pp. 197–198, 202–203.

ployed between the sessions of the convention to transact business which cannot be wisely entrusted to the executive board, yet can be postponed only with grave inconvenience until the next convention."[2] In other words, they were intended to control the executive rather than the legislative arm of the national union. In support of this view, one can point to the struggles which took place within the Carpenters' and Molders' unions to liberalize the initiative.

When the Carpenters first provided for amendment by initiative and referendum (in 1886),[3] they vested the initiative solely in the convention, since only those measures which had secured a two-thirds majority of the convention could be submitted to referendum vote. In 1890, a simple majority was declared sufficient, and, in 1894, the convention was obliged to share the power of initiative with the general executive board, when it was provided that, "At any time the G.E.B. deems a new law or amendment is necessary to govern the U. B., they may recommend a clause to the Local Unions to be voted on . . ."[4] This restored the formal authority of the executive in legislative matters to its prereferendum level.

Before amendment by referendum was adopted, the chief executive (i.e. the general secretary) possessed, in effect, the power to initiate legislation through the institution of his report to the convention which embodied recommendations for legislation that were subsequently voted upon by the delegates. It was the usual practice in American unions for the chief executive to appoint a committee on the president's (and/or secretary's) report which would then report either favorably or unfavorably on the proposals in the president's (and/or secretary's) report. The convention would then vote either to accept or reject the committee's recommendations. This procedure remained after adoption of the referendum, but the executive's power to initiate was now diluted, since the body to which the secretary could present his recommendations no longer possessed final authority to pass upon them. The amendment of 1894, therefore, restored to the executive branch its power to propose changes directly to the group with power to make the final decision. In so doing, it also increased the authority of the executive vis à vis the convention, since the latter was no longer able to block popular consideration of the board's legislative proposals by refusing to ratify them.

This amendment also widened the field of choice open to the membership by eliminating the convention's monopoly over the proposals submitted to referendum. It failed to satisfy the proponents of the popular vote, however, for without the ability to initiate, the grass roots merely possessed the passive authority of the veto. Finally, in 1900, the initiative was extended to the local unions in a law which was obviously intended to curb the power of the executive:

2. Glocker, *Government of Unions*, p. 207.
3. *Constitution*, 1886, Art. VII, Sec. 1.
4. *Constitution*, 1890, Sec. 183; 1894, Sec. 39.

Any Local Union may submit an amendment to the Constitution and Local Rules as a new law. The proposed amendment must be sent to the G.S.-T. (General Secretary-Treasurer) who shall publish it in *The Carpenter* one month prior to the next regular meeting of the G.E.B. and if approved by that body, it shall be submitted to a general vote. If the amendment is endorsed by five Unions in as many States, *approval of the G.E.B. shall not be required.*[5]

The Molders, too, ultimately strengthened their initiative and referendum at the expense of their executive board. Unlike the Carpenters, however, they had provided for what might be termed, "popular initiative," at the outset, subsequently surrendered it to their executive, and finally restored it. When the referendum was first introduced in 1868, it was provided that an amendment could be initiated if proposed by five or more local unions and that it would be ratified if approved by three-quarters of the members voting. In 1879, approval by a majority of the executive board was substituted for sponsorship of four locals in addition to the local of origin as prerequisite to placing a proposal before the membership. At the same time, the vote required for ratification was reduced from three-quarters to a simple majority, "since it was believed that this plan safeguarded the organization against rash schemes."[6] (The Carpenters, on the other hand, required a two-thirds vote even when the initiative was restricted to the convention and the executive board.)

It appears, however, that what originally had been approved as a safeguard came to be regarded as a straitjacket, for, in 1895, the rules were changed to provide that "in the event of a proposed amendment not receiving the sanction of the executive board, on the appeal of ten local unions, the executive board shall publish in the *Journal* their reasons for disapproval, and the secretary shall send it to local unions in circular form." Subsequently, the requirement was tightened a bit by requiring the support of twelve locals on appeal, not more than five of which could belong to the same local conference board. However, power to block the initiative was not restored to the executive board, nor was the vote required for ratification raised above the simple majority to which it had been reduced when executive approval was first required.[7] The executive, indeed, attempted to reëstablish some measure of its erstwhile control, and, prodded by President Fox, the convention of 1899 adopted the following as a standing resolution:

That when a local Union contemplates issuing a circular to the other locals of the I.M.U. of N.A., its text shall first be submitted to the President of this

---

5. *Constitution,* 1900, Sec. 183 (b). (Italics mine.)

6. Frank T. Stockton, *The International Molders Union of North America* (Baltimore: Johns Hopkins, 1921), p. 31. See also *Constitution,* 1879, Art. XIV, Sec. 2.

7. See *Constitution,* 1895, Art. XIV, Sec. 1. In 1888, however, an attempt had been made to foster mature deliberation through a requirement that proposed amendments "be left open for discussion in the *Journal* for three successive issues" before a vote was taken. (*Constitution,* 1888, Art. 16, Sec. 1.)

Union, who shall append, over his signature, the word "Approved" or "Disapproved." In the event of disapproval he shall point out the objectionable features to the issuing local, and upon their modification, disapproval shall be withdrawn.[8]

Standing resolutions, however, did not carry the force of law, and no penalty was attached for violation. As a result, we find that the president informed the convention in 1902 that, "Unfortunately, our local unions encourage the ignoring of Resolution 40 by responding to circulars which do not bear evidence of having been submitted to the President as required."[9]

It is a matter of common knowledge that the referendum appeared nobler in prospect than it proved in performance. It suffices here to record that the experiment was no more successful in this country than it had been in Britain, and that the defects discussed by the Webbs were not absent on this side of the Atlantic. Even so devoted an admirer as Glocker—whose enthusiasm prompted an endorsement of the institution which was hardly supported by the facts which he presented—conceded that amendment by referendum was attended by grave shortcomings, which we might summarize under the following headings:

Reluctance to Increase Dues

Glocker contrasts the Carpenters, who refused to increase their dues and to create a central strike fund, with the Molders whose convention adopted a system of high dues without submission to popular vote and whose president later declared that, "Had such a proposition been submitted to referendum vote there is not the slightest doubt that the change would have been overwhelmingly defeated."[10]

Failure to Vote

When the Molders held a referendum on seven important amendments in 1897, 66 out of 223 locals failed to submit returns."[11] Previously, less than one-third of the membership had voted on an amendment which would have enabled local unions, at their discretion, to raise their initiation fees. As a result, the president complained that, "While the referendum is, without doubt, nearest to the true democratic principle, it is subject to some very serious drawbacks." His point was given added emphasis when, in 1899, only one-quarter of the membership voted on the question of concluding a national arbitration agreement with the National Founders' Association.[12]

The Bricklayers' executive officers were similarly frustrated by the failure of repeated attempts to secure popular assent to affiliation with the American

8. *Standing Resolution No. 40,* 1899.
9. *Proceedings,* 1902, p. 624.
10. Glocker, *Government of Unions,* pp. 220, 225.
11. *Journal,* October 1897, pp. 478–479; February 1894, p. 6.
12. *Journal,* April 1897, p. 172; June 1899, p. 286.

Federation of Labor. Although the Bricklayers did not provide for amendment by referendum, division of opinion between the larger locals, which favored affiliation, and the smaller unions, in opposition, was so great that the executive officer and the conventions sought a mandate directly from the membership. In 1899, the measure obtained a majority vote, but the vote cast was so light that Secretary O'Dea, while passionately in favor of the verdict, accepted it with misgivings:

The very important matter of AFFILIATION with the AMERICAN FEDERATION OF LABOR, was ordered by the last Convention to be submitted to the Subordinate Unions for a vote, the same to be returned and printed in the Semi-annual Report. The question was submitted, the vote returned, and the result is YES, that we affiliate. The vote will be found in the accompanying table.

In giving the result of this vote we are not to be held as voicing the *full* sentiment of the organization by the announcement of such result.

Neither does the result on this important question come up to the expectation intended, for it was with the direct purpose of getting a *full and decisive vote* from *all* of the Subordinate Unions, that the question was submitted to them by the last Convention. Of the total number of Unions on the roll to whom the question was submitted, upwards of one-third of the number refused to vote, thus letting the matter go by default. Of the Unions who have voted, the number who voted in the negative were double to those who voted in the affirmative, and if the defaulting Unions had voted in the same proportion as those who had voted, the question would have been defeated by a large majority.

The result is not satisfactory, but we must accept it. A majority of the Unions have voted, but a minority of Unions by their silence has allowed the proposition to be carried, thus committing the organization to a measure which it apparently does not want. It must now abide by it for the time being, though the force and sense of it will not go into practical effect until formally ratified by the next Convention.

There is no use of kicking, shouting or howling. The vote is cast. The result is announced.

There can be no excuses received of not knowing anything about it. That won't go. Everything connected with the matter was presented to you in Circular No. 10, dated April 26th. Was again mentioned in Circular No. 12, dated June 10th, and again in Circular No. 13, dated June 20th. In each of these notices the *importance* of voting either YES or NO was forcibly called to your attention, and you were likewise notified that all Unions who did not send in a vote would be counted in the *affirmative*.

You accepted the circulars and instructions, and now you must accept the result. Take your medicine and stop kicking.

In all this matter you were left to your own free will and judgment, without interference in any shape for or against by your executive officers, so that a full and honest expression of sentiment on the matter could be obtained.

Excuses of ignorance of the matter will not avail. Of the 85 Unions represented at the last Convention, the delegates of which were fully cognizant of what action had been taken, 16 of said Unions returned no vote.

It was claimed at the Convention that owing to the small number of Unions represented that a momentous question of this nature should not be acted on by them, as they represented a small minority of the organization and that the matter should go to the organization at large, so that the real and full voice of the members should be heard and counted.

It was so done. You have the result. We could have done as well and saved six months' time and expense, had the Convention settled the matter there and then.

Each Union is on record as to its vote on the matter, but official action by your executive officers will be withheld until the assembling of the next Convention, for the last Convention made no provision as to expense, representation, demands or form of policy to be adopted.

So the matter now stands, and will stand, unless the Executive Board brings the matter again before you in a different light and purpose, which in all probability it may have to do perhaps in a very short time.

THE PROPOSITION TO AFFILIATE WITH THE AMERICAN FEDERATION OF LABOR, IS CARRIED.[13]

O'Dea, however, spoke prematurely; it was decided that the proposition was not carried, and subsequent referenda were held. In all these the motion was rejected, but now the low vote cast prompted the officers to continue the polling, for frequently the margin of rejection was exceeded by the number of locals and/or members not voting. Thus, in 1903, the motion was rejected by a majority of forty locals (it is not clear whether a majority of locals or of members was required; from O'Dea's remarks one might judge that both were sought), but sixty-eight failed to send in returns. In 1913, while the majority both of members and organizations voting was decisively against affiliation, of 82,351 members, only 20,351 voted, with a majority of 5,601 opposed. And while 525 of 750 locals voted in the negative, 186 locals failed to vote at all. The upshot was that ratification was finally secured in 1916 by action of the convention alone, with President Bowen apparently playing an active role in preventing another submission to referendum.[14]

Excessive and Inconsistent Legislation [15]

Because the local unions threatened to clog the official mails with their proposals, and because the voting membership was wont either to approve legislation which conflicted with other laws which they had also approved or to disapprove measures which were necessary to the execution of other measures which they had ratified, attempts were made to require that the assent of the executive be obtained before a proposal could be submitted to referendum. Thus the Molders' Standing Resolution of 1899, referred to

13. *Proceedings,* 1899, p. 175.
14. *Proceedings,* 1903, pp. 466–472; 1913, pp. 516–530; 1916, pp. 121–140.
15. Glocker, *Government of Unions,* pp. 228–229, 231.

above, which modestly required only that the president be permitted to read proposals and append his opinion in case of dissent before their submission to the membership, was prompted by President Fox's objection to the issuing of circulars "containing erroneous statements, and sometimes malicious insinuations, or a suppression of fact." [16] This was strong language for the cautious Fox, but it did not measure up to the indictment issued by an ex-Socialist and friend of the referendum, Secretary McGuire of the Carpenters:

While I yield to no man in my faith of a general vote upon questions of importance and my admiration for the referendum vote, still I believe the time has come when I should speak out and recommend a radical change in the method of passing upon the work of the general convention by our members at large. My observation has been that very often a constitution coming from the delegates assembled together, and hearing each section and amendment thoroughly debated pro and con, is definite and clear upon the questions or principles dealt with. But after being passed upon by a general vote of our members it is usually as clear as mud—often conflicting, always indefinite, scarcely ever understood by any two members alike—and likely to impede the progress of our organization and ultimately to weaken our influence among thoughtful men.

It must not be inferred that I would recommend the abolition of a referendum vote, but I do recommend the adoption of a change in this one respect, and that is that only general principles or definite questions, or a section of the constitution, having no direct connection with the preceding or following section, shall be submitted for a general vote as, for example, in our constitution we are called upon to determine whether we shall have a member's funeral benefit. Let us suppose that it is necessary to have, say, six sections dealing with the necessary details, all those sections may be absolutely necessary to an intelligent working of this particular benefit, and dovetail together perfectly. But when the sections are submitted for a general vote, suppose (as often happens) that one or two sections are defeated and the rest carried, you can easily see that the whole question is turned into a farce and a cheap one at that, or it is left to one or two men to determine what the remaining sections mean. This makes me feel very strongly that only the question, *shall we have a certain thing* (should be submitted to referendum—L.U.) and then the details to carry it out, should be left to the convention.[17]

Benefit and Strike Referenda

It will be recalled that availability of the referendum to appeal adverse rulings on eligibility threatened the solvency of some of the benefit funds maintained by British unions, because the membership tended uncritically to uphold such appeals. In this country, the benefit system maintained by the Carpenters' Brotherhood was endangered by some referendum votes, although the Carpenters did not allow individual cases to be appealed to

16. *Proceedings,* 1899, p. 12.
17. *Proceedings,* 1898, p. 8.

popular vote from the decisions of the general executive board. Their wisdom in this respect was evidenced by the fact that the secretary complained that the locals "out of sympathy to financially aid the claimant, or, as we know of in some cases, to avoid the responsibility of . . . disapproving the claim . . ." passed on to the general executive board "the disagreeable and unpleasant duty of rejecting a large number of claims which naturally has aroused, more or less, the hostility of some local Unions, where otherwise there would be no grounds of complaint."[18] In 1895, McGuire informed the convention that with "membership decreasing, and our liabilities for benefits growing greater as we grow older, we must strive to place our system of benefits on a solvent basis." In accordance with his recommendations, the convention reduced the scale of benefits and passed a rule whereby each new member would have had to pay a registration fee of fifty cents. "The adoption of the first would have decreased our liabilities, and the second would have added considerably to our income." But both these measures were defeated in referendum. As a result, the benefit fund ran into the red. The union was obliged to levy a special *per capita* assessment of thirty cents on its entire membership and also to borrow seven thousand dollars from its strike fund and over twelve thousand from its organizing fund.[19]

Since the American unions devoted a smaller portion of their energies and resources to benefit activities, and a larger portion to strike support, we find that the referendum's proneness to fiscal irresponsibility was evidenced chiefly in the latter field of endeavor. According to Glocker, "The tendency of the local unions to approve all strike applications without discrimination may at times be exceedingly disastrous."[20] As a result, some national unions eliminated the strike referendum after they had provided for substantial strike aid. This was observed in our discussion of the relationship between the establishment of such funds and the emergence of the chief executive.

When, in 1881, the Carpenters provided that each local maintain a strike fund in its own treasury by setting aside 10 per cent of its monthly receipts, they also provided that any decision by the executive board of the Brotherhood not to sanction a local "difficulty" could be reversed by a simple "majority of all members voting."[21] In 1886, however, when the locals were

---

18. *Proceedings,* 1888, p. 16. Also, *Proceedings,* 1894, p. 23, wherein McGuire announced that, "Again and again the G.S. and G.T. have been compelled to perform the unpleasant but imperative duty of disapproving claims that on their very face were clearly illegal, so that in the last two years 184 claims, amounting to $24,455, were disapproved." He admonished the locals to "conform strictly to every term of our laws, and in claims for benefit every interest of the order should be guarded and considered and not allow the moneys of the U.B. to be frittered away to satisfy mere feelings of personal friendship or empty sentimentality."

19. *Proceedings,* 1896, p. 25.

20. Glocker, *Government of Unions,* p. 223.

21. *Constitution,* 1881, Art. XI.

instructed to divert five cents per member monthly into their funds and the executive board was empowered to levy special assessments in support of an authorized strike upon the depletion of the funds, the majority required to reverse the board's decision on appeal was raised to two-thirds. Furthermore, "The General President, in conjunction with the Executive Board, shall have power, when satisfied from facts and information in their possession that a strike should cease, to declare the same at an end, so far as the financial aid of the Brotherhood is concerned, and shall so notify all Local Unions." In 1890, the strike referendum was discontinued, and the decision of the general executive board was thus made final. Two years later, provision was made for the accumulation of a central strike fund, to be held in the Brotherhood's treasury.[22]

The Molders underwent a similar evolution. At first, the national union merely undertook to solicit funds from the affiliated locals to support strikes of which its executive committee, consisting of the president and vice-presidents, approved.[23] Since each vice-president at this time was a delegate from a local union, this procedure was almost tantamount to ratification by a referendum of the local unions. "No real restraint was thus imposed upon local unions," according to an early observer, "and the financial assistance thus provided was of a kind to encourage rather than to prevent strikes."[24] In 1861, provision was made for the levying of strike assessments, but the requirements with respect to national approval remained unchanged.[25] In 1867 it was provided for the first time that strike benefits of stated amounts be paid, and in 1868 the maximum per capita assessment which the international president could levy was increased from 2 per cent of the members' weekly wages to 5 per cent. At the same time, the vote required for approval was increased from a simple majority to two-thirds of the local unions.[26]

Furthermore, since many of the locals had failed to vote in the past, it was provided that those not voting should be counted in the negative. As a result, virtually no strikes were declared "legal," and the 1870 convention ordered that benefits be paid to two locals which had struck without authorization from the international. This convention then changed the regulations to provide that a failure to vote be counted as an affirmative vote and that a strike would be sanctioned unless the strike circular received a "negative vote of two-thirds." However, it sought to forestall indiscriminate approval

22. *Constitution*, 1886, Art. XX; 1892, Sec. 59.

23. Stockton, *Molders Union*, p. 101. See also p. 27.

24. F. W. Hilbert, "Trade-Union Agreements in the Iron Molders' Union," in *Studies in American Trade Unionism*, ed. by Jacob H. Hollander and George E. Barnett (New York: Henry Holt, 1906), p. 222.

25. Stockton, *Molders Union*, p. 102. In 1867, it was required that approval be secured by a majority vote of the corresponding representatives of the local unions, instead of the vice-presidents who were no longer representatives of local unions, (p. 103).

26. Hilbert, *Studies in Unionism*, p. 223.

by providing that the international president include in each strike circular the weekly amount which each local would be required to contribute. Nevertheless, the local corresponding representatives continued to abstain from voting, and thus virtually all circulars were authorized. Therefore, in 1874, it was once more required that two-thirds of all the locals vote in the affirmative. Moreover, the president was authorized to include in each circular his recommendation as to the merits of the dispute under consideration and also to discontinue aid after he considered that strikes were lost.[27]

These measures proved inadequate, however, since the local unions, instead of levying strike assessments upon their members as they were supposed to do, frequently utilized for strike purpose all their local resources, as a result of which they fell into arrears with the international.[28] Furthermore, a previous regulation, providing that no dispute could be circularized unless it had been first submitted to arbitration, proved ineffective since the employers displayed no interest in arbitration.[29] In 1882, it was sought to remedy the situation, first, by building up the local funds with the proceeds of a special levy of one dollar upon each member, and, second, by eliminating the referendum and vesting in the president and the executive board

absolute control of all strikes and lock-outs. . . It shall be considered a sufficient cause for expulsion from the National Union, should any local Union attempt to assume responsibility of striking without their grievance being considered by the President and having the sanction of the Executive Board before going out. . .[30]

But the funds accumulated by the special levy proved inadequate, and, therefore, in 1890, the Molders finally provided for a central strike fund, financed out of current tax receipts (which were increased for the purpose). Thereafter, the executive board and President Fox (who assumed office in 1890) made it a policy never to authorize a strike unless sufficient resources were available for the disbursement of the prescribed weekly benefits.

The Bricklayers, as we know, at first vested in their national president and vice-president the power to approve all applications for strike aid, but they quickly reconsidered and left the determination of these questions to popular vote. However, it was not long before the national officers began to suggest a return to the original system. Thus, in 1870, after a strike had been approved by referendum and the tax was presumably collected, President Gaul, after having received certain unfavorable information from the president of the striking local "that entirely changed my mind as to levying a tax for the relief of said union, I did not think it expedient or necessary to issue

27. Stockton, *Molders Union*, pp. 103–105.
28. *Proceedings*, 1878, p. 10.
29. Hilbert, *Studies in Unionism*, pp. 224–225.
30. *Constitution*, 1882, Art. VI, Sec. 2; 1890, Art. VI, Secs. 1 and 2. See also Stockton, *Molders Union*, pp. 106–107.

for relief under the circumstances."[31] In 1874, the president was authorized to advise the locals on the merit of each application for aid and also to refuse further aid after he considered that a strike had been lost. But these measures fell considerably short of Gaul's previous recommendation that the decision on financial aid be vested solely in the president "if coincided by either of the Vice-Presidents," "the opinion of the Executive to be based upon the moral and financial condition of the Union interested, and their prospects of success."

The object of this [he explained] is to check the disposition of organized bodies in resorting to these means, in many cases on frivolous and unwarranted pretexts, which in eight cases out of ten result in destruction to the Union engaged and heavy assessments on all connected, as taxation in its most favorable form becomes obnoxious by repetition.[32]

The next suggestion by an international president was that a central strike fund be established. In 1884, local funds were created by a single per capita levy of ten cents (raised to one dollar for new locals in 1887), and in 1891 a central fund was created by a single assessment of twenty-five cents per head, to which there was subsequently added the proceeds of an equal tax upon all new members. The fund grew from $5,870 in 1891 to $14,147 in 1900, and with this growth in the international's combat potential came a repetition of President Gaul's old complaint. According to Secretary O'Dea,

The Bill of Grievance is . . . printed and submitted to the Subordinate Unions to vote upon, and they *always* get the required vote granting them permission to strike. This vote is most generally a sympathy vote, for the majority of unions vote yes on pride so as to have it . . . (said) they never voted against a strike, and they never stop to consider whether the circumstances attending the nature of the strike is justifiable, or whether the state of trade throughout the country, and the conditions of the organization would warrant a recognition of it in supporting such a movement.[33]

In 1903, the strike referendum was discontinued, and final authority to authorize was vested in the executive board.

In addition to the hypergenerosity of the local unions, another serious drawback to the strike referendum was the delay entailed in obtaining authorization.[34] This undoubtedly accounts in part for the widespread disposition on the part of the locals to strike first and seek approval and aid afterwards. One national president, Gaul of the Bricklayers, actually aided his locals in circumventing the referendum. He hit upon the device of requesting contributions, "believing [so he said] that voluntary contributions are far favorable [i.e. preferable] to special taxation and is more generally responded

31. *Proceedings*, 1871, pp. 8–9.
32. *Proceedings*, 1871, p. 15.
33. *Proceedings*, 1893, pp. 25–26.
34. Glocker, *Government of Unions*, pp. 231–232.

to on the part of the members of the organization." When the Philadelphia local called a strike before submitting its "bill of grievance," Gaul informed its officers that their violation of international law made it impossible for him subsequently to distribute their bill but that he would, if requested officially, "cheerfully call for voluntary contributions." He concluded that

The time required for a union to obtain permission to strike being too long. . . I think the question of granting such authority may with safety be invested in the executive officer or in the Judiciary Committee. . .[35]

Direct Election of Officers

In our discussion of the role played by the early convention in the selection of the executive officers of the national union, it was pointed out that the primitive concept of personal membership in the convention imparted to our national unions, while the latter were still in their rudimentary stages, a tradition which favored election of officers by the delegates to the convention. It was really not until the first decade of the present century had passed that elections by vote of the membership gained any degree of popularity, and as late as 1913 Glocker could find only "perhaps eighteen national unions" which had adopted the latter system. He noted, as did the Webbs in England, that

Popular elections are said . . . to result in the reëlection of the officers in power. There may be other candidates who are much better fitted for the positions, but they are comparatively unknown, or possess only a local popularity. On the other hand, the men already holding office have a decided advantage over the other contestants because their names are familiar to every member in the organization.[36]

He went on to observe that, "Officers are repeatedly reëlected by convention as well as by popular vote, and under both systems often continue in office for many years." This is undoubtedly true, and it was suggested above that length of tenure in office was more closely associated with such factors as the growth in power and activity of the national organization, the consequent demand for the services of professionally competent officials, and the establishment of systems of executive compensation, rather than with the manner of selection. Moreover, long incumbency *per se* did not necessarily sap the vitality of the democratic institutions which the founders of the national unions here and in Britain had attempted to erect. Long tenure posed no threat if the power to make high policy was removed from the incumbent's office.

In addition to his comments upon the coincidence of popular elections and lengthy tenure of office, Glocker observed that the movement to conduct popular elections derived its impetus from dissatisfaction with the political

35. *Proceedings*, 1870, pp. 24–25.
36. Glocker, *Government of Unions*, pp. 213, 224.

cliques and factions which developed within conventions and which frequently influenced the course of elections. In quoting a certain trade union official, he implied that the referendum proved fatal to such undesirable alignments.[37]

The history of the Typographical Union sheds a curious light upon this matter. The move to elect officials by popular vote in this union (adopted in 1896) must be considered in connection with certain peculiar conditions obtaining in the printing industry and also in connection with the fact that the I.T.U. admitted to regular membership foremen printers and sought to control their hiring policies. Employment was apt to be irregular in the printing industry, which was characterized, especially in its newspaper branch, by sharp weekly and daily variations in the demand for labor.[38] Hence attached to each establishment was a work force, which was in excess of demand at off-peak intervals. The foreman sought to have available a supply of competent extra hands, or "subs," and, in order to do so, he attempted to retain the more competent subs by favoring them in their assignment of extra work. With the introduction of more expensive machinery, the greater fixed charge on which placed a premium on efficient operation, the foremen's desire to give preference to the more efficient men became more acute.

The nonsupervisory printers, on the other hand, adhered to the original policy of the I.T.U., which stated that each regular worker should control his position, or "sit" (short for "situation") and be entitled to designate his own relief, the understanding being that work would be divided fairly equally among the "subs." When the foremen sought to modify this practice by instituting "sub lists," which contained the names of those subs who were eligible for appointment and thus limited the discretion of the regulars, great rank-and-file opposition, led by the traveling printers, developed. A rule prohibiting "sub lists" was passed at the 1884 convention. When the foremen sought to circumvent this restriction on their hiring activities by employing the printers of their choice for specified periods, such practices were also outlawed by the convention.

At first the foremen's opponents pressed for an equal division of work, which took the form of a rule, passed in 1890, forbidding any member to work more than six days in any one week. However, opposition to the "sub list" was also directed against the foremen's "right to discharge an employee on purely personal grounds," and it ultimately resulted in the passage (in 1890) of the Printers' famous "priority" or seniority, law. This law required the foreman to present proof of incompetency in order to justify the prior

37. Glocker, *Government of Unions,* pp. 213–214.

38. The following summary of events leading up to the passage of the Printer's "priority law" is based upon the account in George E. Barnett, *The Printers* (Cambridge, Mass.: American Economic Association, 1909), pp. 209–242.

discharge of a printer with higher seniority than the man retained. The law also applied to the promotion of subs to regular positions. And, since the foremen themselves were members of the union, authority to determine the propriety of a contested discharge or promotion was vested in the president of the international union. Thus both factions had great incentive to control the international executive.

Although the foremen formed only a minority of the union's membership, they were highly influential because of their power to dispense jobs to their favorites. Professor Taft holds that a definite connection existed between this power of patronage and the emergence of rival cliques, and the record certainly seems to support this position.[39] The first of these groups was referred to as the Brotherhood of the Union of North America, which was formed in the seventies. It was charged by its opponents, who later banded into an organization of their own known as the Progressives, with seeking to dominate the convention and to dictate the choice of officers. The convention of 1880, in a long resolution which was directed at the incumbent administration, made it unlawful for any member to belong to the Brotherhood, which was described as an "oath-bound, sign, grip, and password using organization."[40] This convention also required each delegate to pledge that he would "not, in legislation, election of officers, or otherwise, allow any secret, outside or improper means of any kind whatever to influence my action." They also recommended that a similar pledge be administered by the local unions to their initiates. This pledge contained the following significant clause:

that in the employment of such men unionism will be first considered, competency next, and personal or other preferences last.

But despite this vigorous exorcism, the devil of factionalism remained much in evidence. The next convention (1882) refused to adopt a resolution calling for disciplinary action to be taken against any delegate who joined any "caucus, organized conference, or society" and against any "person or persons who shall accept the nomination" of such a group. It contented itself with a harmless expression of sentiment to the effect "that this International Union deprecates and condemns all meetings of a secret character, held for such purposes (i.e. the nomination of officers), under any form or under any name." Moreover, in 1888, (after the passage of the rule against sublists) the convention "postponed" action on two resolutions, one of which made it "unlawful for a member to associate himself with any society or combination composed exclusively of printers having for their object the manipulation or

39. Philip Taft, "Opposition to Union Officers in Elections," *Quarterly Journal of Economics,* February 1944, pp. 248, 253–262. See also Taft, *The Structure and Government of Labor Unions* (Harvard University Press, 1954), pp. 52–56.

40. Quoted in George A. Tracy, *History of the Typographical Union* (Indianapolis: International Typographical Union, 1913), p 322. See also pp. 323, 354–355, 422–423.

giving out of positions, the shaping of legislation, or the controlling of the offices of the union." But this convention did instruct the locals to prohibit secret groups within their own jurisdictions.[41] And in 1896 a resolution against "one or more secret societies" was passed unanimously and each delegate was required to "solemnly swear, before Almighty God, by everything that I hold sacred and holy" that he would belong to no such group, "whether known by the name of the Brotherhood, Caxton League, Wahnetas, or any other name whatsoever, or any other body, with or without a name, or any such body that may technically dissolve itself at the adjournment of its meetings. . . ."[42]

Since provision was also made for the holding of elections by popular vote at this convention, the record of the Printers bears out Glocker's contention that recourse to direct election was stimulated by aversion to factionalism within the convention. But his implication that such factionalism disappeared after the referendum was installed was disproved by the subsequent course of events within the Typographical Union. In his report to the convention of 1900, a president condemned what Tracy termed, "the decadence of the spirit of brotherhood and fraternity and the development of intense factional feelings among the members of many important unions." Tangible evidence of such "factional feelings" took the form of allegedly scurrilous attacks against certain officers and members of the international. As a result, the president felt obliged to deny the contention of some that "indulgence in the practices complained of had proven the referendum system a failure in the organization."

Nevertheless, factionalism not only persisted; it ultimately became institutionalized within the framework provided by the referendum election of officers. It is an ironic fact that the International Typographical Union owes its unique two-party system to origins which were generally condemned (and which, incidentally, were completely overlooked by its most illustrious biographer, Barnett). But Taft believes that, "The existence of a closely-knit group aiming to secure control seems to have stimulated active political interest in the affairs of the Union."[43] However, since factionalism in other unions failed to produce the same happy result, it would appear that behind the printers' factions there must have existed initially a genuine divergence of opinion over one or more issues which were of vital importance to the individual members and which could not be resolved by the secession of the disaffected group. It appears that the opposition, led by the influential and militant "tramps," did not gain control over the international executive. However, as long as the foremen retained *de facto* control over the allocation of jobs, secession was out of the question; the opposition had to remain "loyal."

41. Taft, "Opposition to Officers," p. 257.
42. Tracy, *Typographical Union*, pp. 518–519. See also pp. 619, 638–639.
43. Taft, *Structure and Government of Labor Unions*, p. 56. Also p. 55.

Loyalty, moreover, ultimately paid off, for the convention did curtail drastically the foremen's control over hiring, discharge, and promotion.

CONTROL BY THE EXECUTIVE BOARD

The object of the referendum was to contain the executive board within a minimum area of discretionary authority. By and large, it failed to accomplish its purpose. (The full story of its failure belongs in an account of a period in the history of American unionism later than the period covered by this study, but we have had occasion to note that some of the most important national unions in the nineteenth century abandoned their strike referenda in favor of control by the executive board.) What did the board's rise to a position of legal power, as the supreme authority of the national union between sessions of the convention, signify?

To begin with, it should be noted that the mission of the board was akin to that of the referendum. Referenda were designed as a check on the power of the national executive boards, and "National executive boards were created to serve as a check on the power of the national officers."[44]

In their attempt to achieve the same purpose, the British unions experimented with a variety of organizational types. From our brief summary of the Webb's findings, we can distinguish four leading types of members on executive councils. There were the unpaid members, chosen by the governing branch. There were the full-time salaried officers of the national union, elected either by the general membership or by the convention. There were the representatives of the district unions, who were either elected by the districts or by the membership of the entire national union. Finally, there were members, other than national or local officials, who were elected by the convention.

In the United States, as in Britain, one or more of these member types entered into the composition of each kind of executive board that was devised. In neither country, of course, were all four types found on the same board.

In Chapter 8, the Carpenters' Brotherhood was referred to as one of the few American unions which had followed, for a while, the British pattern of first seeking to vest control in an executive board selected by a "governing branch" and ultimately transferring power to a full-time executive officer. At first the Carpenters' executive board was composed of the president, three vice-presidents, and the secretary—all of whom were elected by the convention—and of the treasurer and three trustees, who were chosen by the local or locals in the city which had been selected by the convention as the secretary's headquarters.[45] Thus the officers nominated by the governing branch were outnumbered by those chosen by the convention; however, a two-thirds vote was necessary to decide all matters within the board's competence. This

44. Glocker, *Government of Unions*, p. 186.
45. *Constitution*, 1881, Art. II.

board was authorized to approve strike petitions, but its decisions were subject to reversal by referendum vote. It could also decide all points of law, differences among locals, and grievances, but these judicial decisions could be appealed to the convention. At the outset, then, the governing branch did not govern in any final sense; it was an import grafted on to a system in which ultimate authority was shared by the convention and the referendum.

In 1886, the authority of the board was, in some respects, strengthened at the expense of both the convention and the referendum. The composition of the board was changed so that all five of its voting members were chosen by the membership of the headquarters local (or locals, if more than one existed in that city or within a radius of ten miles). It was required that the board hold meetings twice a month, or more often if required. The secretary and treasurer were granted "the right to a voice, but no vote." The board's judicial decisions were still subject to appeal to the convention, but the referendum vote required to overturn its strike rulings was increased from a simple majority to a two-thirds vote. It was also granted the power of initiative, and it was instructed to hold the bonds of the secretary and treasurer and to audit their books monthly. It could appoint state and territorial organizers on recommendation of the appropriate locals and when sanctioned by the president; and it could make "treaties" with other national unions, subject to approval by the local unions.[46]

At the same time, however, the board became less representative of the membership at large, for the convention decided that headquarters be located in one city, Philadelphia, for the next ten years. (This was subject to change by a majority of two-thirds in a referendum, and in 1902 the headquarters was transferred to Indianapolis.) Thus the Carpenters paralleled the experience of the British unions whose governing branches ceased to rotate after a professional administration had been established.

The other locals apparently resented Philadelphia's domination, for, at the following convention, some of its powers were transferred to seven general vice-presidents, each of whom was chosen from a separate geographic district. It was provided that, "The seven General Vice-Presidents shall also act as Organizers, and each must be a member in good standing of some Local Union in the district in which he shall act."[47] Thus the board surrendered its power to appoint organizers. Furthermore, it was established that

The General President and all of the Vice-Presidents shall report in January of each year at the General Office, and shall there act and sit as a board of appeals on all claims and grievances, their decision to be final.

Since the board's judicial powers remained on the books and since the new group's decisions were to be "final," one must conclude that the convention's judicial authority was transferred to the president and vice-presidents. At this

46. *Constitution*, 1886, Art. XXII.
47. *Constitution*, 1888, Art. XIV.

session, also, the board was stripped of its authority to make "treaties" with other unions.

In 1890, the board was reconstituted on a geographic basis. The number of vice-presidents was reduced from seven to two and, unlike their regional predecessors, they were assigned no organizing duties. The new board was composed of five members: one from the New England states, New Brunswick, and Nova Scotia; one from the middle states, Ontario, and Quebec; one from the southern states; and two from the western states. The new board's judicial status was the same as its predecessor's had been, with final appellate authority vested in the convention and with the general secretary and the general treasurer deciding all appeals in the first instance.[48] The power to appoint district organizers, which the old board had possessed prior to the abortive experiment with the seven vice-presidents, was not returned to the new board, however, but was vested in the secretary, subject to approval of the president. But the authority of the new board was increased in one respect, for the strike referendum was discontinued in 1890 and the decisions of the board concerning strike authorizations became final.

The board lost its judicial functions in 1894, when the secretary-treasurer was empowered to decide on all appeals and grievances, subject only to appeal to the convention. On the other hand, its strike authority was further increased in 1896, when it was decided that the president should share his authority to discontinue financial aid to a striking local with the board.[49]

We conclude that the Carpenters were unwilling to allow much authority to remain with their first executive board, the members of which were chosen by the local unions in a city that had been designated as a semipermanent headquarters. On the other hand, they apparently were quite willing to delegate wider powers to groups in which all geographic regions of the Brotherhood were directly represented. But wider representation was purchased at the price of reduced efficiency: whereas the Philadelphia board was instructed to convene at least once every two weeks, the seven vice-presidents were not expected to "sit as a board" more than once every year, and the board which was established in 1890 was hardly in a position to meet more frequently than the vice-presidents had been.

The Molders experimented with virtually all the types of organization identified by the Webbs. Their first "national executive committee" consisted of the president and the vice-presidents of the national union. Since, at that time, each vice-president was chosen by his respective local union, this committee was essentially a trade union senate which provided equal repre-

48. *Constitution*, 1890, Sec. 15. In 1892, it was stipulated that one of the two members from the western states be from west of the Mississippi (*Constitution*, 1892, Sec. 15; *Constitution*, 1890, Sec. 28).

49. *Constitution*, 1894, Sec. 26; 1896, Secs. 135 and 136.

sentation for all local unions. To this group was given the authority to approve requests by striking locals for solicitation of funds on their behalf. In fact, it was "invested with all the authority of the national union, the making of laws excepted."[50] But, since each vice-president served in his home local as corresponding representative, it proved impossible to convene this committee in meeting.

In 1863, therefore, the practice of designating "general" vice-presidents (who were not chosen by particular local unions or districts) was inaugurated, and in 1867 the four general vice-presidents were designated as a board of trustees. Nine years later, the vice-presidents were dropped from the board, which was now to consist of "three members in good standing, elected by the convention, other than officers." Thus, in composition, the Molders' board of trustees now resembled the Webbs' ideal of an executive council of amateurs selected by and responsible to the representative convention. In fact, however, the Webbs would have been quite disappointed with the Molders' board of trustees, for, aside from its authority to fill any office declared vacant by the president—with the exception of the offices of president and local corresponding representative—its functions were restricted to supervision of the financial activities of the president and the treasurer. The president, meanwhile, exercised appellate judicial authority, subject only to appeal to the convention; he passed judgment on the by-laws of new locals; and he was empowered to suspend locals for any violations of international law.[51] Furthermore, the power to approve strikes was still vested in the corresponding representatives of the local unions.

In 1878, the three trustees were included on an executive board, together with the four general vice-presidents. The board had been reconstituted and made stronger as a result of the defalcation of a president; and, as Stockton wrote, "The president's position was made something like that of a corporation head dealing with his board of directors."[52] The president was obliged to share with the new board his judicial functions and his authority to appoint and pay organizers. Henceforth, he could visit local unions and "inspect their proceedings" only after he had secured the board's approval, and he had to "lay all matters of interest to the I.M.U. of N.A. before the executive board." In its report to the special convention held in 1879, the board held

that the controlling power of the Organization should not be left entirely in the hands of one man, as the rulings and actions of one has not given that satisfaction so necessary to our success.[53]

Shortly after the board had been granted this large measure of control over the chief executive, however, it lost its amateur standing, for, in 1879, the

50. *Proceedings*, 1859, p. 10. (Quoted in Stockton, *Molders Union*, p. 28.)
51. *Constitution*, 1876, Art. III.
52. Stockton, *Molders Union*, p. 29; see also *Constitution*, 1876, Art. III.
53. *Proceedings*, 1879, p. 12.

requirement that the trustees be "other than officers" was deleted from the constitution.[54] And in 1882, the trustees (now five in number) were dropped from the board, which thereupon consisted entirely of the president (who had no vote) and the vice-presidents, whose number was increased to five. At the same time, the strike referendum was eliminated, and the president and the new Board received "absolute control of all strikes and lock-outs."

But the lesson of 1878 was not forgotten, and the Molders were not content to entrust the supervision of their president to a group of unsalaried vice-presidents whose duties were largely unspecified, but who presumably were available for organizing work at rates of compensation which they, in their capacity as board members, could establish. The board was reconstituted once more; this time the vice-presidents were removed, and the new board was composed of the president and five trustees. Moreover, the latter were "to be elected from Unions located within one day's travel from the official headquarters."[55] The board exercised appellate authority which was superior to that of the president.

On the other hand, the president was made independent of the board as far as certain organizing and kindred activities were concerned. He was authorized to visit and inspect local unions entirely on his own initiative, and he was empowered to appoint organizers "in such manner as he may deem best calculated to advance the interests of the I.M.U. of N.A." Thus the president possessed authority to enable him to create a corps of paid appointees whose influence could reach every local in the national jurisdiction. Furthermore, in 1888, the one remaining vice-president was made "subordinate to the President; he shall proceed to any section of the country designated by the former." In 1890, two more vice-presidents, with identical assignments, were added, and a fourth was provided in 1899.[56] And, although the Molders sought to implement their intention to police the chief executive with an amateur executive board by providing that no member thereof should be permitted to hold any other elective office in the international union while serving on the board, it is perhaps significant that no rule was passed to prevent board members from serving as appointive officers.

In any event, the experiment with an executive board selected by a governing branch was subsequently abandoned, and the Molders, by now thoroughly frustrated, created a board of trustees chosen by the convention whose members were selected "to represent as nearly as possible every section of our broad jurisdiction and its diversified interests."[57] Since Stockton reported that this board met "frequently, often for sessions lasting for a week or ten days," one wonders how it was possible for members from "every section" to

54. *Constitution*, 1879, Art. IV, Sec. 5.
55. *Constitution*, 1886, Art. III.
56. *Constitution*, 1888, Art. IV; 1890, Art. IV; 1899, Art. IV.
57. *Journal*, August 1913, p. 671. (Quoted in Stockton, *Molders Union*, p. 30, fn. 8.)

maintain both their amateur standing and financial solvency. The trustees were paid only their mileage expenses and a per diem allowance. It is pertinent to quote Glocker (whose observation was not restricted to the Molders' situation) on this point:

Moreover, even when they receive no salary, the members of the executive board are frequently selected for special service by the president, so that the chief executive has the opportunity to create a coterie of adherents by letting fall the plums to those who favor his policies.[58]

The executive board of the Glass Bottle Blowers' Association was similar to the executive council of the English Cotton-spinners, as described by the Webbs. It was chosen by the convention and consisted at first of "such officers and such number selected from the representatives as the Annual Session may so decide." In 1893 the convention terminated its own discretion in this matter by providing that the board would consist henceforth of the vice-president and six members, duly elected by the annual sessions. In 1896, it was provided that the six members be "selected from the trade at large."[59]

The Bottle Blowers stipulated that their executive board should exercise all powers of the association between annual sessions (it will be recalled that this union did not institute amendment by referendum), and proceeded to endow it with rather formidable authority. The board shared with the president the power to interpret the laws of the association whenever a difference of opinion arose in any branch over the meaning and intent of such laws. The president had to secure the consent of a majority of the executive board in order to suspend "any Branch in the Association for any violation of its laws, or for insubordination to any lawful command of himself or the Executive Board." This grant of authority over the president was made at the same time that it was provided that the board be composed of six "members" and only one national officer. The same convention likewise restrained the president in the exercise of his power to suspend officers of the association. Similarly, the consent of the board was required before the president could assemble the convention in a special session. Moreover, the authority previously delegated to the president, of "general supervision within the union" and of ensuring "that the general workings of the Branches are in accordance with the laws of the Association," were deleted from the constitution.[60]

The board also had the power to sanction local strikes and, by a vote of two-thirds, it could levy strike assessments. Furthermore, it was established that "the distribution of assessments be left entirely in the hands of the President and the Executive Board."[61] The president shared with the board the

58. Glocker, *Government of Unions*, p. 192.
59. *Constitution*, 1892, Art. III, Sec. 10; 1893, Art. III, Sec. 11; 1894, Sec. 11; 1896, Art. III, Sec. 11.
60. *Constitution*, 1888, Art. XII, Sec. 72; 1892, Art. III, Sec. 13; 1894, Art. III, Sec. 13.
61. *Constitution*, 1892, Art. III, Sec. 11.

authority to settle disputes with employers concerning the apprentice law and the employment of gathering boys on press work.[62] Finally, the convention, in 1892, decided that

for exigencies not covered by these laws, the President and Executive Board may adopt regulations to govern this Association, which shall have the force of law until reversed by the Annual Session, and all such regulations shall be reported to Annual Session for approval.[63]

Two observations should be made at this point. The first is that the Bottle Blowers were not reluctant to delegate extensive authority to their executive branch; in this repect their achievement is more remarkable than that of the British Cotton-spinners, for the Bottle Blowers, unlike the latter, met only once every year in convention. Second, their willingness to create a powerful executive was premised upon the assumption that the chief executive officers would be controlled by a board of members who worked at the trade. Thus the board received two varieties of power: the first represented a net accrual of authority to the executive wing of the association; the second was gained at the expense of the president and represented a shift of authority within the executive branch.

Special circumstances attended each case. The disappearance and defalcation of a national secretary appears to have preceded the convention of 1894, at which many of the powers of the chief executive officers were made subject to concurrence by the board.[64] Furthermore, the establishment of a system of national collective bargaining created strong sentiment in favor of providing an executive with sufficient flexibility and authority to cope with the changing conditions arising at the conference table. Nevertheless, some uneasiness prevailed among the delegates at the prospect of granting so much authority to a small group of members who could not have represented all the regional interests of the membership. This was illustrated by the following statement in support of a resolution which was designed to prevent the executive board from making any changes in the national trade agreements:

Owing to the dissatisfaction existing throughout the trade in consequence of the power invested in the Executive Board, who can alter or change any and all laws adopted by the annual conventions. And,

Which laws are the result of careful thought and due deliberations on the part of the representatives who are called together from all parts of the country. And,

Whose knowledge we consider paramount (coming, as it does, from so many of the brightest minds in our order) to the few who comprise the Executive Board, Therefore be it

Resolved, That any law or laws agreed upon between the Executive Board

62. By-Laws, 1892, Sec. 24.
63. Constitution, 1892, Art. XII, Sec. 72.
64. Proceedings, 1894, p. 33.

of this Association and the Manufacturers' Wage Committee at the conference be strictly adhered to, and under no circumstances shall the Executive Board make any change or modifications unless approved by a majority vote of the members of the entire trade in good standing.[65]

The convention, however, was unwilling to provide for an appeal to popular vote; it modified the above resolution by substituting the requirement that any change made by the executive board must be approved by the two conference committees (the manufacturers' and the union's). The union committee was chosen by the convention.[66] But ultimately the convention agreed to sacrifice even its control over the annual agreements, for the composition of the union's negotiating committee was changed, and all the association's representatives thereon, with the exception of the president, were members of the executive board. And, according to an early account of collective bargaining in the glass bottle industry, "the union conferees have throughout the conference debates shown unusual independence of judgment. . . . The representatives of the union have full power to settle questions without referring the matter back to their organization. Nor do they go to the conference instructed to take one stand or another."[67]

The Printers, after some early experimentation, finally settled on an executive council composed entirely of national officers, each of whom was elected by the general membership.

The first executive board of the Printers was obviously not intended to act as a restraining influence upon the president, for it was provided

that the President of the National Union shall appoint, before the close of each session, a National Executive Committee, consisting of one representative from each Union, whose especial duty it shall be to correspond, individually, with the printers in the various cities and towns in his neighborhood, and endeavor to secure the formation of Unions in said places.[68]

It was not necessary, however, to restrain the president in those days when the national union had little authority, for, as Barnett tells us, "The officers of the National Union, as constituted during the period from 1851 to 1885, were merely an adjunct to the annual session."[69]

But after the international had embarked upon an independent existence of its own, an executive council was established which, it was hoped, would wield real authority. It consisted of the president, the three vice-presidents,

65. *Proceedings*, 1898, p. 62.
66. *Constitution*, 1896, Art. III.
67. Leo Wolman, "Collective Bargaining in the Glass-Bottle Industry," *American Economic Review*, vol. VI (1916), pp. 549–567.
68. *Constitution*, 1857, "General Laws," p. 44.
69. Barnett, *The Printers*, pp. 60–61. The following account is taken from pp. 68–69.

the secretary-treasurer, and the organizers. There were seven of the latter; each of whom was assigned to a specific geographic district, so that the council was theoretically dominated by these regional representatives. Its specific powers included adjudication of disputes between locals and administration of the strike fund. The council was to meet twice a year, but it did not meet at all during the first year of its existence, because the union was passing through a period of financial stringency. The president's report to the next convention described a familiar problem: The council's membership was too scattered to meet frequently, "and as matters are frequently referred to them which should be decided promptly, much time is lost. It may be worth considering whether a smaller council less scattered would not be an improvement." The convention followed the president's lead and made the council "smaller" and "less scattered" by removing the organizers. The new council thus consisted entirely of the executive officers. Now the only check upon any one executive officer was the necessity that he gain the approval of the majority of his fellows. The only merit in this system was the fact that none of the executive officers was appointed by the chief executive; each received his mandate from the electorate (which consisted, first, in the convention delegates and then, after 1896, in the general membership.) According to the Webbs, this tended to prevent the emergence of a "personal dictatorship." But the alternative to personal dictatorship was "a closely combined and practically irresistible bureaucracy," born of "the close union of all the salaried officials to conduct the business of the society in the way they think best."[70] And, as we know, bureaucracy, in the form of cliques and secret societies, certainly did develop within the ranks of the Printers; that it did not prove "irresistible" was due to the existence of special conditions for which the council was certainly not responsible.

The history of the Bricklayers' executive board differed from that of the Printers' chiefly in the lack of any attempt by the former to include any individuals other than national officers in the membership of the supreme executive organ. The Bricklayers' first "board of trustees" was composed simply of the president, the vice-president, and the secretary. It was instructed only to receive the bond and securities of the treasurer-elect and "to perform such other duties as this Union may require."[71] Supreme appellate jurisdiction and the power to pass upon applications for strike assistance were conferred upon the president and the vice-president. Not until 1882 were any "other duties" specified, and then the presidential power to grant charters was modified by a requirement that the consent of the executive board be secured. However, an elaboration of the board's mission indicated the purpose of its existence:

70. Sidney and Beatrice Webb, *Industrial Democracy* (London: Longmans, Green, new edition, 1911), p. 28.
71. *Constitution*, 1867, Art. VIII.

Should the President fail or neglect to perform such duties as are imposed on him by this Constitution, the Executive Board shall proceed to the performance of such duties themselves.[72]

In other words, the executive board was not regarded primarily as a check on the president, but as a stand-in—a wise precaution, however, since failure to perform official duties was not unknown in the early years of national unionism. Nor was the lack of genuine restraint upon the chief executive a fatal defect in those times, for the Bricklayers, like the Printers, had not yet entrusted any real authority, apart from regulating the traveling card system, to their national organization. Indeed, Glocker notes that before 1875 very few of the national unions had even evolved such rudimentary executive committees as the Printers and Bricklayers then boasted, and, he added, "Luckily the functions of the federated unions were so few that the officers had very little opportunity to display arbitrary power."[73]

As most national unions began to accumulate independent authority, however, they formed executive boards in an attempt to prevent that authority from being concentrated in the hands of the officers, who had hitherto discharged all the functions of the national organizations between sessions of the convention. Not so the Bricklayers. This venerable organization, which had possessed an executive board at a time when locals in most other trades were still striving to form national unions of their own, made few serious attempts to set up a system of checks and balances within its executive wing, even after the latter's duties and prerogatives had been greatly expanded. In some instances new authority was granted to the president; these included the power to suspend local unions (previously vested in a referendum of the locals) and to pass upon the constitutionality of local regulations. In other cases, power was entrusted to the board itself; it may be recalled that the Constitution of 1897 vested "the *entire* control of *all* executive business of this union, when not in session" in the executive board, and that this included concurrence in the appointment of special presidential deputies and the "full and complete control of all strikes." But "all questions relating to laws of I. U. or Subordinate Unions" received final disposition at the hands of another group, the judiciary board, which consisted of the president and the first and second vice-presidents.[74] The only change made in the jurisdiction of the executive officers was that the secretary was relieved of judicial duties, but the president and the first vice-president were on both the executive and the judiciary boards, and the president became the chief executive in fact as well as in name as a result of the changes made in 1897.

Thus the board's powers were acquired primarily as a result of additions to the functions of the executive branch of the union. Nor did the Brick-

72. *Constitution,* 1882, pp. 46–47.
73. Glocker, *Government of Unions,* p. 187.
74. *Constitution,* 1897, Art. I.

layers approve any attempt to broaden the base of its executive board by including members, other than officers, selected by the convention and/or representative of diverse portions of the national territorial jurisdiction.

Although the lines of evolution traced out by executive committees of the first four unions considered above—the Carpenters, Molders, Bottle Blowers, and Printers—were not parallel in all respects, the detailed examination of their careers suggests certain general conclusions. These four American unions sought to endow supreme executive bodies with the following attributes: (1) membership representative of the different geographic districts of the national jurisdiction, (2) amateur control (for members of the board were unsalaried) and (3) efficiency, insofar as this quality could be ensured by holding frequent sessions. Unfortunately, none of the types of organization with which either the British or the American unions experimented could achieve all three of these desiderata simultaneously. A board elected by the governing branch could presumably satisfy the second and third conditions, but at the expense of the first (after the governing branch stopped rotating among the different locals). A board composed exclusively of the full-time salaried executive officers of the national union could function efficiently, but it could not afford direct representation to the various regional interests, and it could hardly provide amateur control over the salaried executive officers of the national union. A board composed of representatives of the various geographic districts (of which the early American board of local union officials was an extreme variant) provided geographic representation, but it could satisfy only one of the two remaining conditions: in the United States, where the board members were unsalaried, meetings were held infrequently; in Britain, where they frequently were paid, frequency of sessions seemed to present no problem. Finally, a board whose members were chosen by the convention could, at best, achieve any two of these three objectives: if the convention chose members "to represent as nearly as possible every section of our broad jurisdiction" and if it did not provide salaries for them, its board was apt to meet infrequently; if it wished a board composed of men at the trade who could meet frequently, geographic representation had to be sacrificed; and if it wished a board which met frequently and at the same time represented a cross-section of the national jurisdiction, compensation had to be provided for these executives.

The story of our four unions suggests that, in this country, the first condition was emphasized: that membership on the board be directly representative of the different geographic sectors of the national jurisdiction.[75] In order to satisfy this condition, the board's operating efficiency was often seriously impaired, for, as Glocker remarked, "Meetings of the executive committee

75. See Glocker, *Government of Unions*, p. 195: "The members in each section of the country and in each division of the trade demand representation on the executive board." See also p. 192.

are held infrequently because of the expense of bringing together its members, who are usually scattered about in various parts of the country." Now the British, too, emphasized the importance of adequate geographic coverage, but in some instances, they also created boards which were able to meet frequently by providing for salaried members who, although representing different geographic districts, resided at the national's headquarters city. (Salaries were paid either by the national union or by the various district unions.) They sacrificed amateur control in such circumstances, however, for, as the Webbs pointed out in the case of the Amalgamated Society of Engineers,

The eight members, who are thus transferred by the vote of their fellows from the engineer's workshop to the Stamford Street office, become by this fundamental change of life completely severed from their constituents.[76]

On the other hand, those unions in which "the members of the representative executive reside in their constituencies and, in some cases, even continue to work at the trade 'failed' to exercise real and continuous authority over the civil service." And since this verdict was visited upon unions whose executive boards met once a month, how much greater was this failure in the United States!

It remains to be added that, for reasons of economy, the American unions did not typically pay their board members salaries and congregate them permanently at headquarters. Therefore, the more frequently they met, the more probable it was that they were financed informally, by being employed by the chief executive as traveling organizers or for other "special service."[77] It need hardly be pointed out that it would have been preferable had they been paid official salaries by the convention, for board members paid by the president could hardly have been expected to exercise real control over their paymaster. Furthermore, even if the best conditions (as prescribed by the Webbs) for the exercise of such control had prevailed—if the president was elected by and truly subordinate to the convention and if the board's members were elected by and responsible to the same body—they would not have been sufficient to have enabled the board member to be independent, let alone vigilantly critical, of the professionally competent full-time official. This, we recall, was the conclusion of the Webbs in England; and Glocker's evidence to the effect that president's judicial decisions tended to be upheld on appeal, suggest that it might well have been valid in this country also.

Having prefaced this account of the development of the principal governing institutions of American national unions with a summary drawn from the Webb's discussion of union government in Britain, it might be well to attempt a summary of the findings in this part of the work by indicat-

76. *Industrial Democracy*, p. 49. See also pp. 50–51.
77. Glocker, *Government of Unions*, p. 192. See also p. 189.

ing certain similarities and contrasts in the evolution of the government of the early national unions in both countries.

Selection of the National Executive

Most of the early British unions provided for direct election of the chief executive; they were unwilling to entrust this task to the governing branch. The early national presidents in this country, on the other hand, were usually elected by the convention. This practice reflected the persistence of localist sentiment, as a result of which the national union was originally regarded as a federation of locals rather than as an organization composed of individual members. Neither method of selecting the executive, however, failed to prevent long tenure in office by the incumbent.

Tenure in Office

The American experience suggests that, in this country at least, reduction in turnover among chief executives was associated with increased compensation as well as with growing awareness by unionists that executive efficiency was an increasing function of tenure in office.

Title and Authority of the Chief Executive

In most British unions, the chief executive was the general secretary; in most American unions, he was called president. While this difference in nomenclature is of no significance in itself, it might be taken as indicating somewhat greater readiness on the part of the Americans to invest their chief executive with certain policy-making powers vested in the national union, in addition to routine administrative duties. These powers grew out of the organizing and advisory activities of many early national presidents, which involved them in extensive traveling and protracted absence from national headquarters. Such duties were increased with the growth of national control over strikes (especially the determination of eligibility for national strike benefits), with the result that the consequent increase in the authority of the national union was lodged, in the first instance, in the national president. In particular, the latter was frequently empowered to appoint traveling deputies, whose descendants are the international representatives, an influential group of officers who are usually responsible directly to and dependent upon the international president.

The Convention

In both countries, an attempt was made to curb the power of the chief executive by vesting superior authority in meetings of delegates from local unions. In both countries such delegates were, at first, "instructed" and without much authority to act on their own, but they were later granted discretionary authority. Despite the liberation of the delegates, however, and despite the fact that the senatorial principle of representation (whereby each local received equal representation, regardless of size) gave way to representation more nearly in proportion to membership, the convention failed as an effective governing institution in the national union in this country.

In part, this failure can be attributed to the fact that, in most cases, unions had to choose between holding frequent conventions and holding conventions which were well attended, especially by delegates from the smaller locals which were frequently unable to defray the expense of sending delegates to the conventions. This dilemma reflected the fact that the great geographic extent of this country, coupled with the relatively wide dispersal of many industries, made transportation costs more of a problem here than in Britain. It also reflected the persistence of a spirit of localism which in large part was responsible for the general failure to adopt the economic alternative of representation by districts, which was practiced more extensively in Britain. District representation might also have reduced the excessive size and unwieldiness of the American conventions; in addition, it might have enabled resources to be diverted to the holding of longer sessions.

The Referendum

In Britain, unlike the United States, the referendum preceded the truly "representative" convention in time. In many British unions referenda were resorted to in lieu of holding conventions; in this country the convention continued in existence after the referendum was introduced, although some of the authority previously reserved to the former was transferred to the latter. Finally, the motive underlying the initial adoption of the referendum was different in each case: the British unionists viewed it as yet another device to restore the governing power to the "voices"; the Americans regarded it at first as a means whereby power would be transferred from the convention, which was coming to be considered an instrument of the national union, back to the local unions. But once the practice of allowing each local one vote was abandoned in favor of allowing each member one vote, the referendum became a truly national institution in the American union movement, as it was in Britain.

As a device for curbing the power of the national executive, however, the referendum failed in both countries, and for largely the same reasons. Union members were reluctant to vote increases in dues at the same time that they were willing to liberalize benefit provisions or to approve strike and benefit petitions; they frequently enacted ill-considered and inconsistent legislation; and they frequently failed to vote at all.

The Executive Board

In both union movements, the executive council proved unable to lead an existence independent of the influence of the full-time executive officers.

Whether the membership of the board consisted in the full-time salaried officers, in representatives chosen by a "governing branch," in representatives chosen by the convention, or in representatives selected by locals in different geographic districts, it could not arm itself with all the virtues which were considered necessary. These were: (1) membership representative of the different geographic districts, (2) control by unsalaried members, (3) the ability to meet at frequent intervals. The Americans chose to emphasize the first requirement, but, in so doing, they were obliged to sacrifice the second and even, on occasion, the third. The British in some cases satisfied the second condition at the expense of the third; in others they reversed the procedure.

THE PROBLEM OF APATHY

It appears that each union movement possessed only a partial inventory of those governing devices, each of which was regarded by someone or other as essential to democratic government. The British, for example, could hold conventions more frequently; they elected delegates by districts in some cases; and they staffed their executive councils with "lay members." The Americans, on the other hand, frequently authorized their conventions to select their national officers, a practice which the Webbs endorsed with enthusiasm. Yet in neither country did the national union discover the secret of curbing the power of the national executive. Although it might be maintained that the British executive council, with its lay representatives, has proved more effective than either the American executive council or convention,[78] centralization appears to characterize British as well as American unionism today.[79] It is possible, of course, that if all the virtues listed above could have been concentrated in a single union, the problem of preventing the excessive enlargement of executive control would have been solved.

Nevertheless, it is not likely that the mere existence of a particular set of governing mechanisms would have sufficed. Without active participation at the local level by the rank and file on a scale sufficient to make the executive board at once responsive to the local constituencies and independent of the professional executive, the influence of the latter was bound to predominate.

In retrospect it might be suggested that the problem of apathy among the

78. See S. H. Slichter, *The Challenge of Industrial Relations* (Ithaca: Cornell, 1947), p. 9.

79. See Joseph Goldstein, *The Government of British Trade Unions* (London: Allen and Unwin, 1952). This study is confined to the Transport and General Workers' Union and has met with criticism on this and other grounds, but there has been little disposition to assert that apathy does not exist. See *Socialist Commentary,* September 1952, v. 16, pp. 199–202. See, on the other hand, the review in *The Economist,* August 2, 1952, v. CLXIV, no. 5684, p. 282, wherein it is claimed that "the average man is simply not a sufficiently political animal," and that, "A permanent atmosphere of conscientious communal fervor is no more natural than a permanent flow of adrenalin at the rate appropriate to life-and-death struggle. The price of liberty is eternal vigilance; but the penalty of insomnia is neurosis and collapse." See also Hugh Clegg, *Industrial Democracy and Nationalization* (Oxford: Blackwell, 1951), pp. 19–22.

membership was foreshadowed in the early history of the trade union movement, which was characterized by the sporadic formation of shop meetings and strike committees, which were essentially temporary institutions designed to cope with immediate problems and doomed to dissolution following disposition of the issue at hand.[80] Barnett describes early meetings of printers as follows:

At these meetings a statement of the demands of the journeymen was formulated; a committee was appointed to deal with the employers, if a new wage list had been framed; and the printers present pledged themselves to stand out for the prices agreed upon. Such temporary organizations were formed naturally in times of general discontent, when the feeling that the prices for work were unsatisfactory was widespread.[81]

In time, of course, the realization grew that passing crises could best be met by permanent organizations, and the "continuous association of wage-earners" replaced the "mass meeting." But there is no reason to believe that the emergence of continuing institutions implied the development of continuing participation by the rank and file. In the course of an address largely given over to a thoughtful and courageous searching of soul, President Prescott of the Printers warned the delegates to the 1898 convention that

it is imperative that we do something to stimulate interest among our members. There is not an earnest worker in our ranks who has not been pained and grieved at the slight interest taken in union meetings, as testified by the attendance, and I am constrained to admit that from the best possible information obtainable this lethargy is becoming more deep seated and widespread, which does not augur well for our future. And, sad to relate, the blight is not peculiar to our organization, but has been responsible for the steady decrease in membership of every considerable American union except ours. . . .[82]

Consideration of the problem of apathy leads us to recall our discussion of the ill-starred referendum. In British and American national unions one reason for the failure of the referendum consisted simply in lack of popular response. To be sure, more enthusiastic participation by the rank and file would not have ensured the success of this institution, for enthusiasm is no substitute for political wisdom, and the Webbs demonstrated that the degree of rank-and-file sophistication required by the referendum was unattainable and, in any case, not essential to the success of representative democracy. The latter, however, does require a certain measure of concern and vigilance on the part of the governed, even if they do delegate the work of government to certain officials. To that extent, the failure of the rank and file to respond to the referendum was symptomatic of something more important than the mere inadequacy of that particular instrument of government.

80. Glocker, *Government of Unions*, pp. 9–10.
81. Barnett, *The Printers*, p. 3.
82. Tracy, *Typographical Union*, p. 545.

PART

V

JURISDICTION AND FEDERATION

CHAPTER ELEVEN

ECONOMIC ASPECTS OF JURISDICTION

THE NATIONAL UNION's jurisdiction was defined with respect to occupation as well as territory; and the former boundary could be as vital to its survival and bargaining power as was the latter. In setting forth the first of "the conditions, under which a check to the supply of . . . a factor of production of some commodity, may cause a very great rise in its price," Marshall identified what was frequently an important (although not an inherent) attribute of jurisdiction, namely "that the factor itself should be essential, or nearly essential to the production of the commodity, no good substitute being available at a moderate price."[1] Now Marshall considered only that type of trade union action which consisted in raising wages by restricting the supply of labor. That this indirect method was in fact rather widely practiced in this country during the nineteenth and early twentieth centuries, however, is indicated by the following statement of Barnett:

The struggles . . . for a mere raising of wages by concerted action, are usually to be found in those unions where the conditions in the trade are such as to depress the wages of the workmen much below the rate of pay prevailing in other trades for workmen of a similar character. In such trades unionism does not ordinarily flourish. Strong unions exist in those trades in which, by a series of rules, competition is made of itself to bring to the individual workmen a higher rate of pay, and the action of the union in increasing the standard rate is almost perfunctory and a matter of course. . . .[2]

Let us suppose for the moment, however, that a union had recourse only to "a mere raising of wages." In that event, it is possible that no "very great rise" could be secured or maintained even if all the Marshallian conditions in fact prevailed, namely, essentiality, inelastic demand for the final product, small proportion of the cost of the factor in question to total direct cost, and elastic supply of coöperant factors. For if the rise in the wage rate was

1. Alfred Marshall, *Principles of Economics* (London: Macmillan, eighth edition, 1947), p. 385.
2. American Economic Association, *Papers and Discussions,* 1909, p. 48.

accompanied by an influx of workers from other occupations to the trade in question, so that an excess supply of labor developed, the situation would have held as little promise, from the union viewpoint, as if the labor supplied by the union's members had not been essential (or, if the other conditions enumerated by Marshall had failed to obtain). Again, the prevalence of the prescribed conditions alone could not ensure that a reduction in demand for a certain class of labor would not result in a "very great" fall in the wage rate if the workers could not turn to alternative occupations at very nearly equal rates of pay. Thus the Marshallian conditions are not sufficient in situations in which unions sought to raise wages without restricting supply, for they relate only to factors making for an inelastic demand for labor and do not specify necessary conditions of supply.

It is apparent from the foregoing that certain conditions of supply must in fact prevail in order that the union's "relative negotiating strength" be sufficiently great to raise wage rates appreciably above the level which would have prevailed in the absence of the union. The term "relative negotiating strength" was coined by a writer in international trade who defined it as "the extent to which the buyer is dependent upon the seller and the seller upon the buyer. Or, as some would say, it is a question of the relative elasticities of demand and supply."[3] Thus it would appear that a union seeking to raise wages without first restricting the supply of labor should seek first, to make the employers in a particular trade dependent upon the union's existing membership for their supply of labor (given other conditions of demand, discussed by Marshall) and secondly, to reduce the dependence of its members upon any one class of employer or job in the industry.

It is apparent that the first objective above was furthered when the union could proceed safely upon the assumption that any increase in the bargained wage would not be followed by an increase in the supply of the type of labor over which it claimed jurisdiction; for any such increment would lessen the employer's dependence upon the present membership of the union and thus make it difficult to enforce the higher wage rate throughout the trade. Now, if in fact this condition of nonentry prevailed, we say that the union in question possessed a clearly defined jurisdiction, although it does not follow that every clearly defined trade jurisdiction implies the existence of such impassable (in the short period, at least) occupational barriers. (Examples of clearly defined trade jurisdictions into which entry has been relatively easy are painting, carpentry, street railway operators).[4]

The second objective above was furthered when the employers could not assume that a reduction in the bargained rate would not be accompanied by a withdrawal from the trade of their unionized employees—for such a withdrawal would make it impossible to enforce the lower wage rate.

3. F. V. Meyer, "Bulk Purchases," *Economica*, February 1948, pp. 51–60.
4. I am indebted to Professor Slichter for calling my attention to this point which is essentially that trade jurisdiction cannot be defined with respect to ease of entry.

In other words, the union's "relative negotiating strength" was greater the less elastic the supply of labor at wage rates in excess of the prevailing "union level" (that is, the greater the difficulty of entry into the trade), and the more elastic it was at wages below the prevailing union level (that is, the greater the ease of exit, or, more precisely, the higher the "transfer earnings").

Although we shall presently consider union policies which were designed to further the two objectives listed above, it is obvious that the latter could be and were achieved, to varying degrees, in the absence of union organization. Moreover, the existence of favoring conditions—evidence of which is furnished by the persistence of a wage differential in favor of a particular occupational group—tended to constitute a "natural" foundation upon which durable unions could be based. Such conditions consisted in disagreeableness of the work and skill required for the work involved.

"DISAGREEABLENESS" AND INDUSTRIAL UNIONISM

Among the conditions which Adam Smith considered sufficient for "inequalities of pecuniary wages" was the "disagreeableness of the employments themselves,"[5] which made outsiders who were capable of entering the trade in question reluctant to do so, even for a wage which was higher than those prevailing in their own occupations.

The United Mine Workers was a union whose trade jurisdiction derived much of what effectiveness it had from the disagreeableness of the employment of its members. Certainly, skill was not a sufficient factor; union officers themselves conceded the case with which coal could be mined by strike-breaking "imports."[6] Furthermore, the United Mine Workers and its predecessors were industrial unions which, making no attempt to restrict their membership to those in the highest paid categories, admitted "all men who are employed in and around the mines of the United States, who will submit to the constitution and by-laws."[7] On the other hand, the unique hazards to which miners were exposed distinguished coal mining from other occupations and enabled the mine workers' unions to carve out an industrial jurisdiction.

5. Adam Smith, *The Wealth of Nations,* ch. I, part I. (The Modern Library Edition, New York, p. 100.)

6. In his discussion of the successful employment of nonminer strikebreakers during the Hocking Valley (Ohio) strike in 1884–1885, Chris Evans conceded that, "While the character of the men, so far as mining coal was concerned, was not near as good as the old miners, the fact remained that those working were producing all the coal needed to supply the trade . . ." Chris Evans, *History of the United Mine Workers of America* (Indianapolis? 1918), v. I, p. 129. Cf. also, pp. 119, 125–126 and v. II, p. 354.

7. *Constitution of the Miners' National Association,* 1873, Art. III. (Reproduced in Evans, *United Mine Workers,* v. I, p. 38.) See also *Constitution: Amalgamated Miners' Association of the United States* (abortive), Preamble (in Evans, p. 109); *National Federation of Miners and Mine Laborers* and its *Constitution,* 1885, Art. III (in Evans, p. 141) and *Third Annual Proceedings,* 1888 (in Evans, p. 267); *Constitution of the United Mine Workers of America,* 1890, Preamble and Art I, Sec. 2 (in Evans, v. II, p. 19).

While the industry experienced a heavy influx of new workers (beginning in the 1880's), the newcomers were predominantly immigrants from abroad rather than native American workers from other industries. On the contrary, native (or naturalized) Americans tended to migrate from coal mining to other occupations. This situation was described by one of the Pittsburgh operators, in the "joint convention" of 1894:

Unless we got labor from Italy and the countries of Central Europe, we would have no men in this country to operate the mines. English and German speaking miners soon enter other avocations.[8]

The mine unions themselves always emphasized the element of danger in formulating their demands,[9] and in 1899 the United Mine Workers declared it their object

To secure an earning fully compatible with the dangers of our calling and the labor performed.[10]

It should be noted, however, that although such conditions as disagreeableness and danger acted to block entry and thus to further the dependence of employers on the union's members, they did not necessarily satisfy the requirement of economic versatility by providing workers with high transfer earnings which might serve as an effective platform for the existing wage. Thus a decline in demand in the disagreeable occupation might be reflected in a severe fall in the wage rate, or in unemployment creating a downward pressure upon the wage rate.

SKILL AND CRAFT UNIONISM

Most early union occupational jurisdictions were based upon skill. The existence of occupational boundaries formed by what Adam Smith termed "the difficulty and expense of learning" served as excellent incubators for trade unionism. A highly skilled and versatile group of workers could not only feel relatively secure against entry into their craft, but, in the event that demand for their services fell in one area of their jurisdiction, wages could fall no further than the level prevailing in other areas in which their skill was also required. Thus while jurisdictions based upon "disagreeableness" drew support only from employer dependence upon the existing membership, jurisdiction based upon skill were buttressed by the economic versatility of the members as well.

If most union jurisdictions in the nineteenth century were in fact based upon skill, the fact that many or, as Barnett claimed and Marshall appears

8. Evans, *United Mine Workers,* v. II, p. 348.
9. For an account of the unions' ceaseless preoccupation with the problem of mine safety, see Evans, v. I, pp. 23, 86, 97, 98, 148, 400–401; v. II, pp. 18, 78, 83, 189, 567, 656.
10. *Constitution,* Preamble (in Evans, v. II, p. 656.).

to have assumed, most of them raised wages "by a series of rules" designed to move the supply curve of labor upward does not detract from the importance of the conditions which determined the shape of that supply curve in its original position. If union rules made union-won wage increases possible, the prior existence of skill or disagreeableness made both unionism and an already high wage level possible; so that, in an ultimate sense, skill or disagreeableness, rather than "a series of rules" was the agent whereby "competition is made of itself to bring the individual workman a higher rate of pay." Skill or disagreeableness affected not only the elasticity of demand for the factor in question—in making for essentiality, but also the elasticity of supply —in making the supply of the factor not easily reproducible.

Moreover, the union rules to which Barnett referred were not confined to devices designed to provide "a check to the supply" of the labor in question; unions also sought to institute rules which were intended to improve upon nature by preserving and/or strengthening those conditions which furthered the achievement of both objectives discussed above and thereby tended to enhance "relative negotiating strength."

Before proceeding to an examination of jurisdictional policies, however, it might be desirable to specify more precisely what is implied by the terms "craft" and "job." For the purpose at hand, a craft may be defined as a number of operations, any one of which can be performed only by a worker (the craftsman) who can perform all of the others. A job, on the other hand, consists of a number of operations which an employer hires a worker to perform. Some or all of the operations which are included in a particular job may be included in the worker's craft; on the other hand, some of the job requirements may not be included in the range of operations embraced by a given craft.

The jurisdictional policies adopted by unions, in seeking to maintain or to increase the dependence of the employers upon the services of their existing membership and to increase the latter's independence of the employers in any one job category, fall into the following categories: restriction of the number of new craftsmen admitted every year; inclusion of all operations which formed part of the craft; inclusion of all workers in the craft. One further policy, which did not bear directly upon the stated objectives, was the exclusion of persons who performed none of the operations included in the craft.

Alternatively, any of the above policies might be classified under one of these two headings: Policies of Exclusion or Policies of Inclusion.

Policies of Exclusion

Restriction of the Number of Craftsmen

Successful prosecution of a restrictive policy would go far in securing a supply of union workers which would be inelastic at wage rates equal to or higher than the prevailing level. Restriction was frequently attempted by union apprenticeship regulations which specified the ratio of apprentices to journeymen allowed in union establishments (or which, in some cases, established a flat maximum number) and which also provided for minimum terms of apprenticeship.[11] There is little doubt that such restrictive policies were considered desirable. Thus the glass bottle blowers (who, at the time, were organized into District Assembly No. 149 of the Knights of Labor) entered into a bitter strike against the employers in the eastern part of the country when the latter refused to promise that they would not employ any additional apprentices during the season (or "blast") of 1886–1887. During the course of the strike, some of the New Jersey locals rebelled and allowed their employers to continue the practice of hiring two apprentices for each furnace with a five-pot capacity. They also acceded to a 15 per cent wage cut. The district assembly had previously accepted a reduction of 10 per cent, but insisted that no additional apprentices be employed. After the defection of the New Jersey locals, the district executive board offered to accept two additional wage reductions—the first, of 5 per cent, in order to grant the other employers the same reduction in wages as that which had been conceded to those in New Jersey, and the second, of 2 per cent, in order to compensate those employers who did not take on new apprentices. According to District Master Workman John Coffey,

We could well afford to sacrifice 7 per cent of our wages at present, aye, and more, if we could only obtain control of that (apprenticeship) system. We could then have a guarantee that good wages for the future would be assured. . . .
This strike was not entered into to prevent manufactures taking apprentices during the blast of 1886 and '87 only; there was a loftier purpose involved, which was to force from manufacturers the admission of the blowers' right to control the system.[12]

Few other unions, however, were able to control entry into the trade as well as the Glass Bottle Blowers. The union's control over the supply of apprentices was reflected in the fact that the growth requirements of the industry could be met only through increases in the allowable ratio of apprentices to journeymen. Thus, in 1899, the president of the union urged his constituents to work diligently in times of prosperity, so that the employers' demands for more apprentices could be resisted. The following year, he reported that he was able to hold the employers off, but only by promising them that all "places" would be filled. He attributed the existence of "idle

11. Some unions also discouraged the employment of apprentices "by pushing their wages so high that employers do not find it economical to train many boys." Sumner H. Slichter, *Union Policies and Industrial Management* (Washington, D. C.: Brookings, 1941), p. 12.
12. *Proceedings,* 1887, p. 13.

places" to the idleness and intemperance of the membership, caused by prosperity earnings. But, whether due to a backward rising supply curve of
bottle-blowing labor or not, the idle places were not filled; and in 1901 the
union agreed to an increase in the ratio from one apprentice to every fifteen
journeymen to one-to-ten.[13] However, few unions had organized their jurisdictions as completely as the Bottle Blowers; and the successful prosecution
of a policy of restriction required a high degree of skill and organization.[14]
This fact was conceded more readily by the officers of the national unions than
by many of the local unions which persisted in quixotic measures aimed at restricting entry into the trade. Although most of the printers' locals provided
ratios of apprentices to journeymen, the International Typographical Union
refused to adopt any limitations upon the number of apprentices, because it
was appreciated that the unorganized printing offices in small communities
could not be prevented from supplying the larger centers with printers.[15] And
while the Iron Molders did establish a national ratio, its executive officers
were impressed with the unionized employers' argument that a more liberal
ratio was necessary in order to allow them to meet the competition of nonunion establishments. Although the national officers pressed repeatedly for
liberalization, thirteen years passed before the membership of the locals agreed
to raise the ratio of apprentices to journeymen from one-to-eight to one-
to-five.[16]

Exclusion of Noncraftsmen

These include workers who were able to perform some, but not all, of the
operations included in the craft (the semiskilled, or "specialists") as well as
those who could perform none of the craft operations. We shall discuss only
the latter category at present, however, reserving consideration of the problem
of specialization for the following section.

Restriction of membership in the national union to those who were
competent, in the opinion of their employers, to perform all or some of the
operations included in its craft jurisdiction raised the issue of industrial
unionism. It was apparent to the craftsmen that they gained little by admitting
the uninitiated into their ranks, just as it seemed apparent to the latter that
their own bargaining power would be increased by forming an industrial

13. *Proceedings,* 1899, p. 37; 1900, pp. 53–56; 1901, p. 12.

14. See Slichter, *Union Policies,* p. 35. Of the 120 national and international unions
affiliated with the American Federation of Labor in 1904, Motley found that "only nineteen actually succeed in enforcing apprenticeship as a prerequisite to membership." These
nineteen were distinguished by the fact that they were "exceedingly well organized."
James M. Motley, *Apprenticeship in American Trade Unions* (Baltimore: Johns Hopkins,
1907), pp. 53, 60–61.

15. George E. Barnett, *The Printers* (Cambridge, Mass.: American Economic Association, 1909), pp. 169, 171–172, 177–178.

16. Motley, *Apprenticeship in American Trade Unions,* pp. 42–50.

union about a nucleus of skilled "key workers."[17] The craftsmen, however, while they occasionally encouraged groups of unskilled in their industry to form their own unions, feared that, if they admitted them into their own craft unions, they would be obliged to go out on strike in the furtherance of alien interests or to open the trade to outsiders. Thus the Bottle Blowers had a longstanding agreement with the Improved Green Glass Pressers' Association whereby the former refused to work with nonunion pressers, but the Blowers steadfastly rebuffed all overtures of amalgamation by the Pressers, including one offer "to sacrifice all our rights and privileges as the Improved Green Glass Pressers' Association to those of the Green Glass Blowers' Association, except such rights as are laid down in our By-Laws respecting the fixing of the price list and of preventing and governing the employment of apprentices."[18] Similarly, the Bottle Blowers accorded recognition to a union of glass gatherers and declared their intention not to work with nonunion gatherers, but, at the same time, the Bottle Blowers had incorporated into their by-laws a prohibition against allowing gathering boys to blow out glass. And finally, in 1901, the Blowers resolved to assist in the formation of a union of Glass Packers.[19]

Although noncraftsmen were frequently excluded from craft unions, the latter themselves were often composed of members of more than one craft. The special circumstances which helped to account for such "compound craft" unions will be discussed in a later section of this chapter; but we might anticipate that discussion by observing that the existence of craft amalgamations did not constitute evidence to refute our earlier statement that skilled workers tended to avoid entangling alliances with groups who could not add appreciably to their own bargaining strength.

Policies of Inclusion

Inclusion of All Work in the Craft Jurisdiction; Opposition to Specialization

The institution of apprenticeship antedated trade unionism, and the original purpose of apprenticeship was to equip newcomers with a thorough mastery of the entire craft. This was the case in the United States, as it had been elsewhere, but, as the extension of markets and the acceleration of the rate of technological change made possible greater division of labor, employers in many industries lost interest in apprenticeship and sought the services of specialized workers. The job, in other words, tended to become narrower

17. Cf. John T. Dunlop, "The Changing Status of Labor," in Harold Williamson, *The Growth of the American Economy* (New York: Prentice-Hall, 1946), *passim*. Also, John T. Dunlop, "The Development of Labor Organization: A Theoretical Framework," in Richard A. Lester and Joseph Shister, *Insights into Labor Issues* (New York: Macmillan, 1948).

18. *Proceedings,* Glass Bottle Blowers' Association, 1897, p. 101. Also, *Proceedings,* 1887, pp. 63–65; 1888, pp. 47–48, 52; 1892, p. 67; 1894, p. 50; 1895, pp. 64–65; and 1896, pp. 41–42.

19. *Proceedings,* 1899, pp. 90–91, 93; *By-Laws,* 1892, Sec. 10; *Proceedings,* 1901, p. 53.

than the craft, and the employers were interested primarily in the job. The skilled workmen, however, were interested primarily in the preservation of their crafts, and hence unions succeeded employers as the guardians of the institution of apprenticeship. Under union sponsorship, however, this institution acquired another purpose:—the restriction of entry into the craft. But the original ends of competence and versatility remained, because they were of as great importance to the members of a craft union as they had been to employers.

The importance of a uniformly competent group of workers to the maintenance of union standards has been well described by Motley:

If every worker in these trades possessed equal ability and sufficient physical strength for a uniform amount of work, a common wage scale could easily be agreed upon. But the presence of a large number of unskilled workmen, both union and non-union, presents serious complications. Those competent to earn the wage scale attempt to maintain a high standard, while the incompetence of the inferior workman tends to lower it, and a wide difference exists between the extremes of these two classes. Since the union rate is a minimum, it is easy for the rapid well-trained workman to earn his wages; but the journeyman just able to command the rate is always hard pressed, and the incompetent is actually paid, if not in excess of his industrial worth, at least a higher proportionate rate than his fellow workmen. Nevertheless, even the stronger unions hesitate to raise the union rate unduly, lest those unable to command it become a powerful force in opposition, as non-union workmen. . . .[20]

For this reason, many unions required that their members be competent to earn the prevailing journeyman wage. (See Chapter 5, p. 121.) Since it was a general union principle that all members in the same occupational and geographic jurisdictions receive the same wage, the purpose of requirements of competence was to equalize labor costs per unit of output as well as wages, by ensuring that every "natural unit" (man-hour) hired would contain the same number of "efficiency units."

The maintenance of traditional craft skills was of especial importance to unions in industries in which the craft was more inclusive than most of the jobs. Under such circumstances, there was a tendency for the craft to be splintered into a number of specialties, each manned by workers who were largely unable to perform the others. Aside from the alleged outrage to its members' instinct of workmanship, this process of splitting the labor force into a number of noncompeting groups redounded to the economic disadvantage of the group as a whole and of each component individually. It will be recalled that one of the factors which determined the "relative negotiating strength" of any seller was the degree to which the seller was

20. James M. Motley, "Apprenticeship in the Building Trades," in Jacob H. Hollander and George E. Barnett, *Studies in American Trade Unionism* (New York: Henry Holt, 1906), pp. 267–268.

independent of the buyer with whom he negotiated. When both buyer and seller are collective entities, the principal means whereby the latter can gain a measure of independence of the former is the existence of a demand for his services by some other type of buyer. Thus an important bargaining asset of a union was the economic versatility of its membership. It was the availability of alternative markets for their services—each market demanding a different "segment" of the entire range of operations in which the craftsmen were proficient—which provided the versatile craftsmen with "transfer earnings," thus ensuring that no one group of employers could set a wage much lower than the wage prevailing in the best-paid of the other employments available to their employees. (This is the significance of the elastic segment of the supply curve of union labor in any one range of occupations.)

In view of the above, it is not surprising that many national unions, which made little attempt to emphasize the restrictive aspects of apprenticeship, did stipulate competence as a prerequisite to membership. Although the International Typographical Union refused to adopt a uniform ratio of apprentices to journeymen, "it has always shown a strong liking for the old system of indenturing or binding the apprentices" and it sought the employers' consent to a thoroughgoing training course for beginners.[21] This opposition to specialization was further reflected in their regulations governing the learning of linotype operation. At first it was provided that the machines could be operated only by journeymen printers. Later, however, local unions were empowered to permit apprentices to work on linotypes, but only during the last six months of their term. The opposition of the officials of the Cigar Makers' International Union (whose constitution stipulated a three-year term of apprenticeship) to "team work," or a system under which division of labor was practiced, was motivated by similar considerations. "The reason advanced . . . is that the tendency of a division of labor is to lower wages, and the aim of the union is to train cigar makers who will be adept in making cigars complete and not merely adept in either bunch making or rolling."[22]

While division of labor could lower wages, it was also true that certain methods of wage payment were conducive to division of labor. Unions frequently opposed such methods; and although, as we shall observe in Part VI, resistance to specialization did not constitute the sole or even always the most important basis of their opposition, it did influence the formulation of certain economic policies. The preference of national officers for uniform minimum as opposed to "average" rates of pay was due in large part to their belief that the average rate encouraged specialization by offering to employers a stimulus to hire less efficient workers at lower rates of pay for the performance of certain operations exclusively, while (it was implied) the minimum rate

21. Barnett, *The Printers*, p. 173. Also pp. 175–176, 198.

22. U. S. Commissioner of Labor, Eleventh Special Report, *Regulation and Restriction of Output* (Washington, 1904), p. 569.

operated to exclude poorer workers from employment. For the same reason, national authorities tended to frown upon the practice of paying different rates to journeymen who were employed at different types of work which allegedly required the same degree of skill.[23] Opposition to the establishment of different rate groups according to differences in individual competence stemmed in part from the belief that this practice tended to encourage retention of a group of inefficient or incompletely trained workers who became specialists at certain tasks. Finally, some unions were opposed to piece work and other systems of payment by result because they were conducive to specialization: low piece rates could be translated into relatively high earnings if the worker remained on one job for a sufficiently long period of time.[24]

At the same time that they asserted jurisdiction over various classes of work, the unions sought, whenever possible, to exclude the employment of specialists. When the Printers decided to include proofreading within their jurisdiction, they admitted nonprinter proofreaders to membership, but, after they had secured control over this work, they required that all proofreaders admitted to membership in the future be "practical printers."[25] Opposition to the admission of women by local unions of printers stemmed in part from the fact that, since girls expected to remain in the trade for only a relatively short period of time, they were employed almost exclusively at setting "straight" matter. Thus they could quickly become proficient as specialists and earn a relatively high weekly wage despite their acceptance of low price rates.[26]

The Bricklayers decided that work on terra cotta must be done by "Union bricklayers and masons, as it makes a demand for just that many more bricklayers or masons who shall engage in that kind of work." Fireproofing was another branch of the trade of which the same union sought exclusive possession; and, although unskilled laborers were actually employed on this work, the Bricklayers sought to exclude them from employment by denying admission to fireproofers who could not qualify as practical bricklayers, masons, and plasterers. Furthermore, in 1892, the Bricklayers resolved

That fireproofing, block arching and Terra Cotta, setting and cutting, be considered bricklayers' work, *and that the regular rate of (bricklaying) wages of the locality be charged.*[27]

23. David A. McCabe, *The Standard Rate in American Trade Unions* (Baltimore: Johns Hopkins, 1912), pp. 89, 94, and 97.

24. Commissioner of Labor, *Regulation of Output*, pp. 114 and 127–128.

25. Commissioner of Labor, *Regulation of Output*, pp. 246–248; George A. Tracy, *History of the Typographical Union* (Indianapolis: International Typographical Union, 1913), pp. 594–595.

26. Barnett, *The Printers*, pp. 315–316.

27. *Proceedings*, 1884, pp. 74 and 111; 1883, p. 13; 1896, p. 2; 1910, p. 163; 1892, p. 32. (Italics mine.)

By the time that the Bricklayers decided to appropriate the work of tuck pointing, they had become proficient indeed in annexing work and in excluding specialists. The work in question had been performed by a group of workers known as tuck pointers, who were organized into a union which was chartered by the A.F. of L. in 1903. Nevertheless, the Bricklayers not only asserted exclusive jurisdiction over pointing; they induced the Federation— which they themselves had not yet joined—to revoke the tuck pointers' charter![28]

One should take note of the fact that unions whose original crafts had been made obsolete in part by technological change were especially anxious to secure control over new job territories. Thus the Printers became interested in proofreading only after the linotype had displaced some of their members, and the Bricklayers sought control over fireproofing, terra cotta, and cement work because the increased use of steel in the construction industry had reduced the demand for brick.[29] The bitter jurisdictional fight between the Carpenters and the Wood Workers over millwork was caused by the introduction of wood working machinery, "the result of which was to transfer from the outside carpenter to the factory larger and larger portions of the work of finishing building material, such as sash, blinds, door and window frames, and the like."[30] The plight of the carpenter was expressed by McGuire in 1894:

Year after year carpenter work is becoming less trouble, and less plentiful owing to recent innovations in architectural construction. With the introduction of iron and stone staircases, tile floors and tile or metal wainscoting, with cornices and bay windows in many cases of other material than wood, and with numerous other changes going on, the chances for steady employment of carpenters, even in best of times, are extremely uncertain. Added to this, the increase and perfection of wood-working machinery, the flood-tide of emigration, the lack of apprentice-ship, the ready influx of men into the trade, all add to the stringency in demand for carpenters.[31]

The reference to "the lack of apprenticeship" and the consequent "ready influx of men into the trade" is especially interesting; it reveals how amorphous the Carpenters' jurisdiction had become. Since, with the introduction of substitute products and new processes, the demand for union carpenters had declined at the going wage rates, it was necessary for the United Brother-

28. *Proceedings,* 1903, pp. 473–483; 1905, p. 124.

29. Fireproofing, moreover, was an excellent alternative occupation for a bricklayer, because it was "inside work" and was done mostly in the winter months, which were traditionally idle periods in the "outside" industry. (See *Proceedings,* 1883, p. 13.)

30. Frederick S. Deibler, *The Amalgamated Wood Workers' International Union of America* (Madison: University of Wisconsin, 1912), No. 511, Economic & Political Science Series, v. 7, no. 3, p. 162.

31. *Proceedings,* 1894, p. 27 (report of the secretary).

hood to make their supply curve as elastic as possible as well as to raise demand by attempting to control as many types of work as its members were capable of performing.

Although the craft union was opposed to specialization, we find that pieceworkers frequently sought to divest themselves of certain nonremunerative work. An agreement between the Window Glass Workers' Local Assembly 300 and the American and Federation Companies for the year 1902–1903 provided that "Cutters are not to carry out glass."[32] The by-laws of the same union forbade blowers and gatherers from building up or turning pots or building up furnace rings; "nor shall any blower or gatherer carry out rollers, whether paid for doing so or not." The Glass Bottle Blowers' Association also excluded certain nonremunerative operations from its craft jurisdiction; its by-laws provided

That blowers will not be allowed to ladle out glass. That we consider ring setting brick layer's work, and unless it is the foreman who is paid for such work, no member shall be allowed to do it.[33]

For the same reason pieceworkers in some trades favored the employment of helpers—men or boys who performed unskilled tasks of the variety mentioned above—thus enabling the skilled pieceworkers to increase their daily earnings. Did the exclusion of nonremunerative work and the employment of helpers constitute specialization? Slichter observed that

Instead of attempting to broaden the operations which are regarded as the skilled mechanics' work and opposing specialization, unions that serve pieceworkers often encourage specialization and seek to transfer as much work as possible from journeymen to helpers because the skilled workers can thus increase their production and earnings.[34]

Now we must recall that the specialization to which the unions were opposed involved reduction in the craftsmen's versatility and in his unique ability to perform certain operations. The abandonment of unskilled operations involved a narrowing of the job but not of the craft; the craftsmen's "relative negotiating strength" was not enhanced by his performance of work which lay within the capability of the uninitiated. The employment of helpers, however, could result in specialization in the sense in which we have defined it—not, however, because the journeyman abandoned control over unskilled work, but because "the helpers in the course of several years may learn how to do the journeyman's work." Thus, while the glass-workers' unions referred to above could insist upon the exclusion of certain work without qualification,

32. Commissioner of Labor, *Regulation of Output*, p. 623. See also pp. 619 and 620.
33. *By-Laws*, 1892, Secs. 12 and 13.
34. Slichter, *Union Policies*, p. 312. Cf. also p. 338.

Unions adopt various policies toward helpers. Some organizations attempt to prevent the use of helpers; others seek to restrict their work so that they will not have an opportunity to learn the journeyman's job; still other organizations accept the helper as a man who is learning the trade and undertake to regulate the number of helpers and their work.[35]

Hence we find that, where the helper system encouraged specialization as we have defined it, it was by no means always accepted by those responsible for the formulation of union policy; the Molders' official opposition to the helper, or "Berkshire," system was prompted in great part by the fact that "the helper appeared . . . to threaten a flood of semi-skilled mechanics who had enough specialized capacity to elbow all-around molders out of jobs."[36] At the same time it should be recalled that piecework itself was opposed by national authorities where it threatened to make specialists out of "practical" journeymen. But where piecework or the exclusion of certain work which was not paid by the piece was not condemned by union authority, genuine specialization was not a threat. Both piecework and the helper system were opposed by national authority on other grounds, however. Thus the Molders' deplored the consequences of greed: journeyman molder's practice of hiring several "bucks" in order to maximize the number of flasks which he could handle tended to increase the supply of journeyman labor and thus to depress the piece rate. Similarly, the incentive effect of the piece rate often either provoked opposition to this method of payment or inspired restriction of output (see Part VI below).

Inclusion of All Personnel in the Trade Jurisdiction

Exclusive control over all workers in the trade was essential to the "negotiating strength" of any union. From the union's viewpoint, it made little difference whether the outsiders were unorganized or were members of some "dual" union, because they were available to the employers as a substitute for the labor sold by the members of the union in question. Thus the Glass Bottle Blowers, who had rejected the Pressers' bid for amalgamation, favored either amalgamation or an exchange of working cards with the Flint Glass Workers, "as the method of working in the Flint and Green branches were in every way identical," following the invention of the tank furnace which enabled flint glass to be made by the same process that was used in producing green glass.[37] After rejecting this offer and then attempting unsuccessfully to maintain the higher piece rates which had been paid to flint blowers before

35. Slichter, *Union Policies,* pp. 45 and 46.

36. Frank T. Stockton, *The International Molders Union of North America* (Baltimore: Johns Hopkins, 1921), p. 181.

37. *Proceedings,* 1892, pp. 23–25; 1901, p. 26. For an account of the jurisdictional struggle between the two unions, see George E. Barnett, *Chapters on Machinery and Labor* (Cambridge, Mass.: Harvard University Press, 1926), pp. 72–79.

innovation made them subject to the competition of green glass blowers, the Flint Glass Workers offered amalgamation to the Bottle Blowers. The Flints, however, were a multicraft union, and their offer specified that their existing craft departments would be preserved and that, after the merger, any member would remain free to transfer from one department to another.[38] But President D. A. Hayes of the Bottle Blowers had previously declared, "I do not believe in the Flint system of organization," and the Bottle Blowers made it clear that they desired amalgamation only with the prescription glass department of the Flints (which contained their blowers). In 1901, this latter group, upon its own request, was admitted to membership in the Glass Bottle Blowers' Association.[39] The jurisdictional purity of the Bottle Blowers was thus preserved on two counts: all (or virtually all) bottle blowers were brought into the ranks of the organization, and all other workers remained excluded from its ranks. In 1914, however, this union began to organize unskilled workers[40]; but, since its craft lines had been all but obliterated by technological innovations in the industry, its jurisdictional logic remained impeccable.

Although the national unions were opposed to specialization and to specialists, on occasion they found themselves obliged to admit some of the latter into their ranks. This occurred primarily when the specialists were capable of performing, however imperfectly, other craft operations, or when the number of members of the craft union in question, who wished to work on the specialty, was small relative to the demand for the specialized labor. In the former case, the specialists had to be admitted in order to avert a threat of dualism; in the latter they had to be admitted in order to protect employment opportunities for those "craftsmen" who wished to take advantage of them. One reason why some of the craft unions felt themselves obliged to retain some of their jurisdictional outposts—at the cost of admitting the garrisons of specialists—was the necessity of preserving the jurisdictions of their members in small communities in which specialization was not as advanced as it was in the larger industrial centers. Thus, the Bricklayers were unwilling to relinquish jurisdiction over plastering, although they wanted no part of "exclusive plasterers," so long as their members in small towns found it "absolutely necessary to work at the two branches in order to make a decent living," and even though many bricklayers in the large cities could do no plastering.[41] And the Molders, although at first they encouraged the Coremakers to organize into a union of their own, later repented their generosity when the latter sought to restrict molder apprentices from learning coremaking. The Molders then insisted on retaining jurisdiction over coremaking,

38. *Proceedings,* Glass Bottle Blowers' Association, 1900, pp. 75–76.

39. *Proceedings,* 1897, p. 24; 1900, p. 79; 1902, p. 14.

40. Barnett, *Chapters on Machinery and Labor,* p. 106.

41. *Proceedings,* 1905, p. X (report of the president). Also *Proceedings,* 1899, pp. 168–172; *Proceedings,* 1903, p. 93.

because, in small shops which employed no regular coremakers, it was necessary that molders make cores.[42]

Logically, it was to the advantage of specialist groups to be annexed by craft unions, provided, of course, that the number of craftsmen who sought employment in the specialized occupation did not overcrowd that trade, but provided also that it was great enough at the same time to exert some appreciable indirect effect upon the specialist's wage. For assuming that all workers in the specialized occupation received the same wage, the "transfer earnings" of the more versatile could exert an elevating effect upon the specialty wage. On the other hand, craft unions tended to be dominated by the higher-paid groups (for instance, the stove molders, the steel puddlers and finishers,[43] the bricklayers, the compositors), so that other groups frequently believed that their special interests were being ignored. This was especially true in the case of the stone masons and the machinery molders, both of whom attempted to secede from their parent organizations.[44]

These and other secession movements were opposed by the parent unions, which were not enthusiastic about including the special groups in their ranks, but which could not afford to let them go. The Bricklayers required that a member who had drawn a traveling card from an "exclusive" masons' (or bricklayers') local and deposited that card in a "mixed" local could be issued only a mason's (or bricklayer's) card by that mixed local.[45] This practice was eloquent of the unhappy marriage between the two trade groups. Indeed, there are several instances of attempts made at secession by high-wage groups, who felt that too much attention was being paid to the problems of the other occupational groups. Such attempts were made by stove molders (by a group of St. Louis locals who claimed that "the different elements that embody the composition of the I.M.U. of N.A. are ignorant of the nature and requirements of stove molding and in a measure antagonistic to our interests"),[46] by bricklayers (who attempted to form an exclusive organization entitled the United Order of American Bricklayers),[47] and, in the steel industry, by the finishers and puddlers.[48] Thus, neither specialist nor craftsman was happy in the other's company, but, where a merger took place, it occurred because the specialists were numerous and competent enough to make their affiliation highly necessary to the craftsman.

42. *Journal,* January 1, 1900, p. 34.

43. See John A. Fitch, *The Steel Workers* (New York: Russell Sage Foundation, 1910), p. 98.

44. *Proceedings,* Bricklayers: 1884, pp. 37–38, 61–62; 1890, p. 45; 1897, p. 58; 1902, p. 3; 1903, pp. 4, 429–435. Stockton, *Molders Union,* p. 48.

45. *Constitution,* 1900, Art. XIII, Sec. 7.

46. *Proceedings,* 1890, pp. 8–10.

47. *Proceedings,* 1873, pp. 6, 17, 21, 22–23; 1874, pp. 5, 7; 1875, p. 7; 1884, p. 11.

48. Jesse S. Robinson, *The Amalgamated Association of Iron, Steel, and Tin Workers* (Baltimore: Johns Hopkins, 1920), pp. 53–55.

We have already observed that national officers tended to oppose wage policies, including the establishment of certain differentials, which were conducive to specialization. Where specialization was an accomplished fact, however, it sometimes became necessary to recognize the necessity of accepting such differentials; the alternative was the establishment of uniform minimum rates at the low levels earned by the specialist, since the latter could not be excluded by the establishment of high minima. Consider the uncomfortable position in which President Fox of the Molders found himself:

(While) I do not wish to be construed as favoring an attempt to grade our membership . . . in establishing minimum rates, especially when they approach the higher ranges, we should be careful to use wise discrimination when there is a class of work of very inferior grade included, and upon which molders are employed who are adapted for that class of work only. . . . Circumstances over which we have no control are creating a class of molders capable of distinct classification from that of the all around mechanic or jobbing molder for whom we have been accustomed to legislate.[49]

He then proceeded to define the uncontrollable circumstances as "the specializing trend."

"COMPOUND CRAFT" UNIONISM

The inclusion in the same union of different occupational groups whose common boundaries were made indistinct by the versatility of an appreciable portion of the membership was a matter of jurisdictional necessity. Some unions, however, were "compounded" of genuinely distinct crafts, since they included "workers who do not engage in the same tasks or occupations.[50] The Printers, Iron and Steel Workers, Machinists, Meat Cutters and Butcher Workmen, and Street and Electric Railway Employees are organizations which have been placed in this category; and, in the opinion of Hoxie, "a large proportion of the unions, local and national, in the United States are today (1924) compounded or amalgamated craft unions, whether or not so designated by title."[51]

The practice of grouping "related" but distinct trades in a single organization has been ascribed to the desire of each craft group for the support of the others in times of strife. An inquiry into the divergent jurisdictional practices of different unions of the period—for some unions excluded all but those who practiced a single calling—must, then, account for the fact that certain highly skilled crafts apparently required sympathetic aid more than did others

49. *Proceedings,* 1895, p. 610.
50. Robert F. Hoxie, *Trade Unionism in the United States* (New York: Appleton, 1924), pp. 42, 43. Hoxie suggested the term, "crafts union," as an alternative to "compound craft union."
51. Theodore W. Glocker, "Amalgamation of Related Trades in American Unions," *American Economic Review,* vol. V, (1915), pp. 554–575; see especially pp. 557–558.

which chose the way of isolation. The explanation appears to lie in the fact that a skilled group's dependence upon outside help varied inversely with the extent to which it had succeeded in organizing the members of its own craft. For if a unionized group in an imperfectly organized trade struck one employer, it was possible for him to contract for the performance in a nonunion firm of the work normally done by his striking employees and thus to maintain operations in the other departments of his plant. Under such circumstances, the striking group would have little chance of success, unless it could persuade other key craftsmen to abstain from work and to make the former's grievance their own. A strike of the unions of iron boilers and puddlers in Pittsburgh in 1875 failed because the struck employers were able to keep the heaters and rollers at work on muck iron produced by nonunion boilers and puddlers in other localities. Convinced that their strike would have been successful had the heaters and rollers supported them, the highly skilled puddlers and boilers abandoned their policy of craft exclusiveness and entered into an "Amalgamated Association" with the other trades in the industry the following year.

The experience of the boilers and puddlers, however, might be contrasted with that of another skilled and more completely organized group, the glass bottle blowers.[52] The latter, it will be recalled, rejected the pressers' offer of alliance and also refused to amalgamate with the Flint Glass Workers because the latter was a multicraft union. Thus, although many of the national unions were compounded of more than one craft, others, like the Glass Bottle Blowers, Locomotive Engineers, Shoe Lasters, and Cotton-mule Spinners, eschewed amalgamation. "There are aristocracies," Glocker observed, "even among the aristocrats."[53]

The degree of aristocracy achieved by any group was largely measured by the extent to which the services offered *by its members* were economically essential to the employers for whom they worked. And, given the availability of alternative methods of production utilizing different resources (labor or nonlabor), the degree of essentiality possessed by a unionized group of workers was largely determined by the degree of organization achieved by the union in question. For the concept of craft jurisdiction, hinging upon the availability to the employers of substitutes for the labor of the union group, implies control over all the workers in the craft in question. Given such control, the need for outside support from other occupational groups in the industry did not appear to be as urgent as it was when the craft's own "jurisdiction" was insufficiently organized—or, at least, the possible gains of amalgamation were then outweighed by its cost, namely, the obligation to reciprocate.

52. The Glass Bottle Blowers' Association claimed two-thirds of the bottle blowers of America as its members in 1896. Warren E. Scoville, *Revolution in Glass-Making* (Cambridge, Mass.: Harvard University Press, 1948).

53. Glocker, "Amalgamation in Unions," p. 573.

But even to those skilled groups which were vulnerable to the competition of nonunion fellow-craftsmen, this "cost" of coalition was a deterrent to amalgamation with other crafts. On the other hand, however, it furnished a powerful incentive to the formation of multicraft unions. This budding paradox is quickly resolved once it is appreciated that the type of coalition sought by the more highly skilled craft was not a partnership of equals but an arrangement whereby it might cast the deciding vote in determining the conditions under which all parties might be called upon to make common cause. For this reason it was often inadvisable for a craft to enter into—or to remain in—a combine in which it was outnumbered, when decisions were made by majority vote and each group was accorded representation proportionate to its numbers. Numerous secessions, both successful and abortive (some of which were referred to in the preceding section), indicate that amalgamation did not end craft "separatism."

Thus Local Assembly 300 of the Knights of Labor, which included flatteners and cutters as well as blowers and gatherers in the window glass industry, proved to be an exceedingly unstable organization, because, "Whichever side controlled the union received advantages in the adjustment of wage scales."[54] In 1895, the blowers and gatherers formed a secret "Protective Association" to vote as a unit in the Local Assembly; this development was soon countered by the emergence of a secret organization of cutters and flatteners. Four years later, after the blowers and gatherers had gained control of the union, the other two groups withdrew to form the Window Glass Workers' Association of North America. The two unions then joined battle, with the local assembly entering into an exclusive agreement with one of the two rival combines in the industry and the association concluding a similar compact with the other. Since each union pledged itself to supply its own employer group with all necessary labor, including that over which the other exercised jurisdiction, the situation remained saturated with unreality until the two craft groupings recombined in 1904. This new union (the Amalgamated Window-Glass Workers of America), however, proved no more satisfactory to the cutters and flatteners than had Local Assembly 300, and they withdrew within a year to form another organization of their own. The four trades were later reunited in still another union (the National Window Glass Workers), but by this time, due to the introduction of new machinery in the industry, the blowers and gatherers had lost much of the jurisdictional foundation upon which their pristine aristocracy had been based, and with it their power any longer to deny equal representation to the cutters and flatteners. As an increasing proportion of the industry's output was machine-made, the demand for blowers and gatherers declined, while the demand for cutters and flatteners increased. Thus the union limited the work week of the former to forty hours, but it imposed no limit upon the cutters and flatteners.

54. H. E. Hoagland, *Report on the Trade Agreements in the Window Glass Industry* (MS. in Johns Hopkins University Library, 1914), pp. 3–4, see also p. 34.

Hence the insistence of many of the more highly skilled trades upon control over the policies of the compound unions set an effective limit to the potentialities of amalgamation—even in industries in which the "competitive menace" of nonunion craftsmen would have made sympathetic help from other groups attractive to the skilled trades. But when the most highly skilled trade was also the most numerous craft in the industry, it frequently favored coalition. However, so that its numerical superiority might secure for it control within the coalition (upon which it insisted), the large skilled group tended to prefer amalgamation to other types of coalition. The most common alternative to amalgamation in a single union as a means of procuring coördinated economic action was federation of independent unions of the different craft groups in the industry. Logically, perhaps, there was no reason why the crafts should have preferred one form to the other. Granted that the more numerous group desired that equal weight be assigned to the vote of each unionist in the coalition, it did not follow that federation implied the senatorial principle of allotting equal representation to each of the independent participating unions. And, on the other hand, it was equally true that numerically inferior groups could obtain representation out of proportion to their numbers as an inducement to enter into or remain in the same unions with larger crafts.

Nevertheless, the price of amalgamation seemed less than the price of federation to the larger and more highly skilled crafts, perhaps because they had been the first organized in many instances and, as a matter of fact, could retain control over a going organization more easily than they could achieve it within a federation of sovereign unions. It was possible, of course, that the degree of autonomy which was necessary to induce the other crafts to remain in the compound union might be so high as to be incompatible with the retention of control by the group in question. In that case—as in the situation in which the highly skilled craft was outnumbered by its potential allies—the costs of amalgamation might be considered to outweigh the benefits therefrom. But when the craft aristocrats did favor coalition, they insisted invariably upon coalition by amalgamation, rejecting coalition by federation.

In summary, the factors determining the nature and extent of craft coalition were: (1) the degree to which each craft in the industry in question stood in need of the support of the others, which in turn can be broken down into: the degree to which it was independent of outside assistance, and the potential helpfulness of each of the other groups; (2) the degree to which each was prepared to make concessions to the others in the form of reciprocal aid; and (3) the degree to which each group was able to extract concessions from the others.

The second and third criteria are not independent of the first. A group's willingness to make concessions in exchange for obtaining outside support from another group depended, in part at least, upon the urgency of its need for that support and upon the other group's ability to render effective aid. Similarly, the terms on which a group could obtain help from another group were determined in part by its own strategic value to that group, which, in turn, reflected qualities that affected its own independence. (In other words, the group best able to bargain for support from other groups on its own terms was, other things being equal, the group which was least dependent upon such help.)

The principal determinants of a craft's need for assistance from the outside were the degree of skill required of its membership and the extent to which its jurisdiction was organized. Skill and organization were, of course, not independent of one another; the degree of skill was one determinant of the degree of organization achieved. While the second and third criteria above hinged upon the first, they were also affected by the relative numerical strength of the various groups. The significance of relative numbers lies in the fact that a minority group might be confronted with the choice of making greater concessions than it would have been willing to make purely on the basis of the economic considerations discussed above or of seceding from (or refusing to enter) the amalgamation.

The necessary condition for successful amalgamation was that all parties stood to gain by alliance, or at least that one or more stood to gain and none was appreciably disadvantaged. This implied that each would be willing to make some concessions in order to enlist the support of the others and that the less independent would be willing to make the larger concessions. This, in turn, required that no great disparities in numerical strength exist among the potential allies. For a relatively small group might be obliged, as a condition of remaining in the union, to concede more than the support of the others was, in its own estimation, worth to it. And a numerically preponderant group could concede less (and demand more) than it would have been willing to concede in order to enjoy the advantages of amalgamation. From the different possible combinations of relative degree of organization, skill, and numerical strength, the following cases may be singled out for analysis because of their historical importance:

The Highly Skilled and Strongly Organized Group

In this case the foundations for "pure," single-craft unionism exist. The prospects for amalgamation with this group were poor, for, having no great need for outside assistance, it was not willing to surrender any of its autonomy in order to secure it.

The Highly Skilled but Insufficiently Organized Group and the Larger, Unskilled, and Poorly Organized Group

Here, again, the prospect for successful amalgamation was remote. The skilled group in this case was not independently strong and could profit from sympathetic assistance. The other group, however, being less skilled and (for that reason) probably even less well organized, was not regarded as a potentially helpful ally. To the unskilled and less independent workers on the other hand, both the need for and the prospective benefit from alliance were greater, but their numerical preponderance would have assured them control in any genuine amalgamation. In this case, the group with less at stake in union would have been outvoted by the group which possessed less economic strength and which probably would have found it advantageous to meet the former's terms of amalgamation, if it had been compelled to do so. As in the previous case, there was no amalgamation because the position of one of the parties (the highly skilled) would not have been improved thereby.

The Larger, Highly Skilled Group and the Smaller Group with Less Skill and Independence

The chance for successful amalgamation was better in this case, because the smaller group which was obliged to make the greater concessions was the one which was the more willing to do so. However, it was possible that the extra bargaining power imparted to the highly skilled group by its numerical strength might lead it to insist upon concessions greater than those which the other group might be willing to make on purely "economic" grounds. In that event, the larger and more independent craft had to decide whether to forego insistence upon terms which it could dictate only by virtue of its majority position or to chance secession by the other group.

This last case was typified by the International Typographical Union, in which one of the most highly skilled craft groups was also the largest. The compound of crafts in this union proved to be unstable insofar as some of the more important groups were concerned. Nevertheless, the record of the jurisdictional vicissitudes of the printers reveals so clearly the motives of a skilled craft group in seeking alliance with other trades in the same industry that we shall conclude this section on "crafts unionism" with a rather lengthy digression upon an unsuccessful attempt at amalgamation.

THE PRINTERS: A DIGRESSION

Like the Glass Bottle Blowers, the Printers were a highly skilled group of craftsmen. But unlike the former, who rejected various offers of amalgamation, the latter made strenuous efforts to include in this organization other groups of workers whose trades were conceded to lie without the bounds of the printing craft. Technological developments during the latter part of the nineteenth century, together with the growing importance of the large newspaper plant—relative to the small-scale book-and-job shop—resulted in extensive specialization and in the emergence of new trade groups. The first of these groups to appear was composed of the pressmen, after the introduction of the power press had effected a clearcut separation between the composing room and the press room in most printing establishments. Some of the pressmen's locals seceded from the International Typographical Union in 1888 and formed an international union of their own the following year. Their example was followed by the bookbinders in 1892, by the stereotypers and electrotypers (whose secession began in 1898 and whose international was established in 1902), and, finally, by the photoengravers (1900).

Each secession was opposed by the typographers, but at no time was their opposition based upon the claim that the secessionists were encroaching upon the jurisdiction of the printers. On the contrary, the typographers sought to retain the affiliation of these splinter groups by offering them successively higher degrees of autonomy within the International Typographical Union as "allied crafts." Thus, the pressmen, who had been regarded originally as "printers," were recognized in 1871 as belonging to a distinct branch of the industry, and provision was made in 1873 for the establishment of separate local unions for pressmen.[55] Furthermore, a constitutional amendment was passed in 1885 providing that the second vice-president of the union be a "practical pressman" who "in addition to his other duties . . . shall decide all questions that may arise between Pressmen and their Union . . . calling into consultation such pressmen as may be selected by the local Union involved . . ." Three years later, it was decided that the stereotypers and electrotypers merited an international vice-president of their own; and, in 1896, three additional vice-presidencies were created, to be filled from the ranks of the photoengravers, mailers, and newspaper writers.[56] The status of these new vice-presidents, however, differed from that of the others in that they were unsalaried and were not regular members of the executive council. They were allowed to vote in the council only "on such matters as appertain to their respective craft." A further step in the direction of autonomy was taken in 1892, when it was provided that the nomination of each vice-president, representing a specific trade group, be restricted to the members in the trade in question.[57]

At the same time, the pressmen's locals were organized into a pressmen's trade district, and the electrotypers' and stereotypers' unions were organized into another trade district. (The pressmen's international vice-president also served as the president of their district trade union, and the vice-president who represented the interests of the electrotypers and stereotypers served in a similar capacity on the governing body of the second trade district union.) Although the typographers eliminated the pressmen's trade district after they had accorded formal recognition to the International Printing Pressmen's Union in 1894, they continued their efforts to prevent the other "allied crafts" from seceding. In 1896 it was provided that one of the I.T.U.'s four delegates to the American Federation of Labor "shall be a member of the allied crafts."

55. Tracy, *Typographical Union,* pp. 172, 257, 268.
56. *Constitution,* 1885, Arts. IV and VI; 1888, Arts. IV and VI; 1896, Arts. IV and VI.
57. *Constitution,* 1892, Arts. IV, XIX, XX.

And two years later the photoengravers "or any other allied trades under the jurisdiction of this organization" were permitted to form trade districts. Furthermore, each trade district was granted exclusive power to charter locals, admit new members, issue traveling cards, and "make all laws necessary for the sole government of" its trade.[58]

In addition to the foregoing, the willingness of the Typographical Union to recognize the jurisdictional claims of the national unions which their "allies" ultimately established is further evidence in support of the contention that its attempts to forestall the establishment of those unions had not been motivated by considerations jurisdictional in nature. In 1895, the I.T.U. recognized "the right of the International Printing Pressmen's Union to charter, regulate and control printing pressmen, pressfeeders and helpers in pressrooms in the United States and Canada; also . . . the right of the International Brotherhood of Bookbinders to charter, legislate and control all branches pertaining to the bookbinding trade . . ."[59] Similar recognition was accorded the International Stereotypers and Electrotypers' Union in 1902 and to the International Photoengravers' Union in 1904.

In the absence of jurisdictional conflict, it appears that the printers' efforts to retain the affiliation of the allied crafts stemmed from their desire to enlist the latter's support in industrial struggles. Thus, after members in each allied craft had been permitted to organize into local unions of their own calling, "joint standing committees" were established, "to whom the several trades shall refer the adjustment of difficulties with their employers."[60] Later, definite provision was made for the authorization and prosecution of joint strikes by local allied printing trades councils. Participation in such strikes by member locals was mandatory.[61] Furthermore, since reluctance to breach collective agreements with employers was advanced frequently as a reason for nonparticipation, it was decided, in 1894, that

No local union shall sign a contract guaranteeing its members to work for any proprietor, firm or corporation unless such contract is sanctioned by the Allied Trades Council.[62]

Nor did the printers' interest in sympathetic action abate after their allies, one by one, chose the way of independence. In the same agreement in which the Typographical Union recognized the jurisdictional claims of the Printing Pressmen's Union and the Bookbinders' Brotherhood, provision was made for the prosecution of "joint strikes and for control of a printing trades label by local joint allied printing trades councils." In 1903 another agreement was

58. *Constitution*, 1896, Art. IV; 1898, Art. XIX.
59. Tracy, *Typographical Union*, pp. 507, 715–718, 783–784.
60. *Constitution*, 1889, Art. XIV.
61. *General Laws*, 1892, Sec. 49.
62. *General Laws*, 1894, Sec. 51.

drawn up, providing for the participation of the Stereotypers and Electrotypers, and in the following year the Photoengravers were included.[63]

The printers' concern with mutual assistance was actuated by the fact that they constituted the largest occupational group in the industry.[64] As long as the other craft groups remained in the Typographical Union, it was possible for the printers' numerical superiority to be translated into political dominance. If the decision to declare a sympathetic strike was made by a simple majority vote of all concerned, the printers, in many instances, could master enough votes to compel other crafts to support them in disputes arising in the composing room, just as they could prevent the occurrence of joint stoppages in situations in which their own immediate interests were not involved. On the other hand, had each craft group been given an equal voice in such matters, the printers would have found themselves in the position of dispensing more sympathy than they received. In the first place, since they occupied a strategic position in the industrial process by virtue of their high degree of skill and essentiality, they were especially desirable allies for the other crafts in times of trouble. Furthermore, if strike expenses were financed on a per capita basis, the more numerous printers' group would be obliged to assume the major portion of the financial burden. Thus it was not improbable to suppose that the other crafts would support one another's grievances as a matter of logrolling strategy, in order to compel the participation of the printers in all disputes.

The printers' interest, then, lay in organizational unity, just as the interest of the allies lay in coöperation among sovereign equals. The attitude of the printers was well illustrated in an amendment to the constitution (passed in 1891), which provided that pressmen, stereotypers, electrotypers, and bookbinders who could join printers' locals where there were not a sufficient number of their own craft in the locality to apply for "independent charters," must "assist and take part in strikes when legally ordered by local (printers') union."[65] This law remained on the books even after the different crafts were permitted to form trade districts within the I.T.U.

But in striving to prevent disunity, the printers were obliged to grant concessions in the direction of craft autonomy which at times made the game seem hardly worth the candle. In 1892, the year in which provision was first made for concerted strike activity by allied trades councils, it was decided that, after attempts at mediation by the district organizer had failed, a sympathetic stop-

63. Tracy, *Typographical Union*, pp. 506–510, 713–718, 783–784. See also Jacob Loft, *The Printing Trades* (New York: Farrar & Rinehart, 1944), p. 191.

64. Tracy, *Typographical Union*, p. 963. In his report to the convention of 1910, President Lynch claimed that, "The International Typographical Union has a membership of more than 50,000, nearly 20,000 more than the combined membership of our allies." In 1909, the I. T. U. had 45,500 members; the printing pressmen, 17,800; the stereotypers and electrotypers, 3500; the bookbinders, 7100; and the photoengravers, 3200.

65. *Constitution*, 1891, Art. I, Sec. 4.

page could be called without authorization from the international's executive council if three-quarters of the members present at the local union meetings (to be convened for the occasion) voted in favor of striking.[66] Now this requirement enabled the large printers' locals to veto proposals for joint strike action when they believed that their own interests would not be substantially furthered thereby, but it also permitted the other craft locals to withhold their support from the printers when the latter sought help more easily than would have been possible had the vote required been a simple majority.

At the next convention, the rules governing strikes were changed once again, and the balance of local power was tipped still further away from the printers. It was provided that, if the district organizer's mediation efforts proved futile and if a majority of the international's executive council approved, a strike vote would be taken only in the local which was a direct party to the grievance at hand. If three-fourths of the members present at the local union meeting voted in favor of a strike and if a majority of the local printing trades unions in the community upheld the position of the aggrieved organization, a joint strike would be called, to "apply alike to each and every union, craft and individual working under said jurisdiction in the office or concerns involved." If, however, the embattled local failed to secure support from the necessary number of its sisters, it could appeal to the executive council. If four-fifths of the members of that body decided that a strike was justified, the president or his proxy was obliged to make another effort to effect a settlement with his employers. This failing, a general strike could finally be called, "and those disregarding this order shall be forthwith expelled."[67] The stages in this procedure, which precede the granting or withholding of approval of the strike vote by the other locals, were identical with the procedure to be followed by individual local unions in obtaining authorization for strikes prosecuted unilaterally.

It is apparent that this new procedure virtually nullified the printers' numerical advantage. They lost their potential veto power, for if an aggrieved local was supported by a majority of the other local unions in the council, the dissenting organizations were obliged to participate in the "general" strike. Furthermore, the printers' powers of initiative were seriously curtailed. As an aggrieved organization which failed to enlist the support of a majority of its fellows, a printers' local could petition the international executive board for authority to call a joint strike. Two of the five members of the board, however, were vice-presidents who represented the interests of the pressmen and of the electrotypers and stereotypers, respectively, and the affirmative votes of four were required for authorization.

The practice of giving each craft group equal voting strength in the authorization of joint strikes was continued in the agreement of 1894, in which

66. *General Laws,* 1892, Sec. 49.
67. *General Laws,* 1893, Secs. 51, 46, 47.

the I.T.U. recognized the national unions which had been established by the pressmen and the bookbinders. At the local level it was agreed that "Grievances requiring joint strikes must be decided by the executive boards or councils of an equal number of each party. . . ." It was also provided that the executive councils of the three signatory international unions "shall for the purposes of this agreement at all times be composed of an equal number of members . . ."; and, although it was hardly necessary to do so, the agreement stipulated that strikes were to be authorized by "a majority of the *bodies*, acting conjointly."[68] Joint strikes could be called by the general officers of the three unions after action had been taken consecutively by (a) the local executive boards, (b) the membership of each local, (c) the presidents (or their representatives) of the three international unions (attempt at mediation), and (d) the executive councils of the three internationals.

The same principle which governed the authorization of joint strikes underlay their termination: "Strikes may be called off by a majority vote of the executive councils." The triumph of craft sovereignty was well-nigh complete, except for the stipulation that strike benefits to all involved be paid by the initiating union, and even here it was provided that, after eight weeks, "beneficiaries shall apply to their respective unions for further relief." The weekly benefits specified were $7 to married men, or the heads of families, and $5 to single men or women.

The printers soon awoke to the fact that, in their attempts, first, to retain the affiliation of the allied crafts and second, to retain their support as sovereign national unions, in disputes with employers, they had conceded too much. The first reaction came in 1896, when the General Laws were expanded to provide that, "In case of strike or lockout where more than one craft [affiliated with the I.T.U.] is involved, settlement shall be made by a majority vote of all crafts involved."[69] The procedure for authorizing such strikes (by assent of either the majority of the locals involved or of four-fifths of the membership of the international executive board) remained unchanged, however, and, in 1898, President Donnelly complained, as Tracy expressed it, that "the obnoxious laws operated to give the allied crafts a weight in the higher councils of the organization entirely out of keeping with their numbers or financial contributions."[70] Under the circumstances, he wondered whether it would not be better to grant the insurgent electrotypers and stereotypers their independence "and cease this ridiculous talk of autonomy, when we know that autonomy means nothing but division and dissension." But the convention refused to follow the president: the laws were not changed, and the stereotypers' and electrotypers' trade district remained in existence. The

68. Agreement reproduced in Tracy, *Typographical Union*, pp. 506–510.

69. *General Laws*, 1896, Sec. 47: It was also provided, however, "That in making settlement all crafts involved shall be parties in the settlement of same; each to have due consideration."

70. Tracy, *Typographical Union*, pp. 580, 581, 600–602.

following year, the convention rejected a proposed international allied trades council (to be composed of the three parties to the tripartite agreement of 1894), and it approved a resolution in favor of "the amalgamation of all crafts pertaining to the printing industry. . . . by which each separate branch would be given complete autonomy, or control over its distinctive technical trade affairs and scale of wages," as an alternative to the working alliance among independent national unions. Thus the printers seemed to favor craft autonomy as a compromise between the desirable extreme of proportional representation of all crafts within the I.T.U., on the one hand, and the undesirable extreme of equal representation of crafts (organized in separate unions) on a supernational allied trades council, on the other—although, as their president had pointed out, autonomy within the I.T.U. was in fact rapidly approaching the latter limit.

The printers' proposal for amalgamation having failed to gain converts among the ranks of the independently organized craftsmen, the former next insisted upon the adoption of a radical alteration of the agreement of 1894.[71] This consisted in the creation of a "joint board of appeals," consisting of the presidents of the three contracting unions. Since the action of any local allied trades council could be reviewed by this new board upon the petition of an aggrieved local union, and since all rules enacted by the board were to be adopted only by unanimous vote of its three members, the Typographers were provided with effective veto power.[72] This arrangement, although it was adopted by all three unions, was unsatisfactory to the two allied crafts involved, with the result that it "was never made effective"; and the tripartite agreement was abrogated later in 1901 (report of President Lynch to the 1910 Convention).

A new agreement was entered into in 1903 which also provided for a system of representation more agreeable to the printers than to their allies. A new joint board was established, on which the printers had three representatives and the pressmen, bookbinders and electro- and stereotypers one each. Tie votes were to be decided by an arbitrator, unanimously chosen by the representatives; and the pressmen and bookbinders were allowed to invoke this procedure if they were jointly dissatisfied with any decision in which the representative of "any other party to this agreement" voted with the Typographical Union.[73] Furthermore, although local trades councils were composed of an equal number (three) of delegates from each local represented, the number of votes granted to each delegate on roll call was made proportional to the number of members in the local union represented.

71. Dispute over control over the allied union label also was a source of discontent. The label was the property of the I. T. U., but the pressmen and the bookbinders wanted equal rights therein. (See Loft, *The Printing Trades*, p. 190.)

72. Tracy, *Typographical Union*, pp. 651–652, 688, 960.

73. Tracy, *Typographical Union*, pp. 715–716, 747, 785, 962, 963, 979–983.

When the Photoengravers were admitted to the agreement the following year (1904) and were allowed to have one representative on the joint board, the I.T.U.'s contingent was increased to four. In 1905, the right of the Bookbinders and Stereotypers to invoke arbitration in the event that another signatory sided with the I.T.U. was rescinded, and the Printers' battle for proportional representation appeared to be won.

In 1909, however, a case came before the council in which the Printers, supported by the Stereotypers, outvoted the other unions. This decision, according to President Lynch, resulted in "estrangement" and "evidently caused considerable resentment on the part of the minority." The "minority" presented two demands: first, that the allied printing trades label, hitherto considered by the I.T.U. to be exclusive property, be owned jointly by the various printing trades unions; and second, that each union receive equal representation on the Joint Conference Board (as the joint board of appeals was now called). The Printers agreed readily enough to the first proposal, but preferred to do without any machinery for strike coöperation on a national level rather than yield their superiority in voting power.

In 1911, an International Allied Printing Trades Association was formed, with a board of governors whose decisions were made effective by unanimous vote only, but this new body was concerned solely with matters concerning the label and with some legislative work.[74] The Printers were no longer willing to share their bargaining power with the other crafts. Their only reaction to the allies' demand for equal representation was the reiteration in 1921 of the suggestion for the amalgamation of all of the unions in the printing trades which they had made in 1899; and the coldness with which this suggestion was received in no wise induced the Printers to proffer any compromise in the interest of sympathetic strike action. They had finally learned that any gains which might have accrued to them in the form of support from other occupational groups—even those in their own industry—were exceeded by the costs involved in the abridgement of their own freedom of action. Their position was stated uncompromisingly by their president in 1910:

It is but natural that the unions of less numerical strength should desire to exercise greater control and power in the Joint Conference Board than they now possess, but when it is considered that the membership of the International Typographical Unions outnumbers the combined membership of our allies by many thousands, it is apparent that we are justified in exercising our right of final word in the policies that shall prevail, even though friction and ill feeling may develop because of that determination. It is to our interest that each of our allies shall become strong, but that strength must not be had solely at our expense and to our undoing.[75]

74. Loft, *The Printing Trades,* pp. 191–194.
75. Tracy, *Typographical Union,* p. 959.

CHAPTER TWELVE

LOCAL AND NATIONAL FEDERATION

THE IMPLICATIONS OF JURISDICTION

THE EXPERIENCE of the national unions in establishing their trade jurisdictions influenced the nature of the wider federation in which they ultimately allied themselves. The working out of these forces of self-interest which were described in the previous chapter resulted in the existence of certain conditions to which any organization which sought to unite the different trade unions in "a community of outlook"[1] was obliged to adapt itself.

In the first place, the national unions found it essential that unitary control be established over all workers following the same trade. In this country, due in part to historical accident (which we shall discuss in the next section) and in part, perhaps, to the overriding spirit of combative individualism which seemed to pervade virtually all aspects of American existence, this came to mean that only one organization operate in a given jurisdiction. Although logically tenable, and even practiced abroad, coöperation among different unions in the same trade was rejected as an unfeasible alternative; and "dualism" achieved, in the post-Civil War period, virtual equality with high treason (which went by such time-honored names as "scabbing" and "ratting") in the American unionist's hierarchy of transgressions. Considering the numerical weakness of even some of the strongest unions at the time—and the corresponding magnitude of their disciplinary problems—this was no mean accomplishment.

Conspicuous lack of success in organizing the unskilled was another arresting phenomenon of the times which was not unrelated to the jurisdictional experience of the skilled trades. While insufficient organization often made it advantageous for the aristocratic elements to enter into amalgamations with other groups in their own industry, the unskilled possessed two peculiar char-

1. The term was used by G. D. H. Cole to distinguish the "labor movement" from the trade union or the coöperative society. See his *A Short History of the British Working-Class Movement, 1789–1947* (London: Allen & Unwin, new revised edition, 1947), pp. 3–4.

acteristics which made them of dubious value as allies. In the first place, their lack of skill reduced their effectiveness during strikes; they could be replaced more easily than other groups—if need be, by recruitment from abroad. Furthermore, their numerical preponderance in many industries made it inadvisable for other groups to enter into the same organization with them; they feared that industrial unionism would mean absorption (see above pp. 321–326).

In some instances, it is true, the unskilled were included in unions which embraced all groups in the trade. The unskilled who were "employed in and around the mines of the United States" were, as we have observed, admitted freely to membership in the United Mine Workers; and all wage earners in the brewing industry were welcomed into the Brewery Workers' union. The relative ease with which the places of the more highly skilled workmen in both of these industries could be filled during strikes by men recruited from lower-paid occupations[2] suggests, however, that industrial unionism in brewing and coal mining owed its existence, at least in part, to the fact that workers in different occupations within each industry could be substituted for one another. The true boundaries of the "craft" encompassed much of the range of occupations in the industry. The various components in the Brewers' union were further united by ties of language and national origin (German) and, more particularly, by that organization's exceptional reliance upon the boycott as an instrument of economic coercion. Our analysis of the occupational structure of the early national unions in terms of the craft group's attempt to maximize its "relative negotiating strength" rests on the assumption—plausible at least in this country over the period with which this study is concerned—that each occupational group relied primarily upon the "method of collective bargaining." The brewing industry, it should be noted, was unusually suited to the employment of the consumer boycott, since the commodity in question was dispensed widely in the establishment which came to be known, with simple justice, as the poor man's club.

And where both the miners and the brewery workers did succeed in establishing jurisdiction over a truly distinct craft group, the operating engineers, amalgamation was facilitated by the presence of rather special conditions which, in both cases, enabled the contribution made by the unskilled to be greater than would otherwise have been the case. The undesirable nature of coal mining endowed the miner with certain unique bargaining advantages, as we have already observed; in addition, the fact that mine villages were isolated communities, composed almost exclusively of miners, made it virtually inevitable that the mine engineers would be organ-

2. See pp. 307 and 308; also Hermann Schluter, *The Brewing Industry and the Brewery Workers' Movement in America* (Cincinnati, 1910). Also John R. Commons and Associates, *History of Labour in the United States* (New York: Macmillan, 1918–1935), v. IV, p. 364.

ized into miner's unions. And where the brewery workers succeeded in organizing the operating engineers, they secured a higher scale from them than the engineers' own international was able to enforce. Thus, in this instance, the less skilled majority induced the strategic minority group to affiliate with it by granting concessions which made affiliation sufficiently attractive to the smaller group.

Moreover, since the miners and the brewery workers were considered unusual because they were organized in industrial unions, it would appear that, when skilled groups were indeed isolated economically from the unskilled in their industries, they did not typically enter into "amalgamations" with them. Hoxie was in error when he classified, albeit "provisionally," the "compound or amalgamated craft unions" as "a mode of transition" between "strict craft unionism" and "industrial unionism."[3] It is doubtless correct not to regard the amalgamation of crafts as an "ideal type," since it probably owed its existence to the organizational weakness of the contracting parties. In that event, however, the compound of crafts must be regarded as a stage of development anterior to "strict craft" rather than to industrial unionism, for alliances might have been expected to disintegrate as each component craft achieved a degree of organization sufficient to eliminate, for all practical purposes, the menace of nonunion competition. In the event of failure to achieve the extent of organization requisite to "strict craft" unionism, however, there was no reason to doubt the stability of the crafts compound, for the organized trades were under no compulsion to admit the unskilled into their unions as long as their own economic jurisdictions remained intact. Of course, the occurrence of technological change has sometimes made the organization of the "unskilled" a condition of the survival of unions of the hitherto "skilled" (witness the Glass Bottle Blowers), and to this extent one might urge that the crafts compound was in fact, if not in theory, a transitional type of trade union, destined to be succeeded either by the industrial union or by no union at all. But Glocker was more nearly correct than Hoxie when he observed that

The chief hope of the unskilled workers rests in an alliance with the skilled, but the skilled gain nothing by such an alliance. On the contrary, such amalgamation entails a sacrifice, since it imposes on the skilled the obligation of fighting battles in behalf of the unskilled. The keynote of the dominant unionism has been self-interest . . . Following this policy, the skilled trades have refused to unite with the unskilled.[4]

Since affiliation with the skilled workers in the various industries was denied to the unskilled, efforts were made to unite them into a single "general" union like those found in Britain (the Transport and General

3. Robert F. Hoxie, *Trade Unionism in the United States* (New York: D. Appleton, 1919), p. 43.
4. Theodore W. Glocker, "Amalgamation of Related Trades in American Unions," *American Economic Review*, v. V (1915), p. 573.

Workers' Union) and Denmark,[5] which really would have amounted to a "craft" union of the unskilled.[6] The National Labor Union, in its first congress (1866), advocated organizing the unskilled into "a general workingmen's association."[7] And twelve years later, a small group of "trade union socialists" (led by J. P. McDonnell and F. A. Sorge) and dedicated disciples of the eight-hour day (Ira Steward, George E. McNeill, and George Gunton), attempted to establish an International Labor Union of the unskilled in all industries. Without the strategic support of the skilled workers, however, these ambitious projects failed, the latter shortening its lines of battle until it finally—and somewhat anticlimactically—emerged as the International Labor Union of Hoboken (New Jersey).

Another factor which restricted the potential development of federation was the traditional reluctance of the national unions to engage in sympathetic strikes. The experience of even the Printers, related above, illustrates the hesitancy of a craft group to pledge strike support to other groups in the same industry, groups with which mutual interests were not strong enough to result in permanent amalgamation. And the refusal of the skilled craft to amalgamate with the unskilled in its own industry can be laid in part to its unwillingness to make the latter's battles its own. Even so altruistic a union as the Glass Bottle Blowers, which actively encouraged the organization of other groups in the industry, refused to unite with them in a single organization.

Thus it was a fact, however deplorable, that for many a national union, sympathy (defined narrowly as the willingness of organized workers in one union to strike in support of men in a different one) began—and ended—at home. This narrow definition of sympathy, however, must not lead one to ignore the existence of other manifestations of a "community of outlook"; for such indeed existed. The most prevalent form of intertrade "solidarity" was the proffering of moral support by noncombatant unions to an embattled sister, as witnessed by the impressive list of resolutions passed

5. In an analysis of Scandinavian trade unionism, Galenson also informs us that similar general workers' unions existed for a time in Norway and Sweden, but that they were obliged to surrender jurisdiction to industrial unions, as the latter developed and grew more powerful. Walter Galenson, "The Labor Movement and Industrial Relations" in *Scandinavia, Between East and West,* ed. by Heming K. Friis (Ithaca: Cornell University Press, 1950), p. 118.

6. The International Hod Carriers and Common Laborers' Union was exceptional in that it was a union of the unskilled which was confined to one industry, the building trades. However, as Glocker points out, in 1915 the international itself "makes no mention of strikes in its constitution . . . pays no strike benefits and rarely declares a strike." These functions were exercised by the constituent locals, which owed whatever strength they possessed to the sympathetic support which the locals in the skilled crafts, affiliated with the laborers in local building trades councils, gave to them. Glocker, "Amalgamation in Unions," p. 576.

7. Commons, *History of Labour,* v. II, pp. 98, 302.

unanimously at the typical annual convention. More tangible support, however, took the form of pecuniary aid, and, considering the extremely narrow financial margins upon which the early national unions were obliged to operate, even a modest gift represented a high degree of sacrifice on the part of the donor organization. Thus even the Bricklayers, then a notoriously self-centered group, received a communication from the Locomotive Engineers who gratefully acknowledged "the kindness and benevolence extended to our Order at the late strike" (in 1874).[8]

But the Bricklayers, along with more altruistic national unions, sought to prevent their local unions from participating in sympathetic strikes. The Carpenters, Iron and Steel Workers, Brewery Workers, Molders, Potters, and Cigar Makers were cited by Janes as unions which forbade their locals to enter into any type of strike without the approval of the national organization;[9] and, it was typically from the national union that most of the opposition to the sympathetic walkout originated.

The opposition of the nationals to sympathetic strikes was inspired by two considerations. The first was desire to conserve their financial resources. The second was disinclination to violate effective trade agreements. When opposition rested primarily on financial grounds, it often manifested itself in a regulation to the effect that the striking local alone pay for its demonstration of sympathy. The Carpenters' executive, in 1886, saw fit to advise the locals that

> In giving grants of money to aid other trades in cases of strikes or trade troubles, it is advisable to exercise care and not make appropriations unless condition of local funds permits and then make it in the form of a donation and avoid any assessment; an assessment levied for such purpose shall be purely voluntary in payment by the members.[10]

In the light of the above, it is interesting to take note of a ruling made two years later by the general executive board, according to which it was (by implication) apparently considered permissible for a union carpenter to cross another union's picket line:

> No member of any Local Union can "scab" it on any other trade by going to work *at such* trade when it is on strike.[11]

When the national union's opposition to sympathetic strikes stemmed from its insistence that affiliated locals uphold the sanctity of the collective bargaining agreements, however, the latter were in some cases flatly forbidden by the national to engage in such stoppages; they were not merely denied

8. *Proceedings,* 1874, pp. 24–25.
9. George M. Janes, *The Control of Strikes in American Trade Unions* (Baltimore: Johns Hopkins, 1916), pp. 50–52.
10. *Decisions of the General Executive Board,* 1886.
11. *Decisions of the General Executive Board,* 1888. My italics.

financial support if they did so. Thus, the Bricklayers, unlike the Carpenters and many other national unions in the building trades, prohibited recourse to sympathetic strikes on the part of their locals,[12] and their action can be explained in part by the desire of the international officers that collective agreements be honored. In 1914 the Bricklayers entered into "offensive and defensive alliances" with both the Steam and Operating Engineers and the Carpenters which were intended to prevent its locals from striking sympathetically without international sanction and to prevent the breaching of trade agreements quite as much as they were aimed at providing effective mutual assistance. Thus, while it was provided

That no member of either organization shall work on any operation where workmen are employed other than those who carry a paid-up working card of each respective International Union. . . .

it was firmly established

That in all "offensive and defensive" movements no subordinate local of either International Union shall be permitted to take any local action whatsoever until the question requiring joint action shall have first been submitted to and determined upon by the Presidents of the International Union of Steam and Operating Engineers and the Bricklayers, Masons and Plasterers' International Union of America. . . . No movement of an "offensive or defensive" character shall be countenanced in cases where such would be in violation of existing agreements that have been submitted to and duly approved by the Presidents of both International Unions as is required by the constitutional laws thereof.[13]

After the Molders' international union became a party to the country's first system of truly national collective bargaining (in 1891), it took steps which restricted the freedom of its locals to participate in sympathetic stoppages. In 1896 the executive board, expressing strong disapproval of sympathetic strikes, warned the locals "that before entering upon a strike of this sort they must consult the best interests of their own trade and obtain the sanction of their recognized international officers.[14] At the 1899 Convention, President Martin Fox reported that the executive board had refused to permit the Denver local to strike a certain employer in support of the Machinists. The Coremakers' local, however, did support the Machinists, and the Molders' local had to seek advice concerning the propriety of making their own cores, since coremaking was an essential step in iron molding. Fox thereupon granted the Molders authority to exceed their jurisdiction in this respect and defended his action by asserting that, "It is not our part to criticize the methods of a sister organization, but we cannot afford to have our members

12. Janes, *Control of Strikes*, p. 50.
13. *Proceedings*, 1915, pp. 508–509. The agreement with the Carpenters is identical with the pact with the Operating Engineers.
14. *Journal*, July 1896, pp. 277–278.

involved whenever the members of a kindred trade upon whom little restraint seems to be exercised choose to make demands upon their employers."[15] The convention later ratified the President's action in a statement of policy which summarizes excellently the position of the national union on this important issue:

Whereas, While we firmly believe in a complete solidarity of all labor interests, and

Whereas, We realize that in no trade can so much be accomplished by a thorough unity of action as among those directly connected with the foundry; therefore be it

Resolved, That it shall be the policy of this organization to render all possible assistance to our sister organizations when in trouble, provided they shall first submit their grievances and request our assistance before entering into a struggle with their employers, and be it further

Resolved, That upon the receipt of a request for aid that might involve our members in a strike, it shall be the duty of the local Union or Conference Board to whom such request is made to at once take action thereon and submit the same to our President and Executive Board for their consideration; and be it further

Resolved, That our members shall be bound to abide by the decision of our President and Executive Board, the same as provided in our Constitution in the case of a grievance of our own members.[16]

That the convention was motivated by its conviction that the locals should respect their trade agreements is made evident in an editorial which subsequently appeared in the union journal. In discussing this resolution, Editor Frey wrote,

Were we to disregard our own laws and ignore every agreement entered into with our employers at the behest or in sympathy with any kindred organization, we would soon lose whatever prestige we have gained as an organization, and would no longer be deemed a *responsible* body with which to enter into an agreement.[17]

The following year, the president was empowered by the executive board to revoke the charter of any local which persisted in conducting a strike in defiance of official orders to the contrary.

Since "business unionism" implied "craft autonomy"—the organization of sovereign unions along craft lines—it is not surprising that sympathetic striking ran counter to it on occasion. For if "solidarity," as the Molders expressed it in their resolution, had been accepted as the ruling principle of American trade unionism, the power of the individual craft group to enter into and/or to abide by the terms of its collective agreements would

15. *Proceedings*, 1899, p. 13 (report of the president).
16. *Proceedings*, 1899, p. 191. My italics.
17. *Journal*, September, 1899, p. 461. See also *Journal*, 1900, p. 414.

have been abridged to some extent. It will be recalled that, when the unwillingness of some of the local unions in "allied crafts" to breach their collective agreements threatened to nullify the Printers' efforts to establish an ironclad system of intercraft coöperation in their industry, the situation was resolved by requiring prior approval by the Allied Trades Council of every agreement involving a member local.[18] Although a perfectly logical inference from the premise, which the Printers adopted at the time, that intercraft "solidarity" was the overriding objective, this arrangement was hardly compatible with craft autonomy and—to the extent that national labor and product markets existed—with a system of autonomous national craft unions. And as the latter assumed an increasing degree of control over their local affiliates, particularly in the spheres of strike activity and collective bargaining, they came to regard appeals to the chivalrous instincts of these subordinate groups as a challenge to their authority and disruptive of discipline.

LOCAL FEDERATION

At this point the national unions came into conflict with another type of parent organization, the local federation of trades. These local federations— or, as they were called, city central trades' unions or trades assemblies or trades councils—antedated the national union as a parent organization with which local craft unions might affiliate themselves, and they appeared with each successive outcropping of local unionism down to the last quarter of the nineteenth century. The first city central was the Mechanics' Union of Trade Associations which was formed in Philadelphia in 1827, the year which, for this reason, was designated as marking the emergence of the labor movement in this country. The vigorous growth of local unionism which began in 1833 and continued until it was blighted by the depression which began in 1837 was characterized by a proliferation of city trades' unions. The state industrial congresses in the forties and fifties, which were political movements of a utopian nature, received questionable support from the underlying population; but the city congresses, which preceded the state organizations, were originally federations of local unions. And with the subsequent revival of local unionism in the early 1850's, fresh attempts to form city centrals were reported, although these apparently did not meet with much success. The first (six) national unions emerged in the fifties, but Andrews tells us that in the Civil War period, "the local trades' assembly, and not the national trade union, was the common unit of labour organisation. . . ." Later, when the national unions were eclipsed during the dark

18. See page 328 above. A similar surrender of craft autonomy in collective bargaining occurred in the railroad industry in 1906, when the first permanent "system federation" was formed on the Southern Railway. It was required that all crafts present uniform bargaining demands and that each agreement contain the same thirty-day notice of termination. Commons, *History of Labour*, v. IV, p. 369.

years following 1873, it appears that some of their protective functions were assumed by some of the surviving city federations. And finally, when the trade union movement emerged once more after 1879, the local federations of diverse trades led all the rest of the parent organizations.[19]

Thus the central labor union continued to function, both as the harbinger of unionism in times of revival and as a rearguard during recessions, well after the national union had emerged to assert its own claim upon the loyalty of the local. The urgency of the national's claim was in proportion to the local's concern with collective bargaining as an instrument for advancing the welfare of its members and also to the degree to which the relevant labor and product markets had become national in scope. Unlike the national union, which was a grouping of local unions of the same craft in different localities, the city central was a grouping of locals of different crafts in the same locality. Since appeal to each craft's sense of "solidarity" could be made more successfully on political than on economic grounds, it is not surprising to find that many central labor unions, whose origin can be traced to the existence of some bread-and-butter problem which confronted one or more of their member locals at the time,[20] emerged in time—often, in a very short time—as political movements.

Thus, the Mechanics' Union of Trade Associations, which grew out of a concerted demand for the ten-hour day, never supported a strike but did plunge forthwith into political activity and wound up as a "Working Men's" party.[21] Some of the city industrial congresses in the 1840's and 1850's owed their existence to specific economic grievances of particular local unions, but control soon passed to political groups espousing legislative programs of varying degrees of implausibility. (So persuasive were the sachems of Tammany Hall at this juncture that, according to Hoagland, the ward replaced the local union as the unit of organization in New York City's Congress.) The city centrals played a considerable part in the intensive political activity by labor groups which characterized the local political campaigns in 1886. In Boston, the Central Labor Union itself formed a complete ticket, and in New York City, the Central Labor Union nominated—and perhaps really elected Henry George for mayor.

19. Commons, *History of Labour,* v. I, pp. 189, 350, 357ff., 551ff., 556, 585–586, 608–610; v. II, pp. 18 and 21ff., 177, 310–311. The quotation in the text comes from pp. 21–22 of the second volume.

20. Significantly enough, the demand for a shorter working day frequently stimulated the formation of city central unions. The issue of shorter hours was one which was common to all trades, even though a uniform reduction in working time, since it was invariably accompanied by a subsidiary demand for maintenance of daily or weekly income, would be reflected in varying absolute increases in wage rates in different trades. Thus we hear of ten-hour and eight-hour "movements," although there were no corresponding "movements" for wage increases—at least prior to the period immediately following the second World War.

21. Commons, *History of Labour,* v. I, pp. 186–195; see also pp. 551–561.

The structure of the central labor unions (regional and embracing many trades) made them well designed for political activity. As a contemporary writer explained,

Let the trade unionists of a city be convinced that their ends can be more effectively advanced by independent political organization, and nothing could suit their purpose better than the system of local unions throughout the city, responsible as they soon would be to the central executive committee, for this is the form which the Central Labor Union would assume.[22]

But when the trade unionists' fancy turned to collective bargaining, they found that their city centrals were not particularly well adapted to this type of activity. To cite the same authority: "the Central Labor Unions are not organized on a plan which will enable them to do this." And where the city centrals did concern themselves with economic matters, they did not engage in collective bargaining, as many of the national unions sought to do, but confined themselves to broader activities which were more suited to their heterogeneous structures. They did occasionally mediate disputes between local unions and employers,[23] but, for the most part, their effectiveness lay in persuading their member locals that an injury to one of them was the concern of all the rest. To this end, the central unions busied themselves in the organization of consumer boycotts and in supporting strikes.

The consumer boycott was a type of activity to which the city central was obviously better adapted than the national union; for this type of boycott required participation by as many people as possible in a given locality, and it required their coöperation as consumers, regardless of their occupational specialties. Again to quote our observer of the time:

Numbers count for more in carrying on a boycott than in any other work of the union. Practically only union men refrain from patronizing a boycotted act, and the merchant fears only when he loses numbers of customers. The general public do not enter into a boycott. They regard it as a quarrel in which they are not interested, and have no time to look into the merits of the case.

Without the Central Labor Union, an effective boycott could not be carried on in the city.[24]

The other principal form of sympathetic support of the embattled local in which the city central engaged fairly extensively was the direct support of strikes. In some instances this actually involved the instigation of sympathetic strikes by local unions not directly concerned with the dispute at hand.[25] Now, from the viewpoint of the national trade union, a sharp distinction

22. William M. Burke, *History and Functions of Central Labor Unions;* Studies in History, Economics and Public Law, ed. by Faculty of Political Science, Columbia University, v. XII, no. 1 (New York: Macmillan, 1899), p. 120; see also p. 118.

23. Commons, *History of Labour,* v. II, p. 311.

24. Burke, *Central Labor Unions,* pp. 82–83.

25. Commons, *History of Labour,* v. I, p. 585.

could be made between a local affiliate's participation in a city-wide consumer boycott and its participation in a sympathetic strike. Since the national union was concerned primarily with maintaining control over the national market for the labor of a particular variety (or set of varieties), it was interested only secondarily in the extraoccupational activities of its own members. Typically, it had no unique interest in their careers as consumers, just as it had no unique interest in their careers as voters. It was true that, in some instances, a national union's welfare depended upon recourse to such methods as political action (the Seamen), the consumer boycott (the Brewery Workers), the secondary labor boycott, or even the sympathetic strike at least as much as it did upon the method of collective bargaining. In such cases, however, success depended primarily upon the number of supporters recruited to the cause; the national union involved was therefore concerned with the relevant extraoccupational activities of all the trade groups in the community (its own included)—and not with those of its own members to a unique degree.

But the national union did assert claim to the prior allegiance of its members in their employment relationships, and it reacted sensitively to any challenge to its authority over the local unions in which they were organized. For this reason the instigation of a sympathetic strike by a city central organization was likely to bring the latter into conflict with one or more national craft organizations. Perhaps the most celebrated example of a sympathetic strike which was instituted by a central labor union was the strike called by the Seattle Central Labor Council in 1919 in support of the demand by that city's shipyard workers for an increase in wages. In this instance, the various local unions supported the city's shipyard workers with impressive unanimity, but a number of international unions applied "pressure" (as the American Federationist termed it) upon their Seattle affiliates to instruct their members to return to work. This intervention by the internationals, incidentally, was prompted by the fact that the striking locals had violated their respective collective agreements when they engaged in the sympathetic walkout.[26]

For the most part, however, the strike activity of the central organization was restricted to the raising of funds, and even this relatively modest function—although performed on occasion with notable success—was limited, in most instances, by the lack of either provision for a continuing central fund or power to levy compulsory assessments upon the member locals.[27] Nevertheless, the existence of a central labor union in a locality was a monument, however humble, to the ideal of a community of interest among union men in all trades; and, whenever a suitable situation arose, it could be counted on

26. Commons, *History of Labour*, v. IV, pp. 439–443.

27. Perlman informs us that during the strike of the New York City freight handlers in 1882, the Central Labor Union in that city raised a fund of $60,000. Commons, *History of Labour*, v. II, pp. 22, 311, and 442.

to press one or more of its affiliates for tangible evidence of their protested faith. The issue between the national craft union and the city central was joined most closely when the latter would request sympathetic support of a striking local only from other locals in the same industry. Against the national's attempt to impress upon their affiliated locals "the sanctity of contracts" would be set the appeal, "not to cross the picket line" of a striking union. Thus, when the Pattern Makers' local in New York City went out on strike for the nine-hour day shortly after the local molders' union had entered into a collective agreement, the latter, in compliance with international policy, refused to violate its agreement by instructing its members to quit work in sympathy with the Pattern Makers. Whereupon the Central Federated Union of New York City suspended the Molders' local, although its president had twice ruled that it had no authority to order sympathetic strikes.[28]

Sympathetic strikes were called more frequently by local building trades councils. These consisted usually of local unions whose members frequently worked on the same projects. Each of these locals, consequently, was confronted with the necessity of deciding whether or not to engage in a sympathetic strike every time any of the others ceased work and picketed the employers in question. But it was not the fact of industrial proximity that accounted for the greater power of the building trades councils; we have noted that, where community of economic interest among the different crafts in an industry was not sufficient to prevent their organization into separate sovereign national unions, as in the printing industry, the latter could be effective in dissuading their locals from engaging in unauthorized stoppages.

Nor could the authority of the building trades councils be attributed to the fact that construction was predominantly (as it remains) a local market industry. From this fact one might be tempted to infer that the attractiveness to a local union of coöperation with locals in other crafts in the same locality might compare favorably with the gain to be derived from coöperation with locals of the same craft in other localities. Nevertheless, although a considerable portion of the printing industry (the newspaper branch especially) was decidedly local in nature, the local allied printing trades councils never succeeded in achieving a position of authority over their local affiliates comparable to that enjoyed by the councils in the building trades.

The most likely explanation of the power of the building trades councils lies in still another peculiarity of the construction industry, the brief duration of the job and, consequently, the crucial importance of the element of time with respect to the prosecution of strikes. For if strikes were delayed by the time-consuming process involved in obtaining sanction from national headquarters, "the building will have been completed and the men scattered."[29] Hence it was often considered expedient to leave discretion in the

28. *Journal,* September 1899, p. 461; October 1899, p. 528; and November 1899, p. 589.
29. Janes, *Control of Strikes,* p. 50.

hands of the locals. Thus, the local character of the industry made initially for less powerful national unions, and the short duration of the job made those national unions peculiarly agreeable to the retention of authority at local levels. These same conditions, furthermore, induced the locals in many communities to cede considerable power to the celebrated "walking delegates," or representatives of the building trades councils, who were often vested with the authority to order workers in all crafts to cease work on a project if a grievance concerning any one group remained unadjusted.

In the case of the Carpenters the relationship between the locals and the various building trades councils was so close that the feeling of intercraft solidarity pervaded even their national organization. Their secretary, P. J. McGuire, was wont to recount with gratitude the contributions made by organizations in other trades to the welfare of various carpenters' locals and then to balance the Brotherhood's ledgers with allusion to numerous instances wherein carpenters' locals had been of service in aiding other building crafts in their organizing efforts. Thus the chief executive officer of a national union was able to note with pride on one occasion that, "It is in this spirit (that) our local unions have affiliated with central labor unions, trades assemblies, building trades councils, or other local central bodies of organized labor, wherever they exist, and have formed them in many instances."[30]

Given the conditions peculiar to the industry, it is not surprising that many national unions in the building trades allowed their locals to strike without their prior consent. Some examples may be cited to support the inference that these concessions were indeed the product of necessity and that no more was conceded in the interest of "sympathy" than was justified by the circumstances described above. Thus the Painters withheld all financial aid from any local union which struck in sympathy with any local union outside of the building trades, without the express consent of the general executive board.[31] And the national unions in those building trades whose relationship to the industry was not defined so narrowly by the peculiar economic characteristics mentioned above were not willing to concede such a large measure of independence to their locals. In 1901, the Stone Cutters' executive board withheld support from one of its locals which had participated in a sympathetic strike which had been called by the building trades council in the community. The action of the board was explained by the general secretary-treasurer, who wrote that, "The executive board does not recognize any organization but a stonecutters'."[32] This assertion of independence should be viewed in the light of the stonecutters' relationship to the other building trades. Although certainly one of the components of the construction industry, the work of stonecutting was typically performed in

30. *Proceedings*, 1890, pp. 18 and 21 (*report of the general secretary*).
31. Janes, *Control of Strikes*, p. 61.
32. Janes, *Control of Strikes*, p. 62.

advance of the entrance of the other trades on the site. Hence the immediate gain which the stonecutters stood to incur from any local intercraft coöperation was not likely to be commensurate with its sacrifice to the general cause—although, by the same token—their potential contribution to the alliance would be appreciable.

The bricklayers and masons were in much the same position as the stonecutters; their "season" also began before those of most of the other crafts in the industry. Like the latter union, their relationship with local trades' councils were by no means as cordial as were those which the Carpenters enjoyed. Indeed, the general secretary of the Carpenters rebuked the Bricklayers for their unusual selfishness and sought to explain this phenomenon with reference to the difference in working seasons.[33] Moreover, the Bricklayers founded their national union earlier than the other building trades and were, at the close of the century, more strongly organized than their sister crafts. Affiliation or close coöperation with building trades councils would have resulted in the Bricklayers giving considerably more than they would have received in the form of sympathetic assistance. The Bricklayers' relationship with other trades was exemplified by a complaint voiced by the Building Laborers' Union of Brockton, Massachusetts, in 1897. While "it has been the custom of the various Unions in the building trades in this city to act in unison whenever trouble existed in any one trade," the stone masons, according to this charge, refused to join the carpenters, painters, and plumbers in declaring a job unfair when the contractor refused "to recognize the Laborers of any other Union."

The excuse offered by the masons of this city has been that the general secretary would not allow the masons to assist the other trades, and as a consequence the masons of this city have always been looked upon with suspicion by the other trades.[34]

The "general secretary" (O'Dea) to whom the Brockton Laborers' Union referred had previously demonstrated his isolationist tendencies by advising the local unions that they could not expect financial aid from the international union if they became embroiled in sympathetic strikes called by building trades councils. Having made it clear that, "If they get themselves into trouble, they must get out of it as they can," he felt justified in issuing a warning the import of which could have been missed by few of his constituents: "Don't squeal if you get bit."[35] The president of the Bricklayers supplemented O'Dea's remarks in a report which clearly emphasized the inability of the building trades council to replace the national union as a source of financial support for the local union:

33. *Proceedings*, 1890, pp. 20 and 21 (*report of the general secretary*). See also Janes, *Control of Strikes*, p. 50.
34. *Proceedings*, 1897, pp. 61–62.
35. *Proceedings*, 1890, pp. 5 and 6 (*report of the secretary*).

these Councils are the cause of continual strife, and strikes are brought on our people *when they have no grievance at all* and are drawn into them by carpenters, painters, slaters, electricians and by any trade connected with the construction of a building, and at times threaten the Subordinate Unions with destruction, *as they cannot be supported financially by the International Union, and do not receive any aid from any source whatever.*[36]

The low esteem in which the local building trades councils were held by the national unions of the stonecutters and of the bricklayers, masons, and plasterers was significant on two counts. It demonstrates, first, that the authority of these powerful local organizations could be challenged success-fully even by national unions in an industry composed of product markets which were segregated economically as well as geographically. Second, it lends support to the view that, quite apart from the emphasis which the city central might have placed upon political activity, the sympathetic activities in which they engaged could have been sufficient in themselves to arouse the antagonism of the national unions. For the organizations against which the Stonecutters and the Bricklayers directed their enmity were the building trades councils, which were unlike the central labor unions in that they included only "allied" trades and devoted the greater part of their energies to economic activities of a sympathetic nature. Furthermore, the Bricklayers' campaign against the building trades councils proceeded along the same lines taken by other national unions in their resistance to the authority claimed by the central labor unions: opposition to depletion of the national treasury for sympathetic purposes and opposition to violation of local collective agreements.

In the previous section the national union's disapproval of sympathetic strikes was listed as a basic condition which any successful federation of nationals would have to accept as a fact of life, or, to put it more formally, as a datum in its environment. In this section a direct relationship was established between the national's opposition to sympathetic strikes and its frequent opposition to the central labor unions. Therefore, in order to assure the national union continuance of its freedom from participation in sympathetic action, any federation which sought to attract and retain its affiliation had to be so constituted that the wishes of the national would prevail over those of the city central in the formulation of federation policy.

NATIONAL FEDERATION—THE KNIGHTS

The story of the Noble and Holy Order of the Knights of Labor has been set forth comprehensively and, if not definitively, at least most per-suasively from two opposing points of view.[37] This should hardly occasion

36. *Report of the President,* 1890, pp. V. and VII. My italics.

37. Selig Perlman, "Upheaval and Reorganisation," part VI in Commons, *History of Labour,* v. II and Norman J. Ware, *The Labor Movement in the United States, 1860–1895* (New York: D. Appleton and Company, 1929).

surprise, for the Knights were not only a phenomenon without parallel in the history of American labor[38] and, as such, richly deserving of the biographical attention which they receive; they also meant many things to many men and thus could easily mean different things to different historians. Our own interest in the Knights of Labor is limited to that organization's relationships with the national craft unions of the time insofar as these relationships bear upon the appropriateness of the Knights as a federation in which the nationals could be included. That these relations were in most cases hostile is a matter of record. But whether this hostility was due to the organizational peculiarity of the Knights or whether it was due to some set of circumstances, which (for our purposes) could be designated as "historical accident," is the question at hand. Could the requirements of national unionism have been guaranteed by this type of parent organization if personalities and chance events had been different? According to one school of thought led by Norman J. Ware this question must be answered in the affirmative, but Commons and Perlman disagreed, maintaining that the interests of the national unions could not have been reconciled with those of the Order under any conceivable set of historical circumstances.

The requirements of the national union in the area of "external affairs" were, in summary: first, the establishment of unified and comprehensive control over each occupational jurisdiction, and, second, independence of all groups outside of the jurisdiction of the national union. The first of these requirements implied an appropriate degree of control by the national over the activities of its "subordinates," which meant, as a minimum, that these latter were to owe paramount allegiance to the national union. From the second requirement was derived the corollary that the national union was privileged not only to exclude from membership the unskilled in its own industry but also to withhold sympathetic aid from any group which it considered to lie outside of its own jurisdictional bounds. It is apparent, therefore, that the preservation of a trade jurisdiction required that the national union be a sovereign organization.

Now the avowed aim of the Knights of Labor was "to raise the wage-earner above the narrow view of his class, or trade, or job."[39] In furtherance of this objective, the Order sought to persuade all components of what Veblen was pleased to term the underlying population that an injury to one was the concern of all; and in its *Adelphon Kruptos,* or initiation ceremony, it was declared that

---

38. The Webbs, however, drew a parallel between the Knights and the earlier "Grand National Consolidated Trades Union," which had been projected in their own country by Robert Owen. Sidney and Beatrice Webb, *The History of Trade Unionism* (London: Longmans, Green and Company, 1894), p. 120, n. 1.

39. John R. Commons, *Documentary History of American Industrial Society* (Cleveland: H. H. Clark, 1910–1911), v. IX, p. 49. For quotation below see v. X, p. 24.

without approving of general strikes among artisans, yet should it become necessary to enjoin an oppressor, we will protect and aid any of our number who thereby may suffer loss, and as opportunity offers, extend a helping hand to all branches of honorable toil.

The constitution of the Order's general assembly was another testimonial to the ideal of intercraft solidarity. In the first place, the unit of membership in the Order was the individual and not the local, district, or trade assembly to which he belonged, although the representatives to the general assembly were apportioned among the latter organizations. Consistent with this concept of individual membership in the parent body was another provision which empowered the general assembly—representing all trades—to issue travel and transfer cards.[40] It was further authorized to establish a maximum initiation fee, in contrast to the minima which some of the national craft unions were seeking to legislate; and membership was declared open to everyone—doctors, lawyers, bankers, and purveyors of intoxicants excepted—who at any time had worked for a wage.[41] Furthermore, the general assembly was considered the supreme tribunal of the Order and it was provided that any individual who had been convicted by any District Court could appeal to the General Assembly.[42] Thus when the Glass Bottle Blowers' union was organized as District Assembly 149 (a so-called "trade district"), its constitution provided for appeal from the highest judicial authority of this national union—a "district court" whose three judges, together with a prosecutor, were elected by the national convention—to the general assembly of the entire Order.[43]

Rejection of the concept of trade jurisdiction and abridgement of the autonomy of national unions erected on trade jurisdictions were implicit in these constitutional provisions, which regarded the individual knight as owing ultimate fealty to the General Assembly rather than to any powerful baronial groups within the labor movement. Moreover, replacement of the ritual by a comprehensive set of legislative demands—which was, in fact, the preamble and platform of the defunct Industrial Brotherhood—was evidence to some of the ascendancy which political activity had achieved over collective bargaining in the eyes of the Knights and, therefore, of the incompatibility of the Order with national unionism. This view was reinforced by the discovery that, although the Knights had adopted the Brotherhood's program without addition, they had indeed made one deletion: the latter's demand for the enactment of legislative standards of apprenticeship was nowhere to be found in the Knights' political platform.[44] In the same

40. *Constitution of the General Assembly,* 1887, Art. I.
41. Commons *et al., History of Labour,* v. II, p. 337.
42. *Constitution,* 1887, Art. IV.
43. *Constitution of District Assembly No. 149,* 1888, Art. X.
44. Commons, *History of Labour,* v. II, pp. 336–337.

manner, it was urged that the voluble devotion of the Knights' leaders to the cause of producers' coöperation hardly qualified this movement to serve as a host to a group of business unions. Finally, the establishment (on two occasions) of general strike funds and of various constitutional provisions aimed at regulating the activities of affiliates in connection with the initiation, prosecution, and termination of strikes[45] was regarded as an abridgment of the authority of the national trade union in a vital sector. This was true regardless of the direction of official policy. On some occasions the policy adopted reflected adherence to the ideal of support of an "injured" trade by all its sisters; on others, it appeared to reflect adherence, at least by some of the leaders of the Order, to the doctrine that the strike was, as far as possible, to be renounced as a weapon of economic warfare. Implementation   of either course implied some surrender of the affiliates' autonomy.[46]

In assessing the significance of this documentary evidence, however, we have been cautioned against taking constitutional provisions more seriously than the Knights themselves were in the habit of doing. Ware concluded that "the Order moved from local to centralized control in theory, and after the first General Assembly from central to local control in fact."[47] Indeed, what distinguished the Knights from earlier labor movements, the same authority justly observed, was the fact that "it began from the ground and worked up," and that its vitality derived from the fact that real authority derived from the grass roots and was not gathered in the withering hands of professional reformers.

In point of fact, this account continues, the Knights were originally an organization which was pure and simple enough to satisfy the most unreconstructed American craft unionist. The early local assemblies were specialized along trade lines. Members of other occupations were admitted, but only for the purpose of indoctrination (or "education") into the principles of the Order, and it was assumed that these "sojourners" would ultimately "swarm," or form trade locals of their own. Moreover, sojourners neither paid dues nor were allowed to participate in discussions relating to the trade. In theory, then, the original local assembly, with its sojourners, must be distinguished sharply from the so-called "mixed local," which was composed of members from different trades, all of whom enjoyed equal rights and privileges. These mixed locals were not logical outgrowths of the sojourner system, but, on the contrary, represented a perversion of pristine principles of organization along trade lines, according to Ware. They became numerous only after the first General Assembly met in 1878, when the executive officers sought to graft upon the Order certain practices inherited from the old Industrial Congresses

45. Ware, *Labor Movement*, pp. 117–154.
46. This conclusion is suggested by Ware's account of the principal developments in the Knights' legislation on the support and control of the strike activities of its affiliates. See Ware, *Labor Movement*, chapter VII.
47. Ware, *Labor Movement*, pp. 63, 64.

which, unlike the early Knights, had attempted to organize workers "from the top down." The mixed local assemblies, furthermore, did not appear to be prevalent in the older, eastern districts, but were largely concentrated in the newer and less industrialized districts in the west in which the number of workers attached to a given trade in any one locality was frequently too small to permit their organization into a separate trade local.[48]

From the rural west, also, came the major pressure for political activity, but as long as the Knights remained active among the industrial wage earners, the Order was never officially committed to political action.[49] It did endorse the platform of the Southern Farmers' Alliance in 1889, and the following year it participated in efforts directed toward the formation of a farmer labor party, but, by that time, the Knights represented very few wage earners. Hence it is possible to conclude that "from its beginning throughout its active career the order as such kept out of politics and can in no sense be considered a political organization."[50]

As far as coöperation was concerned, the Knights' record presented a characteristic dichotomy between legislation and performance. Interest in coöperation was always high and funds were authorized, but no proceeds ever became available for the initiation of central projects. Uriah Stephens, the founder of the Order, did envisage the replacement of the "wages system" with an order of producer coöperation, but in this respect he differed not at all from many of his contemporaries who counted themselves as good trade-union leaders. Included among the latter was William H. Sylvis, the talented founder of the Iron Molders' union, whose organization engaged in far greater experimentation with producers' coöperatives than did the Order which Stephens originated. The Order itself attempted only one such experiment—an unsuccessful coöperative coal mining enterprise—and, interestingly enough, the funds for the project were donated by a national union, the Window Glass Workers, which at the time (1884) was affiliated with the Knights as a local assembly.[51]

Finally, the same disparity between theory and practice which was observed in the case of coöperation persisted with respect to the strike policies of the Order. At the height of their numerical strength, the Knights were associated with some of the largest and most dramatic strikes in the country's history; yet the Order itself "never called a strike and seldom supported one."[52] It was mentioned above that official philosophy swung nervously between the one extreme of supporting strikes in the interest of "solidarity" and the other of deprecating strikes in the interest either of "arbitration" or of renunciation of the wage economy. Actually, neither type

48. Ware, *Labor Movement,* pp. 25–26, 156–160, 350–370.
49. See Commons, *History of Labour,* v. II, p. 341.
50. Ware, *Labor Movement,* p. 43.
51. Ware, *Labor Movement,* pp. 329–333.
52. Ware, *Labor Movement,* p. 63.

of policy was enforced to an important extent, and what is more interesting, failure to enforce central policy seems to have had little effect upon the course of events. This latter peculiarity was characteristic of the "grass roots" nature of the Knights' movement. Thus while central strike funds were legislated, they were seldom collected, but this did not prevent the strikes of 1884 and 1885 (which included the famous contests with the railroad managements) from being prosecuted to a successful conclusion. Nor, on the other hand, did the promulgation by the General Assembly of rules designed to discourage unions from striking deter them in the least. On the contrary, it seemed that the Knights owed a large measure of their popularity with the rank and file of employees to a widespread conviction that membership in the Order was a crucial ingredient in the formula for successful strike activity. Hence dissatisfied groups "struck first and joined the Knights of Labor afterward,"[53] thereby presenting the Order's leadership with a succession of *faits accomplis*.

The remarkably ineffectual nature of the Order's leadership was described succinctly by Terence Powderly, the controversial figure who succeeded Stephens as Grand Master Workman and remained in office during the period of the Knights' extraordinarily rapid growth and, later, of its equally rapid decline. In a letter, quoted by Ware, Powderly wrote a fitting epitaph to his organization:

Whatever may be or may not have been the faults and virtues of the General Officers it is a conviction with me that no act of theirs could avert the impending fate of the Order. Teacher of important and much-needed reforms, she has been obliged to practice differently from her teachings. Advocating arbitration and conciliation as first steps in labor disputes she has been forced to take upon her shoulders the responsibility of the aggressor first and, when hope of arbitrating and conciliation failed, to beg of the opposing side to do what we should have applied for in the first instance. Advising against strikes we have been in the midst of them. Urging important reforms we have been forced to yield our time and attention to petty disputes until we were placed in a position where we have frequently been misunderstood by the employee as well as the employer. While not a political party we have been forced into the attitude of taking political action. . . .[54]

With departures in structure from the Knights' trade-union origins inspired by, and more or less restricted to, nonindustrial elements, and with departures in objective from the requirements of business unionism owing their origin in some instances to the same elements and, in any event, largely frustrated in execution, one could urge that there was no fundamental irreconcilability between the Knights and the national unions. And since the constitutional provisions which centralized authority in the General Assembly were never translated into practice, Ware believed that a parallel could be

53. Commons, *History of Labour*, v. II, p. 368.
54. Quoted in Ware, *Labor Movement*, p. 375. See also pp. 171–190.

drawn between that organization and the later American Federation of Labor. In the first place, it was made possible (in 1879) for Knights in any particular calling to organize themselves into an autonomous "national trade district"; and, althought western opposition succeeded in securing the repeal of this law the following year, in 1882 the General Assembly once more provided for the establishment of trade districts.

The general officers, it is true, were on the whole opposed to the formation of trade units, some claiming that such organizations were contrary to the philosophy on which the Order was founded, but their negative attitude did not necessarily interfere with this type of organization. An outstanding example of insubordination involved the Window Glass Workers, which was able to secure recognition as a trade organization within the Order in 1880, the year in which the early legislation which had encouraged the formation of trade assemblies was repealed. Since, at the time that the first general assemblies were held, most of the organized trades were organized in communities and regions which were specialized industrially (for example, coal mining), a precedent was established for organizing many national unions within the Order as trade district assemblies.[55] The Glass Bottle Blowers, for example, were organized into an eastern and a western district, the Knights' union of coal miners was known as National Trade District 135, and the Brewers formed National Trade District 35. Thus the "district" in many instances lost its geographic significance when it became organized along "trade" lines. Organization by trade could not be expected to effect the same distinction between the mixed and the trade assemblies at the local level as it did at the district, of course, for the local trade assembly was typically as much of a geographic unit as the local mixed assembly. There was one notable exception, however: the aforementioned national union of Window Glass Workers was enrolled in the Knights as Local Assembly 300!

If one elects to emphasize the ability of separate trades to form autonomous national unions within the Knights, however, and to dismiss as insignificant or superficial the violence worked thereby upon the Order's original geographic pattern of organization, it is possible to draw an analogy between the Knights and the Federation. This was the approach taken by Ware. He was of the opinion that

Structurally the Knights contained every form conceivable and in this respect differed not at all from the American Federation of Labor. The mixed local of the Knights is the same thing as the federal union;[56] the mixed district and state

55. Commons, *History of Labour*, v. II, p. 343.

56. The analogy between the mixed assembly of the Knights and the "federal trade and local labor union" of the Federation was also made by Commons (*History of Labour*, v. II, p. 347) and by Hoxie (*Trade Unionism*, p. 119). Originally the two types of organization were dissimilar, because the A.F. of L.'s constitution had provided that a Federal Labor Union could be formed only by workers (seven or more in number) in

assemblies corresponding to the trades' assemblies or city centrals and the state federations; the National Trade Assemblies to the national unions, and the General Assembly to the annual convention of the American Federation of Labor. As for federalism, the autonomy of the district was in fact as great as now is the autonomy of the national union. In theory, the General Assembly was over all. In practice, the districts and even the locals did as they pleased. . . . If the strength of the American Federation of Labor lies in its weakness, the weakness of the Knights certainly did not lie in the strength of the General Assembly or its officers.[57]

The analogy, however, was not complete, for, as Ware saw it, the Knights possessed three unique characteristics which distinguished that organization from the A.F. of L. The first concerned the locus of power; in the Knights, the District Assembly was the most powerful organization; in the Federation, the national trade union was dominant. Second, the Order differed from the A.F. of L. "in its ambition to include all trades," or, more specifically, the unskilled trades. Finally, the Knights, in emphasizing the solidarity of all crafts, placed less emphasis on collective bargaining. Since they did not devote

---

"one trade." Not until 1893 was the constitution amended so as to permit organization by men in "any trade" (*Constitution,* 1890, Art. X, Sec. III). The change was suggested by Chris Evans, then secretary of the Federation, who claimed that it would enable Federal Labor Unions to be organized "in accordance with the original idea which called them into practice." (American Federation of Labor, *Proceedings,* 1893, p. 23). Similarity between these two types of organization was probably greatest in the small community where, as Ware has pointed out, most of the mixed locals of the Knights were found and where, in accordance with A.F. of L. constitutional provision, "federal labor" (as distinguished from "local trade") unions could be formed if there were fewer than seven workers in one trade. In more populous localities, however, the existence of "local trade" unions, composed of workers in the same trade and thus corresponding to the local trade assembly, on the one hand, and of several federal labor unions, some of which were composed of workers in different occupations but in the same industry, on the other, was not uncommon. Neither of these two types corresponded to the mixed local assembly, the former because it was not "mixed" and the latter because it was confined in some cases to trades in the same industry. Furthermore, although some local assemblies were attached directly to the General Assembly, this was not true of many mixed local assemblies which, like trade locals, were subordinated to the authority of their respective district assemblies. All local trade and federal labor unions, on the other hand, were (and still are) chartered by the Executive Council of the Federation. Finally and most important, the federal labor unions of the A.F. of L. have been regarded, in theory at least, as essentially temporary organizations whose function has been to hold the fort until the national craft unions arrive, each to claim its own members and to effect, in the process, the dismemberment of the federal union. Only in the small community, where the number of members in any trade is too small to interest the national trade unions in establishing their own locals, could the federal union be regarded—without enthusiasm—as other than temporary in nature. The mixed local assembly of the Knights, on the other hand, was considered by its supporters to be a fully mature organization, alternative and allegedly superior to the union of men in one trade or compound of related crafts.

57. Ware, *Labor Movement,* p. 164. See also pp. xii, 42, 295.

the major part of their energy to political action or to coöperation either, it is rather difficult to specify what they did emphasize, but Ware was persuaded that "the Knights tried to do a much bigger thing than the Federation—bigger and vaguer."

Nevertheless, Ware did not consider that these differences in "emphasis and center of authority" (as he described them) disqualified the Order as a federation of national unions; he interpreted the animosity which developed between the Knights and the unions in terms of personality conflicts—involving especially Powderly and the "Home Club," on one side, and Samuel Gompers, on the other—and of the attitude of the Knights from the more lightly industrialized regions in the West, which he regarded as a somewhat extraneous influence. Commons, on the other hand, believed that the interests of the Knights were fundamentally opposed to those of the national unions, because the former's "ambition to include all trades" really implied what he described as "a constantly growing effort to absorb the existing trade unions for the purpose of making them subservient of the less skilled elements."[58] Regarded in this light, the Knights' celebrated emphasis upon solidarity was evidence not of a *bona fide* concern for all "producing classes" but merely of the familiar phenomenon of attempting to speak for one faction (although perhaps the most numerous one) in the name of the community at large:

From the viewpoint of a struggle between principles, this was indeed a clash between the principle of solidarity of labour and that of trade separatism, but, in reality, each of the principles reflected only the special interest of a certain portion of the working class. Just as the trade unions, when they fought for trade autonomy, really refused to consider the unskilled men, so the Knights of Labor were insensible to the fact that their scheme would retard the progress of the skilled trades.

But Ware, as we have suggested, saw nothing incompatible between the organization of the unskilled and the maintenance of cordial relations with autonomous national unions. He claimed, in effect, that the question of organizing the unskilled was irrelevant to the issue at hand. First, the fact that the national craft unions had largely ignored the unskilled when organizing in their respective industries was held to reveal their lack of interest in these hitherto unorganized groups. Hence no jurisdictional difficulties could have arisen when the Knights accepted the unskilled as members. And second, there was a continuing class of unskilled or semiskilled workers which the craft union was not at all well adapted to organize: this was the group of workers whose skills were being rendered obsolete by technological changes. Thus, since the national unions were neither willing nor able to organize the unskilled, their interests could not have been affected adversely by the Order's efforts in this direction. "No realist can imagine Strasser, McGuire, Weihe,

58. Commons, *History of Labour*, v. II, pp. 396, 397; see also Ware, *Labor Movement*, pp. xviii, 71–72.

and other signers of the 'treaty' which the unions presented to the Knights at Cleveland being interested in the 'unskilled.' "

While the unions did not object to the inclusion of the unskilled within the Knights, however, they did fear the latter's missionary work among skilled workers, and it was this latter activity—and not the issue of the unskilled—which, according to Ware, was the real source of contention between the unions and the Knights. The unions accused the Knights of providing a haven for individuals who had been disciplined by their local unions and for local unions which had been disciplined by their internationals; and it further charged them with inciting other individuals and locals to renounce their traditional affiliations and join dual organizations within the Knights, a practice to whch the Order's custom of remunerating their organizers on a piece-work basis might have contributed substantially. In short, the Knights were engaging in a practice which was at once superfluous and mischievous, the practice of organizing the organized. Ware's contention that this was the major source of friction receives support from the following excerpt from a circular letter of April 26, 1886, in which a conference of national and international unions was first proposed:

The object of the conference is to devise ways and means to protect our respective organizations from the malicious work of an element who openly boast "that Trades Unions must be destroyed." This element urges our local Unions to disband, and it is doing incalculable mischief by arousing antagonisms and dissensions in the labor movement. Under cover of the Knights of Labor, and, as far as we can learn, without authority from that body, this element pursues its evil work. "Rats," "scabs," and unfair employers are backed up by this element. Suspended and expelled members of Trades Unions are welcomed into their ranks. And these elements use the Knights of Labor as an instrument through which to vent their spite against Trades Unions. That this has been the case can be amply demonstrated by the Cigarmakers' and Typographical International Unions. Other Trades Unions have been more or less affected.[59]

This version of the cause of hostilities was in part accepted, in part rejected by Ware, but in no way did it indicate to him the existence of any fundamental incompatibility. The charge that the Order received into its ranks expelled union members was dismissed as "disingenuous" on two counts. First, the number involved "was insignificant enough to throw grave doubts upon the sincerity of the complaint."[60] And second, since "the mere fact that a craftsman or a local left the national union made it 'unfair,' " Ware apparently implied that in some cases discipline had been visited upon individuals and locals by national unions after and because withdrawals had taken place. Such cases of "unfairness" obviously merited special classification, since they were distinct from any instances in which men and organizations were

59. See Bricklayers' and Masons' International Union, *Proceedings,* 1887, p. 63.
60. Ware, *Labor Movement,* p. 70.

admitted by the Knights after they had been disciplined by the unions with which they previously had been associated. This distinction was important, because the former group of converts—those who had withdrawn from the unions on their own initiative while in good standing—was sizeable. Thus, while Ware saw little merit in the union's claim that the Knights were admitting "unfair" men and organizations, he conceded that their other charge was correct: good unionists had indeed been lured away from the fold. But he maintained that this was not so much the product of human design as the by-product of impersonal forces of economic change which, by the last quarter of the century, had become so pervasive that no labor organization patterned on traditional craft lines could regard its jurisdictional future with assurance.

In the case of the national unions against the Knights, the defense thus rested upon the validity of the following propositions:

(1) Centralization of authority in the general assembly was not a distinguishing feature of the Order, because such centralization existed only on paper.

(2) Structurally, the Knights and the American Federation were not dissimilar. The principal difference lay in the fact that, in the former organization, the power was concentrated in the district assembly, while, in the latter, the national union was the center of authority.

(3) National unions could, however, be formed as autonomous units within the Order, most frequently as trade districts. Thus the ascendancy of the district in the Knights was of secondary importance only.

(4) The relative lack of emphasis by the Order on collective bargaining was not itself a distinguishing feature, since the Knights, at least in the period of their "virginal simplicity" (*circa* 1876), did not emphasize political activity or coöperation at the expense of collective bargaining, as earlier movements had done.

(5) The Knights' efforts to organize the unskilled constituted no threat to the unions, which for the most part were predominantly not interested in organizing these workers themselves.

(6) The unions' charge that the Knights harbored members and locals who had fallen from grace, while perhaps justified in isolated instances, was unimportant, since the numbers affected were insignificant.

(7) The defections from membership which the national unions suffered in the period in which the Knights experienced their dramatic growth were basically unrelated to the rival unionism fostered by the Order. They could be ascribed more properly to what Ware termed the Industrial Revolution in this country which, by making established skills obsolete, created a new class of the "semiskilled" for whose organization the national craft unions were inadequate. The Knights of Labor, on the other hand, was designed

for the organization of the members of this newly created group; this was its distinguishing feature.

The case for the Order, as presented by Ware, can be challenged at some points on matters of fact; at others, on inferences drawn from the evidence at hand. Questions of fact arise, not because the accuracy of the factual material was brought into question, but because, in one important instance, at least, some relevant detail was omitted. The omission occurred in the account of the unions' grievances against the Knights. It will be recalled that Ware implied that the charge of admitting expelled members and locals was not in itself serious enough to account for the deep and bitter hostility which was manifested by the unions. The latter, however, did not confine themselves to this specific complaint; they charged further that, in many cases, the dual organizations fostered by the Knights had sought to undermine the established unions by charging lower initiation fees (a practice which national unions had sought to discourage among their own locals, when more than one existed in the same labor market area), by working for lower wages and longer hours, and even by overt strikebreaking. A questionnaire sent from the office of the Bricklayers' international secretary to the locals of that union is suggestive of the nature of the relations between the trade unions and the Knights at the local levels, although it was drawn up and circulated in 1886 after formal relationships had begun to deteriorate badly. These questions were included:

7th. In what relation to your Union do the members of this Assembly (in the locality) stand? Are they all, or a majority of them, "scabs," or expelled members of your Union?
8th. Are there any very notable cases among them? If so, give their history?
9th. What is the per diem wage received by the members of your Union?
10th. What is the per diem wage received by members of the Assembly?
11th. How many hours per day do members of your Union work?
12th. How many hours per day do members of the Assembly work?
13th. How are the members of the Assembly considered by master builders and by the Union as to mechanical ability: superior or inferior?
14th. What is the initiation fee of your Union, and that of the Assembly?[61]

Of eighty-seven locals whose secretaries replied to the questionnaire, only eight reported that there were local assemblies of bricklayers and masons within their jurisdictions. Four reported that the Knights were working for lower pay than the international members. Three claimed that the Knights were working longer hours. Four reported no difference as to wages and hours, although one of these complained that "the K. of L. working ten hours per day compelled our Union to violate our laws of nine hours." Elsewhere, there were mixed local assemblies whose bricklayer and mason members,

61. *Proceedings,* 1886, pp. 70–71, 73–75.

according to Secretary O'Dea—who, it must be added, had his axe to grind—
were inferior workers, working longer hours and for lower wages, not above
scabbing on jobs struck by the international, and, while paying initiation fees
from three to twenty-five times lower than the international men, "insist(ed)
that the Unions must give them the same recognition and privilege that they
do their own members." Every one of the eighty-seven locals, furthermore,
replied in the negative to a question which solicited their views on consolidation with the Order, and all but one submitted an affirmative answer to
another question, which read, "Is your Union in favor of National and International Trades Unions retaining their distinct autonomy, and not be amalgamated with the Knights of Labor?"[62] (One correspondent apparently
drew, to his own satisfaction, a distinction between "consolidation" of the
Bricklayers with the Order, which he opposed, and "amalgamation" of
national unions in general with the same Order, which he did not oppose.)

The Carpenters also reported instances of friction with members of their
craft who were enrolled in either trade or mixed local assemblies of the
Knights. A case which drew particular attention involved the Chicago local
of the Brotherhood which, for a while, was allied with a Local Assembly of
the Knights and a local of another carpenters' national union, the Amalgamated Society, in a United Carpenters' Council. The council was empowered to levy assessments, to call strikes without consulting the constituent
locals, and to establish uniform trade rules and initiation fees. Difficulties
arose, however, when the United Brotherhood's local began to outstrip the
others in membership, and the Carpenters' council suffered the same fate
that threatened many of the allied printing trades' councils, in which the
typographers' locals often possessed numerical dominance. When the Knights
and the Amalgamated were outvoted, they refused to comply, with the
result that the United Brotherhood group held one final vote which ad-
journed the Council "sine die." Meanwhile, it was alleged, the regulations
governing the establishment of uniform fees and conditions were violated
rather consistently. While the dues paid by the Amalgamated exceeded those
charged by the United local, the former diverted a greater portion of their
revenues to "special benefits and consequently not contributing in any way
towards the expense of forcing up the wages. . . ." The dues paid by the
Knights, on the other hand, were less than half the amount which their colleagues in the United were charged. Moreover,

Prior to the adjournment of the U.C.C., they had violated every rule in existence
in this district; they had taken ex-members of our unions at one dollar per head;
and in some cases as much as they could get out of the applicant, whilst our
regular fee was $10.00 and would have been $25.00, if they had not taken such
a course.

To-day they are working with scabs for any rate of wages, and have repeatedly

62. *Proceedings*, 1886, p. 76.

offered to supply all men needed in cases where we have had strikes, for thirty cents per hour, as this was the only way they would hold their job, knowing that when a settlement was effected they would have to go.[63]

There is some indication that the experience of the Chicago carpenters was duplicated, on a wider scale, by the coal miners. Prior to the amalgamation of the two factions into the United Mine Workers in 1890 (which ultimately resulted in the absorption and atrophy of the Knights' National Trade District 135), many of the "open" (nonsecret) unions accused the Knights' miners of undermining their standards and even, on one occasion, of "black-legging," as strikebreaking was termed by the miners of the period. The Knights, on the other hand, frequently advanced as the reason for their refusal to honor the standards proclaimed by the other unions the unwillingness of the latter to admit them as full equals into proposed bargaining coalitions. Thus, on the eve of a scheduled meeting between some of the operators and the National Federation of Miners and Mine Laborers in 1887, the executive board of the rival Knights of Labor resolved

That we, the executive board of said Miners and Mine Laborers National District Assembly No. 135 have determined that, in case of a refusal upon part of said convention to admit the representatives of said National District Assembly No. 135 on an equal basis with other organizations, we shall not consider our portion of the craft under any obligation to abide by or conform to any scale of prices that may be adopted or any agreement entered into by said convention.[64]

The unions, however, were not disposed to weigh the merits of equal representation against those of proportional representation. It was sufficient for them that, in the competition for membership, the Knights chose to adopt a scorched-earth policy which did not spare such standards of membership and employment as the national unions had striven painfully to establish. Had these standards been respected by both sides, it might have been possible to evolve a *modus vivendi,* with more than one organization existing in any given trade jurisdiction. For, as we have seen, effective unionism required only that unitary control be established throughout an economic jurisdiction, and unitary control could be exercised jointly by two or more unions, if each agreed not to undercut the conditions of employment which the other (or others) had established. "Dualism," considered as an intolerable state of affairs, was not a logical implication drawn from the premise of unitary control; it was an historical phenomenon and indigenous to the American trade union movement. The British, although union rivalry was not unknown to them, muddled through with dual, and even multiple unionism.

One must not rely too heavily, however, upon a comparison between the

63. *Proceedings,* 1894, pp. 15–17.
64. Chris Evans, *History of the Mine Workers of America* (Indianapolis, 1918), v. I, pp. 209–210. This resolution is reproduced in a section which Evans captioned, "Further Pungent Letters." See also pp. 196, 208–210, 228, 235, 254, 275–276, 450–451, 455–457.

experience of the British and the American trade union movements in an attempt to distinguish between "dualism" and what we have termed unitary control; for there were important differences, as well as striking similarities, both in the character of the two movements and in the environments in which they existed. As far as character is concerned, it has been observed frequently that, as a rule, unions in Great Britain emphasized political action and beneficiary activities to a greater extent than did unions in this country, while the latter concentrated more intensely upon collective bargaining than did their British counterparts, although the early trade union leaders in this country derived considerable inspiration from the English in erecting constitutional structures for their own organizations.[65] Moreover, the rank and file were more class conscious in Britain than in the United States (as evidenced by the British labor movement's greater emphasis upon political activity) and, as we indicated in Chapter 8, the influence of the rank and file in union affairs was possibly stronger in Britain. This militated against any undercutting of union standards and discouraged "raiding" of membership. As a result, the urgency to establish unitary control throughout the market area—a prerequisite to effective collective bargaining—might not have been so great; and, therefore, the need to eliminate dualism might not have been so intense.[66]

Among the differences in environment, two emerge as directly relevant to the problem of dualism. The first is the more leisurely pace and less highly competitive nature of capitalist enterprise in Britain (a phenomenon of particular interest to contemporary observers), which paralleled the more leisurely pace at which collective bargaining was pursued by the British unions. In some instances this seems to have been reflected in—or related to— a greater persistence of independent local markets, characterized by noncom-

---

65. Cf., Theodore W. Glocker, *The Government of American Trade Unions* (Baltimore: Johns Hopkins, 1913), pp. 137–140 for a discussion of this British influence. Ware, on the other hand, emphasized the differences between the "new unionism" of the British and the American versions thereof. Whereas British unionism "was more benefit than bargaining and more political than thought" (*Labor Movement,* p. 54), "the new American unionism was different than the old English unionism it copied. It was more aggressively a bargaining affair. . . ." (p. 169).

66. Emphasis on benefits, however, disclosed an alternative reason for the elimination of rival unionism. Competition between rival unions in the same jurisdiction often took the form of offering prospective members either lower rates of contribution and/or higher benefits than did one's competitor. (Sidney and Beatrice Webb, *Industrial Democracy* [London: Longmans, Green, Second Edition, 1911], p. 113.) On the other hand, differences between benefit rates and contributions charged by different unions in the same industry or trade could provide barriers to amalgamation. Thus, the fact that the coal miners' regional union in Yorkshire had established a comprehensive system of benefits, while the South Wales Miners Association had none at all, resulted in a discrepancy in the amount of dues collected by each organization, which was a considerable factor in delaying the amalgamation of the independent district unions into what has been known only since 1945 as the National Union of Mineworkers. (N. Barou, *British Trade Unions* [London: Gollancz, 1947], p. 237. See also p. 51.)

petitive (to a greater or lesser degree) producing regions and, sometimes, by geographic differentiation of products. Thus, what sometimes appeared to be dual unions were, in reality, organizations separated from one another by rather well-defined jurisdictional lines, trade and geographic in nature. For this reason the Webbs, while maintaining that national unions must prevail where national product and labor markets exist in fact, nevertheless refused to lend uncritical support to amalgamation as an end in itself and argued the merits of federation (alliances of sovereign units) on the grounds that "the degree of union between the constituent bodies should correspond strictly with the degree of their unity of interest."[67]

The second point of dissimilarity can be found in the legal environments of the two countries: in Britain no amalgamation between two unions could take place unless an affirmative vote of two-thirds of their total membership had been secured.[68] This law was retained on the books until 1917, and, even then it was not repealed, but only amended so that the required majority vote was reduced.[69] No similar legislation was enacted in the United States, with the result that, prior to the passage of the National Labor Relations Act in 1935, under which the determination of the appropriate bargaining unit was made by a governmental agency and the representation of the workers therein was determined in effect by majority vote, matters of jurisdiction were left to the immediate parties concerned and no other legal restraints were imposed upon the process of amalgamation.

Notwithstanding these and others elements of dissimilarity, however, it is a fact that interunion rivalry existed in the British Isles and that it was carried on with the same lack of discrimination in the choice of weapons that prevailed in the New World.[70] In both countries, furthermore, "amalgamation movements" took place, with some consequent reduction in "overlap-

67. *Industrial Democracy*, pp. 122–141. It is not implied that the allegedly less vigorous forms of competition prevailing in British industry constitute an ultimate causal agent. To a considerable degree, they might have been the result of the geographic limitations imposed on market areas by the natural boundaries of the country, which, taken in conjunction with conditions of technology, might have precluded the existence of more competitive situations. On the other hand, local variations in taste persisted in Britain to a greater extent than they did in this country. As a result, it is probable that, despite the much smaller geographic area of the United Kingdom, her markets were not "nationalized" to the same extent as were markets in the United States. (See T. Balogh, "European Unification and the Dollar Problem," *Quarterly Journal of Economics*, v. LXV, no. 1, February 1951, p. 114.)

68. G. D. H. Cole, *A Short History of the British Working-Class Movement 1789–1947* (London: Allen and Unwin, new edition, 1947), p. 369.

69. Barou, *British Trade Unions*, p. 51.

70. Referring to the situation in Great Britain, the Webbs wrote, "It is no exaggeration to say that to competition between overlapping unions is to be attributed nine-tenths of the ineffectiveness of the Trade Union world." (*Industrial Democracy*, p. 121.) See also their *The History of Trade Unionism*, pp. 338–341.

ping" (as the Webbs termed what was referred to here as dualism).[71] At this point, however, similarity ceased, and the British trade union movement assumed two distinguishing and related characteristics. First, the process of amalgamation was much less rapid than it was in this country, and, second, the degree of coöperation among sovereign unions with overlapping jurisdictions was far greater. Since coöperation is a logical alternative to exclusive jurisdiction as a mechanism for the establishment of a uniform set of union standards throughout a single market area, it would appear that successful adoption of schemes of coöperation—which have ranged from powerful federations to informal "understandings" with respect to "spheres of influence"—was, with due regard for the peculiarities in the British temper and environment above noted, in part responsible for the slow progress of "amalgamation." Indeed, support for "amalgamation" as a principle came largely from adherents of the "New Unionism" who considered it essential to the establishment of trade unions which were at once industrial in structure and revolutionary (syndicalist) in spirit. On this side of the Atlantic, the supporters of "exclusive jurisdiction" were interested primarily in furthering a type of unionism which was predominantly craft, as opposed to industrial, and "business," rather than radical. Their conservative counterparts in Britain, on the other hand, made no especial fetish of exclusive jurisdiction, for they were trying to compose their differences by compromising amalgamation with coöperation. And although it was the official policy of the Trades Union Congress to regard federation as "a half-way house" on the road which ended in full amalgamation, it has advocated certain "main principles" of "good trade union practice," adoption of which might well have the effect of retarding, rather than accelerating, progress to the avowed destination by improving accommodations *en route*. The following proposals were urged as *"merely an acceleration of the developments which are already taking place"*:[72]

(A) Unions should consider the possibility of joint working agreements (with unions with whom they are in frequent contact) in regard to: (1) Spheres of influence, (2) Recognition of cards, (3) Machinery for composing difficulties, (4) Conditions of transfer of members.

(B) No member of another union should be accepted without inquiry from that union.

(C) No member of another union should be accepted where inquiry shows that the member is (1) under discipline, (2) engaged in a trade dispute, (3) in arrears with contributions.

(D) No union should commence organising activities at any establishment or undertaking in respect of any grade or grades of worker in which another

71. Barou, *British Trade Unions,* pp. 51–52, and Cole, *British Working-Class Movement,* pp. 324, 337, 369–370, 385.

72. Trades Union Congress, *Final Report: Trade Union Structure and Closer Unity* (London: Trades Union Congress, 1947), p. 33.

union has the majority of workers employed and negotiates wages and conditions, unless by arrangement with that union.

(E) Each union should include in its membership form questions on the lines of the T.U.C. Model Form in regard to past or present membership of another union.[73]

Now these recommendations, which were a distillation of British experience in many trades, bear a curious likeness to the counter-proposals which the Knights made to the "trades unions" after some of the latter had held a "conference" in Philadelphia in May of 1886, at which a committee was chosen to present to the Knights of Labor the terms on which the national unions represented believed that they could live in peace with the Order. Mindful of past grievances, the unions had demanded

That no person shall be admitted to the Knights of Labor who works for less than the regular scale of wages fixed by the Union of his craft; and that none shall be admitted to membership in the Knights of Labor who has ever been convicted of scabbing, ratting, embezzlement, or any other offense against the Union of his trade or calling, until exonerated by the same. . . .

That whenever a strike or lock-out of any Trades Union is in progress, no Assembly or District Assembly of the Knights of Labor, shall interfere until settled to the satisfaction of the Trades Union affected.[74]

In their reply, the Knights—acknowledging by implication the validity of the unions' accusations—agreed that

The basis upon which we believe an agreement can be reached would necessarily include the adoption of some plan by which all labor organizations could be protected from unfair men, men expelled, suspended, under fine, or guilty of taking the places of Union men or Knights of Labor while on strike or while locked out from work, and that as far as possible a uniform standard of hours of labor and wages should be adopted, so that men of any trade enrolled in our order and members of Trades Unions may not come in conflict because of the differences in wages and hours.[75]

73. Trades Union Congress, *Interim Report,* pp. 367–368, as quoted in Barou, *British Trade Unions,* pp. 52–53. It should be noted, in connection with (B) and (C) above, that the British, without insisting upon exclusive jurisdiction, were strongly opposed to secession. "To break away from the group to form a dissident, rival association is one of the worst sins in the Trade Union calendar," according to W. Milne-Bailey, in *Trade Unions and the State* (London: Allen and Unwin, 1934), p. 107. " 'Breakaway Unions,' " he continues, "are accordingly fought bitterly and relentlessly." The Trades Union Congress in 1927 "pledge(s) itself to discourage in every possible way the formation of new Trade Unions, and directs the General Council to refuse to accept the affiliation of any Trade Union which is composed of members who have broken away from an existing Union affiliated to Congress."

74. General Assembly, *Proceedings,* 1886, p. 12. Reproduced in Ware, *Labor Movement,* pp. 283–284.

75. "Address to the Trades Unions," 1886. Reproduced in Bricklayers' *Proceedings,* 1886, pp. 68–70.

So far, the Knights' proposal ran parallel not only to the unions' scheme, which contemplated the supersession of rival unionism by a regime of exclusive jurisdiction, but also with the British program, which regarded mutual respect for standards of membership and employment as essential to the peaceable coexistence of "overlapping organizations." The Knights chose the British way. That they sought (at this late stage in their existence) a system of coöperation and, possibly, federation similar to that which the British evolved was evident in further proposals (in the same "Address") which contemplated both interchange of working cards (see British proposal above) and joint negotiations with employers:

We also believe that a system of exchanging working cards should be adopted, so that a member of any craft belonging to different organizations could work in harmony together, the card of any member of this order admitting to work in any union shop, and the card of any Union man admitting him to work in any Knight of Labor shop.

We further believe that upon a demand for increase of wages or shorter hours of labor, made by either organization, a conference should be held with the organized labor men employed in the establishment where the demand for increase of wages or reduction of hours is contemplated, action upon a proposed reduction of wages or other difficulty to be agreed upon in like manner, and that in the settlement of any difficulties between employers and employees the organizations represented in the establishment shall be parties to the terms of settlement.

But the majority of the national trade unions refused to concede that their standards of admission, discipline, and employment could be protected if more than one organization shared the same geographic and occupational jurisdiction. They had demanded

That in any branch of labor having a national or international organization, the Knights of Labor shall not initiate any person or form any assembly of persons following said organized craft or calling without the consent of the nearest National or International Union affected. . . .

The charter of any Knights of Labor Assembly of any trade having a National or International Union shall be revoked, and the members of the same be requested to join a mixed Assembly or form a local Union under the jurisdiction of their respective National or International Trades Union.

That, any organizer of the Knights of Labor who endeavors to induce Trades Unions to disband, or tampers with their growth or privileges, shall have his commission forthwith revoked. . . .

That the Knights of Labor shall not establish nor issue any trade-mark or label in competition with any trade-mark or label now issued, or that may hereafter be issued, by any National or International Trades Union.[76]

Although the principle of exclusive jurisdiction was spelled out uncompromisingly in these demands, it applied only to dual unionism in specific

76. American Federation of Labor, *Proceedings,* 1886, p. 8.

jurisdictions. While, as Ware observed, the unions' terms, to the extent that they did not constitute an initial bargaining offer, were more a "declaration of war" than a "treaty,"[77] the Order itself was not branded as a "dual" organization. The union demands were aimed only at dual bodies within the Order; no hostility was expressed or implied with respect to any assembly of the Knights "in any branch of labor" not "having a national or international organization" already in existence. Nor were friendly relations ruled out in any case in which a national union outside the Order was not paralleled by a dual organization within the Knights. Gompers himself declared that "There is no conflict necessary between the trades unions and the Knights of Labor"; and this statement, which was applauded by the delegates to the 1887 convention of the Federation, was not inconsistent with a later recommendation of the Committee on Organization that "mutual interchange and recognition of working cards shall cease."[78] When the two national unions of coal miners finally merged, in 1890, into the United Mine Workers of America, the President of the American Federation of Labor addressed a telegram of congratulations to the newly amalgamated organization.[79]

But when the new Mine Workers' union sought, at their first convention, to effect a reconciliation between its two parent organizations by proposing an interchange of cards, mutual recognition of labels, and agreement not to admit one another's expelled members without first securing specific consent, it found that the Federation was no more disposed to consider such coöperation as a way of life in 1891 than its founders had been when the Knights offered coöperation as a counterproposal to the national unions' "treaty" in 1886.

Justified or not, these unions drew from experience the lesson that "overlapping" unionism inevitably meant rival unionism, especially so far as the Knights were concerned. It was no accident that, of all the major national unions, only the glass workers enjoyed really satisfactory relations with the Order: their exceptionally high degree of skill and organization ensured them a monopoly over their jurisdictions and immunity from dualism. But the national unions in less highly skilled or less thoroughly organized trades held the Knights in genuine fear, and their experience with rival dualism made them completely unreceptive to the type of dualism based upon "harmony" which the Knights finally submitted as an alternative to the unions' demand for exclusive jurisdiction. As a result, the British experience with "spheres of influence" was reproduced here only on a minute scale and only under special circumstances. For where "a tacit division of the field," as

77. Ware, *Labor Movement,* p. 284.
78. American Federation of Labor, *Proceedings,* 1887, p. 10; and 1889, p. 20.
79. Evans, *History of Mine Workers,* v. II, pp. 11, 70, 87. It should be noted that the amalgamation of the National Progressive Union and National District Assembly 135 in no sense implied an absorption of the latter union by the former, for the District Assembly contributed about 60 per cent of the new organization's membership.

Saposs termed it, did occur in this country, the "field" itself was invariably marked by "a comparatively clear-cut division of the trade or industry," so that relatively little overlapping of jurisdictions took place.[80]

Ware's observation, therefore, that, "The destruction of the Knights did not end jurisdictional disputes"[81] is true beyond the peradventure of a doubt, but his implied conclusion that the unions' struggle with the Order had little or no bearing upon the American attitude toward dual unionism does not follow. Cause and effect were confused, for the emotional nature of the Federation's later insistence upon jurisdiction can be traced in large part to the traumata inflicted upon the national unions by the overlapping organizations which were sponsored by the Knights. Given the emotional content which the cause of exclusive jurisdiction had thus acquired, it is hardly surprising that "the destruction of the Knights did not end jurisdictional disputes"; on the contrary, the hostilities which eventuated in that destruction virtually ensured that subsequent appearances of dual unionism would invariably generate conflict instead of coöperation. Since exclusive jurisdiction and tacit understanding are, logically, alternative arrangements, adoption of the former to the virtual exclusion of the latter must be explained on historical grounds; and the Knights helped to provide such grounds. In a recent report to the Trades Union Congress, it was declared that, "It would be of no use the General Council inviting unions to dismember themselves in order to conform to one or other theory of organisation."[82] But it need hardly be added that the Congress' American counterpart frequently found it necessary to issue invitations of precisely this nature. Thus when the Webbs prophesied that

So long as the craft or occupation is fairly uniform from one end of the kingdom to the other, the geographical boundaries of the autonomous state must, in the Trade Union world, ultimately coincide with those of the nation itself[83]

they were more deserving of honor in the United States than in their native land.

Ware's interpretation of the Knights of Labor rests upon two propositions: (1) that the hostility which arose between the Knights and the national unions was not necessarily induced by any peculiarities in structure or objective which were characteristic of the Order, and (2) that this hostility, for all its sound and fury, worked little change upon the essential features of the trade union movement. In rebuttal to the latter argument, we have suggested that it was based upon insufficient evidence, that this conflict was in fact considerably more intense than Ware judged, and that, as a result, it did leave a lasting impression upon the labor movement. The validity of the first propo-

80. David J. Saposs, *Left Wing Unionism: A Study of Radical Policies and Tactics* (New York: International Publishers, 1926), pp. 123–126.

81. Ware, *Labor Movement,* p. 207.

82. T. U. C., *Final Report,* p. 13.

83. *Industrial Democracy,* p. 138.

sition can likewise be questioned, not with respect to sufficiency of the evidence presented, but on account of certain inferences drawn therefrom. Essentially it rests upon an interpretation of those facts which Ware identified as distinguishing the Knights from the American Federation of Labor: the District Assembly as the repository of authority in the Order, organization and support of men in unskilled occupations, and relatively less emphasis upon collective bargaining. It was claimed by the Knights and later by Ware that these *differentia* did not make the Order unsuitable as a federation in which autonomous national unions might find membership congenial. It was asserted by the autonomous national unions and later by Commons and Perlman, however, that one of these hallmarks of the Knights—their insistence upon the organization and support of the unskilled—made them completely unacceptable as bedfellows. Examination of these differentiating characteristics reveals merit in the latter contention, and it indicates further the existence of substantial interrelationship among the three traits.

To begin with, the mixed district assemblies were no better adapted to collective bargaining than the city centrals of earlier periods had been (see pp. 343ff. above), and for the same reasons: they were regional, rather than national, in jurisdiction, and they embraced (theoretically) all occupations. Ware himself emphasized this in pointing to the failure of a mixed District to support a group of shoemakers in an organizing strike and its willingness to accept a "settlement" whereby the employer agreed to dismiss his strikebreakers and rehire the strikers "as individuals."[84] He held, however, that this merely proved the case for trade districts. The mixed district assemblies, however, never took kindly to the idea of organizing national trade districts, constitutional provisions to the contrary notwithstanding. For the formation of national trade assemblies implied detaching the locals of the trade in question from the various mixed districts to which they had hitherto belonged; carried to its logical extreme, the establishment of national trade assemblies in every trade would have resulted in the total disappearance of the mixed regional districts. The latter were vigorously opposed to the surrender of their locals to trade districts, and, when the mixed district assemblies were powerful enough, they were able to block the issuing of national trade charters. When, for example, the Philadelphia District Assembly objected, the General Assembly refused to issue a national trade charter to the bricklayers of Philadelphia; and when the strongly antitrade District Assembly No. 49 of New York City would not permit a blacksmiths' local to withdraw its affiliation in order to join a duly chartered national trade district of machinists (in whose jurisdictions blacksmiths were specifically included), it was upheld by the General Assembly. Ware emphasized the fact that it was possible to form national trades assemblies even in the period when it was unconstitutional to do so, but here is evidence (presented by the same author) which indicates that it was not always possible to form them when the constitution specifi-

84. Ware, *Labor Movement,* p. 203. See also pp. 175–176, 187, 193–195.

cally provided for the chartering of national unions as trade districts.

Nor was Ware's inference that any group of craftsmen could organize themselves into a trade district simply by confronting the general executive board with an accomplished fact warranted by the examples which he offered. The Window Glass Workers, having organized as a national organization in 1880—a year in which the formation of trade districts was outlawed by constitutional amendment—before requesting authority, was recognized as Local Assembly 300; but when the window glass layers-out requested similar authority to form a national union within the Order, their petition was rejected summarily on constitutional grounds. "The unfortunate layers-out," said Ware, "suffered for their regularity." It is more probable, however, that the misfortune of this group was caused by the fact that the skill of their calling and the extent of their organization were considerably below the levels enjoyed by the Window Glass Workers who were, at the time, one of the most highly skilled and the most thoroughly organized of any body of craftsmen in the country. It would appear that national trade districts could be formed and recognized when the workers in question were powerful enough to organize national unions on their own resources, but that less advantageously situated trades had to reckon with the hostility of the mixed districts.

The reluctance of the mixed districts to surrender local affiliates to trade districts reflects the incompatibility which existed between the two types of organization. For the economic power of the mixed district lay in recourse to sympathetic action, while the strength of the national trade district was measured by the degree of craft autonomy which it possessed. Conflict between the two "districts"—the local federation and the national trade union—was as inevitable within the Knights of Labor as it had been before that organization came into existence; one need not, as Ware did, scrutinize personalities in order to explain it. For the national trade assembly to be really autonomous, it had to be free to refuse sympathetic assistance to other crafts. But if trade autonomy were countenanced, what would become of the Order's celebrated emphasis upon "solidarity," the brotherhood of industrial mankind? The conflict could never be resolved satisfactorily: as a matter of fact, solidarity won out over autonomy where the mixed district was strong; while autonomy prevailed where the trade district was powerful. Thus, in 1887, New York's District Assembly No. 49 was powerful enough to call a sympathetic strike of thousands of men in many trades in support of a dispute involving eighty-five coal handlers; but the Brewers, then organized as a national trade district, refused to obey the order to quit work. This episode was in part responsible for their subsequent withdrawal from the Order.[85]

From the viewpoint of the skilled groups, the mixed district assemblies were frequently useful as incubators of craft unionism which, following the depression of 1873–1879, performed the same functions as had earlier local

85. Commons, *History of Labour*, v. II, pp. 420–422.

federations in previous periods of revival: namely, "gather(ing) together the various unattached local unions that had sprung into existence, and help(ing) to resuscitate local unions that had been abandoned by their own national trade unions."[86] But once they had achieved a fair degree of organization in the important producing regions, the crafts turned their backs on the mixed districts and looked to national trade organization. Thus Ware observed that, "As the Brewers gained strength they left the Order . . ."[87] Not all groups, however, possessed sufficient natural bargaining advantages to enable them to achieve such self-sufficiency; they looked to the more powerful trades for sympathy and they looked to the mixed assemblies as the type of organization best designed to enlist such support in their behalf. It was observed above that, if every trade group had been able to form a national trade district, the mixed district assemblies could not have been regarded as permanent organizations; now it is evident that the latter found a claim to permanence in the existence of local assemblies of unskilled workers who were unable to form national organizations along trade lines. Furthermore, it was in the interest of these unskilled affiliates that the district assemblies sought to prevent their skilled member locals from leaving them for national trade assemblies. Without the power to order the skilled locals in a community to engage in demonstrations of sympathy, the district assembly was unable to support those groups which depended on it for help; and without the power to help those unable to help themselves, it lost its excuse for being.

Undoubtedly the Knights believed that, since an injury to the skilled craftsman was the concern of the unskilled worker, as well as the other way around, general adoption of the concept of "solidarity" would work to the advantage of all. But the skilled crafts knew better; they knew that it was best to avoid certain entangling alliances, and it was for this reason that they insisted upon trade autonomy and thus came into conflict with the mixed districts.

Thus the distinguishing characteristics of the Knights were not nearly so innocuous as Ware had protested. The mere fact that the Order designated both local federations and national unions as "districts" could not obscure their incompatibility. The structural peculiarity of the Knights lay not in the dominance of the district assembly; it was found in the dominance of the mixed district assembly. It was necessary to choose between the mixed and the trade assembly, and the Knights chose the former. In so doing they created an organization within which trade groups which desired to concentrate on the work of organization and collective bargaining could not function efficiently. The dominance of the mixed assembly implied the sacrifice of collective bargaining to other objectives (the third distinctive feature of the Order), for the choice between forms of organization implied, or reflected, a choice between objectives. The Knights may indeed have elected to do some-

86. Commons, *History of Labour,* v. II, p. 344.
87. Ware, *Labor Movement,* p. 223.

thing "bigger" than the Federation, but in so choosing, they materially impaired their ability to do the smaller thing.[88] Their larger goal was presumably the organization of the unskilled (the second hallmark of the Order), and the dominance of the mixed district meant nothing in fact if it did not imply the subordination of the selfish interests of the crafts to the selfish interests of the unskilled groups, although, as we have noted, this hard fact apparently was not appreciated by the Knights. Ware's theory of the neutrality of the unskilled is hardly tenable. It is refuted, rather than substantiated, by the fact that the national unions had evidenced no desire to organize the unskilled. That lack of inclusion meant, not indifference, but the desire to exclude is apparent when it is recalled that the unskilled were eager for amalgamation with these groups of "key" workers. Thus the layers-out of window glass were doubly unfortunate in their failure to organize a national trade district of their own, for they attempted self-organization only after they had been rebuffed by the powerful and exclusive trade assembly of the Window Glass Workers. Failure to organize independently and need for support by the more powerful went hand in hand. The Window Glass Workers, incidentally, were cited by Ware as having provided "the best example of trade unionism within the Knights."[89] This episode suggests that their good relationship rested on something other than adherence by this Assembly to the Order's principle of solidarity. Perhaps the foundation was provided by its strength, which was great enough to allow it to violate that principle without challenge by the district assemblies.

Again it should be noted that craft exclusiveness did not imply callous indifference to the misfortunes of others. The same Assembly of Window Glass Workers which had rejected the overtures of the layers-out financed the only coöperative venture in which the Order itself was ever directly involved,

88. The founders of the Industrial Workers of the World, successor to the Knights as champion of the unskilled, more clearly recognized the incompatibility between "sympathy" and collective bargaining. In their eyes, any trade union which failed to break its trade agreement and strike in sympathy with another group in the same industry— that is, any union which failed to respect another's picket line—was guilty of "union scabbing." (See Paul F. Brissenden, *The I.W.W., A Study of American Syndicalism* [New York: Columbia University, 1919], pp. 85–86, 115.) It is significant, therefore, that, although both organizations were singularly unsuccessful in their bargaining activities—a distinguishing characteristic of American grass-roots radicalism in the labor movement—the I. W. W. was more deliberately opposed to collective bargaining as a matter of principle than was the Order, whose leaders seemed to regard it more as a necessary, but temporary, evil to be endured until a new society could be ushered in. "To the I.W.W., agreements—particularly all *time* agreements—are in themselves evil," wrote Brissenden. This was not true of the Knights. In their recognition of the inconsistency between bargaining and sympathy, the Wobblies were more sophisticated than the Knights, who sought to implement both solidarity and autonomy within their organization. The latter, however, appreciated the degree to which the welfare of the unskilled depended upon the support of the skilled to a greater extent than did Haywood and other leaders of the I.W.W. See also Brissenden, pp. 194, 198, 201, 324.

89. Brissenden, *The I.W.W.,* p. 191.

namely, the Cannelburg coal mine, in 1883.[90] Indeed, the following rhymed tribute to the Knights' credo came from the pen of one of the founders of the American Federation of Labor, Secretary McGuire of the Carpenters:

> For working people the world over,
> Have one glory and one shame;
> What hurts one of them in any part
> Injures all of them the same.[91]

Yet the Carpenters, although more "class conscious" than most crafts (under the leadership of McGuire, who had sowed Socialist oats in his youth) never joined the Knights of Labor and were embroiled in a fair share of disputes with that Order. McGuire, indeed, had offered the Knights an interchange of cards with his organization early in 1886 (to which he received no reply), but when the unions later rejected a similar offer from the Knights, the Carpenters chose without hesitation to assist in the formation of a Federation based upon the principle of exclusive jurisdiction. The poetic effort which appears above was written in 1890, and the writer doubtless saw nothing in it which was inconsistent with a statement concerning the Knights that he had made two years earlier:

> I maintain most firmly that while we should be ever ready to help all other sister organizations, and do *practically* (sic) recognize the common fraternity of interests that exist between all branches of honorable toil, yet, *in the management of our trade affairs,* we should never make ourselves subordinate to any other organization. . . .[92]

Altruism assumes discretion on the part of the philanthropist, and the unions had no intention of relinquishing their power to do good by affiliating with an organization which assigned priority to solidarity over autonomy. In their final appeal to the national unions, the Order's General Executive Board wrote,

> We recognize the services rendered to humanity and the cause of labor by Trades Union organizations, but believe that the time has come, or is fast approaching, when *all* who earn their bread by the sweat of their brow shall be enrolled under one general head, as we are controlled by one common law—the law of our necessities.[93]

Now organizations of skilled workers have never been averse to holding membership in a federation which included unions of unskilled workers, but they were not prepared to surrender their autonomy as a condition of membership, for they stood to lose far more than they could gain by so doing. Powderly was condemned by Joseph R. Buchanan, the Knights' celebrated

90. See Ware, *Labor Movement,* pp. 329–333.
91. *Proceedings,* 1890, p. 21.
92. *Proceedings,* 1888, p. 18. My italics.
93. Bricklayers, *Proceedings,* 1886, p. 69. My italics.

organizer and leader of the strikes against the Union Pacific railroad in 1884, who claimed that

He did not see that the unionists who were members of the order were so because they loved its principles and not because they needed its protection; they had all the protection in trade matters that they required in their unions.[94]

But Powderly's alleged ignorance merely reflected the Knights' dilemma, for even if he had appreciated the unionists' independence of the Order, he could not have guaranteed them autonomy in their crafts without jettisoning the interests of the craftless. Hence his appeal was essentially directed to the higher nature of the skilled, to which no one could really expect a more favorable reply than McGuire's. The latter's observations on the "fraternity of interests" were in the tradition of another man of letters, la Rochefoucauld, who, two centuries before the Carpenters' secretary led his constituents into an American Federation of Labor, had observed that, in the final analysis, we all have sufficient fortitude to bear up under the adversity of others. One must concur, then, in the judgment of Carroll Wright (which, since it was written in 1887, near the height of the Order's power and notoriety, bore witness to his talent as an observer of the labor movement):

It stands to-day as an organization representing the opposite of the trades-union, and is bending all its energies to preserve the broad principle of harmonious interworking of all interests, as against the trades-union idea, which comes closer to human nature, of the preservation of individual interests.[95]

The argument that the Knights of Labor was an organization compatible with autonomous national unionism was no more tenable than the assumption upon which it rested—the assumption that the interests of the unskilled were not opposed to those of the skilled union members. Let us now consider the other main line of apology for the Order, one which, it might be noted, is alternative rather than complementary to the first. It will be recalled that Ware distinguished between two classes of unskilled workers—those who never had acquired any skill and those who had, but whose training was later made obsolete by the onward march of innovation (a distinction also made by Commons)[96]—and that he attributed most of the rivalry between the Knights and the unions to the exodus of members of the second group from trade unions to the Order. According to this analysis it really mattered little whether the Order was suitable for the affiliation of trade unions, since the latter were bound to become obsolete with the skills which had once delimited their craft jurisdictions. Furthermore, the alleged leveling influence of the "Industrial Revolution"—that of reducing all workers to the categories of

94. Joseph R. Buchanan, *The Story of A Labor Agitator* (New York: The Outlook Company, 1903), pp. 316–317.

95. Carroll D. Wright, "An Historical Sketch of the Knights of Labor," *Quarterly Journal of Economics,* v. I, no. 2, January 1887.

96. Commons, *History of Labour,* v. II, p. 382.

unskilled or "semiskilled"—lent substance to Powderly's contention that all wage earners were "controlled by one common law," that their interests were identical and that, presumably, they should, for that reason, all "be enrolled under one general head."

Both theoretically and historically this second line of reasoning is more attractive than the first. By stressing the disintegrating effects of technological change upon the economic underpinnings of the craft unions, the Knights and their historian after them laid bare the static assumptions of trade unionism. The unions themselves, of course, were far from oblivious to the menace presented by mechanical and human substitutes for skilled labor and, in their "Address" to the Knights in 1886, defiantly proclaimed as one of their vital functions the protection of the craftsman's skill and the higher standard of life which set him apart from the masses with whom the Order had invited them to make common cause.

the various trades have been affected by the introduction of machinery, the sub-division of labor, the use of women's and child's labor, and the lack of an apprentice system, so that the skilled trades were rapidly sinking to the level of pauper labor. To protect the skilled labor of America from being reduced to beggary, and to sustain the standard of American workmanship and skill, the Trades Unions of America have been established.[97]

It cannot be held that trade union jurisdiction, as defined in the last chapter, is premised upon a given and unchanging state of the industrial arts, for not all economic innovation results in the obsolescence of existing and traditional craft skills. In some instances, innovations actually increased the demand for skills which had been used in connection with superseded methods or equipment; and, in other cases, the growth of product demand sometimes made it profitable for old processes and machines and skills to be utilized for a considerable period of time after the new techniques had come into operation. In order that a given economic jurisdiction persist, it is required only that the economic importance of the trade upon which it is based persist, despite the occurrence of technical change. But it can be urged that a highly dynamic economy did not provide the most favorable conditions for the entrenchment of craft unions, for economic change has in fact made many skills obsolete and, in so doing, has deprived the organizations of the skilled workers in question of the superior bargaining positions which they had previously enjoyed by presenting employers with the availability of alternative resources. Thus the dynamic process of innovation worked the same effect upon union monopolies as it did upon business monopolies; the former, as well as the latter, were and still are exposed to what Schumpeter termed, "the perennial gale of creative destruction."[98] In both cases,

97. Reproduced in Bricklayers' *Proceedings*, 1886, pp. 67–68.
98. Joseph A. Schumpeter, *Capitalism, Socialism, and Democracy* (New York: Harper, second edition, 1947), p. 87; also chapters VII and VIII. See also Sumner H. Slichter, *The American Economy* (New York: Knopf, 1948), p. 15.

the ability to extract monopoly returns for a protracted period of time was severely limited: businessmen found that innovation opened their markets to competitors; unions found that the destructive gale sometimes blew their jurisdictional foundations out from under them.

But innovation was only one element in the process of economic development, another ingredient of which—and often a necessary condition of innovation—was the widening of markets (see Chapter 1 above). And if the trade union was inferior to the mixed union of the Knights in coping with innovation, the district union, dominant in the Order, was certainly unsatisfactory in dealing with issues arising out of interregional competition. Powderly himself was not unaware of this problem. While he advocated achieving the eight-hour day by statutory enactment, he opposed the efforts of the Chicago packing house employees (and of all other trades as well) to secure this result by striking; and Ware (disapprovingly) quotes him as maintaining that "it would be but a question of time until the trade would leave Chicago and go to other points where men were working ten hours. The laws of business cannot lightly be tampered with. . . ."[99]

The Knights' concern with technological change bore implications for its structural development which should prompt one to reassess the significance of the general assembly's constitution. In view of their insistence upon the inclusion of all groups, including the unskilled, and of their conviction that the Industrial Revolution would make a necessity of the virtue of solidarity, the Knights could not have succeeded without transferring power from their mixed districts to their general assembly. It is true, as Ware established, that the Order was centralized only in theory; but it is equally true that it was not a successful organization, and it is possible that its failure to survive was related to its failure to achieve the transfer of authority from local federation to national federation, just as the national unions' ability to survive depended upon the transfer of authority from local trade union to national trade union.

Given an extension of markets sufficient to disqualify regional unions as efficient bargaining organizations and assuming a continuing process of "economic mutation" sufficient to disqualify trade jurisdiction as a basis of bargaining power, One Big Union was the only type of organization which theoretically could establish the conditions required for a high degree of "relative negotiating strength." The latter requires control by the bargaining union of all classes of labor required by any employer for the performance of those operations over which the union claims jurisdiction. If all classes of labor could be substituted for one another, the union, in order to confront the employer with an inelastic demand or an inelastic supply curve of labor at wage rates in excess of the prevailing level, would have to control all relevant occupations. (This is analogous to the case of perfect monopoly in the product market, which, according to Chamberlin, "would be one embracing the supply

99. Ware, *Labor Movement*, p. 154.

of everything, since all things are more or less imperfect substitutes for each other."[100]) However, although considerations of bargaining strategy might have furnished the original impulse for centralization of authority in a general assembly of all trades, it is doubtful whether such a union, once established, would have placed primary emphasis upon collective bargaining. It is more probable that a union of all workers, confronted with the limitations on its ability to further the welfare of all its members by economic action, would have turned to political action. Such action might have been limited either to the espousal of specific programs designed to increase the per capita income of its membership at the expense of other groups in the country or to the advocacy of governmental guarantees of full employment (which a regime of full unionism probably would have insisted upon), or both; but it is probable that the political programs to which One Big Union would have devoted most of its energies would have been of the radical or utopian variety which Powderly and some of his colleagues actually preached. Thus, in their effort to minimize the importance of certain peculiarities found in the constitution of the general assembly and in the utterances of its leaders—notably the centralization of power in the general executive board and the subordination of collective bargaining to other methods and broader objectives—by emphasizing that they were never translated into practice, the apologists for the Order failed to appreciate that these peculiar features nevertheless spelled out the only conditions under which the admittedly unique goal of the Knights could be realized—"the thorough unification of labor."

In theory, both the Knights and the national trade union were unsuited to the total dynamic environment, because each was adapted to only one aspect of that environment and was not well equipped to cope with the other. In fact, however, it seemed that a labor organization's failure to orient itself to the extension of market areas, as exemplified by the district-dominated Knights, was fatal; while failure to be oriented to the possibility that changes in products and methods would uproot existing craft jurisdictions was not necessarily fatal, since craft obsolescence was not an inevitable concomitant of economic change, at least in the short run. The Knights, relying for their strength upon the solidarity of all trades, were obliged to gamble that the leveling influence of technological change would be great enough to make membership in the Order a matter of self-interest to the unions' members. The trade union, on the other hand, relying for its strength upon the economic isolation of its membership, was obliged to gamble on the permanence of that isolation. The Knights lost this bet.

100. Edward H. Chamberlin, *The Theory of Monopolistic Competition* (Cambridge, Mass.: Harvard University, fifth edition, 1936), p. 65. See also Robert Triffin, *Monopolistic Competition and General Equilibrium Theory* (Cambridge, Mass.: Harvard University, 1941), pp. 103, 128, 132–133.

CHAPTER THIRTEEN

NATIONAL FEDERATION:
THE AMERICAN FEDERATION OF LABOR

MANY TRADE unionists believed that the only type of international order which the national union could find to its liking was one in which it was free to follow isolationist foreign policies if it chose to do so. These policies, it will be recalled (pp. 334ff.) emerged from the efforts of the national unions to establish trade and geographical jurisdictions which were designed to maintain or improve the negotiating power of their constituents. The national union typically sought, first, to define its own jurisdiction; second, to exercise exclusive control over that jurisdiction; and, finally, to deny any obligation on its part to meddle in affairs outside its own jurisdiction. Neglect of the unskilled and reluctance to sanction sympathetic strikes were specific consequences of the last of these three objectives. Having persuaded themselves that the Knights of Labor did not provide an atmosphere in which their goals could be recognized and generally accepted—having convinced themselves, on the contrary, that the Knights jeopardized their very existence—the national unions proceeded to fashion a federation to their own specifications.

The American Federation of Labor, as Slichter pointed out, "was based on two principles: (1) the principle of autonomy . . . and (2) the principle of exclusive jurisdiction, that there can be only one legitimate union in one recognized field of jurisdiction."[1] Let us consider now the implications of the first of these two principles.

AUTONOMY

The principle of autonomy underlies two of the jurisdictional objectives of the national union—establishment of exclusive control over its own jurisdiction and freedom to limit its economic activities to the confines of that jurisdiction. Under the Knights of Labor, the sovereignty of the national union had been disputed in theory by the general assembly, or national fed-

---

1. Sumner H. Slichter, *The Challenge of Industrial Relations* (Ithaca: Cornell University, 1947), p. 8.

eration, and in fact by the district assemblies, or local federations. The latter frequently had contended with the national union for the allegiance of the local unions in its trade in order to enlist the strength of that craft in support of groups or issues outside of the national union's jurisdiction. They had weakened the national's control over its own jurisdiction in the interest of obliging or persuading its members to embark upon adventures foreign to their immediate self-interest (that is, trade jurisdiction). Thus, for national autonomy to emerge as the ruling principle in a new federation, it was necessary that the national union achieve a position of power within that federation. Historically, acceptance of the principle of autonomy meant "the dominance of the national union"[2] over the local federation, on the one hand, and the national federation on the other.

Dominance Over the Local Federation

The foundation for the supremacy of the national unions over the local federations was laid at the first convention of the Federation of Organized Trades and Labor Unions (the immediate predecessor of the American Federation of Labor) in 1881. At that meeting it was established that the number of delegates allowed each national or international union vary directly with membership, but that each local trades assembly or council be represented by one delegate, regardless of the size of the membership of its affiliated locals.[3] This system of representation was opposed by the local bodies. At the preliminary meeting in Terre Haute, on August 2, 1881, they had been represented on the same basis as the national unions—one delegate for each organization. After the dual system had been voted by the convention, they sought to substitute for it another plan whereby nationals, trade assemblies, and unaffiliated locals alike would be granted delegate representation in proportion to membership—namely, one delegate for each hundred members or less and one additional delegate for each additional five hundred members or major fraction thereof. This represented a compromise between the system of allowing an equal number of delegates to all groups, which they preferred, and the system which the convention had adopted; but, despite the numerical strength of the local federations, it was voted down. The system was altered the following year to admit two delegates from each state or

2. The phrase comes from the title of a penetrating article on this subject by George E. Barnett, "The Dominance of the National Union in American Labor Organization," *Quarterly Journal of Economics,* v. XXVII (1913), pp. 455–481.

3. *Proceedings,* 1881. The original basis for representation from national or international unions was as follows:

1 delegate for 1,000 members or less (in 1885 this number was changed to 4,000)
2 delegates for 4,000 members
3 delegates for 8,000 members
4 delegates for 16,000 members
5 delegates for 32,000 members, "and so on."

provincial federation, but the number of delegates allowed each city federation of locals remained fixed at one.[4]

This dual system of representation was carried over when the Federation was rechristened in 1886. The essential difference between the old and the new organizations, however, is the fact that the steps necessary to effect the definite and irrevocable shift in power from local federation to national union were taken after the present American Federation of Labor had been formed. For even the dual plan of representation which the first Federation had adopted could not prevent the delegates from the city federations and local unions from outnumbering the delegates from the national unions in several of its sessions.[5] In some cases local unions which were affiliated with but possibly very imperfectly subordinate to national unions sent their own representatives to the first Federation's meetings. In 1886, this practice was ended with the passage of a regulation which restricted representation to "each Local or District Trades Union, not connected with, or having a National or International head. . . ."[6] But national unions, at this time, were few in number relative to the local federations and the local unions in trades over which no national had yet claimed jurisdiction. Thus the delegations from the national unions still were not secure; Barnett quotes a delegate to the 1886 convention of the A.F. of L. who later reported to his own international union (the Printers) that "local organizations in a single large city could be so strongly represented as to outnumber all the duly accredited delegates from distinctive national and international bodies."[7]

But at the next convention the ascendancy of the national unions was made secure by the adoption of a constitutional provision which authorized the deciding of questions by roll call upon demand and which provided that, in roll-call votes, each delegate of a national or international union should cast one vote for every hundred members (or major fraction thereof) he represented, but that no city or state federation should receive more than one vote. Representatives of the federations sought to modify this provision, but the most that they were able to accomplish was the passage of an amendment in 1888 requiring the concurrence of one-fifth of the delegates present before roll could be called. Even this modest gain was largely neutralized the fol-

4. *Proceedings,* 1882. Also Barnett, "Dominance of the National Union," p. 461. District Assemblies of the Knights of Labor were also allowed representation on the same basis as the local federations. Gompers had opposed granting any representation to the assemblies affiliated with the Order, but his recommendation was not followed by the convention.

5. Barnett, "Dominance of the National Union," p. 462. Gompers, in his report to the Convention of 1900, said, "Nor is it out of place to call attention to the fact that, though our Federation was formed in 1881, the records demonstrate that a large preponderance of those who were in attendance were not its friends . . ." (*Proceedings,* 1900, p. 17.)

6. *Constitution,* 1886, Art. IV.

7. Barnett, "Dominance of the National Union," p. 462, n. 3.

lowing year, however, when the proportion was reduced to one-tenth.[8] In 1900, the local federations launched their final counterattack. One amendment was introduced which provided that each delegate be allowed only one vote on roll call as on show of hands, and another proposal was advanced whereby delegates from city centrals would have been permitted to cast the votes of local trade and federal labor unions which were affiliated with them. Both were rejected;[9] for, with the adoption in 1887 of the roll-call procedure suggested by the national unions, the latter had settled so securely in the seat of power that it was impossible to unhorse them thereafter without their own consent.

Behind all this parliamentary legerdemain lay the objectives of the national unions: first, to destroy the city centrals' ability to compete with the nationals for control over the local unions and to confine them largely to the sphere of political activity; second, to require them to render active support in the campaigns to bring all of the locals in each trade jurisdiction under the authority of the appropriate national union. Since political activity was regarded by the founders of both federations as a primary function of the organization,[10] "the encouragement and formation of Trades and Labor Assemblies or Councils" was ranked with "the encouragement and formation of National and International Trade Unions" as "objects" of the Federation.[11] "To secure legislation favorable to the interests of the industrial classes" was also made a constitutional objective, and this latter object presumably explains the founders' interest in promoting the formation of trades and labor assemblies, since they were organizations which, as we have observed, were best adapted to political activity.

It soon became apparent that majority sentiment favored the enforcement of a division of labor between the national unions and the local federations, at least to the extent of reserving to the former such economic prerogatives as they wished to exercise. For the 1885 convention of the old Federation amended the constitution so as to make it an object of the organization not only to encourage and form national and international trade unions but also to *"secure their autonomy."* [12] No similar addendum was appended to the section dealing with the encouragement and formation of local federations. On the contrary, after the problem of representation had been resolved to the satisfaction of the national unions, the Federation proceeded to implement its stated object of securing the autonomy of the nationals by abridging the autonomy of the local federations.

8. *Constitution*, 1887, Art. IV, Sec. 2; 1888, Art. IV, Sec. 2; 1889, Art. IV, Sec. 2.

9. Barnett, "Dominance of the National Union," pp. 463–464.

10. Some of the delegates to the 1881 convention believed that their course had been charted for them by the British Trades' Union Congress which was engaged primarily in political activity. (*Proceedings*, 1881, p. 6.)

11. *Constitution*, 1881, Art. II, Secs. 2, 3, and 4.

12. *Constitution*, 1885, Art. II, Sec. 4. Italics mine.

A test of strength between the two types of organization arose over attempts by central labor unions to compel their affiliated local unions to participate in sympathetic strikes which the former had authorized. As in the past, the national unions were opposed to this practice, holding in effect that the good union doctrine of "sanctity of contracts" should take working precedence over the good union doctrine that "an injury to one is the concern of all." The Knights of Labor, it will be recalled, supported a contrary interpretation and sought to assign priority to the local federations when they clashed with the trade groups over this issue. The American Federation of Labor, on the other hand, sided with the national unions, and it supported them more powerfully than the Knights had supported their "mixed" district organizations. The position of the A.F. of L. was first spelled out by President John McBride in his report to the 1895 Convention:

> In the past year several instances are recorded in which members of local unions, working under contracts with employers, were ordered by the central organization to cease work and go out on strike for the purpose of aiding members of some other union who had a dispute with the same employer. The members thus ordered out on strike were placed in an embarrassing position. To quit work and violate the terms of their contract, without any provocation from their employer with whom the contract was made, was to act dishonorably, while to continue at work and disobey the order of the central body was to court denunciation and expulsion from membership in the latter body.
>
> It is clearly evident that if a trade union possesses the right to make contracts upon trade matters, no central union should either assume or be delegated the right to ask for or insist upon the violation of such contracts. It is here that the work of the trade union and the central body conflicts.
>
> Whether contracts are made by a local union direct, or through its national union, proper and careful consideration should be given to the effect of such contract upon those who labor for the same employer, but not included in the contract terms.
>
> In 1894, the Executive Council tried to remedy the defect here referred to, by the adoption of a resolution which provided, "That contracts made by unions with their employers should be faithfully lived up to by the unions so long as they are not violated by their employers; and the occurrence of any trade dispute with such employer by other unions than those having contracts shall not be the cause for the violation of agreements by such unions as have regular contracts."
>
> If this rule or something similar was made the law, much future trouble could be avoided.[13]

The resolution to which McBride referred was tabled by the convention after lively debate on the respective merits of sympathetic striking and the

13. *Proceedings*, 1895, p. 13; also pp. 63–64. In 1893, President Gompers reported that the executive council had adopted a resolution almost identical with the resolution of 1894. It was prompted by the efforts of striking unions to induce the executive council to order other unions to strike in sympathy with them. No reference was made at that time to the role played by the local federations in organizing sympathetic strikes. (*Proceedings*, 1893, pp. 15–16.)

honoring of contractual obligations, but "something similar" was passed three years later. Neither McBride nor the measure which he urged upon the convention distinguished between local unions which were members of national unions in their trades or locals not so affiliated. In 1898, however, this distinction—irrelevant to the questions of union morality which had been the subject of debate—was drawn, and the following amendment to the constitution was adopted:

> No Central Labor Union, or other central body of delegates, shall have the authority or power to order any organization, affiliated with such Central Labor Union, or other central labor body on a strike, where such organization has a National organization, until the proper authorities of such National organization have been consulted and agreed to such action.[14]

Thus the convention was unwilling to abridge the authority of the city centrals in the interest either of the principle of inviolability of contracts or of the local unions affiliated with the central labor organizations. But it was willing to infringe upon the authority of the city centrals in the interest of the national unions "to secure their autonomy."

The A.F. of L. proceeded further to secure the autonomy of its national affiliates at the expense of its affiliated central federations. In 1897, the convention had been advised of several disputes which had arisen between national unions and central labor unions when the latter had attempted to resolve, on a local basis, jurisdictional differences among locals which were affiliated with national unions. It was proposed that a special committee be appointed "to define the powers of central bodies in settling such disputes." This recommendation was rejected, however, in favor of a flat denial of "the right (of the central bodies) to interfere between national organizations."[15]

> Del. Bennett said he was opposed to central bodies being invested with any more power than they now possess.
> Del. Doyle said he did not believe that the central bodies should have the right to interfere between national organizations.
> Concurred in.

In 1901, the Federation stripped the city centrals of their important and time-honored power of originating boycotts, because delegates from some of the national unions had complained that locally originated boycotts had embarrassed the nationals in their relations with employers. Barnett observed that, "On several occasions city federations have been forced, on complaint of national unions, to call off boycotts."[16]

Finally, the local federations were forbidden to intervene in collective bargaining activities—"the adjustment of wage contracts, wage disputes, or

14. *Constitution,* 1898, Art. XII, Sec. 5.
15. *Proceedings,* 1897, pp. 76, 91.
16. Barnett, "Dominance of the National Union," p. 472.

working rules" of local unions affiliated with national unions without the consent of the latter.[17]

It was necessary, from the viewpoint of the national unions, that the ability of the city centrals to compete with them for authority over the local unions be eliminated. Relegation of the central bodies to the rank of second-rate powers did not, however, ensure that the locals would automatically transfer their banners to the camps of the nationals. Therefore, in their effort to bring the local unions under their authority and also to strike at "dual" locals affiliated with the Knights, the nationals were not content with disarming their old rivals; they were determined to press them into service as recruiting and enforcement agents in this campaign.

The first step in this direction consisted in the passage in 1886 of an amendment to the Federation's constitution which forbade any central body to admit to its ranks delegates "from any local organization that is hostile to the objects of this Federation, or that has been suspended or expelled by a National or International organization" upon pain of "being denied representation in general conventions of this Federation."[18] Under this law, a Trades and Labor Assembly was subsequently suspended from representation until it, in turn, suspended one of its affiliates, a local of brewery workers, "for insubordination to the National Union of Brewery Workmen."[19] In 1889, it was resolved "That it is the wish of this Convention that the various Central Labor Unions and State Federations, and all the organizers connected therewith, as well as the organizers of this Federation, be requested to urge upon the various local trade unions represented therein, to affiliate themselves with their National and International Unions when such exist." In 1895, the following resolution, proposed by Treasurer Lennon, was passed:

That it shall be the duty of all state federations and local central trade organizations affiliated with the A.F. of L. to insist that local unions affiliated with them shall, if not attached to the national or international union of their trade, do so within six months from January 1, 1898, or be suspended from said state federations or central labor bodies, and shall remain suspended until they affiliate with their respective general organizations.

The following year the Federation forbade the city centrals to admit any local unions which were "not connected with" an affiliated national or inter-

---

17. *Proceedings,* 1906, p. 245. Cited in Barnett, "Dominance of the National Union," pp. 473–474.

18. *Constitution,* 1887, Art. IV, Sec. 5. The following year, this section was expanded by the addition of organizations owing their "allegiance to any other body, National or International, not connected with this Federation, (or) hostile to any affiliated organization," to the list of groups to which the local federations were commanded to refuse admission.

19. *Proceedings,* 1890, pp. 41, 29–30. The local's "insubordination" consisted in refusal to pay a per capita assessment which had been levied by the national union.

national union.[20] On the other hand, it was provided (in 1902) that a city central could withhold membership from a local union in good standing with an affiliated national union only if it could prove charges against the local—and, in that case, the latter could appeal to the executive council of the Federation.[21]

No similar obligations were imposed upon the national unions. It was merely proclaimed to be their "duty . . . to instruct their Local Unions to join chartered Central Labor Unions in their vicinity where such exist"; and, if their locals chose not to do so or to withdraw from the local federations, the nationals were not required to discipline them. This double standard was also manifested in provisions governing the organization of new national unions and city centrals. It was stipulated that "Local Central Labor Unions shall use all possible means to organize and connect as Local Unions to National or International Unions the organizations in their vicinity; to aid the formation of National or International Unions where none exist. . . ." But a companion injunction upon local unions to form central labor unions was watered down to a mere suggestion. Originally (in 1890), it had been proclaimed "the duty of local unions of the American Federation of Labor to organize Central Labor Organizations in the localities where none exist, or to join those already existing, to secure the affiliation of the same with the American Federation of Labor, that there may be unity of action for the purpose of advancing the interest of each other and establishing the principles of this Federation."[22] But later on, at the same time that the city centrals were enjoined to "use all possible means" to urge their member locals either to affiliate themselves with or participate in the formation of national unions in their respective trades, the Federation superseded these direct instructions to local unions with the following innocuous reminder:

Where there are one or more Local Unions in any city *belonging to the National or International Unions,* affiliated with this Federation, they may organize a Trades Association or Central Labor Union, or join such body, if already in existence.[23]

The clue to this change in tone is found in the changed conception of the local union, a change which was induced by the steady growth in numbers and influence of the national unions. The 1890 regulation, which made the organization of central labor unions mandatory upon the locals, referred to the latter as "local unions *of the American Federation of Labor,*" implying a line of authority running directly from the Federation to the local. But the

20. *Proceedings,* 1889, p. 38; 1895, p. 57; 1896, Art. XII, Sec. 1.
21. Barnett, "Dominance of the National Union," p. 398. Writing in 1913, Barnett observed that, "This right (of appeal) has been freely used. . . ."
22. See *Constitution,* 1894, Art. XII, Sec. 2; 1894, Art. XII, Sec. 4; 1890, Art. IV, Sec. 5.
23. *Constitution,* 1894, Art. XII, Sec. 3. My italics.

amendment of 1894 was restricted to local unions "belonging to the national or International Unions, affiliated with this Federation"; and in this case the A.F. of L. did not presume even to advise or urge the constituents of the national unions to form or join local federations.

Let us summarize the results of the successful efforts of the national unions to achieve dominance within the American Federation of Labor over their historical rivals, the city federations:

(1) While the number of delegates allowed to each national union in the conventions of the A.F. of L. was determined with reference to its membership, no city federation could be represented by more than one delegate. And while each delegate from a national union could cast one ballot for every hundred members whom he represented on roll-call votes (which could be demanded by a very small fraction of the delegates), no local federation could cast more than one vote.

(2) Central labor unions were not permitted to admit or retain in affiliation any local unions which were suspended from, expelled by, or otherwise "not connected with" an affiliated national union.

(3) On the other hand, central labor unions were not permitted to refuse admission to locals which were in good standing with their national unions, unless they preferred specific charges against them; the Executive Council of the Federation passed final judgment on the merit of such charges.

(4) No obligations governed the national unions in their relationships with locals which paralleled those regulating the local city central relationship. The nationals were not obliged to discipline any of their locals which had been suspended or expelled by city centrals—or which simply refused to join them; nor were they required to admit local unions in their respective trades solely because the latter were acceptable to central labor organizations.

(5) Finally, the city centrals were shorn of some of their most important economic prerogatives: the power to order local unions to strike without prior consent of the national unions in question, the power to originate boycotts without similar authorization, the power to intervene on their own initiative in collective bargaining between employers and member local unions, and the power to impose or negotiate local settlement of jurisdictional disputes without consulting the national unions whose jurisdictions were involved.

The earliest concessions to the national unions were made at conventions in which delegates from the latter organizations had not yet achieved numerical dominance. Following our earlier discussion of the principles governing the formation of federations and amalgamations, it is apparent that these conditions were demanded by the nationals as the price of their participation in the new federation, a price which other organizations represented at the conventions were willing to pay. Later concessions were made by the local federations when they were outvoted (they were outvoted partly as a result of earlier concessions whereby they had consented to be outvoted), but they nevertheless remained within the Federation.[24] The dominance achieved by the national unions over the local federations was an example of "revolution by consent." The city centrals in a real sense consented to their surrender of autonomy, since they were free to secede from the A.F. of L. That they chose to remain within that organization indicated their awareness that economic development had reached a stage which made federation with the national unions more important to them than it was to the nationals. Hence their acceptance (although by no means prompt) of their changed status and mission, which was best described by John McBride of the Miners in his only report to the A.F. of L. as its president in 1895:

> The central labor organizations and state federations were intended to serve as auxiliaries to the trade and labor movement, but in no sense were they intended to interfere either with the autonomy of the trades or encroach upon matters under the jurisdiction of the trade unions, except in a way of lending a helping hand when called upon by a trade union in distress.[25]

Dominance Over the National Federation

Since "the American Federation of Labor was formed to protect the national unions from losing their independence to the Knights of Labor,"[26] it could hardly be expected that those national unions, in view of their economic objectives, would surrender to their own creature prerogatives which they considered essential to their independent existence. Hence the frequently repeated assertion that the A.F. of L.'s strength lay in its weakness, which meant that the national unions' strength was reflected in the A.F. of L.'s weakness. In order to evaluate this weakness, we shall contrast the authority (or lack thereof) possessed by the Federation with that possessed by its affiliated national unions, on the one hand, and with the formal constitutional power of the General Assembly of the Knights of Labor, on the other, in the following areas: affiliation of the individual, standards of admission, standards of discipline, standards of government, control over strikes, and collective bargaining.

24. Barnett ("Dominance of the National Union,") records an abortive attempt by the Milwaukee city federation to call a nationwide convention of delegates of city centrals in 1902. Even this movement, according to a spokesman, "had no design to organize a body antagonistic to the A.F. of L." (p. 464) The spokesman was Victor Berger; and since his reassuring remarks were typical of the gentlemanly tactics adopted by the Socialist Party in its dealings with the national unions (see David J. Saposs, *Left Wing Unionism: A Study of Radical Policies and Tactics* [New York: International Publishers, 1926], pp. 33–47), it is probable that the proposed federation of city centrals would have been a preponderantly political body with no real desire to challenge the autonomy of the national unions and their control over their own locals.

25. *Proceedings*, 1895, p. 13.

26. Slichter, *Challenge of Industrial Relations*, p. 8.

Affiliation of the Individual

From its inception, the A.F. of L. was a federation in the literal sense of the word: its members were sovereign organizations. At the first meeting of old Federation of Organized Trades and Labor Unions, it was decided that "This association . . . shall consist of such Trade and Labor Unions as shall . . . conform to its rules and regulations, and pay all contributions required to carry out the objects of this Federation."[27] The unit of membership was thus the sovereign union rather than the individual unionist. This contrasted with the practice of the national unions and with the theory of the Knights of Labor (see p. 350 above). The national unions, like the Federation, began their careers as federations of independent unions, their only "members" being delegates from the local unions and the national officers whom the latter elected (and who, themselves, were frequently required to be accredited delegates from their own locals). The national unions, however, evolved from unions of unions to unions of individuals; the individual trade unionist became a member of his national union directly. Thus the printer was a member of the International Typographical Union as well as of, let us say, Typographical Union No. 6, in New York City where he lived and worked; but he was not a member of the American Federation of Labor, nor did he ever become directly affiliated with that organization. Because of his membership in the national union, the individual could, upon presentation of a traveling card, transfer his membership from one local to another without the payment of an initiation fee to his new local. He could not, however, transfer from one national trade union to another without charge and as a matter of right; the Federation possessed no authority over the national unions equivalent to the latter's power to enforce recognition by the locals of the traveling card, or, in certain cases, to issue cards directly.

The power to issue travel and transfer cards was a constitutional privilege of the General Assembly of the Knights of Labor, however, for, unlike the A.F. of L., the Order was regarded as one big union of individual Knights. The unit of membership in the Order was the individual just as it was in the national union; whereas, in the Federation, the unit of membership was the trade union.

Standards of Admission

Many national unions stipulated standards of admission, which their affiliated locals were obliged to respect, in one or more of the following areas: initiation fees (specifying uniform, maximum and/or minimum amounts to be charged); apprenticeship and/or competence; certain classes of workers whose eligibility to membership was a matter of controversy, especially women and negroes. Theoretically, the Knights' General Assembly also regulated standards of admission: it was authorized to establish a maximum

27. *Constitution*, 1881, Art. I.

initiation fee to be charged by the district and local assemblies; and membership in the Order could not be denied to anyone who had ever worked for a wage—provided that he was not a member of the legal, medical, or banking fraternities, or a seller of intoxicants. The Federation, on the other hand, possessed no comparable authority. This was revealed most clearly when later attempts to induce the A.F. of L. to compel its affiliated national unions to admit negroes to membership on equal terms with white workers were defeated. The successful opposition invariably rested its case upon the inability of the Federation to meddle in the internal affairs of its autonomous affiliates.[28]

Standards of Discipline

Some national unions specified offenses for which locals were obliged to punish their members and even stipulated the punishment to be meted out for each specified offense. Similar power over the disciplinary activities of affiliated organizations was never ceded to the American Federation of Labor. The extent to which such cession of power from the national to the Federation could have abridged the autonomy of the nationals in a vital respect can be illustrated by one example. One of the offenses most commonly specified in the constitutions of the early national unions was "scabbing" or "ratting," which included working on any job struck against by the national union or any of its locals. Aside from considerations of union equity, mandatory punishment for this offense was of considerable help to the national union in establishing and maintaining control within its trade jurisdiction. But if the A.F. of L. had been able to specify and stipulate punishment for an offense comparable to (but not identical with) the type of action outlawed by the national union, the latter's own freedom of action would have been curtailed rather severely. For the comparable A.F. of L. measure would have been a requirement that any union member be punished for crossing any picket line established by any union affiliated with the A.F. of L.; and such a requirement would have imposed upon the national unions the obligation to participate sympathetically in affairs outside their own respective jurisdictions—an obligation which they were determined to avoid.

28. When the question of organizing negro workers was first brought before the convention in 1900, it was recommended that they be organized in separate federal labor unions. Thus, provision was made only for organizing these workers in local unions directly affiliated with the A.F. of L. (Herbert R. Northrup, *Organized Labor and the Negro* [New York: Harper, 1944], pp. 8–9.) These federal labor unions were conceived of as essentially temporary in nature, ultimately to serve as the nuclei of new nationals, whereupon their direct relationship with the Federation would be terminated. Hence they were ill-adapted to the organization of negroes, since no action was taken to ensure that negro federal labor unions would be assured affiliation with national unions in their trade; and, even if the formation of negro national trade unions paralleling the jurisdiction of established counterparts had been feasible, it is not likely that the Federation would have agreed to charter new groups in jurisdictions in which the incumbents were already organized. Thus the Gompers-inspired expedient of providing separate federal labor unions for negroes was no solution at all.

In addition to—or, as we have seen in some cases, in lieu of—prescribing disciplinary standards, national unions curtailed the authority of their "subordinate" locals by establishing the right of the individual to appeal to national authority from the sentence imposed in the local union. On the federation level, the general assembly of the Knights had been regarded as a tribunal to which individuals who had been sentenced by district courts could appeal; and, since some of the "districts" were "trade" in nature—that is, national trade unions, this meant that, theoretically, the national union within the Order did not possess final disciplinary authority over its individual members. This was not true in the A.F. of L.; no provision was made for appeal from national authority to the Federation. The judiciary of the national union remained a supreme court.

Standards of Government

The national unions required periodic submission by their locals of detailed information concerning membership and financial status. National officers were empowered to investigate the accounts kept by the local unions. In some cases, the dues charged by the local unions and the frequency with which local elections were conducted were prescribed by national regulations. Comparable powers were not possessed by the Federation, which specified only the per capita payments which its affiliates were obliged to pay to it in order to retain their good standing. The only penalty visited upon an affiliate which misrepresented its membership in order to reduce its financial obligation to the Federation was the proportionate reduction in representation at the A.F. of L. conventions which such a course of action—by no means uncommon—automatically entailed. It might be added a local union which misrepresented its membership status to the national with which it was affiliated suffered a similar reduction in representation at the latter's conventions. However, the nationals' concern with local membership and financial resources was usually more intense than the Federation's interest in the veracity of the data presented to it by the nationals. Unlike the Federation, national unions, to a greater or lesser extent, performed economic functions which were intended directly to increase the bargaining power of their affiliates. Hence information concerning the local situation and the need to maximize national revenues (which depended upon the accuracy of that information) were of such great importance to the national unions that they were unwilling to rely solely upon the relationship between the veracity of the reporting local and the size of its delegation to the national convention as a guarantee of accuracy.

Control Over Strikes; Financial Resources.

One reason why some of the national unions sought more closely to examine the basis upon which the financial accounts of their affiliates rested than the Federation did was that part of the proceeds were earmarked for disbursement as aid to striking locals. It will be recalled that the power to grant aid invariably was accompanied by the power to prescribe conditions under which the applicant was eligible to receive aid and that it was also associated with the power to regulate strike activities of local unions even apart from their eligibility for financial assistance.

Now the issue of strike support presented a peculiarly delicate problem to the founders of the Federation. On the one hand, the national unions, with the example of their relations with their own locals before them, were well aware of the close association between power and purse, and they feared that a wealthy and benevolent Federation would be a potential menace to national autonomy. On the other hand, they, and Gompers in particular, were also aware that a Federation was in the final analysis a monument to the fraternity of organized labor, that the average member of the rank-and-file was prone to judge a labor organization by results, and that the most tangible of results was the effective support it could render to a group of men on strike. We have seen that the leaders of the Knights of Labor had also been made aware of this popularly accepted criterion and that the wavering policies which they adopted reflected some embarrassment on their part. The inability of the Knights to establish an effective central strike fund and their ultimate rejection of such an institution did not originate in any reluctance to implement the principle of mutual aid at the expense of trade autonomy. On the contrary, those who opposed the strike fund in principle (as contrasted with the unions who apparently voted for the establishment of funds and then refused to support them by levying assessments upon their membership) combined their opposition to the funds with attempts to curtail local strike autonomy. They held that strikes were to be discountenanced as a dissipation of energy in futile pursuit of short-term objectives at the expense of an alternative program which consisted in replacing the wage economy with a utopian alternative (presumably coöperation).

It was the other way around with the national unions in the American Federation of Labor. The dominant elements in their leadership entertained no serious thought of replacing the wage system; therefore they were committed to the strike as an indispensable instrument of a policy characterized by the pursuit of immediate and measurable economic gain. Yet the A.F. of L. succeeded no more than the K. of L. in creating a strike treasury, for its largest members were fearful of unfavorable repercussions upon both their freedom to regulate strike activity within their own jurisdictions and their own exchequers. The first Federation had indeed taken steps in the direction of establishing a central system of strike benefits. In 1883, the convention passed a resolution recommending the establishment of "a fund sufficient to cope successfully with concentrated capital." The following year, a constitutional amendment was passed by the convention, to be effective if approved by a two-thirds vote in a referendum of "the actual membership of this Federation," which empowered the Federation's Legislative Committee to approve any strike or lockout for payment of benefits, provided that prior approval had been obtained from the district, state or national organization involved, then to levy an assessment not to exceed two cents weekly "upon the members under the jurisdiction of this Federation," and finally to disburse benefits not to exceed three dollars per week to each striker.[29]

Despite this brave show of specifying maximum payments and benefits, however, the work of the 1884 Convention, providing only for *ad hoc* assessments, marked a retrogression from the previous attempt to establish a permanent fund. Clues to the motive underlying this retreat are furnished by the requirement of prior approval by the affiliated organization with which the striking local was attached, and also by the provision that the entire amendment required ratification by two-thirds of "the actual membership"—a proviso which gave the larger national unions a number of votes in precise proportion to their membership. This section of the constitution was modified in 1885, however, by omission of any requirements of prior approval by the district, state, or national body of which the applicant local was a member, by the omission of the specified maximum per capita benefit payments, and also by omission of a previous requirement that a strike could not be approved by the Legislative Committee until it had been in progress at least sixty days. At the same time, the delegates referred to referendum a new constitutional provision according to which the committee was to act "as a general Board of Arbitration and Boycotting to whom shall be referred all classes of arbitration and boycotting." Thus it appeared that the Legislative Committee (the most prominent committee in the old Federation) was to receive power to terminate disputes, as a complement to its authority to approve them and to tax the Federation's affiliates in support of them. However, the delegates sought to make this amendment palatable to the affiliated organizations by providing that the Legislative Committee would assume jurisdiction only upon the application of the union involved and, further, "that they (i.e., the committee) shall not interfere with the action of any union taken on their own responsibility, nor shall they consider the request of any union which has already taken action on such responsibility."[30]

The general accommodation of the Federation, in 1886, to the requirements of the national unions was promptly reflected in a drastic change in the laws governing strikes and lockouts of affiliated unions or their own subordinates. The nationals, undoing the paper work of the old Federation, wrote their sentiment into law in the following amendment to the constitution:

While we recognize the right of each trade to manage its own affairs, it shall be the duty of the Executive Council to secure the unification of all labor organiza-

29. *Proceedings*, 1883, p. 15; 1884, p. 5.
30. *Constitution*, 1885, Art. IX; 1885, Art. X.

tions, so far as to assist each other in any justifiable boycott, and with voluntary financial help in the event of a strike or lock-out when duly approved by the Executive Council.[31]

Following this interesting definition of "unification"—and in keeping with the spirit of the occasion—was a provision for the amassing of war chests by voluntary contributions of local unions connected with national affiliates!

> When a strike has been duly approved by the Executive Council, the particulars of the difficulty, even if it be a lock-out, shall be explained in a circular issued by the President of the Federation to the unions affiliated therewith. It shall then be the duty of all affiliated societies to urge their Local Unions to make liberal financial donations in aid of the working people involved.

This virtual denial to the Federation of the opportunity to intervene decisively in labor disputes drew fire from an unexpected quarter. Samuel Gompers, the individual who had done more than any other to ensure that the integrity of the national union would pass unblemished through the process of federation, deplored this apparent lack of generosity. In 1887, a measure which would have empowered the secretary of the Federation to call for a weekly assessment of no more than five cents per capita to support a striking union, upon application of its "general officers," was passed by the convention and referred to a referendum of the membership. Since it provided that no local union could be aided without the request of its national executive, and since it further and perhaps redundantly provided that Federation assistance would be forthcoming only if the laws of the national union "have been strictly complied with" by the local in question, it appeared that the authority of the national union had been afforded every reasonable safeguard. Nevertheless, the measure was defeated in referendum; and Gompers, who thought that he could distinguish between self-interest and selfishness, concluded that

> It is evident that either the principle of the identity of interests of the toiling masses of our country have not been sufficiently encouraged, or the unions are acting upon the belief that each should help itself before attempting to aid the other. In truth, however, the establishment of the former would successfully accomplish the latter.[32]

He thereupon recommended the creation of "an Assistance Fund, to be disbursed by vote of the Executive Council upon an appeal for aid, approved by it, from an affiliated *national* or *international* trade union." The fund was to be amassed from the proceeds of a single per capita assessment of two cents; but he also suggested that further assessments in the same amount could be levied, for not more than five successive weeks, by the executive coun-

31. *Constitution,* 1886, Art. VI, Secs. 3 and 4.
32. *Proceedings,* 1887, p. 22; 1888, pp. 10–11, 17–18. Italics mine in following quotation.

cil in case of necessity. The convention refused to approve this plan for submission to referendum.

Finally (in 1889), the convention did approve of an arrangement whereby the executive council was empowered to levy a special strike assessment of two cents per head on all affiliated national and international unions on the first of January 1890. This was undertaken in support of the Federation's projected drive for the nationwide adoption of the eight-hour day (about which more presently). However, the convention also proposed the adoption of a permanent system whereby the executive council could order assessments (as usual, not to exceed two cents per capita per week) if the following conditions were satisfied: the strikes or lockouts in question had been ordered by affiliated national unions (no mention was made of strikes ordered by state or local federations, as had been the case in the legislation proposed by the first Federation); the said national unions made application for aid from the A.F. of L. "by reason of financial distress"; and the executive council "deem that such organization is entitled to receive such assistance." Such assessments were to remain in effect for periods no longer than five weeks in duration, "unless otherwise ordered by a general vote of all National or International Unions affiliated." Finally, it was provided that "Accompanying a call for an assessment shall be a circular from the President of the Federation, giving a detailed account of the strike or lockout."[33]

This constitutional amendment was approved by referendum and became law. In pressing on to victory in the convention, its proponents overcame a "minority contending it was beyond the authority of the Convention and foreign to the federal character of the organization to permit it to levy assessments on the affiliated unions." Gompers, commenting upon the outcome, replied to this group by calling their attention to the poor response to appeals for voluntary assistance which had been the only method available to him in the past. He then proceeded to reaffirm his contention that there was nothing in a program of federational support of strikes which was incompatible with the principle of national union autonomy:

We insist upon the autonomy and independence of the Trades Unions. In the contest to maintain this principle, I take second position to no man. Yet in its advocacy and to further the high mission with which that Trade Union movement is charged, we, each of our organizations, should stand ready and prepared to render every assistance to protect and advance the interest of any of our fellows with the same fervor and enthusiasm as if we were the ones the blow was directed against.

One for all and all for one is a principle long ago recognized; it is cherished in the hearts of Trade Unionists.[34]

Opposition, however, was not silenced by this eloquence; it persisted, even in high places. Treasurer Lennon of the A.F. of L. announced to the conven-

33. *Proceedings*, 1889, p. 5. (Also *Constitution*, 1889, Art. VIII.)
34. *Proceedings*, 1889, pp. 16, 31.

tion of 1891 his reasons for regarding the system of strike assessments with displeasure:

First. Because I believe said article to be in direct conflict with the fundamental principle of the Federation guaranteeing the autonomy of each affiliated organization.

Second. Because the collection of such assessments can only be made from a few of the strongest organizations.

Third. Because the amount that can be so collected is so small that it is only a delusion to organizations that depend upon it for assistance in case of any great strike or lock-out.

Fourth. Because so long as the Federation has such a law most of the Unions in trouble will apply for assistance, and the necessity of refusal by the Federation Council causes discontent and lukewarmness in the fealty toward the Federation of the Unions refused assistance. . . .[35]

Gompers, too, was impatient with the assessment system, but, whereas the treasurer believed that no aid at all was to be preferred to insufficient resources, the president (who obviously did not subscribe to the treasurer's first and nonfinancial objection) drew the conclusion that sufficient benefits could be paid out if measures were taken to increase resources. To this end he urged upon the convention of 1892 the authorization of "a series of small assessments" which would be used to build up a fund "to be placed at the disposition of the Executive Council" for the disbursement of strike loans. Four years before, the convention had refused to submit an earlier Gompers proposal for an "Assistance Fund" to the membership, but, on this occasion it softened to the point of directing the executive council to submit a plan to the affiliated unions for their consideration.[36] It is possible that one factor which contributed to this change in heart was the loan feature, which in effect meant that the proposed fund would be of the revolving or self-perpetuating variety so that, once built up, it would require no continuing assessments for its maintenance.

In any event, Gompers' victory was but a parliamentary triumph, for the major downswing which began in 1893 followed hard on the convention's action, and the executive council decided not to submit a plan to referendum. This decision might well have been motivated by a reluctance to press for any plan which called for an outlay of money by the unions in a time of financial distress, when dues-paying membership was falling off. But it is also possible that it was the prospect of success, rather than failure, which deterred Gompers and the council. For, while a union which was not contemplating a strike might well have voted against a plan under which it would have been subjected to additional taxation in a period of fiscal stringency, a union which expected to conduct a strike would have regarded itself primarily as a beneficiary of, rather than a contributor to such an arrangement. If most of the

35. Proceedings, 1891, p. 20.
36. Proceedings, 1892, p. 15.

unions polled contemplated strike action, two consequences were easily fore-seeable: (a) that the Assistance Fund scheme would receive a thumping endorsement, and (b) that, after endorsement, it would be drained and bank-rupt with singular dispatch. Now, as Gompers was well aware, the tendency of unions to embark upon strikes against wage cuts in times of depression was apparently as unfailing as the annual migrations of the lemmings into the sea, and invariably bore the same result. And Gompers himself, in 1888, had lectured the delegates upon the art of striking:

To know when to strike, [he told them] and particularly when not to strike is a science not yet fully understood. To strike upon a falling market, or being in-sufficiently organized, or if organized, not yet properly equipped with the ammu-nition so necessary to a successful strike—funds—is unquestionably the height of ignorance.[37]

In 1888 he had used this argument to support his position in favor of the assessment plan which had been defeated by a referendum vote; in 1893, it served to dissuade him from pressing for the creation of a strike fund, which, under the circumstances, might well have had the effect of inducing the affiliated unions "to strike upon a falling market," without being able to pro-vide all—or even any—of them with the necessary ammunition. It will be recalled that his colleague, the treasurer, had predicted that the existence of any fund raised by the Federation would induce all its embattled affiliates to apply for assistance, while the fund so accumulated would be inadequate in size to subsidize "any great strike or lockout" (or, for that matter, a large number of lesser stoppages occurring simultaneously). Gompers might not have placed much weight on these objections when they were raised in 1891; in 1893, however, it is probable that he entertained a much higher opinion of their relevance.

But Gompers' retreat had been orderly; he soon returned to the good fight. In 1896, a new administration proposal for a defense fund was put for-ward, but it was rejected, as was a similar amendment, whose sponsorship was not calculated to improve its chances of endorsement, since it was proposed by a Central Labor Union (of Toledo).[38] Why this move for the creation of a strike fund was not reported out to a referendum we do not know; perhaps the national unions felt that they had been thoroughly "deflated" by the strong business downswing and lacked either the will or the resources to coöperate in financial resistance to further deflationary pressures.

Two years later, however, the Federation adopted what was essentially a voluntary form of strike insurance, whereby payment of a per capita tax of five cents per month into "a common defense fund" was optional with each affiliated union, but "no organization shall receive assistance from the

37. *Proceedings,* 1888, p. 11.
38. *Proceedings,* 1896, pp. 70, 72.

defense fund unless it has contributed to the same, for a period of at least one year." Since assistance was specified on a per capita basis—three dollars per week for a maximum of ten weeks in any one year—it was also provided that no individual in a participant organization could be entitled to benefits "unless he was a member prior to the date on which the strike or lockout began." The executive council's authority, under this plan, was somewhat restricted: upon a request for help from any member of the plan, the council had "the right" to investigate the dispute and essay a settlement (in which case it was provided that "the expense of such investigation shall be charged to the defense fund"); and, after it chose to exercise that right, it had the further "right to refuse assistance from the defense fund." But it was also "provided . . . that the Union so refused shall have the right of appeal to the next convention." However, in the case of local unions directly affiliated with the Federation (local trade or federal labor unions) which participated in this scheme, approval of the executive council prior to the commencement of a stoppage was made a prerequisite for the granting of aid.[39]

Gompers' reaction to this arrangement was characteristic. He requested that the law be modified in order that weaker organizations, which might not have contributed sufficiently to the fund to be eligible for benefits, be permitted to draw on the fund. This suggestion, clearly implying subsidization of the smaller and weaker unions by those greater in numerical and financial strength, ran counter to the principle underlying the scheme which had been adopted, and it apparently received scant consideration from the convention. But the administration succeeded in forcing a compromise the following year when the voluntary plan was abandoned by the convention, and provision was made once more for assessment:

> The Executive Council shall have power to declare a levy of one cent per member per week on all affiliated unions for a period not exceeding ten weeks in any one year, to assist in the support of an affiliated organization engaged in a protracted strike or lockout.

The passage of this amendment represented a victory for the "means test" over "mutual insurance" in the determination of the basic principle governing the disbursement of strike benefits by the Federation. But, in order to gain this important point, Gompers had to abandon his cherished fund in favor of the less desirable method of raising money by *ad hoc* assessment. For, although the adoption of legislation to create a continuing fund was moved in 1900[40] and again in 1909 and 1914, these attempts all failed.[41] The majority apparently were willing to create a fund only if disbursements were to be made on an insurance basis; this point was illustrated in the establish-

39. *Constitution*, 1898, Art. X; see also *Proceedings*, 1898, p. 12; 1899, p. xii.
40. *Proceedings*, 1900, pp. 53, 126.
41. Lewis L. Lorwin, *The American Federation of Labor* (Washington: Brookings, 1933), p. 112; see also pp. 71–72.

ment in 1902 of a fund which was made available only to the local trade and federal labor unions and which was created and maintained solely by revenue diverted from their per capita payments to the Federation.

Furthermore, Gompers' half-victory was not exploited with vigor, for the executive council was reluctant to put its constitutional power of assessment to the test. When he appeared before the convention of the Bricklayers in 1903 to convince that reluctant group of the desirability of affiliation with the A.F. of L., Gompers assured them that the financial sacrifice implied in the assessment authority of the executive council was in fact insufficient to dissuade even the most prudent from membership in the Federation:

> The Executive Council of the A.F. of L. has power to levy an assessment of one cent per member per week for ten weeks in any one year. In the history of the A.F. of L. there have been but three assessments levied, in all amounting to about twelve cents. Even during the great strike of the Miners in the Anthracite region in Pennsylvania last year, no assessment was levied.[42]

Over the following decade (1904 to 1914), according to Lorwin, the Federation levied assessments in the amount of only $169,553.[43] Over the thirty-year period, 1900 to 1931, about $250,000 was assessed; and, since some of the assessments were raised for organizing purposes and others were earmarked for legal expenses in connection with the Danbury Hatters' case, "the total collected for purely strike aid in 30 years is thus less than $140,000." Indeed, an alternative method of raising funds, that of appealing to the generosity of the affiliated unions, was resorted to more frequently than the method of mandatory assessment. This might, with justice, be regarded as a tribute to the altruism of the unions; it is also a measure of the Federation's lack of power.

The outcome was as the president had foreseen. Without a continuing strike fund, failure of a program of Federation strike aid was virtually assured. Under a fund plan, collections were not intimately associated with disbursements, whereas, under the assessment system, the Federation was obliged to test the compliance of its affiliates each time a crisis arose and at such times the danger of embarrassment to the executive council through lack of response by the unions was most acute. Rather than risk noncompliance, the leadership of the Federation chose the way of discretion and left the question to the conscience of each affiliated union.

It is almost superfluous to add that the Federation received no authority over the strike activities of its national affiliates comparable to that which some of the latter possessed with respect to their locals. The nationals jealously guarded their power to initiate, conduct, and terminate strikes; indeed, as we have seen, their concern in this direction largely motivated their steadfast refusal to build up the financial strength of the Federation, for their spokesmen feared that the power to dispense aid was both a necessary and suf-

42. *Proceedings,* Bricklayers, 1903, p. 468.
43. Lorwin, *A. F. of L.,* p. 125. See also pp. 362–363.

ficient condition of the power to regulate activity. Gompers, of course, denied that it was a sufficient condition; whether or not it was a necessary one was of indifference to him, because he had no desire to extend the power of the Federation over its affiliates. Indeed, what demand for such power did exist originated on the side of the affiliated unions themselves. Thus while Gompers favored the creation of a fund and the nationals opposed it, he opposed the assumption of authority over strike activities—a position for which he was bitterly attacked by some of the national unions. Opposition to this manifestation of abstinence on the part of the A.F. of L. came chiefly from embattled affiliates, however, who were willing, as an emergency measure, to lower the standard of autonomy before the ensign of solidarity, since they stood to gain (or so they believed) from a policy favorable to sympathetic striking. But the national unions had fought the city centrals on this issue, and it was hardly possible that they would cede to a national federation what they had successfully denied to the local groups. This basic attitude of the national unions supported Gompers in his refusal to attempt to initiate sympathetic action in support of striking unions; and it enabled him to stick to his guns when appeals for aid became numerous with the onset of depression in 1893 and striking organizations were "insisting that . . . (other unions) should be ordered to strike by the Executive Council on pain of having their charters revoked and denied fraternal recognition."[44] Perhaps the most celebrated of Gompers' refusals to pledge the strike support of the affiliates of the Federation occurred in the Pullman strike of 1894 and the steel strike in 1901.[45]

44. *Proceedings*, 1893, pp. 15–16.
45. In the former case, it appeared that the strike was lost by the time that Debs requested the A.F. of L. to call a sympathetic strike; and the executive council in fact advised "that all connected with the American Federation of Labor now on sympathetic strike should return to work, and those who contemplate going out on sympathetic strike are advised to remain at their usual vocations." This refusal to commit reserves to a lost cause, however, did not prevent the A.F. of L. from later contributing nearly eight hundred dollars to the legal fund of the vanquished American Railway Union whose leaders were charged with contempt for having violated an injunction. (Ray Ginger, *The Bending Cross* [New Brunswick: Rutgers University, 1949], pp. 149, 153–154; also John R. Commons and Associates, *History of Labour in the United States* [New York: Macmillan, 1935], v. II, p. 503.) In the steel strike, also, Gompers, although he offered "moral and financial support" (according to Perlman and Taft), appeared not to have considered the cause—a closed shop in all the plants of the newly formed United States Steel Corporation—attainable. "When the steel corporation was organized by J. Pierpont Morgan and Company, Shaffer, then president of the Amalgamated, contrary to my advice, made a demand upon Morgan for the establishment of the closed union shop. Morgan resented Shaffer's demand and flatly declared he would oppose him and break him if it took five years." (Samuel Gompers, *Seventy Years of Life and Labor* [New York: Dutton, reissued in 1943], v. II, pp. 127–128.) Gompers apparently believed that a strike could not be won; but there is evidence that he failed to appreciate—or to concede—that the union could not survive as an efficient bargaining organization unless it succeeded in organizing all the plants in the new corporation. (See Commons *et al.*, *History of Labour*, v. IV, ch. IX; also, Ch. 2, above.) In both instances, Gompers refused to

Collective Bargaining

The intervention of the national union in the field of collective bargaining ranged from the virtual supersession (in a few cases) of local discretion in the negotiation and administration of industry-wide trade agreements, through prescription of union standards of employment to which the locals were required to adhere in their own trade negotiations, down to the dispatching of expert negotiators (usually in the persons of officers of the national unions) to aid locals with bargaining problems. The American Federation of Labor, however, was granted no authority to prescribe economic standards for its affiliates. Its activity in this area was confined to the last type of service activity, the most ambitious instances of which were the attempts by Gompers and other important labor leaders (especially John Mitchell of the Miners) to intervene in the steel and anthracite coal strikes (1900–1902). Gompers and Mitchell sought to win both unions and employers to an acceptance of moderation and arbitration in place of striking. (Like outstanding American labor leaders of previous generations, Gompers was opposed to the strike. But, whereas men like Sylvis, Stephens, Powderly, and Debs based their opposition to striking upon their conviction that it was impossible for labor's gains to be at all commensurate with its sacrifices under the "wages system," Gompers opposed the strike because he believed that superior results could be achieved through peaceful measures and within the existing institutional order.)

The results of this activity, however, were frequently considered negligible by the unions, and, on one notable occasion at least (the steel strike of 1901), it was implied that Gompers and his colleagues had subordinated ends to means, that in stressing the peaceful approach, they had failed to press for a favorable resolution of specific issues as vigorously as they might have. For this reason, Gompers' favorite vehicle of coöperation, the National Civic Federation, became suspect in many labor circles. There might well have been some merit in these charges (scholarly and sympathetic authority sides with the accusers),[46] but it must be remembered that, however ineffectual the

---

advocate a sympathetic strike and in both instances he pledged "moral and financial support"—even when it was apparent to him that victory was highly improbable. This would indicate that his refusal to espouse the sympathetic strike (he had no authority, in any event, to order sovereign national unions to strike) was based, not upon the probability of success in the instance at hand, but rather upon opposition to this weapon in principle and upon his determination to protect national autonomy in this vital area of activity.

46. Perlman and Taft believe that Gompers was so anxious to secure recognition in principle of the Amalgamated Association of Iron, Steel and Tin Workers by the newly formed United States Steel Corporation that he failed to appreciate the position of the union's president, who insisted that his organization could not be secure until all of the plants of the corporation were recognized. (Commons *et al.*, *History of Labour*, v. IV, p. 108.)

method of persuasion proved in the opening years of this century, no alternative was available to its exponents in the executive councils of the A.F. of L.

For a while, however, it appeared that both the old Federation and its successor might play a far more direct role in the economic fortunes of their constituents. It was believed that a Federation was the proper agency to secure the adoption of the eight-hour day in all industries. When the old Federation appeared to be moribund, some sought to transform it from an unexciting lobbying organization into an economic body by placing it at the vanguard of a new shorter-hours movement in 1884. A similar demand was made at the A.F. of L. convention of 1888, which went on record as endorsing a demand for the general adoption of the eight-hour day in 1890. In 1889, however, the strategy of piecemeal attack was substituted for the concept of a general and simultaneous advance. It was decided to select one union, the Carpenters, for the first test, to support them with the resources of the other affiliates until they had gained their objective, then to support another group, and so on. The Carpenters did achieve notable progress in 1890, but the A.F. of L.'s second choice, the Miners, was unfortunate, since they were too weakly organized to stand any chance of success.

The failure of these Federation-led "movements" can be laid primarily to the inertia of the national unions, or at least to their unwillingness to grant sufficient funds to the Federation. The old Federation, it will be recalled, did submit to referendum a provision which would have empowered the legislative committee to levy special assessments for and to disburse benefits to the members of unions whose strikes it approved. But it rejected a proposal from the Cigar Makers whereby each affiliate would have contributed 2 per cent of its revenues toward a strike fund. "In consequence the Federation was unable to expend a dollar in aid of the strike."[47] The record of the present A.F. of L. was better. As reported above, the Convention of 1889 did empower the executive council to levy strike assessments on all national affiliates, and it did supply the Carpenters with funds. While grateful for this assistance, however, the Carpenters' secretary, who was also the secretary of the Federation, obviously believed that the sum raised was not as great as expected. In reporting to his own convention in 1890, he noted that

The American Federation of Labor did all in its power to aid us, and furnished us with over $12,000. We also got efficient help in local cases from the unions connected with the Federation. But the system of assessment provided for by the Federation was entirely new to the national trade unions affiliated, and many of them could not and cannot pay the assessment until their national conventions meet. Hence the Federation was crippled to quite an extent, and the amount levied on the unions was so small that the results were not what they will be in the future after the system is perfected by the next convention of the Federation.

47. Commons et al., History of Labour, v. II, p. 377.

Still the amounts received at various times came when they were indeed badly needed.[48]

There is no evidence of what McGuire had in mind when he referred to perfecting the system of assessments. It is possible that he meant the establishment of a strike fund which Gompers did propose to the convention. The latter empowered the executive council to submit such a plan to referendum, but, as noted above, the subsequent advent of depression made it unwise to press for adoption. Under the imperfect system of which McGuire complained, the sum received by the A.F. of L. during the one-year period 1889–1890 ($12,060.64) actually constituted about one-sixth of all moneys paid to striking locals by the United Brotherhood for the two years, July 1, 1888—July 24, 1890 ($72,119.98). Had an equal amount been received from the Federation in the first year and had the contributions from the Brotherhood's own resources remained unchanged, the Federation's share of the total strike aid expended would have amounted to about one-third. (Actually, the net contribution of the A.F. of L. was reduced by the amount of the Brotherhood's assessments paid to the Federation over the two-year period, which totaled $3,200.80.) This, in relative terms, would have constituted a substantial contribution, but it is apparent that the efficiency of Federation aid was dependent upon the internal strength of the organization aided.

This was illustrated in the case of the coal miners, who had been selected by the A.F. of L. convention to make their bid for the eight-hour day as soon as the Carpenters' movement had been terminated. The United Mine Workers, however, had organized no more than 10 per cent of the workers in their jurisdiction at the time, and, thus being convinced that they "were not in a condition to ask for eight hours . . . let the matter drop for another year."[49] But the next convention of the A.F. of L., according to Chris Evans, a leading figure in the miners' union and also secretary of the Federation at the time, "reaffirmed the conclusion that we should demand eight hours, and, to the extent they had the power to do so, ordered us to make the demand at this time." The miners were to demand eight hours on May 1, 1891. The miners' employers in the Connellsville coke region seized the initiative, however, by demanding that the union accept a reduction in wages and also "agree to work not less than nine hours per day, to continue for three years." Thus the miners had the struggle forced upon them prematurely, and their President, John Rae, appealed to Gompers for financial aid by levying immediately the assessment which the convention had approved. But Gompers refused to do this, probably because he realized that the strike had no chance of success. Subsequently, when the official starting date of May 1 approached, the miners once again refused to strike. This episode reveals clearly that the aid contem-

48. *Proceedings,* 1890, pp. 18 and 19.
49. Commons *et al., History of Labour,* v. II, p. 477; Chris Evans, *History of the Mine Workers of America* (Indianapolis, 1918), v. II, p. 106; p. 95.

plated by the Federation in its version of a shorter-hours movement was in effect so limited in amount that it could not prove decisive if the union aided was not sufficiently strong to win on its own. Under such circumstances, the Federation was hardly in a position to "order" any sovereign union to strike.

In electing not to assume a dominant position in the movements for shorter hours in which various national and local unions were engaged, the Federation passed up an opportunity to intervene actively in the collective bargaining activities of its affiliates. The demand for increased leisure had played a significant role in uniting unionists in diverse trades into virtually all the "movements," local and national, which had preceded the American Federation and its immediate predecessor. This was true for reasons both psychological and economic in nature. The various "shorter hours movements" seem always to have borne deep emotional significance for the country's workers, who consistently demonstrated their willingness to forego an increment to their incomes in favor of an increment to their weekly stores of leisure. Thus, despite the aloofness of the leadership of both the trade unions and the Knights, the old Federation's attempt to inaugurate a national eight-hour movement in 1884–1885 derived great impetus from the enthusiastic response of the men in the "shipyard, shop, and mill" (to quote from a well-known jingle on the eight-hour day).[50] The popularity of "greater comforts, shorter hours" was further demonstrated in the Federation's second campaign, launched by the convention of 1889. Two years later, Gompers reported that

It is worthy of note that, in all the answers received upon the statistical blanks sent to the Trade Unions in this country, three blank spaces were provided for answers to the question: "What, in the opinion of your Union, are the three most important questions that the A.F. of L. should concentrate its efforts to secure?" While the two other answers differ materially, every Union answered: "A reduction in the hours of labor."[51]

In addition to its unusual popularity, moreover, the shorter-hours movement possessed the merit of being peculiarly well suited for adoption by a federation of different trades. It was a denominator of economic interest com-

---

50.   Ship-yard, shop and mill:
                               Eight hours for work,
                               Eight hours for rest,
                           Eight hours for what we will.

This was written by George E. McNeill, who, with George Gunton and Ira Steward, formed a trio which worked with the singlemindedness of dedicated zealots for the cause of Eight Hours. Rhyme seems to have been one of their favorite vehicles of persuasion. The jingles of Steward and his wife are well known, and McNeill progressed from the specimen quoted above (which appeared in the report of the Federation's Special Committee on the eight-hour question in 1890) to a more ambitious and distressing effort which followed faithfully the rhythms of Longfellow's "Evangeline."

51. *Proceedings*, 1891, p. 13.

mon to men in otherwise unrelated occupations (see above, Chapter 13, fn. 28). Furthermore, since the demand for a reduction in hours commonly was linked with the requirement that wage rates be raised sufficiently to maintain weekly income, adoption of a uniform reduction in hours would have resulted in equal percentage increases in wage rates, so that the national wage structure would have remained unaltered in this respect. Thus, the early movements for shorter hours were somewhat akin to the later phenomenon of uniform, or "pattern," increases in wages with which the present generation of trade unionists became familiar in the period following the end of the second World War.

But, despite the undeniable popularity and apparent feasibility of the demand for shorter hours, the national unions in the A.F. of L. refused to support it effectively as a Federation program. For although a general movement for shorter hours might have been feasible, it was not a matter of vital concern to the dominant national affiliates. While maintenance (or reduction) of wage differentials between various localities or regions was a matter of such importance to the local unions in the same trade that it frequently induced them to surrender important economic and administrative prerogatives to the national union in that trade, the preservation of existing wage differences between relatively "unrelated" industries (which, to repeat, could have been ensured by a uniform reduction of hours with maintenance of weekly income) was of relatively little concern to the national unions in those industries. Achievement of the eight-hour day in one trade was not conditioned upon its achievement in others. Furthermore, raising funds for a Federation-led drive by per capita assessment meant that the larger national affiliates would have borne the brunt of the pecuniary sacrifice involved. The larger unions were unwilling to assent to such an arrangement, since they were in a better position to achieve a reduction in hours by their own efforts than were the smaller organizations which stood to benefit financially from a Federation-supported "movement." And since, in the A.F. of L., representation, as well as taxation, was in proportion to numbers, the larger unions were able to prevent passage of revenue-raising provisions which were necessary to the expansion of the Federation's economic activities.

EXCLUSIVE JURISDICTION

In addition to respecting the autonomy of its national affiliates, the Federation was committed to the principle of exclusive jurisdiction, which was implied in the authority of the national union to exercise exclusive control over its own jurisdiction.

Exclusive control had been threatened from various directions. The most immediate and serious challenge was presented by the dual organizations established by the Knights of Labor, which, in their effort to bring the skilled trades under the aegis of the Knights, admitted into their ranks individuals and locals which had been expelled from national unions and which, on occasion, undermined the standards of employment which the national unions were striving to secure. Indeed, as we have seen, it was the struggle with the Knights which elevated the principle of exclusive jurisdiction to its position of unchallenged eminence in the American trade union movement, eliminating as a practical alternative the possibility of peaceful sharing of a trade jurisdiction by two or more sovereign organizations.

Another menace was presented by local and regional federations of local unions (including the District Assemblies of the Knights), which challenged, not the administrative jurisdiction of the national union, but its economic control over the relevant trade area. For the local federation sought to establish prior control over the local union, which ran counter to the fact that exclusive jurisdiction implied unchallenged control by the national union over all the local unions in its trade.

Furthermore, the national union itself frequently threatened the concept of exclusive jurisdiction. This occurred when one national union sought to organize all or part of a trade area to which another national claimed exclusive right. In such situations, of course, each disputant accused the other of dualism. The forces of innovation which blurred and, at times, completely erased "natural" craft barriers to "free entry," frequently led to boundary disputes between affected unions. In addition to such examples of "opportunistic dualism," to use Saposs' terminology, dual national unions were occasionally created by radical leaders for political purposes (notably in the cigar industry), although, in this country, "ideologic dualism" was much less important than it was abroad.[52]

To some extent, the A.F. of L. demonstrated its adherence to the principle of exclusive jurisdiction by virtue of its acceptance of the principles of national autonomy and dominance. Thus, the menace of the local federation was efficiently removed as a result of the development of the system of representation which the nationals insisted on as a condition of their participation in the Federation. Furthermore, by its lack of authority over such "internal" affairs of the national unions as policies governing the individual's affiliation, admission, discipline, striking and collective bargaining, the Federation itself was eliminated as a fifth challenger to exclusive control by the national union over its own jurisdiction.

But the A.F. of L. did not confine itself to a passive respect for national autonomy. It was committed, by virtue of two resolutions passed in 1899,[53] to guarantee to each national affiliate not only self-government but also exclusive control over its own jurisdiction. One resolution provided that, in order to reduce "strife and bitterness" between affiliated national unions, each new applicant for a charter shall henceforth

clearly state and define in its laws all the branches of trade over which it claims jurisdiction, and should such laws cover branches of trades already chartered by

52. Saposs, *Left-Wing Unionism*, pp. 10–12, Chapters V–VIII.
53. *Proceedings*, 1899, pp. 156 and 136.

the American Federation of Labor, then such charter shall be denied until passed upon by the American Federation in convention assembled, when the claims of all parties shall receive a hearing.

The other resolution proclaimed that "this principle of trade autonomy guarantees to the weaker crafts the same measure of protection that the stronger bodies can maintain for themselves."

We shall presently consider situations in which, in order to guarantee exclusive jurisdiction to one union, it was necessary to abridge the autonomy of another; but at this point it is pertinent to note that, whereas adherence to the principle of national autonomy implied an essentially negative policy for the Federation, support of the principle of exclusive jurisdiction implied affirmative action as well.

The method whereby the Federation sought to implement the latter principle consisted in the issuing of a charter or "certificate of affiliation" to each union, in which the latter's jurisdiction was rather carefully spelled out, and in reserving that charter to the union in question exclusively. Most frequently this consisted in merely accepting the organization's own definition of its area of operations. By either withholding or withdrawing charters from rebellious or rival groups, the Federation sought to strengthen the control of the "legitimate" jurisdiction against (1) secession from within or independent local unionism and (2) aggression from outside rivals.

Secession or Independent Local Unionism

In 1885, the first Federation declared as one of its objects that "No organization which has seceded from any State, national, or international organization shall be allowed a representation or recognition from this Federation." The following year, its successor reënacted this bit of legislation and in 1887 added unions which were "suspended or expelled from" Federation affiliates to the proscribed list. In the early years of the new Federation's existence, enforcement of this provision took the form of aiding the national union to maintain or establish control over its various local jurisdictions. This is illustrated in the case of the New York local which seceded from the National Alliance of Stage Employees in 1894 and declared its intention of preventing members of the latter organization from working in New York by striking any theater in which they might be employed. Whereupon the A.F. of L. convention passed a resolution "to aid and support, by all proper means, any and all members of said National Alliance finding employment in the theatres of the city of New York," and resolved further, "That the organizer of the American Federation of Labor for New York City be and is hereby instructed to lend his assistance to the National Alliance in organizing a local of that craft in the city of New York."[54]

54. *Constitution,* 1885, Art. IV, Sec. 3; 1886, Art. IV, Sec. 2 ("Local" were substituted for "State" organizations; 1887, Art. IV, Sec. 2; *Proceedings,* 1894, p. 31.

The Federation sought also to bring under the control of national unions local unions in their respective jurisdictions which had been organized by the Federation itself. These "federal trade or local labor unions" were chartered directly by the A.F. of L., but the latter made it understood that their independent existence was conditioned upon the absence of a national union in their jurisdiction. At the very first convention of the old Federation, it was established that "No local Trades or Labor Union shall be entitled to a representation in the sessions of this Federation where International or National Unions of said craft exist, or where there are Trades Assemblies or Councils in the locality."[55] There was some reluctance on the part of the locals to join the appropriate national unions, however. The reasons were not discussed, but it may be assumed that financial considerations were important, for the per capita taxes which the local trades unions paid to the A.F. of L. were considerably lower than those which other locals were required to pay to their national unions.[56] Nevertheless, Gompers announced his determination to place each directly affiliated local in its proper national jurisdiction, and he did not hesitate to revoke the Federation charters in order to enforce compliance:

There have been cases of local unions of certain trades that were directly affiliated to the American Federation of Labor, which, when a National Union of their trade was organized, desired to retain their direct affiliation with us and refused to join the National Union. After repeated attempts to persuade them to attach themselves to the National Union, and their failure to comply, I have felt it incumbent upon me to revoke their charters.[57]

That Gompers' assertion of authority in this particular area met with the approval of the affiliated national unions is reflected in the passage of the following constitutional amendment in 1893:

When a National or International Union has been formed the President shall notify all Local Unions of that trade to affiliate with such National or International Union, and unless said notification be complied with within three months, their charter shall be revoked.[58]

55. *Proceedings*, 1881, p. 17.
56. The per capita tax of the local trades and federal labor unions was fixed at three cents annually in 1881. In 1882, each local union's annual assessment was set at ten dollars plus a per capita tax of one cent on membership over five hundred. In 1888, the assessment was changed to a monthly per capita tax of one cent. In 1897, this was raised to two cents. In 1899, Gompers reported that "the local unions are usually required to pay a higher per capita tax to their national organization than is required by the American Federation of Labor from the locals which had no national head. The officers of the nationals largely perform duties toward their respective locals that the officers of the American Federation of Labor perform to the locals holding charters direct from it." (*Proceedings*, 1899, p. 8.)
57. *Proceedings*, 1890, p. 14.
58. *Constitution*, 1893, Art. VII, Sec. 2. See also *Proceedings*, 1895, p. 72; *Constitution*, 1896, Art. IV, Sec. 1.

Even where the independent existence of a directly affiliated local was justified, however, some control by a national union over its jurisdiction could be threatened if some of its members, presumably not in good standing, could find asylum within the local trade or federal labor union. Hence the Federation's next step was to ensure to the best of its ability that its affiliated locals did not give aid and comfort to the enemy of the national union. To this end, it provided, first that "no federal labor union shall be recognized as affiliated if its membership consists of a majority of active members of trade unions," and, second, that "Only *bona fide* wage workers who are not members of, or eligible to membership in, other trade unions shall be eligible as delegates from Federal Trade Unions."

Rival National Unionism

Federation policy was designed to protect the approved national jurisdiction from encroachment by unauthorized national unions as well as from fragmentation by insubordinate or reluctant local groups. Jurisdictional disputes involving national unions exclusively may be classified, from one point of view, into two groups: those in which one party to the dispute—whether complainant or alleged aggressor—was not affiliated with the Federation, and those cases in which both parties were affiliated.

In jurisdictional disputes to which unaffiliated unions were parties, Federation policy consisted in denying charters to the outsiders if their applications were opposed by affiliates. Thus, on the objection of the United Brotherhood of Carpenters and Joiners, the convention of 1888 withheld a certificate of affiliation from the Amalgamated Society of Carpenters (the American branch of the British union) because "it has been proved to a demonstration that it is detrimental to the interests of labor to have more than one organization in any trade . . ."[59] In 1896, the Federation refused to charter the United Order of Box Makers because the Amalgamated Wood Workers objected. And two years later the dissent of the Brotherhood of Painters and Decorators served to disqualify the National Paper Hangers' Protective and Beneficial Association of America. In the latter case, the convention, while expressing sympathy with the objective of organizing the group of workers in question, carefully confined itself to the recommendation that the Brotherhood of Painters and Decorators "be urged to grant the Paper Hangers of the country the fullest possible jurisdiction of their craft, but as members of the Brotherhood. . . ."

Complaints did not originate solely in affiliated unions; it was not uncommon for outside organizations to protest the chartering by the A.F. of L. of

59. *Proceedings,* 1888, p. 19. In 1891, however, the Amalgamated Society was admitted. (*Proceedings,* 1891, p. 6.) Following a series of disputes with the Brotherhood, it was finally ordered to amalgamate with the latter in 1924. See also *Proceedings,* 1896, pp. 66–67; 1898, pp. 51 and 131.

groups which, in their opinion, encroached upon their own jurisdictions, even though the latter were not legitimatized by certificates of affiliation. In such cases, Federation practice was usually determined by the nature of the relationship existing between the A.F. of L. and the complainant. If the protest emanated from a hostile source, it merely served as an additional inducement to grant the disputed charter. Thus a certificate was issued by the executive council to the Tile Layers' union over the objection of some of the local and district assemblies of the Knights of Labor.[60] To the latter it doubtless appeared that this procedure of granting charters to unions whose jurisdictions were disputed by unaffiliated groups was nothing but Federation-sponsored dualism—especially since, on other occasions, the executive committee withheld charters from unions upon the request of certain organizations which, like the Knights, were unaffiliated but which, unlike the Knights, were considered friendly by the Federation.

By refusing to authorize others to organize the jurisdictions of such friendly outsiders, the Federation made possible future affiliation by the latter unions. The Bricklayers are an outstanding example of an outside union which was wooed—for twenty years—by the Federation in this manner. Mention has been made of instances in which Federation charters to local unions of tuck pointers were revoked on complaint of the Bricklayers. It remains to add that, in these and some other cases, the reaction of the Bricklayers was solicited by Secretary Morrison of the Federation, who corresponded with Secretary Dobson of the Bricklayers in order to determine whether the latter's organization had any objection to action either proposed or taken by the executive council of the A.F. of L. The officers of the union appreciated this consideration, and, on one occasion, the editor of their Journal, in an editorial entitled, *WHY WE SHOULD AFFILIATE,* wrote:

Because during the past few years (and especially do I refer to this present year) the A.F. of L. has refused charters at our request where titles were sought which covered the jurisdiction of workers we claim control of.[61]

60. *Proceedings,* 1888, p. 33. So high a priority did the Federation eventually assign to the elimination of trade-union activity by the Knights that it was even willing to side with an insubordinate local against a national affiliate in order to further this prime objective. The United Brewery Workmen, a union which was affiliated with both the Federation and the Knights at the time, requested the Executive Committee of the A.F. of L. to compel the Chicago Trades and Labor Assembly to expel a Chicago local because the latter had refused to pay assessments to the national. The local, however, was opposed to the national's policy of affiliation with the Order and for that reason refused to honor its financial obligations. Since the national union also attempted to coerce its two Boston locals into joining the Order, the Federation's executive council "voted that while the assessment on Local 18, of Chicago, was regularly levied, it would refuse to support the national union in this instance, unless it withdrew from the K. of L." (*Report of Executive Committee,* 1895, p. 27.)

61. *Proceedings,* 1903, p. 468. Also, pp. 478–483.

Gompers' action in urging the return of members who had left the un-affiliated Railroad Brotherhoods to join Eugene Debs' American Railway Union in the Pullman strike of 1894 is likewise indicative of the Federation's penchant for playing favorites among outsiders in matters of jurisdiction.

In his autobiography, Gompers asserted that "I have never been willing to sacrifice fundamental principles for mere growth."[62] If we are to accept this statement at face value, we must reconcile his Federation's practice of chartering unions charged with dualism by some outside groups, not only with its stated adherence to the principle of exclusive jurisdiction, but also with its contrary practice of withholding charters at the behest of other out-side organizations. One could reconcile these practices with each other by assuming first, that only chartered unions were legitimate, second, that every trade jurisdiction, including those yet unborn and hence undefined, was owned in the first instance by the Federation, and, third, that the Federation possessed full and final authority to issue or to withhold charters at its dis-cretion.

The Federation's affirmative policy of seeking to guarantee exclusive rights of jurisdiction to the "legitimate" national union by virtue of its con-trol of the charter was especially significant in disputes in which both parties were affiliates. In such cases mere passive respect for national autonomy was not helpful in dealing jurisdictional justice. Since jurisdictional disputes were essentially conflicts involving boundary definitions, it was inevitable that one side's autonomy be abridged in favor of the other's. To avoid inter-national anarchy it was necessary that the Federation possess sufficient au-thority to interpret the charters which it had issued, to make awards and, if necessary, to revoke its charters.

Now this implied that the Federation did not pass title to a jurisdiction in conferring a charter upon a national union; it retained some powers after the charter had been issued. Yet it could not be maintained that the affiliated union merely held its charter in tenure. The jealously cultivated autonomy of the national union ensured that its charter could not be revoked by the issuing agency because of failure to satisfy certain standards of behavior and per-formance, since no authority except the union itself could determine such standards. For example, while one of the stated objects of the Federation in granting the charter was the extension of union organization throughout the jurisdiction in question, failure of the chartered union to organize its jurisdic-tion thoroughly did not constitute grounds for revocation of the "certificate." The union's control over its jurisdiction was based less upon stewardship than upon property right, which included the right to abuse as well as to use.[63]

---

62. Gompers, *Seventy Years*, v. I, p. 414; v. II, p. 138.

63. The later Congress of Industrial Organizations appears to have evolved a some-what different approach to this subject. In revoking (at its 1949 convention) charters from some of its affiliated national unions for their failure to comply with certain cri-

But, while the Federation, both in theory and in practice, observed a policy of *laissez-faire* regarding these and other "internal" activities of the national unions, it was apparently granted some power over the conduct of their "foreign" affairs. It will be recalled that the national union regarded the power to define its own jurisdiction as an attribute of its autonomy; but the authority of the A.F. of L. superseded that of the national at this point. The latter's right in its charter could not be construed as absolute if the Federation was to honor its obligation to reserve exclusive control over each jurisdiction to the appropriate union.

The Federation, nevertheless, was markedly reluctant to exercise its jurisdictional authority. This was illustrated notably in its approach to the jurisdictional problems raised by technological innovation and the development of large-scale industry. The founders of the Federation were aware of this menace to established skill; but, in their "Address" to the Knights, they asserted that the "Trades Unions" were the appropriate organizations "to protect the skilled labor of America from being reduced to beggary, and to sustain the standard of American workmanship and skill."[64] Changing technology, however, often led to jurisdictional disputes between "Trades Unions," as noted above (p. 405, in our third "challenge" to exclusive jurisdiction). Gompers apparently was concerned with the inadequacy of the traditional basis of jurisdiction in the light of the changing industrial environment. To the convention of 1888 he proposed—in highly tentative fashion, to be sure—a scheme whereby direct representation in the convention would be transferred to "industrial divisions." His remarks, which seem to have been

---

teria of satisfactory performance in their "internal" affairs, it seems to be adopting the "tenure" approach to the issued charter. The most widely publicized grounds for revocation was Communist domination of the union executive, but one union on the right also lost its affiliation at that convention: the Retail, Wholesale, and Department Store Employees' union was stripped of its charter for failure to make appreciable headway in organizing its jurisdiction.

The action of the 1953 convention in expelling the allegedly gangster-dominated International Longshoremen's Association and in issuing a charter to a new group marks an interesting reversal of traditional Federation policy. However, this action was influenced by public opinion and cannot, at this time, be held to constitute an important precedent for future policy.

64. The sensitiveness of the founding fathers on the subject of skill was reflected in an exchange in the first convention of the old Federation. As Chairman on the Committee of the Plan on Organization, Gompers moved that the name of the group be "The Federation of Organized Trades Unions of the United States and Canada." Some delegates protested, claiming that the title would exclude the unskilled "laborers." Despite denials by Gompers and Powers of the Lake Seamen (who defended the title because he held that it would exclude "political bodies which might try to force themselves into our future deliberations"), the name was changed to the "Federation of Organized Trades and Labor Unions." (*Proceedings,* 1881, pp. 15–16.) In view of this debate, it is a matter of interest that the title of its successor, The American Federation of Labor, omitted reference to "trades," which in the minds of some carried a connotation of skill.

based upon his own conviction of the desirability of an evolution to industrial unionism, follow:

The thought has frequently occurred to me whether in the near future the basis of our Federation should be modelled upon a somewhat different basis from the present one, by having the various industries classified by the divisions of these industries; such as, for instance, the iron, steel, or metal industry to have a convention of the representatives of all the trade unions in that industry; the building trades to have their convention of the representatives of the unions in their trade, the railroad employees theirs, and so on, each legislating upon the questions that affect the general interests of their particular trades and interests; these industrial divisions to be in turn represented by their proportionate number of delegates in the convention of the American Federation of Labor, and a representative of each industry elected a member of the Executive Council.
The idea may not be practical for immediate adoption, but discussion of it can only lead to good results. One thing is certain—the autonomy of each trade and industrial division would thus be more firmly secured.[65]

But the delegates were not likely to rejoice at the prospect of securing the autonomy of "each trade and industrial division." They were intent on maintaining the autonomy of each national union as it was then constituted, industrial change or no. Strangely enough, however, the first approximation to an "industrial division" was organized at the insistence of the national unions involved—and was accepted only reluctantly by the executive council of the Federation. The organization in question was fashioned by some of the national unions in the building trades. It originated in response to the challenge to their authority over their respective jurisdictions which the local building trades councils presented by virtue of their practice of resolving jurisdictional issues at the community level. As a result, the national union's jurisdiction tended to vary from locality to locality in rough proportion to the strength of its local union in each place. When many of the local councils united in 1897 to form a federation, the National Building Trades Council, in which the representation granted to the local councils was greater than that allowed the national unions, the latter, in opposition, formed an organization of their own, the Structural Building Trades Alliance (1903). The A.F. of L.'s executive council at first viewed with suspicion the formation, outside the Federation, of this industrial division. It was finally legitimatized, however, when, in 1908, it became the Building Trades Department of the American Federation of Labor.

Two departments in other industries were formed shortly thereafter, the Metal Trades Department (1908) and the Railway Employees' Department (1909). The fears of the executive council (which included the president, who apparently entertained second thoughts on the scheme which he had proposed in 1888) were never realized: according to Lorwin, "The departments

65. *Proceedings,* 1888, p. 14.

have not changed the essential character of the Federation."[66] The department never constituted an independent entity; it was dominated by its constituent national unions, and it never was represented directly in either the convention or the executive council of the Federation. The guiding philosophy of the department was well expressed in a report of the executive council of the Building Trades Department, made in 1909, in which

Your Executive Council has taken the position that jurisdiction lines are laid down by International organizations, and as such they can be altered, amended, or waived by duly accredited representatives appointed by each International Union acting in a general way, and thereafter such amendments, changes, or conditions must be ratified by the Executive Committees of the Internationals in interest.[67]

In view of this philosophy, it is not surprising that the original objectives of the departments were never satisfactorily achieved. Departmental action was not instrumental in promoting amalgamations in situations where traditional craft jurisdictions had been made obsolete by economic change,[68] nor did the department give evidence of independent authority in the settlement of jurisdictional disputes.[69]

Furthermore, while the passage quoted above referred to the relationship between the national union and the local council within the framework of a department (note the phrase "acting in a general way"—that is, to prevail uniformly throughout an international jurisdiction) it was equally relevant to the relationship between the national union and the Federation itself. For it was eloquent of a highly proprietary attitude on the part of the national union toward the charter; it was quite evident that the definition of its jurisdiction ("amendments, changes, or conditions") was considered by the national to be within its own province. In instances of conflicting interpretations, therefore, the Federation's action betrayed its lack of *de facto* authority. Awards were indeed made and, on some occasions, charters were withdrawn, but the outcome in most cases could have been predicted by prior knowledge of the relative strength of the contestants.

The triumph of expediency over principle was made apparent in the Federation's relation to disputes occurring between its two "industrial" affiliates—the Mine Workers and the Brewery Workmen—and sundry affiliated crafts. The principle involved was "trade" or craft jurisdiction, the integrity of which was violated in specific instances when the industrial unions sought to extend control over their own jurisdictions. The first breach of principle occurred in 1901, when, in the well-known Scranton Declaration,[70]

66. Lorwin, *A.F. of L.,* p. 395.
67. Quoted in Barnett, "Dominance of the National Union," p. 402.
68. Lorwin, *A.F. of L.,* p. 395.
69. Commons *et al., History of Labour,* v. IV, p. 368.
70. *Proceedings,* 1901, p. 240.

the United Mine Workers were authorized to organize craftsmen of all trades employed in or around the coal mines. This declaration implemented the Miners' jurisdiction at the expense of those of the craft unions involved, but it was pointed out that this was an exceptional case,

owing to the isolation of some few industries from thickly populated centers where the overwhelming number follow one branch thereof, and owing to the fact that in some industries comparatively few workers are engaged over whom separate organizations claim jurisdiction. . . .

Under such peculiar circumstances, technical violations of jurisdictions could be tolerated because of their negligible significance to the craft organizations involved; it will be recalled that the Operative Plasterers finally consented of their own accord to the organization of members of their trade in small towns by the Bricklayers, while the latter disclaimed interest in "exclusive plasterers" in the larger communities. Thus the convention which passed the Scranton Declaration could, in subscribing to this doctrine of "paramount organization," at the same time reaffirm its adherence to the principle from which it was a departure:

As the magnificent growth of the A.F. of L. is conceded by all students of economic thought to be the result of organization on trade lines, and believing it neither necessary nor expedient to make any radical departure from this fundamental principle, we declare that as a general proposition the interests of the workers will be best served by adhering as closely to that doctrine as the recent great changes in methods of production and employment make practicable.

The Scranton Declaration really begged the question, of course, for what was to become of the "fundamental principle" when the changes referred to above were so "great" that adoption of a policy of paramount organization would constitute a serious threat to craft jurisdictions? In the struggles of the United Brewery Workmen to exercise exclusive control over their industrial jurisdiction—which led them to cut across craft lines maintained by the Coopers, Stationary Engineers, Firemen, and Teamsters, the Federation was confronted with a challenge to craft jurisdictions which was not confined to the industrial back country. At the 1900 convention, the Federation upheld the claims of the Coopers to jurisdiction over men in their trade employed in the breweries. It rejected similiar arguments advanced by the other crafts, however, possibly because they were organized and chartered more than a decade after the Brewers had received their certificate of affiliation. But in 1902 the convention ordered the Brewers to surrender their locals of engineers and firemen. The Brewers refused to comply with this directive, just as they had withheld compliance with the earlier order to relinquish control over the coopers. In 1906, the crafts involved, led by the Teamsters, induced the Federation to pass a resolution providing that the Brewers' charter would be revoked unless they surrendered the craftsmen belonging to the contending unions within ninety days. The Brewers once more ignored the will of the convention, and, in 1907, their charter was actually revoked. But the Federation found that it could ill afford to lose the affiliation of a relatively large and powerful national union, and the next year, contrary though its action was to the "fundamental principle" of craft jurisdiction, the executive council reissued its charter to the insubordinate organization.[71]

The Brewers' triumph, needless to add, did not represent a triumph of paramount organization over craft jurisdiction. It represented nothing but the triumph of expediency and the (virtual) abdication of the Federation as an independent influence in the settlement of jurisdictional disputes involving its large and influential affiliates. Its inglorious role was well described by Perlman and Taft:

The Federation, when implored for aid by the weaker union with right on its side would at first sincerely come to its defense, but being extremely reluctant to apply force to any of its constituent unions, to say nothing of a strong and belligerent one unwilling to abide by arbitration awards that went against it, it would end by accepting what it saw was inevitable, and then turn to persuade the weaker union to accept its fate.[72]

This situation came about, not because the unions questioned the legal right of the Federation to make awards and to revoke charters, but because they—or the larger and stronger among them—were quite willing to face the consequence of noncompliance. The conflict between the authority of the Federation to interpret or revoke charters which it had issued and the autonomy of the union in defining and redefining its own jurisdiction was resolved in a simple manner. The Federation could make its award; the disaffected union could refuse to accept the award; and, finally, the Federation could expel the latter for disobedience. The reason that the Federation so frequently adopted the interpretation of the stronger disputant was that the latter was capable of functioning, without noticeable loss in efficiency, outside the Federation, whereas the former frequently was not.

The Bricklayers furnished an impressive example of a powerful union's ability to go it alone. One of the oldest of the national unions (it was founded in 1865), it did not affiliate with the American Federation of Labor until 1916. Its isolationism, further, antedated the A.F. of L., for, although it had apparently sent a delegate to the congress of 1867, it had refused to send a delegate to the National Labor Union in 1869. A year later, it authorized its president to represent the union at the National Labor Congress in 1870, but he was unable to attend; in reporting to the convention, however, he observed that some of the Bricklayers' locals did send representatives to the congress. In 1876, the convention refused to participate in the formation of a proposed Industrial Congress, and its relations with the Knights of Labor

71. Hermann Schluter, *The Brewing Industry and the Brewery Workers' Movement in America* (Cincinnati: International Union of Brewery Workmen of America, 1910), pp. 219–227.

72. Commons *et al.*, *History of Labour*, v. IV, p. 358.

were sufficiently hostile so that the president of the Bricklayers warned the delegates to the 1890 Convention that "we have abroad in our land an organization whose object I believe to be to absorb all National and International bodies, and failing in this object, some of these men will attempt to sow discord and discontent among the members. I beseech you, be on your guard."[73]

The Bricklayers' ability, as well as their desire, to remain unaffiliated can be traced to their unique position in the construction industry. Because of the highly skilled nature of their craft relative to the other building trades (it was generally the most highly paid craft in the industry), because of their earlier and, for a considerable time, more complete organization, and because, as mentioned previously, their "season" preceded that of most of the others, they enjoyed a rather high degree of economic independence. On the other hand, the same factors which accounted for their self-sufficiency made alliance with them peculiarly desirable to the neighboring trades. Hence the Bricklayers' hostility to entangling alliances was identical with the aversion of a highly skilled craft to amalgamation with other groups which were less skilled and, in the aggregate, more numerous: the sacrifices involved in sympathetic support of the others would have been considerably outweighed by the gains derived from sympathetic support by the others. Their opposition to affiliation with the A.F. of L. was based on the persistent suspicion that affiliation on the national level would be reflected in commitment to participation in local sympathetic strikes.

Gompers sought to reassure them on this point. Appearing before the Bricklayers' convention in 1888, he characterized the Federation as an organization "which, while solidifying the strength of all Trades Unions and Central Labor Bodies into one grand Federation, yet recognized the complete autonomy of each and every trade, and permitted no other branch to interfere with its domestic and internal government."[74] Repeated assurances along this line were made by the president and other representatives of the Federation (including P. J. McGuire) either in personal appearances at the Bricklayers' conventions or in written communications.[75] The national officers, led by Secretary O'Dea, strongly favored affiliation; thus in 1891, a resolution was presented which noted that

In affiliating with the A.F. of L. we maintain the autonomy and independence to conduct all our local or international trade disputes as best suit the views and interests of our members. . . .[76]

73. *Proceedings,* 1869, pp. 93 and 94; 1870, pp. 11 and 89; 1876, pp. 19–21; 1890, p. 4. In 1884, the Bricklayers had accused the Knights of attempting to induce their local in Washington, D. C. to secede and join the Order. (*Proceedings,* 1884, p. 9.)

74. *Proceedings,* 1888, p. 81.

75. Cf. *Proceedings,* 1889, p. 45; 1899, pp. 5 and 38–39; 1900, p. 38; 1902, p. 38; 1904, p. 24; 1905, p. 42; 1912, pp. 136–137.

76. *Proceedings,* 1891, p. 130.

But bricklaying was predominantly a local trade, and, consequently, the persuasion of the local unions on this subject was decisive. The national conventions would not take it upon themselves to make a final determination; instead they submitted the question of affiliation to referenda of the locals. Such referenda were held in 1891, 1899, 1900, 1903, 1904, 1906, and 1913.[77] In all cases except one, the number of locals opposing affiliation exceeded the number favoring it; and in the one referendum where the reverse was true, such a large number of locals failed to vote (122 out of 325) that, despite O'Dea's warning that failure to vote would be counted as voting in the affirmative, the executive council decided to refer the matter back to the convention. When the decision to affiliate was finally reached in 1916, it was taken as a result of a vote of the convention delegates, President Bowen having blocked the introduction of a motion to submit the matter to another referendum.[78] Referral to referendum was favored by the smaller locals, most of which were opposed to affiliation, because the referendum allowed only one vote to each local, regardless of membership; whereas the proponents of federation favored the convention vote, which gave greater representation to the larger locals, in favor of affiliation.

The smaller locals supported their opposition to affiliation with two arguments. First, they claimed that affiliation was not essential to the well-being of the Bricklayers, or, as one delegate expressed it, "that the I.U. could well afford to maintain its present position."[79] Second, they claimed that, especially in the smaller communities, the local Building Trades Councils were seeking to utilize the Bricklayers' strategic position for their own ends, and that affiliation with the Federation would entail an obligation to support the other trades. This position was well put by one delegate in the final debate on affiliation:

The building trades in Indianapolis hate us, Mr. Chairman. They will not have anything to do with us. With the aid of the Executive Board, twice we went down the line and beat them. It was simply through the strength of the Executive Board. I appeal to the small organizations in this convention; are you going to hand us over to the enemy? Affiliation can do no harm in the larger cities as I see it; in cities like Chicago, like San Francisco, like New York, like Boston, if you will, where practically the entire building trades are on a par with the bricklayers; but in the majority of the smaller towns of this country the building trades are not on a par with the bricklayers, with the result that the bricklayer is compelled constantly to go down the line in an endeavor to lift up to

77. *Proceedings*, 1891, p. 27; 1892, p. 19; 1899, pp. 38–39, 5 (*Report of the President*); 1900, p. 39; 1903, p. 91; 1904, p. 132; 1906, p. 154; 1913, pp. 516–530.

78. *Proceedings*, 1916, pp. 121–140. A convention vote favored representation of the International at the 1884 convention of the Federation of Organized Trades and Labor Unions, but, due to the defection of the Bricklayers' president and vice-president that year, no delegation was sent. (*Proceedings*, 1884, p. 15; 1885, p. 29.)

79. *Proceedings*, 1906, p. 154.

his level those who have had the same opportunity to organize as he has had but have refused to do so. . . .[80]

Hence an earlier observation by Secretary Dobson that, "If their relations with the local trades are friendly their vote is favorable; if unfriendly, their vote is against the proposition."[81] But if opposition at the local level for a long while prevented affiliation, the ultimate necessity for many of the locals to be admitted to their local Building Trades Councils finally ensured it. For, although the Bricklayers' jurisdiction was a key one in the industry, it was not airtight. Members of other crafts could, with varying degrees of proficiency, lay brick, and thus the Bricklayers' International was faced with the necessity of protecting its jurisdiction against encroachment by such groups as the Plasterers, Stonemasons, and Marble Workers. The chief mechanism of protection was support by the local Building Trades Councils. (Thus, in 1902, the Bricklayers' local in Alton, Ohio, reported that it had been able to wipe out a rival local of Stonemasons because it was supported by the local Building Trades Council.)[82] Conversely, the chief mechanism of aggression was opposition by the Building Trades Councils, for the latter could—and did—implement their local jurisdictional awards by refusing to work for contractors unless they hired members of the approved local for the work in question. Now the A.F. of L., of course, possessed no powers comparable to those of these local councils, but it did apparently utilize the latter's coercive authority in its campaign to recruit the Bricklayers. Having observed that its initial policy of refusing to charter unions with which the Bricklayers were engaged in jurisdictional controversy had failed to secure the latter's affiliation, the Federation ceased to honor the latter's requests so scrupulously.

In 1908, the Building Trades Department of the Federation decided that no local union could affiliate with a local Building Trades Council unless its parent national union was affiliated with the Federation. And, according to the Bricklayers' president, "the Bricklayers was the union that was referred to throughout the discussion of the matter."[83] Since the current rivals of the Bricklayers, especially the Plasterers and the Stonecutters, were affiliated with the Federation, the Bricklayers could be placed at a serious disadvantage at the local level.[84] In a letters to the Bricklayers in 1912, in which he again urged affiliation, Gompers reminded them that membership in the A.F. of L. was prerequisite to membership in the Building Trades Department, and he also implied rather obliquely that the ability to obtain redress against jurisdictional aggression was a prerogative reserved to affiliates.[85] This point was under-

80. *Proceedings,* 1916, p. 121.
81. *Proceedings,* 1913, p. 516.
82. *Proceedings,* 1902, p. 37.
83. *Report of the President,* 1909, p. v.
84. *Report of the President,* 1906, p. vi.
85. *Proceedings,* 1912, pp. 136–137.

scored when, in 1902, the Federation issued a charter to the International Association of Marble Workers, whose jurisdiction the Bricklayers promptly claimed as part of their own. The Bricklayers were powerful enough to defeat most of the locals of the new union, but it was duly noted that the support of the Federation, represented by the Building Trades Department, was on the other side this time and that no move was made to withdraw the charter of the offending group.[86] It is impossible, from the available data, to assess the effect of these developments, but it is a fact that the international officers were able to induce the convention to take the matter into its own hands only after the Federation, stiffened by its Building Trades Department, had abandoned its policy of deference to the unaffiliated international.

Ironically, the coercive power which was partly instrumental in inducing the Bricklayers to affiliate was possessed, not by the Federation itself, but by the leading species of a genus whose influence the national-dominated Federation was striving successfully to reduce, the local federation. Had the A.F. of L. relied on its own resources, it is doubtful whether the pressure exerted by it upon an unaffiliated national union would have been decisive or whether, by parity of reasoning, the threat of revocation of its charter would have sufficed to deter a relatively strong and well-organized national union from refusing to comply with an award which ran counter to its own definition of its jurisdiction. In practice it would appear that neither the Federation's services to nor its authority over the affiliated national union were sufficient to accomplish that purpose.

Following the economist's distinction between fixed, or overhead, costs and direct, or variable, expenses, the services of the Federation might be classified under two heads: the type of service which benefited the particular union because it helped to create a more favorable environment for the entire trade union movement and hence could be termed "overhead service," and the type of service which bore a direct relationship to the welfare of the specific union and could be allocated "directly" to that union's account. In practice, it would be difficult to classify specific activities in one or the other category, since many contained elements of both, but it might be presumed that the Federation's political activity and President Gompers' celebrated attempts to induce public acceptance of trade unionism as an institution thoroughly compatible with the American way of life could be placed in the former group as "overhead" services. Now the unfortunate aspect of this class of services, from the Federation's point of view, was that, by their nature, benefits accruing from them could not be withheld from a specific trade union upon termination of its affiliation (or, as in the case of the Bricklayers, failure to affiliate in the first place) with the American Federation of Labor. Nothing could prevent the unaffiliated union from deriving gain from such Federation

86. *Report of the President,* 1915, p. vi; *Report of the Secretary* (same year), pp. 481–500.

activities without incurring the obligations (and these included financial contributions) of affiliation; like the nonmember in a partly unionized firm, they enjoyed what has been known in the union terminology as a free ride. The Federation on the other hand required the affiliation and support—financial, moral, economic, and political—of the union, for without that support, its ability to engage in such overhead activities would have been curtailed. The degree of curtailment—the dependence of the Federation upon the union in question—moreover, varied directly with the numerical and financial strength of that union. Hence the Federation's tendency to range itself on the side of the bigger battalions when it became necessary to choose among its minions.

Some of the Federation's services, however, were of such a nature that they could be withheld from some unions at the same time that they were made available to others. Intervention in negotiations with employers and financial aid in support of strikes belonged to this category, but perhaps the most important of such services were the organizing activities of the Federation. At the 1886 convention, it was decided that

The Executive Council shall use every possible means to organize new National or International Trades Unions, and to organize local Trades Unions and connect them with the Federation, until such time as there are a sufficient number to form a National or International Union, when it shall be the duty of the President of the Federation to see that such organization is formed.[87]

Despite the fact that the organizers whom the executive council commissioned were unsalaried in this early period of Federation history,[88] their efforts met with considerable success. This was true especially in "small towns, and even in large cities, which furnish(ed) employment to only a small number of people" in each trade.[89] There the procedure was to organize all trades into federal labor unions, which, being temporary organizations, presumably awaited subsequent fragmentation by the appropriate national craft unions. The service thus rendered to the national unions must have

87. *Constitution*, 1886, Art. VI, Sec. 2.

88. A move to elect a salaried general organizer was defeated in 1886. (*Proceedings*, 1886, p. 24.) In 1888, a suggestion that each organizer be paid an annual salary of one hundred dollars went unheeded. (*Proceedings*, 1888, p. 20.) By the end of the century, however, the president was able to report that "For the first time in the history of our Federation we have not been closely pressed for means to carry on the work of organization," and that the seventeen special organizers in the field were "paid from the funds of the American Federation of Labor" for "time and expenses." (*Proceedings*, 1899, p. 9.) For some time previously, it appeared that the organizers of the A.F. of L.—like their predecessors in the Knights—had been reimbursed indirectly by the local unions which they had organized, a certain percentage of the proceeds from the issue of charters, official supplies, and subscriptions to the *American Federationist* having been devoted to this purpose. (*Proceedings*, 1896, p. 23.)

89. *Proceedings*, 1887, p. 10.

been appreciable, for official acknowledgments and protestations of gratitude were not lacking in their official records. As early as 1883, the president of the first Federation reported that "The National Union of Journeymen Plasterers has tendered thanks to your committee for efforts which have served to strengthen their organization. We have endeavored to add branches to the National Association of Wood Carvers . . ." In 1898 Secretary McGuire of the Carpenters referred to the "invaluable" services rendered by the Federation's local and district organizers. And the national executive of the Bricklayers, in urging affiliation upon the reluctant locals, did not hesitate to point to the work of the A.F. of L. organizers in their field in 1903 and to draw a pointed conclusion:

We will simply add that while the healthy growth of the B. & M.I.U. during the past few years has been owing in a measure to the general prosperity of business, still the hustling organizers of the A.F. of L. have done magnificent work in hundreds of cities and towns in getting our unorganized craftsmen together and imbuing them with the needs of organization. Through their efforts alone we have been able to save several thousand dollars in this special line of work, and it is almost safe to assert that 35 per cent of the new Unions we have added during the time alluded to is to be credited to A.F. of L. organizers, costing us comparatively nothing, and this in the face of being a non-affiliated body.

President Gompers and Secretary Morrison, when any doubts have arisen with their organizers as to helping us in this work, have upon every occasion hastened to the rescue, saying, "the B. & M.I.U. is not an hostile organization; we hope to secure them some day." Can any one say that this hope has not been born of patience? How much longer shall it last? [90]

Despite the apparent popularity of this activity and the requests for aid which various national and local unions directed to the executive council,[91] there is reason to believe that the organizing efforts and achievements of the Federation did not constitute an unmixed blessing to the national unions involved. It will be recalled that, for financial reasons, the local trade and federal labor unions were often reluctant to surrender their direct relationship with the Federation and submit to absorption by national unions. But if the per capita tax which the directly affiliated locals paid to the Federation was lower than the taxes paid by locals to parent national unions, it was higher than the per capita tax paid by the latter to the A.F. of L.[92] Gompers, on several occasions, ascribed the failure of Federation-organized locals to form or join national unions in their own trades to their financial incentive to remain directly affiliated with the A.F. of L.; and, in 1899, he opposed a

90. See *Proceedings*, 1883, p. 8; 1898, p. 31; 1903, p. 468.

91. Cf. *Proceedings*, 1893, p. 39; 1895, pp. 80–81.

92. In 1897, the per capita paid by the national unions to the Federation was one-third cent per month (previously, one-fourth cent), while the per capita contribution of the local trade and federal labor unions was two cents per month (previously, one cent). (*Proceedings*, 1897, p. xii.)

reduction in the per capita paid by the federal locals on the grounds that the existing differential "is a preventive against the formation of nationals and is in itself detrimental to the advancement and progress necessary."[93] However, the attraction between the Federation and the local unions affiliated directly to it was a mutual one, and national officers frequently found it difficult to persuade the parent organization to sever the umbilical cord. This was a matter of common, if unofficial knowledge.[94] The executive council of the Federation appeared somewhat on the defensive with respect to this matter; in 1898 the secretary reported somewhat defensively that

many letters have been received from our organizers informing us that they have organized local unions and sent the applications for charters direct to the officers of the National Unions of their respective trades, showing conclusively that the advancement of trade unionism has been the object our organizers had in view.[95]

The Federation could not achieve by coercion what it sometimes failed to accomplish by service—the assurance that its affiliates would always find it to their advantage to comply with A.F. of L. directives. The degree of authority over such vital activities as the admission and discipline of members, strikes, and economic policies ceded by a local union to a national union in its economic jurisdiction measured the value which the local placed upon affiliation with the national. It also measured, therefore, the degree to which the penalty of expulsion from the national could serve as a deterrent to local disobedience. Since the American Federation of Labor was not granted control over its affiliated national unions comparable to the authority of the latter over their own locals, the penalty of expulsion from the Federation could not be the same deterrent to insubordination as was the penalty of expulsion from the national union. Thus the Federation's power to implement its awards in cases of jurisdictional dispute—which was implied in its subscription to the principle of exclusive jurisdiction—was substantially impaired by virtue of its adherence to the other fundamental tenet on which it was based, the principle of autonomy.

93. *Proceedings,* 1899, p. 8. See also *Proceedings,* 1890, p. 14; 1897, p. 6.

94. I am indebted for this information to Mr. John P. Frey, President of the Metal Trades Department of the American Federation of Labor. During the period under discussion in this study, Mr. Frey was the editor of the Iron Molders' *Journal.* His information was corroborated by Mr. William Schoenberg, President of the United Cement, Lime, Gypsum and Allied Workers, American Federation of Labor.

95. *Proceedings,* 1892, p. 18. At the same convention, however, a resolution calling upon the executive council to unite the federal labor unions of laundry workers into a national union "as soon as possible" was not voted on. Instead the convention concurred in a substitute resolution, "That the form of such National Unions as far as the A.F. of L. is concerned, be left to the discretion of the Executive Council." (p. 41.)

PART
VI

RELATIONS WITH EMPLOYERS

CHAPTER FOURTEEN

NATIONAL STRIKE POLICIES

ALTHOUGH many of the rules affecting union jurisdiction were established in collective bargaining, this study has thus far been concerned primarily with the internal development of national unions and with their relations with other labor organizations and with one another. In this part, however, we shall consider certain aspects of the national unions' relations with employers. This chapter will deal with some aspects of national strike policy, and the following chapters will be devoted to some economic policies of the national unions and their local affiliates.

National and local unions were alike in sanctioning the strike as a device for improving the conditions of employment. To be sure, some of the most outstanding national officers of the post-Civil War era—and William Sylvis was among them—did not hesitate to make public their skepticism concerning the efficiency of trade unionism in achieving a significant measure of progress for the membership. The grand scribe of the Order of the Knights of St. Crispin declared that, "The present demand of the Crispin is steady employment and fair wages, but his future is self-employment,"[1] and the Molders at one time (1868) changed their name to the Iron Molders' International Cooperative and Protective Union. Nevertheless, most of these union officers were tough-minded men who, pending the materialization of the best of all possible worlds, were quite willing to make shift in the one in which they lived. Indeed, the same philosophy which led them to doubt the efficacy of union remedies left them with a strong conviction that coercion was required for the achievement of whatever progress could be attained within the confines of the "wages system." This viewpoint was well expressed by a president of the Glass Bottle Blowers' Association who urged the creation of a strike fund because

I believe we will have periodical strikes as long as we are wage workers. There never will occur a time when the relationship between the employer and em-

1. John R. Commons and Associates, *History of Labour in the United States* (New York: Macmillan, 1936), v. II, p. 79.

ployee will be of such a close, friendly or fraternal character as to preclude the possibility of a strike, except it be where both are jointly interested in a financial sense in a business.[2]

Thus, the circuitous route over which he traveled led the national officer first away from and finally back to the prosaic line of battle which his more humble brethren in the local unions had formed; and he was quite willing to take his place at their head once the action had commenced. However, national strike policy did differ from the local viewpoint in one important respect. The local was almost always willing to support a strike; indeed, as we have observed in our discussion of strike referenda, it was even invariably willing to support strikes entered into by other locals (see above, pp. 278–281). Past failures seldom proved effective in checking this impetuosity; local memories, it seems, were short. This might have been due to the fact that local unions themselves were often short-lived. The failure of a strike was frequently attended by the dissolution of the striking organization and the dispersal of its leading spirits. Thus when, after the passage of time, a new organization arose, it started *de novo,* with its native impulsiveness uninhibited by recollection of ancestral reverses.

The national officers, however, had longer memories; and, although the recollection of past defeats seldom persuaded them that the strike should be abandoned altogether as an implement to enforce economic demands, it did instill in them a nice sense of discrimination which was lacking in the lower echelons. Unlike many locals, the nationals distinguished between two classes of strikes—those which probably could be won and those which probably could not. As a result, national policy was characterized, first, by an attempt to dissuade locals from engaging in strikes in which the odds were not favorable to success, and, second, by the desire to make effective financial assistance available to striking locals, so that a greater proportion of strikes could be classed as probable victories. Thus, achievement of the second objective would have the desired effect of reducing the number of strikes which would fall beyond the pale of national approval; at the same time, however, it was predicated upon acceptance of the first objective, for, as we observed in Chapter 8, considerations of fiscal solvency made it imperative that the national union be authorized to restrain to some degree the local's instinctive pugnacity. Let us turn now to this first attribute of national strike policy and consider the principles of selection which underlay the advance approval of some strikes and the condemnation of others.

STRIKES IN DEPRESSION AND IN PROSPERITY

As a rule, national officers sought to dissuade locals from striking in what some of them termed "unfavorable trade seasons." "Trade seasons" included not only conventional chronological periods within the calendar year but the longer swings of prosperity and depression as well.

2. *Proceedings,* 1887, p. 15.

It was difficult to persuade the local unions not to strike in bad times for two reasons. In the first place, employers frequently sought to reduce wages, and, since existing wage scales were generally regarded as minima and union members usually pledged not to work for wages less than "the scale of prices for labor, appended to this constitution" (see p. 73), strikes against wage reductions implied the defense of union "standards." In the second place, employers not infrequently coupled wage reductions with attempts to unseat the locals to which their employees belonged, for they were under no legal obligation to bargain with them "in good faith" and, when the demand for labor was slack, they were under no economic compulsion to recognize them. Thus, a larger proportion of work stoppages consisted in lockouts—as distinguished from strikes—in quiet times than in brisk periods, and resistance to wage reductions was often linked with a defense of the local's bargaining status and, indeed, of its very existence.

Hence strikes against wage reductions acquired initially a status higher than that accorded to strikes for wage increases. The Glass Bottle Blowers imposed a fine of one hundred dollars upon any member who was guilty of accepting employment "where difficulties have arisen in consequence of any question involving rights, privileges and general usages of the Association, or on account of prices or wages, or a reduction thereof. . ."[3] While the Molders provided that payment of strike benefits to their members commence on the date that the strike was sanctioned, they also stipulated "when the members of any local Union are recognized as being locked out on account of Union principles, they shall be paid from the date of lockout." When they initially established conditions under which strikes could be sanctioned by national authority, they referred only to cases wherein "a difficulty occurs under the jurisdiction of any local Union, through a reduction in wages or through the principles of our organization being jeopardized in any manner. . ." Not until a considerable period of time had elapsed did they specify that approval might be granted "should any Union desire to make a demand for an increase of wages."[4]

The Bricklayers' national executive could hardly have expected the affiliated locals to refrain from striking during slack seasons, since the following definition was enshrined in the national constitution in 1869:

Whenever the word "scab" appears in this Constitution, it shall signify an employer who has violated the laws of this or local unions, whom the members of this Union are debarred from working for or with, until he or they have complied with the laws of said Unions.[5]

The extent to which the locals of this national union were committed, as a matter of principle, to resistance to employers' attempts to undercut union

3. *Constitution,* 1892, Art. IX, Sec. 49.
4. *Constitution,* 1879, Art. VI, Sec. 2; 1882, Art. VI, Sec. 2; 1890, Art. VI, Sec. 2.
5. *Constitution,* 1869, Sec. 7.

standards is revealed in the following resolution, which was presented to the convention of 1885 by a New York local:

That any Union that strikes against a reduction of wages, or an increase of hours, shall be exempt from assessments to support any Union who may be previously on strike, but shall pay all assessments due to the time up to date of their own strike.[6]

As a final example, we might cite the Piano Workers who, while they did not countenance strikes for an increase in wages between the first of June and the first of August and between January first and March first, nevertheless did sanction strikes during those dull seasons if the object was either to resist a reduction in wages or the imposition of the contract system of employment or payment by truck.[7]

Nevertheless, many national unions ultimately adopted policies which were opposed to the calling of strikes, for whatever reason, in times of depression. The gallant local union, striking for its "standard" in the face of hopeless odds, must have presented, to the older and wiser heads at national headquarters, a striking resemblance to the celebrated engineer who died defending his right of way. National leadership was rarely quixotic. Men who had renounced—often with genuine reluctance—the unattainable in favor of the practicable when they turned from the Coöperative Commonwealth to the Business Union were not likely to approve the sacrifice of the latter, as an organization in being, to an ideal, considerably less exciting (although genuinely professed) than the former, which was expressed in so many cents per hour or in so many hours per day or per week. Indeed, even the national leader to whom business unionism had always been an end in itself was no more obliged—provided that he was sufficiently sophisticated—to defend the specific terms of a particular wage bargain than the puritanical captain of industry, who regarded the pursuit of gain as a worthy end in itself, was obliged to insist upon some specific rate of return. Adherence to the cause, in both cases, simply meant doing the best one could under the circumstances, it being tacitly appreciated that survival was an essential condition of success.

We need allude only briefly and in a general way to those factors, characteristic of periods of trade slump, which stacked the odds against the success of local strikes. Recessions and depressions were characterized by a reduction in the demand for union labor and an increase in the supply of nonunion labor. Reduction in demand came from two sources. First, the employer's demand for labor in general was reduced as a result of the reduction in demand for his product. Second, his demand for union labor in particular was

6. *Proceedings,* 1885, p. 69.
7. Cf. George Milton Janes, *The Control of Strikes in American Trade Unions* (Baltimore: Johns Hopkins, 1916), pp. 45–46.

reduced. We may suppose that, as a result of union-conducted strikes in opposition to wage reductions, differentials between the supply prices of union and nonunion labor tended to increase, so that the latter became cheaper relative to the former. In that situation the employer, without experiencing any cyclical increase in his native preference for nonunion over union workers (or, more typically, any decline in a preference for union over nonunion workers) would find it advantageous to substitute nonunion for union labor. Indeed, he would do so as a matter of competitive necessity, for if he could not reduce his own labor costs while his nonunion competitors were reducing theirs, his competitive disadvantage would increase—at a time when selling prices were being driven down by decline in product demand.

As far as the increase in the supply of nonunion labor was concerned, its origin was easily traced, for it was accompanied by a decline in union membership. Unemployment and reduced wages led many members to economize on their consumption outlays by discontinuing their payment of union dues and assessments. Furthermore, fear of being replaced by unemployed nonunion workers frequently induced workers to relinquish their union membership, while unemployed members were often willing to take the "ironclad oath" in order to get jobs.

On the other hand, despite their favorable chances of winning, some employers probably sought to avoid protracted shutdowns because they believed that the cost of victory outweighed the gains from victory:—the reductions in cost due to wage cuts. The cost of shutdown varied directly with the volume of business lost due to shutdown and with the urgency of the employer's need for cash to defray continuing expenses (assuming that their output could be sold at prices in excess of prime costs). In many cases it might be presumed that the need for liquidity was higher in depression than in prosperity.[8] At the same time, however, profits lost due to shutdown were lower in bad times, when "time" lost on account of a strike might have been considerably less than the total period elapsing between the beginning and the termination of the strike. Thus one cannot determine, *a priori,* whether the cost of victory to employers increased or decreased in bad times, since the components of that cost varied in opposite directions.

However, if the employer's willingness to incur strikes depended upon the probable chances of victory and the necessity to achieve victory (to reduce wages or to prevent them from rising) as well as upon the cost of victory, it is likely that, during the depressions of the late nineteenth century, the cost of stoppages declined relative to the prospective gains therefrom.

8. Slichter maintained, that in the depression of 1920–1921 many employers sought to avoid labor trouble because, having speculated in raw materials during the preceding boom, they had to liquidate inventories. (Sumner H. Slichter, "The Current Labor Policies of American Industries," *Quarterly Journal of Economics,* v. XLIII, May 1929, pp. 398–399.)

Confronted with an increase in the supply of nonunion labor and a reduction in the demand for the services of their constituents, the national leaders urged measures which were designed to alleviate both conditions. To hold their membership, they urged a policy of amnesty upon the local unions (see above, pp. 140ff.); since every nonunionist was a potential "rat" who threatened union standards, it was better to have delinquent members than no members at all.

Now, since the suspension of discipline for delinquency might have induced some members who otherwise would have remained in good standing to fall in arrears themselves, the policy of amnesty was not calculated to place the local and national unions in a strong financial position for the support of strikes to maintain union standards of employment. From the national viewpoint, however, this was not too great a drawback, for, in addition to their advocacy of measures to check the increase in the supply of nonunionists, the national officers favored a policy of opposition to strikes in bad times. In addition to the obvious merit of deterring the locals from committing suicide, this policy might have offset, to some extent, the reduction in the demand for union labor, for, if the union members did not resist wage cuts, employers had less incentive to replace them with nonunion labor. Thus the national leadership was not necessarily averse, in hard times, to sacrificing the sinews of war in order to avoid giving offense to the financial sensibilities of the rank and file. When the Bricklayer's president sought to defend his policy of refusing international support to local petitions for strike aid during the depression year 1895, he claimed that, "It was our duty that we owed the general organization to discountenance any attempt to saddle any further expense or tax on our membership."[9]

Given, then, the undesirable conditions of demand and supply which prevailed in "unfavorable trade seasons," it is not surprising that the national officers sought to impress upon the local membership the advisability of sacrificing what the latter often regarded as principle to expediency. Chief Arthur told the Locomotive Engineers (in 1894) that, "There is a time to strike if you have a good cause and there is a time not to strike"; and, although the chief's remarks must be considered in the context of the industrial pacifism for which he was renowned (or notorious), this statement can stand as an adequate summary of prevailing sentiment among the national leadership. President Heartz of the Bricklayers informed the convention of 1893 that

The Executive Board had quite a number of applications during the year, from Unions desiring strike privileges. A great many of the applications were not in accordance with your laws regulating such matters, and we necessarily refused to countenance them, to the great disappointment of the applicants. And

9. *Report of the President,* 1895, p. 3.

we felt, that it was a duty we owed to the entire organization to discountenance strikes during a season like the one we are passing through, as it would be courting disaster for any of our organization to go on strike at the present time, or in fact since the first of July.[10]

Then, after referring to a strike which ended unsuccessfully after having been authorized by referendum, the president tendered some advice which must have grated upon the ears of at least some of the local union representatives:

And I would advise all Unions to vote on strike privileges, not through sympathy or on the spur of the moment, but to consider the condition of trade, and the chances of success, and from a business standpoint.

With the passage of time and the accumulation of central funds, the national unions became better able to control the strike activities of the locals and thus to enforce the type of advice of which a sample was quoted above. We mentioned at the beginning of this study that it was not until the end of the nineteenth century that the national unions could be regarded as relatively permanent institutions and that this stability was manifested by the fact that the ratio of expirations to new national unions was markedly lower during the depressed decade of the nineties than it had been during the depressed decade of the seventies (see p. 4). The higher survival rate of the national unions was undoubtedly associated with a higher survival rate of their constituent locals, and the latter might well have owed their life, in many cases, to the restraining influence of their parent organizations. This is suggested by the following excerpt from Secretary O'Dea's annual report in 1895:

For the first time in twelve years we have passed through the season without a strike of an international character, or one legalized by the I.U. This is something remarkable, and is without a parallel in the history of trade unions in this country for the same time.

It goes to show that the members of our organization are awakening to the fact that there is a time for strikes as for anything else, and that strikes in times of depression are not the right thing and should be avoided if possible.[11]

The same businesslike viewpoint was expounded with considerable lucidity by General Secretary Sherman of the National Brotherhood of Electrical Workers who testified before the United States Industrial Commission in 1899. The Brotherhood was then a new organization (it had been founded in 1891), and the following excerpts from the secretary's testimony reveals the contrast between the national and the local viewpoints and the national's

10. *Proceedings*, 1893, p. 3.
11. *Proceedings*, 1895, p. 34.

preoccupation with the problem of nonunion workers as potential strike-breakers in bad times:

(A) Taking it from a personal standpoint, if I was working for an employer and he proved to me that it was absolutely necessary, in order for him to make a fair percentage on the money invested by him, that my wages should be reduced until times became better, I would accept it. But whether the rank and file in labor organizations would do the same thing, I cannot say. . . .

(Q) Were not nearly all strikes that we have had within the last few years, on the part of organized workmen, strikes to recover the loss in wages? (A) Yes. . . .

(Q) Do you consider strikes at this period a sign of prosperity? (A) I do. I think the prosperity has something to do with it. . . .

(Q) If an equal number of strikes, or any number of strikes occurred to resist reductions or attempts to lengthen the hours of labor, that might be taken as the opposite of good times? (A) Yes. Well, the strike question can be put down into a nutshell. If 500 men walk out of this building on a strike and the manufacturers can get 500 men to replace them, they will beat them. If they cannot get 500 men to replace the 500, they have a battle. . . .

(A) In my brotherhood, a local cannot go on a strike without the sanction of the executive board of the brotherhood. That has to go through a certain routine, and we have to know before they go out that they have a good show to win the strike, or we will not allow them to go out, and we look the ground over pretty carefully and if we find that there is a chance to beat them with nonunion men, we do not go on with the battle.[12]

But if the national officers sought to shun the strike in depression, they were confident of its effectiveness in prosperity. It appears to follow from Secretary Sherman's testimony on the crucial importance of the availability of strikebreakers that, if strikes could not be won in bad times because employers could easily recruit strikebreakers from the ranks of the unemployed, strikers had "a good show" to win in good times, when there were no (or many fewer) unemployed to furnish the strikebreaking service. Hence he considered that "the prosperity has something to do with" the recent wave of strikes "to recover the loss in wages."

Furthermore, statistical data presented by the Industrial Commission invite inferences which would suggest, at first blush, that the confidence of the union leaders in the strike in good times was not misplaced. For the commission's analysis of strikes over the period 1881 to 1900 reveal that strikes for increases in wages and for reduction in hours (most of which might be presumed to have occurred in business upswings) were relatively more successful than were strikes against wage reductions (the incidence of which

12. United States Industrial Commission, *Report on the Relations and Conditions of Capital and Labor Employed in Manufactures and General Business*, v. VII of the Commission's Reports (Washington: Government Printing Office, 1901), p. 375.

was greatest in depression). This is revealed in the following excerpts from the tabular presentation of the commission's data:

TABLE 10

RESULTS OF STRIKES ACCORDING TO CAUSES, 1881–1900.[a]

Causes	No. of establish- ments struck	Per cent of establishments in which strikes were—		
		Successful	Partly Successful	Unsuc- cessful
For increases of wages and adoption of scales	64,321	53.2	18.2	28.6
For reduction of hours, over- time pay, holidays, etc.	40,228	59.3	14.2	26.5
Against decrease of wages	10,843	41.3	12.1	46.5

[a] U. S. Industrial Commission, *Reports on Labor Organizations, Labor Disputes, and Arbitration, and on Railway Labor*, v. XVII of the Commission's Reports, (Washington, D. C.: Government Printing Office, 1901). See also Alvin H. Hansen, "Cycles of Strikes," *American Economic Review*, v. XI, December 1921, no. 4, pp. 616–621 wherein it is observed that the percentage of strikes against wage cuts was twice as great in the depression years 1883–1885 and 1893–1897 as in the relatively prosperous years 1881–1882 and 1886–1892.

Periods of business recovery were characterized by growth in the demand for labor and by a relative decrease in the supply of nonunion labor. Although Secretary Sherman sought to explain his Brotherhood's position on "the strike question" solely with respect to the cyclical fluctuation in the supply of non-union labor, the movement in demand was also a most important factor underlying the successful strike records achieved by the unions in periods of recovery and prosperity.

Indeed, since growing demand for labor could of itself generate increases in money wages, is it not possible that the unions owed their success to the fact that the wage increases which they "won" would have come about in any event? It is understandable that national officers were prompt to point to favorable strike records and, while helping the membership to count their blessings, invariably took full credit (in the name of their organizations) for wage increases achieved. The following statement, taken from the report of Secretary McGuire to the 1888 convention of the Carpenters' Brotherhood is an excellent example of the usual claim:

Taken all in all, we can safely say that through the instrumentality of our Organization, we have succeeded in securing certain advantages and benefits which would not have been obtained for our members, had our Brotherhood and its local unions not been in existence. Not alone have we obtained higher wages and reduced hours of labor for our own members in many cities, but in all such cases, a large proportion of the non-union men have equally profited with union men in all that has been achieved.

For instance, in two years we have advanced wages from 25 to 75 cents per day in 268 cities under our jurisdiction. This affected fully 26,000 members, which, at an average of 50 cents advance per day, would make a gain of $13,000 per day to those members; or on a basis of 9 months' work per year, $2,808,000 more wages annually for these 26,000 members. When we also add the non-union men who have shared in this advance, it will bring the amount to fully four million and a half dollars more wages per year that have been secured for and placed in the pockets of the union and non-union carpenters through the agency and work of our Brotherhood.[13]

But it has been argued that wage increases which actually were granted after strikes would have occurred in the absence of strikes and unions.[14] However, the hypothesis that unions did not establish wage levels appreciably higher than the levels which would have ruled in the absence of unions does not easily square with the fact that the number of strikes for increases in wages and reductions in hours, most of which probably occurred in prosperous periods, was nearly ten times the number of strikes against decreases in wages during the period 1881–1900 (see Table 10 above). Why should employers have been willing to incur strikes for wage increases which they would have granted anyway? Granted that the hypothesis is consistent with the higher percent of union victories during good times, can it be reconciled with the fact that there were more strikes to be won?

One answer might be that, although a strike might have been settled by the granting of a wage increase no greater than the increase which would have occurred in the absence of the strike, the union's initial demand was for a wage increase considerably in excess of the final settlement. In such instances, strikes were necessary to achieve wage increases no greater than those which would have occurred without strikes. That such strikes could plausibly be regarded as union "victories" by the membership and the general public was due to the fact that the final settlements were for figures in excess of the employers' initial offers just as they were below initial union demands. Whether or not employers also regarded the outcome as union victories depended largely on whether they realized that they would have

13. *Proceedings,* 1888, p. 18. Slichter pointed to the wage increase which occurred in the steel industry in 1952 "only after a prolonged strike" as evidence in support of the thesis that the United Steelworkers did secure wage increases in excess of those increases which might have been expected to occur "in the absence of unions or in the absence of strong unions." ("Wage Policies Since World War II," an address before the Economic Conference of the Chicago Association of Commerce and Industry, November 24, 1952.)

14. Milton Friedman, "Some Comments on the Significance of Labor Unions for Economic Policy," in David McCord Wright, ed., *The Impact of the Union* (New York: Harcourt, Brace, 1951), p. 222.

been obliged to grant the bargained increases in order to retain as many workers in their employ as they required.

The possibility that employers were not aware of the purely competitive necessity for raising wages suggests another explanation of the increase in the incidence of strikes and in union victories, if it is assumed that the unions typically struck to support demands for increases no greater than those which would have been granted anyway. If employers would not have become aware of the necessity for raising wages until they found that they were either losing workers or unable to hire additional workers at the old wage rates, they would have initially resisted any increases demanded by unions. However, such resistance would have presumably diminished once their "ability to pay" the union wage became apparent to them, provided that the union was willing to settle at the true competitive level; hence the union "victories." In that event, however, it would not be true to regard unions as "simply thermometers registering the heat rather than furnaces producing the heat."

Thus the union could have enhanced the economic welfare of its membership, even though the wage increase which it "won" would have been achieved without its efforts. By "demanding" such a wage increase from the employer to the point of striking for it, the union "won" it for the members of the employer's existing force. By demanding immediately the wage which the employer would have paid eventually, the union spared its members the cost—pecuniary and otherwise—of changing jobs. Furthermore, if the union's demand could be won without recourse to a strike, the union could claim credit for reducing the social, as well as the private, cost involved in frictional unemployment.

In this connection, Gompers' remarks on the allegedly beneficial effect of strikes are somewhat pertinent:

If the workers, say, have struck for an increase in wages, and the employers refuse to concede them, and finally defeat the workmen, yet as a matter of fact it is almost invariably the case that those who have taken the places of the men who went on strike were themselves receiving less wages before doing so. It is seldom, if ever, that a workman will go from a position where he receives higher wages to take the place of a striker at lower wages. . . . It is asserted that those who strike are compelled to look out for other positions, which is naturally true; but in only isolated cases do they accept positions which pay them less than those they struck against.[15]

The impact of the union thus would have consisted merely in the anticipation of demand-induced wage increases and in the elimination of "cobweb" movements of supply and demand converging on the new competitive equilibrium. Moreover, the union lead would have tended to dwindle over

15. Testimony before Industrial Commission, *Reports on Labor*, v. VII, p. 608.

time. In the first place, nonunion firms would ultimately have been obliged to raise wages to levels which union action had anticipated. In the second place, union firms might have reacted more sluggishly than their nonunion competitors to subsequent increases in demand if they had entered into annual agreements with the unions who represented their employees. Union agreements, as we shall observe in the following chapter, usually specified minimum and not maximum rates of pay, and employers did in fact exceed union scales; but it may still be argued that, where annual negotiation of collective agreements was conventional, some retardation in the rate of adjustment was involved. However, despite the fact that this cobweb effect, fortified by reference to the firm annual agreement, tended to be only short-run in nature, it does imply some impact upon the process of wage adjustment which must be directly attributed to the trade unions.

In fact, some impact ought to be assumed, whether or not one accepts the hypotheses suggested in the preceding two paragraphs as plausible explanations of the occurrence of strikes and of union victories under the thermometer theory. For that theory cannot be squared with evidence (referred to in Chapter 1) which would indicate that wages were generally higher in unionized firms than they were in nonunion establishments. One must add that the same evidence suggests that such differential union effects upon wages were likely to be more pronounced in the short-run than in the long-run, for the nonunion, low-cost firms frequently expanded either more rapidly than or at the expense of the unionized firms. (Our cobweb hypothesis, as we have noted, would also indicate a dwindling effect, although it could account for instances where union firms did not lose business to nonunion firms.) But a cyclical upswing is usually treated as a short period; therefore we should inquire into conditions under which strikes for wages in excess of nonunion levels could have been won as over-all demand increased.

If we assume that the wage demanded by the union was higher than the wage which would have ruled in its absence, then granting the union's demand could have meant either that total profits were reduced or that their rate of increase was reduced. Output and employment might well have been curtailed in union firms, and one expects that both the will and the ability of employers to resist the union wage would have been considerably greater than the unions' relatively favorable strike record indicates that they actually were. But if union demands resulted only in braking the rate at which profits were increasing during the upswing, the effect upon output and employment, other things being equal, might have been to prevent them from expanding as rapidly as they otherwise would have done, rather than to depress their existing levels.

This effect would hold whether the increase in the demand for labor was derived entirely from a prior increase in the demand for the product which it helped to produce or whether it proceeded from other sources as well. The former case was typically characterized by a lag of wages behind prices during the business upswing. Presumably, and especially if the previous depression had been severe, a reserve of unemployed prevented wages from rising as rapidly as prices in response to an expansion of demand; while diminishing returns from the increase in output and employment and higher labor costs incurred "by breaking in new hands" could account for increasing marginal costs and, therefore, prices, in the absence of a significant rise in wages. To the extent that a union could reduce the wage lag in a given industry, it would dampen the employer's willingness to expand output and employment, but it would not necessarily oblige him to curtail the scope of his present operations. If unions could have raised wages as rapidly as prices moved upward, then, assuming productivity unchanged and assuming that prices began to rise before full employment was reached, no expansion would have taken place. Unions, under such instantaneous cost-of-living adjustments (if such are conceivable) would have prevented real wages from falling.[16]

When the wage lag became generalized throughout the entire economy, it appeared as a decline in real wage rates and a corresponding increase in real profit rates (unless the decline in real wage rates proceeded entirely from the rise in the prices of farm products).[17] Hence workers were under special incentive to obtain increases in money wages, while employers were not too averse to granting their demands. As the chairman of the New York State Board of Mediation testified in 1900,

The great increase in the number of strikes in the last 20 months, in my opinion, did not indicate more than usual seriousness or difference between labor and capital. As I have said, they took place on a rising labor market, and as wages

16. Cf., J. M. Keynes, *The General Theory of Employment Interest and Money* (New York: Harcourt, Brace, 1935), p. 284 and especially Vera Lutz, "Real and Monetary Factors in Determination of Employment Levels," *Quarterly Journal of Economics*, v. LXVI, May 1952, no. 2, pp. 258–259.

17. It has been suggested that the wage lag might act to reduce the length of the cyclical upswing, despite the buoyant effect which it exerts via increased profits. In *A Contribution to the Theory of the Trade Cycle* (Oxford: Clarendon Press, 1950), J. R. Hicks argues that, by damping down the inflation in money incomes, the wage lag allows the check to the expansion in real output—due either to the achievement by the economy of the "ceiling" of full employment or to the inability of the combined forces of induced consumption and induced investment (the "supermultiplier") to achieve that ceiling—to take precedence over the purely monetary boom (pp. 126–127). By parity of reasoning, therefore, it might be suggested that, insofar as unions can reduce the lag of money wages behind prices, they succeed, *ceteris paribus,* in prolonging the upswing and postponing the "real" downturn. But since strong unionism was not nearly so pervasive throughout the economy in the nineteenth century as it is today, we must conclude that whatever reductions in wage lag the early unions were able to achieve in the industries in which they were organized were not attended by the over-all indirect effect of sustaining aggregate demand. On the other hand, it follows that union activity in the period under study was less instrumental in inducing further price rises and/or curtailing the expansion by forcing the economy against a monetary ceiling. On the latter point, see Gottfried Haberler, "Wage Policy, Employment, and Economic Stability," in Wright, *The Impact of The Union,* p. 49.

are the last thing to rise, the laborers became very anxious and eager to get higher wages and forced the issue all along the line.[18]

On the other hand, not all upswings were characterized by the wage lag in the period which extended from the end of the Civil War until the beginning of the twentieth century. During most of the upswings in that period, as we have noted (pp. 18–19), real wage rates did not fall. This does not necessarily imply, however, that prices in the manufacturing sector of the economy failed to outrun industrial wage rates, for agricultural prices entered into the cost-of-living index and might have been a factor in preventing real wage rates from falling. Nevertheless, one can readily account for the fact that, even within any given industry, it was not necessary that activity be curtailed when money wages rose as rapidly as—or even more rapidly than—product price. If innovations and/or new investment increased the physical productivity of labor, higher money wage rates need not have been reflected in (proportionately) increased costs.

It is possible, moreover, to conceive of instances wherein a union-won wage rise need not even have been instrumental in checking further expansion. For one thing, if further expansion were impossible in any event, the union's wage increase would not—because it could not—act as a brake upon progress under the first set of conditions outlined above. If full employment of the particular class of labor in question had been reached prior to the union's wage demand (which could have been the case if the preceding depression had not been characterized by severe unemployment) and if the demand for labor had been in excess of the (fixed) supply at the hitherto prevailing wage, a wage increase, while it might have reduced the quantity of labor demanded, would not necessarily have reduced employment. In such cases, however, if the wage would have risen to the indicated level in the absence of unionism, the role of the union would be confined to possibly reducing the time interval in which the demand for labor is in excess of supply.

Furthermore, if one admits the possibility that excess demand in the market for the product under consideration was not automatically self-correcting and would not necessarily result in a rise in price, but that, if the price did rise in response to an increase in costs, consumers would increase their spending on this product in order to buy the same quantity as before, then the effect of the union's wage rise would be, first, to push up the product price and, second, to stimulate increased consumer money demand.[19]

18. Industrial Commission, *Reports on Labor*, v. VII, p. 876.

19. John Maurice Clark, "Criteria of Sound Wage Adjustment," in Wright, *The Impact of The Union*, pp. 4–5; also p. 63. Also, Sumner H. Slichter, "What Have We Learned from Our Experience With Inflation?" (address before the Iowa Bankers Association, October 22, 1951), p. 5. The assumptions, as stated by Clark, are some discretion on the part of the seller in setting the price of the product and a "flexible credit system." Again,

Moreover, if union-won wage increases had been sufficiently widespread, they could have induced increased business borrowing and thus accelerated the upswing in demand.

Under circumstances similar to those described above, then, it was possible for wages to rise by union action and, therefore, for a larger proportion of strikes to be prosecuted to a successful conclusion in good times than in bad. Such increases, while encroaching upon prospective profits, need not have done so to an extent sufficient to induce employers to incur the costs involved in stoppages of sufficient duration to overcome the endurance of the strikers. It is also possible, of course, that vigorous union wage policies, even if not seriously contested by employers, were attended by repercussions which, from the union viewpoint, were unfavorable. In the first place, the rise in the cost of union labor might well have been conducive to the substitution of other resources for that labor, where such substitution was technologically feasible, provided that the cost of the union labor in question was rising relative to the cost of the substitutes. In the second place, as we have been assuming, it is conceivable that union gains, while not resulting in absolute curtailment of operations, might have braked the rate of recovery and expansion and, consequently, the rate at which the unemployed—including unemployed union members—were reabsorbed by business enterprise.

To what extent these repercussions might have inhibited unions in formulating demands during general upswings is, however, beside the point at issue. We are here investigating, not how strikes were avoided by unions, but the conditions under which they could be won by unions which were pressing demands for increases in excess of those which would have been granted by employers solely out of competitive necessity. We have observed that the reduction in the supply of nonunion labor and the increase in product demand tended to reduce the employer's willingness to incur strikes, since the former reduced the employer's prospects for victory and the latter made the avoidance of increases in labor costs less imperative.

On the other hand, the cost of incurring strikes tended to decline in good times insofar as cash reserves increased and could be tapped to defray continuing expenses during the shutdown period. But to the extent that shutdown costs varied directly with profits lost due to the strike, those costs rose in good times. Thus, since the chances of victory were less favorable and the necessity to resist union demands less urgent, it might be reasonably concluded that the cost of incurring strikes outweighed potential benefits therefrom more frequently in periods of expansion than in recessions and depressions.

---

however, it might be noted that, if the supply of the product in question had reached its "ceiling," a rise in price need not necessarily result in a reduction in sales volume and output, even though it failed to touch off a compensating increase in money demand.

SEASONAL STRIKES AND THE ANNUAL AGREEMENT

The tendency of workers with little experience in unionism to strike was in evidence not only in times of depression throughout industry generally, but in all phases of the cycle in those trades in which the demand for labor followed a pronounced seasonal pattern. Locals, by striking during slack seasons, endangered their existence, just as they did when they struck during cyclical downswings. Strikes in the readymade garment industry were concentrated in the dull seasons,[20] and it was reported that the most highly skilled group, the cutters, "are only organized when they are out of work."[21] And a president of the Bricklayers noted that

even if the strike (in winter) be successful, there are always some regrets on the part of members, who having taken a prominent part in the strike by their official position or otherwise, are sacrificed to the bitterness of the employers who, feeling sore, take this method of revenge.[22]

Accordingly, it was national policy to discourage locals from striking during dull seasons as well as during the longer periods of general depression. After receiving the president's report, from which the above quotation is taken, the Bricklayers' convention of 1871 passed a resolution which provided that, "no aid be given by the National Union to any Local Union striking from the 15th of November to the 15th of March." Similar laws were passed by the Cigar Makers, Sheet Metal Workers, Piano Workers, and Carpenters.[23] The Piano Workers, as noted previously, did not go so far as to forbid all strikes during the dull season: they allowed strikes against wage cuts in opposition to the contract system of employment or to payment by truck. The Cigar Makers provided only that no applications for increases in wages be tendered during the dull seasons, and the periods of suspension of such applications were made to vary from region to region, the dull season occurring between April and October in the South and between November and April elsewhere.

20. Industrial Commission, *Reports on Labor*, v. XVII, p. 638.

21. Industrial Commission, *Reports on.Labor*, v. VII, p. 308. It appears that workers in all the needle trades were too volatile in temperament during this early period to be good union material. (Cf. the testimony of Secretary White of the United Garment Workers before the Industrial Commission, v. VII, pp. 182–184.) The tendency of their local unions to disband following the termination, whether successful or not, of the particular crisis which had previously prompted their formation, is reminiscent of the pre-union stage of worker organization, which Glocker designated as the "shop meeting." (Theodore W. Glocker, *The Government of American Trade Unions* [Baltimore: Johns Hopkins, 1913], ch. I.) It is noteworthy that the Webbs, in their classic definition, insisted that a trade union was a "*continuous* association of wage earners." (Sidney and Beatrice Webb, *The History of Trade Unionism* [London: Longmans, Green, 1894], p. 1. My italics.)

22. *Proceedings,* 1871, pp. 9–10.

23. Janes, *Control of Strikes,* pp. 44–46.

The influence of the national officers in securing these periods of abstinence is demonstrated in the case of the Carpenters. Two years before, the Brotherhood decided not to sanction any "general strike" (involving all the employers in a given locality) between April first and October first in any year, and it had been reported that the general executive board had "discountenanced all trade movements earlier in the season, advising a later date." And the convention of 1890, which finally imposed a policy of restraint on the locals, took legislative action after having heard Secretary McGuire warn them that

No greater danger at present confronts our organization than to have local unions undertake strikes on their own authority early in the season—sometimes in March or April—before the work is in the market. Carpenters cannot and should not strike at the same time in the season as masons and bricklayers. Our work comes after theirs, and our demands should not be made until the new work is well under way. Early strikes are attended almost universally by defeat, and in the few cases where we have not had complete success it has been where we have had premature or unauthorized strikes, or where long notice was given to the employers and opportunities given them to prepare for the struggle. Unions desiring to strike hereafter should take warning from this and act advisedly.[24]

But if the employer had his workers over the barrel "before the work is in the market," the situation was reversed after the busy season had begun; and if it was conceded that there was "a time to strike" as well as "a time not to strike," should we expect to find the national officers calling off the local dogs of war once work was under way? The crucial importance of the element of timing to the outcome of a strike was implied by Gompers in his testimony before the Industrial Commission. He attempted to demonstrate that Ben Franklin's old saw about the time lost being never found again did not apply to time lost on strike in seasonal trades. According to Gompers,

the time which is lost in the strike is always made up in a greater continuity of industry after the strike is closed. It is seldom, if ever, workmen are continually employed throughout the entire year. *A strike is simply a transferring of the time when idleness shall occur from the advantage of the employer to the advantage of the employees.*[25]

What made "a transferring of the time when idleness shall occur" from the slack season to the busy season "to the advantage of the employees"? It was reported of even the poorly organized garment workers, whose strikes,

24. *Proceedings,* 1888, p. 17; 1890, p. 20. The secretary's remarks and the convention's subsequent action were apparently prompted by unsuccessful strikes in Buffalo, Denver, and Dayton. (The dissimilarity between the busy season of the Bricklayers and that of the Carpenters was referred to in Chapter 12 in explaining the reluctance of the former to ally themselves with the latter.)

25. Industrial Commission, *Reports on Labor,* v. VII, p. 608; for quote below, v. XVII, p. 638. My italics.

it will be recalled, occurred most frequently during "times of great dullness," that, "if they are extended into the period of busy work, the result is likely to be that that period will last longer than would otherwise have been the case, or that work will be rushed more rapidly, *with perhaps consequent higher pay.*"

Transition from slack to busy season, like transition from depression to prosperity, was characterized by an increase in employer demand for the labor in question and by a decrease in the supply of nonunion labor. Seasonal variation in the supply of nonunion labor was probably not as sharp as cyclical variation, for, granted the case of the garment workers and other groups which had yet to establish really "continuing associations," cyclical variations in the mortality rates of local unions and in paid-up membership was probably greater than seasonal swings therein.

On the other hand, seasonal changes in the demand for labor may well have been greater than cyclical variations. Furthermore, seasonal upswings in demand differed somewhat from cyclical recoveries in that the former were characterized by changes in the shape, as well as in the position, of the employers' demand curves. Two factors were primarily responsible for the fact that the elasticity of the demand for labor typically underwent considerable reduction during the busy season, and both stem from the short duration of that period. The first consists in the fact that, since the year's work was concentrated in a short period of time, businessmen in many trades frequently sought to schedule their production prior to the commencement of the busy season and entered in contracts with customers in which both prices and quantities were specified. In addition, the shortness of the busy period restricted the range of technical alternatives to "fixed technical coefficients of production," so that it was not feasible to substitute other resources for labor, or *vice versa* within a given season.

Given these two conditions, it was not impossible for unionists to proceed with a fair degree of safety on the "lump of labor" assumption—namely, that the amount of labor demanded by the employer was fixed and hence invariant with respect to the wage rate. The shortness of the busy season made it unlikely that employers could substitute other factors for labor in response to a rise in the wage rate before the end of the season. And the prior existence of contracts fixing both product prices and quantities—to say nothing of the desirability of completing construction projects already begun—made it unlikely that union-won wage increases would result in any immediate reduction in output and employment. Thus, an "all-or-none" choice might be forced upon the employer: confronted with wage demands after the busy season had started, they were without the traditional alternatives of adjusting price and output so as to maximize profits under the higher cost conditions; they either had to produce the agreed-upon quantity at the agreed-upon price or not produce at all. On one occasion a group of glass bottle manufacturers requested a negotiating committee of the Glass Bottle Blowers' Associaion to defer their demands for a while because

they claimed that they had taken orders based upon their reduced blowing scale, and to increase the blowing cost at that time would seriously endanger their position as business men.[26]

At the same time, the Bottle Blowers were engaged in a bitter organizing strike against the nonunion employers in Bridgeton, New Jersey, and the strategic importance of the seasonal element to the union's high command is revealed in the following statement by President Hayes:

August and September are the months in which contracts are usually made, and if we can keep the factories in their present crippled condition they will not only lose the large orders which they hitherto held, but will not be in a position to make any new contracts.

The reader might discern in the nineteenth-century employer's dilemma a situation akin to that with which the latter's descendant might be confronted under a guaranteed-annual-wage contract. Under traditional collective bargaining procedure, the union contents itself with a wage demand, and the employer is free to adjust his hiring accordingly. Under the guarantee, however, this freedom could be denied to the employer, the union's demand specifying both wage rate and employment.[27] Now the early unions, by taking advantage of the alternation of dull and busy seasons, could succeed in imposing the all-or-none condition, which we regard as characteristic of the "ideal" guaranteed wage contract, through the medium of the traditional bargain—that is, a demand confined to wages only. Under the terms of the "wage bargain," the employer was technically free to reduce his employment of labor in order to maximize his profits at the higher labor costs, but he was effectively prevented from so doing either by the prior existence of a "price bargain" with his customers or by the necessity to conclude a given piece of work, already started, within a time limit prescribed by the length of the unexpired portion of the busy season, less, perhaps, the time required for subsequent projects scheduled after the completion of the current one. Theoretically, the result could be the same under the seasonally timed wage demand as under the guaranteed wage contract (see Appendix II below). Thus, by making nature work for them, early local unions could, in the short run, achieve results out of proportion to their long-run powers of adhesiveness and coercion, just as a swimmer, not powerful in his own right, can make good progress shoreward if he knows how to ride the surf.

Under the circumstances, it is not surprising to find the Carpenters'

26. Glass Bottle Blowers, *Proceedings*, 1899, pp. 17–18, 21.
27. Cf. Wassily Leontief, "The Pure Theory of the Guaranteed Annual Wage Contract," *Journal of Political Economy*, v. LIV, February 1946, no. 1, pp. 76–79.

general executive board "advising a later date" after refusing to recognize strikes called "early in the season." Combined with this line of advice was the injunction to strike without giving the employer any inkling of what was coming. Thus President Saffin of the Molders had recommended that a law requiring that locals request employers to arbitrate be changed in view of the latter's refusal to arbitrate and because "such notice gives the employer time to prepare for such strikes."[28] Apart from denying to the employer the opportunity to recruit a force of strikebreakers in advance, the tactic of surprise could prove advantageous insofar as the employer might be caught with a project or order only partly completed and, as in the case of a seasonally timed wage demand, with terms of sale fixed by prior commitment. This latter aspect of the element of surprise is implicit in a formula which McGuire prescribed for his Carpenters:

> At all times our policy should be first to secure conferences with the employers, and, by negotiation or conciliation, endeavor to secure a settlement, only resorting to a strike as a last alternative. But when we do strike let us strike to win, and give little notice of our intention to strike. And strike only when carpenter work is plentiful and let our strikes be short and decisive.[29]

But although national officers were not averse to authorizing strikes during the busy season—just as they were not averse to authorizing strikes in good times—they stopped considerably short of urging the locals to strike whenever circumstances were favorable to success. Certainly, in McGuire's plan of battle the strike was conceived of as a weapon of last resort, although, judging from the Molders' experience, it might not prove easy for an obedient local executive committee both to take the prior step of requesting negotiations and to retain the element of surprise.

One reason why the nationals were reluctant to advocate a policy of attack without reservation suggests itself immediately. If the union had the employer at a disadvantage during the busy season, the tables were turned once that season was past. The Molders were especially troubled in this respect. The national executive, on one occasion, sanctioned a strike against an employer who, during a shutdown for repairs and inventory announced that he would reëmploy his help on a piecework, instead of a time, basis. The strike was lost.[30] National approval, however, had been made mandatory, for as far back as 1876, the international's constitution had provided that

> When a shop or shops have been closed for one or more weeks, and a notice is given that when such shops resume operations it will be at a reduction of wages, or that the men shall sign contracts, or work Bucks, . . . such notice will be con-

28. *Proceedings,* 1876, p. 10.
29. *Proceedings,* 1892, p. 17.
30. *Proceedings,* 1895, p. 22.

sidered a lockout, provided such (local) Union, by a two-thirds vote, shall declare it a lock-out.[31]

If adequate data on molders' wages were available, they might reveal a marked seasonal pattern, for, if the local union were top dog during the busy season, it was the underdog when the foundries were closed down. The situation was very well described in an article by John P. Frey and John R. Commons, in which the authors noted that

There were two periods in the year, midsummer and midwinter, when it was customary to close the foundry for from one to two months, as this was the period between seasons. If the foundryman desired to force a low price on a *new* stove, the patterns would not be sent to the foundry until the closing-down period had arrived. While the shop was closed the molders would be shown the new patterns and notified of the molding price the firm was willing to pay. A refusal on the molders' part to accept these would generally lead to a statement that the shop would remain closed until they were willing to accept them, and on many occasions an extremely low molding price was secured under these circumstances. Again, when a strike occurred and was lost the foundryman changed the former prices, and when union molders returned they were forced to work for lower piece prices. It would happen also that the foundrymen waited until periods of depression had arrived before setting a new molding price. Conversely, when trade was brisk and the conditions favorable, the molders would succeed in forcing a higher price on certain pieces or upon an entire set of stoves. . . .[32]

The employer's bargaining position improved in two respects during the dull season. In the first place, since he had no unfilled or partially completed orders outstanding, labor ceased to be a "fixed" cost in the special sense that output itself could not be varied. Thus, even though there might have been but little possibility of substituting other factors for labor in the short period under contemplation, future prices and, therefore, output could be adjusted in response to changes in wages. Demand for labor, in other words, became more elastic.

On the other hand, after the busy period had given way to the slack season, the cost of labor to the worker became less variable in nature and assumed more of the characteristics of a fixed charge. Following J. M. Clark, one might divide total labor cost to the worker into a fixed component and a part which varies with output. "The necessary maintenance of labor" is a fixed cost, in that it "goes on whether the laborer is employed or not."[33] The

31. *Constitution,* 1876, Art. VI, Sec. 5. "Working Bucks," or "Berkshires" referred to the practice of employing helpers. (See Sumner H. Slichter, *Union Policies and Industrial Management* [Washington: Brookings, 1941], pp. 46–47, n. 71.)

32. John P. Frey and John R. Commons, "Conciliation in the Stove Industry," *Bulletin No. 62* of the U. S. Bureau of Labor (Washington: Government Printing Office, 1906), v. XII, p. 156.

33. J. Maurice Clark, *Studies in the Economics of Overhead Costs* (Chicago: University of Chicago, 1932), pp. 360–364, 377.

variable component consists in the surrender of leisure, which, of course, must increase with employment and, other things being equal, with output. Now until the worker earned an income sufficient to defray his "necessary maintenance," the cost of working was not variable to him, for the time devoted to work did not represent any alternative foregone. Income and leisure, at very low income levels, are complements rather than substitutes. But, if the worker's wage rate was sufficiently high, periods of steady employment yielded him an income in excess of necessary maintenance, which, as Ricardo conceded, could be defined only as a function of "the habits and customs of the people" in the period specified. In busy seasons, therefore, leisure was valued as an alternative to income and the variable element in the cost of working to the worker was significant. However, with the reduction of employment in the dull season, income was reduced to a level near or below necessary maintenance. The result, according to Clark, was that "when an unemployed worker finds a job, the leisure he gives up has no very material value and costs him no very material sacrifice." For, "when labor is laid off, no material human cost is avoided, and if work is found to fill up the gaps, human costs do not increase in proportion to work done." To put it more formally, at sufficiently low levels of income and employment, the marginal rate of substitution of income for leisure approaches infinity.

Hence, during the dull season, the cost to the worker became more of an overhead than a direct charge. Since such cost does not "increase in proportion to work done . . . the differential cost of labor is negligible." And if differential (or marginal) costs of labor to workers declined drastically during seasons of reduced employment, their "reservation prices" were reduced accordingly. Like the employer, who, in the middle of a busy season, was virtually obliged (within the limits of the all-or-none choice available to him) to pay the wage demanded by the union, the worker, during a dull season, was obliged to work for whatever wage was offered. Furthermore, if the worker's aptitude was specialized, he was obliged to take whatever wage (above the level paid to unskilled labor) was offered by the employer in question; thus specialization of the worker's skill was analogous to the employer's inability to substitute other resources for the labor in question. Thus the return to the worker, who was "denied" both the alternative of working in some other trade and the alternative of not working at all, was akin to the return on "sunk" capital; it assumed the nature of a quasi-rent.

The danger in selling different units of the same article (in this case, labor) at difference prices (in the dull and brisk seasons) lies in the fact that acceptance of a lower price might set a precedent and tend to "spoil the market." Now, in terms of this discussion, the superiority in the long run bargaining power of either party consisted in its greater ability to hold the other party to terms of employment to which the latter had agreed under duress. Although (if we can take contemporary reports at face value) it appears that local unions, in some instances, were able to raise wages by timing their demands strategically during the busy season, employers were able to impose their will upon their employees during the following lull, when competition for labor was reduced. This indicates that the employer was not obliged (as a buyer) to spoil his market for labor. And since wages frequently rose seasonally during the busy months, it appears that workers did not necessarily spoil their market as sellers of labor. Indeed, in the absence of any constraints upon the free market for labor, it is not conceivable that the workers' market would be spoiled, for, without other changes, a subsequent rise in the demand for labor would ensure a rise in wages in the next busy season.

In some cases, however, employers succeeded in imposing restraints upon the labor market which made it impossible for the men to renegotiate the terms on which their labor was sold after demand had increased. When the Molders authorized strikes against employers who insisted that "the men shall sign contracts" as a condition of reëmployment following a shutdown, they were referring to an arrangement whereby molders were obliged to sign individual agreements obliging them to remain with the same employer for one year, at a stipulated wage. Contracts were presented to the men during the slack season, when many were out of work. The following episode, reported by President Martin Fox, is typical of this practice:

In midwinter the stove manufacturers of Hamilton, Ontario, demanded a reduction of 10 per cent in the scale, which the members of Union No. 26, rather than become involved in a strike, agreed to accept. Announcing themselves ready to go to work, the firms demanded that they should first sign a contract binding themselves to work one year at the reduction.[34]

In the 1870's, hiring in the iron and steel industry was characterized by a "contract system," under which the first four weeks' wages and 25 per cent of all subsequent wages were withheld until the end of the year, to be paid only if profits were sufficient to "justify such payment."[35] Such contracts were not binding, for breach of the labor contract was not a criminal offense in this country, as it had been in Great Britain, prior to the passage of the Master and Servant Act of 1867. Employers put teeth into the contract, however,—or achieved the same result without the formality of a contract— through supplementary devices such as the withholding of a portion of the employee's wages which would be forfeited if he failed to complete the term of employment specified in the contract. Wage withholding had long been characteristic of the employment relationship in the iron foundry trade. According to one writer, the most notable achievement of the first permanent

34. *Proceedings,* 1895, p. 12.
35. Industrial Commission, *Reports on Labor,* v. XVII, p. 213.

local union of molders (about 1855) was the elimination, in the city of Philadelphia, of the individual contract and the practice of withholding 10 per
cent of the season's wages until the end of the year in order to assure compliance therewith.[36] In some instances, as much as one-third of the earned
wages was withheld.[37] The deep resentment of the rank-and-file against this
practice was shared by the national officers, as is revealed in the following
episode:

Union No. 12 of Rochester, New York, submitted a grievance, . . . involving
one hundred and eleven members who were working for the Co-operative Stove
Company, Sill's Stove Company, and Galusha's Stove and Jobbing Foundry, who,
at the beginning of each year, insisted on the molders to sign an agreement (sic)
binding them to work for the year at such prices and under such systems and
rules as the employers saw fit to make, and that in order to enforce compliance
with the agreement, the men must leave back 10 per cent of their earnings as a
forfeit, should any molder violate the agreement. The members had, for several
years, with consent of the Union, been reluctantly signing these agreements, but
had also been quietly working to strengthen themselves with a view to taking a
stand against the obnoxious system, which the Union finally did. When the firms
wanted the molders to sign for the year 1890, the shops, with the exception of
Galusha's, were closed, and they refused to open until the molders signed. This
they refused to do, but instead sent in a grievance, asking the sanction and support of the I.M.U. of N.A., which was granted. Galusha's molders who, by consent of the Union, had remained at work, were also called out, and the Union
continued the fight until Sill's and Galusha's came to terms, and put their men to
work according to Union rules. While the Coöperative Foundry still holds out,
and is being run by boys, suspended members, non-Union and "scab" molders,
with the Union keeping up the fight against them, which will be continued until
the firm cries: Enough!

Since the workers, during the slack season, were in substantially the same
unfavorable bargaining position as the employer found himself once the busy
season had started, the results achieved by the latter through his offer of
reëmployment were identical in principle to the results achieved by the
former through their seasonally timed wage demands. In both cases, the
proffer of a conventional price bargain generated consequences similar to
results which could issue from a guaranteed-wage bargain, a type of guarantee the imposition of which requires considerably greater negotiating strength.
In obliging the individual worker to sign a contract whereby he pledged himself to work for an entire year at a given wage rate, however, the employer
superimposed upon the exploitation of the opportunities presented to him

36. F. W. Hilbert, "Trade-Union Agreements in the Iron Molders' Union," in Jacob
H. Hollander and George E. Barnett, editors, *Studies in American Trade Unionism*
(New York: Holt, 1906), p. 22.
37. *Proceedings*, 1890, p. 29.

by the dull season a type of bargain which was the precise equivalent of the sort of guaranteed annual wage agreement yet to be achieved by the contemporary trade union. Because of his disadvantageous "overhead" position, the worker might have been willing to work at the prescribed rate, but he would have been willing to do so only for the duration of the dull season. As soon as work became plentiful and his weekly income, at the given rate, increased with the seasonal increase in the number of hours of employment available to him at that rate, the cost of his labor to him became progressively less "fixed" in nature and more "direct." The higher the level of income, the more attractive leisure became as an alternative and, therefore, the higher the wage rate required to induce him to work the same length of time in any given period. The contractual arrangement, then, obliged the worker to work longer than he desired to at the given wage rate, just as the guaranteed annual wage contract could oblige the employer to hire more labor than he would be willing to hire, at the given rate of wages, if he were free to hire only as much as he wished. Thus, just as the combination of labor and wage income resulting from a wage guarantee might not lie on the employer's demand curve, so the combination of months of labor and yearly wage income resulting from the nineteenth-century individual contract did not lie on the worker's supply curve.

This arrangement, needless to say, was not devised by employers with malice aforethought; if one was going to enter into contractual commitments with one's customers, it was desirable first (to put it mildly) to enter into contractual agreements with one's employees. Nor does it imply that employers were able to depress wages to any "subsistence level," uncritically defined, and to keep them at that level. Competition for labor—which, in its long-run aspects, was assigned so important a role in the nation's economic development in the first chapter of this study—was operative even during dull seasons when employers were looking ahead and seeking to contract for future work. Moreover, workers were free to leave during the busy season if wages offered by other employers were sufficiently high to induce them to forfeit the portion of their wages that was withheld. However, granted the operation of competition, it is nevertheless plausible that wages, during the dull season, were depressed to levels which, according to the rapidly changing "habits and customs" of the workers themselves, were considered below the level of maintenance and secondly, that the existence of contracts, reinforced by wage-withholding and allied devices, did serve to postpone increases.

The unions, certainly, possessed no power comparable to the reinforced individual contract. They could, at best, succeed in breaching the individual agreements after the busy season had commenced and in taking advantage of the employers' greater vulnerability. However, competition among employers during the busy season was sufficient to induce adoption of the labor contract in the absence of strong unions; it was noted that, in the New York garment industry

if a manufacturer of clothing secures a good cutter he generally agrees to pay him good wages, but he will certainly want him to stay in his employment throughout the season, because otherwise he might stay so long as the demand for cutters is not so large and then quit him just in the height of the season, when he can get a better position at better terms; so as security the employer in this case generally withholds a portion of the wages from week to week, which is paid over at the expiration of the contractual term. Now, that is generally sufficient security, and that, of course, can also be done in case of a contract with labor organizations.[38]

But the labor organizations in question could not match the employer's frequently successful attempts to compel observance on a year-around basis of terms most favorable to their side. The best they could hope for was that there be as many "wage reopenings" as there were trade seasons within each year. But the more frequently terms of employment were altered, the greater the number of strikes. And the greater the number of strikes, the greater the strain on local and national treasuries and the higher the mortality rate of local unions.

There is evidence that some local unions in the construction industry (a highly seasonal trade), confronted with superior opposition, were content to forego the transient advantage which they enjoyed during the busy season and to settle for an arrangement whereby the employers would, they hoped, forego the less transient advantages presented to them by the off season. They sought annual contracts which they were willing to enter into before the busy season had begun. An incident reported by Bricklayers Local No. 6 of New York to the convention of 1871 reveals both the nature of the concession made and the compelling reason for making it:

It has always been customary, since the foundation of our Union, for us to set our wages for the ensuing year about the middle of February, which custom gives our employers an opportunity to know how to figure for their work for the season. We never had any trouble in regard to wages until last February, when the boss masons of our city, with very few exceptions, formed a combination among themselves to procure a reduction of our wages. . . .[39]

The local unions in the building trades regarded the firm collective agreement as a desirable alternative to the strike during the busy season. According to the testimony of a representative of the National Building Trades Council (an organization of the local councils, formed in 1897) before the Industrial

38. Industrial Commission, *Reports on Labor,* v. XIV, p. 56. (Testimony of Dr. Isaac A. Hourwich.)

39. *Proceedings,* 1871, p. 27. Although the national president, upon the urging of No. 6, petitioned the other locals for contributions, the response was nil, since "several of them are in pretty much the same condition as ourselves."

Commission, the locals would not press for a revision of terms of employment once work had started if they had entered into an annual agreement with the employers, but they might well strike in the middle of their work if no such agreement were in effect:

Q. What guaranty would a contractor have in taking a contract and in employing your union labor, in regard to wages on that contract? For instance, he is paying to-day so much an hour to those various trade unions of the employees; he takes a contract and has to pay wages in all sorts of lines; how would he be able to know when he took a contract whether he was going to make or lose money unless he allowed a wide margin for that kind of contingency?

A. It is presumed that if he agrees to employ union labor that he understands that the union rate of wages will be paid to his employees. In the case which you cite, if an organization having a regular rate of wages would be employed by a contractor, and after their being employed they would attempt to take undue advantage, perhaps of some conditions of his work, and make a demand for a higher rate of wages, it would be so manifestly unjust that in this central body, to which I have referred in the matter of the grievance, they would not be supported by any of the local organizations. I do not know of an instance. It would be manifestly unjust.

Q. Your rate of wages is established for certain lengths of time, or can it be changed at any moment?

A. Yes; we can change our rate of wages at any time we desire. In localities—for instance, New York, Chicago, and in St. Louis, I believe, and in several other cities of the country where the employers are organized, and where the organized employers are found in a condition in which they can deal with the employees—they enter into yearly agreements, I believe, usually on the 1st of May, and all those matters are understood. But there are other localities, for instance, Washington, where the employers are not organized, and we can not enter into such an agreement as that with the employers of the District.

Q. Do the various branches of labor that go to make up the building trades council fix a rate of wages that shall govern throughout the season in each locality? . . .

A. It does not obtain throughout the season. They establish a rate of wages, and, as I stated, they can change that rate of wages; they can either advance or reduce it, as far as that is concerned, unless in the case where they enter into an agreement with the employer relative to the rate of wages. At the time at which they enter into the agreement they are bound by it and always have abided by it.[40]

It will be noted that, according to the testimony above, given in the year 1899, the first of May was the date on which annual agreements were entered into most frequently. That was a fairly "neutral" date, coming before most work had begun in the busy season and, at the same time, sufficiently near the end of the dull season so that competition among employers for labor more nearly reflected "average" conditions. It was certainly a more advantageous time for the union to negotiate over wages than "about the middle of

40. Industrial Commission, *Reports on Labor,* v. VII, pp. 143–144.

February," which was the contract date with which the New York bricklayers had to content themselves back in 1871. With the contract date delayed until May, it was undoubtedly more difficult for the employers to withstand a strike which might ensue from their insistence upon a reduction of wages, as they had done on that occasion. Indeed, the president of the national union, beset with appeals for aid from local unions on strike at the wrong time, would have been willing to settle for even an earlier contract date—if only the employers would consent to contracts:

I would therefore advise that some steps be taken to compel Unions under our jurisdiction to notify employers, at the first meeting in January of their respective Unions, to establish wages for the ensuing year, and notify the employers of such action, thereby enabling them to contract for work to suit the wages of journeymen, and at the same time take from the employer his great arm of defense in the spring, namely, that he was not notified before taking his contract.[41]

The Granite Cutters' National Union required its locals to surrender the element of surprise by giving employers not less than three months' notice in advance of their intention to strike for wage increases, provided that the employers gave them the same notice of any proposed reduction.[42]

Nevertheless, there were those at the grass roots who preferred not to surrender a quid for their quo; they wanted a firm contract in January, but they wanted to improve the terms a bit in June or July. The national executive of the Bricklayers, however, stuck by its guns; on one occasion, Secretary O'Dea was outspokenly critical of the strategic manoeuvres of some of the international's local affiliates:

Some of these Unions who had applied, did so, late in the season when there was not a possibility of a chance to enforce the new order of hour work and when it would have been a matter of the greatest absurdity to attempt to do so. Every intelligent and fairminded person will admit, that for any Union, be it old or new, that will attempt to take advantage of employers, whether it be in the middle or latter part of a season, either in trying to get a reduction of hours or an increase of wages, after said employer had duly entered into and had contracts upon their hands made in accordance with previous agreements and rules, and had up to such time lived in fair unison and terms with their employes, to take such advantage without warning or timely notice, or the giving of something in return as equivalent for such a demand, would be unjust, unwise and injudicious, and would result in distrust, discord, ill feeling and defeat to the Union or party who tried it and place a barrier in the way of future progress.[43]

The Molder's national executive was also in favor of the annual contract; in 1899, the president was pleased to announce that the locals in Cincinnati

41. *Proceedings*, 1871, pp. 9–10.
42. Industrial Commission, *Reports on Labor*, v. XVII, p. 148.
43. *Proceedings*, 1888, p. 5.

and Cleveland, "both well organized centers," not only had secured wage increases during the past year, but "what was better still, *with the assistance of your officers,* succeeded in securing an agreement for one year at these rates, with a further provision for annual conferences to determine the wage rate for the following year."[44] Indeed, it was possible for this national union, which had succeeded in establishing a system of national collective bargaining with the employers' association in the stove industry, to urge upon the locals the extension of the principle of substituting contracts for strikes to the longer period covered by the business cycle. This educational task was nevertheless formidable, and, on one occasion, President Martin Fox assured the delegates from the local unions that

We are alive to the fact that there is still a large number of our membership who feel as if their privileges were unduly abridged, because these conference agreements prevent them from entering upon a strike immediately upon a grievance arising. But if they will only reflect for a moment and study our experiences previous to the year 1890, and consider how manufacturers and molders in the stove trade stood as two opposing forces in the field, each ready to seize upon the slightest advantage they could gain over the other. If conditions inclined to the one side, wages would go up, but as soon as they inclined to the other, down they would go. When periods of depression came, such advantage would be taken of our members that they would become discouraged and demoralized; our membership would decrease and our power be so weakened that months of the subsequent good times would have gone by before we were ready for the next encounter. With that state of affairs contrast the present. In March it was agreed by representatives of the two organizations that there should be an advance of 10 per cent in wages on April 1, and when that date came, the advance ran like magic all along the line, and within thirty days the stove manufacturers, with but few exceptions, granted the advance. This could not have been so generally accomplished, with months of effort, under the old method, even in the best of times.[45]

WHERE TO STRIKE

National unions were sometimes obliged to decide not only when to strike but also where or whom to strike. We know from Chapter 6 that national unions frequently required authorization by the national executive and that, in some cases, they prohibited more than a given number of local unions from striking simultaneously. Now, while national officers were thus endowed with the authority to pass judgment upon strike applications submitted by local unions, they were rarely obliged to adhere to any specified principle of selection in choosing among competing applicants for authorization. Knowledge of the circumstances surrounding each application, combined with knowledge of the decision made in each case, might, therefore, reveal whether the national officers had evolved any discernible principles of selection on their own.

In particular, one would like to learn whether or under what circumstances it was the practice to assign priority to proposed strikes against low-wage firms or firms in low-wage regions over proposed strikes against high-wage firms or firms in high-wage regions. This would help to clarify certain aspects of national wage policy, to which we shall turn our attention in the following chapter. Did the national officers ever believe that the resources of all the locals should be used first to help the low-paid constituents catch up with the others? Did they ever believe that those resources should be used first to enable workers in high-wage and possibly more profitable firms to push even further ahead than the rest? Did a concept of the "general welfare" underlie such decisions—for example, if it was decided to support strikes in high-wage regions or against high-wage firms, was the decision made in the belief that settlements in such regions or with such firms would serve as "key bargains," to borrow Dunlop's phrase, and would spread to other sectors of the national jurisdiction?[46]

Unfortunately the data required to answer these questions definitely are not available. Certain relevant hypotheses, however, are suggested by some fragmentary evidence at hand and might be put forward.

In the first place, it is suggested that some organizations intended that the national union should support only those strikes which could be reconciled either with common national objectives or with the welfare of more than a small group of members. Thus the Bricklayers' constitution stipulated that

A strike will not be considered unless it be for a demand to maintain the standard hour work-time, or for a decrease in the hours of labor, a demand for an increase in wages, or to resist a reduction thereof, and all strikes must be of a general character in which the (local) Union is arrayed against the employers as a whole, and *vice versa*. Any strike by a Subordinate Union against an individual, firm, or a minority of the employers of its locality, shall not be considered an I.U. matter. . . .[47]

It is also suggested that decisions to authorize or support strikes against either high-wage firms or low-wage firms were often made with the "general welfare" in mind. Strikes against firms paying wages notably below the average in the community or against firms in low-wage areas were sometimes

46. See John T. Dunlop, "American Wage Determination: the Trend and its Significance," in *Economic Institute on Wage Determination and The Economics of Liberalism* (Washington: Chamber of Commerce, 1947), pp. 41–43; "Wage-Price Relations at High Level Employment," *American Economic Review*, v. XXXVII, May 1947, no. 2, Papers and Proceedings, pp. 250–251.

47. *Constitution*, 1897, Art. XVII. This provision apparently acted to bar from consideration any local strikes in support of restrictions on apprenticeships.

given priority over other applications. Thus the Carpenters, in one instance, refused to support a local's opposition to wage cuts by a firm which was paying higher wages than its competitors, and, in another case, it refused to sanction a grievance against an employer who had reduced wages below the prevailing level in the locality. Both episodes occurred during the depression in the 1890's, and in both instances the executive board referred to its policy of discouraging strikes during the severe downswing. But the board did sanction a strike against a wage cut by a firm whose "wages already paid were very poor."[48] The Molders' executive board refused, on one occasion, to sanction a strike for a wage increase in Chicago. The board noted that it had also received petitions for strike support from locals in eleven other cities and it had decided that it was necessary to "redeem" the low-paid districts first.[49]

However, when the national authorities did come to the aid of low-paid workers, they frequently made it clear that they were moved as much by regard for the well-being of the more well-to-do as they were by the plight of the less affluent jurisdictions. When competition prevailed between firms in high-wage localities and firms in low-wage localities, national support of strikes in the latter was justified on the grounds that such support was necessary in order to protect the higher levels in effect elsewhere. The president of the Typographical Union explained the necessity of assigning priority to the task of organizing the book-and-job trade more thoroughly in the low-wage towns which were in competition with the larger cities: "When we complete this work of organization, it will be possible for us to increase the wage rates, enforce union rules, and thereby minimize any advantages which these towns at present enjoy."[50] But when the high-wage locals did not perceive that deferment of their own strike plans and support of strikes by low-wage locals was in their own true interest, the national official was placed in a most uncomfortable position. Consider the following excerpts from a sermon which a president of the Molders was obliged to deliver:

But it must be apparent to every intelligent thinker in our jurisdiction that it does not suffice to secure advances in the larger and better organized centers, but that it is equally our duty to attend to the interests of those who have not been so fortunate. Not only have the National officers esteemed that to be their duty, but have been strong in the belief that the large centers could not long maintain their advantages unless the smaller and lower paid localities were brought up more nearly to an equality with them. Imbued with the soundness of that reasoning it has been my endeavor to advise the distribution of the support of the organization as equitably as circumstances would permit in order, as it were, to preserve the balance and remove those inequalities in labor cost which are an important factor in the intense competition of the present day. It is with some regret, I have

48. *Proceedings,* 1895, p. 38; also, pp. 33–34, 36.
49. *Proceedings,* 1902, p. 612.
50. *Proceedings,* 1899, p. 65.

to say that there is not yet that strong community of interest and sympathy between local unions of the Iron Molders' Union of North America which is necessary for the fullest success of that policy. It has been difficult to convince our members in some localities, of their duty in this direction. Self-interest is strong within all of us—and in some respects, it is a desirable attribute—but when the interest of an individual or a locality is sought to be promoted and advanced regardless of the interest of all other persons or localities, it becomes the duty of those vested with the authority to interpose a restraining hand.[51]

The Molders' national executive also favored coming to the aid of locals which struck low-wage firms in their jurisdictions in order to protect the standard rates paid by other firms in the same area. On one occasion the secretary reported that

On June 16, 1899, grievances were submitted wherein the Conference Boards of New York and vicinity and Chicago requested the authority to strike one shop in each locality to enforce the minimum wage rate in order to hold those in line who are paying the rate. Grievances were sanctioned.[52]

Approval of strikes in high-wage jurisdictions were also justified with reference to the greater good. In 1898 the carpenters' locals of New York City struck certain contractors, builders, and architects in order to oblige them to cease awarding contracts for wood trim and interior decorations to non-union, out-of-town manufacturers. The strikes were supported by the United Brotherhood, whose secretary took pains to point out the extralocal implications of the contest:

The action prosecuted by our New York Locals against cheap, unfair, non-union trim, made in outside towns, has been beneficial in organizing the mills of Stamford, Conn.; Batavia, N. Y., and Rochester, N. Y. Added to that it has aided very materially in upholding the standard wages in New York City.[53]

Where competition existed between high-wage and low-wage firms, it was frequently not judged expedient to strike the former. In 1872 Saffin warned the Molders not to strike for a reduction in hours because reductions could be secured primarily in the best-organized establishments which were already paying higher wages than their competitors. "If then . . . we do not at the same time compel their competitors also to reduce the hours of labor . . . , we will drive some of our employers either out of business, or force them to move their establishments."[54]

But where competition was not so keen, was not the national union in a position to give priority to strikes against certain firms or localities which

51. *Proceedings*, 1902, p. 602.
52. *Proceedings*, 1899, p. 31.
53. *Proceedings*, 1898, p. 32.
54. Quoted in F. W. Hilbert, "Trade-Union Agreements in the Iron Molders' Union," pp. 240, 242.

might have served as "wage leaders"? For if it was possible to conclude certain "key bargains" which, with relatively little additional effort, could be duplicated in the other firms in the national jurisdiction, it was not the best strategy to strike the substandard "followers" first. The Molders attempted to follow a "key bargain" pattern of strategy for a while in the machine foundry branch of their jurisdiction. In 1899, they first negotiated a 10 per cent increase (following a wage increase of that amount in the stove foundry industry) in the larger centers and then demanded and received increases in the smaller outlying localities which brought wage rates paid therein to equality with rates in the cities.

Two years later, however, a similar move failed, and the Molders' failure reveals why the "key bargain" strategy was not practicable for many unions in the nineteenth century. The Molders were attempting to duplicate in the machine branch the national bargaining institutions which they had successfully helped to erect in the stove industry. The National Founders' Association, however, proved much more difficult to bargain with than the Stove Founders' National Defense Association (for reasons which we shall consider in Chapter 16), and, after it had passed certain resolutions (the so-called "Detroit Resolutions") which opened membership to nonunion as well as union firms and then rejected union demands for a wage increase, the Molders decided to call a strike (in 1900). The national executive instructed locals in Chicago, Cincinnati, and St. Louis to withhold their strike petitions and decided to concentrate the entire national effort in the Cleveland area. The Cleveland local struck all of the local foundries which belonged to the National Founders' Association; six hundred molders quit work. But the Association came to the aid of its Cleveland membership; the latter received funds in the amount of $125,000 from the Association. The strike lasted seven and one-half months and terminated in a compromise, with the union receiving some increase in pay but conceding certain differentials to which they had been opposed. But the Cleveland settlement failed to develop into a pattern for the entire industry; indeed, some Cleveland employers refused to abide by the settlement, and the Association refused to terminate their membership.[55]

It might be argued that one usual ingredient in the "key bargain" strategy, imperfection of competition, was not present in sufficient strength in this case. Nevertheless, it was not so much the presence of competition as it was the willingness of the members of the employers' association to coöperate with one another in resistance to the union that resulted in the failure of the union's strategy. In the stove branch, the Molders had observed the same phenomenon of united resistance as early as 1849—well before the national union was formed—when, according to Hoagland, the Pittsburgh employers,

55. *Proceedings,* 1902, p. 610; Hilbert, "Trade-Union Agreements," pp. 234–235, 240–241.

prompted by a convention of "ironmasters of the United States," decided to cut wages in order to provoke a strike which they hoped would mobilize public opinion in support of a tariff increase.[56] Moreover, whereas prior to 1850 the Molders' locals had conducted strikes against individual employers only, after 1855 "strikes . . . extended to the entire trade. . . Instead of dealing with individual employers, the unions began to deal with representatives of employers' associations. . ."

On two occasions the Molders were involved in strikes which covered major portions of the stove industry. In 1866 the employers formed the "Iron Founders' Association" and initiated "the great lockout" which involved ten cities; their objects were to compel the hiring of helpers (or "bucks"), to eliminate restrictions on the hiring of apprentices, and to withdraw recognition of the union.[57] The second widespread stoppage took place in 1887. After the St. Louis Molders struck the Bridge and Beach Manufacturing Company for a wage increase, the Stove Founders' National Defense Association, in accordance with certain provisions in its constitution, extended the shutdown. Bridge and Beach molding patterns were sent to shops of other association members both in St. Louis and in fourteen other molding centers, both east and west. When the Molders in these Association shops refused to handle the struck work, they were locked out by their respective employers.

Thus united action by employers could on occasion frustrate the "key bargain" strategy or, indeed, any attempt by the national union to support one or a few strikes at a time. It might be added that the Stove Founders' group also provided for the procurement of strikebreakers to replace up to 70 per cent of the employer's normal force, if feasible, as well as for compensation for loss of production up to two dollars per day for each worker formerly employed and the assumption of any expenses incurred in connection with police protection and litigation.[58] Other employer groups which were effective in dealing with unions were characterized by (a) the establishment of "defense funds," and (b) willingness to discipline (by fine or expulsion) members who tended to backslide and reach settlements with their unions which were not sanctioned by the associations to which they belonged.

It should be noted that neither in 1866 nor in 1887 did the Molders seek a showdown. The "great lockout" was not successful, from the employers' viewpoint, and the Iron Founders' Associations disbanded. Nevertheless, the national union did not rejoice at the demise of its foe, for Sylvis had written

56. *International Molders' Journal*, November 1911, pp. 822, 823.

57. John P. Frey and John R. Commons, "Conciliation in the Stove Industry," pp. 133–134.

58. F. W. Hilbert, "Employers' Associations in the United States," in Hollander and Barnett, *Studies in Unionism*, pp. 185–208.

to the employer's association "to congratulate you upon coming together for the purpose of organization, and to say that we have long held that organization on your part was necessary, because we felt that organization on both sides would result in such a mutual understanding as would prevent the unpleasant differences which so frequently exist between us."[59] In the Bridge and Beach affair, the union at one point sought to prevent the strike from spreading by ordering the molders in other shops to work on the struck patterns and by requesting a conference with the executive council of the Defense Association. Although the union's request was ignored, the fact that the outcome of the strike was indecisive (both sides claimed victory) made both sides amenable to the ultimate establishment of national collective bargaining in 1891.

The conditions underlying both the success and the failure of industry-wide bargaining will be discussed in Chapter 16; we are here concerned only with its relation to national strike strategy. The experience of the Molders suggests that a national union which preferred to conduct its strikes a few at a time and to concentrate on "key" areas when feasible was willing to accept national negotiation as an alternative to industry-wide strikes. Indeed the success of national bargaining in the stove industry was predicated upon the success of the key bargain approach. Although only about 50 per cent of the country's stove molders and 60 of a total of about 300 employers were initially covered by the agreement,[60] the Molders chose to serve demands for changes in conditions of employment first upon members of the Association, "knowing that as an organized body it could act more quickly and effectively, and that if granted by its members a similar advance would be conceded at once by every other manufacturer, especially by those running open and nonunion shops."[61] On one occasion, when a firm which was not a member of the association but which was the largest manufacturer of a particular type of stove, reduced its piece rates and announced its intention to reduce selling prices by 10 per cent, an officer of the national union informed the employer that, if the firm did not rescind its cut, the national union would grant an equal reduction throughout the country. The cut was rescinded. When the union and the association negotiated increases in 1899, 1900, and 1902, nonmember employers uniformly followed suit.

59. Quoted in Frey and Commons, "Conciliation in the Stove Industry," p. 134.
60. Hilbert, "Employers' Associations in the United States," p. 195.
61. Frey and Commons, "Conciliation in the Stove Industry," pp. 159, 160, 162.

CHAPTER FIFTEEN

SOME EMPLOYER WAGE POLICIES

IN THE last chapter we observed that a strike called by the union during the busy season was, analytically, the equivalent of the individual labor contract offered by the employer during the dull season, when such contract specified not only the wage rate to be paid but also the length of time which the prospective employee would be required to work, and when it also provided that a certain portion of total wages be withheld, subject to forfeiture in the event that the worker quit before the specified terminal date. Both practices were, in principle, variants of the all-or-none bargain, in which the moving party stipulated that the other party buy (or sell) a given number of units of the good or service in question at a given unit price or none at all.

This type of arrangement was the equivalent of discriminatory selling or buying, under which different units are sold at different prices.[1] The seller (in this instance, the worker) who would have preferred to sell more than the specified amount of labor at the specified wage rate under an all-or-none arrangement was in the same position as the seller who, under discrimination, chose not to sell more than that amount because any additional units could fetch only wage rates which were lower than the corresponding marginal rates of substitution between leisure and income. On the other hand, the worker who would have preferred to sell less than the amount of

---

1. A. C. Pigou, *The Economics of Welfare* (London: Macmillan, fourth edition, 1948), pp. 279–280. Pigou termed the practice of charging a different price for each unit of a commodity "discrimination of the first degree." He held, however, that "an analysis of the method is of academic interest only." Joan Robinson concurs: "He (Pigou) envisages the monopolist as dividing, not the individual buyers, but the separate units of the commodity, between the different markets, but he does not make it clear how this can be done." (*The Economics of Imperfect Competition* [London: Macmillan, 1933], pp. 186–187, fn. 1.) Leontief, however, has demonstrated that the guaranteed wage bargain (like bulk purchasing and selling in international trade) is, in effect, "discrimination of the first degree," although he did not specifically identify it as such. ("The Pure Theory of the Guaranteed Annual Wage Contract," *Journal of Political Economy*, v. LIV, February 1946, no. 1, pp. 76–79.) It is our contention that the wage guarantee is but one species of a considerably larger genus in the market for labor.

labor which he was obliged to sell at the specified rate under the terms of an all-or-none bargain was in the same position as a seller who was induced to sell a certain total quantity under conditions such that each successive unit fetched a higher price than the preceding unit—that is, no more was paid for each unit than was required to induce the worker to offer that unit of work.

Thus it can be seen that employer practices which involved the all-or-none offer can be classed with other employer practices which provided "extra pay for extra work." Similarly, it can be appreciated that union policies which were intended to oblige the employer to hire more labor than he desired to at the prevailing wage rate were the forbears of the "pure" guaranteed annual wage contract. Other union policies obliged the worker to sell less labor than he desired to at the prevailing wage rate. These are similar to "extra pay for extra work" policies in that the worker was unable to sell just the amount of labor he would have been willing to offer if the earnings per unit of time or output which emerged from the all-or-none or discriminatory bargain had been quoted on the more conventional basis under which the seller was free to adjust his supply. However, the purpose of the union policies which we will discuss was to maintain the wage rate above the competitive level and thus was in what the union considered to be the higher interest of the worker.

Since all the employer practices and union policies referred to in the previous paragraph can be included in the class of bargains which are characterized by the purchase at different wage rates of different units of effort from the seller or by the sale at different wage rates of different units of effort to the buyer, they can be regarded as examples of intrapersonal discrimination. Another method of payment which was encountered by unionists in the nineteenth century consisted in what might be termed interpersonal discrimination. Whereas the imposition of the type of wage bargain described in the preceding paragraph obliged the individual, in effect, to sell different "units" of his labor at different rates of pay, interpersonal discrimination consisted simply in paying different rates to different individuals for labor of uniform skill and efficiency. (Pigou referred to this practice as "discrimination of the third degree".) We will eventually consider union reaction to such practices.

Discrimination, whether among different individuals or among different units of work sold by a single individual, produced wage differentials, or, more precisely, differentials in effort earnings. But not all differentials, of course, indicated the presence of discrimination. Thus different wages were frequently paid by different employers for identical work. Such differentials did not imply discriminatory purchase, although they would have indicated the existence of discriminatory sale of labor if the different wage levels had resulted from decisions made by a single union authority. Geographic differences in wages, with which many of the early national unions were much preoccupied, fall in the same category. Similarly, interpersonal wage differences arose from the worker's ignorance of wages paid in other establishments in the same locality or even from his lack of knowledge of wages paid to his fellow employees, although this latter practice indicated the presence of discriminatory purchase. Moreover, as we shall presently observe, the policy or attitude adopted by a national union with respect to any given wage differential was not determined exclusively by the presence or absence of the element of discrimination. In the following discussion, we shall classify union policies merely with respect to the types of wage differential—or the analytic equivalent thereof—to which they were appropriate. In instances where the same union policy was relevant to more than one class of differential, it is discussed more than once.

It should also be noted that the desire to eliminate or to impose differentials did not always account in full for the adoption of the union policies discussed; we shall, therefore, call attention to other motivating factors where present, especially in the cases of wage-withholding, labor grading, and restriction of output. The following discussion will draw upon the work of David A. McCabe, George E. Barnett, and Sumner H. Slichter. The latter's monumental treatise, *Union Policies and Industrial Management,* has provided students of American unionism with a source of analysis and information which is a fitting companion work to the Webb's classic *Industrial Democracy.*

In this chapter we shall discuss union reactions to two broad categories of employer practice; the first consists in payment on other than a straight piecework or timework basis; the second, in paying different workers unequal wages for work of the same variety and of equal efficiency. Employer practices under the second heading include geographic wage differentials, but that will be the subject of Chapter 16. In Chapter 17 we shall consider some union policies which implied an attempt to oblige the employer to hire more labor than he desired to at the prevailing wage rate (the guarantee of work or wages), and some union policies which consisted in obliging the worker to work less than he desired to at the prevailing wage rate.

EMPLOYER PRACTICES

Failure to Pay on a Specified Straight Piecework or Timework Basis
The Basis of Calculation

In some piecework industries, employers either withheld from their workers detailed information of individual production records or they falsified such records. Since daily and weekly earnings depended upon the amount of work of acceptable quality which was performed, it was possible, by understating an employee's actual output, to reduce the actual piece wage below the stated rate. And since the worker was guided by the latter when he accepted employment, this type of reduction obliged him, in effect, to offer the same amount of his labor at a lower wage rate than he had agreed to do. Assuming that he would have been willing to offer either more or less work at the lower rate if he had been quoted that rate at the outset, the practice of understanding output was the equivalent of discriminatory hiring which worked to the employee's disadvantage.

The molders and the coal miners were especially concerned with this matter. The former were sometimes not credited with good castings which were subsequently broken by workers in other departments of the foundry; moreover, as Frey and Commons observed, "The removal of castings from the foundry to the cleaning room was often done in a slipshod manner, and an opportunity was afforded dishonest foremen to give credit for less work than had been made.[2] The first president of the employers' association, the Stove Founders' National Defense Association, remarked that, "the systems then (before the establishment of the Association) in practice in many of the stove foundries of the country were but little better than petit larceny." To remedy the situation, the Molders demanded that each man's work be counted, at the end of the day, before it was moved from his work space, or "floor," down the gangway. This practice was termed the "gangway count."

The Miners' National Association (1873–1876), an early and short-lived forerunner of the United Mine Workers, made it one of their objects, "To secure the true weight of the miners' material at the mine, thus giving to them and the operators their legitimate dues."[3] The Miners demanded state legislation which required that output be verified by checkweighmen, who were to be selected by the Miners. This practice was finally adopted throughout the industry, but only after prolonged resistance by the operators, despite the fact that the Miners were willing to pay for the wages of the checkweighmen and did so where the latter were allowed.[4] In 1898, the Eighth (Indiana) District of the United Mine Workers wrote into their constitution a provision which called for payment of both dues and checkweighmen's wages by check-off.

The national union, it should be added, had its own institutional axe to grind; the checkweighmen could be utilized as excellent sources of information which would be exceedingly useful to district and national officers in formulating wage demands. Thus, the following resolution was adopted at the national convention of 1891:

2. John P. Frey and John R. Commons, "Conciliation in the Stove Industry," in *Bulletin No. 62* of the U. S. Bureau of Labor, v. XII (Washington: Government Printing Office, 1906), pp. 128–129.

3. *Constitution of the Miners' National Association,* Art. II, Sec. 5. Reproduced in Chris Evans, *History of the United Mine Workers of America* (Indianapolis, 1918) v. I, p. 38. See also pp. 91–92; v. II, pp. 355, 483.

4. Evans, *United Mine Workers,* v. II, pp. 91, 92, 485, 582.

Whereas, Our organization has no definite manner of knowing the exact amount of coal going into market and the general statistics as to the average wages per man; therefore be it

Resolved, That this Convention demand that every checkweighman be required to keep an account of all coal mined in their respective mines; number of days run in month; number of hours worked per day; number of cars per man; average weight per car; average wages per man, and report monthly to the secretary of their district on blanks furnished him for that purpose from district to National Secretary.[5]

The demand was not confined to the two trades discussed above; it was widespread among pieceworkers. Thus some agreements which involved a New York local of cloak makers provided that individual record books be furnished to workers by the employer, who agreed to enter therein piecerates and the number of pieces credited to the holder.[6] And, in 1901, a longshoremen's contract provided that, "The Dock Managers or Owners shall at all times give to the men interested an opportunity to inspect bills of lading or orders for receiving cargoes for the purpose of learning or verifying the tonnage to be loaded or unloaded."

The individual contract

In the preceding chapter, mention was made of union opposition to individual labor contracts which provided for wage withholding and forfeiture. Some national unions sought to prevent their members from entering into such arrangements.[7] Thus, the constitution of both rival unions of window-glass workers—Local Assembly 300 of the Knights of Labor and the Window Glass Workers' Association—contained an identical provision to the effect that

no person . . . leaving part of his wages stand in the hands of his employer in order to secure him against loss or to retain a position shall be allowed to retain a membership.[8]

5. Evans, *United Mine Workers,* v. II, p. 88. Cf. also p. 426 for a later district resolution calling upon all local presidents to see to it that the checkweighmen submitted their reports.

6. U. S. Industrial Commission, *Report on Labor Organizations, Labor Disputes, and Arbitration, and on Railway Labor* (Washington: Government Printing Office, 1901), v. XVII, p. 413. See also p. 371.

7. It would appear that, in some industries at least, the individual contract not only provided for the withholding of wages, but also "bound" the worker not to join a trade union. The latter obligation came to be known as the "yellow-dog contract," but originally it was referred to in some trades as the "iron-clad" oath or contract. In his testimony before the Industrial Commission in 1901 (*Reports on Labor,* v. XII, p. 33), President John Mitchell of the United Mine Workers referred to an agreement providing for the withholding and forfeiture of wages as "an iron-clad contract." Thus it may be inferred that the individual worker may have been bound, by the same document, both to work at a specified wage for a specified time and not to join a union.

8. Quoted in U. S. Commissioner of Labor, *Eleventh Special Report: Regulation, and Restriction of Output* (Washington: Government Printing Office, 1904), p. 616.

The national unions also pressed for frequent and regular paydays. In the glass container industry, the Glass Bottle Blowers' Association secured an industry-wide collective agreement with the National Green Glass Vial and Bottle Manufacturers' Association, which provided that

All members shall be compelled to receive not less than twenty (20) dollars a week in cash, or forty (40) dollars every two in cash, and all settlements shall be in cash. . . . The second pay day of each month shall be designated as the day to ask for and receive extra money when due, provided three days' previous notice be given.

Each firm shall make a cash settlement within two weeks after the fire goes out.[9]

The Carpenters also stressed frequent paydays. The Carpenters' executive council of Chicago secured agreements which proscribed the withholding of wages more thoroughly than did the Bottle Blowers, whose contract provided only for minimum cash payments on regular paydays. The Chicago Carpenters insisted that

Every journeyman carpenter shall receive his pay in full each week on Tuesday, not later than 5 p.m., but in case of discharge he must be paid at once on the job or waiting time paid. In case of a temporary lay off for any cause whatever he shall be paid in full if he so demands.

The Bricklayers' locals in the boroughs of Manhattan and the Bronx, New York City, inserted a similar clause into their agreement with the Mason Builders' Association. Later, the Bottle Blowers provided that "All members shall be compelled to receive, and the manufacturers must pay in full in cash every two weeks, and not more than one week's earnings shall remain unpaid."[10]

In addition to bargaining directly for frequent payment, unions secured the passage of state laws which made mandatory payment at weekly, semi-monthly, or monthly intervals. They also were instrumental in securing legislation which dealt with payment in kind. Some state laws prohibited the "truck system" outright; others regulated the prices charged and the quality offered in company stores (for the unions charged that employers deliberately reduced real wages by raising prices in company stores); and still others attempted to prevent workers from being obliged to patronize company stores.[11]

9. Reproduced in Industrial Commission, *Reports on Labor,* v. VII, p. 921; see also v. XVII, pp. 380–381, 384.

10. Quoted in Leo Wolman, "Collective Bargaining in the Glass-Bottle Industry," *American Economic Review,* vol. VI (1916), pp. 549–567.

11. John R. Commons and John B. Andrews, *Principles of Labor Legislation* (New York: Harper, 1916), pp. 55–56 (first edition).

It should be observed that such practices as payment in kind (company stores and dwellings) and wage withholding did not have the effect of forcing the workers into an all-or-none bargain. As we observed in the previous chapter, even forfeiture of wages could not effectively oblige the worker to offer more labor than he desired to at the given wage rate if he was able and willing to work for another employer at a higher rate of wages. Such devices as wage-withholding and payment in kind did, however, tend to tie the worker to his job, and, to that extent, they made the all-or-none type of arrangement, where the latter did exist, more effective.

In some cases it is reasonable to infer that employers deliberately exploited payment in kind as a device for either tying the worker to the job through the extension of credit[12] or for reducing his real wages by charging high prices at the company store. Thus when coal miners who traded at stores which were not owned by the mine operators were given an insufficient number of empty cars to fill,[13] thereby suffering a reduction in daily earnings, one might conclude that employers did not regard the company store merely as an "employee service." But even where employers simply sought to provide better facilities for their workers than the latter could have obtained through purchase, such facilities (as Commons and Andrews wrote) "have counteracting disadvantages in contractual ties of dependence."[14] "Cash means freedom," according to Commons and Andrews, and there is no doubt that trade unionists concurred without reservation (although their more secure descendants would deny this proposition).

Opposition to timework; subcontracting

Although, for reasons which will be discussed under another heading, officers of many national unions frequently opposed piecework and preferred payment by the hour or day, sentiment among the rank and file often favored the former system under which earnings varied directly with effort, if not always in equal proportion thereto. In some trades, however, timework was opposed primarily because it offered the employer an inducement to increase the pace of work, since, by so doing, unit labor (as well as overhead) costs

12. See Industrial Commission, *Reports on Labor*, v. VII, p. 109 (testimony of Denis A. Hayes, President of the Glass Bottle Blowers' Association).

13. Industrial Commission, *Reports on Labor*, v. XII, p. 43 (testimony of John Mitchell, President of the United Mine Workers); v. VII, p. 46 (testimony of James Campbell, Chief Factory Inspector of the State of Pennsylvania). According to Mitchell, the miners' union in Pennsylvania offered to accept a reduction of five cents per ton if the operators agreed to eliminate their stores. See also Commissioner of Labor, *Regulation of Output*, p. 451, in which it is stated that the interest which miners' unions displayed in seeking to ensure that "no miner shall have a 'free turn,' either day or night, or more than his share of cars" is alleged to stem from the practice of discriminating against men who did not deal at company stores.

14. Commons and Andrews, *Principles of Labor Legislation*, pp. 53, 55.

could be reduced. Union officials, in such instances, were prone to oppose timework, because, as custodians of the union wage rate, they pointed out that an increased expenditure in effort on the job, unaccompanied by a proportionate increase in hourly or daily earnings, constituted, in effect, a reduction of the "standard rate."[15] According to McCabe, preference for piecework in the garment and textile trades could be traced in considerable part to fear of "speeding up" under timework.[16]

The speed-up under the time system of payment is classified under methods of payment wherein the individual is obliged to work more than he would have been willing to under a given wage rate, because, in the timework bargain, the worker's expenditure of effort was not specified. Furthermore, if the pace was accelerated after the worker had accepted the position and had begun to work, he was confronted with the alternative of accepting a reduction in his effort wage or of quitting the job and seeking another—and with no better prospect either of foreknowledge of the pace of work in another establishment or of insurance against subsequent acceleration in tempo in the new place of work. This point is made by the Webbs in a passage on the "indeterminateness" of the labor contract in their *Industrial Democracy,* wherein it was also observed that a worker was not at liberty even to leave his job following such a change in the conditions of employment, for, if he did not give "the notice expressed or implied in his contract, he could be sued for damages"—"and such actions by the employer are frequent, especially in the coal-mining industry."[17] The worker, in short, was confronted with a choice of the all-or-none variety.

Timeworkers, in both Britain and the United States, were exposed to the speed-up, especially in trades in which timeworkers were hired by subcontractors who, since they were paid according to quantity produced and since their own costs consisted virtually entirely in the wages which they paid to their employees, were under strong incentive to drive the timeworkers whom they hired. Thus, in the coal mines of Britain, work was contracted out to "butty masters" whose income varied directly with output and who hired

15. Cf. George E. Barnett, *The Printers, A Study in American Trade Unionism,* (Cambridge, Mass.: American Economic Association, 1909), pp. 132–133. In the case of the printers, the introduction of the linotype stimulated transition from piecework to timework, partly because the printers' unfamiliarity with the new process made it desirable for them to receive a minimum time wage. Employers sought to hire fast workers primarily to minimize unit overhead costs, which had been greatly increased by investment in the new machines.

16. David A. McCabe, *The Standard Rate in American Trade Unions* (Baltimore: Johns Hopkins, 1912), pp. 231–232; also p. 212.

17. Sidney and Beatrice Webb, *The History of Trade Unionism* (London: Longmans, Green, 1894), pp. 658–659; fn., p. 659. Cf. also pp. 306 and 664. Sumner H. Slichter, *Union Policies and Industrial Management* (Washington: Brookings, 1941), p. 282, also observes that "payment by time leaves an important item of the labor contract undetermined, namely, how much the worker is expected to do in a given time."

miners at given daily wages. This system was vigorously opposed by the miners' unions. The same arrangement prevailed in the construction industry where bricklayers, whose wages were set on a time basis, were hired by subcontractors, known as "piece-masters."[18]

In the United States, the butty system, in modified form, was confined to the Pennsylvania anthracite coal fields, where it was the practice for a contracting miner, on piece work, to hire up to as many as ten day laborers, to whom he furnished tools, powder, and other supplies, and whom he paid one-third of their earnings. This system was drastically modified in 1900 when, after a strike led by the United Mine Workers, it was agreed that no contract miner hire more than two assistants.[19]

The longshoremen on the Great Lakes originally worked for day wages under contractors. After their union became established, however, the system of contracting stevedores was abolished, and the longshoremen were hired directly by the dock managers or the owners of the ships on a group piecework basis. "The local union arranges to load or unload the vessels, charging so much per ton, and divides the proceeds among the members of the union who are engaged in the work, while the different members are allowed work in rotation."

The introduction of the so-called "task system," which occurred only in the garment industry in New York City, involved a change from piecework to week work, a change which was induced by the intense competition prevailing among both "manufacturers" (really merchant-capitalists who invested in raw materials, let out the work to contractors, and sold the finished product) and contractors. This system was well described in the special report of the Commissioner of Labor entitled *Regulation and Restriction of Output:*

The contractor, who was, perhaps, himself a member of the team on a kind of coöperative basis with the others, would go to the manufacturer and ask for work. Finding that there was but little work to be had, he would offer to take coats cheaper than the price theretofore paid. When he went home, he would tell his men that there was not much work; that he had been obliged to take it cheaper, and that since he did not want to reduce their wages and pay them less per day all they would have to do would be to make another coat in the task—that is, if they were accustomed to make nine coats in the task, they would be required to make ten, then eleven, and so on. The wages were always reduced on the theory that they were not reduced at all, but the amount of labor increased. In this way speed was developed.[20]

In such cases the contractors neither possessed capital of their own nor provided the workplace in which their employees worked. They were, in fact,

---

18. The Webbs, *Trade Unionism,* pp. 290, 298.

19. Industrial Commission, *Reports on Labor,* v. XVII, pp. LV, 370.

20. Commissioner of Labor, *Regulation of Output,* p. 545. Cf. also pp. 543–544 and Industrial Commission, *Reports on Labor,* v. XVII, pp. 186, 192–193, and 195.

little more than foremen, hired on a piecework basis, who paid the workers whom they hired out of their own earnings. In some trades the contractors themselves were members of a union; where they were, the workers whom they hired were generally termed "helpers." Hence there was no important economic difference between the contracting system, described above and the helper system, to which we have already referred in the discussion of jurisdiction. Where the contractor himself was a member of the union, however, union officers could attempt to eliminate the helper system by urging the promulgation of appropriate work rules which would be binding upon the membership as well as by agreement with the employer.

But in such instances the national officers frequently encountered opposition among the employing membership to the adoption of regulations which the latter regarded as tending to alter their economic status and to reduce their earnings. This appears to have been the case in the Molders' union which, although it "emphatically discountenance(d) the Helper or Bucksheer system" in 1860, had to deal with numerous disciplinary cases involving "running bucks" as late as the 1890's.[21] Local Assembly 300, the powerful national union of the Window Glass Workers, ruled that, "No flattener shall be allowed to pay any part of layer-out's wages or any help that may be employed about the flattening house."[22] The Steel Workers, on the other hand, declared in favor of the institution, although, at the same time, they sought to protect the helper; their constitution provided that "all men are to have the privilege of hiring their own helpers without dictation from the management, and no member shall be permitted to discharge a helper, except for just cause, nor shall a member reduce the wages of a helper during the scale year."[23]

It should be noted that the Molders and the Window Glass Workers did not admit helpers to membership, whereas the Iron and Steel Workers did. Of the unions cited in the preceding paragraph only the Steel Workers sought to regulate the employment of timeworkers by pieceworkers with reference to the interests of the latter group as well as the former. The Molders and the Window Glass Workers, composed exclusively of the employing elite, legislated against the helper system solely in the interest of their own membership. In their opposition to the helper system, the national officers were seeking to defend the standard piece rate against the depressing influence of the cupidity of the rank and file. In that respect, union opposition to the helper system was similar to union opposition to piecework: in each case an attempt was made to restrict individual output in the ultimate interest of each

21. Frank T. Stockton, *The International Molders Union of North America* (Baltimore: Johns Hopkins, 1921), pp. 182–183.

22. Quoted in Commissioner of Labor, *Regulation of Output,* p. 621.

23. *Constitution,* 1905, Art. XVII, Sec. 22.

member.[24] Thus, while there existed no appreciable economic distinction between labor contracting and the helper system, an important difference did exist with respect to the nature of union regulations in each case. In attempting to regulate or eliminate subcontracting, national unions sought to prevent the individual member from working more intensely, at the existing time wage, than he would have been willing to had it not been for the "indeterminateness" of the employment contract; in attempting to regulate or eliminate the helper system, national unions sought to prevent union members from producing as much as they would have desired to at the existing piece wage. In this section we are concerned only with the former type of regulation.

The incentive wage

Two major types of "payment by result" were in use at the end of the nineteenth century: the piece rate, under which the worker was compensated at the same rate for each unit of output of acceptable quality which he produced, and the "bonus" or "premium plan" of one type or another, under which successive units of output fetched successively lower prices after a certain ("standard") number had been produced within a given time period. Both systems encountered union opposition, on one occasion or another, on one, some, or all of the following grounds:[25]

(1) The product did not lend itself to accurate measurement; the job was not sufficiently standardized because product specifications were frequently changed; materials varied in quality, or the flow of materials to the workbench was uneven, causing unavoidable loss in time.

24. The attitude of the Carpenters is interesting in this respect, for, while they were not opposed to their members acting in the capacity of employers, they were opposed to members accepting piecework as employees. Thus they were opposed to contracting only where it was considered to be the equivalent of piecework. This resulted in approval of contracting but prohibition against subcontracting, as is illustrated in the following regulations:

"A member taking direct contract from owner, where the latter furnishes the material and the member contracting hires Union men and pays Union wages by the day, is not piece-work; but if the owner is an employing contractor, it is piece-work . . ."

"No member shall lump, sub-contract, or work at piece-work for any builder, speculator, or contractor, but may do work by the day, or contract for a friend, who is not a builder, speculator or contractor, and shall not remain in business longer than three months, without permission from his L. U. (Local Union), or by withdrawing from the U. B. (United Brotherhood). . . ."

"Where a member contracts work or becomes a foreman, he must comply with Union rules and hire none but members of the U. B."

Standing Decisions of the General Executive Board, 1887; *Constitution* 1888, Art. VI, Sec. 5; 1896, Art. VI, Sec. 7.

25. Cf. McCabe, *Standard Rate,* pp. 71–72, 112–113, 213–216; Slichter, *Union Policies,* pp. 283–311.

(2) The increase in output induced by payment by result occasioned, directly or indirectly, a reduction in the basic rate of pay.

(3) The induced increase in output overtaxed the individual worker and tended to shorten his productive career.

(4) Payment by result stimulated specialization of the worker, thereby fragmenting established craft skills.

In this section, we shall be concerned solely with the "bonus" type of payment because, as we shall see presently, it was more effective than straight piecework in inducing extra output. Although the objections enumerated above applied to bonus as well as to piecework, we shall not comment upon them—or upon the union policies to which they gave rise—in this section, since we are here interested primarily in practices or policies which were related to a situation in which the individual was induced to offer more work than he would have been willing to offer at a given wage rate under more conventional or less sophisticated methods of payment. The first objection will be discussed below in this chapter; the second and third, in the chapter in which restriction on individual output is discussed (Chapter 17); and the fourth has already been referred to in the chapter dealing with jurisdiction (Chapter 11).

There was, however, one union argument against bonus or premium pay which was not—and could not be—invoked against straight piecework; it was objected that, under the former system, extra work commanded a lower piece rate than did regular work. This reason assumes special significance when we consider, first, that, while all unions which opposed piecework were also opposed to bonus premium pay—such as the Boot and Shoe Workers, the Garment Workers, and the Printers—some unions which accepted piecework rejected the bonus or premium; and second, that the superiority of the latter over piecework as an incentive device was closely related to the fact that it provided for the compensation of different units of output (or effort) at different rates of reward. Under both straight piecework and premium a given increase in output per hour resulted, *ceteris paribus,* in higher hourly earnings, but in the latter case the increase in hourly earnings was lower than in the former because earnings rose proportionately less than output, that is, piece rates were reduced as output increased (see Appendix III). The worker had to work harder and produce more, under the premium system, to earn the same daily wage. Thus Slichter wrote, "It is true . . . that almost all unions are opposed to premium or bonus plans because these plans are essentially devices by which the fast workers are compelled automatically to cut their own piece rates."

It should be noted that a comparison between the straight time rate and the straight piece rate is not identical with a comparison between the straight piece rate and the variable piece rate (or premium rate). Under straight time, any increase in effort expended per hour results in a reduction in effort earnings, since the hourly wage is given; under straight piece rate, any increase in effort expended per hour does not necessarily result in a reduction in effort earnings, since hourly wages vary in exact proportion to output per hour;[26] under premium rates, any increase in effort expended per hour necessarily results in some reduction in effort earnings, for, although hourly earnings vary in the same direction as output per hour, they do not do so in exact proportion. Thus union tolerance of piece rates in some situations can be reconciled with opposition to the various premium and bonus plans which began to appear in this country toward the end of the nineteenth century on the basis of the unionist's desire to defend his effort wage. Moreover, union opposition, where it occurred, to time work (discussed in the previous section) bore the same family resemblance to the opposition to premium or bonus plans as "rushing" did to "incentive."

The inclusion in this section of the employer practices discussed in the three preceding sections follows from the observation made at the outset that obliging a worker, as a condition of employment, to work longer or more intensively than he would desire to at a given wage was equivalent to buying different units of his resource at different rates of compensation. Now we find that the practice of buying different units of that resource at different rates of compensation results in inducing the worker to work longer or more intensively than he would have desired to had the resulting wage been offered on a straight time or piece basis (see Appendix III).

In practice, the two methods—compulsion and incentive—tended to merge into one when, as was not infrequently the case, the increased supply of labor induced by premium pay made it possible for the employer to raise the "standard," that is, to increase the minimum output on which no bonus rate was paid. Then, in order to earn the same income as before, the individual was obliged to work still harder; conversely, if he worked no harder, his income for the same output was reduced. Moreover, while akin to the tendency of the employer, under straight piecework, to reduce the rate following an increase in output and hourly earnings, increasing the standard worked even greater hardship on the individual concerned, for he would then be expected to produce the new standard as a condition of retaining employment.[27] Raising the standard could confront the worker with an all-or-none type choice, which was equivalent to reducing the base rate on such output as he was willing to produce short of the new standard to zero and then offering a higher rate of pay for the remaining output up to the new standard; beyond the

26. This assumes an invariant relationship between effort and output. Actually it might require more "effort" to produce a standard unit of output when the worker is tired than when he is fresh; it can be argued that, after a certain output has been achieved, effort per unit of output varies directly with output. This supports the argument advanced in some contemporary unions that, for incentive plans to win acceptance, earnings should increase proportionally more than output.

27. Commissioner of Labor, *Regulation of Output*, pp. 124–125.

new standard, extra output was rewarded at higher rates under an explicit incentive arrangement. Thus President Fox of the Molders opposed an institution known as the "set day's work":

Another bad feature in the trade is the establishing of a set day's work, with the privilege of allowing the molder to make increased amount, for which additional pay from twenty-five to fifty cents per day above the regular rate is allowed.

In some foundries, for doing a piece of work in ten hours that would ordinarily take a day and a half, time and a half is paid, with which no fault can be found; yet it must be admitted that it leads to this, that while times are good the one molder makes a day and a half in ten hours, but when times are slack the molder is compelled to make the same piece of work in ten hours for a regular day's pay.

This is even worse than a reduction, and a rule should be established not to allow any member to work under such a system. If a piece of work that would ordinarily take a day and a half, must be made in ten hours, an additional molder should be employed to complete the job in the required time.[28]

The Printers' opposition to the bonus was based on similar grounds. When the linotype was first introduced, the International Typographical Union persuaded employers to give journeymen compositors the opportunity to operate the new machines if they proved their efficiency on the new job. The locals themselves established minimum standards of competency, expressed as a given number of ems per hour, which were known as "dead lines." At the same time, it was agreed that piecework would be eliminated in offices where the linotype was installed. As printers became accustomed to the linotype, the dead lines became virtually inoperative as devices for weeding out the incompetent, but employers sought to employ them as output standards in conjunction with bonus systems. From the viewpoint of the union, this was tantamount to a reëstablishment of payment by result, and, since they feared that the work of the more efficient operators would tend to induce employers to raise the minimum required for employment, the I.T.U. adopted legislation forbidding linotype operators to work "where a task, stint, or dead line is imposed by the employer . . ."[29]

As a result of the operation of the task system, workers tended to make the standard their maximum; this was the case in the machinery and pottery trades. In machinery, restriction of output prevailed among union and non-union workers alike where incentive systems, which were built upon standards of output, were introduced. Restriction of output will be discussed below as a union device for restraining the individual from producing as much as he might wish to produce; we mention it here only to point out that it was believed necessary to restrain individuals from producing as much as they

28. *Proceedings,* 1895, p. 20. My italics.
29. Barnett, *The Printers,* pp. 202–203; Commissioner of Labor, *Regulation of Output,* pp. 52–57, 139–140, 689–692.

wished in order to forestall circumstances in which they would be obliged, as a condition of employment, to produce more than they wished.

The record of union opposition to certain types of incentive payment permits us to clarify the concept of a "union" or "standard" wage in two respects. In the first place, since the base rate was considered a minimum, this concept ruled out any incentive system under which a given percentage increase in output over a standard amount was not rewarded by at least an equal percentage increase in pay. And second, the concept of a "standard" ruled out any system of compensation which tended strongly to reduce either the base rate itself or the average hourly or daily earnings—in the present case by raising the standard output.

Paying different workers different wages for work of the same variety and of equal efficiency

The basis of calculation

In the previous section it was observed that, by withholding from the worker information concerning his output, the actual piece wage could be reduced below the stated rate. It is also pertinent to point out that information concerning the rate of pay, as distinct from output, was also withheld, not in the sense that the individual was unaware of the stated rate per piece at which he was hired, but in as much as, under an early variant of individual bargaining, he did not know the rate at which his fellow worker was hired. It was possible, therefore, that different workers in the same establishment received different wages for work of the same variety and of equal efficiency. This situation gave rise in the stove industry to a demand by the Molders' unions that the employer list the piece rates on each line of work in a "price book," which should be available for general inspection. According to Frey and Commons,

Many firms were unwilling to furnish their molders with a list of the prices they were paying for their work, and frequently there would be two or three prices on the same piece in the same foundry. This condition easily led to abuses which were the cause of much friction, suspicion, and bitter feeling. For the purpose of safeguarding their interests the molders would demand that the foundryman should furnish them with a price book in which all piece prices would be indicated. Should the foundryman decline to do so a strike might follow.[30]

Some time after national collective bargaining had been established in the industry (1891), the employers agreed that

Firms composing the membership of the S.F.N.D.A. should furnish in their respective foundries a book containing the piece prices for molding, the same to be placed in the hands of a responsible person.[31]

30. Frey and Commons, "Conciliation in the Stove Industry," p. 128.
31. Conference Agreement between the Iron Molders' Union of North America and the Stove Founders' National Defense Association, 1896, Clause 9.

Some employers, however, did not acquiesce graciously in this stripping of the veil of privacy from the employment relationship; one offender (whom the Association threatened not to support in the event of a strike) refused to comply on the grounds that "he did not intend to pay negroes the book price or he never would have put the foundry where he did."[32] And some foundrymen sought to evade the intent of the agreement by means of a liberal interpretation of "responsible person"; they entrusted their price books to their own superintendents or clerks.[33] Finally, on the insistence of the union, the employers agreed to a revision of the agreement, in 1896, whereby custody of the price book was specified more narrowly; instead of placing the book "in the hands of a responsible person," it was provided that it "be placed in the care of the foreman of the foundry and a responsible molder agreeable to both employer and employees, said book to be placed in a locker on molding floor, to which the foreman and the molder so elected shall each carry a key."[34]

It is not claimed that, in their insistence upon secrecy, employers were motivated solely or even primarily by a desire to discriminate among their own employees; for, "if his molding price was lower than that paid by his competitors, it apparently gave him an advantage in the open market,"[35] and this in itself was sufficient to commend a policy of secrecy. But the advantages of interpersonal discrimination were not lost upon the employers, if one can place credence in the following excerpt from an editorial in the Molders' *Journal*:

The molder must make an individual contract, which will be private, so that the employer can use it to bull-doze the next who applies for work. The molders, instead of working in harmony with one another, must be made suspicious of each other. . . .[36]

The upshot, according to Frey and Commons, was that "molding prices were far from equal on similar work made in the same shop and district."

Piecework

Slichter and McCabe agree that union opposition to piecework is likely to be encountered when, to quote the former, "the unit of performance is difficult to define or measure; . . . when operations in various shops are very different and when new operations are numerous and not closely comparable with the old ones; or . . . when it is difficult to compel the employer to maintain standard working conditions."[37] Opposition to piecework on these

32. Commissioner of Labor, *Regulation of Output*, pp. 184–185.
33. *Journal*, October 1898, p. 475.
34. Conference Agreement, 1899, Clause 15.
35. Frey and Commons, "Conciliation in the Stove Industry," pp. 156, 157.
36. *Journal*, February 1877, p. 226.
37. Slichter, *Union Policies*, p. 296.

grounds should be mentioned in this section because these conditions frequently resulted in interpersonal differentials and because unionists complained of piecework for that reason. The Webbs claimed that the strongest opposition to piecework by British unions originated in trades where variation in product resulted in inequality of effort-earnings; they further made the point—which, in the light of the previous subsection, is of particular interest to us—that such inequality was caused by individual bargaining which resulted inevitably from the nature of the work:

The engineers have always protested that the introduction of piecework into their trade almost necessarily implied a reversion to Individual Bargaining. The work of a skilled mechanic in an engineering shop differs from job to job in such a way as to make, under a piecework system, a new contract necessary for each job. Each man, too, will be employed at an operation differing, if only slightly, from those of his fellows. If they are all working by the hour, a collective bargain can easily be made and adhered to. But where each successive job differs from the last, if only in small details, it is impossible to work out in advance any list of prices to which all the men can agree to adhere. The settlement for each job must necessarily be left to be made between the foreman and the workman concerned. Collective Bargaining becomes, therefore, impossible.[38]

McCabe, however, denied that this was true in the United States, where, he claimed, "The fixing of prices even under these conditions (i.e., where the unit of work was difficult to measure) is not individual bargaining or subcontracting. The prices are fixed, or at least subject to ratification, by a shop committee which represented the union, not determined finally by the employer or foreman and the workman or workmen who are to make the particular pattern."[39] Nevertheless, in Britain, the application of piecework to a nonstandardized output resulted in differences in effort wages. Indeed, if local unions assumed responsibility for the setting of the rates, as well as for bargaining in general, under such circumstances, they became more intimately concerned with conflicts of interest within their membership.

The Machinists in this country, as in Britain, were opposed to piecework because, as Ethelbert Stewart wrote, "there is such a wide diversity of work, so many pieces to be made, so few of a kind, that the piece-price system is not adapted to the industry."[40] In order to "earn wages" a machinist either had to become a specialist at one type of work or he had to exert himself on the job, since, in the typical job shop, a single run of work seldom was long enough to permit the worker, in time, to substitute acquired proficiency for physical effort. According to a former president of the I.A.M.,

Piecework in the Norfolk and Western shops here has made bitter enemies of men in the shop. It has made bitter enemies between the man who rushes and

38. *Trade Unionism,* p. 291.
39. McCabe, *Standard Rate,* p. 229, fn. 1.
40. Commissioner of Labor, *Regulation of Output,* pp. 114, 115.

pushes in order to do all that his strength and durability will permit him and his fellow-workman, who possibly may be capable of doing as good work but may not have the physical endurance to keep it up. It is bound to create an enmity and stir up discord between men of that class in the shops, consequently the men cannot be as friendly as they should be; and I care not what kind of a shop men work in or what branch of industry, unless a fellow-feeling of humanity exists among them they can not possibly accomplish the results that their employers desire unless they have a good will toward each other.

Thus the Machinists' opposition to piecework was not based upon resistance to specialization or even to differences in earnings per unit of effort; they objected to inequality in earnings which resulted from differences in the amount of effort put forth per unit of time by different individuals.

The Printers also sought to minimize inequality in earnings, but they were not opposed to piecework in principle. When compositors were paid according to the piece—that is, by the number of ems of type, a partially blank page was paid for at the same rate as a page which was filled with "straight" matter although it usually required considerably less time and effort to complete. The employers wished to divert some of the "display" matter, which contained a high proportion of "fat" to time workers, but they were opposed vigorously, at first, by the local unions. As a result, there was keen competition among the compositors in each office for work which consisted in a high proportion of "fat" matter. That justice might prevail, fat was distributed by lot, by rotation, or merely by requiring that all copy be placed on a "hook" and that the compositors should draw their work in order. Employers, however, frequently desired that certain work, especially advertising copy, be restricted to a few highly competent compositors. Since this precluded the above method, it was next agreed that such matter be auctioned off to the highest bidder and that the latter, in turn, distribute a certain portion of his earnings to the other compositors in the office. But this ingenious method failed to satisfy the employers, since the highest bidder was not necessarily the most competent journeyman in the office. Finally the locals, in exchange for an increase in the piece rate on "straight" matter, agreed to permit advertisements to be set by time workers. It should be noted that the national union was concerned only with the problem of dividing work among the pieceworkers. It opposed, although in a tentative fashion, a practice whereby some employers, in attempting to obtain the desired degree of skill on "display" work, created "departments" to which certain pieceworkers were assigned and to which all the work of this variety was sent; these pieceworkers were thus afforded an excellent opportunity to earn more than their fellows. But the national union did not disapprove of the method of auctioning the "fat," nor did it oppose the final step whereby the locals began to allow this work to be performed on a time basis.[41]

41. Barnett, *The Printers*, pp. 116–122.

Thus the Printers were not averse to the practice of rewarding equal units of effort unequally (namely, paying for fat at the same rate as straight matter), for such discrimination increased the employer's total wage bill. (Note the fact that the actual transfer of fat to timework was accompanied by a rise in piece rates on straight matter.) Nor were they opposed to their members receiving unequal earnings under piecework as long as the gains from discrimination could be distributed among the membership in a manner acceptable to all. Their opposition to the department system probably was based on the belief that it would be virtually impossible for the union to devise a system of compensation to the lower-paid members if membership in the high-income group was determined (a) by the employers, (b) on a nonrotating basis

The experience of the Potters was similar to that of the Printers, except that the former remained firm in their opposition to allowing employers freedom to place the best paying work on a time wage basis. They also objected to the practice of placing some potters on piecework and others, in the same shop, on timework, holding that, while the employer was free to employ either method, one method chosen should apply to all in the same shop.[42]

"Equalizing" and other differentials versus "labor grading"

Although the nineteenth-century unions were opposed to interpersonal differences in both rates and earnings under some circumstances, they were quite willing to tolerate and even to advocate them in other situations. Even individual bargaining was permitted in some cases, and, although each member was expected not to accept a wage under the union minimum, he was free to secure more advantageous terms if he could. The early printers' locals adopted this method, although they were shortly to learn that, as long as a substantial number of journeymen were willing to work for less than the union scale, individual bargaining was as ineffective as collective bargaining was unattainable.[43] The Watch Case Engravers' International Association of America might be cited as a curiosum; not only did it tolerate individual bargaining, but it also dispensed entirely with the prescription of a minimum wage.[44] According to McCabe, however, failure to provide for a minimum was merely

---

42. David A. McCabe, *National Collective Bargaining in the Pottery Industry* (Baltimore: Johns Hopkins, 1932), pp. 178–179.

43. Barnett, *The Printers,* pp. 279–282.

44. Industrial Commission, *Reports on Labor,* v. VII, p. 299. This organization was of late origin (1900), and it was formed expressly as an attempt to cope with the problems created by technological change which threatened the skill of its membership with obsolescence. The preamble of its constitution stated that, "Our profession has been reduced by unjust means—by subtraction of the art therefrom—leaving it simply as a mechanical labor. Therefore let us pride ourselves in elevating it to its proper stand as an art, demand the proper time for the execution of same, and increase the compensation thereof."

evidence of weakness on the part of the local unions concerned; national unions invariably favored the establishment of minima even when they were content with a system of individual bargaining.[45] The attitude of the Plumbers, as reflected in the following excerpt from the testimony of President John S. Kelley before the Industrial Commission, was typical:

Q. Do the individual members of your unions make contracts for their own employment, or is that regulated by the union so that the business agent does the business?
A. No; nobody makes a contract for the men. He simply goes and hires out at the stipulated rate of wages demanded by the organization. I do not know of any that have ever had a contract made for them. They have all been interested enough in themselves to ask for the prevailing rate of wages.
Q. Then all the members possess the same liberty of contract as they did when they did not belong to the union?
A. Oh, yes.[46]

Even where collective bargaining and the minimum rate prevailed, some unions sought to protect the interests of those members who were earning more than the minimum. McCabe mentions three devices which were employed to this end: (1) provision for the payment of a commission on sales in addition to a minimum weekly wage (barbers, milk drivers, brewery drivers, retail clerks), (2) retention of existing differentials, whether percentage or absolute, above the minimum, following a rise in the latter (machinists, molders, and, less frequently, blacksmiths, carpenters, woodworkers), (3) prohibiting reduction of wages of members who had been receiving wage rates in excess of the level now designated as a minimum (building trades).[47]

Moreover, it should be noted that differences in earnings which were based solely upon differences in wage rates, as distinct from those which resulted entirely from individual differences in output, given the same wage rate, frequently met with approval. Such differences in earnings were approved by national authority on the one hand, where certain jobs were more undesirable or difficult than others, and, on the other, where certain groups of members were less efficient than the rest.

In some instances unions demanded higher rates for unusually unpleasant or hazardous work. The Granite Cutters set higher rates for outside work than for inside work because of the greater exposure to the elements; they also set higher rates for work with surface machines because of exposure to dust. In such cases, however, differences in money rates of pay, whether piece rates or time rates, did not imply differences in effort earnings; since the higher paid jobs were more disagreeable, the differentials were required to

45. McCabe, *The Standard Rate*, pp. 81–82.
46. Industrial Commission, *Reports on Labor*, v. XVII, pp. 968–969.
47. McCabe, *The Standard Rate*, pp. 83, 86–88, 106–108.

induce workers to put forth the extra effort or to undergo the extra disagreeableness involved. Thus, in tolerating these wage differences, the trade unionists were merely acquiescing in the equality of what Adam Smith termed "the whole of the advantages and disadvantages, real or imaginary."

Nor did they object when wages varied "with the easiness or cheapness, or the difficulty and expense of learning the business." Evidence of this consists in the fact that differences in wages paid to different groups of members within multicraft unions were accepted in principle; unions presented different minimum rates for each distinct craft group. Thus, at one time when the International Typographical Union still included all the printing crafts, the compositors were regarded as the most highly skilled group and received higher wages. Other unions recognized that certain groups of their members who, although not in separate crafts, possessed unique skills which enabled them alone to work at certain jobs, were "entitled" (from the union viewpoint) to demand and receive higher minimum rates. McCabe cites, as example, tool makers and die sinkers among the Machinists, linotype operators among the Typographers, decorators in the Brotherhood of Painters and Decorators, molders in the Stereotypers and Electrotypers, carvers in the Granite Cutters, sewer-builders in the Bricklayers, and mortar makers and cement mixers in the Hod Carriers' and Building Laborers' Union.

On the other hand, certain classes of members who were recognized as possessing less skill than that required of a competent journeyman were allowed to accept lower rates. The unions did not acquiesce in the payment of differentials based upon skill in all cases, however, as we shall see below; only when a particular class of member was specialized on a particular type of work which required either more skill (as described in the above paragraph) or less skill than that possessed by a competent journeyman was such dispensation granted. Apprentices and helpers received lower rates of pay, but frequently care was taken that they did not perform journeyman work. Thus apprentices to pressers in the pottery trade were restricted, for many years, to turning out small pitchers at a low piece rate, while the journeymen refused to make apprentice ware.[48] Some unions sanctioned the employment of helpers who were paid lower wages than were the journeymen. And some even accepted the practice of placing different groups of journeymen in different wage brackets, when each group performed work which lower paid journeymen were unable to do. McCabe cited the case of the printing pressmen whose pay varied directly with the size of the press which they were able to operate.

In the case of older workers many unions were willing to permit lower wages to be paid for work of the same variety but of lower than average efficiency. In a memorandum submitted to the National Founders' Association, the Iron Molders proposed

48. Commissioner of Labor, *Regulation of Output*, pp. 694–695.

That an aged molder not competent to perform the average day's work, with the consent of the local union, be privileged to work for such a rate of wages as can be agreed to between himself and the foundryman or his representative.[49]

The Printers' locals permitted their older members to work for less than the union time rate, provided they were below average in efficiency.[50] The Stone-cutters issued "exempt cards" to members over fifty years of age who satisfied local investigating committees that they were unable to earn the standard rate; and the Painters elected physically disqualified or aged journeymen to honorary membership, which relieved them of the obligation not to work under the union rate. Some locals of the Granite Cutters and other unions which maintained both time and piece scales provided that older members be paid by the piece.[51] Slichter maintained that under piecework the older worker's pay automatically reflected his diminished efficiency and it was not necessary for the union to relax its standard in order to enable the super-annuated member to retain his job.[52] It should be noted, however, that, since the older worker had to expend more time and energy to produce a unit of product than did the journeyman of "standard" competence, equality in piece rates, like inequality in time rates, implied unequal effort earnings.

Nevertheless, there were many instances in which wage differences were not tolerated. Although the Printers permitted their older members to work for lower rates if they were in fact of less than average efficiency, they insisted that their female members not offer their services for less than the standard rate, although the efficiency of the latter was recognized to be lower than that of the average journeyman. Their motive was suspect; after an initial policy of exclusion from membership (down to the late eighteen-sixties) had failed to halt the employment of women as printers, and since they were employed at lower wages than men, the union apparently thought it best to join the ladies. Accordingly, it admitted them to membership, but it refused to permit them to be segregated in separate locals; in that way it could enforce payment of the same rate to both sexes.[53] Comparison between this union's wage policies with respect to older journeymen, on the one hand, and women, on the other, reveals something of a paradox: insistence that the full "standard" rate, or "the rate for the job," be paid to a class of workers whose economic inter-

49. Commissioner of Labor, *Regulation of Output,* p. 176. A similar clause in a local agreement is reproduced on p. 173: "It is understood that when a molder through old age or other physical inability becomes unable to put up or perform the average day's work that he shall be free to work for a rate below that of the minimum, provided said rate be agreeable to the molder and the committee in the shop." See also pp. 268, 324, 343.

50. Barnett, *The Printers,* p. 135.

51. McCabe, *The Standard Rate,* p. 105.

52. Slichter, *Union Policies,* p. 295.

53. Barnett, *The Printers,* pp. 311–316. According to Barnett, "The mass of women compositors cannot earn the union rate; and the union prefers to leave them unorganized rather than to permit them to work for less than men" (p. 316).

ests the union did not really take to heart and the toleration of lower ("substandard") pay for a group with whose welfare the union was genuinely concerned.

Diversity of motive also underlay acquiescence in the lower rate for apprentices. A beginning apprentice could not perform journeyman work and thus could not replace those more highly paid workers, but an apprentice who was near the end of his term frequently performed journeymen's work at apprentice pay and thus could constitute a "competitive menace" to the standard rate. Raising the apprentice rate would tend to discourage the substitution of apprentices for journeymen where it could be effected, but it would also encourage more boys to enter the trade and thereby possibly menace the standard from another direction.[54] Employers in the pottery industry charged that the union deliberately depressed the wages of apprentices "in order to discourage girls from starting in the business."[55] But although there existed strong reasons for tolerating or insisting upon the apprentice differential, to the extent to which apprentices could perform journeyman work the union was obliged to restrict the magnitude of that differential.

Grading employees according to seniority was opposed where it was believed that junior workers could perform the same tasks as well as their seniors. The Machinists and Molders permitted the employment of young journeymen, who had just risen from apprenticeship, at rates below the journeyman's minimum,[56] but the Locomotive Engineers refused to permit grading according to seniority because that system enabled the railroads to obtain "first class service . . . for less than the first class rate of wages."

Although opposition to grading in accordance with seniority was based on the denial that junior men were necessarily less competent than long-service employees, it did not follow by any means that unions agreed to the practice of paying lower wages to workers who were acknowledged to be less efficient than the run of journeymen. Although such differentials were tolerated in the case of both old and very young workers, unions sought to secure their standard rates against the competition of lower-rated labor—in the case of older workers, by ascertaining that they really could not perform journeyman work with fair efficiency; in the case of apprentices, by seeking to dissuade employers from placing them, or from placing too many of them, on such work.

The same considerations governed unions in their attitude toward the grading of labor not in accordance with seniority but in accordance with individual proficiency. Where grading was approved, unionists advanced the same argument that won the case for the differential based upon age: it was necessary to permit less efficient members to accept lower wages in order that they

54. Cf. Slichter, *Union Policies*, pp. 12–13.
55. Commissioner of Labor, *Regulation of Output*, p. 675.
56. McCabe, *The Standard Rate*, pp. 95, 97–101, 103–105.

might secure employment at all as union members. Yet many unions which tolerated grading sought to minimize competition between lower-paid and higher-paid men by making their different occupational compartments as watertight as possible. Among the Photo-Engravers, the half-tone etcher worked for a higher rate than did the line etcher, but the latter was not permitted to do half-tone work even if he could perform such work.[57] The Lathers concluded agreements which divided their members into "first-class men" and "second-class men"; the former received $4 a day and the latter were paid only $3.50. The first-class man had to nail 1600 laths a day and the second-class man, 1300; but, while both could exceed the minimum output, the second-class man was never permitted to nail 1600 laths. The New York Stonecutters' local enforced a rule which provided that, "Every employer must employ at least one-third of first-grade men, and as many second-grade men as there are third-grade men in his employ." Apropos of this last regulation, we should note that, while some unions, mostly in the building trades, sanctioned the formation of groups of undertrained and lower paid journeymen who had passed the maximum age of apprenticeship, they curtailed sharply the number of such "improvers" and permitted them to work at a lower rate for only a specified period of time.

But where grading was opposed, it was claimed that it tended to depress the standard wage because the different grades were not well insulated from one another. Employers would find it possible to substitute inefficient but relatively cheap labor for more efficient but better paid journeymen. The latter, in turn, might be willing to work below standard, so that they would now take work away from less competent members. Although it was reported that some stonecutters suffered unemployment because they had graded themselves too high, it was equally true that others had undergraded themselves in order to obtain work. Undergrading appears to have been particularly acute in periods of unemployment. The Painters complained that its effects were especially severe "when work is scarce"; McCabe notes that opposition to grading among the Stonecutters increased "from about 1895," which followed the onset of a severe depression in 1893. Opposition to an improved system was also stimulated by the tendency of competent journeymen to work below the union minimum. It is interesting that, at least in the cases of the granite cutters and the stonecutters, national unions objected to labor grading while the same locals were still sanctioning this practice.

Even where it was impossible for employers to use men in different grades on the same work, grading tended to lower union standards by encouraging specialization. Less efficient workers would be employed exclusively on certain jobs; more efficient workers, on others. Thus the demand for more highly skilled or efficient labor would, in effect, be reduced; this would create a

57. Commissioner of Labor, *Regulation of Output*, pp. 94, 321–322, 343, 345.

pressure upon the standard.[58] If, on the other hand, a uniform rate had been rigidly adhered to, the less efficient or poorly-trained workers would have been excluded from the trade, and employers would have been obliged to hire competent journeymen on jobs for which it would have been economical to hire less efficient workers at lower rates of pay. This point has been discussed in connection with the concept of craft jurisdiction, where it was noted that rules against labor grading were intended in part to protect the union's economic jurisdiction.

To the extent that the union permitted wages to vary with competence among men in the same line of work, it widened employment opportunities for its members—or, more realistically, it expanded its potential membership among those employed at the trade. But by the same token it gaited the pace to the slowest and thus held down the average rate. By insisting upon an inviolable minimum rate based upon average competence, however, the average rate was raised; but now those whose efficiency did not make their employment at the union minimum rate profitable were excluded—from employment or membership or both. Weak locals sometimes accepted "average" rates with individual adjustments above and below the "average," but national officers stressed the desirability of securing a minimum based upon the efficiency of a competent journeyman[59]—and the longer the term of apprenticeship, the higher the possible "standard" rate.[60] This point is put excellently by McCabe:

Occasionally unions have sought for a solution in the direction of standardizing the workers by dividing them into groups according to competency. But the usual basis of grouping is the kind of work done, not the efficiency with which it is done. An appreciable tendency toward standardization of men engaged in the same kind of work or subject to the same minimum, at least toward the elimination of those below a somewhat variable level of capacity, is fostered in many unions by the requirements as to competency insisted on for admission to membership. In the great majority of cases, however, the same rate applies to workers of appreciably differing capacities, and the establishment of the standard leaves

58. Specialization could also make the more highly skilled worker less efficient than the less skilled worker on the latter's own job. Thus, in the pottery trades, apprentices made only jugs and journeymen pressers did not make jugs because the piece rate on such ware was lower than the piece rates on other products. As a result, the apprentices grew more proficient than journeymen at turning out jugs, and "it is generally conceded that few all-round pressers could make as many small jugs in a day as an apprentice could make." (Commissioner of Labor, *Regulation of Output*, p. 695.)

59. McCabe, *The Standard Rate*, p. 81.

60. The optimum term of apprenticeship fell short of the maximum, however, for two reasons: (1) the longer the term, the greater the number of boys hired, because it is profitable to pay apprentice wages for near-journeyman skill; and (2) the greater the employment of apprentices, the less the employment of journeymen and the greater the temptation for journeymen to work in nonunion shops. (Slichter, *Union Policies*, p. 12.)

some members of more than average efficiency under the necessity of individual contracting to secure wages higher than their less efficient fellow members.[61]

We might digress briefly to assess the import, to our concept of jurisdiction, of the tolerance of wage differentials based upon differences in skill as opposed to the tolerance of differentials based upon differences in competence. To the extent that specialization is actually discouraged within a craft union, one should not expect to find marked differentials in effort or efficiency rates (except those required to "equalize" jobs of different unattractiveness) —and to the extent that such differentials are absent, one should not expect to find specialized subcraftsmen. Between distinct crafts, however, one would expect to find variations in wages. It would be tempting to add that the existence of such wage differences could suffice to distinguish a multiple craft union from a craft union, but this criterion would hold only if the craft union's jurisdiction was so well organized that it could enforce a uniform minimum rate upon the labor market.

In addition to fearing the depressing effect of labor grading upon the standard rate, some unions found that grading was productive of division and dissension among the membership. The secretary of the Coopers claimed that, "If the union is a party to classifying some of its members as second or third class mechanics, they will not be satisfied, and will work against the union."[62] Now the Webbs cautioned against identifying the unionist's demand for a standard rate with "yearnings for equal division of unequal earnings."[63] Their interpretation, however, has recently been challenged and the position taken (a) that unionists insist "upon a uniform wage rate throughout their jurisdiction"[64] and (b) that such insistence stems from the making of comparisons which were described (by Professor Ross) as "equitable" in nature (but which the perverse Veblenian might regard as "invidious").

The evidence presented in this section does not support these propositions. Unions did not insist upon uniform wage rates under all circumstances; and where uniformity was considered desirable, it is necessary to specify what type of rate was to be made uniform—whether time rate, effort rate, or efficiency rate. Where genuine differences in skill were involved, differentials in all three rates were accepted. For work involving the same skill but varying with respect to nonfinancial inducements, efficiency and time differentials might be accepted, but it was implied that effort earnings should be equal-

61. McCabe, *The Standard Rate*, p. 16.

62. Industrial Commission, *Reports on Labor*, v. XVII, p. XLIII. The journeymen Stonecutters passed a resolution to the effect that grading tended "to destroy that friendship which is essential to true unionism," as the Report of the Commissioner of Labor paraphrased it (pp. 342–343).

63. *Trade Unionism*, p. 282.

64. Arthur M. Ross, *Trade Union Wage Policy* (Berkeley: University of California, 1948), pp. 48, 50, 51.

ized. Among workers with similar training but of varying proficiency, uniform efficiency rates were demanded, but inequality in time and effort earnings could ensue and were sometimes accepted. Thus, none of the three rates was required to be uniform under all circumstances; where differences in skill existed, differentials in all three were permitted; and differences in time earnings—which Ross apparently accepts as relevant for his purposes—were frequently accepted under all three sets of circumstances.

It may be that some trade unionists in nineteenth-century America were powerfully motivated by considerations of an egalitarian or "leveling" nature; there is no reason to suppose that the Coopers' secretary erred in his estimate of the state of opinion in his own union, or that the Coopers were unusual in that respect. Nor is there reason to believe that national officers were not concerned with avoiding dissension in the ranks and that union policies were not designed to promote internal solidarity. Why, then, were not uniform wage policies uniformly adopted?

One reason might well be that such policies were not in the interest of internal cohesion. Granted that the low-paid membership were in favor of an upward revision in their earnings relative to the earnings of the high-paid groups, there is nevertheless equal reason to believe that the latter were quite as strongly committed to the maintenance of existing differentials in their own favor. And, in the interest of internal cohesion, it was as necessary that the more highly skilled or proficient workers remain in the union as it was that the less highly skilled or proficient remain. We might recall from our discussion of jurisdiction and amalgamation that secessions were threatened by high-paid as well as by low-paid groups; nor were amalgamations formed solely in the interests of the high-income workers. The possibility (not to imply the ultimate feasibility) of secession was sufficient to underwrite the continuance of certain occupational differentials. But even where secession was not practicable—as in cases involving workers of varying efficiency in the same craft—it did not follow that the cause of solidarity was served by uniform wage policies; as Slichter pointed out, "the highest earners in the union may be quite reluctant to support demands for higher wages,"[65] especially when most of the gains would go to the lower-paid members.

Thus we note that "political" considerations relating to the need to maintain organizational unity could not be expected to produce uniform wage policies. Moreover, our examination of union attitudes with respect to interpersonal differentials up to this point suggests that, where the national union did seek to enforce uniformity, it was motivated by a desire to protect the standard rate, conceived of as a minimum, against downward pressure exerted by the employment of workers paid less than the minimum or by the specialization of work or worker. Now it has been objected that protection of the standard does not require uniformity, but merely the elimination of nonunion competition and a policy of downward inflexibility. But the elimi-

65. Slichter, *Union Policies*, p. 303.

nation of nonunion competition is only a necessary condition of such protection; it is not a sufficient condition thereof. Competition by lower-paid labor, to which we have been referring in this section, may come from within the union's ranks if the union permits some of its members to accept substandard wages; indeed adoption of the priniciple of the "average," as distinguished from the "minimum," wage, might ensure that the competition from lower paid workers would be union competition. Enforcement of the principle of the "minimum," on the other hand, implies elimination of both union and nonunion competition. It also explains the observed variations in policy with respect to differentials; the latter were discouraged where their existence would result in competitive pressure upon the "standard"; where they were permitted, such pressure was absent. Where uniformity was the policy, it was adopted as a means, not as an end in itself. All this is implied in a "policy of downward inflexibility." It is also implied in a report by President Fox to the Molders' Convention of 1899 on a conference with representatives of the National Founders' Association:

And finally, we see no good that would come of an attempt to grade the wages of our members according to the work they do. It would open the way to too many abuses and dangers and invite a general gravitation to the lowest level. Hence it was your representatives stood firmly by the principle of a minimum wage, believing that the wages of the more skilled workmen can well be left to adjust to themselves, as they do at present.[66]

It should also be pointed out that, even where the union sought to equalize time earnings, as distinct from effort or efficiency rates, its policy could better be regarded as a measure to protect the standard rate than as a manifestation of any egalitarian impulses of the membership. Opposition to incentives (discussed above) and restriction of output (to be discussed later), which in effect precluded earnings above the standard under certain conditions, support the former explanation.

We have said that where interpersonal differentials were not permitted, the possibility of competitive pressure upon the minimum rate was present; we should now add that, where such pressure was absent, differences in rates and earnings were frequently protected, or at least tolerated by union authority. As we have observed in this section and elsewhere, differentials based upon skill and job content were frequently protected by national unions; so were differentials which were created by individual bargaining or by labor grading, where it was feasible to establish "noncompeting groups."

Thus it has been observed that, so far as can be inferred from its policies with respect to certain interpersonal differentials, the national union sought (a) to establish uniform rates or earnings where uniformity was required to protect union minimum rates from competitive pressure, and (b) to protect

66. *Proceedings,* 1899, p. 7.

certain interpersonal differences where no such competitive pressures existed—that is, where cheaper labor could not readily be substituted for higher-paid labor. Such behavior would also be characteristic of a seller who is bent on obtaining the greatest possible monetary return from the sale of some resource or commodity: he too is represented as charging a uniform price for all units sold in each single market but, at the same time, discriminating among different economically isolated markets. Nevertheless, we cannot infer on the basis of evidence presented thus far that the national union invariably chose wage policies designed to maximize the wage bill over its entire jurisdiction. While the "political" considerations discussed above did not preclude discrimination with an aim to maximum returns on the basis of skill, job content, or worker efficiency, such "rational" discrimination among different employers—especially among employers in different localities—was not always politically practicable, as we shall discover in the following chapter.

CHAPTER SIXTEEN

POLICIES ON GEOGRAPHIC DIFFERENTIALS

UNION ATTITUDES AND POLICIES

McCABE TERMED "the area of the standard rate" that area over which an attempt was made to establish either a uniform piece rate or time rate. Whether it merely covered all the shops in a given locality or whether it extended beyond city limits to embrace an entire local market, a "district," or a nation-wide jurisdiction, it appears that the area of the standard rate coincided with "the area of competition."[1] Since we have already considered the tendency to establish uniform rates throughout local markets in our discussion of local jurisdiction, we shall confine our attention in this chapter to the policies adopted by national unions with respect to wage differences among different producing areas.

First we must take note of the fact that, where no competition prevailed among local producing regions, national unions were not interested in altering or removing geographic wage differentials. McCabe noted that the Shirt, Waist and Laundry Workers adopted a national minimum—which was, however, a very low rate and applied to only a few locals—and that the Printers and the Carpenters required that a minimum time rate be paid by any employer who was permitted to use the union label. But he also pointed out that

The Granite Cutters' Union is the only important union among the building trades which maintains a national minimum rate that is high enough to exert influence upon any considerable number of local standard rates. It is also one of the very few among the building-trade unions in which competition between localities has long presented a difficult problem in fixing rates.

In local market trades, however, where no economic compulsion to equalize costs existed, no action was taken to establish uniform wages throughout the national jurisdiction. (Although such local product market unions as the Theatrical Stage Employees, the Bill Posters, and the Bridge and Structural

1. David A. McCabe, *The Standard Rate in American Trade Unions* (Baltimore: Johns Hopkins, 1912), p. 126. Cf. also pp. 123, 172, 173.

Iron Workers established national rates, they applied only to work "done by members travelling from city to city in continuous employment of one firm or individual.")

The Bricklayers

Bricklaying may be taken as an example of a more conventional building trade, because it has always been a local occupation. Despite some show of interest on the floor of the convention, there is no evidence that the Bricklayers considered seriously proposals to establish uniform wages in the various local markets within their national jurisdiction. In 1867, when the national organization was two years old, the convention was informed that "The rate of wages ranged from $3.50 to $7. per day . . .";[2] and the Committee on General Good recommended that the locals adopt a standard rate of wages for the period March 1-November 1. After considerable discussion, the Committee's advice was rejected, and no further attempt to regulate local wage policies is recorded until 1885 when the delegation from a local union in Michigan introduced a resolution to the effect that the national union should insist that henceforth Bricklayers' wages be not less than three dollars per day. The resolution was defeated.

But the delegates' sentiment for a national policy with respect to hours was much stronger than their interest in uniform wages. In 1866 a resolution was adopted which called for the reduction of daily working hours from ten to eight by the enactment of state legislation. Two years later, the president observed that

The Plasterers of the City of New York and Brooklyn are working the 8 hour day without any difficulty. Such examples are worthy of imitation.

Urging action by the convention on "the 8 Hour Question of momentous interest to our trade and the working men in general," he noted that, "This is no longer a theoretical question, but a practical one,—having been made so by some trades unions."[3] The subject was debated with great animation by the convention whose interest appeared to swing from "the method of legal enactment" to "the method of collective bargaining." The convention tabled a motion calling upon the president to appoint a special committee to petition the Senate and the House for the passage of a national eight-hour law. It heard a petition from a New York local which requested financial assistance in direct support of a strike "in case they demanded the eight-hour day." It also received both a majority report from the Committee on General Good,

2. *Proceedings,* 1867, pp. 38, 42–45; 1885, pp. 66–67; 1866, pp. 23–26. In 1889, the Constitution was amended to require that all locals take action "in their respective Towns, Cities, Counties, and States" to secure the passage of laws "with reference to the shortening of the hours of labor in all branches of labor." (Art. XII, Sec. 12.)

3. *Proceedings,* 1868, pp. 25, 71–72, 94; 1869, pp. 80–87; 1870, pp. 29–30.

which warned that "we deem it (the eight-hour day) inexpedient at the present time and impossible to be obtained by the local unions throughout the country," and a minority report from the same committee which declared, "That we will recognize any local union who may strike for 8 hours." The next convention (1869) was almost evenly divided; the majority report was tabled when the president cast the tie-breaking vote, but the minority report was rejected by six votes. Subsequently, however, it was unanimously resolved "to support any locals that might strike for eight hours." But the convention refused to grant compensation to three New York locals which had struck for eight hours during the preceding year; and it also limited the support of the national union to striking locals in states which had passed eight-hour legislation. Moreover, President Gaul later pointed out that in the case of the New York law, it was "unwise for us to enforce it by strikes," since the type of law which was passed in this period had no enforcement clauses.

The depressions of 1873–1879 and 1882–1885 made the shorter work day appear more appealing, since it could be utilized as a work-spreading device, but national leadership continued to grow more realistic in its estimate of its own capabilities.[4] Although, in 1884, the convention called upon all locals "to adopt such a measure (the eight-hour day) without regard to wages," the president informed the delegates that he was "of the opinion that the time has not come that we, as an organization, should demand eight hours as a legal day's work. I would, therefore, suggest that the feasibility of establishing a nine-hour law be discussed." Two years later, the convention repealed its so-called eight-hour law on the grounds that "it was deemed unwise and inexpedient at this time to adopt that system" and substituted in its place a "nine-hour law, the same to go into effect on May 1, 1886, by all subordinate unions . . . , at nine hours' pay for nine hours' work." This appears to have been a successful tactic, for other trades adhered to the demand for an eight-hour day, and, according to Secretary O'Dea,

In order to successfully cope with the eight-hour movement, Capital practically acknowledged the nine-hour system as presented by our organization, and therefore accepted it without strife, for the time being, so that it could devote its entire attention to the eight-hour system, believing, no doubt, that when it had crashed the other movement, in the state of disorganization which it had created, it could then turn its force upon the nine-hour movement also.

It will be noted that the nine-hour law of 1886 went beyond a pledge of international support to striking locals; it obliged all locals to achieve the nine-hour day by a certain date. Shortly thereafter, however, six locals informed the executive board that it would be utterly impossible for them to make the deadline and that, if the board insisted upon compliance, they would be obliged to withdraw from the international union.

4. *Proceedings*, 1874, p. 5; 1884, pp. 16, 79; 1886, pp. 96–97; 1887, pp. 39–40, 47–48.

The Executive Board were at a loss as to the best course to pursue in the case, and finally decided that it would be better to grant them an extension of time than to force them to surrender their charter.

Two of the six locals subsequently achieved the nine-hour day, but the incident revealed to the national executive that the adoption of a mandatory rule of this nature confronted the union's leadership with a painfully familiar choice. The choice was between enforcement of the uniform law and maintenance and extension of the sovereignty of the national union over its jurisdiction. The willingness of the national leadership in this union to sacrifice discipline in the interest of organization was demonstrated when it opposed attempts to apply the sanction of expulsion to a broad range of individual offenses against union regulations (see Chapter 5). The temporizing of the executive board in the case of the six unions which failed to establish within their respective jurisdictions the conditions of employment which the convention had prescribed seems to provide further evidence of their preference for organization over discipline. In any event they were aware that any gains which might result from the application of the uniform rule were not to be obtained without cost.

The convention, however, was unaware of the necessity for making a choice, unwilling to acknowledge the existence of the problem, or more willing than the board to pay the price of uniformity. For it proceeded to deprive the board of even its limited area of maneuver by adopting a constitutional amendment which provided that

All Unions working under the jurisdiction of the Bricklayers and Masons International Union are notified not to work more than nine hours for a day's work.[5]

The result of the passage of this "Compulsory Act," according to Secretary O'Dea, was that twenty-four local unions were obliged to surrender their charters the following year. In addition the secretary pointed to the

loss of numerous other Unions who craved admission to our ranks, but who, being new and freshly organized, could not without the experience had by our more fortunate bodies, hope to obtain in a month that which we, as an effective organization, took years of hard and persistent work to secure.

The result of such legislation foreseen in Boston has been only too bitterly realized, and the hasty action of a few moments has set back the growth of our order for at least two years. . . .

It seems very strange that a national organization, as ours is, will refuse to accept into its ranks kindred associations of like crafts when it is their wish and desire to be with us, but such has really been the case. . . . Such being our position, all that was left us was to encourage such organizations into local Unions and to await healthful developments in the future.[6]

5. *Constitution*, 1887, Art. XIII, Sec. 5.
6. *Proceedings*, 1888, pp. 1–5.

Thus, under the "Compulsory Law," the relationship between the international union and the locals in the trade approximated the relationship between patron and protege as interpreted by Dr. Johnson. If a local could not gain admission to the international union until it had achieved certain economic benefits for its members by its own efforts, it might well question the desirability of affiliation once it did qualify. Aside from such considerations, however, the loss of membership by locals which struck unsuccessfully for the nine-hour day apparently prompted the convention of 1889 to rescind the Compulsory Law to the extent of empowering the executive board to grant new locals an extension of time if they were unable to comply with the nine-hour requirement. The convention also rejected a reaffirmation of the prohibition against working more than nine hours.[7]

But in 1892 the constitution was again amended to read that "the Executive Board shall not have the power to grant charters to any Union who may not be able to comply with the nine-hour law." At the following convention, President Heartz complained that the new amendment compelled him to return "a great many applications" and, in four cases, fees for charters. Following his recommendation, the convention modified the rule so as to allow the board "to grant charters to any Union who may not be able to comply with the nine-hour law and allow said Unions three months from the time of their installment to secure nine hours, or, return their charters to the Executive Board."[8]

By this time, however, the nine-hour day had been achieved in most communities, and the delegates proceeded to revive their old demands for an eight-hour day. In 1893, the convention modified the constitution to authorize international financial assistance to any local which might strike to resist the efforts of employers to lengthen the working day beyond eight hours, provided that the striking local had been "successfully working under the eight hour day for one year previous to asking aid or assistance from the International."[9] As on previous occasions, interest in the reduction of working hours was stimulated by the onset of a downswing in employment, which prompted the convention to demand that the locals press for shorter hours without demanding compensating increases in hourly wage rates. In 1884, the convention had called upon the locals "to adopt such a measure without regard to wages"; in 1886 the convention adopted its nine-hour law, "the same to go into effect on May 1, 1886, by all subordinate Unions . . . at nine hours' pay for nine hours' work"; in 1893, all locals "who may be able to make new and additional demands" were urged to press for "a reduction of the hours before asking for a rise in wages." In 1895, it was resolved "That hereafter, any Union demanding the eight-hour day, shall drop one hour's pay,

7. *Proceedings,* 1889, pp. 18, 43, 97, 86, 95.
8. *Constitution,* 1892, Art. XIII, Sec. 6; *Proceedings,* 1892, p. 3; *Constitution,* 1893, Art. XIII, Sec. 6.
9. *Constitution,* 1893, Art. XII, Sec. 2.

or forfeit the privilege of asking contributions from subordinates." The Convention took no action on this resolution. And in that same year the convention rejected a proposed constitutional amendment which would have permitted members to work, at a minimum of time and one-half, more than nine hours "in case of extreme necessity."[10]

Nevertheless the convention moved more cautiously in pursuit of its objective this time than it had on previous occasions. Although it passed a general rule prohibiting overtime work, it subsequently permitted certain members to work such number of hours "as will tend to hold and control . . . work in Rolling Mills, Smelting Works, Blast Furnaces, or Corporation work held or controlled by scab or non-Union men . . ."[11] And although it revived the notion of setting a target date—a Quixotic custom which smacked of syndicalism in its impracticability—it contented itself with ordering all locals to try to secure "by means of arbitration" the eight-hour day before January 1st, 1897. The following year a resolution was passed which instructed the delegates, upon returning to their locals, "to use all honorable means to obtain the eight-hour work day."[12] Indeed, it appears that, after three years of depression, the Bricklayers were more concerned with the preservation of the nine-hour day than with the achievement of the shorter work period. The revised version of the constitution, which appeared in 1897, provided that "The International Union shall have power . . . to regulate the standard hour working day," repeated the prohibition against any local or member working "more than nine hours in twenty-four hours," and authorized the executive board "to grant charters to any Union that may be able *at once* to comply with the nine-hour law" (my italics).

As for the eight-hour day, the constitution merely held that

The above named standard work-time does not prohibit Unions, from securing the eight-hour work times, and any such Union that has been successfully working under the eight-hour day system for a period of one year or more is entitled to all the aid or assistance of the International Union to maintain the same, in the same manner as is granted to nine-hour Unions. . . .[13]

With the improvement of business conditions in 1898 came a spate of eight-hour resolutions and the passage of one of them which called for a referendum of the locals "for or against the establishment of a universal eight-hour work day, starting May 1st, 1899."[14] In his letter of transmittal to the

10. *Proceedings,* 1884, p. 79; 1886, p. 97; 1893, p. 77; 1895, pp. 72, 75.

11. *Constitution,* 1897, Art. X, Sec. 3.

12. *Proceedings,* 1896, p. 60; 1897, p. 79.

13. *Constitution,* 1897, Art. X; Art. XI, Sec. 3; Art. XII. "This can be departed from only in cases of *extreme* emergency which must be reported to and receive the sanction of the Executive Board. In *sudden* cases of emergency, the Subordinate Unions can act at once, especially where life is at stake."

14. *Proceedings,* 1890, pp. 48–49.

locals, the International secretary observed that while everyone of course favored the eight-hour day, the resolution "does not say how it shall be put into operation," whether or not locals which were unable to achieve it would be allowed to retain their charters, and whether the International was expected to finance local strikes for reduced hours.

To accomplish this movement successfully we must be backed by the sinews of war, which is finance. Are we prepared for that now? Are we preparing for it? [15]

This referendum appears to have suffered the usual fate of referenda: only 134 locals out of 300 replied. At the next convention, however, the executive board was empowered "to grant financial assistance to any Subordinate Union who may apply for said assistance, with proof, that with said assistance they can secure the 8 hours without regard to wages." [16] But this was far from a compulsory law, to which the international executive remained opposed. The attitude of the latter stands revealed in the following excerpt from the report of the secretary in 1900:

During the year 55 unions have reported as securing the eight hour work day, and with very few exceptions an increase of pay going with it, this coupled with the fact that no trouble of a very serious nature occurred in order to secure its observance makes it highly gratifying to all concerned. This silent and peaceful method of securing a shorter work day deserves the highest commendation, a constant agitation within our own ranks and direct conference in a quiet manner with our employers is by far preferable to open agitation and warfare. [17]

The Printers

The experience of the Printers ran remarkably parallel to that of the Bricklayers in that both national organizations made little or no attempt to establish uniform wages but did adopt mandatory rules governing the length of the work day or work week. Barnett noted that

The standard rates among the Printers are entirely local, although from a very early time the local unions have felt to some extent the effect of the lower rates in other cities. [18]

At the first convention (1850) of the national union, it was resolved that one of the principles underlying the establishment of local unions be the "Regu-

15. *Report of the Secretary,* 1898, pp. 83–85.
16. *Constitution,* 1899, Art. X. The proviso "without regard to wages" apparently reflects one motive behind the eight-hour drive, which was to "reaffirm the principle that the lessening of the hours of labor in ratio as the army of unemployed increases, is the basic stone upon which the Trades Union movement rests." (*Proceedings,* 1898, pp. 48–49).
17. *Proceedings,* 1900, p. 229.
18. George E. Barnett, *The Printers* (Cambridge, Mass.: American Economic Association, 1909), pp. 113–114, 139.

lation and adjustment of the different scales of prices so as not to conflict with each other"; this objective was granted at least formal priority over "giving traveling certificates to their members."[19] Intercommunity competition was experienced primarily in the book and job branch of the industry, but, although different piece rates for "extra" work of the same variety were established in different cities, the convention, in 1858, declined to adopt uniform rates. The national union adhered to its position, although one president was aware of the undesirability of competition from the poorly organized smaller communities and noted that further organizing work would improve the situation. He also pointed out that

The question of wage equalization in competitive districts is a subject which has been considered to a greater extent by the United Mine Workers of America, the Glass Workers, and the Iron Workers, than by the printing trades-unions.[20]

But the question of hours was considered seriously by the Printers, just as it was by the Bricklayers. Although the Printers subscribed to the shorter-hour sentiment which prevailed during the eighties, the national union refused to urge the locals to participate in the proposed general movement for the eight-hour day which was to be launched in 1886.[21] Like the Bricklayers, the Printers played a lone hand, and, furthermore, prudently adopted a nine-hour law (in 1887). Their interest in shorter hours was stimulated primarily by three develepoments—first, an increasing proportion of time workers to piece workers in the trade; second, the introduction of the linotype which resulted initially in considerable unemployment; and third, the depression in the 1890's, which intensified unemployment in the trade.

A further resemblance to the Bricklayers can be discerned in the reluctance on the part of the Printers' national executive to countenance a "compulsory" nine-hour rule in the face of a persistent refusal on the part of the membership to vote an assessment for the accumulation of a war chest. However, the nine-hour day was actually secured in the absence of such a rule; following the reduction of the work week in Boston and New York, the United Typothetae (the national organization of employers in the book and job branch) entered into the so-called Syracuse Agreement with the national union in 1898, whereby weekly hours were to be reduced to fifty-seven by November 21 of that year and to fifty-four one year later.

Shortly thereafter the Printers began to press for the eight-hour day, but the Typothetae refused to concede a second reduction without a struggle, holding that the Syracuse Agreement was still in effect and that the union was bound under its terms not to seek a further shortening of the work

19. George A. Tracy, *History of the Typographical Union* (Indianapolis: International Typographical Union, 1913), p. 118.
20. *Proceedings*, 1899, p. 65.
21. Barnett, *The Printers*, pp. 145–147, 149, 152, 153.

period.[22] This time, however, the membership, upon the recommendation of the convention, adopted a resolution which provided both that the eight-hour day must become effective on January 1, 1906 and that an assessment be levied to support striking locals.[23] This action had been strongly advocated by the national executive who were motivated, not merely—as in the case of the Bricklayers—by the knowledge that national strike funds were a necessary condition of the success of the movement, but also by the belief that those locals which had already achieved the eight-hour day would not be able to retain it unless their sister locals were granted sufficient assistance to enable them to reduce the working periods within their own jurisdictions to the same length.[24] Presumably it was believed that demands by employers for a return to nine hours were incited by the dissemination of information concerning the existence of longer hours in other communities; when the Pittsburgh employers defeated a nine-hour strike in 1891, they were aided by the United Typothetae, which recruited strikebreakers in other cities and sent them to Pittsburgh.[25]

The adopted resolution stipulated that "in each instance where the eight-hour day is refused work shall cease."[26] As a result, the Printers became engaged, for the first time, in strikes which simultaneously involved all their locals (with the exception of those in whose jurisdictions the eight-hour day had already been established). In most instances the operation was successful, but in many cases the patient died. Barnett reports that in the period from May 31, 1905 to May 31, 1907—a prosperous period in the trade—200 locals with 2153 members surrendered their charters or were suspended for nonpayment of dues. But there is no reason to believe that, once the strike assessment had been levied, this high mortality rate caused the Printers' national executive to entertain any doubts concerning the wisdom of the undertaking; in this respect they differed considerably from the executive officers of the Bricklayers who, as we have observed, consistently ranked organization above "compulsory" movements. Many of the locals lost were small in numbers; but their importance must not be underestimated, for it will be recalled that the smaller communities constituted a significant source of young—and frequently nonunion—printers.

Moreover, the international executive council did not hesitate to take punitive action against its larger affiliates. When the membership of the St. Louis Typographical Union instructed its officers to sign a three-year

22. Tracy, *Typographical Union,* pp. 778–780, 783.

23. Barnett, *The Printers,* pp. 155–156.

24. Cf. the report of President Lynch to the 1904 convention. Reproduced in Tracy, *Typographical Union,* p. 780. "Those who enjoy the shorter workday jeopardize it by non-action."

25. For an example of such a demand, cf. Barnett, *The Printers,* pp. 155–156, fn. 25; p. 157.

26. Tracy, *Typographical Union,* p. 783.

contract, which provided for the nine-hour day, with the local Typothetae, the secretary-treasurer of the international visited St. Louis and explained that the proposed contract was in violation of international law. The executive council then sent telegrams to both parties, warning them that it would not countenance a nine-hour contract; and the entire council later proceeded to St. Louis and attended a special meeting of the local union. The membership, however, repeated their instructions to their officers; whereupon the executive council, by unanimous decision, suspended the charter of the St. Louis union. The president of the local then requested the council to modify the suspension order so as to permit the local to issue traveling cards and to pay per capita dues to the international, but the council was adamant. President Lynch notified the local's president that the suspension would be lifted only if "St. Louis Union repudiates the illegal nine-hour contract with the St. Louis typothetae and reaffirms its allegiance to International law, the eight-hour demand and the eight-hour plan endorsed by the referendum of the International Typographical Union, and serves written notice on the St. Louis typothetae that this action has been taken." He then wrote, "Permit me to reiterate that if trouble should occur in St. Louis because of this action by the union, . . . then the executive council will support the reinstated union." The St. Louis local promptly yielded to the international's insistence, and its charter was reinstated.[27]

It may be inferred that the local union feared deprivation of the traveling card more than the international feared an influx into other jurisdictions of traveling printers from St. Louis who did not carry cards. To this extent a relatively high degree of organization in the most important centers of the trade served to strengthen the authority of the national union in a predominantly local product market jurisdiction. Indeed, in this respect a national union in this type of jurisdiction was more fortunate than a national union organized in a national product market, for, in the latter case, stronger local unions could not be encouraged to secure "standards" which might place their employers in an unfavorable competitive relationship with employers in producing regions where lower "standards" and costs still prevailed. Where vigorous competition among producing regions existed, the national union was in the position of a convoy commodore; since all ships in the convoy had to proceed at the same speed, the common pace could not exceed the speed of the slowest ship. But where local markets were better insulated, stragglers could be left to their fate, provided that there were not too many stragglers. Now Lynch and his fellow executive officers apparently believed (a) that a minority of the local unions could not maintain the eight-hour day if a substantial portion of the remainder did not make similar progress, (b) that, with the financial aid of the former, the latter could, in most cases, successfully effect a similar reduction in hours, if they were obliged to do so as a

27. Tracy, *Typographical Union*, pp. 801–808.

condition of maintaining their good standing in the International Typographical Union, and, finally (c), that such good standing was so essential to the members of each local union—many of who were in the habit of traveling about in search of work—that each local would prefer to fight for the compulsory standard rather than to accept the alternative of expulsion from the international.

President Lynch appears to have been an exceptionally shrewd judge of the capabilities of the Printers' locals. In 1907, the convention's Eight-Hour Committee reported that

We agree with the statement made by the International president in his report that there never has been brought forward an adequate and indisputable reason why our book and job members who are skilled in their branch of the trade should not be adequately paid and enjoy reasonable hours. We also believe that the apathy and neglect of self-interest that have characterized the book and job printers in the past is now changed, and that we have at least aroused these members to a realization of what they can accomplish and what they are entitled to if they only will.[28]

The accuracy of this appraisal was substantiated by the fact that although losses in membership and locals were not negligible, they were rather quickly recouped. At the following convention Lynch was able to report that

The membership of the International Typographical Union at the present time is perhaps the best indication of results secured, and proof that the work has been effective. The membership today is but a trifle less than at the time the eight-hour difficulty occurred, when it was about 47,000. Today the membership is about 46,000.

There was little doubt in the president's mind concerning the factor responsible for the success of the movement:

No organization involved in difficulty with employers carried its members on strike and benefit rolls as long as the International Typographical Union in the eight-hour difficulty.

Finally, Lynch was perhaps willing to incur some loss—or at least the risk of loss—because the printers in the very smallest communities could never be well organized and also because he had discovered that the presence of such unorganized groups, if numerically insignificant, was not necessarily fatal to the maintenance of higher standards in well organized centers.

In the St. Louis case referred to above, the disciplinary action taken by the executive board was sanctioned by an international rule, adopted in 1902, which provided that "No local union shall sign a contract guaranteeing its members to work for any proprietor, firm, or corporation, unless such con-

28. Tracy, *Typographical Union*, pp. 900–901, 916. Cf. also Barnett, *The Printers*, p. 157.

tract is in accordance with the International law and approved by the International president."[29] Although the suspension of the St. Louis local constituted the first important application of that rule, international authority had begun to encroach upon local autonomy in the eighties and had prevailed in many areas other than hours of work. Several reasons for this interesting extension of national power in a union whose jurisdiction was predominantly characterized by the persistence of local markets might be—and some have been—advanced.

In the first place, it should be noted that the extension of international control began about the same time that the central organization began to grant financial aid to striking locals.[30] In one respect the establishment of certain international regulations governing conditions of employment prevented the depletion of international funds, for if a local wished to strike for other conditions or for conditions superior to those specified in international law, it could not assume that aid from the parent organization would necessarily be forthcoming. We have already noted how the international executive had insisted upon provision for a strike assessment as a condition for the proclamation of an eight-hour rule. On a previous occasion, an international president had complained that "There is a growing tendency on the part of local unions to petition the international for support and assistance which the locals are competent and able to handle."[31] On the other hand, the existence of international laws strengthened the bargaining power of the locals which could refuse to consider any modification of a demand for conditions which were included in the work rules of the international; they were assured of international aid in the event of employer resistance—and the employers were aware of this fact. But international regulations were also mandatory in character, since the locals were obliged to establish the conditions specified therein; and the mere existence of international funds fails to explain the mandatory nature of these laws.

We have already observed that technological change played an important part in the establishment of a uniform-hours rule. The international also adopted other regulations which governed local policy with respect to the machine—for example, requiring that it be manned by printers and stipulating the conditions under which apprentices could work on it. However, although "The evident necessity for adoption of a common machine policy was a powerful influence in hastening the movement toward centralization in the Typographical Union,"[32] it is doubtful that technological change by itself could have produced that movement. Thus the introduction of the stone-planer did not result in strengthening the authority of the weak jour-

29. Barnett, *The Printers*, pp. 351–352.
30. Barnett, *The Printers*, pp. 39, 40.
31. Tracy, *Typographical Union*, p. 616.
32. George E. Barnett, *Chapters on Machinery and Labor* (Cambridge, Mass.: Harvard, 1926), p. 9, n. 1. Also pp. 11–13, 19, 30–59, especially pp. 45–51.

neymen Stone Cutters' Association over its affiliated locals; although various national regulations governing the transportation of planer-cut stone and the introduction of the planer were adopted, those which were intended to be mandatory upon the local unions were subsequently repealed.

In some instances, general laws, although challenged by the employers, pertained to internal jurisdictional matters. Thus the employers were opposed to the I.T.U.'s assertion of jurisdiction over linotype machinists and proofreaders.[33] Refusal to arbitrate such laws might be distinguished from refusal to arbitrate rules directly specifying conditions of employment. In this respect, the Printers treated the employers no differently than they treated the president of the American Federation of Labor; when Gompers sought to intervene in the jurisdictional dispute with the Machinists over the machine tenders, the convention of 1900 blandly instructed President Donnelly to inform him that the international union could not submit its own laws to arbitration.

International law requiring that foremen be members of the union was, however, much less an "internal" jurisdictional affair. The extension of international control in this area might be traced—legitimately if indirectly—to the extralocal nature of the labor markets in the printing industry; for rules governing the membership and the hiring practices of foremen were adopted, as we have noted elsewhere, largely in the interests of the "tramp" membership who were anxious to protect their employment opportunities as "subs" or extra men.[34] Regulations governing the affiliation and activities of foremen might well have constituted the most important area of international law. It was the refusal of the executive council of the international to agree to arbitration of the foreman membership rule, after the New York local had agreed to arbitration by the international and the United Typothetae, which prompted the 1902 convention to pass the general rule forbidding arbitration of any international laws. And when, one year later, a resurgence of local sentiment resulted in the adoption of a constitutional amendment which prohibited the international from enacting and enforcing laws "relative to the internal affairs of printing offices,"[35] repeal was promptly obtained after the secretary-treasurer pointed out to the delegates to the following convention that retention of the new amendment implied repeal of those international laws which regulated the hiring practices of the foremen, of which one was the celebrated "priority" law.

But, according to Barnett, "The increasing centralization of power is due chiefly to the gradual realization that many functions can be better discharged by a central organization than by the local unions."[36] This well-considered statement seems to imply that centralization was not so much a matter of

33. Tracy, *Typographical Union*, pp. 622, 639, 641–643.
34. Barnett, *The Printers*, pp. 215, 339.
35. Tracy, *Typographical Union*, pp. 766, 768–770.
36. Barnett, *The Printers*, p. 40.

necessity as of advisability in this predominantly local product market jurisdiction. We would suggest that, as indicated above, the impetus toward centralization came from the international's executive officers who realized that a combination of persuasion, aid, and coercion could increase bargaining strength at the local level. The larger and more powerful and affluent locals had to be persuaded originally that it was in their interest to make contributions to causes for which their weaker sisters were striving; and all locals had to realize that if they struck out to achieve the minimum international standards they would be supported, that if they did not, they would be dropped, and that the degree of organization throughout the trade was sufficiently high to make expulsion from the I.T.U. (with concomitant loss of the traveling card privilege) a prospect virtually as painful as failure in a contest with local employers.

Although the degree of national control over the economic standards of local unions was obviously higher in the case of the Printers than it was in the case of the Bricklayers in this early period, the two national organizations were similar in their indifference to the existence of geographic wage differences. And even where uniform standards in other areas existed, their mandatory character suggests that they were not proposed exclusively or even primarily on behalf of the laggard locals in a spirit of egalitarianism. For they served the interest of those locals whose standards were higher, and who chose either to aid the others because they feared that poorer conditions elsewhere menaced better conditions at home (the case of the Printers) or to avoid aiding weaker locals by requiring that the possession of standards equal to their own be a prior condition of eligibility for national affiliation and support (the case of the Bricklayers).

Where market boundaries did coincide with national jurisdictions, however, national unions were interested in establishing standards with respect to wage rates as well as other conditions of employment. Indeed, the desire to establish national wage standards was in large part responsible for the formation of national unions in several notable instances. This was true not only of the Coal Miners, as noted in the first chapter, but also of the Flint Glass Workers, the Glass Bottle Blowers, the Potters, the Granite Cutters,[37] and, as we shall see presently, the Molders. Like the two local-product-market unions discussed above, these and other national market organizations were impelled, in establishing uniform national policy, not so much by egalitarian sentiment as by a lively awareness of the conditions of economic survival. The nature of the motivation underlying the formulation of national wage policy stands revealed in the experience of the unions in the iron foundry, glass, pottery, and coal mining industries.

Moreover, apart from any information concerning the intent behind national wage policies, examination of the records of these unions sheds some

37. McCabe, *The Standard Rate*, pp. 150, 155, 158, 173–174.

light in two additional areas. The first of these concerns the type of differential which it was proposed to eliminate or reduce. Was the object to establish "uniformity in pay in proportion to effort and skill expended"? Was it to establish uniform labor costs? Was it to "take wages out of competition"— and, if so, what did that imply?

The second area of darkness consists in the nature of the economic impact which might be expected to ensue from the elimination of geographic wage differences. Classical theory holds that the imposition of a wage above the competitive level excludes some workers from employment in the occupation involved; from this it has been inferred that the imposition by a union of geographic uniformity bars from the trade workers in hitherto low-wage areas and obstructs the process whereby a desirable reallocation of resources would ultimately be achieved.

In the following brief case studies, an attempt will be made to provide information concerning, first, the motivation underlying the adoption of geographic wage policies, second, the nature of the magnitude, if any, which the union sought to make uniform, and third, the direction of economic change which might be expected to issue from the type of policy advocated or adopted.

The Molders

The Molders' concern over wage differentials was in large part responsible for the formation of their national union in 1859.[38] Nor did they swerve from their original intent in subsequent years; in 1887 we find President Fox welcoming a newly-formed employers' association as a partner in the project of equalizing piece rates—a task which, he pointed out, the union had hitherto been attempting to perform alone[39]; and in 1890 a "conference committee," which was organized to conduct joint negotiations on an industry-wide basis, awarded wage "adjustments" to certain firms, although no general advance was allowed at all.[40]

The Molders, however, were not interested in equality for its own sake but were concerned primarily with softening the impact of interregional competition upon wage rates. Thus, when the secretary of the employers' association in Cincinnati complained, in a letter to Sylvis dated February 2, 1867, that piece rates were "60 to 70 per cent higher here" than in the east and that "there is no reason why we should not be entitled to obtain our labor at the

38. John P. Frey and John R. Commons, "Conciliation in the Stove Industry," *Bulletin No. 62* of the U. S. Bureau of Labor, v. XII (1906), p. 132. Frey and Commons wrote of "This idea of equalizing competitive prices, appearing for the first time as a reason for organizing a national union. . . ."

39. F. W. Hilbert, "Trade Union Agreements in the Iron Molders' Union," *Studies in American Trade Unionism,* ed. by Jacob H. Hollander and George E. Barnett (New York: Henry Holt, 1906), p. 227.

40. *Proceedings,* 1895, pp. 15–16.

same price, and thus be enabled to compete successfully for the trade that legitimately belongs to the West," Sylvis replied that

You say the prices for labor should be the same in the West as in the East. We think a difference of 20 per cent. between the East and the West should be no disadvantage to the employers of the West.[41]

The Molders refused, in normal times, to eliminate wage differences by permitting firms in high-wage regions (the west) to reduce their rates. Such a policy, according to an article which appeared in the *Journal,* would merely invite retaliation by the low-wage area and the inequality would be restored, "giving the dealer and purchaser the profit, who but for the reduction in wages would have been content to pay and buy for prices that would afford all concerned in the trade fair and reasonable profits, and satisfactory wages."[42]

Instead, the Molders proposed to raise wages in lower-paid areas. Replying to the Cincinnati employers in a letter following the one which we have already quoted, Sylvis wrote (in 1867):

We must again call your attention to the important fact, that the preamble to your printed circular of the 2d instant, is a misstatement—known to be such by you. In that preamble you say: "There is no reliance to be placed in the repeated promises made to us by the Molders' Union Association for the regulation and equalization of the prices East and West." At the beginning of the last year we undertook to raise prices in the East. The work was begun in Troy. We wanted an equalization of price, taking the highest shop as standard, and an advance of 25 per cent upon the equalization. This would have given us an advance of 50 per cent in Troy. We were obliged to give up the advance because you made common cause with the Eastern employers in an attack upon the life of our organization. But for your opposition, prices would now be fully 50 per cent above the present standard in Troy and other points East, and you would have no cause for complaint.

The same philosophy was held, at a later date, by President Fox with respect to differentials between large and small producing regions:

It may be that in one or two cities in a certain district molders' wages might seem too high by comparison with those paid in the outlying districts, but that is largely because the scale of the latter is too low. Our efforts are therefore devoted to bringing these as nearly as possible up to the standard; but to agree that they should enter into the computation when an equitable basis is to be established, seems unreasonable.[43]

It was mentioned above that wage rates were higher in the west than in the east. In the 1870's, the eastern centers of production were apparently larger than those in the west, for it was observed that "Stoves made in the

41. Frey and Commons, "Conciliation in the Stove Industry," pp. 136, 137.
42. *Journal,* April 30, 1889, p. 5.
43. *Proceedings,* 1899, p. 7. Cf. also *Proceedings,* 1902, p. 602.

East are sold extensively in the West; but few Western stoves are sold in the East, simply because there is but little, if any surplus production over home demand."[44] Originally the Albany-Troy district was the greatest stove manufacturing center, but, by the end of the century, Detroit was the largest producing region. Thus the geographic wage differential was the result and not the cause of the movement of industry. High wages in the west reflected growing demand for labor in that region; they did not result in an exodus of industry to the low-wage area, for they were a symptom of the movement in the opposite direction.

Thus the union's preferred policy of raising wages in low-wage areas would have tended to stimulate the westward movement of capital by raising labor costs in the region where demand was undergoing relative decline. Union wage policy in this instance would not have tended to reverse the "right" direction of economic change; one can hold that it would have induced the adjustment to proceed at greater speed and, possibly, that it would have resulted in a greater westward movement than would have occurred otherwise. An actual instance of the operation of this wage policy was recorded in the pages of the Molders' *Journal:*

Rathbone, Sard & Co. (Albany) alleges that as a result of certain unfavorable conditions it had become handicapped in marketing its wares in the West, and that as a consequence it must manufacture at a western point for its western trade or receive a reduction in cost of production at its eastern plant to offset the cost of transportation of its products west. It requested a reduction in the price of molding. Opinion divided among the molders as to course to pursue. Many regarding it as subterfuge to obtain a reduction in wage scale and the threat to move as a "bluff." Vote of all molders in plant of firm taken in No. 2 foundry and by a vote of approximately 200 against to 100 in favor, the molders decided against granting the reduction. . . . Matters thus rested until the close of the year, when shops Nos. 4 and 5 closed permanently; firm announcing that it would locate its western foundries at Aurora, Ill.[45]

The effect of this type of wage policy upon the migration of labor is more problematical than its effect upon the movement of capital; it depends upon the relative importance of wage levels and of job opportunities as determinants of labor mobility. On the one hand, raising wages in the east might have tended to maintain an excess supply of labor in that region; on the other, the decline of employment in the east and the expansion of demand for labor in the west might have tended to accelerate the westward migration of labor. Had the union not sought to interfere with the geographic wage pattern, both the wage incentive and the employment incentive would have stimulated westward migration. The union policy, had it been adopted, would have eliminated the former.

44. *Journal,* March 10, 1875, p. 228.
45. *Journal,* July 1909, p. 503.

Actually, however, this policy was not carried out to the extent required to eliminate geographic differentials altogether. As a result of collective bargaining with the Stove Founders' National Defense Association, an arrangement was worked out in 1892 whereby equalization of wages was to take place only within each of several regional districts, while provision for uniform percentage changes on a nationwide basis tended to freeze the broader geographic wage relationships.[46]

The Glass Workers

Competition between high-wage and low-wage producers also accounted for the Glass Workers' interest in uniform wage policies. The Glass Bottle Blowers maintained that it was their object "to thoroughly unite all green glass workers for their mutual benefit and protection; to regulate and maintain a uniform price-list throughout the trade. . ."[47] Their national officers perceived more clearly than the membership the importance of thoroughgoing organization in a competitive industry. In 1894, Vice-President Troth complained that

The conduct of a portion of our membership toward those taken out of scab houses is not what it should be. The annual conventions orders (sic) the executive officers to use all efforts and honorable means to get control of the non-union or scab workmen and factories. Your officers have complied with said orders and have taken them out. In doing so it became necessary to guarantee them the support and protection of the Association which is guaranteed to every man who takes the obligation of the Association. They were accorded the right and privilege of going out in the trade to secure employment in union factories, which were their right and privilege as members. Instead of receiving that treatment that should be accorded to them as union men they have been hooted at and driven back into the scab dens. Others have been denied the financial aid promised them while loyal to the organization and unable to secure employment in a union factory. How can you get control of the scab factories and workmen if you do not give the workmen all the rights, privileges and protection of the Association? I have no love for a man that will scab on his trade, but self-preservation compels me to seek his friendship and fellowship. I can only get him with me by treating hm as a man. The men taken out of the scab houses are on strike and are entitled to strike benefits. . . .[48]

In 1897, President Hayes observed that "Those of our members who are far removed from non-union localities cannot realize the magnitude of this evil as can those who are brought into personal contact with it, yet there is not a man in our trade but daily feels its influence." The following year he tried once again to expose the delegates to some basic economics for trade unionists:

46. McCabe, *The Standard Rate*, pp. 136–140.
47. *Constitution*, 1892, Art. I, Sec. 2.
48. *Proceedings*, 1894, p. 21. See also *Proceedings*, 1897, p. 10; 1898, p. 22.

from the nature of some of the resolutions sent out this year one would imagine we had no non-union competitors in America; and I sincerely hope that the members representing the branches from which come these resolutions demanding the suspension of apprentices, abolishment of Saturday night work and an increase in wages will be kind enough to explain to this Convention how such things are going to be secured ALL AT ONCE. . . .

My desire and aim has been to hold our present position until the non-union men shall have been organized into an association by themselves. . . .

Geographic wage differences between unionized regions could be as troublesome as differentials between unionized and unorganized areas. Like the Molders, the three national unions in the glass industry before the end of the century, the Bottle Blowers, the Flint Glass Workers, and Local Assembly 300 (the national union of skilled window-glass workers) were confronted by a situation in which wages in western manufacturing centers were higher than those in the east. This was due in part to the fact that the eastern centers were more exposed to the competition of foreign producers (whose lower costs, in turn, resulted largely from an international wage differential; the wages of skilled American glass workers were much greater than the wages received by their colleagues abroad). Higher wages in the west were also made possible by lower fuel costs in that part of the country.[49]

All three unions sought to equalize wages by raising wage rates in the lower-paid regions relative to those in high-wage areas. The Bottle Blowers approached their objective of maintaining "a uniform price list throughout the trade" as a result of two early strikes; the first, in 1878, established a uniform price list throughout the Pittsburgh area, and the second, in 1883, brought the firms in the Ohio valley up to the Pittsburgh wage levels.[50] In 1899, the President of the Association was asked, "Have you different scales of wages in different sections where your work is done?" He was able to reply, "No; in the union they have a uniform list."[51] In the national agreement with the National Bottle Manufacturers' Association in 1903, the following rule, illustrative of national control over collective bargaining, was adopted:

Section 1. Prices, rules, and regulations established by the joint committee can not be changed or deviated from in any manner by the action of any branch, individual blower, or manufacturer offering or accepting a higher or lower price, or ignoring any of the rules.[52]

49. Pearce Davis, *The Development of the American Glass Industry* (Cambridge: Harvard, 1949), pp. 41–42, 71, 74, 120, 128; Warren C. Scoville, *Revolution in Glassmaking* (Cambridge: Harvard, 1948), pp. 33, 59, 91.

50. Milton Derber, "Glass," in *How Collective Bargaining Works* (New York: Twentieth Century Fund, 1945), pp. 703–704.

51. United States Industrial Commission, *Report on the Relations and Conditions of Capital and Labor Employed in Manufactures and General Business* (Washington: Government Printing Office, 1901), v. VII, p. 108.

52. Quoted in Eleventh Special Report of the Commission of Labor, *Regulation and Restriction of Output* (Washington: Government Printing Office, 1904), p. 637.

The pronouncements of the national officials of the Bottle Blowers (quoted above) concerning the necessity to organize nonunion sectors of the association's jurisdiction (the most important of which was the southern part of New Jersey) suggest strongly that their interest in establishing geographic wage uniformity stemmed primarily from a desire to eliminate competitive pressures upon union standards rather than from any insistence upon "equal pay for equal work" as an end in itself. The record of the Window Glass Workers invites a similar conclusion. In 1867, the New York Window Glass Workers lost a strike for higher wages, "primarily because of lack of aid from the Pittsburgh unions"; as a result the New York manufacturers could reduce prices and compete more successfully with the western manufacturers, whose fuel costs were lower.[53] When the locals in the east and the west merged in 1879 as Local Assembly 300 of the Knights of Labor, the new national union sought to eliminate competitive whipsawing by equalizing total, rather than labor costs; "it gave a differential to the localities where coal was most expensive, so as to even up conditions as much as possible."[54] In 1882, however, as the result of a strike, wages in the east were raised almost to equality with wages in the west. But it is significant that, in convention, the delegates from many locals in the east had demanded that the prevailing geographic differential (of 10 per cent) should be increased rather than reduced, since it did not suffice to overcome the west's competitive advantage.[55] Thus the drive for "equal pay" originated with the high-paid, not the low-paid members.

The Flint Glass Workers in the east, like their colleagues in the window glass and bottle trades, had been paid less than their opposite numbers farther west in order to compensate for the higher cost of coal and other materials in the east. The American Flint Glass Workers' Union, in 1888, followed the example set by the other two national unions in the glass trades and succeeded in obtaining wage increases in the low-paid east, thus eliminating existing differentials.[56] Since the industry was moving west in search of lower fuel costs,[57] the high-wage region was expanding. By favoring wage increases in the low-wage areas, the wage policy of this national union probably tended to accelerate, rather than to arrest, the westward migration of both capital and labor. Thus, after some western representatives, who had gained control of the Flint Glass Workers, had prevailed upon his workers to strike for higher wages (in 1888), E. D. Libbey shut down the works of the New England Glass Company in Cambridge, Massachusetts and moved to Toledo, Ohio. Moreover, 115 men who had been employed in the Cambridge works followed Libbey to Toledo, although 35 of these subsequently returned East.

53. Davis, *American Glass*, p. 132.
54. Commissioner of Labor, *Regulation of Output*, pp. 600–601.
55. Commissioner of Labor, *Regulation of Output*, p. 615.
56. Scoville, *Revolution in Glassmaking*, pp. 91–93, 235.
57. Davis, *American Glass*, pp. 73–74.

Thus these unions in the glass industries followed the example set by the Molders in attempting to eliminate geographic wage differences by raising wages in the low-paid areas rather than by reducing them in the high-paid areas. In all four cases, industry was migrating to the high-wage regions, so that union policy probably tended to reinforce, rather than to arrest, the movement of resources which had been induced initially by changing patterns of demand although it also tended to prevent any ultimate tendency of western wages to fall. This type of national wage policy tended to work to the advantage of the high-wage locals in the west just as it threatened to undermine the employment position of the (originally) lower-paid eastern locals. Both geographic factions in the Window Glass Workers were highly sophisticated concerning their respective local interests: the eastern locals resisted national efforts to raise wages in their regions relative to western levels, while the adoption of this national policy reflected the dominance of the western locals within the national union. (It might also be noted that the decision to strike the Libbey works in New England was traced to western influence in the Flint Glass Workers' organization.)

The Potters

Further evidence of sectional sophistication can be found in the record of the Potters. Prior to 1897 the pottery workers in the east were not united with those in the west in a single labor organization. Piece rates were higher in the east, although daily earnings were higher in the west, due primarily to more extensive employment of modern machinery and, according to some, greater expenditure of effort required of the workers in the western potteries.[58] In 1894 a strike which was called in the west by the National Brotherhood of Operative Potters in opposition to a reduction in wages was lost after the eastern union (which had recently severed its relationship with the Knights of Labor and was still in a formative stage) had conceded defeat in a similar struggle.[59] Originally both groups had been organized as a national trade district within the Knights. The westerners withdrew in 1890 and formed the Brotherhood. Following overtures from the Brotherhood and assistance from its national officers in another wage dispute in which the eastern employers sought to narrow the geographic differential, the eastern locals entered the Brotherhood in 1897.[60] The western locals pressed for a uniform wage scale, and, in 1900, the Brotherhood almost achieved this objective. Uniformity was to be obtained, however, by adopting "an average of prices East and West," with the result that piece rates in the east were re-

58. Industrial Commission, *Reports on Labor*, v. XIV, pp. 644, 652, 654; v. XVIII, p. 373.

59. David A. McCabe, *National Collective Bargaining in the Pottery Industry* (Baltimore: Johns Hopkins, 1932), pp. 28–34; Commissioner of Labor, *Regulation of Output*, p. 66.

60. Commissioner of Labor, *Regulation of Output*, p. 666.

duced. But the Trenton, New Jersey local of jiggermen and dishmakers had notified the convention of the Brotherhood of its opposition to "averaging," and, after the uniform list was negotiated, it seceded from the Brotherhood; and it was joined by some kilnmen, turners, and handlers. It then became necessary to abandon the attempt to form a national scale, but after reorganizing in the east, the Brotherhood in 1904 secured from the manufacturers an agreement to extend the western list to the east. The Brotherhood's officers agreed to replace any jiggermen who might quit work in protest over the new scale; thus coerced, the latter surrendered and a national joint agreement was signed in 1905.[61]

The Potters thus secured uniform piece rates by reducing rates in the high-wage region as well as by raising them in the low-wage region. Since the western locals controlled the national organization,[62] this strategy was adopted at their insistence. Had national policy reflected the eastern interests, however, an attempt would have been made to eliminate geographic differences solely by raising wages in the west. The eastern position was well stated in testimony given by a representative of the Trenton local of Jiggermen and Dishmakers' which had seceded from the Brotherhood in protest against the uniform agreement:

Q: Why are you disconnected both locally and nationally with the organized labor of other industries?

A: Because the national organization, that is, the National Brotherhood of Operative Potters, operated to our hurt, so as to effect a reduction in our wages, and as a consequence we would not have anything to do with them. They gave out a list or a scale of pay for goods, of products, that very materially reduced the wages of Trenton Potters. Consequently we refused to have anything further to do with them, believing that this was not a time when wages should be reduced. . . .

Q: That is something unique in the history of labor unions to reduce wages.

A: I should think it is.

Q: How do you explain it?

A: I can't explain it.

Q: Were they composed largely of representatives from other parts of the country?

A: Yes; largely of representatives from the West.

Q: Was the scale of wages lower in the West than here?

A: Yes.

Q: Was it an attempt to equalize wages between the West and the East?

A: Yes; by bringing the wages of the East down to those of the West.

Q: You thought the equalization ought to have been made by bringing the wages of the West up to those of the East, did you?

A: Yes.

61. McCabe, *Pottery Industry*, pp. 36–43, 190–193.
62. Industrial Commission, *Reports on Labor*, v. XIV, p. 641.

Thus the eastern locals would have preferred to raise wages in the low-wage (piece rate) region. This policy was adopted by the Molders and the unions in the glass trades, but, whereas the low-wage areas were, at least relatively, the declining centers of production in the foundry and glass industries, they were the expanding centers in pottery. Adoption of this program in pottery, therefore, would have implied quite different effects from those it tended to produce in other trades: instead of tending initially to reinforce the actual movement of capital to the low-cost west,[63] it would have tended to inhibit such movement by raising western labor costs; instead of tending to stimulate any westward migration of labor by reducing job opportunities in the east, it would have discouraged that migration by tending to reduce job opportunities in the west. The eastern program, in short, furnishes a good illustration of the classic case against institutional imposition of wage uniformity.[64]

But western rather than eastern views prevailed in the Brotherhood; and a policy of reducing wages in the high-rate region might be expected to produce changes in the opposite direction. Little migration had been taking place; none from west to east, because, although piece rates were higher in the east, earnings were higher in the west; and none from east to west, because, although time earnings were higher in the west, the extra effort required apparently deterred Trenton potters from moving to Ohio (East Liverpool was the center of the western branch of the industry),[65] just as the greater pace of work in the United States prompted some English-born potters to return, disillusioned, to their native land.[66] Nevertheless, by insisting upon a reduction in eastern piece rates, the low-rated western unionists were hardly acting to discourage migration into their area.

Nor was their policy calculated to attract industry into their region, for reducing wage rates in the east relative to those in the west would tend to arrest the westward movement of the industry. Moreover, the Brotherhood, unlike some of the old eastern locals, advocated the installation of more modern machinery in the east, presumably in order to make a reduction in piece rates more acceptable to the eastern potters, whose productivity would be improved by the new machines, thereby maintaining or even increasing their time earnings. And since the traditional union justification for the higher eastern rates had been that they were necessary to compensate for lower productivity of capital, it was expected that the reduction in eastern rates would result in greater investment in modern equipment. In order to

63. Industrial Commission, *Reports on Labor,* v. XIV, p. 654.

64. Cf. Henry C. Simons, "Some Reflections on Syndicalism," *Journal of Political Economy,* v. LII, no. 1, March 1944, pp. 1–25. Reprinted in Henry C. Simons, *Economic Policy for a Free Society* (Chicago: University of Chicago, 1948), pp. 121–159, especially, pp. 133–139.

65. Commissioner of Labor, *Regulation of Output,* pp. 685, 688, 694.

66. Industrial Commission, *Reports on Labor,* v. XIV, pp. 647, 652.

encourage such investment, moreover, the agreement provided that, "where unusual conditions or inconveniences exist beyond the average the jiggerman shall receive a percentage extra," although the procedure to be followed was first to impose the uniform list and later to restore differentials if "inconveniences beyond the average" had not been eliminated.[67]

Thus the Potters' policy of "averaging"—that is, reducing wage rates in the high-rate areas and raising them in the low-rate regions differed, on the one hand, from the policy advocated by their eastern locals and, on the other, from the policy adopted by the unions in the foundry and glass industries. It differed from the former in that it did not tend to arrest the movement of industry; it differed from the latter in that it did not tend initially to accelerate the rate of migration. Instead it approximated the type of adjustment which the free market might be expected to produce:—a fall in eastern rates and a rise in western rates; but since this union policy tended to anticipate the verdict of the market place, it may be that the westward movement of the industry proceeded less rapidly than otherwise would have been the case.

The object of the union was not to protect the higher rate by excluding lower-paid workers from the industry (cf. Simons), but to protect the standards of the lower-rated westerners from downward pressure originating in the inability of the eastern workers to maintain their higher rates. With one exception, the parties involved were reasonably satisfied with the transaction —western unionists, whose rates were protected, and even raised, by the averaging process; western manufacturers, whose unit costs still remained below those of their eastern competitors; and eastern manufacturers whose position was improved. The exception, of course, was the group of eastern unionists, the reduction in whose wage rates apparently outweighed, in their estimation, any improvement in their employment prospects. But from their viewpoint, of course, it should not have been necessary to make that choice at all; the solution which they preferred was the classic policy of raising low rates elsewhere.

Although the establishment of uniform piece rates served a most pragmatic purpose for the western locals, the president of the Brotherhood advocated, as a matter of principle,

that there should be a price set for doing a certain kind of work according to regular methods and under ordinary conditions. This is to be our price regardless of the section . . . if it is clearly shown that the methods employed and the conditions and facilities prevailing are not up to the ordinary, then there should be extras so as to enable the men to earn equally as good wages as are earned under ordinary conditions.[68]

Thus the agreement provided for the establishment of "extras" where "conditions and facilities" had not been raised to average. But although very

67. McCabe, *The Standard Rate*, pp. 190–191, 199–200.
68. *Proceedings*, 1903, pp. 117–118.

little modernization took place in the east, subsequent negotiations "left many actual differences beyond the boundary of extra compensation." Instead, uniform piece rates were established in order to reduce competition between the two regions.[69] Hence the union, in assigning to uniformity in piece rates priority over uniformity in time rates, demonstrated that the true objective of its wage policy was economic in nature.

The Miners

The Miners, like the Potters, pledged allegiance to the ideal of equality in effort earnings; like the Potters, also, they suffered this principle to be honored in the breach when strict adherence would have resulted in competitive pressure upon the union standard. In Chapter II we referred to the fact that intense competition between different producing areas was largely instrumental in inducing the different district unions of coal miners to form a national union in order to eliminate downward pressure on wage rates. Mine operators were persuaded to enter into collective bargaining arrangements with the United Mine Workers on the theory that industry-wide (or, at least, extralocal) bargaining would help to eliminate wage competition and to place all regions on a basis of what was termed "competitive equality." By "competitive equality" they meant an approximation to equality in total costs, so that operators in all producing areas might live and let live. Competitive equality thus implied inequality in wage rates; or, as an operator from southern Illinois put it,

We have banded together here so that the operators in every district might exist, notwithstanding the different conditions that prevail; and so long as we work on those lines some miners will have to accept less wages than others.[70]

For that reason, uniform rates were not established throughout the unionized sector of the industry, nor even throughout the "central competitive field," which included the bituminous mines in western Pennsylvania, Ohio, Illinois, and Indiana, and which formed the area over which the agreements emerging from the Interstate Joint Conferences extended. A separate base rate was established in each of these states, or, as they were termed, "districts." Each district served as a basing point for other districts which were outside the central competitive field, and any changes in the basing-point rates were reflected, insofar as it was possible to do so, in equal changes in outside base rates. Nor were rates always uniform even within districts; within each district, state conferences were held and local rates were set by applying accepted differentials to the district base.[71]

69. McCabe, *The Standard Rate*, p. 374.

70. Commissioner of Labor, *Regulation of Output*, pp. 391–392.

71. McCabe, *The Standard Rate*, pp. 134–136; Isadore Lubin, *Miners' Wages and the Cost of Coal* (New York: McGraw-Hill, 1924), pp. 45–49, 88–92, 101–104, 185–186, 259–260.

The wage differentials which emerged from—or survived—collective bargaining were intended, in some instances, to offset competitive inequalities. Thus operators whose mines were further removed from a common market might be awarded wage differentials which tended to offset their higher freight charges. The union did not object to these "freight differentials" in wages; indeed, it sought to apply the principle which governed their establishment to the solution of another problem which arose by virtue of the fact that some operators had installed machines in their mines while others retained the hand, or pick, method. By insisting that the piece rate on machine work should be reduced below the pick rate by an amount no greater than that required to defray the cost of installation, maintenance, depreciation, and a "fair" profit, the union attempted to protect the pick miners from machine competition. The operators, however, departed from the principle of "competitive equality"; they wanted to reduce the piece rate on machine work to the point where the daily earnings of pick and machine miners would be equal.

The union matched the operators' inconsistency, however, in another area. It demanded (successfully) that the daily wage rates for inside company men, who were paid on a time basis, be made uniform throughout the central competitive field. Since different mines utilized differing proportions of inside men (for transportation and maintenance) to total labor force, establishment of the uniform time rate meant that the per ton cost to mines employing relatively large numbers of inside men would be higher than unit costs in mines employing relatively little maintenance help.[72]

Now there was some question whether the union was inconsistent in its policy on time wages or in its piece rate policy. For, according to Lubin, while the national officers endorsed "competitive equality" as a desirable objective, they really did not define the term as the employers did. Instead they considered it to mean uniformity of wage rates, which, in the opinion of Secretary William Green, would "bring about as near as possible equal competitive opportunities." And since the unionists also insisted that piece rates be higher in thin-vein mines (where output per manshift was low) than in thick-vein mines, it might appear that the wage rates which they sought to equalize were earnings per unit of effort.

Yet that interpretation of the union's underlying policy would leave unexplained their acquiescence in piece rate differentials. It is plausible to believe, in this writer's opinion, that the national officers, for all their egalitarian professions, were at least as unwilling as were the operators to force mines to close down, that they wished to protect existing standards against competitive encroachments, that they were willing to tolerate wage rate differentials where differentials were necessary to forestall these two eventuali-

72. For the following discussion on wages in the coal mining industry, see Lubin, *Miners' Wages*, pp. 78–79, 92–100, 139, 144, 191–197.

ties, and that they were willing to contemplate cost differentials, resulting from rate uniformities or otherwise,[73] only where such differentials were not of appreciable magnitude. Even union policy on vein differentials can be explained on these grounds, for although the higher rates in the thin-vein mines raised labor costs in those mines, the latter could remain in operation. And although the higher rates were intended to compensate the thin-vein miners for lower productivity, they did not do so completely, and their earnings were not as great as earnings in thick veins; as Lubin wrote, "they are willing to bear an appreciable part of the cost of keeping the thin-vein mines in operation."

Our case studies furnish information in the three areas to which reference has been made above: (1) the economic effect of geographic wage policies, (2) the types of rate which unions sought to make uniform, and (3) the motives underlying the adoption of geographic wage policies.

(1) The direction of economic change induced by the wage policies of the unions selected for examination depends upon the type of policy selected—whether to raise wages in the low-rate areas (iron molding, glass) or to reduce wages in the high-rate areas (pottery); and upon the nature of the industrial relocation—whether capital is moving to the low-wage region (under stimulus of lower labor costs) or to the high-wage region (in response to lower costs of other resources or to changing patterns of demands). Static analysis assumes other things equal and considers the case in which only wage rates are unequal; it also assumes the adoption of a policy designed to raise wages in the lower area to an equality with those in the high-wage region. Neither assumption need in fact prevail, and where these conditions are altered, the indicated effect of union policy is of course different from the solution to the original problem. Specifically, we have observed that where wage differentials were the result rather than the cause of industrial migration, union policy might tend to reinforce rather than to inhibit such migration, although it cannot be claimed that it would effect an "optimum" geographic allocation of resources, since it would prevent the higher (e.g. western) rates from falling and thus tend to damp down the industry's growth. Moreover, we have noticed that national policy need not take the form assumed; the Potters' policy of reducing high wage rates, in the interest of their low-rate locals, was just as "rational" as the policy of raising low-wage rates, advocated by the high-rate locals. The policy actually adopted de-

73. Lubin pointed out that failure to establish any policy with respect to yardage and dead-work rates was consistent with neither philosophy. Since the amount of work of this nature per ton of coal varied from section to section, equalization of unit costs would require that piece rates would be lower where the proportion of dead work was high. Or, if it were desired to equalize effort earnings, dead-work rates would have to be made equal to mining rates.

pended, in the case of the Potters and the Flints, upon which group of locals was in control of the national organization.

(2) Before proceeding to any information which our case studies might provide concerning the type of rate which the national unions sought to make uniform when they advocated uniformity, let us summarize and comment briefly upon McCabe's conclusions on this subject. With respect to piece-working unions, he held that the object was the equalization of the "real rate of remuneration . . . over as much as possible of the union jurisdiction"; by "real rate" was meant "not so much one standard rate over the whole competitive area or over the whole jurisdiction . . . as . . . pay in proportion to effort and skill expended."[74] However, he also observed that equalization of this rate was desired "more particularly over such parts as lie within the same competitive district"; and previously he had characterized the early policy of the Molders as evidence of their desire to achieve "uniformity in labor cost." Moreover, he subsequently made the interesting observation that time-working unions tended to establish narrower areas of uniformity than did piece-working organizations; and he attributed this phenomenon, first, to "the more local character of competition in most time-working trades," and, second, to the fact that "where minimum time rates differ, proportional differences in labor cost do not necessarily follow." The latter result is explained in part by the fact that differences in minima did not always signify differences in time rates actually paid, but a more important explanation consists in the fact that "the higher rates of wages are often paid in the localities which have men of higher than average efficiency."

In view of the importance which he attributed to the desire of the national unions to "take wages out of competition" it might appear surprising that McCabe formulated the objective of the piece-working unions in terms of "pay in proportion to effort and skill expended" rather than, simply, as the desire to remove inequalities in labor costs. But he was correct in drawing this distinction, since some unions (the Garment Workers, the Hatters, and the United Mine Workers) insisted upon the payment of higher piece rates where productivity was lower due to inferior equipment or the unfavorable conditions of work. In such cases inequality in piece rates implied inequality in unit labor costs, but equal earnings in proportion to effort and skill.

Three of our case studies, however, revealed attitudes or policies which seemed not to imply insistence either upon uniform effort earnings (given the level of skill) or upon uniform unit labor costs. In all three cases, national authorities tolerated inequalities in piece rates which were unrelated to differences in worker productivity. The Molders agreed to the maintenance of regional differentials in piece rates. Local Assembly 300, the union of the window-glass workers, tolerated lower piece rates in regions in which the

74. McCabe, *The Standard Rate*, p. 163. See also pp. 138, 160–162, 181–183.

cost of fuel was relatively high. Finally, the Miners, whose policies with respect to day rates for inside men and with respect to vein differentials in piece rates implied inequalities in unit labor costs in the interest of equal effort earnings, agreed upon freight differentials in piece rates which meant that both effort earnings and labor costs would be unequal. Now the policies described in all three cases, while consistent with neither of the two objectives identified by McCabe, are nevertheless consistent with the desire to minimize interregional competition; but they imply equality, not of unit labor costs, but of unit total costs. No claim of generality is made of course; the avowed policies of the miners with respect to vein differentials and of the potters with respect to "extras" would have implied unequal total unit costs (and equal effort earnings) if they had been pushed sufficiently hard. Thus we find here, as we did in the last chapter, that unions did not invariably require that either time or effort or efficiency rates be made uniform.

(3) With respect to the motivation of union wage policy, this examination of geographic wage policies supports another conclusion reached in the last chapter—that wage differences were opposed by unions when their existence tended to exert downward competitive pressures upon union standards. The Bottle Blowers sought "to regulate and maintain a uniform price-list throughout the trade" for the same reason that they attempted "to thoroughly unite all green glass workers"—that is, "for their mutual benefit and protection." Moreover, the fact that the impetus to uniformity was furnished by the high-paid locals in the Bottle Blowers' Association suggests that it reflected a desire not so much for "equity" as for "protection." This was also the case, it will be recalled, with the Printers; and, although the Potters' national organization chose to impose uniformity by reducing wages in the high-rate east as well as by raising them in the low-rate west, the easterners in that union did advocate exclusive reliance upon the latter course. In this connection, it is pertinent to note also that, according to McCabe, the high-wage locals in the Cigar Makers favored the establishment of uniform wages because of the "depressing effect exerted upon prices by competition from places with low price lists."[75]

Where, however, competition between different producing regions existed but was characterized by differences in nonlabor costs, some national unions favored the establishment of "equalizing" differences in wage rates. Finally, where competition was not present to a marked extent, geographic (and other interfirm) inequalities were not opposed by union authority; in this respect also geographic wage policies were consistent with the attitudes of national officials to other types of interpersonal differentials.

However, the geographic wage differentials which the national unions did protect or encourage in the absence of competition do not appear to have reflected necessarily the existence of a policy aimed at maximizing the wage

75. McCabe, *The Standard Rate*, pp. 127–128.

bill throughout the national jurisdiction. While the protection of interpersonal differentials based upon skill, job content, or worker efficiency was consistent with such maximizing psychology, the advocacy of higher wage rates in high-cost (or low-productivity) firms or areas was not. The vein differentials favored by the Miners and the "extras" demanded by the Potters constituted discrimination against high-cost rather than against low-cost employers. The hands-off policy of the national unions in local market jurisdictions might have indeed resulted in the establishment of higher wages in low-cost regions; this, however, can hardly be held to reflect the over-all design of a single seller—unless one holds that, in making central strike funds available to the high-wage locals, the national executive intended them to preserve or increase existing geographic differentials in the interest of maximizing the total industry wage bill.

In theory, of course, there is no reason why a union should not have elected always to maximize total money income (or some combination of income and leisure) by judicious discrimination in the sale of its members' labor; for, by selecting some "politically" appropriate principle of compensation, it could have redistributed the total "receipts" among the membership in any manner desired. In fact, however, unions were not able to redistribute their members' wage incomes. (The Printers, in their advocacy of bidding for the "fat" were an exception, but, when employers declined to sanction this practice, the I.T.U. would not accept as an alternative a system of piecework under which certain members would always receive higher earnings than the rest.) It appears that discrimination was feasible only when the pattern of wage rates and incomes which it produced directly was acceptable to the membership, in the sense that it did not alienate any influential segment thereof. It is therefore possible that, while differentials based upon differences in skill, job content, and even efficiency could win acceptance, differentials based upon geographical location alone (from the workers' viewpoint) were not acceptable—unless it was agreed that they were necessary in order to "protect the standard," or unless the different local markets were well isolated.

In the discussion of interpersonal wage differences in the last chapter, we found that national union policy was consistent with the maximizing hypothesis both in situations characterized by the presence of product competition and in situations in which such competition was lacking. In the former case, uniformity in wage rates was sought after; in the latter, differentials were tolerated or promoted, the effect of which was to maximize wage income throughout the occupational jurisdiction. In this discussion of geographic wage differences, however, we found that the national union policy was clearly consistent with maximizing behavior only to the extent that it was necessary to protect existing union levels from interfirm competition.

But it is a risky undertaking to try to infer intent from policy, for stated policies represented a compromise between what the national unions would have desired under ideal conditions and what they could realistically hope to attain. Although the national unions did not, for the most part, discriminate among firms in the sense that certain firms discriminated among customers,[76] we do not know whether they would have engaged in this type of practice if they had been free to do exactly as they pleased. We do know that they typically were not able to impose their will upon the employers with whom they dealt and that any agreements entered into by both sides presumably reflected the outcome of negotiations in which the employers' views carried some weight. Moreover, there is reason to believe that the geographic wage patterns which emerged under national collective bargaining conformed closely to the desires of the employers who were parties to such agreements, as we shall find in the next section.

EMPLOYER INFLUENCE: NATIONAL COLLECTIVE BARGAINING

McCabe cites instances in which employer influence upon national collective bargaining is apparent. Coöperation on the part of the employers made possible the establishment of a uniform price list in the Pressed Ware and Iron Mold department of the Flint Glass Workers in 1888, for previous efforts in this direction by the union alone had not been successful.[77] A uniform wage scale, established in the iron and steel finishing mills west of the Alleghanies in 1885 "was . . . obviously brought about by the refusal of manufacturers in one district to pay more than those in another and by the union's bringing up the lower-priced districts to the level of the higher in order to prevent reductions in the latter."

The influence of the employers in the pottery industry was evident; according to McCabe, "the fact that the majority of the employers regarded uniformity in wage rates as a desirable thing for the industry was of great assistance in bringing about national collective bargaining and giving the agreement system valuable momentum in the earlier years."[78] When the western manufacturers, in 1897, agreed to raise wages to levels which had prevailed in 1893, they did so at a time when the Brotherhood was numerically too weak to have secured the raise without the voluntary coöperation of these employers. (The upswing in business conditions might have produced the wage increase in the absence of a strong union, but the employers were not obliged thereby to recognize this weak union in order to grant the increase.) Moreover, as a result of the prestige gained by its recognition and by the wage increase in the west, eastern locals joined the Brotherhood, making

76. Richard A. Lester, "Labor Monopoly and Business Monopoly: A Faulty Analogy," *Journal of Political Economy,* December 1947, pp. 513–536. Arthur M. Ross, *Trade Union Wage Policy* (Berkeley and Los Angeles: University of California, 1948), p. 49.

77. McCabe, *The Standard Rate,* pp. 147, 152.

78. McCabe, *National Collective Bargaining in the Pottery Industry,* pp. 33, 35, 37, 43, 93–94, 373.

it a truly national union and doubling its membership within a year. Shortly thereafter the Brotherhood secured a national wage-scale agreement with the general ware division of the United States Potters' Association. This development, too, proved to be a cause rather than an effect of the union's strength, for McCabe reported that the favorable attitude of the manufacturers towards a uniform list enabled the union to attain an objective "which it is very doubtful that it could have secured by force." Subsequent refusal by the eastern locals to accept the uniform agreement of 1900 was followed by withdrawal from that agreement by the United States Potters' Association. But the western manufacturers did not hesitate to return to sectional bargaining with the western locals, and, after the Brotherhood finally forced the dissident eastern locals into line, national bargaining was promptly resumed (1905).

Why were employers in some industries interested in entering into national collective agreements? According to McCabe, "The disinclination of the manufacturers in the higher-rated districts to continue to pay more than was paid in other districts was one of the reasons for the desire of the union to bring the lower-rated districts up to the level of the higher."[79] This interpretation implies that the early systems of national collective bargaining were established upon the insistence of the unions involved, which, therefore, had to be strong enough to impose their will upon at least some of the employers concerned. Thus McCabe points out that "The unions which first attained national scales were unions in highly skilled trades, concentrated in a comparatively small number of localities, such as the iron and steel, and glass trades. These characteristics were important sources of union strength, and made possible vigorous agitation for uniformity in wage scales." Barnett had previously come to a similar conclusion, although, taking note of the fact that the movement toward the adoption of national and district systems of collective bargaining began with the emergence of prosperity in 1898 and subsided in the panic year of 1907, he attributed the necessary union strength to the employers' "need for labor" and to their desire for industrial peace.[80]

While evidence was cited in support of each of these theories, neither theory squares with McCabe's interpretation of national bargaining in pottery, which he ascribed to employer acquiescence in the face of union weakness. Moreover, McCabe's emphasis upon the factors of skill and industrial concentration should be regarded primarily as indicating necessary conditions for the success of national collective bargaining rather than as establishing originating causes thereof.

Thus neither theory is completely general. Moreover, the historical timing of the national bargaining movement suggests an additional explanation. For the period 1898-1905, which witnessed widespread adoption of national

79. McCabe, *The Standard Rate*, p. 143.

80. George E. Barnett, "National and District Systems of Collective Bargaining in the United States," *Quarterly Journal of Economics*, v. XXVI, 1912, pp. 430–431.

and district bargaining (26 such multiemployer agreements were inaugurated in that interval, according to Barnett), also included a period of intense "trustification" in industry. Although the combination movement became significant in the 1870's, it was after 1897 that the very large business unit became prominent and that "there came five years of abnormal activity in the organization of trusts."[81] While no attempt will be made to determine whether national or district bargaining was accompanied by restrictive arrangements, or the attempt to form such arrangements, among enterprises in every case in which national or district bargaining over wages occurred, it should be noted that such a relationship did exist in each case of national or district bargaining which we examined in the previous section of this chapter.

Pottery

The general ware division of the pottery industry was concentrated in two main centers: Trenton, New Jersey, in the east, and Canton, Ohio, in the west. McCabe assigns to this localization an important role in the preservation of amicable industrial relations on a national scale.[82] Nevertheless, he also points out that the employers' interest in national collective bargaining was stimulated initially by their endeavor to restrict product competition, both foreign and domestic. The negotiations which took place in 1897 followed an apparently chance meeting of representatives of the Brotherhood and some western manufacturers in the nation's capital, whither each group had repaired to press for higher tariff duties. The union delegation suggested that, if their common mission could be accomplished successfully, it would be possible both to raise wages and to establish uniform piece rates. The manufacturers were interested and in turn suggested that the union, as a condition of the establishment of equal "working prices," organize nonunion potteries and insist that all manufacturers establish uniform selling prices. The union refused to police the price agreement by itself, but it did agree to "do all we could to help the manufacturers to maintain a uniform selling price for their products, even to the calling out of such manufacturers as tried to undersell; they in return agreeing to pay a proportionate share of such expense."

In the other branch of the pottery industry, the sanitary ware division, the manufacturers' association which entered into a national agreement with the Brotherhood in 1902 had originated as an output cartel, formed after a series of price wars had convinced the manufacturers that

It might be cheaper to kill off one batch of competitors, but it is not cheaper to kill a new crop (which emerged after prices were raised following the termination

81. Chester W. Wright, *Economic History of the United States* (New York: McGraw-Hill, 1949, second edition), pp. 560–562.

82. McCabe, *National Collective Bargaining in the Pottery Industry*, pp. 89–91, 369–370, 372, 381.

of hostilities) every few years. It is cheaper and better to divide up the business so long as anybody can live.[83]

The manufacturers were also apparently convinced that the demand for their product was highly inelastic and that existing excess capacity would prevail at any price. A representative of the union sought to defend his own organization from charges of restricting output by observing that

The big concern is to the association what the hogger-in is to the workmen; he must be controlled in his production or he will do it all and the average man will get nothing—hence a working list and a monthly allotment. The association limits production as much as we do.

Bituminous coal

In bituminous coal the intense competition generated by excess capacity (for the creation of which railroad freight differentials were in part responsible) prompted operators in the unionized fields to enter into industry-wide bargaining with an eye to establishing "competitive equality." Their interest in so doing was heightened by the fact that labor costs were equal to about two-thirds of total costs[84] and also by the low price elasticity of demand for their product (in the period before the emergence of petroleum as a major substitute fuel). According to a contemporary British scholar,

It was the feeling that it was only the action of the men which could set limits to a competition which most operators hated even while they felt driven to it, which caused so many of the operators to sympathise with the strike of 1897. The Pittsburg operators had lately endeavoured, without the aid of their men, to carry through a so-called "uniformity" scheme, but had failed to secure the adhesion of the 95 per cent of the operators which was considered necessary.[85]

Stoves

Early employer associations in the stove industry were hostile to the Molders' union. In 1876 a contributor to the union journal complained that "the association (the National Association of Stove Manufacturers, founded in 1872) never meets but immediately after war is declared against the molders in some section, and the incidents connected therewith are proof positive of some secret arrangement between the bosses arrived at while attending their convention."[86] Later, in 1885, some employers formed the Stove Founders' National Defense Association in order "to rid themselves of the tyranny of the Iron Molders' Union, and to run their several works un-

83. Commissioner of Labor, *Regulation of Output*, p. 701.
84. Lubin, *Miners' Wages*, p. 235.
85. W. J. Ashley, *The Adjustment of Wages* (London: Longmans, Green, 1903), pp. 103–104.
86. *Journal*, June 1876, p. 712.

hampered by its restrictive influences."[87] They sought to live up to the letter and the spirit of their prospectus, for in 1887 the Association conducted what was virtually an industry-wide lockout to counter the unions' refusal to handle struck work which the association had circulated among its member shops.

But failure to achieve better than a draw in this struggle was followed, in 1891, by the inauguration of industry-wide bargaining. Yet this development cannot be interpreted simply as a gesture of surrender on the part of the employers, for as we know, the employers had long been interested in eliminating differences in labor cost among competing firms. (This, incidentally, had been one of the avowed objectives of the Defense Association.) Moreover, their concern with wage differentials stemmed from a desire to inject an element of monopoly into the industry. Although the National Association of Stove Manufacturers might have facilitated concerted antiunion activity, its primary purpose apparently had been to stabilize prices.[88] An early manufacturer urged his colleagues

Not to delude ourselves with the idea that we can by low prices drive other manufacturers out of the market; this plan has often been attempted, but without much success. . . .

There are about 200 manufacturers of stoves in our land, but the business is regulated by less than 150. Can not this small number agree upon and maintain such a course as shall produce the result that each is so desirous to attain? We have, by united action, partially achieved this, and it can be increased and perpetuated by the cultivation of faith in each other, and the putting in experience of our common sense.[89]

Competitive price reductions would have tended to reduce sales receipts to the industry, for, if we are to believe Mr. Perry of Albany, the employer quoted above, the demand for stoves was quite inelastic with respect to price:

Stoves are an article of prime necessity; in a large number of dwellings they become the most essential article of furniture; a good cooking stove is the delight of a housekeeper and she will make sacrifices to obtain it. The public do not buy stoves because they are cheap, but because they want them, and they generally want the best kind. There will be about the same number annually sold, whether we realize half a cent per pound more or less, and this half cent represents to most of us a larger sum than the actual profits.

Hence the following essay in sarcasm from an early issue of the Molders' *Journal:*

87. Quoted in Hilbert, "Trade Union Agreements," p. 227.
88. Russell S. Bauder, "National Collective Bargaining in the Foundry Industry," *American Economic Review*, v. 24, September 1934, p. 465.
89. *Journal,* July 1875, p. 358. The formation of the American Radiator Company and the Pittsburgh Stove and Range Company in 1899, like the formation of the first Association, was prompted by the desire to regulate competition.

They (the manufacturers) acknowledge that stoves are a prime necessity; there is no foreign competition; the stove manufacturers have a national organization; they fix prices, to which all agree, and as they are "all, all honorable men," we know they do not undersell each other.[90]

Inelastic product demand must be considered in connection with the fact that the molders' wages constituted 40 to 50 per cent of direct costs.[91] In the depression of 1893-1897, it was reported that the members of the National Association of Stove Manufacturers "preferred to maintain the price of stoves and pay their workmen the same rate of wages as was paid when times were good, believing that no more stoves would be sold in the aggregate even if prices were cut."

Russell S. Bauder claimed that, shortly after 1850, "the industry expanded beyond the possibility of the market to absorb its product at profitable prices and cutthroat competition became common."[92] In view of the belief that demand was inelastic, the drive to stabilize prices becomes readily understandable; and, when one considers the importance of labor costs, it is plausible that employers should have sought to prevent competitive reductions in prices by attempting to stabilize wages.

According to Bauder, it was the "relatively static and over-developed" condition of the stove industry which was mainly responsible for the success of national collective bargaining therein, whereas the fact that the jobbing- and machinery-foundry industry was "expanding rapidly" accounted for the failure of the union's attempt to duplicate in this latter branch the feat which it had performed in the former. In the stove industry "the Union was able to intervene and indirectly to control price competition through its policy of uniform rate setting which it was able to extend throughout the industry." Since only about 25 per cent of the stove foundries in the country were members of the association by 1900, the union's police function was a significant one. It is also noteworthy that the union agreed to enforce in non-association foundries wage changes which were instituted by agreement with the association.

But no similar role existed for the union in the rapidly growing machine and job foundry industry. Moreover, since skilled molders were in short supply in this branch, the National Founders' Association was unalterably opposed to such union practices as restriction of apprentices, limitation of output, and opposition to piece rates. Indeed, it is difficult to explain why the employers should have assented to industry-wide bargaining in the first place. Bauder believed that their intent was to utilize collective bargaining as a device to restrain union wage demands. Since the union president reported

90. *Journal,* April 1876, p. 610.

91. Frey and Commons, "Conciliation in the Stove Industry," pp. 125, 160–161. *Journal,* April 1876, p. 616.

92. Bauder, "The Foundry Industry," p. 465. See also pp. 464, 466, 467, 469, 470.

that, in 1898, "we could not find molders enough for the foundries of this country,"[93] it is possible that the wage rate which the two parties had agreed to in conference was lower than that which would have emerged if collective bargaining and unionism had then been removed from the industry. But the union, of course, could not be expected to endorse a sacrificial wage policy indefinitely, if such a policy it really was.

Bauder's hypothesis, however, succeeds in explaining the success of industry-wide bargaining in stoves better in the early period than in the period (beginning shortly after 1900) in which substitute methods of heating and cooking emerged. The rise of substitutes did restrict further the potentialities of the industry for growth, as Bauder pointed out, but, at the same time that the demand curve shifted downward, it became more elastic (or less inelastic). It might now have been possible to increase sales appreciably by reducing prices—and this might have involved reducing wages. At the same time, the emergence of substitutes destroyed the role of price stabilizer, which, Bauder declared, had been assumed by the union.

The union's own explanation for its success in stoves and its failure elsewhere called attention to the fact that

In the Defense Association we are dealing with a class of men engaged in the manufacture of the same line of goods, men who have a great deal in common in their business methods and necessities and whose relations with labor can be governed by general rules; in the Founders' Association, on the other hand, we are dealing with men engaged in the manufacture of anything from a marine engine to a plow point, men whose businesses are so entirely dissimilar that in determining their relations to labor it has been found impossible to formulate a plan that would give general satisfaction. . . .

At the Cleveland Conference last June, it will be remembered that the representatives of the N.F.A. would not even concede the equity of the principle of a minimum wage in their foundries. That position has been abandoned, however, and now the equity of a minimum wage is not questioned but we find them off on another track and this time we are asked to give countenance to the employment of a class of unskilled (?) men on the rougher work of the foundry. Here again we find an evidence of the diversified membership of the National Founders' Association, for this proviso has evidently been added to the general proposition to meet the views of that part of their constituency making the most inferior grade of foundry work. But it is clear, were it agreed to as a general proposition, it could legitimately be taken advantage of in every foundry in the country. Where would the employment of this class of labor end? . . .[94]

This explanation, however, is not unrelated to the theory discussed above, for if demand had been as static and inelastic in the machine and job foundry

93. U. S. Commission on Industrial Relations, *Final Report and Testimony*, quoted in Bauder, "The Foundry Industry," p. 469.

94. *Journal*, 1899, p. 642.

branch as it had been in the stove branch, skilled foundry labor probably would not have been represented as scarce, and the drive to reduce costs by the employment of "specialists" and unskilled labor on operations requiring less skill would not have been so intense. The same difference in conditions helps to explain the greater impatience of employers in the job and machine foundries to install the molding machine, which utilized unskilled labor to advantage. What the union was really objecting to was not the diversity of products turned out but rather the desire of some employers to avail themselves of substitutes for union labor. If all the employers in the machinery branch of the industry had turned out identical products, but, at the same time, if they all had desired to effect this substitution with uniform intensity, the union would have been no better off.

Glass

In window glass, industry-wide bargaining was but part of a larger arrangement under which the union was to police the operation of output and sales cartels. The first manufacturers' organization with which the newly formed Local Assembly 300 dealt was the American Window Glass Manufacturers' Association, which was formed in 1880 in order to control output. Previous attempts to restrict output had proved unsuccessful, but, with the coöperation of the union, the new association succeeded where predecessors had failed. Local Assembly 300 limited both the supply of skilled workers and output per worker. It restricted the supply of workers by refusing to admit to apprenticeship anyone "whose father is not a full-fledged citizen"; and only sons or brothers of blowers or gatherers could become apprentices in those crafts.[95] And later, having suffered from the immigration of foreign craftsmen, Local Assembly 300 sent organizers abroad and stimulated the formation of the "Universal Federation of Window Glass Workers of the World" in 1885 in an effort to control migration to this country. Apprenticeship and admission regulations were made more restrictive with respect to aliens and their sons than they were with respect to native-born candidates.

The Local Assembly also restricted individual output. It set a maximum hourly output for gatherers and blowers (nine rollers) and cutters.[96] It also regulated the monthly output of each blower, and penalties for exceeding the maxima were severe. Excess output had to be paid for at regular piece rates, but the proceeds therefrom went to the union and not to the blower or gatherer concerned. While this rule applied to "any blower, gatherer, pot, or place making more than the specified amount of glass," it was the worker, rather than the employer, who bore the penalty. Furthermore, it was provided that

95. Commissioner of Labor, *Regulation of Output,* pp. 615–617, 619–621.
96. *By-Laws,* 1899, Art. VII, Secs. 15, 21, 23, 36, 55.

Any blower or gatherer making their quota in less than the given number of days in a settlement, the company shall have the privilege of filling the place for each day the regular blower and gatherer works ahead. The regular blower or gatherer must pay all overproduction made in the place.

The union also converted the traditional summer vacation, or "summer stop," in the industry into a device for the restriction of output. At first the union insisted upon a stop which was to be uniform throughout all establishments; later, the length of the stop—and, therefore, the length of the work year, or "fire"—was determined by collective bargaining at the annual conferences at which other conditions of employment were established.

Initially the union's rules "approximated practicable maxima," according to Pearce Davis, but after the tank furnace and other technical improvements had been introduced, they became genuinely restrictive.[97] In the Eleventh Special Report of the Commissioner of Labor, *Regulation and Restriction of Output,* it is stated that window glass "is the only industry where the workmen, through their organization, have attempted to join with their employers to regulate the total output of the industry according to the varying states of the market."[98] What circumstances made such regulation peculiarly desirable to the employers in this industry? Why did they come to regard the participation of the union as essential to the success of their endeavors? And why did it appear that Local Assembly 300 might be able to police these restrictive arrangements?

(1) Restriction of output appeared essential to profitable operation because, in the opinion of many, the industry suffered chronically from excess capacity which stimulated vigorous price competition and because the demand for the product was inelastic, so that falling prices meant declining revenue. According to one unpublished report,

> For at least forty years the manufacture of window glass has been an overbuilt industry. The demand for its products is inelastic since the total cost of the glass used in the construction of a building is usually less than one per cent of the cost of the building. Hence a considerable increase or decrease in the price of glass would affect its consumption but little. . . . Since the market has been restricted to American producers and since the industry during all this time has been overbuilt, the history of the window glass trade is a succession of demoralizing competition, price and production agreements, large profits, new competition, price cutting, more demoralization of the trade and the cycle is repeated.[99]

(2) Since attempts by the manufacturers themselves to restrict output failed to achieve enduring success (high prices established by cartel arrange-

97. Davis, *American Glass,* pp. 136–137.
98. Commissioner of Labor, *Regulation of Output,* p. 599.
99. H. E. Hoagland, "Report on the Trade Agreements in the Window Glass Industry" (December 9, 1914; MS in The Johns Hopkins University Library), p. 5.

ments merely induced the entry of additional concerns), the contribution of the union was a crucial one. The union was to underwrite monopoly arrangements by denying to potential entrants access to the skilled labor of its members, for, although little capital was required to establish a glass factory, the services of skilled blowers, gatherers, flatteners, and cutters were indispensable. The union's ability to police trade agreements thus required the unusually high degree of organization which it had achieved.

(3) Union-management collusion, however, also required the passage of highly protective tariff legislation. According to Davis,

The control of prices and production achieved and exercised by L.A. 300 and by the association of manufacturers would have been impossible had protection been absent. The union would have had no power to set maximum hourly, monthly, and yearly output had foreign window glass been less heavily handicapped. Likewise, control of output, of plants in operation, and of prices would have been dependent upon factors other than the decisions of an association of manufacturers had a protective tariff been nonexistent.

Finally, it is evident that the cost of tariff protection to the window-glass industry from 1860 to 1890 was in a large part paid by American consumers. Domestic costs and prices were higher than foreign costs and prices.[100]

Of the factors discussed above, employer interest in coalition (due to excess capacity and inelastic demand) and in union participation in monopolistic arrangements, union willingness to restrict output and "take wages out of competition," and the presence of protective tariffs were not restricted to this industry. They were observed elsewhere in situations which were not, however, characterized by the working arrangements which prevailed in the window-glass industry. What was unique in the latter case was the exceptionally high degree of control which the union in question maintained over its jurisdiction, which permitted it, on occasion, to give effect to exclusive arrangements with a given association of manufacturers. The most celebrated of these arrangements was the contract which Local Assembly 300 entered into with the American Window Glass Company (the successor to the American Glass Company which was formed during the price wars that erupted in the depression period and wiped out previous cartel organizations) in 1899. In return for a block of stock, of par value $500,000, and a seat on the company's board of directors, the union agreed to furnish the corporation with a number of skilled workers sufficient to run its plants at capacity during the stipulated "fire," or work year. Since skilled labor was scarce following the long and severe depression, this arrangement was intended to force nonmembers of the combine out of business.

Nevertheless, the monopolistic arrangements in this industry did not prove to be stable. Although the four skilled jurisdictions in the industry were well

---

100. Davis, *American Glass*, pp. 138–139.

organized, ranks were divided within the local assembly. The cutters and flatteners vied with the blowers and gatherers for control of the national union; and, according to Hoagland, "whichever side controlled the union received advantages in the adjustment of wage scales.[101] In 1895, the blowers and gatherers formed a secret Protective Association within Local Assembly 300. These two groups controlled the national union, although the cutters and flatteners later countered with the formation of an unofficial organization of their own within Local Assembly 300. In 1899, the uneasy alliance was terminated by the withdrawal of the cutters and flatteners, who then formed the Window Glass Workers' Association of North America.

The struggle between the two groups of workers continued after the secession, however; it was converted from intramural antagonism into a jurisdictional dispute and, as such, virtually ensured the failure of any exclusive agreement between union and management. It will be recalled that, in 1899, Local Assembly 300 guaranteed to supply the American Glass Company with all the skilled workers required to operate its factories. When the cutters and flatteners left, however, the local assembly was hardly in a position to carry out its end of the bargain. The cutters and flatteners, moreover, promptly signed an agreement with the Independent Glass Company, a selling agency representing manufacturers outside the American Glass Company, in which they agreed to a longer working year than that which Local Assembly 300 had established. A price war broke out, which was terminated in 1900 because neither side could obtain a monopoly of all types of skilled labor. Peace was apparently negotiated by the jobbers who had suffered heavy losses during the period of price cutting and who now sought to stabilize conditions by forming a single purchasing agency, the National Wholesale Glass Jobbers' Association, which bought glass from both manufacturers' associations. In order to raise the price of glass, the "fire" was shortened once again.

But higher prices attracted new capital into the industry. So did the shorter fire, for some members of Local Assembly 300 rebelled against the shorter fire and established coöperative foundries (the cost of erecting a "pot" was only $2500) under the aegis of the Federation Window Glass Company, a sales organization. Thus, under the umbrella of high prices, capacity was increased in the classic manner, and the new arrangement quickly gave way. The Federation and the American combined forces with the object of driving the Independent out of business, the latter having left the pool in 1902 because it was dissatisfied with its assigned share in total output. Once again the opposing interests of the two groups of workers determined the composition of the alliances formed among the manufacturers.

In 1903, another truce was arranged and another selling agency (the Manu-

101. Hoagland, "Report on the Window Glass Industry," pp. 3–4. The following account is taken largely from this source and also from Commissioner of Labor, *Regulation of Output,* pp. 601–606.

facturers' Window Glass Company) was erected as a monument to concord, but, according to Hoagland, the priceless ingredient was sadly lacking:

Wage scales were published and then cancelled by private agreement. New ones with lower terms were secretly accepted. Finally L.A. 300 agreed with the American to go 5 per cent below the scale of the Window Glass Workers' Association "no matter how far they go, said reduction to take effect on same day and date as their reduction."[102]

Interunion competition also facilitated the introduction of the blowing machine. Originally both organizations forbade machine operation, but, after the American Company had perfected the machine in 1903, both the Local Assembly, in its contract with the coöperatives, and the Window Glass Workers, in its agreement with the Independent, agreed to accept wage cuts in order to meet machine competition. Apparently the introduction of the machine redressed the balance of power among the skilled groups in the industry in favor of the cutters and flatteners; it created an excess supply of blowers and gatherers and an increased demand for the services of the other craftsmen.[103] In any event, after another secession from Local Assembly 300 had occurred in 1904 (due to "mismanagement, misuse of funds and dictatorial methods used by the officials"), a new organization, the Amalgamated Window Glass Workers, was formed which embraced all four crafts. It was dissolved as a result of an antitrust suit in 1908, but a successor organization emerged which was able to include blowers, gatherers, cutters, and flatteners. Its activities, however, were confined to the hand plants. In the machine branch of the industry, such unionism as survived was dominated by the cutters and flatteners.

After the American Company discontinued hand blowing in 1904, Local Assembly 300 ceased to exist as an organization of any importance. Hand blowers and gatherers were organized in the United Window Glass Workers, composed of members in all four trades, and in two other unions (the Blowers' and Gatherers' Independent Association and the Blowers' and Gatherers' Protective Association), which excluded cutters and flatteners, until the formation of the National Window Glass Workers in 1908. Meanwhile, the American Company had recognized a new union of machine cutters and flatteners, The Window Glass Cutters' and Flatteners' Association, which it granted a differential over hand rates in recognition of the poorer quality of glass produced by the machine in the period immediately following its introduction. But the differential was progressively reduced as the machines proved their ability to produce better glass, until it was entirely eliminated in 1910. In that year, the association demanded a 12 per cent differential over the hand workers, and the company withdrew recognition and formed a company-dominated union with which it negotiated thereafter.

102. Hoagland, "Report on the Window Glass Industry," pp. 7, 12–13.
103. Scoville, *Revolution in Glass Making,* p. 227.

Thus the experience of the Window Glass Workers reveals that their national union was able effectively to police arrangements designed to restrict output only so long as it possessed exclusive control over a highly essential sector of the labor supply in the industry. At the same time the manufacturers were able to exclude competition only to the extent that the union possessed such control, for otherwise they were unable to prevent the entry of new firms. Jurisdictional disputes, refusal of individual membership to abide by union restrictions upon individual output, and, finally, technical change which rendered an important part of the union's jurisdiction (glass blowing, formerly the highest-paid craft in the industry) virtually obsolete— each of these developments could weaken the union's control sufficiently to result in the dissolution of the monopolistic institutions which were erected upon the foundation of union power.

The Window Glass Workers have been contrasted with the Glass Bottle Blowers and the Flint Glass Workers, since, in the jurisdictions of the latter two organizations, there existed no direct limitation upon individual output[104] and employer organizations apparently had not originated as monopolistic organizations.[105] While granting the historical accuracy of these observations, however, one must not infer difference in motive from divergence in recorded actions. Thus, while the Bottle Blowers and the prescription branch of the Flints abandoned restrictions upon daily output per member, they sought vigorously, as we have noted elsewhere, to restrict the number of apprentices in the industry; and the abandonment of the "move system" in the flint industry, which came shortly after bottle-making was transferred from a piece-work to a time-work basis in the early 1860's, was instigated by the employers "against the protest of the workmen," although it is believed that no strikes resulted from the change. And while, as Professor Wolman observed in an unpublished report,[106] the extent and jurisdiction of the employers' associations in the glass bottle industry were determined by the jurisdictional bounds of the union, it is well to recall that when the Flints, in their first national convention (1878), demanded a uniform move list for the Pittsburgh district, they were acting upon previous information that the manufacturers themselves desired uniformity.[107]

When the bottle blowers were organized into an Eastern League and a Western League, the manufacturers were organized into a Western Association and an Eastern Association; but, after the two Leagues had coalesced in

---

104. Commissioner of Labor, *Regulation of Output*, p. 625.

105. Derber, "Glass," p. 694; Davis, *American Glass*, p. 148.

106. Leo Wolman, "Collective Bargaining in the Glass-Bottle Industry," *American Economic Review*, vol. VI (1916), pp. 549–567.

107. Commissioner of Labor, *Regulation of Output*, pp. 627, 632.

1890, the two manufacturers' organizations merged into one. The two manufacturers' associations had been antagonistic before the creation of a national union, but it does not follow that the latter phenomenon was an independent cause of the merger of the employer groups. Increasing interregional competition produced the national union, and there is some reason to believe that it also was productive of a receptive attitude to industry-wide bargaining on the part of the manufacturers. While the National Glass Vial and Bottle Manufacurers' Association concentrated primarily upon collective bargaining, at least at the outset,[108] it did have committees on tariffs and on railroad rates; and it was dissolved in 1924 after the Attorney-General had declared that it was a price-fixing agency. Moreover, in 1899 the National Glass Company was formed as a trust which, according to testimony before the Industrial Commission, controlled 75 per cent of national output and which was designed to eliminate cutthroat competition.[109] Reduction of nonunion competition was an important objective in its formation. In this connection, the testimony of President Hayes before the Commission is highly interesting. It suggests that any difference between the organized bottle manufacturers and their colleagues in the window glass trade was not one of spirit.

Q. Is there any indication that glass manufacturers in this country will form a trust?
A. Yes; the indications point that way; the conditions of trade almost force them into a combine. . . .
Q. Is the inability of organized glass blowers to restore that 15 per cent because of competition from glass manufacturers who employ nonunion labor?
A. Domestic competition, yes; it has kept down the market.
Q. Is that one of the conditions that you spoke of that would force the trade into combines?
A. That is a part of it; yes.
Q. Is the only way you can get this 15 per cent in wages restored by your association organizing the nonunion workmen or the employers organizing themselves into a trust?
A. If we succeed in organizing all blowers in the bottle trade, and find conditions favorable, we may get that 15 per cent. I am not sure our trade would strike for it. In regard to the trust, that would not do it at all. I will tell you why. All the manufacturers in this country are now organized into a national association—
Q. Employing union and nonunion labor?
A. Yes; there is a national association including all. There is a Western association composed of men employing union labor exclusively. They make a uniform selling price in markets in which they can establish it. The manufacturers who have no uniform price among their men state they can never keep it up to an agreement because there is no basis on which to form a selling price. If necessary, he will make a sale by cutting below the agreement.

108. Wolman, "Report on the Glass Bottle Blowers," pp. 40–41.
109. Industrial Commission, *Reports on Labor,* v. VII, pp. 838–840.

Q. Does he cut his employees, too?

A. Certainly.

Q. In the case of the formation of a trust, would the nonunion labor be taken up with the union labor, and a uniform trust scale made?

A. They have, as I understand it, often made selling agreements, but they have never been able to keep them, for this reason: The wages in the trade were not uniform; if they were controlled by a trust, of course, they would become more perfect, but where only a part of the manufacturers had no basis, and could cut indiscriminately, they have been unable to maintain a uniform selling price.

Q. Have the manufacturers recognized in your association an organization that has the effect of maintaining wages among the workingmen and a uniformity of prices and conditions, to the end that competition among them may be less fierce?

A. That is it, precisely.

Q. You think that is the principle reason why the manufacturers encouraged the building up of your association?

A. Yes; in order that they may know where their competitors stand.[110]

Longshoremen on the Great Lakes

Commons' account of industry-wide bargaining between the Longshoremen's Association and the employers' associations known as the Lumber Carriers, Lake Carriers, the Great Lakes Towing Company, and the Dock Managers reveals the presence of rate-fixing arrangements in the relevant "product" markets and stresses the relationship between the maintenance of shipping rates and industry-wide collective bargaining in the case of lumber.[111] In 1898 the president and secretary of a lumber carriers' association appeared before the Longshoremen's convention and complained that, due to the competition of the railroads and the railroad steamers, carrying charges were being driven below costs. They then put this interesting proposition to the union:

The ship-owners or vesselmen, having carried lumber at a loss for the past two years, and witnessing the effect and success of your efforts and organization, decided last winter to follow your example,—organize for a living hire, and appeal to your body so closely identified with us for aid and assistance. At a meeting held in Detroit in February last the vessel-owners did succeed in effecting a voluntary association for the purpose of maintaining a uniform minimum rate which should cover the cost of transporting lumber and forest products. They succeeded in enlisting a large majority of all the vessels on the lakes. Unfortunately there were a few who did not come in. They threaten to disrupt our association, and we therefore, the Executive Committee of the Lumber Carriers' Association, come before your honorable body, asking and appealing for the coöperation which is

110. Industrial Commission, *Reports on Labor*, v. VII, p. 108.

111. John R. Commons, *Labor and Administration* (New York: Macmillan, 1913), pp. 277–294, esp. p. 278.

necessary for our existence, for our success as well as yours. This assistance which we request is that you should either refuse to load boats not belonging to the association, or boats belonging to the association that cut rates, or impose a heavy fine, heavy enough to prevent such suicidal business or to drive them all into the association. This we recommend be done on the entire chain of lakes, or more especially the Lake Superior districts. . . . Whatever action you may take, it should be taken as soon as possible, for the reason that members and nonmembers are cutting the rates, and we fear that, if some action is not taken promptly, it will become general and the association will go to pieces.

The convention rejected the proposal because they did not wish the national union to oblige the locals to impose fines upon nonassociation boats, and the association disbanded shortly thereafter. In 1900 a new association was formed which entered into a contractual relationship with the union. No provision was made for the fining of nonassociation boats as such by the international union. However, a constitutional clause (adopted in 1893) providing for the fining of boats which hired nonunion longshoremen was invoked by some locals which did fine boats because they had not joined the association. Since fining took the form of charging the vessel involved a higher hourly rate for labor than the contract rate, "the nonassociation owner, having no agreement, may be charged any price that the local wishes and can enforce. If he protests, the answer is that he can get the association price by joining the association. This opportunity to make extra earnings is enough of an inducement to the locals to lead them to put a higher price on nonassociation boats, without any request to do so from the association or its representatives." Furthermore, the locals assigned priority in loading and unloading to association boats over nonassociation boats; this discriminatory treatment was of considerable importance during the busy seasons.

Commons concludes that "the present Lumber Carriers' Association has been able to hold its members and to enforce its scale of freight rates" only because the union accorded it the preferential treatment described above. The Association of Dock Managers, on the other hand, "do not depend upon the union to maintain their organization"; nevertheless it "has been in existence since 1874, for the purpose of establishing uniform scales of charges for loading and unloading boats." (In 1900 this association entered into a trade agreement with the Longshoremen.)

These examples do not, of course, warrant the conclusion that industrial concentration invariably implied the development of industry-wide bargaining. The anthracite coal industry is an outstanding example of a highly concentrated—and highly localized—industry in which a policy of restriction of output ran parallel with a policy of unremitting opposition to unionism.[112]

112. Commissioner of Labor, *Regulation of Output*, pp. 485–502. Not until 1920 did the operators recognize the United Mine Workers as the official bargaining agent of the anthracite miners. As the result of a strike in 1902, President Theodore Roosevelt ap-

The steel industry is another case in point; we have already recalled that the formation of the United States Steel Corporation resulted in the elimination of the Amalgamated Association as a powerful bargaining agent in this industy. In these cases, monopoly power facilitated resistance to collective bargaining. The ability of the large business unit either to acquiesce graciously in collective bargaining arrangements or to withstand union demands is analyzed in Chapter 2 above.

But where such factors as excess capacity and inelastic demand were instrumental in the formation of cartels, the philosophy underlying which was one of "live and let live," employers believed, in some important instances, that centralized collective bargaining could be of considerable assistance in "stabilizing" competition. In such cases, employers advocated policies which called for taking wages out of competition. Hence, where multiemployer bargaining actually resulted in a movement in the direction of equalizing "pay in proportion to effort and skill expended," one cannot infer from this knowledge alone that such equalization represented the "ultimate" objective of the national union which was but one party to the agreement.

pointed an Anthracite Coal Strike Commission to arbitrate the dispute, both sides having agreed to accept its recommendations. But the Commission, although granting an increase in wages and a reduction in hours, did not compel the operators to recognize the union. As a result, relations proceeded under the terms of the Commission's award. (Waldo E. Fisher, "Anthracite," in *How Collective Bargaining Works* [New York: Twentieth Century Fund, 1945], pp. 288–297.)

CHAPTER SEVENTEEN

WORK RULES

GUARANTEEING WORK AND WAGES

The minimum guarantee

ALTHOUGH the passing of the long-term individual contract, under which wages were withheld, meant the abandonment of one arrangement whereby the worker was compelled to work longer than he desired to at a given rate of wages, it did not represent unalloyed gain to the employee. For the long-term contract had implied security as well as coercion, and its abandonment liberated the employer from what, in some cases, amounted to a traditional obligation to provide steady work for his employee at the same time that it freed the latter from any obligation to remain on the job.[1] President Kelley of the Plumbers compared some jurisdictions in the United States unfavorably with jurisdictions in Canada in this respect. In reply to the question, "Are they very steadily employed generally (in Canada)?" Kelley said

> More so than in the larger cities of the United States. They employ so many men and they keep the men steady. In the United States the employment of plumbers has got down to the hourly system. They hire you for an hour, and if you come in and they have nothing for you to do they lay you off; whereas in Canada they will keep you around the shop doing odds and ends and getting up material. That used to be in vogue in the United States 10 or 12 years ago, but now all the material that used to be made in the shops by the journeymen when there was no work outside is manufactured by machinery, and all that employment is taken away from them.

Q. Do the journeymen plumbers now get as much by the hour system per day, week, and month as they formerly did by the day, week, or month?

A. No. I can not say as to the conditions all over the country, but I am more

---

1. Oscar Handlin dwells in some detail upon the immigrant worker's sense of economic insecurity which he attributed in large part to "the steady decline in the span of the labor contract." *The Uprooted* (Boston: Little, Brown, 1952), pp. 73–74. His account, however, fails to call attenion to the economic disadvantages to the worker of the longer contract, although he does add that "Piecework brought the consolation of independence . . . and the illusion that additional effort would bring additional returns."

familiar with Chicago, and I feel safe in saying that the journeymen plumbers do not average over $2 a day the year round.[2]

In some instances unions in the building trades obtained the payment of "waiting time," that is, pay for the time elapsed between a member's notification of discharge and the payment of his wages. Provision for payment of "waiting time," however, was merely intended to ensure prompt payment of wages upon termination of employment; as such, it was a device which was related more closely to policies designed to eliminate wage-withholding than to policies designed to oblige employers to guarantee some minimum amount of employment or income. "Waiting time" was not an ancestral form of the modern institution known as "call-in time," which does guarantee a minimum payment (a half or a full day's pay). The Potters, however, did attempt to insist that employers, in effect, "keep you around the shop doing odds and ends . . ."; on one occasion, they protested against the hiring of "odd help," instead of journeymen dippers, to carry unfinished ware from one workplace to another.[3]

Where members were on piecework, however, unions sought to prevent employers from assigning such nonremunerative "odds and ends" to them. Their object was to rid themselves of nonremunerative work. Thus McCabe notes that the dippers referred to above sought to penalize employers for assigning to journeymen on piecework the task of carrying work, by obliging the employer to pay extra for "the carry." The union's attitude changed after piecework gave way to day work.

But attempts by pieceworkers to exclude nonremunerative work obviously were not at all inconsistent with the desire to secure some minimum guarantee of income, and pieceworkers were at least as insistent as timeworkers on this point. The Flint Glass Workers, the sheet and tin division of the Amalgamated Association of Iron, Steel, and Tin Workers, and the kiln-work branch of the Potters espoused the so-called "turn" system, under which the worker was paid by the piece for output in excess of the "move" or standard but was guaranteed the wage for the "move" even if, through no fault of his own, he failed to produce the prescribed output. Originally, the Flints' move constituted a maximum limit upon output which was set by the union; later, when this limit was abandoned and the average actual output per turn substantially exceeded the "move," "the latter lost its efficiency as a guarantee of average wages."[4]

2. United States Industrial Commission, *Report on the Relations and Conditions of Capital and Labor Employed in Manufactures and General Business* (Washington: Government Printing Office, 1901), v. VII, p. 970.

3. David A. McCabe, *National Collective Bargaining in the Pottery Industry* (Baltimore: Johns Hopkins, 1932), pp. 271–272.

4. David A. McCabe, *The Standard Rate in American Trade Unions* (Baltimore: Johns Hopkins, 1912), p. 71. Also, pp. 69–72, 74. Cf. also Sumner H. Slichter, *Union Policies and Industrial Management* (Washington: Brookings, 1941), p. 314.

On the railroads, all operating employees on freight trains and engineers and firemen on passenger trains worked under what amounted to a piece system with a minimum guarantee. They were paid on a mileage basis, but were credited with one hundred miles for each completed trip (that is, a run between two terminal points). A trip of one hundred miles was considered a day's run; thus it was possible for a man who made two trips, each under one hundred miles, in one day, to receive pay for two day's runs. Moreover, as McCabe pointed out,

The day's run guarantee sometimes operates to give 100 miles to a crew which is sent out a few miles and brought back and released in a very few hours.

"Such occurrences," he added, "are, however, very rare."

When the printers were on piecework, they charged their employers for "standing time," or periods when no work was available for men on the job. Instead of establishing a minimum time rate, however, the employers and unions adopted the practice of furnishing printers with "bogus" copy, which the latter duly set up and were compensated for at regular piece rates. With the advent of the machine, the bogus rule became less prevalent for two reasons: in the first place, high overhead costs constituted a stimulus to employers to provide for continuous operation and, therefore, steady work; and, secondly, the piece rate system largely gave way to time work.[5]

Under certain circumstances, the guarantee of minimum income under piecework was the equivalent of devices which were designed to oblige the employer to hire more labor than he wished to under timework. This is apparent if one considers that piecework might be regarded as a variant of timework under which the wage per unit of time varies directly as output per unit of time in such a manner that the wage per unit of output—the piece rate—remains constant. Under a minimum guarantee, however, the time rate remains unaltered if output falls below some "standard"; namely, the piece rate rises. Given a reduction in productivity, the employer would purchase fewer hours of work at the same time rate if he were free to do so. Since he must guarantee a time income, however, he is in effect obliged to hire more labor than he desires to at a given (time) wage rate. Conversely, under the modern device of "call-in" pay under timework, the employer might be regarded as paying an infinitely high piece rate if he is obliged to pay for idle time.

By insisting upon a minimum guarantee of income, some unions were able to replace one form of discrimination with another. Under straight piecework, as we have noted, earnings per unit of time varied directly as output per unit of time. Under the minimum guarantee, for all output under the standard, earnings per unit of output varied inversely as output per unit of time. But output per unit of time could vary either because of some change

5. George E. Barnett, *The Printers* (Cambridge, Mass.: American Economic Association, October 1909, pp. 209–212.

in effort supplied by the worker or because of some change in output per unit of effort offered or expended. From our earlier summary of the conditions under which unions were opposed to piecework and incentive pay and from the above discussion of the demand for the guaranteed minimum, it might be concluded that unionists did not necessarily object to payment per hour which varied in direct proportion to effort offered or expended per hour, but that they did object to hourly payment being reduced in proportion to output per unit of effort—that is, "due to circumstances beyond our control." Under such circumstances, different units of effort were paid for at different rates; thus the same conditions underlay the demand for the minimum guarantee and opposition to incentive pay.

Some makework rules

Some of the types of makework regulation identified by Slichter were also intended to oblige employers to hire more labor than they would otherwise have been willing to hire at a given wage rate. These consisted in: "controlling the quality of work," "requiring time-consuming methods of doing the work," "requiring that unnecessary work be done or that work be done more than once," "regulating the number of men in a crew or on a machine or requiring the employment of unnecessary men," "requiring that the work be done by members of a given skilled craft or occupation," and, in some instances, "limiting daily or weekly output."[6] If, under such rules, an employer desired to produce as much as he would have produced in their absence, he would have been obliged to hire more labor. However, if conditions underlying the demand for labor, such as consumer demand for the finished product and the state of technology, had been the same after the imposition of the makework rule as before, the employer would presumably have chosen to produce a lower output in response to the increase in unit labor costs resulting from the makework regulation. Given the lower output, the number of employees hired would be determined by the fixed proportions of labor to other resources implied by the rule; this number might be greater, less, or even precisely the same as the employer would have hired, in the absence of the rule but at the same wage rate, to produce the larger output under the technologically optimum proportion of labor to other resources at that output. The intent of the union in establishing the work rule was evidently to oblige the employer to hire more labor than he would have otherwise employed at the given rate. But imposition of the makework rule could not ensure this outcome in every situation since this type of rule specified only the proportion in which labor can be combined with other resources, leaving the employer free to vary output and, therefore, total employment. In contrast, it will be recalled that the short run bargaining advantage imparted by the seasonally timed strike resulted not only from the employer's inability

6. Slichter, *Union Policies*, p. 166.

significantly to substitute other resources for labor within the short time period involved, but also from the fact that contracts with customers frequently made it impossible for him to alter output in response to wage changes. And it is interesting that some of the most successful experimentation with makework rules occurred in the building trades, a highly seasonal industry.

Slichter attributed the adoption of such rules "primarily to the insecurity of employment in modern industry."[7] Two lines of evidence might be adduced in support of this explanation.

Makework and technological change; opposition to rushing

In the first place, attempts to make work were frequently inspired by the displacement of labor due to technological change. Thus the Steel Workers sought to cope with the automatic nail-making machine, which rendered the nailer's skill obsolescent, by attempting to limit to four the number of machines which a nailer might operate, although one man could run six machines at least.[8] The Printing Pressmen forbade any member to run more than two single-cylinder presses, one flat-bed rotary press, or one perfecting press.[9] In addition, locals established minimum crews by collective agreement in different cities, but not all of these minima were considered excessive by publishers.[10] On the other hand, union regulations designed to force the employment of hand feeders after the introduction of automatic feeding devices were genuinely restrictive.[11]

The response of the New York Housesmiths' Union to technological change—in this instance, the pneumatic riveter—also took the form of a minimum-crew requirement. Under hand riveting, a team of four men was required, whereas pneumatic riveting required only three—a heater, a holder-on, and a driver. Nevertheless, the union required the retention of the fourth man—to "spell off" the others.[12] The Chicago and New York locals of stonecutters attempted to cope with unemployment of hand stonecutters by the planer by insisting that excessively high ratios of stonecutters to planers be employed.[13]

Restrictive regulations like the foregoing tended, if enforced, to make the installation of new devices unprofitable. According to a Chicago publisher,

---

7. Slichter, *Union Policies*, p. 164. See also pp. 198, 263.

8. See also Jesse S. Robinson, *The Amalgamated Association of Iron, Steel and Tin Workers* (Baltimore: Johns Hopkins, 1920), pp. 126–127.

9. Industrial Commission, *Reports on Labor*, v. XVII, p. XIX.

10. United States Commissioner of Labor, Eleventh Special Report on *Regulation and Restriction of Output* (Washington: Government Printing Office, 1904), pp. 91–93.

11. Slichter, *Union Policies*, pp. 263–264.

12. Commissioner of Labor, *Regulation of Labor*, p. 311.

13. George E. Barnett, *Chapters on Machinery and Labor* (Cambridge, Mass.: Harvard University, 1926), pp. 37, 47, 49, 93–94.

It is certain that by improved machinery for handling the rolls and various devices now on the market the number of men required about a press could be greatly reduced. After our present contract expires we expect to put in all of these improvements. It would be useless to put in the machinery now, because the union would compel the employment of the same number of men whether there was anything for them to do or not. . . .

The union's position, however, implicitly denied any intent to prevent the introduction of the new presses or even to compel the hiring of unnecessary labor. Indeed, it rested on the premise that its required minimum was simply a safeguard against "rushing," or excessive strain on the individual pressman. Thus, instead of constituting an arrangement whereby the employer was obliged to hire an excessive amount of labor, it was a defense against the practice of obliging an employee to work harder than was desirable. In practice, however, it is often difficult to determine whether a specific union practice constitutes an effort to prevent the worker from being forced off his supply curve or whether it constitutes an effort to force the employer off his demand curve.[14] In the latter case, the practice constitutes restriction of output under timework in that it implies an excess supply of labor and a wage rate above the competitive level; in the former case, the practice would result in raising the wage rate from a subcompetitive level. Thus the labor contract under timework is akin to an "all-or-none" agreement. The difficulty of distinguishing "restriction" from opposition to an "unfair" or "excessive" work pace is due to the fact that the timework contract does not specify the amount of work to be performed. Thus, the fact that crews were smaller in the nonunion press rooms in Chicago than in the union establishments did not prevent a union official from urging his case as follows:

You know Sandow could lift a horse. Now, if a publisher can get a lot of horse lifters into his press room I suppose five of them would consider it a snap to run a sextuple press. The pressmen's rules are not adjusted on a horse-lifter basis. That is all I have to say.[15]

14. On the difficulty of determining a socially optimum pace of work, see Slichter, *Union Policies,* p. 166, n. 5. See also pp. 199–200.

15. Commissioner of Labor, *Regulation of Output,* pp. 94, 300–301. Insistence upon "good workmanship" also could be used as a device for making work, as Slichter pointed out, when the union's prescribed standards were higher than those required by the employer. In one instance at least the two lines of defense—the protection of the consumer against poor quality and the protection of the worker against overwork—were joined. The Operative Plasterers' Society of New York specified in detail the amount of labor (in terms of both men and time) to be hired in the erection of tenement houses, claiming, "with a good show of reason . . . that there is a tendency to rush men on tenement houses and speculative work, and that the limitation provided for in the agreement prevents rushing, and, therefore, causes better work to be done."

The Machinists ruled that "any member . . . running two machines in any shop where they do not exist shall be subject to expulsion."[16] The rule also sought to prevent the member from "introducing or accepting piece-work." Although this union, like the Pressmen, claimed that its rule was intended primarily to prevent excessive physical strain, it is evident from the following excerpt from a circular issued in 1901 wherein its primary interest lay:

To the machinists—greeting:

Here are some of the gains made and benefits received by the members of the International Association of Machinists during the last two years:

We prevented the introduction of the two-machine system in 137 shops, employing 9,500 men. It is safe to say that if this system had been introduced the force of men would be reduced one-eighth; hence, in this we have saved the positions of 1,188 men, whose daily wages would amount to $2,613.60 per day or $818,056.80 per year.[17]

Union opposition to "pace-setting" was invariably defended on the grounds that it constituted a legitimate defense against an excessive pace of work. Pace-setting occurred in timework trades where, since pay did not vary with individual output, a worker's ability to secure and maintain employment depended upon whether or not he qualified as "competent." Hence, given the time rate, employers sought to maximize requirements of efficiency. Not infrequently they attempted to raise the general level of efficiency by bribing more able employees to set a faster pace in return for a higher wage; thus, by paying some employees an incentive wage, they attempted to raise the qualifying level of efficiency for the rest who remained under a time system of payment. The result was that slower employees would either be barred from employment (the loss of their services would presumably be balanced by increased productivity of those remaining at work) or would have to exert themselves to a greater extent in order to qualify. In the latter event, according to one union argument, they would be obliged to hasten the onset of occupational senility, both because they would burn themselves out by increased exertion and because, as "old" (less efficient) employees, they would find it impossible to obtain employment later on.[18] Some unions, therefore, sought to establish standards of competence; Slichter cites the "deadline" clause in local agreements between newspapers and printers' unions as an outstanding example.[19] Some unions forbade members to

16. Industrial Commission, *Reports on Labor*, v. XVII, p. XIX.

17. Commissioner of Labor, *Regulation of Output*, p. 143. In fact, it apparently proved impossible to enforce the two-machine rule. The fact that two-machine operation was sanctioned where it already existed when the rule quoted in the text above was adopted (1901) is indicative of the union's lack of power in this area, for originally the prohibition was unqualified. (Cf. Slichter, *Union Policies*, p. 184 and n. 49.)

18. Cf., Commissioner of Labor, *Regulation of Output*, p. 272.

19. Slichter, *Union Policies*, pp. 168–169, 175 and fn. 24.

accept wages in excess of the standard, and their purpose in so doing was the prevention of pace-setting. Others forbade their members to rush the work. Pace-setting was practiced rather widely in the building trades[20]; and the following rule of the Boston Bricklayers' local eloquently reflects the union objective of protecting the slower workman:

Members shall work together in a spirit of brotherly love. There shall be no rushing or driving that will injure or jeopardize the interests of a fellow-member, such as spreading mortar on the wall before the line is put up, repeatedly slacking the line before it is laid out its entire length, or putting up the line more than one course at a time, unless obstacles interfere with the same, or the laying of brick above the line except on a lead or ´ting.[21]

Makework and the level of wages

Slichter's concept of the makework rule as a reaction to "the insecurity of employment in modern industry" is further supported by his observation that

Make-work rules are likely to be paid for by wages lower than the union could otherwise obtain, because the disadvantages which the union can afford to impose upon employers are limited.[22]

But the fact that the cost to a union of enforcing a makework regulation could be measured in terms of a wage increase foregone does not imply that, in an effort to cope with unemployment, the union adopted a policy designed simply to maximize employment. For such a policy implied nothing but acceptance of the competitive wage. At the competitive wage the demand for and supply of jobholders are brought to equality; since there are no excess jobholders, "making work" is unnecessary. Under such circumstances, if rules of the makework variety did appear in collective agreements, they could not work real hardship upon the employers involved. The Eleventh Special Report of the Commissioner of Labor, *Regulation and Restriction of Output,* cites many examples of regulations which employers themselves regarded as "reasonable"; in such instances it is possible that the "union wage" was not substantially above the level which would have prevailed in the absence of collective bargaining.

But where employers complained that makework regulations did oblige them to hire more labor than they wished to, we can conclude that the unions with whom they bargained had succeeded in pushing wages above competitive levels. In such cases employers were pushed off their demand curves by union action which was aimed either at securing a wage increase without

20. Cf., Industrial Commission, *Reports on Labor,* v. XVII, p. LIX. In Britain pace-setters were known as "bell horses." Cf., Sidney and Beatrice Webb, *The History of Trade Unionism* (London: Longmans, Green, 1894), p. 305.

21. Commissioner of Labor, *Regulation of Output,* p. 286.

22. Slichter, *Union Policies,* p. 197.

suffering the consequence of a loss in employment or—perhaps more realistically in the light of the relationship observed between makework regulations and technological change—at preventing a reduction in wages without loss of employment. In principle, then, the effective makework demand was the equivalent of the guaranteed minimum demand discussed above; it was the practice of a discriminating monopolist. It might appear from the foregoing that, contrary to Slichter's statement, a strong union need not choose between jobs and employment, but that it could raise wages while enforcing its makework regulations. Obviously, however, each wage increase of this nature would result in a worsening of the employer's position; and if the union was either unable or unwilling (for example, through fear of driving the employer out of business) to effect a further deterioration of that position, it would be confronted with a choice between maintenance of jobs through makework rules and "wages lower than the union could otherwise obtain." Put in formal jargon, the union's choice between wages and employment refers, not to a movement along the employer's demand curve for labor, but to a movement along one of his indifference curves (see Appendix IV); this is the sense in which we interpret Professor Slichter's important explanatory clause, "because the disadvantages which the union can afford to impose on employers are limited."

That makework rules were inspired by insecurity of employment was undoubtedly the case, but the adoption of these devices was not at all inconsistent with an underlying attitude of resolute optimism. Exclusive concern with job protection would have been inconsistent with the adoption of such regulations. As it was, the unions were unwilling to jettison their wage standards, even when confronted by declining demand for the labor of their members.

But if it was true that the unions were not exclusively concerned with job opportunities, it was equally the case that they were not wholly preoccupied with maintaining standard rates. The adoption of makework rules implied concern with employment as well as with "standards." However, the insistence of the Webbs upon the "protection of the standard" is not, in one sense, questioned by our analysis of the makework rule; it is, on the contrary, sustained. In the first place, since the "standard" has been regarded generally as a going rate rather than a rate which might lie within the ability of the union to attain but which is not yet attained, the union's willingness to forego an increase in favor of a makework policy could not be considered a betrayal of the "standard." Second, although, on the above assumption, protection of the standard would rule out the acceptance of wage cuts (save as a matter of expediency, when advocated by officers as a tactical move), enforcement of makework rules involved the maintenance of rates. Maintenance of rates in the face of declining demand might be achieved without makework rules, of course, but such exclusive concentration on wage rates implied the acceptance of loss of employment. Makework of the variety here under discussion (which under these circumstances might be interpreted as adherence to a point on the employer's old demand curve after it had been replaced by a lower one) was clearly a superior alternative method of protecting the standard rate.

But while the enforcement of makework rules, and minimum earnings, discussed in the previous chapter, facilitated the protection of the "standard rate," it also necessitated a redefinition of the protected object. For what the union was interested in protecting with makework was a given combination of employment and wage income. By dividing the latter by the former, a "wage rate" emerged, to be sure, but it was not this rate alone which the union sought to protect. Had it been concerned only with this or any other rate, it would have permitted the employer to hire only as much labor as he wished to at that rate; just as if it had been solely preoccupied with maintaining a given volume of employment, it would have permitted the employer to purchase it at whatever wage rate he chose to pay.

RESTRAINING THE WORKER

Work-sharing and restriction of output under piecework

Policies which consisted simply in opposing wage cuts without attempting to maintain employment were, we have suggested, inferior to the types of makework regulations discussed in the preceding section, for they were unlikely to achieve their objective in the face of unemployment among the membership. But if it proved impossible to avoid declining employment, another alternative was open, in some cases. By obliging members to share the work available at the going wage, by "limiting daily or weekly output," and by "indirectly limiting the speed of work,"[23] unions were able to keep each member at least partly satisfied—although at the expense of preventing a great number from working as long or producing as much as they wished at the prevailing wage rate. Slichter lists limitation on output and on speed of work as makework rules, for he defines the latter as "efforts of unions to make work for their members." They are different, however, from his other makework categories which were discussed in the previous section; the latter were designed to enlarge or maintain the number of jobs available to the membership, whereas restrictions on output and speed were essentially intended to ration among the membership whatever jobs the employers made available at the union wage rate.

The Printers' "sub" rule was a celebrated work-sharing institution. We discussed this rule in connection with the emergence of the two-party system in the International Typographical Union; under it, a regularly employed member might be obliged to share his work week with a substitute. Thus "Big Six," the New York local, required that any member who had worked

23. Slichter, *Union Policies,* p. 166.

eight hours' overtime in any week (forty hours constituted a regular work week) "lay off" for one day and surrender his place to a "sub."[24]

Employer reactions to work-sharing and restriction

Although such rules obliged each individual to work fewer hours or at a slower pace than he would have done in their absence, and thus had the effect of reducing the total labor supply at the prevailing wage rate, they did not always meet with employer resistance. Thus, when the Jewish-language typographical local in New York cut the daily shift from eight to four hours following the introduction of the machine, the employers raised no objection, because the machines were allowed to run twelve hours each day. This attitude was well expressed by an employer in the pottery industry who had been requested by one of his dishmakers to hire an unemployed man instead of assigning some extra work to the employee in question. The employer complied with this request apparently without any reluctance, for he said,

Besides, I do not see where we are out anything by the transaction. We do not pay any more per dozen for dishes when made by two men than when made by one.[25]

Employers in the bituminous coal industry, however, objected to the union practice of "equalizing the turns," that is, limiting the number of cars which any one miner could load, despite the fact that, according to one union spokesman, union officials

were always careful to figure the output of the mine and then divide it between the number of men working in that mine, thereby guaranteeing that while every man got an equal turn the output of that mine was not reduced one ton. That is why restrictions have been placed in a few mines. Wherever restrictions were placed for any other purpose our organization has always taken a stand against it and compelled the men to wipe it off their books if passed by their locals.

But the miners also limited cutting by machine operators, and, in some instances, they limited the number of loaders assigned to each mining machine. In each case, the employers claimed that output was restricted. The union denied that it was its intention to restrict output, but its defense rested largely upon an attempt to distinguish between restriction of output and maintenance of wage rates:

We limit the number of loaders to protect the earning power of the men, not to decrease the output either of the machine or the mine. They could, and some of the mine managers would, pack the mines with men behind these machines until a man could not earn $1 a day as a loader. We have got to protect ourselves and we do it.

24. Commissioner of Labor, *Regulation of Output*, p. 85.
25. Commissioner of Labor, *Regulation of Output*, p. 696. For discussion and quotes below see also pp. 430–448, 450–458.

The kinship between work-sharing devices (exemplified by equalization of turns) and restriction of output under piecework is revealed by the origin of the former practice. Originally, active union members or men who did not live in company houses or deal at company stores were discriminated against by operators who withheld cars from them, so that, according to the Commissioner of Labor, "There have been times in Illinois, and elsewhere, when a miner would stay all day in a mine and never get a pit car to load." Thus, in a very real sense, equalization of turns, as well as restriction, was prompted by a desire to secure the union wage rate.

Under the type of makework regulation discussed in the previous section, employers were sometimes obliged not only to pay the union wage but to pay that wage to more workers than they otherwise would have been willing to hire. Under work-sharing and restriction of output under piecework, they were not obliged to hire more labor than they wished to at the prevailing wage (for the amount of work supplied by the members was restricted to the amount demanded), but the prevailing wage was higher than the wage which would have ruled in the absence of these regulations. Whether or not the employers accepted such regulations depended on whether or not they acquiesced in the union wage and not, for the most part, on the type of regulation involved (whether work-sharing or restriction of output). For, just as some employers (the mine operators) were opposed to work-sharing, others accepted restriction upon individual output.

Examples of such acquiescence may be found in situations characterized by multi-employer bargaining. Although the existence of industry-wide bargaining did not invariably imply assent to restrictive practices, the latter could and did characterize monopolistic arrangements. Thus we have already noted that Local Assembly 300 policed restriction of output in the window-glass industry and that, in so doing, it enforced individual production quotas and varied the length of the "summer stop," or idle season. At the local level, it was reported that "the plumbers have never undertaken to limit the amount of work a man shall do, except in Chicago." In Chicago there existed a Master Plumbers Association which enforced collusive bidding for contracts upon its membership through an exclusive contract with the local union; upon notification that a particular employer was no longer considered in good standing in the association, the local would withhold labor from him.

In the sanitary ware division of their jurisdiction, the Potters enforced restrictions on output in the form of detailed "rules governing the day's work" and forbade the making up of lost time. The Sanitary Manufacturing Potters' Association was not a "trust"; the Trenton Potteries Company, however, was regarded by the union as a "trust," although its members claimed that the total of the output quotas established by the company exceeded market demands. Nevertheless, it is interesting to note that, whereas western manufacturers were strongly opposed to union restrictions, the president of the association claimed that the members of his organization tacitly acquiesced in such practices.[26]

It will be recalled that the miners imposed a piece rate differential in favor of members working in thin-vein mines despite the fact that this tended to aggravate the unfavorable competitive condition of those mines. Now we must add that the unions sought to "equalize" competitive conditions by restricting output in the thick-vein mines in Illinois; since machines could be employed more profitably in the latter, the unions accomplished their purpose by restricting machine operation. The thick-vein operators were not happy about the arrangement, but, as one operator explained,

The operators were whipped to a standstill. Impoverished by our insane price-cutting and the long period of hard times, threatened with a total loss of all our markets on the very eve of returning good times, we simply had to take our medicine. We were compelled to submit not only to any terms the miners' union saw fit to impose, but to join the Illinois Coal Operators' Association, where we are outvoted and made to seem unanimously opposed to ourselves.[27]

A miner was equally forthright:

Of course you can get more coal from an undercut in an 8-foot seam than you can in a 5 or 6 foot seam. The thick-vein fellows were whipped into the competition agreement by a strike. Some of them thought to best the game on the sly by virtue of natural advantages, and are mad because they met with obstructions and are forced to give the other properties a chance. Did you ever think that God Almighty restricts the output of sunshine 50 per cent to give the moon a chance?

Where employers were not opposed to genuine restrictions on output or to work-sharing, they were in effect acquiescing in the maintenance of a union wage. Indeed, maintenance of a union wage might be considered the cost of enforcing sufficient restriction of output in order to assure a monopoly price, as in the case of the Window Glass Workers or the Chicago Plumbers. We have already observed, however, that union recognition did not always accompany "trustification"; anthracite coal was a case in point. In that industry output was restricted and rationed among the different mines by a judicious allocation of railroad cars. In each colliery, therefore, output was fixed. The Miners' union, in its turn, rationed this fixed output among the miners by requiring an equal distribution of cars among them and by preventing men from cutting coal on days when the mine was not hoisting. The union's role, however, was not that of enforcer of a collusive agreement among employers; for, although such an agreement was in effect, the employers apparently

26. Commissioner of Labor, *Regulation of Output,* pp. 364, 365. See also pp. 700–701, 707–708; McCabe, *National Collective Bargaining in the Pottery Industry,* pp. 395, 397–398.

27. Commissioner of Labor, *Regulation of Output,* pp. 413, 414.

were not in need of any methods of enforcement other than the rationing of cars among the collieries and did not wish to bargain with the union at all. Instead of tolerating or welcoming the union's share-work rules, the operators opposed them because it deprived them of their ability to play favorites among the miners, as in the case of the bituminous industry. Since one object of playing favorites was to prevent either the raising or the maintenance of wages by union activity, it is apparent that the anthracite operators did not intend to sanction restriction of individual output among the miners, despite the fact that they practiced it themselves.

"Rushing" and opposition to restriction under piecework

In seeking either to eliminate piecework or to restrict individual output under piecework, some unionists availed themselves of the same arguments which were invoked against pace-setting on timework. The Printers, for example, opposed piecework on machine operation because it induced rushing and overstrain.[28] The president of the Machinists claimed that, "In many instances the rapidity with which the workingmen have been driven under the piecework and similar systems have been the means of driving the mechanics to the insane asylum."[29] The bituminous coal miners, as noted above, sought to limit output under piecework; they restricted machine output by limiting the number of loaders per machine and by limiting the number of runs. Their officers claimed that such restriction was necessary in order to protect the health of the machine operator, whose work was extremely rigorous.

But the argument against rushing was not always identical with the argument against piecework—or in behalf of restriction of output under piecework. It could not be argued that all or even most individuals were obliged to work harder than they wished to under piecework, for, since the worker was paid in proportion to his output, there was frequently no need for the employer to seek to force the worker to work more than he wished to.

To complain, therefore, that the worker's health was jeopardized by piecework sometimes implied that the worker himself was not the best judge of his own true interests. To urge that individual output under piecework be restricted on the grounds of physical or mental well-being was not always to advocate that the worker be moved to a position on his supply curve from a position off that curve to its right; it could mean that he be moved from a position on the curve to one off it to the left. Thus Ethelbert Stewart noted that the business agent of a machinists' district council objected to a premium wage system in one of the plants in his jurisdiction because

there was a certain percentage of men who had no judgment about taking care of themselves; they had no ideas as to when they were really abusing their own

28. Barnett, *The Printers*, p. 133.
29. **Commissioner of Labor**, *Regulation of Output*, pp. 121, 135, 430, 439, 450.

bodies, and when you give such men an opportunity to earn 50 or 60 cents an hour, where before they have been earning 26 cents, the only thing they can see or think of is the money, and they will rush in at a high-speed rate, never thinking of their physical condition at all, until they have reached the point of breakdown, and then it is too late.

The Glass Bottle Blowers' short-lived *Preamble and Resolution as to Limitation of Day's Work* (1894) held that

No man can continue long working at high pressure without impairing his physical vitality. Naturally stimulants are resorted to to restore exhausted nature. Fuel must be added to keep up the steam, with a result that is too often seen and which we all deplore. And how often do we find that at an age when men are in the prime of life and ought to be in the highest physical condition, they are simply broken down wrecks and good candidates for an early grave. It is no wonder that from nearly every part of the country, for many years past, the evil has been watched with increasing interest, and the clearest thinking minds in our Association are convinced that something must be done to save us from ourselves. . . .

Now it is certainly possible that one might work in present haste and repent in future leisure. One reason why it is held that, if a consumer can and does choose freely among alternative possibilities, he is better off than if he cannot or does not, is that, if he makes a mistake about his own well-being on one occasion, he can profit thereby the next time he exercises his free choice. But if the choice is between income and leisure (including "leisure on the job") and if too much income is chosen (too much work performed), with the consequences of the variety described in the above quotation, it is not possible to profit by the mistake; one cannot have one's working life to live over again.[30] The man who overworks bears a close family resemblance to the man who overspends; in both instances there is probably excessive preference for present over future money income. Under the circumstances, obliging the worker to work less than he wishes to at the going rate— denying him a preferred choice—might well be in his own best interest.[31] It might also, therefore, be in the best interest of the community. Or, rather, it might be held that the exercise of free choice between work and leisure in a free market does not guarantee an optimum result over time to the community.

But people seldom appreciate being told what is good for them, whether or not they know what is good for them; and union policies aimed at enforcing restriction of output frequently encountered opposition from the rank and file. In this connection the Industrial Commission observed, "The principal officers of many of the most important American unions, whose

30. The above remarks were suggested by an argument in I. M. D. Little, *A Critique of Welfare Economics* (Oxford: Clarendon Press, 1950), pp. 44–45.

31. See Slichter, *Union Policies,* pp. 161ff. and especially p. 166, n. 5.

members habitually work by the piece, would, if they had the power, instantly abolish the system."[32]

Indeed, one need not dig deep in order to uncover ruins of attempts either to abandon piecework outright or to enforce restriction of output under piecework. Thus the New York local of the Mosaic and Encaustic Tile Layers' Union adopted in 1895 a set of rules defining in detail "a day's work" and establishing fines for infringement thereof; but it was abandoned after a few months because the members claimed that under certain conditions it failed to provide them with "a full day's work."[33] The Potters experienced considerable difficulty in enforcing legislation designed to restrict the output of pieceworkers in the general ware division of the industry, although, as we have observed, restriction was practiced in the sanitary ware branch. According to McCabe, resolutions and rules which attempted to eliminate the so-called "contract system," under which journeymen pieceworkers employed journeymen time workers, to set a maximum working day for pieceworkers, and to enforce certain standards of quality (which did not carry extra pay) were largely ignored.[34] In fact, the union found greater support for the latter type of regulation among the employers than in the ranks of its own membership; thus did restriction on this occasion make strange bedfellows. According to one manufacturer in the industry,

In our conferences when we jump on to the union representatives because the work is not done so well as formerly we are met by the protest that we are never satisfied with quantity; that output has been nearly doubled per jigger, and that it is up to us to decide somewhere between quantity and quality.[35]

In 1894 the Glass Bottle Blowers' convention, on the urging of its national executive, passed the following rules, which were obviously designed to restrict output and earnings under piecework:

No member of this Association who is engaged in the blowing or finishing of vials, bottles, fruit jars, or oil cans, 36 oz. wt. or under, whether made on the plate, stone, block, twisted ware, jericho, or combination shop, will be permitted to make more ware in one day than will pay him seven dollars per day.

On all ware over 36 oz. wt. and up to and including two-gallon bottles or jars, members are restricted to such numbers as will pay them not more than eight dollars per day.

On all ware over two gallons and up to and including five gallons, all members are restricted to such numbers as will pay them not more than nine dollars per day.

32. Industrial Commission, *Reports on Labor*, v. XVII, p. LVIII.
33. Commissioner of Labor, *Regulation of Output*, pp. 353–354, 357.
34. McCabe, *National Collective Bargaining in the Pottery Industry*, pp. 172–174, 384–385, and 162–163.
35. Commissioner of Labor, *Regulation of Output*, p. 687.

On all ware over five gallons, no member shall make more ware than will pay over ten dollars per day, which will be the extreme limit allowed to be made by any member of the Association.

Section 1. Any member of the Association making over the above amounts according to the class of ware upon which they work, must forfeit and pay over to the local treasurer, on the first pay day immediately following being found guilty of the offense, the full amount made over the limit to which they are restricted; and all branches shall adopt such measures as will secure the enforcement of this law.

Section 2. No shop will be allowed to quit work more than ten minutes before the usual time of quitting on the plea that they have made the required amount to which they are restricted. Any shop violating this law shall be fined 50 cents per man for such offense.

The purpose of this law is to compel members to work at such a rate as will keep them within the limit to which they are restricted.

Section 3. No shop will be allowed to make more ware than the limit fixed by the law, for the purpose of making up losses on previous days. Each day's work must stand for that day only.

Section 4. In each factory two clerks or supervisors shall be appointed by the President of the local Branch for the purpose of carrying out the objects of this measure. They must report all violations of the law to the Branch officers, watch the workings of the law in their locality, and at the end of their term report or suggest such alterations or improvements that they may deem advisable for the betterment of this measure. They shall hold office for the entire season.

Section 5. It shall be the duty of every member of the Association to see that any violation of the law that may come within their knowledge shall be reported to their Branch.

Section 6. It shall be the duty of the National President when notified by any local that difficulties have arisen which interferes with the enforcement of these laws, to visit such local, or appoint some competent member for that purpose, to convince and compel all refractory members to live up to the laws, and shall have full power to use all the strength of the Association to enforce them.[36]

The following year all these laws were repealed, and subsequent attempts to revive restriction were defeated.[37]

Few employers were agreeable or even amenable to either restriction or work-sharing; for their support or acquiescence implied, as we have observed, acceptance of the going wage rate. On the other hand, not all attempts to restrict output were unsuccessful; indeed both the propensity and the ability of even unorganized workers to practice such restriction are matters of common knowledge. Nevertheless, even where successful, restrictive policies tended to promote some dissatisfaction among the membership. To a greater

36. *Proceedings,* 1894, pp. 92–93.

37. Leo Wolman, "Collective Bargaining in the Glass-Bottle Industry," *American Economic Review,* vol. VI (1916), pp. 549–567.

or lesser extent, they forced the union which adopted them into a third-party position, unenviably situated between the employer and the membership. Granted that the union was acting in the true interests of the members, so long as that true interest remained unperceived by them, a potentially danger-ous line of distinction was drawn between the leaders and the led. It would appear that, if the desire, discussed above, to save the latter from themselves had been the only reason for the existence of restriction, the game would hardly have been worth the candle. What other conditions, then, might have led unions to adopt rules which obliged members to work less than they would otherwise have desired?

Other reasons for adoption of sharework or restriction

UNEMPLOYMENT OR OVERWORK OF CERTAIN MEMBERS. It was stated at the outset that restriction or work-sharing was frequently regarded as a device to diffuse the incidence of a reduction in demand. Similarly, it was believed that such devices were helpful in avoiding situations which were character-ized by an increase in the supply of labor, conditions of demand remaining unchanged. This type of situation frequently developed with the introduc-tion of piecework, as a result of which some individuals tended to increase their rate of output, now that it was no longer made unprofitable for them to do so. Increased productivity under piecework resulted from the change in method of payment; it did not imply a change in the worker's valuation of income as against leisure, as is illustrated in Appendix III. But increased output by some workers sometimes tended to oblige others to work harder than they desired; for, it was claimed,

the employer very soon becomes dissatisfied with his slower workmen, and comes to the conclusion that he might as well have all fast workmen as only a part. Slowly, perhaps, but surely the older and slower workmen are weeded out. If they can't stand the pressure, they must give way to those who can. All fraternal feeling is lost sight of in the mad rush; self-interest alone too often seems to be the mainspring of our actions.[38]

The complaint is akin to the protest against pace-setting under timework; here we find that, under piecework, some individuals were obliged to work harder than they would have been willing to. The remedy, as in the case of pace-setting, was to oblige the others to work less than they desired to; but, whereas the latter group was, almost by definition, a tiny minority among the membership in the case of pace-setting, under piecework those frustrated by union restrictions could well outnumber those who were "rushed" as a result of management employment policies. Thus the Bottle Blowers, from whose "Preamble" the above quotation was taken, went on to state uneasily—but prophetically—that

38. *Proceedings,* Glass Bottle Blowers, 1894, p. 91.

To alter or remedy this state of affairs can only be accomplished by each man agreeing willingly to abide by such restrictive laws as this convention may adopt. It is no easy or simple matter to formulate any plan that will apply successfully to the different places and conditions throughout the trade. . . .

Thus, while piecework might have created conflicts of interest within the union, restrictive rules certainly failed to eliminate them. If piecework discriminated against the slower man, restriction discriminated against the faster worker. But it is possible that the argument in favor of restriction which was based upon acknowledged overwork or unemployment among one particular group within the membership was more effective than the argument based upon the alleged but unperceived self-interest of all. For at least the older members favored restriction; and although numerical support for restriction under piecework was not as impressive as support of rules to eliminate rushing or pace-setting under timework, the influence of the older members within the union was not negligible.

TECHNOLOGICAL CHANGE. In this connection, we might consider again "the insecurity of employment in modern industry"; and we might inquire whether technological displacement stimulated the adoption of working rules. As Barnett and Slichter pointed out, unions which were confronted with technical changes attempted either to obstruct them, to compete with them, or to control them. If the method of obstruction was adopted, one means of implementing it was to increase the cost of machine operation to the point where it became uneconomical to substitute it for the older methods. This could be done by insisting upon very high piece rates on machine work.[39] Insistence upon makework rules which required employers to hire more workers per machine than they desired also tended to make machine operation expensive, as noted in the preceding section. Now we may add that limitation of output by machine operators produced the same effect. Thus, as Barnett and Slichter pointed out, the Flint Glass Workers attempted to limit output per worker in the pressed ware (machine) branch to the average level of output per worker on hand-blown ware of similar nature in the prescription branch; this tended to equalize costs under both methods of production.[40] The Stonecutters combined makework with restriction of output; in addition to some local rules demanding that a given number of stone-

39. Slichter, *Union Policies*, pp. 208–209.
40. See also Barnett, *The Printers*, pp. 73–74. The Flints also pursued a high piecework policy in the lamp chimney division.
The manufacturers in the sanitary division of the pottery industry accused the Potters of attempting to obstruct the development of the casting process by limiting output. The union, however, claimed that this practice resulted (1) from the manufacturers' practice of charging for defective ware (especially since the new process apparently increased the probability that unacceptable work would be turned out) and (2) from the manufacturers' refusal to accept the union's proposal to put casting on a day-wage basis. (McCabe, *Pottery Industry*, pp. 409–410.)

cutters be employed for each planer, the national union passed a rule which held that "In no case shall planers be allowed to run or work more than the number of hours per day worked by stonecutters of said branch."[41]

The policy of competition also involved the creation of a cost differential in favor of the old process. But whereas, under obstruction, this could be achieved merely by equalizing unit labor costs under the two methods, the policy of competition implied reduction of wage rates under the old method. (It would pay to install a new machine only if the operating costs under the old process exceeded both operating and installation costs under the new method.) Since both restriction of output and work-sharing attempted to restrict the supply of labor and thus to maintain wage rates, the policy of competition, unlike obstruction, therefore implied the abandonment, rather than the adoption, of such devices. Thus the Glass Bottle Blowers, in addition to accepting reductions in piece rates, abandoned the summer stop in an attempt to enable the semi-automatic machine, which employed the skilled men who were members of this union, to compete with the Owens automatic, which dispensed with their services.[42] It should be stated that the institution of the summer stop was one form of restricting hours of work and that the latter, since it resulted in a reduction of the rate of labor supply, was akin to work-sharing devices. (Reduction of the work period was sometimes undertaken in order to share work; in the case of the Bricklayers, we observed that the shorter hours movement took an extra impetus during periods of business depression.)

Unlike either obstruction or competition, the policy of control did not imply intent to prevent unemployment among the membership by making it unprofitable for the employer to install the labor-displacing device. Granted the introduction of the machine, however, the extent of the ensuing unemployment among the membership depended on two things: (1) the number of jobs remaining in the industry, and (2) the identity of the jobholders. By seeking to control the jobs, the union, following the policy of control, thereby sought to minimize unemployment among its members. Now if the union did succeed in retaining control over the machine, but if the number of jobs was reduced by the innovation, the union might have resorted to some device for sharing the work. Hence the reduction in hours enforced by the Jewish printers' local, which, it will be recalled, was acceptable to the employers as well as to the workers.

It must not be assumed, however, that such a device would have won employer acceptance in all situations, for it did tend to maintain the wage rate. It may be presumed that the employing printers were content to continue paying the established rate because hand compositors proved superior to other types of labor as machine operators.

41. Barnett, *Chapters on Machinery and Labor,* p. 47. Also pp. 36–37.
42. Slichter, *Union Policies,* pp. 232–233. Also Barnett, *The Printers,* pp. 99–103.

This was not true in the case of the Molders. The introduction of the molding machine in the 1890's resulted in little if any displacement of labor:

The molder is generally a factor in producing all labor-saving machinery, even that which is introduced into the foundry, and that, together with the increased demand for iron goods consequent upon the cheapening of production, has served to offset to a considerable extent the displacement that would otherwise have occurred, owing to the introduction of foundry improvements.[43]

Nevertheless, molders were displaced. The union at first appeared to ignore the machine, probably because its potentialities were underrated by the membership during the early stages of its development and because they found that machine work was harder and more disagreeable than hand work.[44] In other words, they neither feared nor wanted control over the machine. As a result, unskilled labor was hired for machine operation; and, as the machine proved increasingly capable of performing work formerly done by skilled molders alone, the latter were menaced by technological unemployment. As a result, the convention of 1899, at the urging of President Fox, passed the resolution which is quoted in part below:

First, That it be accepted as the future policy of the Iron Molders' Union of North America that we should seek to establish our jurisdiction over the molding machine operator and all those who work at molding in the numerous subdivisions into which the specialization of our trade has divided it.

Second, That we advise and instruct our members to accept jobs upon any molding machine when the opportunity is afforded and to endeavor to bring out its best possibilities.[45]

There is some question as to whether the molder's special skill and training counted sufficiently in machine operation to compensate for the greater physical strength of the unskilled laborer who was hired to operate the machine.[46] The issue is not crucial, however, for, given their respective rates of pay and efficiencies, it paid to hire laborers. The union's policy with respect to pay had been set forth in 1892 as follows:

Whenever by improved appliances, new or different methods, or superior facilities introduced by the manufacturers, an increase in the quantity of work

43. *Journal*, July 1898, p. 330.
44. *Proceedings*, 1899, pp. 4, 11; Commissioner of Labor, *Regulation of Output*, p. 168.
45. *Journal*, August 1899, pp. 396–397.
46. Margaret L. Stecker ("The Founders, The Molders, and the Molding Machine," *Quarterly Journal of Economics*, 1918, p. 278) claimed that the huskier unskilled workers made the best machine operators. This viewpoint was not shared, however, by union spokesmen and by some employers. Cf. *Journal*, October, 1900, pp. 575–597. Cf. also Frank T. Stockton, *The International Molders Union of North America* (Baltimore: Johns Hopkins, 1921), p. 194.

produced can be made, the price of molding may be decreased proportionately. Provided that the new price shall not reduce the average wages of the molder who makes it.[47]

Since the daily wage paid to the unskilled operators was less than that received by the hand molders, application of this policy would have resulted in an increase in piece rates on machine operation. The employers were naturally opposed—not only to the union's wage policy but to the entire program of control, for without the latter, which included admission to union membership of the semiskilled operators, the wage policy could not have been implemented.[48]

The employers, organized in the National Founders' Association, also interpreted the Molders' resolution on controlling the machine to mean that the ultimate purpose of such control, aside from raising wages, was to restrict output.[49] The union had denied that the phrase "to endeavor to bring out its best possibilities" lent itself to this interpretation; it was agreed, however, that laborers actually operating the machines worked harder than molders and for lower wages and also that some locals pursued an unofficial policy of restriction in order to obstruct the machine's progress. On the other hand, the union maintained that some employers had pursued a policy of pace-setting by bribing laborers to put forth "a temporary burst of speed." Therefore, said President Fox, "Foundrymen should not expect too much and molders should not do too little."[50] Vice-President John P. Frey maintained that the national union disavowed any limitation on output (the so-called "set day's work") and added that "We will require any local union to repeal any such by-law or rescind any such resolution whenever our attention is called to it."[51] As a proof of the Iron Molders' true intentions, he referred to local collective agreements which specifically outlawed restriction. The following excerpts from an agreement with the Twin City Foundrymen's Association might be cited as an example:

Clause 5. Machine molding as at present carried on shall not be disturbed during the life of this agreement. . . .
Clause 8. It is agreed that restriction of output shall not be countenanced in any way.

We might at this point summarize our discussion of the influence of technical change upon the adoption of restrictive practices. Adoption was most likely to occur if the union followed a policy of obstruction. If a policy of competing with the machine was selected, however, restriction was ruled

47. *Journal*, February 1892, p. 5.
48. *Iron Trade Review*, August 17, 1899.
49. *Proceedings*, 1902, p. 616.
50. *Proceedings*, 1900, p. 575.
51. Commissioner of Labor, *Regulation of Output*, pp. 170, 172.

out; indeed, if restrictive rules had been in effect prior to the selection of this policy, their abandonment became necessary as part of a general program of reducing union standards. Under a policy of control, maintenance of standards depended upon the availability of substitute labor. If substitutes were not readily available, the union wage might have been maintained and restriction or work-sharing might have been feasible. If, on the other hand, alternative sources of efficient labor were at hand, it might have proved impossible to maintain the standard wage—and to restrict output by individual members. Thus we find that restriction was feasible when it proved possible to prevent technological unemployment by obstruction; it was not feasible if the object was to prevent such unemployment by competition either with the innovation itself or with other groups of workers whom the innovation made available to the employers as a substitute for the labor of the union's members. When it was not possible to prevent displacement of labor by the machine, but when, at the same time, it was unnecessary to guard against substitution of other labor on the machine, restriction proved feasible as a work-sharing device.

One further distinction is in order. We have been considering work-sharing and restriction of output under piecework as devices which obliged the individual to offer less work than he would have been willing to supply at the going wage. In this respect, both work-sharing and restriction were alike insofar as they intended to restrict the supply of labor available to union employers and thus to maintain (or increase) the wage rate. But when one considers these practices in connection with union policy with respect to technological change, it becomes apparent that "restriction of output" could be more restrictive of output than "work-sharing." This would be the case if a union combined restriction of individual output—or a reduction in the individual's workday—with restriction of machine output. The Stonecutter's rule, which was intended to govern the operation of the planer is a case in point; it will be recalled that this rule was one component of an over-all policy of obstruction. It might be contrasted with the practice of the New York printers, who restricted hours of work but allowed three-shift operation, which formed part of a policy of control. Similarly the Glass Bottle Blowers permitted three-shift operation on the semiautomatics as part of its policy of competition with the Owens automatic machine and in order to make work for unemployed blowers.[52] And the Chicago Brickmakers, while stipulating the size and number of gangs per 100,000 bricks produced and the division of the total piece rate among the members of the gang, made no attempt to limit the output of the pressed-brick machine.[53]

RATE-SETTING UNDER PIECEWORK. Union rules restricting individual output were adopted even in situations in which "uncertainty of employment" was not a major consideration. Restriction of output under piecework was cer-

52. Slichter, *Union Policies*, p. 233.
53. Commissioner of Labor, *Regulation of Output*, pp. 380–381.

tainly understandable. In the absence either of restriction or of an increase in demand, increased output would have tended to depress piece rates and, possibly, hourly earnings. (For a more complete canvassing of the possibilities under the situation described above, see Appendix III.) An argument along these lines would have constituted an appeal to one's immediate self-interest, but it was unlike the argument for restriction on the grounds of overwork, which constituted an appeal to consideration of one's ultimate wellbeing. It would have been identical with the arguments used by businessmen who, in those less inhibited times, frequently did not hesitate to defend "trusts" and "rings" on the grounds that these institutions made it possible to do what each firm wished to be done but was unable to accomplish individually.

Indeed, the behavior of some employers tended to support this union model of rate setting in piecework trades.[54] Thus the general superintendent of a lamp factory reported,

If men earn more than the established wage rate as fixed by the rate of workmen on the outside—that is, in other factories—we would of course cut the piece price. Where the piece price has been fixed, using the number of pieces per hour as gotten out by the foreman and the base rate of 15 cents per hour, for instance, as the department's permissible earning, we then would permit 10 per cent of the pressers in these rooms to earn more than the hourly rate at the piece price. But if much over 10 per cent of the employees in a given room were earning more than that hourly rate we would cut the piece price.[55]

Hence it is not surprising that the president of a potters' local should complain that

All our trouble is with the speedy man, or hogger-in. At our conferences the bosses pick out two or three men from their pay rolls to show what men can earn at present prices. I believe a limit would be a good thing. . . . As it is we have no control over the hogger-in. We would not care for him if the manufacturer did not use him or his earnings as a club to beat down our prices, or keep them down. But if they will use him we must control him.

It was mentioned earlier that the miners defended their practice of limiting the number of loaders to each machine on the grounds that it was necessary "to protect the earning power of the men. . . ." The miners in the Bellville district of Illinois also enforced a maximum day's earnings for a while. According to one union official,

The rank and file of the miners believed that the operators would use high earnings to beat down the mining rate in the conventions. They did not believe

---

54. Slichter (*Union Policies,* p. 312) cited as one cause of limitation of output of piece-workers "the desire of the workers to protect themselves against the tendency of the employers to cut piece rates when the earnings of some workers became large. . . ."

55. Commissioner of Labor, *Regulation of Output,* pp. 194, 437–438, 686.

that District 12 was strong enough to uphold its mining rates regardless of the earning power of the men. . . .

An editorial in the Iron Molders' *Journal* combined this line of argument (which, despite an apparent confusion in terminology is very well put forth) with the appeal to unperceived self-interest on the grounds of physical overstrain:

It may be possible in the enactment of the law limiting the amount that piece-workers shall put up as a day's work, that, to those who are and have been making and putting up over the amount, an injustice has been done, by what, they say, is reducing their wages. Well, perhaps if we look at the question in a selfish light it might be so construed. But what about the whole membership? Does it not benefit more members by an equitable distribution of the jobs and work? Does it not lighten the burden of the overworked and avaricious member, who, in his efforts to make big wages, is daily overexerting himself and prematurely breaking himself down to not only the injury of himself, but that of his family and his fellow-workman? And do not our employers continually contrast the greatest with the smallest wages made and make that one of their arguments for cutting prices? In this age of machinery the proprietors do not look at the quantity of work produced, but at the cost of production; and where a man is making more money than they think he ought to, they never refer to the amount of work done, but to the amount of money made. . . .[56]

In reply, we might quote from an interview with a foundryman which took place some eighteen years after that editorial had been written:

We do not cut piece prices where a few exceptional men earn too much money on certain patterns, and in such cases to prevent the discontent that is bound to spring up in a shop where some men are earning a great deal more than anyone else, we ask these men to make fewer pieces and put on more men when the men are obtainable. Of course if all the men, or even most of the men, were making very high wages on piece rate we should probably cut them. Unscrupulous manufacturers who use the speed of the fastest men to scale down the rates have made piecework very unpopular with all workmen, and we all have to suffer from their mistakes.[57]

The defense of both the lamp manufacturer and the foundryman amounted to a disavowal of the practice of pace-setting, but it was acknowledged candidly that where hourly earnings were generally higher than the "standard" with respect to which management had set the piece rates, the rates were reduced. Both employers, however, indicated that this procedure was necessitated by the pressure of competition, which suggests that the union interpretation betrayed ignorance of the fact that piece rates were

56. John P. Frey and John R. Commons, "Conciliation in the Stove Industry," *Bulletin No. 62* of the Bureau of Labor, v. XII (Washington: Government Printing Office, 1906), p. 178.

57. Commissioner of Labor, *Regulation of Output,* p. 168.

ultimately determined in the wider market. Nevertheless, the unionists were certainly correct in claiming that an inverse relationship existed between the wage rate and the amount of labor supplied by their members. Thus it is very interesting to find that, once the stove manufacturers agreed to accept the union wage, the Molders were willing to abandon restrictions on individual output. National collective bargaining in the stove industry began in 1891; in 1902, the two parties added the following clause to their agreement:

> Inasmuch as it is conceded by the members of the S.F.N.D.A. (i.e. the employers) that the earnings of a molder should exercise no influence upon the molding price of work, which is set, according to well-established precedent and rule of conference agreements, by comparison with other work of a like kind, the placing of a limit upon the earnings of a molder in the seven hours of molding should be discontinued in shops of members of the S.F.N.D.A.[58]

It is apparent that the Molders agreed to terminate restriction because they were no longer in the position of the Miners who "did not believe that District 12 was strong enough to uphold its mining rates regardless of the earning power of the men." In our discussion of the relationship between technological change and restriction of individual output, we observed that unions abandoned restriction when they no longer wished to maintain the wage rate at existing levels. Now, in discussing the relationship between maintenance of the piece rate and restriction of output, we find that an important union was willing to abandon restriction, not because it did not wish to maintain the wage rate, but because it was no longer obliged to restrict output in order to maintain the rate. It was clearly to the advantage of the union to exchange restriction for a guarantee of the rate which had prevailed under restriction, for it eliminated the conflict between the union and those members who had chafed under the restrictions which the union had imposed upon them. Employers also stood to gain when union rules resulted in limiting the utilization of machinery. Thus the New York garment manufacturers granted a reduction in the work week of two and three-quarter hours in exchange for removal of restriction on output. This bargain, incidentally, was quite acceptable to the other party to the transaction. "The officers of the union have not objected to raising the limit or abolishing it as a matter of principle, but have held it as a possible asset in case of negotiations for increase of wages or reduction of hours."[59]

Relaxation or surrender of work rules

Examples of the abandonment of restrictions on output in exchange for higher wages or shorter hours illustrate a special case of a proposition developed by Barnett and Slichter. According to the latter,

58. Quoted in Frey and Commons, "Conciliation in the Stove Industry," pp. 179 and 193.

59. Commissioner of Labor, *Regulation of Output*, p. 536.

If the union can get something in exchange for abandoning a burdensome rule, it will naturally do so. Likewise the best opportunity for employers to insist that a restrictive rule be dropped is when the union wants something—a wage increase, a reduction in hours, or something else.[60]

"Burdensome rules" thus abandoned were not restricted to limitations upon output of individual workers. The Chicago Brickmakers accepted an increase in the day's stint (under timework) during the depression of the 1890's rather than submit to a reduction in the daily wage.[61] The national executive of the Molders agreed that stove molders put up a deposit for their tools. When the Quincy, Massachusetts local objected that this agreement obligated molders who never had to buy their tools previously to incur this expenditure henceforth, the national executive replied that this concession was necessary in order to obtain the employers' consent to make "price books" available for inspection, to establish piece rates for new work "within a reasonable time" (ordinarily, two weeks), and to pay for work lost on account of "dull iron."[62]

But it was on the question of liberalizing the apprentice-journeyman ratio that the impact of collective bargaining upon the modification of union rules can be observed most dramatically in the stove industry. At their first convention in 1859, the Molders adopted a constitutional provision specifying a ratio of one apprentice to every ten journeymen, plus an allowance of one apprentice to each shop. The ratio was excessive, and Sylvis urged its replacement by a ratio of one to five; whereupon the convention of 1867 established the ratio of one to eight. The latter ratio was never uniformly enforced, however; and after national collective bargaining had been established with the employers in the Stove Founders' National Defense Association in 1891, the employers pressed for liberalization, calling attention to the fact that the rule penalized those employers who were obliged to comply with the union rule. The association refused to acknowledge the one-to-eight ratio as binding upon its members, but its president pointed out that, whereas in the past employers had recruited nonunion apprentices during strikes, this source of supply was now denied to the members of the S.F.N.D.A. who were parties to an agreement which adopted "the principle of arbitration in the settlement of any dispute." Thus the employers who recognized the union were now placed at a disadvantage with their competitors. Moreover, he added, liberalization of the apprentice ratio would facilitate the abandonment of the "berkshire," or helper, system, which the union opposed. The representatives of the union had previously evidenced their willingness to liberalize the ratio in exchange for the abandonment of the berkshire system (although the latter

60. Slichter, *Union Policies,* p. 390.

61. Commissioner of Labor, *Regulation of Output,* p. 380.

62. *Journal,* July 1896, pp. 321–323; November 1896, p. 472; Frey and Commons, "Conciliation," pp. 192 and 181; see also pp. 162–176.

apparently was on the wane), but the membership declined repeatedly to modify the constitutional restriction on the employment of apprentices. In 1902, however, the union's representatives agreed that, if both parties found that the ratio of one to eight resulted in any employer's being "injuriously affected by his inability to secure a sufficient supply of journeymen molders," the latter would be allowed to employ "such additional number of apprentices as may be required and mutually agreed to." Finally (in 1905), without amending their constitution, the membership empowered their conference representatives to consent to a ratio of one-to-five, with safeguards designed to avoid the unemployment of journeymen or apprentices.

Thus it was only after national collective bargaining was established that the national officers could persuade the membership to consent to a *de facto* increase in the apprentice ratio. That the acceptable *quid pro quo* consisted in the assurance of a wage level which the membership had sought to protect by restriction of numbers stands revealed by the following proviso in the agreement of 1902 which empowered the presidents of the two signatory groups to grant relief under the one-to-eight ratio:

If it be found that inability to secure and hold journeymen molders is due to an inequality or low standard of molding prices or undesirable shop conditions, it shall devolve upon the two presidents or their representatives to at once take steps to remedy these prices or conditions in accordance with the standard prevailing in the district.

Barnett pointed out that national employers' associations could obtain concessions with respect to work rules only when they were in a position to negotiate over wages or hours[63]; thus the agreement between Local Assembly 300 and the American and Federation Companies for 1902-1903 provided for arbitration "in case of any controversy arising in the factory in reference to this wage scale, rules or usages. . ."[64] But where employer groups were either unwilling or unable to bargain over wages or hours, they could not hope to obtain modification of union work rules. M. L. Stecker attributed the breakdown of national collective bargaining in the stove foundry industry to the refusal by the Molders' representatives to agree to any modification of work rules which had been adopted by the union[65]; but we know that the executive of the same union was perfectly willing to modify such rules in the stove branch of the trade—even to the extent of opposing some of the most deepseated prejudices of the membership. Barnett attributed the difference in the two cases to the fact that the Molders' agreement with the Stove Founders' provided that "The general rate of molders' wages should be established for

63. George E. Barnett, "National and District Systems of Collective Bargaining in the United States," *Quarterly Journal of Economics,* v. XXVI, 1912, pp. 425–443.
64. Commissioner of Labor, *Regulation of Output,* p. 623.
65. Stockton, *The Molders Union,* pp. 129–131.

each year without change,"[66] whereas the National Founders' Association refused to assent to the establishment of a national minimum wage. Indeed, the foundrymen, in refusing to negotiate on certain issues, defended a position which, in more recent terminology, might be described as "refusal to surrender management prerogatives." The Molders' president noted that

there has developed a disposition among the members of the Association to insist upon certain privileges as a matter of right, and to regard the carrying out of their will in these matters as no violation of the spirit of the agreement.[67]

Whereas, Stockton observed, the Molders and the Stove Founders never discussed "abstract questions of the rights or obligations of either side."[68]

Even where both parties were able and willing to bargain over wages or hours, however, it did not follow that management could obtain modification of work rules or customs. We have had occasion to call attention to the unwillingness of the International Typographical Union to permit its affiliated locals to accede to proposals by local employer groups to relax regulations specified by international law in exchange for concessions on wages or hours. Thus local employers' associations were not able to "buy" liberalization of restrictive practices. Yet when the book-and-job printers entered into a national arbitration agreement with the international itself, they found that "the International Typographical Union takes the exalted ground that after they have passed a law it is as irrevocable as the laws of the Medes and Persians."[69] But Barnett called attention to the fact that this agreement did not provide for the determination of wages; and he concluded from this and other examples, "that the success of a national or district system of collective bargaining is far more probable when the scale of wages is a national or district scale, since only then is it likely that working rules will become subject to joint determination."

Barnett's analysis did not imply, of course, that national collective bargaining over wages and hours was a prerequisite to joint determination of "other conditions of employment." He did note, however, that "the national union tends, even in the absence of a nationally uniform rate of wages, to build up a series of national working rules . . . which are enforced upon local unions in their dealings with employers." And he further noted that, partly as a result, local employer associations organized national groups in order to bring work rules under joint determination. But the establishment —or the strict enforcement—of work rules by the national union did not

66. Conference Agreements, Clause 5, 1892. Quoted in Frey and Commons, "Conciliation," p. 191.

67. *Proceedings,* 1902, p. 610. Cf. also F. W. Hilbert, "Trade Union Agreements in the Iron Molders' Union," *Studies in American Trade Unionism,* ed. by Jacob H. Hollander and George E. Barnett (New York: Henry Holt, 1906), p. 236.

68. Stockton, *The Molders Union,* p. 125.

69. Barnett, *The Printers,* pp. 435, 437, 440–441.

always occur "in the absence of a nationally uniform rate of wages," as it did among the Printers. Thus, following a lockout in 1900, the Chicago Carpenters, in exchange for the maintenance of the eight-hour day and the stipulation of an hourly wage rate, agreed (a) that there be no restriction of output or restriction upon the use of machinery and (b) that all differences arising under the agreement be settled by arbitration.[70] This agreement remained in force, despite the fact that it ran counter to the following standing decision of the general executive board of the United Brotherhood:

A joint arbitration committee of contractors and journeymen cannot be allowed to try members of U.B. for violation of trade rules.[71]

In summary, work rules could be liberalized when the following conditions prevailed:

(1) The willingness and ability of employers to enter into joint negotiations over wages and hours were essential to the joint determination of work rules.

(2) Where union work rules were liberalized, they were liberalized only by units of union government, whether national or local, which had the *de facto* power to bargain over both work rules and wages and hours.

(3) Where the first two conditions obtained, unions were willing, in principle, to trade work rules for employer adherence to union "standards," and specifically,

(4) Where the national union was empowered to establish both work rules and wages and hours, it was willing to bargain over the terms of both with competent employer representatives. The position of the national union was well stated by President Denis A. Hayes of the Glass Bottle Blowers:

It is charged that trade unions at their annual conventions pass arbitrary measures intended to control the actions and limit the rights of the manufacturer, and that their executive officers go about demanding the enforcement of these measures. As a matter of fact, the modern trade union makes no absolute rules excepting such as relate to the internal government of the organization, and all matters, such as wages, hours, apprentices, etc., requiring the consent of the manufacturers are settled by voluntary arbitration at the wage conferences held annually between the representatives of the manufacturers and the executive committee of the union.[72]

(5) Finally, just as the national union was prepared to dissuade its locals from "bargaining away" work rules established by national authority, as in the case of the Printers, so it was prepared to persuade them to abandon both national and local restrictions when the first condition listed above was

70. Industrial Commission, *Reports on Labor*, v. XVII, p. 386.
71. General Executive Board, *Standing Decisions*, 1897.
72. Commissioner of Labor, *Regulation of Output*, p. 641.

satisfied. After Editor Frey had explained to the readers of the Molders' *Journal* the advantages which accrued to the union from the agreement which pledged all Molders to put up a deposit for their tools, he added,

And above all arguments is the one that collective interests should at all times be placed before local interests, and the latter should be willing to accede to a minor point, that the general welfare might be promoted.[73]

73. *Journal,* August 1896, p. 323.

THE NATIONAL UNION IN THE AMERICAN LABOR MOVEMENT

CHAPTER EIGHTEEN

SOME THEORIES OF THE LABOR MOVEMENT

IN DISCUSSING union policies on certain issues connected with strikes and collective bargaining, we have restricted ourselves to a consideration of what might be regarded as the economic outlook of the national union, for we did not deal with its political or utopian programs. Our choice might be justified by reference to the primary purpose of this study, which is to account for the "dominance of the national union" (the phrase is Barnett's) in the American labor movement; for the ascendancy of the national union reflected the rise of the economic outlook to a position of preëminence in that labor movement. It was suggested in the analysis of jurisdiction that the triumph of the national union over the local federation reflected the victory of business unionism over political reform; given the primacy of collective bargaining, the relevant environment to which union structure conformed was the economic environment. As product or labor markets became nationwide in extent, power passed from the local union to the national union in the relevant trade or congeries of trades, and within the national union, authority became concentrated in the executive branch. Union structure conformed also to the occupational, as distinct from the geographic bounds of the relevant market; thus there arose the typically American concept of "exclusive jurisdiction," to be contrasted with acceptance of plural unionism, based upon political or religious differences, abroad.

It is not our primary purpose to inquire into the reasons which underlay the primacy in this country of the set of values which came to be known as business unionism. However, some of the findings in this account of the rise of the national union are relevant to that broader and deeper problem. In the first place, they constitute evidence in the light of which some theories óf the labor movement in the United States might be reviewed; in this connection we shall consider the interpretations advanced by Commons and Perlman. In addition, material presented in previous chapters should enable us to identify a set of environmental phenomena which were sufficient to account for both the strong preference for collective bargaining found in the

American labor movement and for certain occurrences and practices which are more difficult to explain with reference to the other hypotheses.

According to John R. Commons, "Labour movements in America have arisen from peculiar American conditions, and it is by understanding these conditions that we shall be able to distinguish the movements and methods of organization from those of other countries."[1] The American worker was confronted with certain peculiarities in his physical, economic, and institutional environments; these consisted in "the wide expanse of free land," "the historical extension of markets over this broad expanse," exposure to successive waves of immigration, business fluctuations which "have touched higher peaks and lower depths" than in other countries, easily won political equality, and a system of government characterized by both federalism and autonomy of the three functional branches.

The existence of free land was held to have contributed heavily to the individualistic flavor of the early American labor movements. Since "free land was not a mere bounty of nature," political activity was necessary to wrest the land from the forces of "monopoly and slavery"; hence it was productive of a "movement." But the movement was not characterized by "aggression on the property rights or political power of others," because "the poor and industrious . . . (could) escape from the conditions which render(ed) them subject to other classes." Hence the crusade for free land produced "a labour movement based on the ideas of a 'middle class' or the 'producing classes' rather than the 'wage-class' "; "it was individualism rather than socialism, individual labour rather than trade unionism."

But participation in the nation's political life was made possible only because the poor and industrious in this country were granted "with scarcely a struggle" what their counterparts in other lands could not secure, despite heroic exertion," until "two or three generations" later—"the boon of universal manhood suffrage."

Thus entry into politics was easy, but it is often the case that where admission is free few prizes are awarded. Workingmen found that, in order to secure the passage of desired legislation, it was necessary to prevail upon state as well as federal legislative bodies. Possession of the ballot frequently did result in courtship of the labor vote by the major parties, but such overtures also proved fatal to budding indigenous labor parties.[2] Moreover, even in cases where their efforts met with success, federal and state courts frequently undid their legislative labors. As a result, "our Federal and judicial system of government added its pressure on labour and forced it to acquire

1. John R. Commons and Associates, *History of Labour in the United States* (New York: Macmillan, 1936), v. I, pp. 3–5.

2. John R. Commons, *Labor and Administration* (New York: Macmillan, 1913), p. 149.

by trade union action what in other countries has been granted by legislation."[3]

Alongside these deterrents to political activity, there existed an incentive to "trade union action" in the form of the "extension of markets" which, in the New World as in the Old, was a concomitant of economic development. The extension of markets was characterized by specialization and division of labor in production, enterprise, and sale. With the emergence of the local market, the itinerant journeyman gave way to the urban self-employed master craftsman who produced to order ("bespoke ware") and who later hired journeymen to produce for stock and eventual sale in the local retail market. Although a separate employee class emerged in this retail stage, functional specialization failed to produce "antagonism" between the "merchant-master" and his hired hands; as a local monopolist, the former could "pass the (wage) increase along to the consumers."[4]

But the development of canals threatened the entrenched position of the local merchant-master by exposing him to competition from other producing regions. At the same time, of course, he was afforded the opportunity of selling in other markets. It was necessary, however, that goods destined for the "wholesale" market be produced at a lower cost per unit; this was apparently accomplished (in the case of shoes, at any rate) by reducing the piece rate on this ware and producing goods of possibly inferior quality but designed to sell at a reduced price. Production of wholesale ware for "export" was carried on at first by "inferior workmen who could not command the wages demanded" and received by journeymen on "bespoke" and "shop" work. The latter nevertheless suffered from the competition of wholesale work, for their employers, formerly local monopolists, had been reduced to the status of monopolistic competitors selling a somewhat differentiated product. As a result, sales of the higher quality ware fell, the more highly skilled workers were obliged increasingly to turn to wholesale work, and their piece rates were thus reduced. They no longer considered their interests identical with those of their employers; it was at the "wholesale order stage," therefore, that, according to Commons, "the wage-bargain assumes importance" and "the conflict of capital and labor begins."

It was, however, little more than a beginning. The amount of "export" trade carried on by the merchant-employer could not have been great, for such trade required more financing than did local retailing, and capital was hard to come by in the post-Revolutionary War era. As a result the merchant-employer was not well able to compete with imports from foreign nations.[5] Where domestic "export" (interregional) trade did flourish, it was controlled

3. Commons, *History of Labour*, v. I, p. 9.

4. John R. Commons, "American Shoemakers, 1648–1895: A Sketch of Industrial Evolution," *Quarterly Journal of Economics*, v. XXIV, November 1909, pp. 53–59.

5. Commons, *History of Labour*, v. I, pp. 90–93 (Saposs); "American Shoemakers," pp. 59–69. See also p. 79.

by merchant-capitalists, who had access to credit, rather than by merchant-employers. The latter increasingly surrendered their merchandising activities and remained as small contractors, hiring labor and bidding for orders from the merchant-capitalist. Since the merchant-capitalist apparently enjoyed something in the way of a regional monopoly of capital in the trade, he was also able (it was implied) to exploit a position of monopsony with respect to the small employers and thus indirectly with respect to their hired journeymen.[6] Hence to the competition of less efficient labor and ware of poorer quality there was added the element of monopsony (once removed) as a depressant on the wage rate of the skilled journeyman.

The merchant-capitalists also intensified the process of substitution, for, by further widening market areas, they encouraged the utilization of less skilled labor. The merchant-capitalist tapped the supply of cheap convict labor; and, in order to compete with the latter, the small masters resorted to job dilution and speed-up. Thus the skilled journeyman's place of work was converted into a sweatshop. Finally, with the introduction of machinery, employers were able to utilize unskilled immigrant (Chinese as well as European) labor; it was in this connection that the merchant-capitalist himself was driven to the wall and that organized labor's "immigrant problem" arose. Commons, however, takes pains to point out that the employment of power machinery, identified by Marx as the source of "exploitation" in modern capitalist society, was but a later symptom of the historically and logically antecedent process of the extension of markets.

Although the merchant-capitalist might have been a local-market monopsonist, he was not a monopolist as well, since he frequently was subjected to the competition of his fellows from other producing regions.[7] Thus the interests of the consumer were served by the process of development; and Commons concluded

that the ever-widening market from the custom-order stage, through the retail-shop and wholesale-order to the wholesale-speculative stage, removes the journeyman more and more from his market, diverts attention to price rather than quality and shifts the advantage in the series of bargains from the journeymen to the consumers and their intermediaries.

In one respect Commons' theory of the extension of markets is incompatible with his adaptation of the "Turner doctrine" concerning the role of free land in the west. The former was credited with producing the modern trade union; the latter with inhibiting its development. Yet both developments proceeded simultaneously in this country; improvements in transportation linked eastern producing regions with western markets (as early as the post-

6. Commons, *History of Labour,* v. I, p. 7.
7. Commons, *History of Labour,* v. I, pp. 61, 88, 95, 102. Louis M. Hacker, *The Triumph of American Capitalism* (New York: Columbia University, 1940), p. 255.

Revolutionary War period in Commons' "wholesale-order" stage and in the subsequent "merchant-capitalist" era as well) at the same time that different producing centers were brought into competition with one another in their respective local markets. Now trade unionism existed in the 1820's and 1830's, but since the famous "safety-valve" was not turned off until over a half century later, Commons was not free to admit the existence of trade unions until the last decade of the nineteenth century. He attempted to extricate himself from this embarrassing dilemma by implying that the early unions really were not unions at all; the unions of the thirties, he contended, were

not based on a permanent change in industry or markets but on a temporary rise of prices and cost of living. Hence, here our problem in detail is to distinguish the forms and policies of labor organisations not having a reason for endurance but a reason only for keeping wages from lagging behind the prices of commodities.[8]

Yet in his discussion of the influence of the business cycle, he holds that upswings were characterized by "trade unionism" and downswings by "politics, panaceas, or schemes of universal reform." Undoubtedly Commons was impressed by the ability of the national unions to survive the depression of the nineties, but if he chose to identify ability to survive depressions as the criterion of trade unionism, his choice implied rejection of the analysis involving the extension of markets, which apparently entailed the conclusion that unionism emerged at the "wholesale-order" stage. In any event, from the account in the *History* of unionism in the thirties, late forties, and early fifties—to say nothing of unionism, including national unionism, in the post-Civil War period—there emerges the picture of a labor organization which does not differ appreciably in form or spirit from the trade union of the late nineteenth and early twentieth centuries. One wonders whether Commons, had he written after the appearance of the work of Goodrich and Davison, which indicated that very few wage earners had in fact been able to "escape" to the land, would still have sought to cast doubt upon the legitimacy of the early union movements.

The fact that few, if any, eastern workers were able to metamorphose themselves into frontier farmers did not, of course, prevent the majority from ardently desiring to free the western domain from the grasp of "monopolists"; but one can accept Commons' conclusion that the existence of the West produced a unique political movement without subscribing to the view that it prevented the emergence of "genuine" trade unionism.

It is evident, therefore, that Commons' theory of the extension of markets provides a better fit for the historical facts when it is unburdened by his interpretation of the Turner thesis of the frontier. However, this theory, the most brilliant and ambitious attempt to account for the development of the American labor movement, appears deficient in two important respects, al-

8. Commons, *History of Labour*, v. I, p. 20. See also pp. 11, 12, 18.

though once freed from loose interpretation and some extraneous matter, it can perhaps be rehabilitated and made to serve as a special case (possibly the most important special case) of a more general hypothesis.

The theory has been interpreted to hold that "the widening of the labour market" (to use Commons' phrase) tended to depress "wages" and that workers responded by forming unions.[9] It is apparently implied that unions emerged as a response to a reduction in wage incomes. If this were the case, however, difficulty might be encountered in reconciling a theory which sought to explain the rise of unionism by invoking a variant of "increasing misery" with a rising trend of real and money wage income in a high-wage country. In fact, Commons himself did not claim that reductions in wage income necessarily resulted from the evolutionary process which he described. That process did involve reduction in the amount of skilled labor employed per unit of output, primarily at the "wholesale-order" and later stages, either through dilution of quality or specialization, which made it possible to utilize less skilled labor. Hence piece rates were reduced, as noted above, but this by no means implied that earnings also fell; if product demand was sufficiently elastic, reduction in unit labor costs and prices might well have been accompanied by increased earnings by skilled journeymen. Another factor which tended to produce the same effect was the growth of the internal market, due to the rapid increase in population which coincided with the extension of market areas (see Chapter I).

Although the "widening of the labour market" did not necessarily entail, as an immediate consequence, a reduction in the income of the skilled journeyman, is it not possible that the emergence of merchant capitalism, which, according to Commons, was itself a product of the extension of markets, provided an impetus in that direction? For the merchant-capitalist, as we have already observed, was alleged to have been a monopsonist (once removed) in the local labor market. (Since the merchant-capitalists competed with one another in local product markets, they could not have been monopsonists in the strict sense of the word, the sole buyer of a given resource in a closed economy.) Thus, it was claimed, at this advanced stage in the expansion of markets, monopsony was added to dilution of the skill-content of the job as a pressure on wage income. Saposs claimed that the real earnings of the skilled workers declined under merchant-capitalism, while "the wages of the unskilled were going up"; this divergence, in his opinion, accounted for the fact that "the early unions were composed exclusively of skilled workers while "no traces of organisation can be found among the unskilled."[10]

9. Cf. Selig Perlman, *The History of Trade Unionism in the United States* (New York: Augustus M. Kelley, 1950 reprint), pp. 266–278; Philip Taft, "Theories of the Labor Movement," in *Interpreting the Labor Movement* (Industrial Relations Research Association, 1952), p. 13.

10. Commons, *History of Labour,* v. I, pp. 104 and 105.

Local monopsony, however, was not always found in industries characterized by the merchant-capitalist system. In the clothing industry of New York or Chicago, many "manufacturers" were located in the same business district, so that the contractor had access to more than one buyer. These industries were notoriously sweated, but the sweating resulted, not from monopolistic buying, but from "excessive competition among the manufacturers."[11] And even in the boot and shoe industry, in which one might infer, from Commons' account, the existence of monopsonistic conditions in the local market, pressure on journeyman wage rates did not necessarily result in reduced earnings. The Journeymen Cordwainers of Philadelphia claimed that the merchant-capitalists (referred to as "the cunning men of the East") "realized large fortunes, by reducing our wages, making large quantities of work, and selling at a reduced price." The reduction of "wages," however, referred to a reduction in piece rates, for they went on to explain that this process did not involve "any positive reduction of our wages."

The answer is plain and simple—by making cheap work, triple the quantity has to be made to obtain a living. . . .[12]

When the introduction of the McKay machine in the 1860's made possible the utilization of "green hands," or unskilled labor, journeymen's piece rates were cut, and this time, "Neither the journeyman's devices nor his foot-power machines yielded a sufficient increase of output to offset his wage reductions." This occurred at the so-called "factory-order" stage, however, which succeeded merchant capitalism.

If then, reduction in wage income was not necessarily associated with merchant capitalism and if reduction in wage rates was characteristic of the earlier "wholesale-order" stage as well as of later stages, the merchant-capitalist would appear to have little or no unique significance for an explanation of the rise of the union movement in this country. It is true that, under merchant capitalism, many small master craftsmen lost their independent status or became labor contractors, but Commons does not claim that trade unions were formed by frustrated craftsmen who were no longer able to achieve or retain the status of merchant-master;[13] on the contrary, unions were formed by the employees of these small contractors in protest against reductions in wage rates administered by their employers. What emerges as

11. United States Commissioner of Labor, Eleventh Special Report, *Regulation and Restriction of Output* (Washington: Government Printing Office, 1904), p. 187. Cf. also p. 193.

12. Commons, "American Shoemakers," pp. 60, 68, 74.

13. Commons, *History of Labour*, v. I, pp. 67–68, 104. In attempting to draw a line between the boss contractor and the pieceworker whom he employed, Saposs sought to distinguish between "contract work" and piece work. His effort was not conspicuously successful. The reader will recall that it was not uncommon for journeymen piece workers to hire helpers—and the former were frequently good union members.

the truly significant consequence of the extension of markets, therefore, is not the succession of "classes" and "stages," so much as the forces of specialization and dilution. The debt which Commons acknowledged to Schmoller and Bücher was of much less consequence than his debt, unacknowledged, to Adam Smith.

Ironically, Commons denies significance to the one "stage" which the reader might well regard as strategic. This is the "retail shop" stage in which distinct classes of employers and employees first arose. Commons does not attribute great importance to this development, so far as the development of trade unionism is concerned, for two reasons. In the first place, the merchant-master's local monopoly allegedly made it possible for him to grant wage demands by raising prices. To this it might be objected that local organizations of wage earners did characterize the retail-shop stage and that they did attempt to bargain with employers.

In anticipation of this line of argument, however, Commons presents his second reason for rejecting the retail-shop stage—and, indeed, all local market stages—as the incubators of modern unionism. Trade organizations in all local market stages, he contends,

included, often in the same individual, all of the economic functions of wage-earning, price-fixing, and profit-making. Such was the typical organisation of the guild, whose occasional appearance is noted in our colonial period, and of the charitable and benevolent societies of the early decades of the nineteenth century.[14]

Commons cites the teamsters and musicians of his own day as "so-called trade-unions, supplying a narrow local market. . . ." But surely the phenomenon of employer membership was not confined to organizations "supplying a narrow local market"; such national market unions as the Molders, the Iron and Steel Workers, and the Window Glass Workers legislated extensively on this subject, and there is no evidence that they made more rapid progress in the direction of elimination of the employer relationship within the union than did unions in local market industries. Furthermore, not all local market unions were composed of full-time employers as well as employees; the unions in the printing trades are a case in point, for the foreman printer did not negotiate over conditions of employment.

But the most serious objection to Commons' attempt to classify local market unions as "guilds" is suggested by the fact that these unions—especially those in the building trades—frequently engaged in strikes to reduce hours, to raise wages, or to prevent reductions in wages. If these local unions really did resemble the medieval guild, it is difficult to explain why they should have engaged in strikes against the employers in question. The strike record in the 1820's and 1830's hardly suggests the existence of a community of interest between union member and employer similar to that which

14. Commons, *History of Labour*, v. I, p. 7.

characterized the guild organization. On the contrary, it suggests that the mere existence of monopoly in the local product market (where it in fact occurred) was not a sufficient condition for the payment of wages above equilibrium levels, but that it merely made the payment of such wages more feasible—if unions were on hand to demand them. Commons does not attribute great importance to this development, it will be recalled, because the merchant-master's local monopoly allegedly made it possible for him to grant wage demands by raising prices.

But even where, in Commons' opinion, the theory of the extension of markets can be applied, it falls short of our objective, which is to explain why the American labor movement placed relatively more emphasis upon collective bargaining and relied upon "the method of legislative enactment" to a lesser extent than did other labor movements. Pressure upon wage rates (which was generated by the process described by Commons as "widening of the labour market") might well serve as a plausible explanation of the origin of "the conflict of capital and labor," but Commons does not demonstrate how it could explain American labor's choice of weapons. Commons himself merely claimed that unions were formed to eliminate "competitive menaces . . . through a protective organization or protective legislation."[15]

To explain why protective organization ultimately proved more acceptable than protective legislation, Commons relied upon another line of argument; it is at this point that his analysis of American governing institutions assumes strategic significance. "Our Federal and judicial system of government" operated to make the attainment of legislative protection so difficult that labor turned to collective bargaining. One weapon was chosen because the other was largely inaccessible.

But one can agree that the early political labor movements were destined to frustration without attributing this outcome to the nature and character of American government. It did prove less difficult to secure the enactment of legislative restraints upon wages and hours abroad, and it is true that courts in other countries could not strike down legislation as readily as courts in the United States could. However, state legislatures were induced to pass laws providing for "free education supported by taxes on property, mechanics' liens on property in order to secure the wage-earner as a creditor, prohibition of seizure for debt by the capitalist creditor of the body of the propertyless debtor, followed in the next decade by the actual exemption of wages and tools from execution for the wage-earners' debts."[16] These laws must be distinguished from legislation on wages and hours, but, in the light of such achievements, can we hold that failure to achieve and secure the latter (until relatively late in the history of the American labor movement) by the method of legislation was really due to certain structural peculiarities of American

15. Commons, *Labor and Administration*, p. 261.
16. Commons, *History of Labour*, v. I, p. 12.

government and not to the exercise of some principle of choice by the American community? Suspicion grows when we turn to the negative influence of the American courts: that they overruled the legislative branch in some areas of concern to the labor movement but not in others suggests that the source of labor's frustration in the judicial sphere lay not in the existence of certain unique judicial powers but rather in the principles which governed the manner in which those were exercised.

Moreover, Commons observed that "our Federal and judicial system of government . . . forced it (labor) to acquire by trade union action what in other countries has been granted by legislation," and this is really the crux of the matter. For suppose that the American labor movement had been unable to achieve its objectives by collective bargaining. Would further political activity have been ruled out? Failure to achieve certain objects by political action by no means implied abandonment of the method of legislation; it could plausibly result in the substitution of radical politics for programs of piecemeal reform. It appears, then, that the subordination of political activity to collective bargaining was due to the success of the latter as well as to the failures of the former. But if this is true, we obviously cannot explain the popularity of collective bargaining solely by reference to the unsuitability of political activity, for political activity was unsuitable in part because collective bargaining proved effective.

PERLMAN'S THEORY

Professor Perlman's explanation of American labor's ultimate choice of collective bargaining stresses "the psychology of the laboring man,"[17] although in conjunction with roughly the same environmental factors which Commons had isolated and upon which he had relied exclusively. The essence of unionism, according to Perlman, is "ownership" and extension by the group of the relevant area of "opportunity" and rationing among the membership of available work by union authority. Unionism thus defined involves submission by the membership "to an almost military union discipline," but such submission is "cheerfully" forthcoming because it is a manifestation of "economic pessimism of the manual group," arising from a deep-seated "consciousness of scarcity of opportunity." "Scarcity consciousness,"

17. Selig Perlman, *A Theory of the Labor Movement* (New York: August M. Kelley, 1949), pp. 237, 239, 240, 242. This discussion of the Perlman theory was presented in condensed form in a paper presented by the writer, entitled, "The Growth of the National Union in the United States" (*Proceedings* of the Fifth Annual Meeting of the Industrial Relations Research Association, 1952, Madison, Wis.). It agrees with the contention of Charles A. Gulick and Melvin K. Bers ("Insight and Illusions in Perlman's Theory of the Labor Movement," *Industrial and Labor Relations Review*, v. 6, no. 4, July 1953, pp. 511–531) that Perlman's argument postulates a unique working-class psychology but, save in some places which will be noted below, the two investigations follow considerably different paths.

in turn, is produced by the interaction between a set of psychological propensities peculiar to the manualist personality and a particular type of economic environment. Concerning the first, Perlman writes:

The typical manualist is aware of his lack of native capacity for availing himself of economic opportunities as they lie amidst the complex and ever shifting situations of modern business. He knows himself neither for a born taker of risks nor for the possessor of a sufficiently agile mind ever to feel at home in the midst of the uncertain game of competitive business.

Awareness of these limitations will produce consciousness of scarcity, economic pessimism, and ultimate amenity to union discipline, but only if the worker is also convinced that his economic horizons are restricted either by institutional or "natural" barriers, which include a shortage of land and an increase in population.

Before we investigate these interesting propositions, it might be well to indicate the type of evidence which Perlman adduces in their support. In general, it appears that support for the proposition that the proper type of environment is essential to the dominance of trade unionism is claimed to emerge from a comparison of labor and other group "movements" in Russia, Germany, Britain, and the United States. The nature of unionism itself, however, is inferred from an analysis of certain union rules and policies, and from a comparison between the latter and certain practices of medieval guilds, on the one hand, and of modern businessmen, on the other.

Can we agree that group ownership and expansion of the area of economic "opportunity" are primary objectives of the trade union? Our discussion of jurisdiction emphasized the importance of job control; the nineteenth-century union sought to reserve to its members the exclusive right to perform all jobs which knowledge of their craft enabled them to perform. This implied the exclusion of noncraftsmen, or "specialists," as well as the inclusion of all relevant jobs within the jurisdiction; Perlman speaks of "the power to keep out undesirables." Less frequently, it sought actively to enlarge this sphere of opportunity by holding down the number of qualified craftsmen through restrictive apprenticeship regulations, but the relatively less frequent occurrence of this type of regulation was due primarily to lack of opportunity rather than to any inherent reluctance to restrict numbers.[18]

It is likewise true that many unions sought to increase the total number of jobs within their jurisdiction. However, this type of activity did not necessarily increase the number of jobs available to the members of the original group exclusively; for unions frequently sought to include in their member-

18. Perlman cites the apprenticeship regulations of the International Typographical Union; but this national union did not—and could not—restrict the supply of apprentices. The apprenticeship regulations in question were designed primarily to ensure versatility and competence. See *Theory of the Labor Movement,* pp. 241, n. 2; 243; 269; 270.

ship the holders of the "new" jobs which they attempted to add to their jurisdiction. Yet this type of practice, which did not increase the number of jobs reserved for the original members could be just as valuable to them as policies which contemplated extending the job jurisdiction without increasing membership. Inclusion as well as exclusion of persons could maintain or increase "relative negotiating strength"; indeed, inclusion of all qualified workers was essential to the preservation of economic jurisdiction, whereas exclusion was not. In this context it might be noted that Professor Perlman cites the closed shop as an institution designed "as much . . . to 'conserve' the jobs as it is to make the bargaining solidarity with the employer treason-proof." It might well be maintained, on the other hand, that the closed shop was primarily designed to force qualified nonunionists into the fold in the interest of the faithful flock, and was therefore a policy of inclusion rather than one of exclusion; unions typically desired not the death of the sinner but only that he turn unto them—and unions suffered considerably at the hands of the judges for this worthy objective. But if the foregoing is correct and if unions which annexed new job territories also offered citizenship to the squatters already on the premises, it would appear that the object of jurisdictional policy—whether or not it involved increasing the number of jobs available to a given number of members—was not to maintain or increase the number of available jobs so much as it was to maintain or increase "relative negotiating strength." "Ownership" of, or control over the appropriate job territory was a means to that end; expansion of the area actually under control occurred only when it was essential to the same purpose. That job expansion occurred frequently is not denied at all; what is denied is that it proceeded from any "job expansion motive."

Can we accept Professor Perlman's interpretation of another union activity, the rationing of jobs, the importance of which he emphasizes together with that of job control and expansion? According to Perlman, this "communism of opportunity" emerged because the "economic opportunity" communized was "limited" in the sense that "the number of jobs available . . . (was) almost always fewer than the number of job seekers." To Professor Perlman, job rationing furnishes evidence of "scarcity consciousness," which in turn implies "economic pessimism of the manual group."

One might wonder how this alleged excess of supply over demand was in fact produced. If we accept our own conclusion that the union sought to maximize "relative negotiating strength" and that, as a result, it succeeded in raising wages in its jurisdiction above the competitive level, existence of excess supply could be readily understood. As we observed in our discussion of restriction of output and share-work rules, rationing of work by the union could be explained only as a device to protect the union wage. If wages were allowed to reach competitive levels, "rationing" would be unnecessary: some workers would have left the trade rather than remain at the lower wage, and the number of jobs at the lower wage would have increased, so that there would have been enough work in the trade for all who remained to work as hard or as long as they desired to. Thus "communism of opportunity" (rationing) was not consistent with maximization of opportunity, if opportunity for the worker is defined "only as jobs in his own occupation." Maximization of employment, as Professor Dunlop points out, implies acceptance of a wage rate "designated by the intersection of the employment and demand functions."[19]

Job rationing, then, might well have been associated with "scarcity consciousness," but the scarcity of which the worker was conscious might have been induced by the wage policies of the union which rationed out his work opportunities to him. Under such circumstances could consciousness of scarcity have implied "economic pessimism"? The answer depends in part upon whether or not the unionist realized that the scarcity of which he was aware was produced by his own hand—a much debated question in recent times. If he did believe that such a causal relationship existed, then job rationing might well have appeared as the essential means to a desirable end rather than as the least undesirable mode of accommodation to an environment the meagreness of which was regarded as a datum. The latter attitude, on the other hand, might well have proceeded from ignorance of the tie between wage policy and job rationing.

Pessimism might also have resulted, in certain instances, either from observation that the demand for labor of the relevant variety was highly inelastic in fact or from the belief that it was inelastic (the "lump of labor" assumption). In either case, it could be assumed that a reduction in wages, although it might eliminate excess supply and the necessity for work-sharing or restriction of output, could hardly bring cheer to the membership. The latter, according to Perlman, regarded opportunity as restricted to the number of jobs in their own occupation, it will be recalled; according to this criterion, it must be concluded that opportunity could not be greatly expanded for the group as a whole.

But even belief in the lump of labor—whether well-founded or not—did not necessarily imply an attitude of pessimism. It is understandable that the prospect of a slide down a near-vertical demand curve—a decline in price (virtually) unrewarded by an increase in "opportunity"—should induce gloom. But the prospect of a ride uphill—a rise in price unpenalized by a shrinkage in opportunity—should inspire optimism even among the innately cautious. And even if the incline departed from the vertical, would the necessity to ration convert the recipient of a wage increase into a pessimist? More-

19. John T. Dunlop, *Wage Determination under Trade Unions* (New York: Augustus M. Kelley, Inc., 1950 edition), p. 40. See also Ulman, "The Growth of the National Union," and Simon Rottenberg, "Wage Effects in the Theory of the Labor Movement," *The Journal of Political Economy,* v. LXI, August 1953, no. 4, pp. 347–348, especially fn. 8.

over, the apparent necessity to ration work and individual earnings carried compensation in the form of increased leisure. The following demand for shorter hours was made by President Lynch of the Typographers, the union whose practices Perlman cites as evidence to support his thesis; it hardly supports the argument that consciousness of scarcity implies a pessimistic appraisal of one's situation:

We do not want the eight-hour day by reason of charity—or philanthropy. We do not want it in order that our physical or mental well-being may be improved. . . . We want the eight-hour day because we are convinced that it suffices for the work there is to do, the work that is to be done, the demand of society for the product of the press. We propose to sell to the employer eight hours of the twenty-four, and we will do as we please with the remaining sixteen.[20]

Perlman himself inclines to the view that workers whose unions enforced work-sharing rules or restriction of output were aware of the relationship between those rules and the union wage. Thus the "opportunity" of which the unionist was so conscious was opportunity to work at a given wage rate; that is the sense in which the restrictive phrase "only as jobs in his own occupation" must be taken. Consider the following statements:

Free competition becomes a sin against one's fellows, antisocial, like a self-indulgent consumption of the stores of a beleaguered city, *and obviously detrimental to the individual as well.*

In practice the same methods employed in solving the internal problem of a fair apportionment of opportunity among the "legitimate" participants are found also to answer the purpose of securing the largest possible return from the outside classes. . . . When the guild or the trade union applies the "common rule" as "working rules" (or "rules for the occupancy and tenure of opportunity," as we might term them), which abolish or check competition for jobs or for patronage of customers, it creates a solid bargaining front against employer or customer, and at the same time tends to bring about a distribution of the opportunity to earn a livelihood, fair to all. Checking the race for employment opportunity tends to equalize security among the members, and simultaneously safeguards or raises the standard of life, establishes industrial liberty, protects future earning power, and increases leisure.[21]

The above hardly implies an underlying attitude of pessimism. Might such an attitude be inferred from other evidence? It will be recalled that Perlman regarded the "manualist" as temperamentally unable and unwilling to take risks. This would appear to imply that workers would prefer, under all circumstances, occupations the pecuniary rewards for which are small but relatively certain, to occupations entailing a high degree of risk but which offer the possibility of very great gains (provided that the actuarial values of the two choices are equal). Economists would probably agree that low-

20. Tracy, *Typographical Union,* p. 811.
21. Perlman, *Theory of the Labor Movement,* pp. 242, 243. My italics.

income groups would make that choice; on the other hand, they would also add that each extreme would be preferred to those occupations "involving a moderate degree of risk but unlikely to lead to either extreme gains or extreme losses."[22] It is difficult, however, to infer innate preference patterns from casual observation, because workers have not in fact been free to choose among occupations. In the first place, lack of education acted as a bar to many occupations, both risky (certain professions and even many lines of entrepreneurial activity) and relatively secure (civil service, teaching, and so on). Second and more important, the worker in modern economic society has had risk thrust upon him. Undoubtedly he has sought to minimize that risk, but it is questionable whether he was willing consciously to sacrifice money income in order to achieve a greater measure of security.

Indeed the trade union might be regarded as evidence of the worker's unwillingness to accept the inevitability of choice. Certainly union work rules cannot be adduced as evidence to support the view that such a choice was in fact made. Work-sharing and restriction of output cannot be regarded simply as forms of social security; they served as devices to maintain high rates of return and—if we grant the assertion that workers viewed the demand for their services as inelastic—to maintain high rates of income as well.[23] We have observed, however, that such rules were regarded with something less than enthusiasm by the membership, Professor Perlman's assertion of cheerful submission to the contrary notwithstanding, and were accepted largely because certain preferred alternatives could not be achieved. Restriction of entry was one such alternative, but, this proving impractical, makework rules were preferable to sharework at the same wage rate. Makework rules indeed involved a surrender of attainable wage levels for attainable employment opportunity, and they might well be taken to reflect a manualist insistence upon security of employment. But, as we have noted, the essential feature of the makework rule was retention of a wage above the competitive level. Can achievement of security by forcing the employer off his demand curve be regarded as evidence of pessimistic resignation to one's economic fate—or might it not be taken simply to signify insistence upon having one's cake and eating it too ?

But perhaps the strongest objection to the imputation of pessimism might be supported by reference to the work of Barnett who, it will be recalled, called attention to the fact that, once secure bargaining relationships had been established, unions were frequently willing to surrender hard-won work rules for wage increases. It is unfortunate that Perlman should have selected

22. For the best discussion of this problem see Milton Friedman and J. L. Savage, "The Utility Analysis of Choices Involving Risk," *The Journal of Political Economy*, v. LVI, 1948, pp. 279–304.

23. On the possibility of financing the unemployed by out-of-work funds accumulated from dues assessed upon the employed members, see Dunlop, *Wage Determination*, pp. 36–39.

as his only example of modern job-conscious unionism the International Typographical Union which was exceptional in its insistence that "international law" could not be arbitrated. Our discussion of the celebrated regulation of 1902 (chapter 16) suggests that its adoption could be ascribed in part to the necessity and desirability of providing each local with the same minimum bargaining power, which could then be exerted to provide it with whatever level of wages it could negotiate in its own jurisdiction. But it is important to recall that, while the I.T.U. did seek to maximize and underwrite local bargaining strength—in part by refusing to permit local unions to relinquish certain regulations, it did not attempt to bargain over wages on a national basis. Where national collective bargaining did occur, however, national unions were willing to bargain over all terms and conditions of employment; and this implied willingness in principle and in practice to make work rules subject to joint negotiation.

Finally, our own examination of union policies and practices is not inconsistent with the view that the nineteenth-century union sought wherever possible to maximize gains as well as to cut losses. This indeed implied Perlmanian "job consciousness" as well as Webbian "protection" of the "standard rate." Both elements are found in Dunlop's hypotheses; the evidence examined in this part of our study (restricted, it must be repeated, to a past period) is not inconsistent with his "vision" of the union as an aggressive institution, intent upon exploiting the possibilities inherent in whatever situation it must contend with, although it was subject to certain internal restraints which were noted in connection with the discussion of geographic wage policies.

Can we accept the parallel which Professor Perlman has drawn between the medieval guild master and the modern union member—and the conclusion that both exhibited a "common fundamental psychology" which stands in contrast to the psychology of the businessman? The Webbs had denied that the trade union was the lineal descendant of the guild; their case rested in part upon the fact that the guild was a quasi-public institution and therefore the representative of the interests of the consuming public as well as of its own membership.[24] Perlman seeks to meet this objection, first, by voicing his suspicion that some guild regulations, although clothed in the language of public interest, were "designed mainly" to increase the bargaining power of the membership,[25] and second, by drawing a comparison between the economic personalities of the guildsman and the trade unionist rather than between their respective institutions.

Nevertheless he does seek to infer the personality of the individual member from an analysis of the regulations adopted by the institution. But it ap-

24. Sidney and Beatrice Webb, *The History of Trade Unionism* (London: Longmans, Green, 1894), pp. 14–18.
25. Perlman, *Theory of the Labor Movement*, p. 260.

pears that the particular examples of guild regulation which he cites actually tend more to support than to refute the Webbs' view that the guild sought to protect the consumer as well as the producer and thus that it must be distinguished from the trade union. Perlman attempted to equate that class of guild regulations which prohibited cornering the market by engrossing, forestalling, and regrating, and which sought to ration available supplies among the guild's members (for example, the "right of lot," the "stint") with union work-sharing regulations. Now, as we have already observed, the effect (if not the purpose) of work-sharing was to maintain the wage rate above the competitive level; thus the wage-earner group benefited (as Commons implied) at the expense of the consuming public, for higher wages in this context meant higher prices. But the "right of lot" and the prohibitions against cornering the market worked to the advantage of the consumer as well as the small producer. These regulations tended to keep prices down—directly, by preventing competitive bidding for the goods offered by the "foreign" supplier (the "right of lot"), and indirectly, by maintaining the number practicing the craft.[26]

It is not difficult to find other examples of institutions and regulations which trade unions inherited from the guilds but which were intended to protect the consuming public as well as the producing group in medieval times. Specification of a minimum term of apprenticeship and regulation of quality of output served a dual purpose, as did the establishment of "just" prices. The necessity to protect the consumer arose from the fact that the relatively isolated local market in the Middle Ages was typically too small to support competitive industries, although the optimum size of the producing unit in a handicraft economy was quite small.[27] (The situation was somewhat analogous to the small village which can "support" no more than one tailor or watchmaker.) Thus, while the alternative to trade unionism in modern times was competitive wages and lower prices, the alternative to guild regulation was not competition but a more thorough exploitation of a monopoly position. Nor must the fact that, in late medieval times, guild regulations were either breached or utilized to strengthen the monopoly power which they had been designed to curb, lead one to ignore the nature of their origin and their reason for being. As Lipson says, "We are apt, in truth, to see everywhere privileges where the men of the thirteenth and fourteenth centuries saw only burdens."

To the extent that medieval Europe was a success, the burdens were

26. Lipson cites an instance of engrossing in order to raise price: E. Lipson, *An Introduction to the Economic History of England* (London: A. and C. Black, 1920), v. I, p. 318.

27. Perlman would appear not to accept this view (p. 261), but it is supported by impressive authority. See Lipson, *Economic History*, pp. 288–289, 294, 296–297, 302, 315, 326, 346, and *passim;* R. H. Tawney, *Religion and the Rise of Capitalism* (New York: Harcourt, Brace, 1926), Ch. I, especially p. 38.

borne, if not willingly, at least in recognition of the existence of certain religious and ethical imperatives and in the belief that the latter should super-
sede and inhibit what Tawney dubbed the "acquisitive appetites." The just
price, while higher than a subsistence wage, was lower than the monopolist's
return; it was supposed to yield a level of income ethically appropriate to the
craftsman's calling. Of course it was not to be expected that the medieval inflationary gap would be bridged completely by spiritual reward—hence the
imposition of legal sanctions by the municipality—but the notion that a given
class of workers was entitled to some specified level of real income survived
the advent of capitalism and emerged as an important characteristic of
British unionism in its early period and, it can be argued, in more mature
phases as well.

Down through the eighteenth century, British unions subscribed to what
the Webbs termed the "Doctrine of Vested Interests," by which they meant
"the assumption that the wages and other conditions of employment hitherto
enjoyed by any section of workmen ought under no circumstances to be
interfered with for the worse."[28] Their programs were characterized by opposition to technological change and by insistence that money wages vary in
direct proportion with changes in the cost of living. Now, in the setting of
the Industrial Revolution, adherence to the "Doctrine of Vested Interests"
might well have infected the sturdiest manualist with a severe enough case
of "economic pessimism." Yet it is an interesting fact that the eighteenth-
century British unionist sought relief from a worsening of his customary
standards not from "economism," or collective bargaining, but from the
"Method of Legislative Enactment," or political activity. When the ancient
guild regulations which had protected their standards in the past ceased to be
operative, the unions petitioned Parliament to enforce them. "In this respect,
and practically in this respect only, do we find any trace of the guild in the
Trade Union."[29]

But Perlman appears to find the counterpart to modern unionism not in
the economic fatalism which was commended to the guildsman by lay and
religious authority but in the well-documented tendency of the guild authorities to backslide by "abusing" the guild regulations. Since, then, both guild
and union employed a similar set of regulations in their own interest, Perlman draws a parallel between guild practice and collective bargaining. And
since he concluded (erroneously) that the guild regulations constituted a defensive reaction to a hostile environment by a group whose bargaining
strength was initially weak, he finds evidence to support the "consciousness
of scarcity" theory of modern unionism.

Collective bargaining characterized that period in the history of British
unionism which followed the failure of early political action and the emerg-

28. Sidney and Beatrice Webb, *Industrial Democracy* (London: Longmans, Green,
second edition, 1911), pp. 562–575. See also pp. 247–250, 596.
29. The Webbs, *The History of Trade Unionism*, p. 20.

ence of new groups of workers who had inherited no traditional standards to support by the "method of legal enforcement." But the new nineteenth-century union engaged in collective bargaining not merely to maintain real wage levels but to advance them; whereas, under the Doctrine of Vested Interests, unions sought to tie money wages to the cost of living, under the Doctrine of Supply and Demand, they sought to tie money wages to product price (the "sliding scale") and profits and, in general, to advance them whenever they could. And, finally, where "Supply and Demand" failed to assure certain groups—for example, the unskilled—of the prospects of security or advancement, unions turned once again to the state to establish by law certain minimum terms of employment, unrelated to their bargaining strength; the Webbs termed this the "Doctrine of the Living Wage." [30]

Thus we return from this brief excursion into British history with the following conclusions: (1) that any similarity between the guildsman and the unionist cannot be inferred from knowledge of their governing regulations alone; (2) that, insofar as the early unionist did resemble the guild master, he accepted and expected no more and no less than a certain customary real income; (3) that the attempt to secure that customary level of income in the eighteenth century was associated with political activity rather than "economism"—hence "pessimism" was not invariably accompanied by collective bargaining; (4) that, on the other hand, the method of collective bargaining was resorted to primarily when the unionist tended to insist upon improving as well as merely maintaining his standard of life; and, finally (5) that if a parallel be drawn between the modern union member and the guildsman of the period of decline of medieval society, it will be recalled that the latter was motivated by a desire to advance his well-being by a more thorough exploitation of his monopoly position than the old laws would allow. He sought, in other words, to create scarcity. Was he, then, a Perlman Pessimist? And if he was not, was his modern brother a Pessimist? Consider the following passage at arms between Samuel Gompers and Morris Hillquit, the noted Socialist attorney, before the Commission on Industrial Relations:

Mr. Gompers (Interrupting): Just a moment. I have not stipulated $4.00 a day or $8.00 a day or any number of dollars a day or 8 hours a day or 7 hours a day or any number of hours a day. The aim is to secure the best conditions obtainable for the workers.

Mr. Hillquit: Yes; and when these conditions are obtained—

Mr. Gompers (Interrupting): Why, then we want better—

Mr. Hillquit (Continuing): You will still strive for better?

Mr. Gompers: Yes.

Mr. Hillquit: Now, my question is, will this effort on the part of organized labor ever stop before the workers receive the full reward for their labor?

Mr. Gompers: It won't stop at all at any particular point, whether it be that towards which you have just stated, or anything else. The working people will

30. *Industrial Democracy*, pp. 575–576, 586–597.

never stop in their effort to obtain a better life for themselves, and for their wives and for their children and for humanity.

Mr. Hillquit: Then the object of the organized workmen is to obtain complete social justice for themselves and for their wives and for their children?

Mr. Gompers: It is the effort to obtain a better life every day.

Mr. Hillquit: Every day, and always—

Mr. Gompers (Interrupting): Every day. That does not limit it.

Mr. Hillquit: Until such time—

Mr. Gompers (Interrupting): Not until any time.

Mr. Hillquit: In other words—

Mr. Gompers (Interrupting): In other words, we go farther than you. (Laughter and applause in the audience.) You have an end; we have not.[31]

Later, during his summary and rebuttal, Gompers added,

I would not want any man to believe that our movement is satisfied. There is not anything satisfying in what we have accomplished. It is gratifying but simply whets our appetite for better and better and still better things.

Although both Perlman and Gompers stand together in their advocacy of "pure and simple" unionism, there is a difference between the defensive, pessimistic brand described by the former and the aggressive, optimistic variety for which Gompers testified. Perlman, to be sure, does state that trade unionism sought "an enlarged opportunity measured in income, security, and liberty in the shop and industry,"[32] but it would appear from the passages quoted above that such enlargement, since it resulted in part from prior attempts to ration scarce opportunity, was a by-product, rather than a prime objective of what he held to be the most distinctive and typical economic activity in which unions engaged. In any event, the case for "economic pessimism" as the mainspring of unionism is hardly strengthened by acknowledging the importance of the aggressive and optimistic characteristics of American unions. We have observed that, in Britain, it was the essentially pessimistic adherent to the doctrine of vested interests who espoused political methods; the supply and demand, or "pure and simple" unionist, was not content with merely holding his own in a hostile environment. Gompers, directly and by implication, testified to the existence of the same parallels in outlook and method in this country. If, then, political activity could be associated with "economic pessimism," and bargaining with optimism, it is not possible to explain the choice of the latter method with reference to an underlying attitude of pessimism.

The foregoing would not deny that economic pessimists could and did form unions for the purpose of collective bargaining. In this connection the distinction which Professor Perlman draws between the personalities of the

31. U. S. Commission on Industrial Relations, *Final Report and Testimony* (Washington: Government Printing Office, 1916), v. II, pp. 1529, 1577.

32. Perlman, *Theory of the Labor Movement,* pp. 5, 6. See also pp. 9, 131, and 197.

union (and guild) member, on the one hand, and the businessman, on the other, is of great interest. It cannot, however, be accepted without reservation. When Perlman tells us that businessmen were invariably reluctant to form and join output cartels because they possessed an attribute which the author terms "abundance consciousness," we recall Adam Smith's celebrated distrust of the gregarious propensities of entrepreneurs.[33] And when, on the other hand, Professor Perlman contrasts that "abundance consciousness" with "the manualist's willingness, nay even burning zeal as shown during strikes, literally to sacrifice his own interest for the good of his group as a whole,"[34] we wonder why there was such great opposition to work-sharing and restriction of output among union members—and such persistent violation of guild restrictions (including the right of lot) in the late Middle Ages.[35]

Nevertheless, there were times when a spirit of venture which animated some entrepreneurs stood out in sharp contrast to the persistent tendency on the part of other groups—including the remainder of the business community as well as the manualists—to seek security with profit. For while the manualist might have had much in common with the merchant of Adam Smith's acquaintance, neither was in the same class as Schumpeter's "innovator" who was "a born taker of risks" and "the possessor of a sufficiently agile mind . . . to feel at home in the midst of the uncertain game of competitive business." In fact the innovator himself contributed greatly to the uncertainty of the game by introducing new products or new techniques which threatened to outflank the prepared positions—"rings," "pools," acquired skills, or union jurisdictions—which had been erected by the ungifted who, denied the rent of ability, pursued monopoly returns after their own fashion. Now, confronted with competition of this variety, the "average" businessman might follow the leader by emulating the innovator; but for the manualist whose skill was threatened with obsolescence that alternative was not available. Under such circumsances, a diagnosis of economic pessimism might indeed be supported by the evidence at hand.

Although Perlman's analysis runs mainly in terms of attitudes and psychological propensities, reference to environmental conditions as determinants of action are not lacking. The businessman is set apart from the manualist because the former alone is a "born taker of risks," but Perlman asserts that

His individualism shows up clearest during periods of great economic expansion. When markets are becoming rapidly extended and technology revolutionized; in other words, when opportunity is expanding by leaps and bounds, then his competitiveness approaches the ruthlessness of a Darwinian struggle for existence.

33. See also Gulick and Bers, "Perlman's Theory," pp. 522-524.
34. Perlman, *Theory of the Labor Movement*, pp. 244-245.
35. Lipson, *Economic History*, p. 244.

At this point Perlman's analysis can be reconciled with Commons' theory. Opportunity for the businessman is defined with respect to extension of markets (and the state of technology); extension of markets and revolutions in technology mean expanding opportunity, including the prospect of rewards greater than the individual would obtain if he continued merely to draw his ration under the terms of some gentleman's agreement. But opportunity for the manualist is defined "only as jobs in his own occupation," and it is apparent that the same dynamic conditions which increased the businessman's (the innovator's) opportunity could decree shrinking opportunity for the manualist. In other words, conditions which implied an excess of demand over supply at going prices for the Schumpeterian entrepreneur could also imply an excess of supply over demand at going wages for the craft worker.

Excess supply could thus be produced under two different sets of circumstances: first, under given conditions of demand, by raising the wage rate above the equilibrium level; and second, following a downward shift in demand, by maintaining the wage rate at the old equilibrium level. Both situations were characterized by monopoly, but, as Tawney observed in his discussion of medieval institutions, "There are, however, monopolists and monopolists." Certainly the "scarcity consciousness" of the bottle blower or the custom shoemaker whose traditional "livelihood" (i.e., "opportunity") was threatened by economic innovation reflected an outlook which differed from that of the building craftsman exploiting a local monopoly. The former attitude might well be described as "economic pessimism," but pessimism could not have been inferred solely from an examination of the practices adopted by the union which was threatened by economic change, for the same practices were adopted by the union which was cheerfully exploring the potentialities inherent in a static situation. The extent, then, to which "economic pessimism" was in fact significant as a causal force in the development of trade unionism in this country cannot be ascertained without reference to the American economic environment.

Thus, as we observed, Perlman joined forces with Commons. But Perlman, although concurring in the historical analysis presented by Commons (to which he himself had of course contributed), supplemented Commons' discussion at several points. These addenda were necessary in part because Perlman, writing in the 1920's, broadened the scope of his investigation. Like Commons, Perlman sought to explain the rise of collective bargaining and its ascendancy within the American labor movement over other forms of activity; but Perlman also asserted, with good reason, that, "The over-shadowing problem of the American labor movement has always been the problem of staying organized."[36] Accordingly, he apparently attempted to explain at

36. Perlman, *Theory of the Labor Movement*, p. 162; also p. 154. For the following discussion refer to pages 8, 155–162, 166–169, 192–198, 207–219.

once the rise of business unionism and its failure to develop into a stable institution.

With the first end in view, Perlman accepted Commons' argument that the existence of the Western frontier stimulated political activity in the labor movement and retarded the development of unionism. Indeed, he wove the Turner doctrine into his own theory by claiming that the existence of the frontier instilled in American manualists the same "abundance consciousness" which allegedly animated American businessmen; it will be noted that the worker, like the innovator, did not measure opportunity in terms of available jobs in his own occupation. The latter definition was not adopted until the frontier had disappeared:

Unionism . . . first became a stabilized movement in America only when the abundance consciousness of the pioneer days had been replaced in the mind of labor by a scarcity consciousness—the consciousness of job scarcity.

But this frontier theory hardly explains the failure of trade unionism to develop into a "stabilized movement" after the frontier had disappeared. Accordingly, Perlman observes elsewhere that "in a sense, the opportunity of the 'West' has never ceased." The worker could seek to better himself by changing occupations, by moving into new and still developing areas, or by taking advantage of free public education to elevate himself into the ranks of the self-employed. As long as opportunity was not defined in terms of one's present occupation, the incentive to form trade unions must remain weak.

It also followed that the incentive to engage in political activity would remain weak in the presence of such alleged opportunity. Thus, while agreeing with Commons that the peculiar nature of the governing institutions, as well as the two-party system, in the United States constituted insuperable barriers to political development, Perlman also observes that the "free gift of the ballot" removed what in other countries had operated as a powerful incentive to support radical political movements. And wherever the political incentive persisted, it would find its outlet in "anti-monopoly" rather than in radicalism, since the former could be interpreted as evidence of a strongly-held conviction that the barriers to opportunity could be removed without drastic institutional change. In particular, "anti-monopoly" did not strike at the institution of private property, and Perlman emphasized the extraordinary devotion to private property as a factor inhibiting both radical political activity and trade unionism in this country.

Perlman's preoccupation with the uncertain position of the trade union in the American community at large, as contrasted with its success within the labor movement, apparently led him largely to ignore, in *A Theory of the Labor Movement*, Commons' extension-of-markets thesis, although, as we have suggested, the phenomenon to which Commons directed our attention could produce precisely the type of "scarcity consciousness" and "economic pessimism" which Perlman had in mind. Instead of dwelling upon the uncertainty and the downward pressure upon the wage rate which economic change could produce and which induced workers to form unions, Perlman emphasized the "welfare capitalism" of the prosperous twenties, which was characterized by the promise of job security, rising real wage rates, and declining union membership. The latter was ascribed to "the dwindling in American labor of a scarcity consciousness and of the feeling of solidarity that follows from such consciousness."

But if "the opportunity of the 'West' . . . never ceased," could "scarcity consciousness" have developed to the point from which it later allegedly dwindled? Since Perlman makes "scarcity consciousness" a prerequisite to unionism, he is in danger of explaining the rise of unionism with reference to the presence of "scarcity consciousness" and the weakness of unionism with reference to the absence of "scarcity consciousness." It is possible, of course, to hold that, with the passing of the frontier, scarcity consciousness became strong enough to account for the emergence of unionism as a more stable institution but not strong enough to enable it to grow into the American institutional fabric more vigorously than it did. Perlman, however, apparently relies upon the phenomenon of immigration (especially German immigration) in accounting for the rise of the modern trade-union movement. While agreeing with Commons that the immigrants constituted a serious "competitive menace" to established unions, Perlman nevertheless credited them with introducing into this country the elements of cohesiveness (which they preserved from their Socialist heritage) and job consciousness which were sadly lacking in the native antimonopolists. If, then, the first champions of stable unionism were found in the ranks of the immigrants and if the latter were denied access to the same range of opportunities which were available to the other members of the community, unionism could be regarded as a "foreign" institution in more than one sense of the word, and its failure to flourish in the American environment should, of course, occasion no surprise.

But when Perlman passed from his historical analysis to an examination of union work rules in order to discover therein "labor's own 'home grown' ideology," he chose as his only subject the International Typographical Union, which institution obviously had not been founded by German immigrants, which antedated the "closing of the frontier" by four decades, but which nevertheless allegedly served as a repository of all the union virtues.[37] One must conclude that Perlman's immigrant argument, like Commons'

---

37. "We are consequently entitled to look to the 'working rules' of the printers' union, since they represent a hundred years' uninterrupted development, for safe guidance as to 'what is on the worker's mind'; at least as to what is on the mind of the American mechanic." (pp. 262–263.)

frontier argument, is of little help in explaining the nature and origin of unionism in the pre-Civil War period which, according to Perlman, resembled unionism of the later Gompers and Strasser variety in most important respects.[38]

Thus it appears that Perlman's historical analysis of the American labor movement (although studded with remarkable evidences of the author's imaginative insight—in particular, the relationship traced between Marxian Socialism and job-conscious unionism) succeeds to no greater extent than his analysis of union work rules in inferring the existence of "economic pessimism" and "scarcity consciousness" and in establishing the proposition that business unionism—invariably and alone—was the product of such a group state of mind. Observing the coincidence of a rapidly expanding economy and a weak union movement, Perlman—unlike Commons—inferred that an inverse relationship existed between the availability of economic "opportunity" and the strength of business unionism. While it was a fact that American unionism appeared unable to stand the prosperity of the twenties, it was equally true that unionism flourished in some trades in the rapidly expanding economy of the pre-Civil War era. And while conditions (for example, technical change) conducive to "economic pessimism" did stimulate the rise of "job conscious" unionism, this was not always the case.

It is reasonable to conclude from Perlman's own account of the Russian and British labor movements that "job conscious" unionism found that an economic and legal environment characterized by the lack of opportunity for economic betterment was as unrewarding as the existence of conditions which were strongly conducive to "abundance consciousness." Thus, according to the author, the failure of "job conscious" unionism to win ascendancy in the Russian labor movement was due to governmental suppression, on the one hand, and to "a rapidly shrinking real wage," on the other. Furthermore, it might be fairly inferred from Perlman's account of the British labor movement that the triumph in that country of Socialism over the "old unionism" (the so-called "New Model"), despite the development of a relatively favorable legal environment, was not unrelated to the deterioration in Britain's economic situation. "No longer could compensation of the laboring class and general labor standards repeat the steady climb as in the period between the fifties and the nineties." In this case it seemed that Socialism, not business unionism, was the product of economic pessimism. For the latter to flourish it was necessary, Perlman claimed elsewhere, "that prospects (were) not wholly hopeless."[39] Thus the reader might gather the

---

38. Perlman (p. 205) denies any great significance to the benefit features which were championed by Gompers and Strasser and were regarded in many quarters at the time as one of the distinguishing characteristics of the "new unionism." See Samuel Gompers, *Seventy Years of Life and Labor* (New York: E. P. Dutton, 1943 edition), pp. 167ff.

39. Perlman, *Theory of the Labor Movement,* pp. 41–49, 146.

impression that the environment most conducive to the growth of collective bargaining and to its supremacy within the labor movement was characterized by some optimum admixture of elements making for enough dissatisfaction to generate labor movement activity and, at the same time, for enough confidence in the potentialities of the economic situation to ensure that such activity would take the form of collective bargaining and not radical politics or, perhaps, syndicalism. In short, the most desirable "manualist" state of mind, from the Gompersian viewpoint, could well have been described by a Yale football coach who announced his intention of losing just enough games "to keep the alumni sullen but not mutinous."

AN ALTERNATIVE HYPOTHESIS

These conditions set forth above were, on the whole, well satisfied in the United States, where the labor movement relied, to a unique degree, upon the method of collective bargaining. The American economy was unusual in that it was characterized by a low ratio of labor to natural resources, by a large and rapidly growing population within an extensive and protected free trading area, and by a business community which harbored a relatively high proportion of individualists bent on exploiting to the full their favorable economic environment. We have already discussed the restraints which these factors directly and indirectly imposed upon the American labor movement —how the dynamic processes of economic growth dissolved craft jurisdictions and made it difficult to form and maintain unions, and how the geographic extension of markets decreed that trade unions, to be successful, become national unions. These and other phenomena examined in this study could be rationalized on the assumption that the American labor movement placed primary emphasis upon collective bargaining (an assumption generally regarded as substantiated by ample historical evidence). In these concluding pages, we shall attempt briefly to sketch the motivating, as distinct from the restraining, influence of the American economic environment and to establish a relationship between that environment and American labor's reliance upon "economism."

The combination of a large and rapidly extending market area and a relative shortage of labor tended, in conjunction with the spirit of enterprise, to induce a high rate of economic growth, which included a high rate of growth in real and money wage incomes and a relatively high level of wage income. These factors also tended both to discourage reliance upon the method of legislative enactment and to stimulate emphasis upon collective bargaining.

Political activity was discouraged as a result of the early abandonment of medieval-mercantilist institutions in the New World; the tradition of government support of a "just" wage, which played such an important role in the shaping of labor movements elsewhere, was virtually nonexistent here.

The abandonment of such regulations—or at least those which were intended to regulate the employment of labor—was due in large part to the greater scarcity of labor in the American Colonies, and, later, Republic. The American settlers imitated the British in decreeing compulsory labor for ablebodied persons; moreover, some colonies obliged regularly employed artificers and handicraftsmen to work on the farms during harvest time.[40] In addition, maximum wages were established by law in various occupations (just as maximum prices were decreed for certain commodities); and refusal to work at statutory rates was prohibited. But the colonies were also making vigorous efforts to encourage the immigration of skilled workers from England, and they soon discovered that they were obliged to choose between a shortage of labor at the legal wage rates and an increased supply of labor. American employers and consumers were not long in making their decision: skilled foreign artisans were hired at wages sufficient to induce them to migrate, although those wages frequently exceeded the statutory maxima; they were even exempted from taxation for a specified number of years and offered land grants or leases; and they were exempted from obligatory labor on the farms in many instances.

Not all legal restraints were removed, however; both immigrant and apprentice labor were held to the terms of their contracts. In both cases the worker was obliged to serve out his period of indenture; this was necessary in order to secure the employer's investment in either the transatlantic passage or the training of the worker involved. Yet competitive bidding for labor resulted in frequent violation of contracts which specified terms of service and in the early legal emancipation of the worker. Moreover, it must be recalled that both apprentice and immigrant received a *quid pro quo:* in return for binding himself over to his employer for a stated (not an indefinite) term, the former was guaranteed training in the trade and the latter was provided with passage to the New World. To the ordinary run of worker who could not benefit from such consideration, this country provided early *de jure* liberation from ties to the employer in the form of the abolition of imprisonment for debt and legislation exempting wages from attachment and execution for debt. While the employee could still be sued for damages and while, as we have observed elsewhere, ingenious employers could find other ways of obliging workers to work longer than they desired to at a given wage, the importance of these early legal ameliorations must not be underrated. Britain, in contrast, enacted a Master and Servant Act (1824) which reinforced the Statute of Artificers and Apprentices of 1563 and subsequent laws and made workers liable to summary arrest and imprisonment for breach of contract and for other causes. Not until 1867 were these

40. Richard B. Morris, *Government and Labor in Early America* (New York: Columbia University Press, 1946), pp. 3ff, 18ff, 22–32, 55ff, 64, 85. Also, "High Wages in Colonial America," *Monthly Labor Review,* v. 28, no. 1, January 1929, pp. 8–13.

provisions modified; not until 1875 did the labor agreement become an entirely civil contract.

In part, these early legal gains resulted from the political fruits of American labor's scarcity, since such scarcity, combined with the individualist temper of the farmer and the employer, facilitated the extension of freedom to the wage-earning sector of the community. Contemporary observers noted that the social position of the American worker was superior to that of his British brother; in a report on colonial town meetings, the American Board of Customs Commissioners wrote, "At these meetings, the lowest Mechanicks discuss upon the most important points of government, with the utmost freedom."[41] Social standing was reflected in political status: labor received the suffrage early in our history (in the 1820's). Thus an incentive to radical political activity, which was potent abroad, did not exist in this country; neither Chartism nor Lasallean Socialism was considered necessary to obtain the vote. On the one hand, having received the ballot as part of his political heritage, the American worker could not be persuaded that political democracy was a unique property of socialism or anarchism; on the other, he was not under the delusion (sometimes held abroad) that achievement of the suffrage was not only necessary but virtually sufficient for the transformation of society into an economic and social utopia.

In one respect, however, the situation of the skilled urban wage-earner was perhaps less favorable in America than it was elsewhere: attempts to establish a permanent craft guild system failed in the colonies. This failure was not surprising in view of the fact that, by the sixteenth century, guilds had come to advance the monopolistic interests of their members at the expense of the consuming public whose interest they had originally been designed to serve. The colonial authorities, while quite willing to protect the consumers—who, since they were largely farmers and in the majority, exerted great influence in public affairs—were determined not to buttress the already formidable economic position of the craft workers. The payment of wages in excess of legal maxima was tolerated as the only way in which the supply of labor could be increased; but payment of monopoly wages—in excess of the equilibrium rates—would not serve the same purpose. Hence discouragement of the guilds was quite consistent with abandonment of legal restraints upon the individual sale of labor. The American criterion was well described by Saposs in the following passage from Commons' *History*:

The agricultural interests, being in control, grudgingly granted protection against the inferior worker and his bad wares. The charters of the Boston coopers and shoemakers, like the monopoly grants, were limited in time, and remained valid only as long as the mechanics fulfilled their part without "enhancing the

41. Morris, *Government and Labor in Early America*, p. 45.

prices. . . or wages, whereby either our own people may suffer." The colonial authorities also took pains to protect the inhabitants from abuse of the powers contained in the charter. Determination of disputes, "in case of difficultie," was placed in the hands of the judges of the county, and appeals were allowed to the county court. Unless the farmer-consumer was certain this protection was to his benefit he refused it. Thus in 1668 the petition of the Boston coopers for a renewal of their charter was denied on the ground that the laws had provided for rectifying many of the evils mentioned and, therefore, there was "no reason to determine anything further at present". . . Likewise in 1672 a company of hatters was promised protection "when they shall make as good hats & sell them as cheap as are afforded from other parts." Similarly when two curriers in 1666 prayed that the General Court do not permit tanners and shoemakers to do currying, their petition was rejected, apparently because there were not enough curriers to do that work.[42]

It should also be noted that the early prohibitions against refusal to work for the statutory wage were accompanied by laws against combinations to raise wages.[43] Now the abandonment of the "artificially" low wage was not accompanied by abandonment of the ban on combinations; wages were to be permitted to rise to competitive but not to monopoly levels. Thus, although the conspiracy doctrine was not enforced here as vigorously as it was in Britain, judicial hostility to trade unions in this country was foreshadowed by these early regulations. Where labor was scarce, monopoly devices, whether designed to depress wages below competitive levels and thus create labor shortage or to raise wages above competitive levels—whether by union bargaining or state minima—were strongly discouraged. The doctrine of vested interests could hold little promise for the American labor movement, in which no traditional interests had been vested by the community. At the same time, however, adherence to the doctrine of supply and demand required recourse to political action, but the principal object of such political action was the implementation of collective bargaining and not the establishment of economic rewards and standards by public authority.

But the persistent scarcity of labor and a rapidly growing economy were not only instrumental in discouraging recourse to radical politics and subordinating the method of legislative enactment to the method of collective bargaining; they also directly encouraged the employment of the latter method. In the first place, the scarcity of labor, especially skilled labor, created an incentive for businessmen to substitute other resources for the scarce factor; and the extension of markets created an opportunity for them to do so by permitting specialization and the consequent reduction of the amount of skilled labor entering into each unit of output. The latter had the effect, as Commons implied, of producing a downward pressure on the effort

42. Commons, *History of Labour*, v. I, pp. 47–48.
43. Morris, *Government and Labor in Early America*, p. 21.

rate of wages and doubtless constituted a sufficient cause for the emergence of unions. The same effect was produced by technological innovation, another facet of economic growth which was stimulated by the shortage of labor. In some instances it was undoubtedly the case that specialization and innovation resulted in a reduction of income as well as effort earnings but such instances were probably characterized by fairly complete obsolescence of the crafts involved; and, although the motive to form a union to defend the jurisdiction against the invasion of the machine and the "green hand" (as in the case of the Crispins) might have been strong indeed, the prospects for success were very poor (see Chapter II). Since we are attempting to account for the emergence and growth of unions, it is necessary to seek out conditions which were consistent with the presence of both motive and opportunity. The existence of downward pressure on the effort rate, in conjunction with the prospect of higher wage incomes, could satisfy both of these conditions; moreover it was consistent with the extension of market areas which characterized the growing American economy.

It is also interesting to observe that trade union activity was apparently provoked by attempts to reduce the effort wage in the building trades, an industry which, because it remained largely local in nature, was not subject to changes in technique to the same extent as were other trades, the markets for which were rapidly expanding in the early nineteenth century. The pressure on rates in the building trades appears to have been produced by the seasonal nature of the industry in conjunction with the efforts of the contracting employers to minimize labor costs during the busy season. In his discussion of the first recorded strike in the building trades, conducted by the journeymen carpenters of Philadelphia in 1791, Saposs observed,

It seems that in the short days of the winter the men were paid by the piece but that in summer the masters instituted pay by the day. This incensed the men and they demanded a specific working day from "six o'clock in the morning to six in the evening."[44]

In their reply to the union, the employers observed that wages were tied to selling prices; we might conclude that their contracts with the landowners were concluded sometime before the onset of the building season when labor was seasonally cheap. Conversion from piecework to timework undoubtedly threatened the efficiency and effort rates; this is what the journeymen undoubtedly had in mind when they complained that "wages (which are, and have been for a long time too low) are meanly attempted to be reduced to a still lower ebb, by every means within the power of avarice to invent." Thus the seasonal nature of the building trades was productive of the same irritant—pressure on the "real" price of labor—which was generated as

44. Commons, *History of Labour,* v. I, p. 110. See also pp. 64–65, 69–71.

a concomitant of economic expansion in other industries. Moreover, their reactions appear to have been similar. The cordwainers waited until their employers had secured orders before they made demands upon them; in so doing, their tactics were identical with those followed by the building crafts-men who struck during the summer months. If it is considered necessary to account for the emergence of trade unionism in terms of a defensive reaction against some external "menace," unionism in both local market and geo-graphically competitive industries can be explained with reference to the same type of phenomenon.

But, as we noted in our discussion of Commons, the existence of a threat to the going rate—or of the simple desire to increase that rate by collective action—merely provided an incentive to labor movement activity; it did not ensure that the method emphasized by the labor movement thus brought into existence would be collective bargaining. Perhaps, then, the primary value of a theory which seeks to relate the peculiar nature of the American labor movement to a combination of factors peculiar to the American economy lies in the ability of the latter to explain or be consistent with the success of collective bargaining in this country. For economic growth in con-junction with a relative scarcity of labor tended to produce relatively high and increasing labor incomes; this in turn frequently ensured that when trade unionists experimented (under the type of stimulus described above and others as well) with collective bargaining, it was not found wanting. Shortly before Samuel Gompers expounded his thesis that the true goal of unionism was perpetual improvement, he had inserted in the record of testimony before the Commission on Industrial Relations a report which listed in proud detail the economic gains achieved by the national unions affiliated with the A.F. of L. during the year 1912. "Results" were forthcoming; whether or not they would have been forthcoming as well in the absence of collective bargaining was beside the point. This does not imply that unions always won their demands or even that it was invariably possible for them thoroughly to organize their jurisdictions as a prerequisite to the achievement of bargaining strength; it means only that collective bargaining paid off frequently enough to establish its position of preëminence in the labor movement.[45]

Economic progress, moreover, created some peculiar problems for the American business union and helped to cast it in a distinctive mold. The American worker rapidly became acclimated to a rising standard of living; moreover, he was frequently willing to work harder to secure progress than were workers in most other countries. Thus, not only was the price he re-ceived per unit of effort high by international standards, but his output of effort was high as well. His willingness to work harder for higher rewards—

45. Ulman, " Growth of the National Union," pp. 168–169; Gulick and Bers, "Perl-man's Theory," pp. 528–529.

notwithstanding his insistence that progress be diverted to greater leisure as well as to higher levels of consumption—is illustrated in the testimony before the Industrial Commission of an official of a local potters' union:

Q. When you say "a killing pace," do you mean that the pace that you work at here impairs your strength and shortens your lives?—A. No, I do not know that it does. It seems to me we live on about the average of potters in other countries. But as the custom of the American citizens is to go ahead in everything, we do the same. Imitation counts for a great deal in this country. For instance, if one person gets a bicycle everybody else wants one.[46] You go to work at 7 o'clock in the morning Monday mornings, while in England and Scotland that would be about breakfast time on Monday morning. Then they quit somewhat earlier than we do. As a rule we keep at it 10 hours a day except Saturday, and quit on Saturday at 4.

Q. You can produce more goods in a day than they are in the habit of producing there?—A. Yes.

Q. But you claim you should be entitled to more earnings when you produce more goods?—A. Yes. We get a better price than the workman does over there for his goods. If we did not we would not be here.

Q. That is, you get a better price per piece or per dozen?—A. Per dozen; yes. . . .

Q. Many employers and many representatives of labor unions have testified that the American workman in any industry turns out a greater amount of finished product than the English worker will do, and they even go so far as to say' that is true of the Englishman transplanted to this country; that there is something in the air or the living that induces him to turn out a greater product. I would like to ask you if it has been your observation that that is true, and if true, what you think are the causes that bring it about?—A. It is true; the causes I do not know.

Q. Is it better living—better conditions under which the people work?—A. I will say we live somewhat better than they do in foreign countries. The opportunities present themselves. I do not think that even the child has the opportunity of living in foreign countries as he does here. He has everything in season, and he lives better. It is a necessity that he does or he could not keep this pace up. I have known men to come to this country and start to work, and found the pace so rapid that they have retired and gone back. The very experience of seeing us with our shirts off scared them into hysterics almost.

Q. You think the operative in your line of business will live as long in this country as he will in the other?—A. I think longer. I believe if I had stayed in England I would not have been living.

Q. (By Mr. Litchman.) How large a proportion of the men who come here become naturalized?—A. I claim that 98 per cent do.

46. Professor Duesenberry, to say nothing of a formidable array of sociological authorities, might derive a measure of satisfaction from this unsolicited testimony in behalf of the "demonstration effect." See James S. Duesenberry, *Income, Saving and the Theory of Consumer Behavior* (Cambridge, Mass.: Harvard University, 1949).

Q. You think it is substantially true that they all do?—A. Yes. They make up their minds to go back, some of them, but in all likelihood they turn up again and come back here. For instance, I came in 1868 and went back in 1871 with the determination of never coming to America any more. I did not like the business much and I wished my time of probation was at an end. Being a bound apprentice there I was wishing that the year was out and the end would come so I could go back. When the time did come I was not long in packing up my traps and getting back to England, I tried for two years and three months to adapt myself to the country of my birth, but I could not do so. It was a failure. I came back to America and have stayed here since, perfectly satisfied.[47]

If our witness at all resembled a typical American unionist, it is not difficult to understand why American unionism was, to use Perlman's term, "wage-conscious." Nor is it difficult to appreciate either why American unionists frequently resisted attempts to insure them to limit output and earnings or why they were willing to forego certain restrictive practices in return for higher wages. For it is a fact that American unionists did not seek to restrict individual output as intensively as did their British colleagues. According to the Commissioner of Labor's Report on *Regulation and Restriction of Output,* the makework "motive" was found chiefly among "older unionists, especially immigrants from England and Wales," and

as regards the intensity of restrictions . . . distinguished from their extent, it is evident that such extreme cases have not been found among trade unions in the United States as in Great Britain.[48]

Thus it would appear that guild-like restrictiveness was more characteristic of trade unionism in Britain than in the United States. On the other hand, there was certainly greater emphasis upon legal enactment as an independent method in Britain than in this country, where collective bargaining achieved supremacy within the labor movement. Must we not conclude that restrictive work practices were not the hallmark of collective bargaining after all, or at least that they were not the outstanding characteristic of a trade union movement which was willing to bargain them away when they could obtain substantial economic gains in return?

The high rate of economic progress in this country also bears implications for the "frontier argument" which holds that the trade union achieved stability as an institution only after the great majority of wage earners had become convinced that they had no opportunity to "escape" from their proletarian status into self-employment as a farmer or a businessman. Despite recently accumulated historical data which suggests that such opportunity

47. U. S. Industrial Commission, *Report on the Relations and Conditions of Capital and Labor Employed in Manufactures and General Business* (Washington: Government Printing Office, 1901), v. XIV, pp. 644, 647.

48. Commissioner of Labor, *Regulation of Output,* p. 28.

was never in fact very great, instances of "upward" mobility were probably great enough to account for the "abundance consciousness" of which Perlman wrote. To the extent, therefore, that belief in the frontier once existed and influenced the labor movement in its choice of methods (namely, anti-monopoly politics), the passing of the dream undoubtedly helped to account for the greater stability of trade unionism. But this result should not be taken as evidence of pessimistic resignation to one's fate. That interpretation might better fit the facts elsewhere, where fixed social status appeared to imply, in the short run at least, invariant living standards; where, as a result, doctrines proclaiming the existence of wages funds and iron laws gained credence in all sectors of the community; and where labor movements turned to political programs which in part reflected the conviction that labor incomes could be increased only through redistribution of the national product and in part simply represented a desire to escape from unpleasant and what was regarded as unpromising actuality. The fact that labor in the United States reacted to the close of the frontier by turning away from excursions into political un-reality and by concentrating its energy upon the eminently pragmatic method of collective bargaining, indicates that acceptance of a permanent wage earn-ing status by no means implied the conviction that economic horizons were narrow or limited. The greater American emphasis upon collective bargain-ing, and the type of bargaining which was chosen, may be regarded as a by-product of this community's greater ability to combine permanence of status as wage earner with rapid improvement in standards of consumption.[49]

It should be added that permanence of wage earning status did not imply permanence of social status in the community. The antimonopoly programs, which aroused considerable interest in labor circles while the frontier was still regarded as "open," assumed that the distinction between the rich and the poor was more significant to wage earners than the distinction between employer and employee, although, as we observed, "class distinctions" were lesser in magnitude in the New World than in the Old. Now, on the heels

49. Perlman observed the persistence of economic "opportunity" after the passing of the frontier and ascribed to it much of the instability which was characteistic of Ameri-can unionism. However, he equated opportunity in this instance with the ability to leave jobs for better ones and thus maintained continuity with the older "opportunity" which consisted in the ability to leave jobs for self employment; in both cases, it was im-plied, the rootless worker did not make good union material. This might have well been true in many instances, but our discussion of the traveling member should certainly caution us against accepting this conclusion as universally valid. In any event, the type of "opportunity" referred to in the paragraph above included the ability to secure an increasing return without being obliged to leave one's job, so that the rolling-stone argu-ment would not necessarily apply. If, however, it be held, for the sake of argument, that the dynamic economy might have filled many workers with such contentment as to re-move all stimulus to labor movement activity, including membership in some "business" union, it follows a fortiori that even more would have been induced to quit the arena of radical or utopian politics.

of the disappearing frontier came the "new immigrant," on the one hand, and the industrial or financial titan, on the other; and it might well have appeared that social and economic distinctions were widening and that, if the appropriate remedy for labor no longer could be found in antimonopoly, neither could it be found in collective bargaining. But the economic community which attracted the immigrant and created the robber baron utilized the peculiar talents of both to introduce a regime of mass production. And mass production, as Schumpeter told us, implied a subtle deterioration in the living standards of the rich, even as it enhanced the material position of the wage earner. The closing of the frontier was thus followed in time by a rise in the economic well-being of the wage earners in a relative as well as an absolute sense. It is possible to maintain that the persistence of the underlying environmental factors which we have singled out for special mention were instrumental in bringing it about that the decline of antimonopoly was not succeeded by a particularly luxuriant flowering of socialism.

While we have been stressing the effect of labor's relative scarcity and a high rate of economic growth in discouraging emphasis upon radical political activity and in encouraging recourse to direct bargaining, it must be recalled that these twin factors assume significance only in conjunction with the strong profit motivation and the individualism which characterized the American community. Without the intensity of the businessman's drive to make money and the necessity for him to do so in competition with his fellows, the low proportion of labor to other resources would not have assumed its historic significance in yielding high economic and social returns to labor; nor, in all probability, could such a high rate of economic progress have been achieved at the same time that the area of political freedom was widening. The individualistic and businesslike temper of the wider community, subjected to certain fortuitous economic constraints, ultimately fashioned a labor movement in its own image.

The hypothesis that "business unionism" in America emerged as a reaction and adaptation to these conditions enables us to establish a more direct relationship between the structural development of the national union and its economic policies. The latter reflect adherence to Gompersian "economism"; the most that can be said about the former on a purely *a priori* basis, however, is that it is consistent with that same philosophy. The mere existence of national unionism does not imply the dominance of the method of collective bargaining. The desire to maintain or improve the conditions of employment in a particular trade or industry by the method of legal enactment could result in the formation of national unions, as it did in England; and the method of mutual insurance also served as a nationalizing influence on occasion (the Brotherhood of Locomotive Engineers). In short, concerted action by any method to secure some objective of particular interest to those in some particular line of work might induce the formation of a national union in that trade. Thus evidence in addition to the existence of national unionism is needed in order to determine which (if any) method was dominant in the labor movement involved.

In the case of the American labor movement, neither mutual insurance nor legal enactment could muster the necessary support. The former failed because labor's primary political demands were not usually formulated with reference to the interests of specific industrial groups; thus the spokesmen for legal enactment advocated the primacy, not of national unions, but of local and regional federations cutting across craft lines. As for mutual insurance, this method never proved as popular in America as it did abroad; and we have observed that, on occasions when the demands of insurance ran counter to the interests of bargaining power, it was not the latter which yielded pride of place.

But the hypothesis that the dynamic character of the American economy, in conjunction with the relative scarcity of labor, induced the working class to concentrate upon the method of collective bargaining does fit the facts. On the one hand, this hypothesis is obviously consistent with the rise and later preëminence of national unionism in an economy in which the extension of labor and product markets was carried out in an unusually workman-like manner. On the other hand, it is consistent with the emergence of a body of policies and regulations which were analyzed in this and the preceding chapters; these include policies with respect to jurisdiction over jobs and men, wage differences (occupational, interpersonal, and geographic), the timing of strikes, methods of wage payment, "making work," "sharing work," and, finally, the "arbitrability" of the above and other policies.

Thus we have an hypothesis which fits the data relating to both the internal structural development and the economic outlook of the national union. It may be tested further by confronting it, as we did, with additional phenomena. It was found to be consistent with the failure of medieval and mercantilist institutions to take root in the New World, and thus with the absence of a tradition of vested interests, which in Britain favored emphasis upon legal enactment. It is likewise consistent with the early termination of specific enforcement under the labor contract and with the "free gift of the ballot," both of which acted as disincentives to radical political activity. It is consistent with the emergence of unionism both in geographically expanding industries and in occupations which remained local in nature. It is consistent with labor's difficulty in "staying organized" and also with the fact that disillusionment with the frontier heightened interest in collective bargaining instead of encouraging excursions into radical politics. Thus we may conclude that national unionism in the United States did reflect the primacy of the method of collective bargaining; by confronting the American worker with a unique combination of opportunity, insecurity, and a relatively high standard of living, the developing economy helped to produce the rise of the national trade union.

LOCAL JURISDICTION

EXAMINATION of the jurisdictional practices of affiliated local unions places in perspective some of the policies and objectives of the national unions which were discussed in Chapter 11 above. Specifically, these were: (1) the inclusion in one organization of all of the members of a given craft in the same market area and (2) the exclusion from that organization of all workers who did not practice the craft in question, provided that organization was complete. The first of these objectives bears a family resemblance to the national union's concern with dual unionism; the second concerns the repercussions upon local organization of the membership in a single national union of different occupational groups.

The doctrine of exclusive jurisdiction, which was widely accepted by trade unionists in this country, implied first, that the geographic jurisdiction of a union of workers in a given craft (as defined in Chapter 11) be coexistent with the relevant product and/or labor markets, and, second, that there be but one trade union operating in the combined trade and geographic jurisdictions.

In some unions, the first of these conditions was more or less faithfully satisfied in the determination of the geographic boundaries of their local bodies. Appreciation of the fact that market boundaries did not necessarily coincide with town or city limits was evidenced by the Bricklayers' Union, which allowed each local union to define its own geographic jurisdiction.[1] The Molders at first restricted the jurisdiction of their local unions to the geographic bounds of their respective communities, but later county and provincial (in Canada) jurisdictions and even areas covering "large parts of American states" were reserved to individual locals.[2] In their attempt to en-

1. Nathaniel R. Whitney, *Jurisdiction in American Building-Trades Unions* (Baltimore: Johns Hopkins, 1914), pp. 25–28. In the convention of 1884, a resolution in favor of making the jurisdictional limits of each local identical with the corporate limits of the community in which it was located was voted down. (*Proceedings,* 1884, p. 66.)

2. Frank T. Stockton, *The International Molders Union of North America* (Baltimore: Johns Hopkins, 1921), p. 44.

sure that local union jurisdiction would be coextensive with the local labor market when workers were hired by large construction firms for out-of-town projects (see Chapter 3, pp. 55–56), the Bricklayers went to the logical extreme of making local jurisdiction completely elastic for economic purposes:

It shall be understood that when a firm or contractor secures work outside of a jurisdiction and brings members from a Union to work upon the same, that fact unionizes that work to all intents and purposes the same as if it was within the established boundary. Subordinate Unions should discourage their members from doing such work unless they can enforce Union rules thereon.[3]

Most national unions, however, restricted the territorial boundaries of their locals to the corporate limits of the communities in which they were established.[4] This practice was resorted to by the Printers in order to prevent the jurisdictional squabbles which frequently took place when larger locals objected to the establishment in newly-settled adjacent communities of sister organizations whose lower union standards threatened to undermine their own. The Printers, however, frequently found it expedient to extend local jurisdictions beyond city limits and even to reject applications for charters from groups in the smaller communities. "Such extensions have been made," according to Barnett, "only when the offices in the annexed territory compete actively with those in the territory under the original jurisdiction of the local union."[5] The Stone Cutters set a maximum radius of twenty-five miles to the jurisdiction of their locals, but "despite the constitutional pronouncement, many branches have been granted jurisdiction over a wider range than twenty-five miles." The Wood, Wire, and Metal Lathers ruled that each local's jurisdiction should extend half the distance to the local adjacent to it, but, in order to appease a group of seceding locals in New York City, one local was awarded exclusive jurisdiction for a radius of twenty-five miles about the city, and the others were amalgamated with it. The extent to which rules which set limits to the areas controlled by local unions without regard to market conditions were honored in the breach is, of course, unknown. But even if it is assumed that the practices of the Printers, the Stone Cutters, and the Lathers were exceptional, one should allow for the possibility that, in some cases, market and municipality were in fact coextensive. In such cases, of course, no local union would have been embarrassed economically by an ordinance forbidding it to cross city limits.

A union whose policy it was to establish unitary organizational control over the local market for a particular type of labor should have provided not

3. *Constitution,* 1897, Art. XVI, Sec. 8.

4. Theodore W. Glocker, *The Government of American Trade Unions* (Baltimore: Johns Hopkins, 1913), p. 16.

5. George E. Barnett, *The Printers* (Cambridge, Mass: American Economic Association, 1909), pp. 44–46.

only that the maximum permissible local union boundaries coincided with the geographical area of the market but also that only one local be chartered in each jurisdictional area. The Molders, for example, ruled that there should be "no more than one Union in each department in any locality."[6] The Printers refused to allow members in the book-and-job branch of the industry to break away from local unions to which their colleagues in the newspaper branch belonged.[7]

Other unions, like the Bricklayers and Carpenters, permitted more than one local in the same trade in one locality. In some instances this policy was inspired by the fear that very large locals could be controlled by cliques and machines. It is also possible, since local union representation at conventions was to some extent proportional to membership, that representatives of some of the smaller locals, as well as some of the national officers, sought to prevent the emergence of powerful blocs of delegates from the larger locals. Thus the Carpenters, in 1886, decided that, "When a Local Union has 400 members in good standing, it should form a second union under separate charter."[8] The Bricklayers refused to adopt a similar rule, although they were strongly urged to do so by Secretary O'Dea:

My reasons are these: The experience of the past two years has shown that where large Unions, like those of the late Unions No. 1, of Chicago, with a membership of 4,000, and No. 4, New York, with a membership of 1,500, that it is almost impossible to govern such large bodies of men, locally *or internationally,* so that the rights of all may be respected. Factions or cliques will form, dissensions will arise, and in the efforts of each to obtain supremacy and rule, the inevitable result would be disaster and ruin, damaging alike to the formation and government of *small* Unions. [Italics mine.][9]

Four years later, O'Dea buttressed his appeal to declare a local union membership of five hundred the maximum allowable under international law by pointing out that no meeting hall could seat that number. A ruling clique could perpetuate itself in power by simple expedient of literally packing the hall with its own henchmen; this situation prevailed in a New York local, a portion of whose membership requested authority to secede and form a separate local union.[10]

But secession, if encouraged, could undermine the position of a local

6. *Constitution,* 1876, Art. IX, Sec. 7.

7. George A. Tracy, *History of the Typographical Union* (Indianapolis: International Typographical Union, 1913), pp. 144, 153, and 168; Barnett, *The Printers,* pp. 42–43.

8. *Constitution,* 1886, Art. III. This provision was repealed in 1890.

9. *Proceedings,* 1886, pp. 48–49 (report of the secretary).

10. *Proceedings,* 1890, pp. 46–47 (report of the secretary). The notorious Sam Parks, walking delegate of the Structural Iron Workers in New York City, received necessary parliamentary support by advising his followers to appear early at union meetings. (Glocker, *Government of Unions,* pp. 29–30.)

organization as well as—or perhaps even more readily than—it could discourage the development of despotic political machines. For if disaffected
members of a local union were permitted either to form or to join other organizations in the locality, the local's power to discipline its membership and,
ultimately, to enforce its standard conditions of employment would be curtailed severely. In 1875 two local unions of Bricklayers in Missouri protested
when the international union granted a charter to a third local; they claimed
that the charter members of the new group were men who had been delinquent in the payment of dues to the older organizations. The Judiciary
Committee revoked the charter of the new group, and its action was unanimously approved by the convention of 1876. Discussing this episode six years
later, the international president said,

If disaffected minorities of the subordinate Unions are to be recognized, fostered
and granted Charters to open new Unions, the principle of secession will have
gained a foothold within your organization, and that principle, if tolerated, would
most assuredly eventuate in the total destruction of the whole fabric of government under which you now exist.[11]

Thus the considerations in favor of limiting the size of each local union—
the discouragement of local cliques and of delegate blocs in the national
convention—was opposed by the familiar spectre of dual unionism, the consequences of which could be quite as disruptive at local levels as it was in the
higher national circles. Confronted with this dilemma, even the sagacious
O'Dea developed a mild case of political schizophrenia. In 1886, the year preceding the convention at which the secretary urged that no local union be
allowed to have more than five hundred members, the executive committee
of the eight New York locals reported that their organizations remained in a
demoralized condition after having called an unsuccessful strike two years
earlier. The international president dispatched O'Dea to the troubled area,
and the secretary remedied the situation by effecting a series of consolida-
tions which reduced the number of New York locals by half. Following this
feat of organizational compression, a committee representing the remaining
locals negotiated a closed-shop agreement with the employers and secured
the nine-hour day. "In my opinion," reported O'Dea, "it is the biggest victory
that has EVER been won by labor in New York City."[12]

Amalgamation, however, was not the only alternative to the evils of
dualism. Some unions permitted the establishment of additional locals in a
community, but only with the consent of the established organizations.[13]
Both the Carpenters and the Bricklayers stipulated that the sentiment of the

11. *Proceedings,* 1882, pp. 14–15 (report of the president).
12. *Proceedings,* 1886, pp. 13–22, 41–42.
13. This was adopted by most of the unions in the building trades. (Whitney,
American Building-Trades, p. 30.)

existing locals be ascertained. The former at first provided simply that "New unions shall not be formed in any city without the consent of the union or unions already existing in such city."[14] Later, however, when the Brotherhood urged its affiliated locals to undergo a process of fission once their membership had exceeded four hundred, it facilitated the formation of new locals by granting charters to more than one local union in the same city if those already established therein "offer(ed) no reasonable objection." But the Carpenters abandoned official advocacy of a maximum limit to local union membership in 1886, and ten years later they reverted to their original requirement that no new local union could be chartered without the specific sanction of the established local union or district council of local unions in the locality.

The Bricklayers, on the other hand, progressively facilitated the creation of additional locals. Their original rule provided that the consent of the existing union must be obtained before another group in the locality could be granted a charter. This was interpreted by Secretary Carpenter to mean that, in cases in which more than one local was established in a community, the unanimous consent of all was required; and his interpretation was promptly incorporated in a constitutional amendment. Four years later, a majority of two-thirds of the existing locals was declared sufficient, and still later (in 1897) a new local could be chartered with the assent of only a simple majority of the established unions.[15]

By requiring the consent of preëxisting locals, the national union could be reasonably certain that it would not be obliged to grant charters to groups of delinquent members. At the same time, the curse of bigness could be mitigated by the establishment of more than one local of the same craft in the same locality. It was still necessary, however, to safeguard against the possibility of uncoördinated economic strategy by the several organizations in the same local labor market and, particularly, against the possibility of interlocal competition for membership (through lowering of dues and initiation fees, and so on) or for employer recognition (through mutual undermining of standards of employment). Thus, as early as 1869, the Bricklayers decided that, "Where there are two or more Unions existing, in any city or town, they shall not have the power to scab an employer or employers without the consent of two-thirds of the several Unions, and the yeas and nays shall be taken, and a true record of the same be kept."[16] And the Carpenters, early in their existence, provided that "All the Local Unions in one city must be governed by the same Trade Rules and the same scale of wages."[17]

14. *Constitution,* 1881, Art. VIII, Sec. 2; 1886, Art. III, Sec. 3; 1896, Sec. 46.

15. *Constitution,* 1875, Art. XIII, Sec. 1; *Proceedings,* 1882, pp. 14–16; *Constitution,* 1882, Art. XIII, Sec. 1; 1890, Art. XIII, Sec. 1; 1897, Art. XI, Sec. 1.

16. *Proceedings,* 1869, pp. 105 and 108.

17. *Constitution,* 1886, Art. III, Sec. 3.

Many national unions found it expedient to insist that the different local unions (affiliated with the same national unions) in each local market area form "district" or "joint" councils to impose the requisite uniformity of conditions and to obtain concerted action in seeking to secure (uniform) union standards. The Bricklayers set forth the duties and powers of their "Committees on General Good" more explicitly than did most unions:

Where there are two or more Unions existing in any city, town, or vicinity, each Union shall be required to elect or appoint three (3) delegates, whose duties shall be to meet and establish a uniform rate of wages, initiation fee, and hours of labor, together with rules and regulations under which all can work in harmony. The body thus convened shall be known as a "Committee on General Good," to which shall be referred the construction of all general working laws for such city, town, or vicinity. No Union shall enact a working law without first referring it to the said committee and through it being placed before the several Unions for their consideration. The several working laws constructed through the operations of this committee shall be known as the "working code" of such city, town, or village, and it will be the duty of each Union to provide its members with a copy of such working code. All communications from this committee to any Union represented in it shall be acted upon and the result communicated as soon as possible. Any Union acting in conflict with the legally-expressed wish of the majority of the Unions in any city, town or vicinity, as reported in and from the Committee on General Good, will be liable to discipline by the Executive Board of the National Union. In case of a majority of Unions undertaking to enforce an unjust measure, or one conflicting with the Constitution of the National Union, the subject in dispute shall be referred to the judiciary of the National Union whose decision shall be final, unless reversed by the National Union in convention assembled.[18]

It is apparent that, in order to achieve the objectives spelled out in the "work codes," the local unions were obliged to surrender some elements of autonomy. The degree of sacrifice required varied considerably from union to union, but some curtailment of local discretion was incurred in the following spheres of activity: the initiation of work stoppages, the determination of initiation fees, and control over jobs.

Strikes

It was the custom that no local in a joint council be permitted to call a strike without the authorization of the members of the other locals. Now if each local were given an equal vote in determining whether or not a strike proposed by one of their number should be authorized, the representation of the larger organizations would be less than proportional to their membership, whereas if the voting power of each local were proportionate to their membership, the smaller locals would be placed at a disadvantage. (This, it will be

18. *Constitution*, 1883, Art. XII, Sec. 8.

recalled, is the same issue which the Printers and the "allied crafts" were unable to resolve.) The Carpenters' Brotherhood presumably left the question to local determination, in providing simply that "Where a D. C. exists, it shall adopt rules for government of strikes and lockouts in that District, subject to the approval of the G. S. and G. T."[19]

The Bricklayers, however, experienced considerable difficulty on this account. On one occasion, the walking delegate of one of the New York locals ordered some members of another local to quit a job, although the consent of two-thirds of the other locals in the locality, required by the international constitution, was not secured. Despite the protest of the local whose men were ordered to strike by the walking delegate, the convention held that the strike was legal.[20] The following year, one of the large New York locals complained that "the system of voting in the Unions separately and transmitting the same to the Committee on General Good is not a thorough and proper manner of getting a majority or two-thirds vote, as may be required . . . it is a continual struggle for supremacy with the large and small Unions, and never resulting in a united action, which is necessary to bring about a successful resistance to any imposition imposed on the members by the bosses." They urged consolidation as a solution, referring to the printers and brown stone cutters as examples worthy of emulation.[21] Their proposal was not accepted, but the Bricklayers did amend their constitution so as to require that "a general meeting of all the Unions should be called, and it shall require a two-thirds vote of all voting, to order any strike."[22] Thus the larger unions were given proportional representation in council, and the freedom of the smaller organizations to call strikes—even strikes involving their own members only—was curtailed severely.

Initiation fees

Local unions in the same community which were affiliated with the Bricklayers', Masons' and Plasterers' International Union were ordered to establish a uniform initiation fee. The Carpenters established a similar requirement—and further provided that the same monthly dues be charged by all locals in a district council.[23] The purpose of these regulations was to prevent the different locals in a district from seeking to attract members away from one another through competitive reductions in the price of admission. So fearful of this type of price war was Secretary O'Dea that, when a local in Jersey City, whose initiation fee was twenty-five dollars, refused to honor the traveling card of a neighboring local, O'Dea upheld the Jersey

19. *Constitution*, 1890, Sec. 125.
20. *Proceedings*, 1884, pp. 36 and 73–74.
21. *Proceedings*, 1885, pp. 52–54.
22. *Constitution*, 1885, Art. XII, Sec. 8.
23. *Constitution*, 1888, Art. III, Sec. 3.

City union and directed the issuing local to revoke its traveling card. The secretary acted without any constitutional authority, but he was determined to stop the "underground railroad business."

You cannot help seeing the necessity of such actions. For instance, any bricklayer by paying a few dollars' car-fare, could go to cities where there is a ten-dollar initiation fee, and immediately take out a traveling card back to where he came from.[24]

Control over jobs

That all employed at the trade in a particular locality be members of the union established therein was adopted as a fundamental assumption of trade unionism in this country before the development of national unions (see Chapter 4 above, pp. 73ff.). And although the need for providing employment for traveling unionists without menacing local union standards was in part responsible for the rise of the national union, this fundamental tenet of local unionism remained unchanged after the locals had united themselves into nationwide organizations. For the instrument which was devised to cope with the problem raised by the migrant member was the traveling card; and, since the act of depositing his traveling card with a local union conferred membership in that local upon the traveler, the principle of restriction of local employment to members of the local union remained inviolate, so long as there existed only one local of a given trade in any local market area.

In some localities in which more than one local appeared, however, the traveling card system proved unworkable. This was true whenever the number of jobs in any one local's bailiwick exceeded the number of its members, so that members of locals in other communities (in which the supply of labor in question exceeded employment) in the district worked in the former jurisdiction. If the locals in the regions of excess labor supply issued traveling cards to their members who wished to work in the region of excess demand (as defined above), they would have lost an important segment of their membership and their very existence as independent organizations might have been threatened. It was to their interest that the craftsmen who resided in their communities but who worked elsewhere retain their membership in their home locals and be admitted to work by other local unions upon presentation of their work cards—which indicated only that they were members in good standing of their home locals. The locals in whose jurisdictions these commuters worked, however, favored the traveling-card system, whereby the commuters became members of the local union in the locality in which they worked, and paid their dues to that local, rather than to the local union in the community in which they merely resided. In 1885 the Bricklayers' locals in New York passed a rule requiring that all bricklayers coming into New York City from localities outside the city limits deposit traveling cards and

24. *Proceedings*, 1887, pp. 29–31.

pay dues to the New York locals. The Brooklyn and Jersey City locals protested this action, but O'Dea upheld the New Yorkers:

And yet these men always got the benefit of the work in the City of New York and never gave anything in return for it. The New York Unions complain of this, and, in my opinion their claim is just.[25]

The convention, however, overruled the secretary and passed the following amendment to the constitution:

Where a member of a Subordinate Union can return home from his work at night, from day to day, he need not take out his Traveling Card, when working in the territory of another Union, provided he observes the rules of work governing said other Union . . .[26]

Dispensing with traveling cards throughout the area of a local market was common practice in unions which permitted the establishment of more than one local in the same trade in a single geographic "district." Thus the ancient rule was set aside in these cases: a local union was obliged to allow its members to work on a job with nonmembers.

Certain observations can be made concerning the experience of American trade unionism in local market areas during the period under discussion:

First, In any trade or industry, the degree of competition prevailing in any local market region was probably greater than the degree of competition which prevailed throughout the entire country. In the first place, competition was probably keener in both product and labor markets—in the latter because of the virtual absence of objective and subjective barriers to travel. In the second place, local areas were subject to both types of competition, even in industries which, on a national scale, were considered as consisting of a number of fairly well insulated local markets.

Second, The extent, therefore, to which trade unions required unitary control over local market areas was greater than the extent to which they sought to impose uniformity over national markets.

Third, In order to achieve uniform union standards throughout any local market, some unions required that no more than one local union in the same craft be chartered in the same locality. And in unions which did permit more than one local union in the same market area, the locals in question were usually organized into "joint" or "district" councils to which they surrendered an appreciable portion of their autonomy.[27] To the extent that

25. *Proceedings*, 1885, pp. 18–21.

26. *Constitution*, 1885, Art. XIV, Sec. 1.

27. The United Mine Workers and its predecessors were in reality amalgamations of district unions, and, in some instances, the latter were more important administrative units than the local unions (one of which was usually established in each mine). Thus delegates to national conventions could be elected from districts and divisions, as well as from local unions. (Chris Evans, *History of the United Mine Workers of America* [Indianapolis, 1918], v. I, pp. 42, 141, 200–201, 381, 404, 406–407; v. II, pp. 20, 92, 223, 237–238, 272 and 375, 331, 662.)

action proposed by a local union required the support of a specified majority of the combined membership of all the locals in the council, the largest locals were the most influential in forming the policies which affected them all. This applied most frequently to the calling of strikes, but, in the case of the Carpenters, it applied equally to the uniform by-laws which all locals had to adopt following the endorsement of a majority of all members voting in all the locals in the district.[28]

Fourth, Despite the loss of certain prerogatives, however, it was possible for more than one local union in the same trade to exist and function in the same market area. And if some practices did not result in ceding power to the larger unions proportionate to their numerical strength, others, like the suspension of the system of exchanging traveling cards, worked frequently to the advantage of the smaller locals and helped to preserve their identity. Even the Bricklayers, when they decided (in 1900) to empower their international executive board to "take such steps as it shall deem proper to bring about a consolidation of said Unions" when they were unable to agree upon a "working code," stipulated that the board could intervene in such a local situation only if two-thirds of the members of all the locals concerned voted to invite this intervention.[29]

This last point illustrates the distinction between the purely economic and the organizational aspects of jurisdiction. Economically, it was necessary to establish unitary union control over the entire market in question (labor and/or product). One way to achieve such control was to insist that one and only one union be given jurisdiction over that market area. This is the method by which the national unions in the United States sought to achieve unitary control; they called it "exclusive jurisdiction" and charged it with high ethical and inspirational content. The doctrine of exclusive jurisdiction has come to be regarded as a hallmark of the American labor movement, partly because of the vigor with which it has been championed, but partly, too, because it failed to achieve like eminence in other lands.[30] Without attempting to explain this peculiarity of national unionism in the United States, one might indicate that "dual unionism" was practiced here—and approved by national authority—on the local level at the same time that it was condemned unsparingly in broader circles.

Too close a parallel between national dualism abroad and local dualism at home should not, perhaps, be drawn; for, while national unions in Great Britain (for example) were autonomous organizations, local unions in this country were distinctly "subordinate" to the national organizations with

28. *Constitution*, 1890, Sec. 43.
29. *Constitution*, 1900, Art. XVII, Sec. 5.
30. In Great Britain, for example, "The Trades Union Congress . . . has consistently taken the stand that no union has an exclusive right to organize any class of worker." (U. S. Department of Labor, *Report of the Commission on Industrial Relations in Great Britain*, 1938, p. 8.)

which they were affiliated. It does not necessarily follow, however, that because the national unions possessed sufficient authority to require their locals to surrender some of their powers to district bodies, the latter would not have been organized in the absence of national authority; the Molders provide an example of spontaneous organization of district boards by local unions.[31] To the extent that such district organizations were in fact the products of local coöperation rather than national coercion, a comparison with some of the British federations of national unions is invited,[32] and the parallel between local dualism in this country and national dualism abroad reëmerges. But

31. The first "conference board" of Iron Molders' locals was formed in the metropolitan area of New York City in 1891, following almost a decade of strife with the local groups affiliated with the Knights of Labor, "with its inevitable consequence—attempts to increase the hours and decrease the wages on the part of the employers." The New York Board raised its own funds through per capita levies, hired salaried business agents as organizers, and affiliated itself directly with different central labor groups in the vicinity. (*Journal,* January 1897, p. 7.) The second board was formed by the Chicago locals in order to "bring about a more harmonious feeling between the members and molders employed at the different branches of the trade"—and especially to cope with the unprecedented influx of out-of-town molders into the city in connection with the erection of the World's Fair. (*Journal,* July 1892, p. 5 and August 1892, p. 3.)

Although President Fox of the International Union was present at the first regular meeting of the New York Board in 1892 and "wished them success and God-speed in their new departure," it was not until 1895 that the International took any action. Then it required that "When more than one local exists in any one locality, a Local Executive Board shall be formed, which shall adjust all differences between the locals and endeavor to agree upon a scale of wages." (*Constitution,* 1895, Art. X, Sec. 7.) Four years later official recognition was extended to any Conference Board which was formed by local unions "within a reasonable radius of a good central point," whose combined membership equalled or exceeded one thousand. The by-laws of such conference boards were made subject to the approval of the President of the I.M.U. It was further provided that when the revenue of any board (to be raised by per capita tax) was found insufficient to meet its running expenses, the international president and executive board were empowered to grant it financial assistance. (In 1902, it was provided that all boards "shall" receive a sum equal to two cents per member per month, upon application. —*Constitution,* 1902, Art. XX, Sec. 3) There is some reason to believe that the interest of the national union was stimulated primarily by its desire to assert control over that important new trade-union official whose rise was associated with the increasing power of the district organization, the business agent. For the amendments of 1895 provided that "The appointment of any Business Agent or employee of such Conference Board shall require the approval of the President of the I.M.U. of N.A.," and that the Business Agent must keep the International Secretary "thoroughly informed as to the workings of the Board, and also submit to him a detailed monthly statement of the expenses incurred." (*Constitution,* 1899, Art. XX.)

Not until 1907 did the International Union empower its president and executive boards to establish conference boards "wherever it will be to the best interests of the I.M.U. of N.A.," to determine their precise jurisdiction, and to require that all local unions located within a board's jurisdiction affiliate with the conference board so established. (*Constitution,* 1907, Art. XX.)

32. Cf. *British Trade Unionism* (London: Political and Economic Planning, 1949), pp. 18–19, 41–43.

even if we grant that the coöperation among the local unions in a market area could not be explained without reference to the coercive authority of the national union, the fact remains that the requisite degree of uniformity throughout the local market was often achieved under dual unionism (however "subordinate" the dual unions might have been), and that the forces of competition operated at least as vigorously within the confines of the local market as they did throughout the national market which the national union claimed as its exclusive preserve.

The fluidity of craft boundaries and the menace of nonunion competition obliged many crafts to compromise one of the principles of pure craft jurisdiction by affiliating with "allied" or "related" trades. In some cases, as we have observed, the craft in question amalgamated with other occupational groups the members of which could perform some of the work of the craft. In other instances, the craft merged with groups of workers who were virtually incapable of substituting for the craftsmen. It is possible to distinguish between these two groups on the locál level: the latter received somewhat greater autonomy than the former.

When the lines separating the "related crafts" were fairly well defined in a particular locality so that the members of one group were not readily available to the employers as substitutes for those of another, the various crafts in the community were often organized into separate local unions. This was the practice of even those national unions which were opposed to "local dualism." Thus the Printers, who refused to charter separate local unions for each of the two printing industries (newspaper and commercial, and book-and-job), did permit the nonprinter, or "allied" crafts to form independent locals when the latter were affiliated with the International Typographical Union.[33] The Amalgamated Association of Iron, Steel, and Tin Workers provided for local affiliation along trade lines (separate locals of boilers, finishers, steel workers, and so on), although it refused to allow members of different nationalities to be segregated in different local unions.[34] And the Molders initially combined interdiction of dualism with toleration of craft sectionalism in a single regulation:

Should the molders in any locality deem it expedient to form Unions of the separate branches of the trade, such Unions will be recognized and respected by this Union; provided there is no more than one Union in each department, *viz:* One Union of Machinery Molders, one Union of Stove and Holloware Molders, and one of Bench Molders, who shall be recognized in any one town or city.[35]

33. Barnett, *The Printers*, pp. 41 (including n. 2) through 43. The allied crafts included, in addition to the pressmen, bookbinders, electrotypers and stereotypers, and photoengravers—all of whom ultimately seceded from the Typographical Union—the mailers, type founders, and newspaper reporters.

34. Jesse S. Robinson, *The Amalgamated Association of Iron, Steel, and Tin Workers* (Baltimore: Johns Hopkins, 1920), pp. 39 and 40.

35. *Constitution*, 1876, Art. IX, Sec. 7.

But when craft boundaries were sufficiently blurred so that the "specialists" could replace craftsmen in certain lines of work, there was some tendency to amalgamate all groups in a community into a single local union, or, that failing, to submit the different locals to the central direction of district councils. The Printers, who allowed the allied crafts to form independent local unions, refused to permit the different occupations in the composing room (the hand compositors, machine operators, machine tenders, and proof readers) to be represented in separate locals.[36] The Molders, some of whose members worked at more than one branch of the trade,[37] qualified their grant of authority to local groups "to form Unions of the separate branches of the trade" by requiring (in 1899) the approval of the international president and executive board before more than one local union could be chartered in any locality. Finally, in 1912, the international executive was empowered to amalgamate different locals wherever it considered amalgamation desirable.[38]

In some cases the extent to which members of one trade division in a union worked at other occupations in the trade varied from community to community. (Versatility, it will be recalled, often varied inversely with the size of the community, with specialization greatest in the larger metropolitan areas.) In such circumstances, the distinction made between substitute and complementary trade groups in the same locality was superseded by a distinction to be drawn between versatile groups in one community and noncompeting groups in another. By requiring that the consent of the existing local union be obtained before any additional locals could be chartered in a community (see pp. 608ff. above), the Bricklayers and the Carpenters in effect allowed their oldest and usually more versatile craft groups to prevent any of the newer branches from gaining recognition as autonomous units with exclusive jurisdiction over their own trades.

Thus, in 1885, unaffiliated local unions of stonemasons in the city of Trenton, New Jersey, were denied charters by Secretary O'Dea because they failed to obtain the consent of the Bricklayers' locals in the city. Three years later, they applied again and were rejected once more. The masons in two other cities (Wilmington, Delaware and Toronto) were also rebuffed when the local groups of bricklayers refused to grant the required permission.[39] On the other hand, the Bricklayers forbade their locals to admit plasterers to membership in localities "where there are exclusive Plasterers' unions of a local or national character," although elsewhere the admission of plasterers

36. Barnett, *The Printers*, pp. 41–43. "The maintenance of a common apprenticeship for all classes of printers has been the chief support of this policy."

37. *Journal*, July 1909, p. 410. (Article by Editor John P. Frey.)

38. Stockton, *Molders Union*, p. 43. After the Molders had forced the secessionist Core Makers' International Union out of existence in 1903, the coremakers' locals were merged with those of the machinery molders.

39. *Proceedings*, 1885, p. 31; 1888, pp. 3–4.

was a matter of local discretion.[40] The distinction was drawn because "exclusive plasterers" did not lay brick, whereas plasterers in many small communities often performed bricklayers' work and consequently jeopardized the security of the Bricklayers' locals if they were not admitted to membership therein. But, with the foregoing exception, the organization's basic policy of local determination was restated and amplified in an enumeration of the "powers reserved to" local unions in 1897:

It has the privilege when being organized, to be installed as an exclusive or a mixed Union, subject to the consent of any other Union or Unions in its city or locality if any there be. It can be a bricklayers', bricklayers' and masons', bricklayers' and plasterers', bricklayers', masons' and plasterers', or stonemasons' Union, as the case may be, upon application, according to its composition . . .[41]

Although all the locals in a community which were affiliated with the same national union were included in the same district council, special status was sometimes granted to noncompeting trade groups, while locals in different branches whose members were to some extent interchangeable were treated as though they were "dual" organizations in the same craft division. Although the Molders allowed only one local union in each "department" in any locality, they insisted that a "Local Executive Board" be formed "to adjust all differences between the locals" in the various branches in each community where more than one local existed and to "endeavor to agree upon a scale of wages."[42] This action was taken because the Molders' subjurisdictions were far from watertight. The Bricklayers, on the other hand, were cognizant of the separateness of trade interests in cities in which "exclusive" locals of the various branches of the trade (as opposed to "mixed" unions) were chartered. Their rule that no local could call a strike unless two-thirds of all the locals (or, later, of the membership, thereof) assented thereto had been passed before they asserted jurisdiction over stonemasons (1883), but after they began to charter "exclusive" masons' unions, they changed the regulation to provide that the referendum be confined to locals "of the same craft."[43]

40. *Constitution,* 1892, Art. XII, Sec. 8. The words "national character" referred to affiliation with the Operative Plasterers' International Union, with which the Bricklayers had a long-standing jurisdictional dispute. The latter, however, did not claim jurisdiction over plasterers in communities in which they were organized into "exclusive" locals by the Operative Plasterers until 1910, when, after attempts to reach a working agreement with the Plasterers failed, the Bricklayers' Union included the word "Plasterers" in its title for the first time.

41. *Constitution,* 1897, Art. XVI.

42. *Constitution,* 1895, Art. X, Sec. 7. It will be recalled that the second "conference board" of molders' locals was formed in Chicago three years before the adoption of this constitutional provision and that its object was to "bring about a more harmonious feeling between the members and molders employed at the different branches of the trade." (See footnote 31.)

43. *Constitution,* 1897, Art. XVII, Sections 2 and 4.

In previous sections, the self-interest of the older—and usually higher-paid —craft groups was invoked in order to explain why these groups joined forces with "related trades," both substitute and complementary. The fact that the Bricklayers allowed the locals of their original craft to determine, in effect, whether separate locals of other branches could be formed in their respective localities reveals that their primary motive in organizing substitute groups was the preservation of primary and alternative sources of employment for bricklayers. This self-interest was made quite conspicuous in a later ruling:

The principles of Brick Masonry and Stone Masonry are plainly defined in Art. 10. But the practical workings of the same are reserved to the Subordinate Unions to define the practice, and where they cannot be readily enforced they must make such concessions in their agreements and Working Codes as will not bring into trouble Bricklayers' Unions, or cause their members to lose employment on account of such disputed work.[44]

Nor was the Bricklayers' unreconstructed selfishness any less in evidence in localities where craft lines were more satisfactorily drawn. When some of the Stonemasons' locals attempted to secede in 1890, O'Dea claimed that the Bricklayers were culpable:

In cities where we have exclusive Bricklayers' and Stonemasons' Unions, there appears to be that want of sympathy on the part of the Bricklayers to assist the Stone-masons, which is contrary to all purposes of Unionism. It was this spirit of non-unionism and dissatisfaction which has caused some of the Stonemasons' Unions to withdraw from our body during the year and form a National Body of their own.[45]

44. *Constitution,* 1897, Art. XVI, Sec. 5.
45. *Proceedings,* 1890, p. 45 (report of the secretary).

THE SEASONAL BARGAIN

SINCE, under the conventional monopoly wage bargain, the employer is free to determine the amount of labor he will hire at the stated union wage, the resulting combination of wage bill and employment lies on the employer's demand curve for labor. The union can do no better than to set a wage such that the resulting combination of wage income and employment will represent the most favorable position for the union (assuming that the union consists of a group of "essentially identical individuals," to quote Leontief) attainable on that demand curve. This combination is described graphically as the point of tangency between the employer's offer curve and a union indifference curve.[1]

Under the "ideal" guaranteed wage contract, however, the union, since it can specify the minimum amount of labor which the employer must hire as well as the wage rate, can conceivably oblige the employer to hire more labor than he would have hired at the union wage if he were free to hire only as much as he wished. Thus the combination of employment and wage bill resulting from the guaranteed wage contract might not lie on the employer's demand curve at all; the union can improve its position by selecting some point to the right of that curve. Since the employer now is restricted to the choice of accepting the union's "package" or of closing his plant, it is possible for the union to establish an employment-income combination which will leave the employer only infinitesimally better off than he would be if he exercised his option of shutting down entirely.

Now, under the seasonally timed conventional (monopoly) wage bargain, as described in Chapter 14, the union can achieve the same result as that made possible under the guarantee of employment. The fact that output is fixed by contract and that the time period is short enough to permit of no substitution of other resources for the labor in question in the production of a unit of product in effect constitute a "guarantee" of employment. The wage rate can

1. Wassily W. Leontief, "The Pure Theory of the Guaranteed Annual Wage Contract," *Journal of Political Economy*, February 1946, pp. 77, 78.

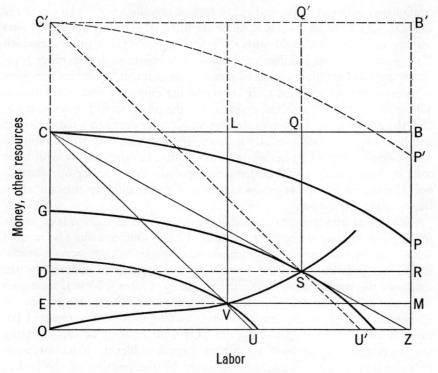

Chart 2. The Seasonal Bargain

be pushed up to any level short of a value at which total costs will exceed total revenues (where the employer might elect not to produce at all). This is demonstrated in Chart 2.

The employer is represented initially as possessing OC units of money before he begins to hire labor from a given work force. The work force (organized into a union) initially possesses BC units of labor (its initial stock of "leisure"). Thus point C represents the initial position of both parties. The employer's indifference curves are convex to the origin at O; the union's are convex to the origin at B. The wage rates are represented by the angles formed by the diagonals radiating from C; the sharper the angle at C, the higher the wage rate. The employer's "offer curve," COVS, connects the points at which the corner points on his indifference curves lie on the wage lines.

Let us assume provisionally that the employer is free to vary the amount of labor units hired, but that he must hire his factors in fixed proportions. Given the latter condition, it is implied that if more labor is hired, output will be increased. The condition of fixed technical coefficients is represented by the employer's L-shaped indifference curves, denoting a complementary relationship between labor and other factors of production. Thus, at wage CO/OZ, CQ (= DS) units of labor are hired in exchange for CD dollars and are combined with OD units of "other factors." (CZ is the wage which is tangent to a union indifference curve and passes through the corner point of an employer indifference curve at the same point. It represents the point of intersection between the offer curves of the employer and of the union. The latter is not drawn on the diagram.) If the union raises the wage, say to CU, the employer will move to the left on his offer curve to V, at which he will hire less labor (EV = CL) for more money (CE) and will combine it with a smaller quantity of other resources (OE). In other words, with labor costs increased, output will be reduced, especially since, under our assumption of fixed coefficients of production other factors cannot be substituted for labor at the same output.

Now let us add the restriction that output is fixed at a given level, corresponding to the employment of CQ units of labor. Output cannot be reduced below this level, because of contractual commitments to customers; it cannot exceed the prescribed amount because of the limitations imposed by the length of the work season (given the efficiency of labor). Now if the union raises the wage from CO/OZ to CO/OU, the employer no longer has the option of reducing output to a level corresponding to the employment of EV units of labor; he must hire DS (= CQ) units or none at all. Assuming that he remains in operation, the higher wage line, like the older one, must pass through S. This situation is indicated by the position of the broken wage line C'U' which passes through the corner point of the employer's indifference curve Q'QSR. But now the employer must pay C'D dollars for CQ (= C'Q' = DS) units of labor at wage OC/OU (= OC'/OU'), whereas, at the lower wage CO/OZ, his wage bill was only CD. The employer is obviously in a less preferred position if he remains (as he must) at S; with price and output fixed, his costs have been increased (by C'C). The initial position has been raised from C to C', with the result that the isoquant Q'QSR is assigned a lower position in the employer's preference scale than QSR had denoted. Q'QSR might, for example, now indicate a "welfare" (but not an output) position equivalent to that assigned to LVM when the wage was CO/OZ, and the starting point was C.

The union's welfare position, on the other hand, has changed for the better. At wage CO/OZ, the union's indifference curve CP represents a series of income-labor combinations which are bargaining minima, in that, if any combination to the right of CP were offered by the employer, the members of the union would elect not to strike a bargain—that is, they would prefer to remain at the starting point, C. But when the starting point is raised to C' (when the wage is raised to C'O/OU' = CO/OU), the union's indifference curve CP no longer passes through the starting point; its officers would be willing to accept a position to the right of CP, for their "final" curve is now C'P'. Now, since the relative position of CP has been raised, the relative position of CU', the curve passing through S, has also been raised. Thus, at position S, the union is relatively better off than it was at the old wage rate; while the employer, by parity of reasoning, is worse off.

It must, of course, be kept in mind that the union cannot raise the wage without limit, for, as stated above, the employer may choose to suspend operations entirely if the union insists on a wage such that total costs would exceed total revenues—that is, he would prefer any position, C, C', and so on to S. At a wage infinitesimally lower than that at which profits are zero, however, he would prefer S to C. In the latter case, S would correspond to the point of tangency between a union indifference curve and the curve of the employer which passes through the starting point in a guaranteed annual wage bargain, as depicted in the Leontief diagram.

The formal similarity between the "pure" guaranteed wage and the seasonally timed conventional bargain can now be demonstrated. Under the conventional bargain, as stated at the outset, the union must choose a position on the employer's demand curve. Under the guaranteed annual wage bargain, the union is not so restricted and maximizes its position by achieving a point of tangency between a union indifference curve and an employer indifference curve. But under the seasonally timed conventional bargain, both of these conditions are achieved simultaneously, since, because of the angularity of the employer's indifference curves (imposed by the assumption of complementarity), whenever a union indifference curve passes through a corner point of an employer indifference curve, it also passes through the employer's offer curve at the same point. Thus, a union, without imposing any guarantee of employment upon an employer, can, in principle, reap the rewards associated with such a guarantee, if it times its ordinary wage demand with sufficient shrewdness.

INCENTIVE PAY

THE FORMAL economic equivalence of "incentive" and "rushing" (or being obliged to work harder than desired at a given time rate of pay) can be illustrated with the aid of conventional indifference curve analysis in Chart 3.

At the effort wage OZ/OL, the individual prefers to offer LN units of effort. Now assume that any extra units of effort will be compensated for at the rate given by the tangent of the angle at M=RP/RM. The individual will now be willing to offer NN' more units for extra income RR', or LN' in all for total income OR'. His average rate of income (income per unit of effort) is OR"/OL. Now if this average rate of income were offered as a straight time rate, the individual would prefer point D; he would prefer to work no more than LN for income ND. Hence by paying him different prices for different units of output, he is "induced" to work NN' extra.

Conversely, suppose that he must produce LN' at wage rate OR"/OL, although he would prefer to offer only LN units. This situation is the equivalent of paying him at the rate of only OZ/OL for the first LN units of his effort and RP/RM for the next NN' units. On the other hand, although our worker would prefer selling LN units to LN' at OR"/OL, he would be willing to sell any amount short of LN" rather than refuse any employment at all at that wage. He would, however, refuse to offer more than LN", for an offer in excess of LN" would correspond to a position on LR" which would be intersected by an indifference curve lying below the curve passing through L, the "starting point," and would thus indicate a preference to retain one's entire initial "stock of leisure." Only under a condition of servitude could the employer oblige the worker to offer more than LN" units of effort at the given wage. Thus, although "incentive" and "rushing" may be equivalent to one another, either is preferable to servitude.

In the above example, the "incentive" wage (RP/RM) had to be higher than the "straight-time" wage (OZ/OL) in order to induce the extra output of effort. This need be the case, however, only when the incentive is applied at a position which is preferred by the individual to all those attainable—

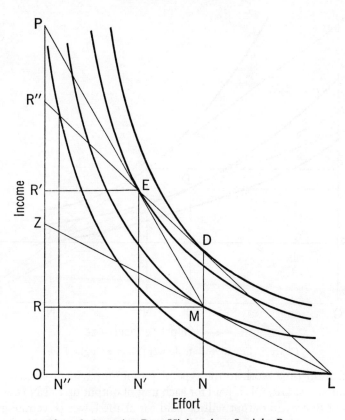

Chart 3. Incentive Rate Higher than Straight Rate

that is, at a point of tangency between the indifference curve and the wage line. If, however, the incentive be applied short of the point at which the worker would have been willing to produce at the given "straight" wage, the incentive could be effective even if it is lower than the straight rate. This proved the case under the early incentive systems referred to in the text, wherein it was possible to induce a given percentage increase in output (and effort) per hour in response to a smaller percentage increase in income per hour. Under such incentive systems, piece (effort) rates were reduced with every increase in output beyond "standard," although income per hour was of course continuously increased. The condition necessary for success here was that the worker be willing to produce more than "standard" output per hour under straight piece-work, computed by dividing the hourly "base" rate by standard output. This is illustrated in Chart 4.

Assume that, under straight time payment, the individual is paid OR income per hour and produces LN units per hour. Then his earnings per unit of output are OP/OL = EN/NL. Now, if the method of payment is

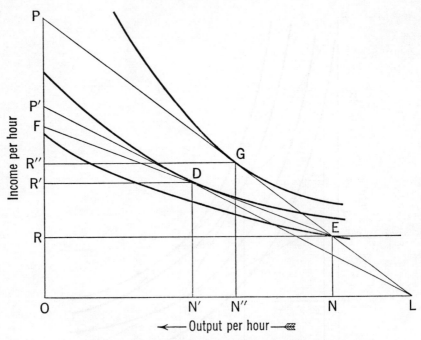

Chart 4. Incentive Rate Lower Than Straight Rate

changed from time work to the type of premium payment discussed in the text, assume that OP/OL is paid for each unit of output up to LN (our "standard") and that extra output will be paid for at the lower piece rate given by the tangent of the angle formed at E (RF/RE). Now the individual will find it profitable to increase his output to LN' pieces per hour, for which he will receive OR' per hour. Although the "average" piece rate has fallen from OP/OL to OP'/OL, the hourly rate has increased from OR to OR' and, given the individual's preference system with respect to income and leisure (or, inversely, to expenditure of effort) the position D is preferred by him to E, so that the incentive is effective in inducing an extra output of NN' per hour.

Under straight piecework, however, the individual would be able to achieve position G, which he prefers not only to E, his position under time-work, but to D as well, for he not only receives a higher hourly rate (OR") but he receives it in return for a smaller output per hour (LN" as compared with LN'). Thus it is apparent why unions which did not oppose piecework were nevertheless strongly opposed to incentive systems which paid proportionally less extra pay for output in excess of standard. It is also apparent why, as mentioned in the text, this type of incentive was more efficient than straight piecework: it elicited greater output per hour (and, of course, at a lower hourly wage).

It will be noted, however, that it was essential to the success of such premium plans, under which extra output was not rewarded by proportionately increased pay per unit, that the worker prefer to produce in excess of "standard," or LN, at straight piece rate. This system probably worked best, in other words, when the worker's preference system was characterized by a relatively high evaluation of income in terms of leisure, as it was in nineteenth-century America.

The second figure can be used to illustrate not only how transition from timework to piecework could result in increased output per unit of time (from LN to LN″) but also how the increased output might result in a worsened position for the workers employed in the trade if it were not accompanied by increasing demand. In our diagram, the demand for labor under piecework can be represented by the diagonal LP. If, however, each employer in a competitive trade hired NN″ more units of labor from each worker under piecework than under timework, the supply of product would increase, price would fall and the value of the marginal product would decline. Demand for labor would now be represented by, for example, diagonal LP′; and each worker might now offer more labor (LN′) at the new and lower wage rate. Even if he offered less labor than before, however, he would still be in a position inferior to G. Hence the attractiveness, in this situation, to a union of a policy of restricting individual output: some output per hour short of LN″, while it would land the worker on an indifference curve lower than the curve passing through point G, would also place him in a position superior to D, for, with the output of each worker less than LN′, the wage rate would not fall to OP′/OL.

MAKE-WORK RULES

In the text (pp. 543ff.), it was pointed out that, if the imposition of make-work rules obliged the employer to hire more labor than he wished, the ruling wage was above the competitive level (at which the number of jobs and the number of job seekers are equated) and the employer was forced to accept a combination of wage rate and number employed which represented a position off his demand curve to the right. Therefore, Slichter's observation that "Makework rules are likely to be paid for by wages lower than the union could otherwise obtain" cannot imply a comparison between two points on the employer's demand curve for labor. Rather, it implies a comparison between two positions, one of which (characterized by the makework demand in addition to a wage rate above the competitive level) is off the curve while the other (characterized solely by the demand for a higher wage rate than that indicated in the first position) is on it.

The wage rate under makework conditions is lower, "because the disadvantages which the union can afford to impose upon employers are limited." Since the employer is obviously worse off under a higher wage rate with makework rules than he is under a low wage rate with makework rules, if the union wishes to impose makework rules and if it cannot "afford" to leave the employer worse off, it must accept a lower rate than it could otherwise obtain. This is illustrated in the following diagram.

At the wage rate PO/OU_1 (the slope of the diagonal PU_1), the employer would desire to employ no more than OV units of labor, since this amount is indicated by the point of tangency (T_1) between his isoquant I_1 and PU_1 (which point also lies on his offer curve PT_2T_1). Assume, however, that the union obliges the employer to hire OM instead of OV units at this wage, so that the employer's position is represented by R. (It may be assumed, to make the example realistic, that at wage PO/OU_1 OM units had previously been hired before the demand curve for labor had been pushed to the left by technological change.) The employer is obviously worse off under the makework rules, since he must spend PC dollars on OM units of labor instead of only PD dollars on OV units; thus the indifference curve tangent to PU_1 at T_1 is higher than the indifference curve I_2 passing through PU_1 at R_1.

If, now, the union wishes to raise the wage from PO/OU_1 and if it cannot "afford" to make the employer worse off than he is at (R), it must accept a combination of wage income and employment, represented by T_2, which is the point at which the wage line PU_2 is tangent to I_2. But since this is a point of tangency and thus lies on the employer's offer curve PT_2T_1, it implies the surrender of all makework rules; that is, the employer, at T_2, is not obliged to hire more labor than he desires to at wage PO/OU_2, or ON. If the union wishes to "make work," it can do so only by accepting a wage lower than PO/OU_2. If, for example, it wishes no less than OV units to be hired, it can do so and charge a wage which is indicated by a diagonal originating at P and passing through I_2 at a point directly above V. Thus when Slichter writes that a union must pay for makework rules by accepting a wage lower than that which it could otherwise obtain if it does not desire to worsen the position of the employer, he is referring to a movement along a

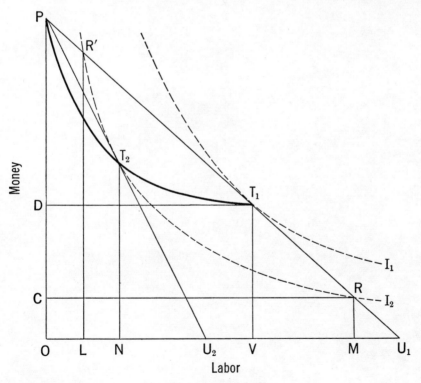

Chart 5. Make-work Rules

given indifference curve of the employer, represented in the diagram by a shift from T_2 to R.

Actually, it is necessary that R represent some position which, from the employer's viewpoint, is slightly preferable to the points on indifference curve I_2. For the employer, under makework rules, is given the alternative of reducing total employment below OV as well as increasing it to OM. If point R′ lies on the same indifference curve as R, the employer is indifferent between employments OL and OM. For him to prefer to employ OM rather than OL units of labor, R should be made slightly preferable to R′. This point was made by Leontief in the reference cited in the text, but it might be pointed out that the probability of reduced employment under makework rules is greater than under the theoretical case in which a union demands either a certain total employment at a given wage rate or zero employment.

INDEX

Wertheim Publications in Industrial Relations

PUBLISHED BY HARVARD UNIVERSITY PRESS

J. D. Houser, *What the Employer Thinks,* 1927*
Wertheim Lectures on Industrial Relations, 1929
William Haber, *Industrial Relations in the Building Industry,* 1930*
Johnson O'Connor, *Psychometrics,* 1934*
Paul H. Norgren, *The Swedish Collective Bargaining System,* 1941*
Leo C. Brown, S.J., *Union Policies in the Leather Industry,* 1947
Walter Galenson, *Labor in Norway,* 1949*
Dorothea de Schweinitz, *Labor and Management in a Common Enterprise,* 1949
Ralph Altman, *Availability for Work: A Study in Unemployment Compensation,* 1950*
John T. Dunlop and Arthur D. Hill, *The Wage Adjustment Board: Wartime Stabilization in the Building and Construction Industry,* 1950
Walter Galenson, *The Danish System of Labor Relations: A Study in Industrial Peace,* 1952
Lloyd H. Fisher, *The Harvest Labor Market in California,* 1953
Theodore V. Purcell, S.J., *The Worker Speaks His Mind on Company and Union,* 1953
Donald J. White, *The New England Fishing Industry,* 1954
Val R. Lorwin, *The French Labor Movement,* 1954
Philip Taft, *The Structure and Government of Labor Unions,* 1954
George B. Baldwin, *Beyond Nationalization: The Labor Problems of British Coal,* 1955
Kenneth F. Walker, *Industrial Relations in Australia,* 1956*
Charles A. Myers, *Labor Problems in the Industrialization of India,* 1958
Herbert J. Spiro, *The Politics of German Codetermination,* 1958*
Mark W. Leiserson, *Wages and Economic Control in Norway, 1945–1957,* 1959
J. Pen, *The Wage Rate Under Collective Bargaining,* 1959
Jack Stieber, *The Steel Industry Wage Structure,* 1959
Theodore V. Purcell, S.J., *Blue Collar Man: Patterns of Dual Allegiance in Industry,* 1960
Carl Erik Knoellinger, *Labor in Finland,* 1960
Sumner H. Slichter, *Potentials of the American Economy: Selected Essays,* edited by John T. Dunlop, 1961
C. L. Christenson, *Economic Redevelopment in Bituminous Coal: The Special Case of Technological Advance in United States Coal Mines, 1930–1960,* 1962
Daniel L. Horowitz, *The Italian Labor Movement,* 1963
Adolf Sturmthal, *Workers Councils: A Study of Workplace Organization on Both Sides of the Iron Curtain,* 1964
Vernon H. Jensen, *Hiring of Dock Workers and Employment Practices in the Ports of New York, Liverpool, London, Rotterdam, and Marseilles,* 1964

STUDIES IN LABOR-MANAGEMENT HISTORY

Lloyd Ulman, *The Rise of the National Trade Union: The Development and Significance of Its Structure, Governing Institutions, and Economic Policies,* 1955; second edition, 1966

Joseph P. Goldberg, *The Maritime Story: A Study in Labor-Management Relations, 1957,* 1958

Walter Galenson, *The CIO Challenge to the AFL: A History of the American Labor Movement, 1935–1941,* 1960

Morris A. Horowitz, *The New York Hotel Industry: A Labor Relations Study,* 1960

Mark Perlman, *The Machinists: A New Study in Trade Unionism,* 1961

Fred C. Munson, *Labor Relations in the Lithographic Industry,* 1963

Garth L. Mangum, *The Operating Engineers: The Economic History of a Trade Union,* 1964

David Brody, *The Butcher Workmen: A Study of Unionization,* 1964

PUBLISHED BY McGRAW-HILL BOOK CO., INC.

Robert J. Alexander, *Labor Relations in Argentina, Brazil, and Chile,* 1961

Carl M. Stevens, *Strategy and Collective Bargaining Negotiations,* 1963

*Out of print